Contemporary Approaches to Activity Theory:

Interdisciplinary Perspectives on Human Behavior

Thomas Hansson
Blekinge Institute of Technology, School of Management (MAM), Sweden

A volume in the Advances in Human and Social
Aspects of Technology (AHSAT) Book Series

An Imprint of IGI Global

Managing Director:	Lindsay Johnston
Acquisitions Editor:	Kayla Wolfe
Production Editor:	Christina Henning
Development Editor:	Erin O'Dea
Typesetter:	Cody Page
Cover Design:	Jason Mull

Published in the United States of America by
Information Science Reference (an imprint of IGI Global)
701 E. Chocolate Avenue
Hershey PA, USA 17033
Tel: 717-533-8845
Fax: 717-533-8661
E-mail: cust@igi-global.com
Web site: http://www.igi-global.com

Library of Congress Cataloging-in-Publication Data

CIP Data

Library of Congress Cataloging-in-Publication Data

Contemporary approaches to activity theory : interdisciplinary perspectives on human behavior / Thomas Hansson, editor.
    pages cm
 Includes bibliographical references and index.
 ISBN 978-1-4666-6603-0 (hardcover) -- ISBN 978-1-4666-6604-7 (ebook) -- ISBN 978-1-4666-6606-1 (print & perpetual access) 1. Active learning. 2. Learning. 3. Learning, Psychology of. I. Hansson, Thomas.
 LB1027.23.C66 2015
 371.3--dc23
                         2014032307

This book is published in the IGI Global book series Advances in Human and Social Aspects of Technology (AHSAT) (ISSN: 2328-1316; eISSN: 2328-1324)

British Cataloguing in Publication Data
A Cataloguing in Publication record for this book is available from the British Library.

Advances in Human and Social Aspects of Technology (AHSAT) Book Series

Ashish Dwivedi
The University of Hull, UK

ISSN: 2328-1316
EISSN: 2328-1324

MISSION

In recent years, the societal impact of technology has been noted as we become increasingly more connected and are presented with more digital tools and devices. With the popularity of digital devices such as cell phones and tablets, it is crucial to consider the implications of our digital dependence and the presence of technology in our everyday lives.

The **Advances in Human and Social Aspects of Technology (AHSAT) Book Series** seeks to explore the ways in which society and human beings have been affected by technology and how the technological revolution has changed the way we conduct our lives as well as our behavior. The AHSAT book series aims to publish the most cutting-edge research on human behavior and interaction with technology and the ways in which the digital age is changing society.

COVERAGE

- Cyber Behavior
- Cyber Bullying
- Philosophy of Technology
- Information Ethics
- Human-Computer Interaction
- Technology and Social Change
- Technology Adoption
- ICTs and Social Change
- Technoself
- Digital Identity

IGI Global is currently accepting manuscripts for publication within this series. To submit a proposal for a volume in this series, please contact our Acquisition Editors at Acquisitions@igi-global.com or visit: http://www.igi-global.com/publish/.

Titles in this Series

For a list of additional titles in this series, please visit: www.igi-global.com

Contemporary Approaches to Activity Theory Interdisciplinary Perspectives on Human Behavior
Thomas Hansson (Blekinge Institute of Technology, School of Management (MAM), Sweden)
Information Science Reference • copyright 2015 • 437pp • H/C (ISBN: 9781466666030) • US $195.00 (our price)

Evolving Issues Surrounding Technoethics and Society in the Digital Age
Rocci Luppicini (University of Ottawa, Canada)
Information Science Reference • copyright 2014 • 317pp • H/C (ISBN: 9781466661226) • US $215.00 (our price)

Technological Advancements and the Impact of Actor-Network Theory
Arthur Tatnall (Victoria University, Australia)
Information Science Reference • copyright 2014 • 331pp • H/C (ISBN: 9781466661264) • US $195.00 (our price)

Gender Considerations and Influence in the Digital Media and Gaming Industry
Julie Prescott (University of Bolton, UK) and Julie Elizabeth McGurren (Codemasters, UK)
Information Science Reference • copyright 2014 • 357pp • H/C (ISBN: 9781466661424) • US $195.00 (our price)

Human-Computer Interfaces and Interactivity Emergent Research and Applications
Pedro Isaías (Universidade Aberta (Portuguese Open University), Portugal) and Katherine Blashki (Noroff University College, Norway)
Information Science Reference • copyright 2014 • 348pp • H/C (ISBN: 9781466662285) • US $200.00 (our price)

Political Campaigning in the Information Age
Ashu M. G. Solo (Maverick Technologies America Inc., USA)
Information Science Reference • copyright 2014 • 359pp • H/C (ISBN: 9781466660625) • US $210.00 (our price)

Handbook of Research on Political Activism in the Information Age
Ashu M. G. Solo (Maverick Technologies America Inc., USA)
Information Science Reference • copyright 2014 • 498pp • H/C (ISBN: 9781466660663) • US $275.00 (our price)

Interdisciplinary Applications of Agent-Based Social Simulation and Modeling
Diana Francisca Adamatti (Universidade Federal do Rio Grande, Brasil) Graçaliz Pereira Dimuro (Universidade Federal do Rio Grande, Brasil) and Helder Coelho (Universidade de Lisboa, Portugal)
Information Science Reference • copyright 2014 • 376pp • H/C (ISBN: 9781466659544) • US $225.00 (our price)

DISSEMINATOR of KNOWLEDGE
www.igi-global.com

701 E. Chocolate Ave., Hershey, PA 17033
Order online at www.igi-global.com or call 717-533-8845 x100
To place a standing order for titles released in this series, contact: cust@igi-global.com
Mon-Fri 8:00 am - 5:00 pm (est) or fax 24 hours a day 717-533-8661

Editorial Advisory Board

Table of Contents

Section 5
Philosophy of Activity Theory

Detailed Table of Contents

Section 1
Information and Communication Technology

Chapter 1
Thurídur Jóhannsdóttir, University of Iceland, Iceland

Thurídur Jóhannsdóttir focuses on mediated behaviour and established practices among Icelandic student teachers. The chapter displays an account of educational challenges and opportunities enabled by the technology bridging geographical and possibly mental distances between pupils, class teachers, and student teachers in rural schools.

Chapter 2
Fia Andersson, Uppsala University, Sweden
Stellan Sundh, Uppsala University, Sweden

Fia Andersson and Stellan Sundh have composed a chapter based on a project on young learners' development, cross-national communication, and the use of digital tools. The purpose of a cross-national project is to bring students together by combining curricular goals with cultural differences. In addition, communication on the Web between students with different cultural backgrounds enables learning English as a foreign language.

Chapter 3
Karen E. Andreasen, Aalborg University, Denmark
Palle Rasmussen, Aalborg University, Denmark

Karen Andreasen and Palle Rasmussen focus on the context of higher education in a chapter that outlines some of the principles of online teaching and learning. This chapter presents a combined approach to studying and developing classroom activity and video-mediated exchanges. Analysis of student behaviors is supported by Etienne Wenger's theory about learning. The impact on teaching and learning by the specifically situated design, distribution, proximity, etc. of educational classroom resources is also analyzed.

Chapter 4
Hans Kyhlbäck, Blekinge Institute of Technology, Sweden

Hans Kyhlbäck provides a comparative analysis of student behavior related to two ICT contexts for game construction. The outcome of students academic design work is artifacts for the players' amusement and joy: two separate but interrelated activities. Effects of the familiar contradiction between school-related grades, marking and examination, and becoming a professional game designer are discussed. Contextualized feedback influences positively the students' feelings of competence, craftsmanship, and professionalism. Expansive learning enables people to learn established knowledge and contribute to new game technology.

Section 2
Education

Chapter 5
Karin Johansson, Lund University, Sweden

Karin Johansson analyzes the planning, rehearsal, and delivery of music by a string quartet and two other constellations as perceived by the author through direct observation. Also included is a comparison between instrumental music making and artistic agency. Aspects of subordination and independence combined with activity theoretical analytical tools, models, and concepts help clarify some of the built-in developmental contradictions of artistic music making in higher education. The chapter covers three explicitly presented and analyzed settings where musical practice is taught and learnt. Contradictions between traditional discipline of music making and deliberative artistic creativity are also analyzed.

Chapter 6
Charlotte Jonasson, Aarhus University, Denmark

Charlotte Jonasson outlines the effects of mediating artifacts in a vocational setting. What is the effect of the student's intentions and motivation for learning? Another interesting aspect is to learn about the developmental relations between the vocational students' urge to compete. Some competitive intentions are productive and others destructive. Timing of food preparation and services plus adequate choice of ingredients for cooking form zones of development for the vocational students. Furthermore, socio-material resources, values, quality of interaction, and social organization of work influence student behavior and performance.

Chapter 7
Juanjuan Zhao, University of Cincinnati, USA

Juanjuan Zhao has written a chapter on the application of Project-Based Instruction (PBI) in a foreign language (Chinese). The chapter covers an outline of action research and cultural-historical activity theory among two groups of students at a US high school. The effect of traditional teacher-centered and PBI-influenced approaches to teaching and learning Chinese are described by means of student commitment, acquisition of cultural knowledge, and communicative skills. The findings suggest that contradictions appear between approaches to teaching and learning of sentence structure, character writing, and recognition.

Chapter 8

Oleg Popov, Umeå University, Sweden

Oleg Popov scrutinizes outdoor science as a potentially useful activity in teacher education. Application of tools, tasks, and measures to management of outdoor lessons help student teachers of Science and Mathematics Education reach curricular goals. Contextual influences, learning objects, and transferability of knowledge are relevant themes related to outdoor science. Results suggest that if properly managed, outdoor science education empowers prospective teachers to learn to deploy a range of mediating pedagogical artifacts and expands their professional competence.

Chapter 9

Anna Linge, Kristianstad University College, Sweden

Anna Linge analyzes creative musical practice in an educational context. Just like in Karin Andersson's chapter, creative tensions between musical conformity and creative musical performance are analyzed from a perspective of teaching and learning. The author introduces Vygotskian concepts of association and dissociation functioning as mental tools for creative music making. Here, the concept of perezhivanie is used for analyzing and explaining tensions between formal education and freedom of artistic expression as defined by individual problem solving.

Section 3
Work Practice

Chapter 10

Laura Seppänen, Finnish Institute of Occupational Health, Finland
Laure Kloetzer, CNAM, France

Laura Seppänen and Laure Kloetzer present an emotionally laden theme exploring the practical design and effect of a using the hybrid concept of worry as a psychological tool for facilitating cross-functional negotiation in meetings between social workers. Professional concepts serve as functional or even cross-functional mediations for improved cross-functional collaboration. The concept of worry seemed to trigger the professionals' attempts to make sense of different contexts. Ambiguity, combined with a formal visual exercise, contributed to the professionals' abilities to elaborate their professional perspectives.

Chapter 11

Päivi Ristimäki, University of Helsinki, Finland

In this chapter, Päivi Ristimäki investigates the interplay between technology-push and demand-pull in a Finnish firm. The purpose of the longitudinal study is to describe influences of re-orientation of the main activity and adaptation to a changing market. Therefore, the firm takes explorative actions in their relation to potential customers. Understanding exploration and exploitation of products and relations for forming and implementing new business logic become the focused activity of research. Dialectic contradictions between sales of a technological product and expertise is another focus of the research.

Riikka Ruotsala examines how client understanding as a way of making generalizations in a collective problem-solving process evolves and changes during a developmental intervention. The intervention focuses on production supervisors' changing work and follows how organizational support functions build collaboration with supervisors. The analysis covers the participants' problem statements, explanation modes and solution ideas. Particular attention is paid to finding indications of evolving theoretical concepts and systemic ways of explaining and solving the problems.

Chapter 13

Hanna Toiviainen reports on development in an international business environment defined as a global workplace. The author analyzes meetings between Asian-Chinese and European-Finnish cultures and describes how different cultures pose challenges and offer solutions for employees who are supposed to collaborate in order to meet market demands for productivity and well-being.

Section 4
Methodology

Chapter 14

Carolina Piccetti Nascimento provides an analysis of educational concepts, clarifying their practical meaning and outlining relations between bodily movement and communication. Subject matter analysis of physical education (Dance and Game) help clarify to teachers, student teachers, and teacher educators how abstract thinking and concrete practices could potentially enhance the quality of teaching and learning. A cultural historical perspective on physical education supported by concepts of essence, movement from abstract to the concrete, historical analysis, and theoretical concepts lies at the heart of the study.

Chapter 15

Thomas Hansson focuses on traditional methodology for collecting data plus analysis of situated influences on people's behaviors, more specifically on behaviors that appear during interviews between students of Pedagogy and missionaries working in the Nordic countries. Complementary data consists of discourses between missionaries interviewing citizens for religious purposes.

B. Ferholt, M. Nilsson, A. Jansson, and K. Alnervik investigate the impact of Vygotskian creativity on exploratory learning during Kindergarten play and imagination. The contents of the chapter cover the findings of three school projects. The authors' approach builds on a combination between cultural-historical activity theory and post-modern writings. A formative intervention into the children's playworlds by researchers and teachers together shows—in one project—that imagination and realistic thinking are related processes.

Chapter 17

Laurie Watts and Beata Gullberg outline European ex-patriots' acculturation processes as they adapt to their employers' workplace cultures during the first years of their employment abroad. Some of the findings clarify the academic functionality of a mixed methods approach and also clarification of the interviewees' practical everyday experiences of food and language.

Inger Eriksson's focus is on developmental work research in general and on constitution of objects in particular. The described context consists of interventionist research displayed as three case studies into teaching and learning of mathematics involving cooperation (designing, testing, and evaluation) between class teachers and researchers.

Section 5
Philosophy of Activity Theory

Leena Kakkori and Rauno Huttunen introduce the concept of hermeneutic zone of proximal development, suggesting affiliation between philosophical "giants" that help explain moral development in man. They say language is something more than a vehicle for communication. Intertwined relations between thought and language are in constant movement back and forth in a dialogical process. Relations between language and thought go from external speech to thinking and from thinking to external speech. Human morality oscillating between an individual internal world and a public external world is a process of play-acting or a happening of truth. The authors' concept of hermeneutic zone of proximal development builds on

Vygotsky's theoy of ZPD, origins of thought and language, and Heidegger's theories. Their conceptions land in similar conclusions or similarities between thoughts.

Chapter 20
Lars Bang, Aalborg University, Denmark

Lars Bang provides an outline of an encounter of thoughts (i.e. a display of the researcher's process of mapping events). The chapter is an attempt at revealing stunted as well as normal games going on between people. In doing so, the author vivisects and reveals inner causality and logic related to late capitalism in contemporary society. The author's ultimate purpose is to integrate capital into psychology and activity theory. A map of capital defines a series of events as a stunted game of locked structures and rigid causalities.

Chapter 21
Regi Theodor Enerstvedt, Oslo University, Norway

Regi Theodor Enerstvedt reflects on past and current theorizing of the "contents" of theory of activity, the historical background of the concept, definitions, spread, and usefulness for critical psychology, and implications. People hold opinions, present arguments, and draw conclusions about the underlying theory and choice of method for making the concept operational to research.

Preface

The title of the book covers a variety of activities, environments, settings, and contexts. The title also suggests a common theoretical-conceptual approach to contemporary cultural-historical activity theory. The topic fits the needs and abilities of modern man because of the impact of activity systems, globalization, and cultural integration. More specifically, the contents of the book unfold contemporary resources of collective endeavors. One reason for choosing a shared individual and collective theme is to learn about the impact of computer-supported instrumentalism. The new technology poses a threat to traditionally acknowledged resources like coordination, cooperation, and co-construction between people. Therefore, there are cultural-historical experiences to share between people who use their ability to communicate as an impetus to systemic innovation of shared activities operating for the good of communities, societies, and nations. From one point of view families, teams, orchestras, courts of law, hospitals, etc. are self-regulating human organizations. From another point of view—which the contents of this book suggests—many approaches to learning enable "change agents" to support, coordinate, study, understand, redesign, manipulate, and improve practices.

General activity theory is a thriving approach to reach highly esteemed objectives, provided they encompass collaboration, learning plus social, and material development. Adding to the wide range of organizational concepts like demand-ability and need-resources, this book contains context-specific methods and empirical cases in 21 chapters on teacher education, modern languages, ICT, music making, vocational training, outdoor science, social work, business activity, industry, global organization, physical education, religious people, Kindergarten, and European expatriates. Other chapters are directed towards relating old philosophy to current approaches and positioning of activity theory in contemporary society.

The target audience of the book consists of theorists and practitioners of organized human activities (i.e. academics and consultants, tutors and doctoral students, teachers and pupils, management and staff, leaders and followers, doctors and patients, therapists and clients, businessmen and customers, plus parents and children).

One section on "Information and Communication Technology" covers the authors' accounts of projects in contexts of Icelandic teacher education, Web-based exchanges between Russian and Swedish school children, classroom designs for learning among Danish pupils, and game construction in Swedish higher education. A section on "Education" contains chapters on music making in higher education, vocational training in upper secondary schools, teaching and learning of a foreign language, and science and mathematics in teacher education. A third section on "Work Practices" displays Finnish examples of adult behavior in predominantly international business activities. One of them is about social work; another chapter is about adaptation to a global market, and then there is a chapter about industrial networking cooperation and supervision. The final contribution on work practices is on the effect of globalization on contents of work. A section on "Methodology" covers a variety of themes and subjects (e.g. initiatives for improving physical education, understanding religious people, creativity in Kindergarten, meetings between European cultures, and teaching and learning in mathematics). A fifth section covers comparison between inspirations to "Philosophy of Activity Theory," introducing a chapter on European "giants" like Vygotsky, Heidegger, and Gadamer by means of a concept alluding to Vygotsky's ZoPD, here called hermeneutic Zone of Proximal Development. There is a similar chapter comparing Marx and Leontjev with Bourdieu and Foucault by focusing on the concept of cultural, political, and scientific capital. A chapter closing this section clarifies the highly esteemed concept of *activity* as traditionally used among proponents of *activity theory*. References and arguments relative to the roots of the concept provide valuable insights to the current meaning of the concept.

The sections and chapters of this book verify the fact that the chosen topic describes a wide scale where people share a deep understanding of human activity. In a section on "Information and Communication Technology," Thurídur Jóhannsdóttir focuses on mediated behaviour and established practices among Icelandic student teachers. The chapter, "Responsive Practices in Online Teacher Education," displays an account of educational challenges and opportunities enabled by the technology bridging geographical and possibly mental distances between pupils, class teachers, and student teachers in rural schools.

In the second chapter, "Young Learners: Communication and Digital Tools," Fia Andersson and Stellan Sundh have composed a chapter based on a project on young learners' development, cross-national communication, and the use of digital tools. The purpose of a cross-national project is to bring students together by combining curricular goals with cultural differences. In addition, communication on the Web between students with different cultural backgrounds enables learning English as a foreign language.

Next, there is a chapter on "Learning in Video-Mediated Classes." Karen Andreasen and Palle Rasmussen focus on the context of higher education in a chapter that outlines some of the principles of online teaching and learning. This chapter presents a combined approach to studying and developing classroom activity and video-mediated exchanges. Analysis of student behaviors is supported by Etienne Wenger's theory about learning. The impact on teaching and learning by the specifically situated design, distribution, proximity, etc. of educational classroom resources is also analyzed.

A chapter on "Game Construction Activity in Higher Education," by Hans Kyhlbäck provides a comparative analysis of student behavior related to two ICT contexts for game construction. Another outcome of students academic design work is artifacts for the players' amusement and joy: two separate but interrelated activities. Effects of the familiar contradiction between school-related grades, marking and examination, and becoming a professional game designer are discussed. Contextualized feedback influences positively the students' feelings of competence, craftsmanship, and professionalism. Expansive learning enables people to learn established knowledge and contribute to new game technology.

The next section is about "Education." Karin Johansson analyzes the planning, rehearsal, and delivery of music by a string quartet and two other constellations as perceived by the author through direct observation. She does so in a chapter called "Collaborative Music-Making and Artistic Agency." Also included is a comparison between instrumental music making and artistic agency. Aspects of subordination and independence combined with activity theoretical analytical tools, models, and concepts help clarify some of the built-in developmental contradictions of artistic music making in higher education. The chapter covers three explicitly presented and analyzed settings where musical practice is taught and learnt. Contradictions between traditional discipline of music making and deliberative artistic creativity are also analyzed.

In "Vocational Learning Mediated by Constructive Competition," Charlotte Jonasson outlines the effects of mediating artifacts in a vocational setting. What is the effect of the student's intentions and motivation for learning? Another interesting aspect is to learn about the developmental relations between the vocational students' urge to compete. Some competitive intentions are productive and others destructive. Timing of food preparation and services plus adequate choice of ingredients for cooking form zones of development for the vocational students. Furthermore, socio-material resources, values, quality of interaction, and social organization of work influence student behavior and performance.

Juanjuan Zhao has written a chapter on "Project-Based Instruction in Teaching Chinese as a Foreign Language." The chapter covers an outline of action research and cultural-historical activity theory among two groups of students at a US high school. The effect of traditional teacher-centered and PBI-influenced approaches to teaching and learning Chinese are described by means of student commitment, acquisition of cultural knowledge, and communicative skills. The findings suggest that contradictions appear between approaches to teaching and learning of sentence structure, character writing, and recognition.

Oleg Popov scrutinizes "Outdoor Science in Teacher Education" as a potentially useful activity. Application of tools, tasks, and measures to management of outdoor lessons combined with cultural historical activity theory help student teachers of Science and Mathematics Education reach curricular goals. Contextual influences, learning objects, and transferability of knowledge are relevant themes related to outdoor science. Results suggest that if properly managed, outdoor science education empowers prospective science teachers to learn to deploy a range of mediating artifacts.

Anna Linge analyzes "Creative Musical Practice in an Educational Context." Just like in Karin Andersson's chapter, creative tensions between musical conformity and creative musical performance are analyzed from a perspective of teaching and learning. The author introduces Vygotskian concepts of association and dissociation functioning as mental tools for creative music making. Here, the concept of *perezhivanie* is used for analyzing and explaining tensions between formal education and freedom of artistic expression as defined by individual problem solving.

In the third section, the authors outline cultural-historical activity theory relative to "Work Practices." Under the title "Micro-Analysis of Concepts for Developing Networking in Social Work," Laura Seppänen and Laure Kloetzer present an emotionally laden theme exploring the practical design and effect of a using the hybrid concept of *worry* as a psychological tool for facilitating negotiation and problem solving in meetings between therapists and divorced families. Professional concepts serve as functional or even cross-functional mediations for improved cross-functional collaboration. The concept of *worry* seemed to trigger the professionals' attempts to make sense of different contexts. Ambiguity, combined with a formal visual exercise, contributed to the professionals' abilities to elaborate their professional perspectives.

In a chapter on work practices Päivi Ristimäki investigates the interplay between technology-push and demand-pull in a Finnish firm. The purpose of the longitudinal study, here labeled "Explorative Actions in Search of a New Logic of Business Activity," is to describe influences of reorientation of the main activity and adaptation to a changing market. Therefore, the firm takes explorative action in their relation to potential customers. Understanding exploration and exploitation of products and relations for forming and implementing new business logic become the focused activity of research. Dialectic contradictions between sales of a technological product and expertise is another focus of the research.

In "Networking around Supervisors in an Industrial Cooperation," Riikka Ruotsala deploys analytical concepts like double stimulation, mediating artifact and agented action in a systemic analysis and explanation of client understandings of workplace support and supervision. The project covers the employees' problem statements, explanation modes, and solution ideas coupled with data collection generated by a developmental intervention. Emphasis is on methodology and the project strategy is to start off by introducing abstract theory and move to concrete practice. Another methodological choice is to distinguish between ontology relative to metaphysics of properties, metaphysics of relations, and dialectics.

Hanna Toiviainen reports on development in an international business environment defined as a global workplace. The title of the chapter is "Interventions for Learning at Global Workplaces." The author analyzes meetings between Asian-Chinese and European-Finnish cultures and describes how different cultures pose challenges and offer solutions for employees who are supposed to collaborate in order to meet market demands for productivity and well-being.

The next section is called "Methodology" and one chapter is about "Subject Matter Analysis in Physical Education." Carolina Piccetti-Nascimento provides an analysis of educational concepts, clarifying their practical meaning and outlining relations between bodily movement and communication. Subject matter analysis of physical education (Dance and Game) help clarify to teachers, student teachers, and teacher educators how abstract thinking and concrete practices potentially enhance the quality of teaching and learning. A cultural historical perspective on physical training supported by concepts of *essence, movement from abstract to the concrete, historical analysis,* and *theoretical concepts* lies at the heart of the study.

Another chapter is titled "Modeling and Analyzing Contextual Influences." Thomas Hansson focuses on traditional methodology for collecting data plus analysis of situated influences on people's behaviors, more specifically on behaviors that appear during interviews between students of Pedagogy and missionaries working in the Nordic countries. Complementary data consists of discourses between missionaries interviewing citizens for religious purposes. Results suggest that the respondents' answers relate to the data collecting context rather than to the agreed topic of the interview (e.g. workplace learning, saving people, or values).

M. Nilsson, B. Ferholt, A. Jansson, and K. Alnervik investigate the impact of Vygotskian creativity on exploratory learning during Kindergarten play and imagination in a chapter called "Creativity in Education: Play and Exploratory Learning." The contents of the chapter cover the findings of three school projects. The authors' approach builds on a combination between cultural-historical activity theory and post-modern writings. A formative intervention into the children's play worlds by researchers and teachers together shows—in one project—that imagination and realistic thinking are related processes.

In a chapter called "Acculturation Processes and Expatriate Behavior," Laurie Watts and Beata Gullberg outline European ex-patriots' acculturation processes as they adapt to their employers' workplace cultures during the first years of their employment abroad. Some of the findings clarify the academic functionality of a mixed methods approach and also clarification of the interviewees' practical everyday experiences of food and language.

Inger Eriksson's focus in a chapter called "Constitution of Objects in DWR Activity" is on developmental methodology in general and on constitution of objects in particular. The described context consists of interventionist research displayed as three case studies into teaching and learning of mathematics involving cooperation (planning, management, and evaluation) between class teachers and researchers.

The last section is on "Philosophy of Activity Theory." Leena Kakkori and Rauno Huttunen introduce the concept of hermeneutic zone of proximal development, suggesting an affiliation between philosophical "giants" that helps explain moral development in man. In a chapter describing "Vygotsky, Heidegger, and Gadamer on Moral Development," they say language is something other than a vehicle for communication. Intertwined relations between thought and language are in constant movement back and forth in a dialogical process. Relations between language and thought go from external speech to thinking and from thinking to external speech. Human morality oscillating between an individual internal world and a public external world is a process of play-acting or a happening of truth. The authors' concept of hermeneutic zone of proximal development builds on Vygotsky's theoy of ZPD, origins of thought and language, and Heidegger's theories.

Lars Bang offers a line of reasoning called "Mapping [Capital v.2.0]: An Encounter of Thoughts." The chapter is an attempt at revealing stunted as well as normal games going on between people. In doing so, the author vivisects and reveals inner causality and logic related to late capitalism in contemporary society. The author's ultimate purpose is to integrate *capital* into psychology and activity theory. A map of *capital* defines a series of events as a *stunted game* of locked structures and rigid causalities.

Regi Theodor Enerstvedt provides an account of past and current theorizing of the "contents" of theory of activity in a chapter called "Reflections on the Theory of Activity." The author scrutinizes the historical background of the concept, definitions, spread, and usefulness for critical psychology, plus implications for productive practices. People hold opinions, present arguments, and draw conclusions about the underlying theory and choice of method for making the concept of activity operational to research.

In conclusion, the impact of general activity theory on the field of organizational development is substantial because of the limited resources for human and material growth offered by mass media, globalization, and information technology. Much too often, current ICT interfaces, designs, and communications build on rigid structures, limiting modes of expression and futile exchanges. Contrary to designs for conservative-superficial cooperation, general activity theory is an operational method for open-ended intervention, as well as for in-depth analysis of human practices. This is where the power of the approach lies, regardless if labeled Vygotskian School, activity theory, general activity theory, cultural-historical activity theory, developmental work research, theory of activity, research on activity, development and learning, or other.

Thomas Hansson
Blekinge Institute of Technology, School of Management, Sweden

Introduction

Expansion is the result of a transition process from actions currently performed by individuals to a new collective activity. A transition from action to activity is considered expansive when it involves the objective transformation of the actions themselves and when subjects become aware of the contradictions in their current activity in the perspective of a new form of activity. In this sense, learning by expanding can be defined as a "thoughtfully mastered learning activity." (Engeström, 1987, p. 210)

I'd like to think that the contents of this book combine soft relational and hard theoretical arguments, qualities and results, all of which characterize aspects of activity theory. Proponents of soft-relational designs like Engeström (1987) focus on individual aspects of activity theory whereas advocates of the hard-theoretical camp like Stetsenko (2005) emphasize the systemic aspects of activity theory. Some questions linger on: What does activity theory contribute to contemporary understanding of development? How do aspects and understandings of activity theory, developmental psychology, action research and anthropology combine? What would be the relations between theory and methodology?

The research community responds to such questions by including contexts, social practices and activity to an overall scheme. Some narrowly defined foci form legitimate responses to Engeström's (2009, p. 303) bold prognosis of the future of activity theory, suggesting application of

formative intervention and virtual change laboratory as a developmental methodology. Engeström's direction of study potentially clarifies mechanisms of productive work, health, communication and attitudes with a more attractive focus than does Bedny and Harris' (2005, p.145) criticism of activity theorists who allegedly fail to use "appropriate analytical principles or methods." From a similar negative focus of research, Hodkinsson, Biesta and James (2008, p. 137-ff) discard of activity theorists' understanding of a "cultural theory of learning."

Personal experience, shared knowledge and empirical-constructivist approaches to reality suggest people choose several lines of research. A common denominator for several kinds of "ethnographical studies and research" so far is that proponents of e.g. action research and activity theory study people operating in/on social systems. However, any definition of social science research takes as starting point a specific ontological and epistemological view of man, people, mankind, humanity etc. Also, it is an acknowledged contention that mental functions of thought, communication and learning relate to cultural, social, and historical operations based on a rather firm epistemological commitment. At the end of the day, natural language, individual learning and cultural development form sustainable influences on material and spiritual progress.

More specifically still, communicative acts carry with them a textual structure, suggesting "natural contradiction" to appear between language and action. A specific linguistic pattern – for example shaped as an utterance in a book on activity theory – inspires behavior in collectively produced social activities among the authors, editor and readers. Put differently, awareness of what it means to become human starts off as a social quality. It is picked up by attention and interaction with the Other, eventually generating subjective awareness of Self and a civilized personality. One consequence of such transformative phenomenological operations is that developmental human activities are conscious, goal directed and co-operative. But it is a futile ambition to separate between social science theory and developmental practices, be it by ethnography, action research, learning organization, change laboratory or other. After all, successful outcomes of research presuppose awareness of the workings of a pedagogical process in which balancing of researcher-subject and practitioner-co-subject generates meaning and truth for others to modify, adopt or discard of. In assessing the quality of such research there is a need to consider pedagogical aspects of R&D in terms of deployed means, motivations and objectives of human behavior.

Initially research for developing activity theory was about the psychology of learning. Then ensued transition of knowledge that emerged from studies in laboratories and moving to educational settings in families, at school in society and at workplaces. Focus shifted from teacher behavior to people and organizations carrying out professional work. Today there is continuity of interest in adaptations of activity theory to information technology (ICT).

The content of this book covers developmental approaches to researching and practicing activity theory. Most practitioners and researchers agree that the totality of life experiences define who we are, awareness of how to perceive of the world and the forming of personality traits. Such a perspective covers cultural, psychological, pedagogical, historical and ecological approaches to thinking, behavior and development. A classical divide between singular subjective and structural-collective influences is another defining theme of the book. For the above applies that relations suited to explaining contemporary and past behavior appear between dialectical pairs like agency and instrumentation, like internalization and appropriation, like creativity and convention and like language and intention.

Activity theory and interdisciplinary research has turned out a productive combination solidly positioned between theoretical consideration and applied methodology. The empirical and conceptual sections, chapters and specific choices made by the authors' the book reflect their application and use of analytical tools, logic of inquiry, thorough argumentation and methodological awareness. The content draws on primary research and empirical data distributed between ICT, Education, Work practice, Methodology, and Philosophy. This rather wide rationale of structured contents covers levels of activity theoretical complexity combined with specific themes, providing a spectrum of basic-elementary and state of the art approaches. The theoretically sound and practically applicable contents illustrate descriptive projects and in-depth analyses of people, settings and activities. Furthermore, the contents cover conceptual studies, theoretical development and appropriation of artifacts.

Some authors discuss the value of present day socio-cultural practices. Others develop concepts and practices by proposing new solutions. There are chapters portraying rarely studied areas of human behavior as an impetus to socio-cultural development. Descriptions of mind and action (Wertsch, 1991, 1998) range over contexts where you are likely to find ICT, education and work. Some authors describe research that unfolds over past, present and future activities. Other chapters contain methodologically sound research in which the authors deploy cultural tools and describe trajectories of individual learning and cultural development. The book provides authoritative background information for deciding on alternative roads of research that enable for creativity, applicability, rigor and motivation.

INFORMATION AND COMMUNICATION TECHNOLOGY (ICT)

Amazingly, most of the scholars committed to either cultural-historical psychology or activity theory do not deal with digitalization. Or at least they underestimate its revolutionary quality and so fail to prove their concepts and methodology. [...] To me, these facts give reasons to ask: Can those automatically and independently functioning technical systems still be called activities or activity systems? (Rückheim, 2009, pp. 88, 91)

Currently, there is a global need for innovation, change, variety and sustainability in ICT. Market oriented phenomena seem to challenge accompanying stabilizing routines for delivering goods and services. One consequence of the battle between stability and change is that as new phenomena see the light of day people adopt new ways of working. Engeström (2010, p. 199 ff.) characterizes new forms of working as "fluid organizations." So ways of acting, thinking and reflecting will emerge. For working life procedures the outcome of the battle between change and stability make up for a major part of current employees' work contents, output and satisfaction.

There are a number of phenomena to study in an emerging world of ICT, e.g. social media, availability of information and netiquette. Rasmussen & Ludvigsen (2009) opt for studies of educational reform. Authors like Barab, et al. (2010) portray videogames and videogame playing as phenomena suited to activity theory inspired analyses. One way of classifying videogaming activity is to establish the use, meaning and effect of affordances "hidden" in rewarding interactions which tend to appear during game-playing. In several of those games the players engage in

transactions and take on a variety of roles. They act as author (source inspiring action), as performer (causing consequences) and as audience (object of reflection). From a research point of view authors define game-playing as dramatic narrative, because game-playing experiences unveil the players' values, ideological contradictions and moral thinking. At other times we define videogames as curricular drama e.g. if used for educational purposes. Based on such considerations Barab, et al. (2010) model and study ICT-environments aiming at integration of moral dimensions with analytical activity on theoretical concepts. They describe game playing in terms of a social community with a shared purpose (objective) in mind. The agents' (subject) of their study initially form one direction of work; another direction covers legitimacy of the content (object); a third direction contains manipulation of the context (developmental change) that ultimately affects the players' objectives, experiences and actions.

In another study which lies outside a tradition of mainstream activity theory Friesen (2009) focuses on the players' cognitions as analyzed and understood by oral-written-verbal rather than gaming operations, acts, interactions and exchanges. Contingent social and discursive ICT-activity defined as transformation by means of natural language is a relevant focus of study at least if compared to old school man-machine (HCI) interactions. Similar to game-playing approaches to activity theory, conversations and discursive practices in social media qualify as worthy of research. Friesen's (2009) activity theoretical approach builds on an objective to apply discursive psychology to his analyses. One conclusion of such studies is that the chosen medium constrains the quality or rather exchange value of Web-based interactions simply because they are limited by the digital design. Suchman (2007) says virtual interactions are asymmetrical with low exchange value because of the flexibility of the system and the agent's lack of responsibility to safeguard against ethical controversies. And also, the quality of interactions are decided by the actual culture which the player/ student brings into the exchanges. The conclusion is that socio-cultural objectives, circumstances and activities verify to the importance of applying an activity theoretical perspective on ICT-related phenomena.

Nardi (2007) suggests collaboration, transformation and learning in "placeless" organizations as a productive ICT theme to study. The argument for focusing on context rather than collectively shared activity as the object of study is that people organize and behave differently in real life exchanges than they do in virtual worlds. For example, they transform practices differently by means of ICT than they do in real life situations. According to Nardi (2007, p. 5) a problem related to current activity theory approaches to ICT is that "the cultural-historical dimensions of activity have been under-theorized [...] much less elaborated than the formal principles." According to Nardi, activity theory viewed from a cultural-historical perspective on ICT should study, describe and explain social change, co-construction and instantiation of ways of managing virtual activities plus attaining objects by means of individual action. In the best of worlds placeless ICT-driven organizations become fluent contexts – or fluid organizations – which reinforce social transformation. Such organizations, interfaces and activities support collaborative learning.

EDUCATION

I am for practicing psychologists, for practical work, and so in the broad sense for boldness and the advance of our branch of science into life. L.S. Vygotsky (Quote in Leontev & Luria, 1968, p. 367)

Several epistemological and philosophical assumptions apply for general activity theory. One assumption relative to education, instruction and teaching and learning suggests that cognitive development equals acquiring of cultural tradi-

tions, behavior and ways of thinking. Another assumption related to teaching and learning is that human psyche and the material world exist prior to the birth of human beings as an empirically given cultural-historical quality. Third, language and relations between subject and object mediate higher mental functions. Four, the functional use of language presupposes an agreed set of socially agreed conventions. Five, the power of collective activity brings forward behavior in individual subjects which eventually manifest as social institutions by internalization of contemporary culture.

A line of theoretical development related to educational practices begins with Vygotsky, suggesting Zone of Proximal Development as a basic concept for understanding teaching and learning plus development of higher mental functions. Shayer (2003) supplies a rare example of negative criticism against Vygotskian theory. Then there are relations between learning and development to follow by arguments on mediation, construction/evolution and use of artifacts. Finally there is application of concepts, signs and psychological instruments. Several activity theory proponents take on board narrowly defined foci on human development and behavior. For example, Leontev introduces activity, needs and motive plus a model for structuring the concepts. Davydov analyzes motives of learning in exploration of theoretical relations saying successfully completed tasks reinforce learning and motivation. Engeström picks up on definitions of activity, characterizing concepts as generators of emerging contexts, implying that e.g. school management, teachers and students actually construct a shared context.

Classrooms are laboratory-like contexts offer conditions for intervention, analysis and change of pedagogical practices and learning outcomes. Also, there are ethical, normative and value-laden aspects of cultural-historical development, schooling and education (Cole 2010) to consider. Contemporary formal education offers identifiable objectives and activities of teaching and learning. Studies into educational practices enables for understanding of activities like therapy, evaluation, grading and examination. Regardless of objective, subject, curriculum, culture or nationality, educational research benefits from studies of classroom behavior among students and teachers. Action research practices and general activity theory shaped as Change Laboratory, Clinic of Change, developmental work research (DWR) or Interactive Research (Svensson, Brulin & Ellström, 2002) benefit from studies in classroom settings, especially if deployed as a Vygotskian laboratory for evaluating the explanatory potential of zone of proximal development, socially constructed knowledge, individual support and scaffolding. By bringing motivation into analyses of education, Hedegaard (2012) provides a complementary view on educational practices. In her context, it matters little if we label context and research object as setting, scene, environment, stage, institution, organization or activity.

A child's life always involves participating in a concrete institutional practice realized by activities and interactions among multiple participants, in recurrent everyday settings; at the same time the child's activity in a concrete practice can be conceptualized from three different planes. (Hedegaard, 2012, p. 129)

Hedegaard's (2012) model includes a formal societal plane on historically evolving traditions, an institutional plane on conventional routines and a narrowly defined plane applicable for any institution. By focusing on educational practices Hedegaard's model of learning builds on key concepts like *activity* and *setting*, including societal influences, cultural tradition, contextualized (home, school, daycare) practices and individual motives.

Rose (2012) provides another example of activity theory applied to US-vocational education. This ethnographic study verifies to the flexibility of activity theory for dealing with types of written data plus analysis of educational practices and contexts. In order to illustrate the span of approaches to activity theory and education, Vandebocoeur

and Collie's (2013) activity theoretical perspective on education applies for social and emotional learning. For research purposes, the authors use concepts like *mediation, unity, unit of analysis, word meaning*. The specific focus of their article on *perezhivanie*, translates as "emotional experience."

These contemporary references have a clear focus on the abstract-theoretical side of learning and development. Based on direct experiences, however, every teacher, pedagogue, mentor, instructor, actor or master holds that education is a practical business. Their experiences imply that the teacher's plan has got to work, i.e. the students must accept the teacher's objectives, planning and performance – in the classroom. Vygotsky (1997) defines schooling contexts as situations for people to explore as accumulated and culturally shared knowledge. According to Vygotsky, schools provide curricula that link everyday verbal knowledge with the proper use of abstract concepts to support aspired deep learning. Furthermore, school contexts offer starting points for authentic problem solving and assessment of learning. Any educational design for studying education, teaching and learning, instruction etc. should contain an account of how-processes related to what-outcomes. Also, teachers act out the double roles of academic expert and social actor. In the lucky cases, the teachers' commitment brings cultural development for individual students and collective societies.

Yet another line of developmental work and research (DWR) in education focuses on adult learning, societal conditions and organizational development. Such initiatives offer a complementary approach to educational studies. The chronological continuity of practical-pedagogical work processes of teaching and learning in such "programs" consists of a mix of Senge's (1990) and Engeström's (1987) conceptualizations of learning organizations. The approach includes studies of collective object of activity and performance in teams. The authors' respective approach cover a comprehensive heap of systemic concepts and processes, conceptual models, leadership, systems thinking, shared visions, personal mastery, evaluation, documentation and publication.

This account of activity theory studies into education suggests a fragmented picture. In adhering to an activity theoretical paradigm in educational research the first day of a university course should cover learning by intervention, teamwork, development and change. Such an introduction includes several stages. They are presented as chronologically organized must-do operations. Valid teaching starts off with (a) the lecturer's introduction; (b) presentation of the pedagogical design, (c) clarification of course objectives, (d) delivery of a presentation of the participants. Before long, there is (e) analysis of what is meant by *activity* and *development*, (f) understanding of holistic thinking and scrutiny of Senge's (1990) disciplines for organizational learning. After lunch there is (g) a presentation of the course literature; (h) explanation of the significance of attitude, awareness, ability and skills for those who contribute to positive development plus (i) presentation of interplay between structure-system and person-profession. After coffee, there is work in teams aims on (j) learning prominent arguments in support of the team members' choice of organization, institution, activity or practice for further study. This is a crucial step because the students will have to pursue their learning object/object of activity for the rest of the term. There will be (k) lessons on Vygotsky, Leontiev, Luria, Davydov and Engeström, clarifying instrumentation, learning, systems thinking and germ cell modeling. The next day the students (l) present an attempt at activity theoretical analysis of their provisional/tentative project by circular and triangular models of development and analysis. At the end of the day the students (m) present the results of their work in learning teams including an account of purpose, objective, internal working procedures and planning of shared activity in the studied company, organization, industry, activity.

Further analysis of (n) the impact of personal ability is accompanied by (o) presentation of the circular model by historical analysis, present situation and construction of new instruments. The students report on (p) the steps they have taken for changing the studied activity. After lunch the students (q) continue work in teams, interpreting homework and asking who has been doing what. They (r) summarize progress in a big group meeting before ending the second day activities.

For the referred (a-r) course on reading-understanding and doing-performing in a developmental activity, there are theoretical and practical consequences to consider. First, there is opportunity for integration between traditional school work assignments like reading course literature, innovative interaction in learning teams plus individual initiative for change based on the needs and opportunities outside traditional educational practices. Find an example relating to the steps that students/team members adhere to as they form a necessary, crucial and proper problem statement. Social science studies of essay writing usually start off with a problem description. Before the learning teams define and solve their combined practical and theoretical problem, they benefit from the university teacher's instruction, guidance and support. Work begins with a mapping of all the practical problems they can possibly imagine. Then the teams decide on a particular problem. Included in their provisional problem statement are prospective solutions to solving natural contradictions. By discussing their choice of activity for further study and intervention, the learning teams delimit and/or reformulate the problem so they can conduct and benefit from an empirical study. They summarize, condense and document the result of their study. But before moving on with the chosen theme they adjust their problem statement. Drawing a time-schedule and a work plan plus preparing for note-taking and signing agreements finalize work in the teams on forming a functional problem statement.

Another example of practical team working among students (in higher education) covers steps for reaching conclusions. For drawing valid conclusions about a studied activity system, the learning teams follow consecutive steps on a ladder of sense-making. They learn to observe relevant data and share experiences; choose relevant data; interpret the data; make assumptions based on ascribed meaning; draw conclusions about the studied activity; form convictions about the world and act on their convictions. They must pass through these steps in their attempts at change and development of a studied activity.

WORK PRACTICE

Social capital is a collective good, not the private property of those who benefit from it. I take a sociocentric view that focuses on what makes communities work. In other words, I search for factors that enable collective actors to sustain themselves, to perform beyond routine expectations, and to reorganize themselves when needed. [...] I suggest that social capital is firmly rooted in and practically inseparable from certain types of tangible material structures and artifacts – including the materiality of human beings as bodily actors. (Engeström, 2008, p. 169)

Modern psychology used to be a Soviet-Russian discipline and workplace learning turned into a favoured Nordic theme. Find titles and disciplinary focus on development of workplace learning for twenty years (1979-1997) in Sweden: *Work* (history), *How do you feel at work* (psycho-social environment), *The workplace* (management), *Competence* (organizational development), *Work oriented design of computer artifacts* (system development), *The practical intellect* (computers and professions), *Learning at work* (applied psychology), *Man at work* (work environment), *Tacit Knowledge* (health care), *The Toolbox* (cultural perspectives on work).

Other lines of research on work practices respond to overarching questions like who is acting in an activity system (Engeström, 2009) and approaches for identifying impact of Self on/in activity systems (Stetsenko & Arievitch, 2004). There are examples related to the pursuit of evolving objects and even critical voices of of activity theory (Martin & Peim, 2009; Bakhurst, 2009). Another line of research relates to the fact that original activity theory first and foremost covers theory. In spite of this fact, contemporary researchers (Foot, 2002) translate activity theory as an empirical method for managing organizational development. Engeström (2009) provides a valid response to Martin & Peim's (2009, p. 131) criticism of "ambivalence over conceptualizations of agentic action" in research of informal learning.

This section of the book covers activity theory related to transformation of work practices, the birth and management of evolving activity systems and weighing of influences on communication, transformation, production and consumption of goods and services. In many examples of activity theory research and development researchers address notions of agency, structure and power operating in large-scale predominantly social rather than industrial structures. In arguing a case for organizational-institutional structures, activity theoretical research needs to draw a clear line between legitimate macro-social (sociology) and illegitimate political (politics) issues. Also status, power, personality plus antagonisms need to be separated from legitimate research on natural contradictions.

By the sheer "nature of things" people seem to assume that routines, products, activities and thinking evolve at a steady pace. This is a globally held contention of progress implying that regardless if spontaneous or planned interventions behaviors form a deviation from what Mother Nature intended about developmental activity. Blasphemy, violation of rules and risk-taking are some of the expressions we use for (dis)connected, (ab)normal and (in)frequent steps that people seem to take at a regular but infrequent basis. Our belief in and support of planned, slow, controlled and steady progress by means of stability rather than innovation is the reason why CHAT-approaches, action research, change laboratory, clinic of activity (Clot, 2009) – well, even problem based learning, consultancy, in-service and lifelong learning - appear as productive approaches to social science. This is true only if compared to hypothesis testing research on quantitative data and natural science traditions of using theory (for interpreting data).

Sudden and surprising deviation from a given norm rarely equals development. At times incremental transition from one stage to another seems to block positive development. The colloquial expression on how to understand and relate to change and development is "why fix it if it isn't broke?" In spite of such Platonic (Taleb, 2007) arguments, and contrary to a generally held contention that progress is slow and predictable, Vygotsky (2004, p. 10) suggests that in improving learning for children, the teacher "imagines, combines, alters and creates something new." Especially on change and understanding related to creativity among employees and researchers, Vygotsky (1994, p. 276) says: "For the first time the formation of concepts brings with it a release from the concrete situation and the likelihood of a creative reworking and transformation of its elements." One might add to the quote, serving as an instrument for sharing an understanding the interplay between theory and practice. Kurt Lewin allegedly described the positive double-bind situation meshed in individual learning processes saying there is nothing as rewarding to development of theory as a good practice and nothing more developmental to an existing practice than a sound theory. According to a contemporary author, Worthen (2008, p. 322) suggests there are generous contemporary contexts and activities for doing so: "a grocery warehouse, steel mill, cleaning company, federal office, an apartment building, public school, and musical instrument factory."

In studying development of work practices through past, current and future innovation, deviation from a norm and dynamic contradiction, there are theoretical and practical approaches to consider. Ellis (2011) mentions scientific concepts that characterize methods for improving theory as well as work practices: *informed-, formative-, developmental-, practice-theory-developing intervention, practitioner and participatory inquiry, reflective practice, activity development and learning plus double stimulation strategy*. Additional examples include on *the job training programs, labor education,* and *community of practice* (Wenger, 1998). On individual learning defined as change that influences ways of understanding collective development, Roth and Lee (2007) argue.

Learning occurs whenever a novel practice, artifact, tool or division of labor at the level of the individual or group within an activity system constitutes new possibilities for others (as resource, form of action to be emulated) leading to an increase in generalized action possibilities and therefore to collective (organizational, societal, cultural) learning. (p. 205)

For Lee and Roth (2008) systemic change and development is a dedicated area of research. So is research on relations between individually and collectively controlled plus culturally and historically evolving behaviors. There is change and development to study within specific here-and-now (space and place) activity systems and there are opportunities to study behavioral patterns in socio-cultural practices. During processes of change, patterns of behavior seem to appear in activity systems and in people. Old contingencies which used to influence and control organizational routines and human behavior seem to fade away with the establishment of research on new work patterns. Laclau (1990) comments on the functionality of behaviors in the operating of effective activity systems, concluding a proposition that contingent conditions of emerging patterns, solutions and behaviors decide how we identify, analyze and understand work practices.

METHODOLOGY

We could review all the opinions offered to explain why an open controversy closes, but we will always stumble on a new controversy dealing with how and why it closed. We will have to learn to live with two contradictory voices talking at once, one about science in the making and, the other about ready made science. The latter produces sentences like 'just do this … just do that … ' the former says 'enough is never enough'. The left side considers that facts and machines are well determined enough. The right side considers that facts and machines in the making are always **under-determined**. *(bold in original) Some little thing is always missing to close the black box once and for all. (Latour, 1987, p. 13)*

Any kind of social science research aims at improving social practices, be it by *Pedagogy of the City* (Freire, 1993), *Critical Education in the Information Age* (Castells, 1999), normative ethics *On Education* (Russell, 1969) or *Rethinking University Teaching* (Laurillard, 2002). One consequence of how academics or fire souls decide on the aim at improving disadvantaged people's life conditions is to help others realize the need for launching interventions into situated practices. Such interactive, democratic and liberating (deliberative) interventionist research is an optimal choice of method which calls for attention to researcher and practitioner goals, values and actions. Having identified the prerequisites for forming a proper methodology, the researcher adopts a balanced approach between argumentative advocacy on the practitioners' behalf and objective rigor for the benefit of the research community. If designed and carried out along those lines, activity theoretical research leads to development of theory just as application of a proper theory leads to design and implementation of socially productive and democratic practices.

Sannino, A., & Sutter, B. (2011) describe interventionist research and development as a coupling between activity theory and interventionist methodology. Others outline the difference between interventionist method and interventionist methodology. It is hard to describe how a practical research method for developing ongoing activity becomes a sound methodology just by labeling the approach cultural historical. If described like this it seems as if the problem were merely a case of contradiction of terms rather than a misunderstanding of the meaning of terms. A title like "Cultural-historical activity theory and interventionist method" might do the trick.

In spite of the risk of mixing up theoretical methodology with practical method, there is conceptual and methodological affinity between generation and interpretation of knowledge, societal development and interventionist research. Social science research, regardless of specific disciplines, lies close to studying and changing of societal practices. One extreme form of research method emanates from materialist cause-effect conceptions of science. Another extreme form of research method orients towards subjective-idealist description and understanding of human experience. Finally, there is a distinction to be made between method, methodology and epistemology. Depending on emphasis on theory, research or practice, the choice of field research methods influence the result. For example, proponents of activity theory say theory and practice form the core of conceptual and practical approaches to studying human behavior. They argue that theory and epistemology make up the constituents of activity theory. They also suggest that ethnography differs from activity theory because the latter contains argued and agreed relations (models, findings, concepts etc.) between theory and practice.

In conducting democratic and theoretically valid research there is a need to apply a proper methodology and adapt it to the objective of a planned study. Kaptelinin and Nardi (2006, p. 71-72) suggest activity theory research should start with a definition of the problem and then focus on selection of a suitable *method*. Finally, the researcher should design, manage and study "the formative experience which combines active participation with monitoring of the developmental changes of the study participants." As to the *methodology* of activity theory defined by problem-solving procedures, Leontev (1977) complements Kaptelinin and Nardi's (2006) stance, emphasizing the influence of the motive (of activity) and narrowing down on individual motivations:

Analysis first identified separate activities, according to the criterion of the difference in their motives. Then the action process obeying conscious goals are identified, and finally, the operations that immediately depend on the conditions for attainment of a specific goal. (p. 7).

There are limitations as to how far the choice of methodology assists the researcher's work. If the researcher's objective were to study historical data, the choice would be limited to hermeneutic method for analyzing textual information. If the researcher's objective were to study human practices there were acknowledged methodological options for analyzing field data. Varying degrees of interventionist methodologies characterize e.g. action research, cultural-historical activity theory and ethnography.

During field research on workplace learning there are levels of researcher involvement in the practitioners' activity. The researcher's actual choice of control depends on the researcher's need for balancing openness and secrecy about research. And it depends on the pre-set agenda for accomplishing change in the researched activity. The researcher's involvement, role-playing, control and commitment basically depend on setting, objective and activity. *Leader, organizer, fly on the*

wall, agitator and *family member* are some of the labels people use for describing levels of researcher involvement. Regardless of appropriateness of the labels the researcher must learn to separate development from change in the studied activity. Then the researcher should be aware of gradual, abrupt, hidden, planned or spontaneous changes, interpret them and finally control future change.

It is an old contention that social practices and academic disciplines constitute a fruitful avenue for exploring society and social science research. However, one might add, this contention holds true only if research is grounded on a theory that helps the researcher to seek the recurring laws, models, concepts and relations that form human behavior. In doing so, researchers draw on relevant inter-disciplinary ideas, models and concepts. A paradigmatic activity theoretical school of research must engage with societal practices. By connecting psychology with human practices a system for furthering research will see the light of day because engagement between theory and practice has a positive effect on social science methodology and epistemology.

PHILOSPHY OF ACTIVITY THEORY

We know more about isolated mental processes and skills, but we seem incapable of generating an overall picture of mental functioning. We can often find regularities under controlled laboratory conditions, but as soon as we move to other, more natural settings these findings seem to disappear in the sea of "real life." (Wertsch, 1991, p. 1)

A colleague of mine asked if general activity theory equals method or theory. I was unable to supply a coherent answer to the question there and then. After reflecting on the theme I realized that activity theory is a theory about human behavior. It is also a method suited for studying organizational development, human nature and life on earth. Finally, it is a methodology based on a comprehensive set of ontological and epistemological understandings.

Since the 80's there has been growth in application, adaption and explanation of activity theory. Three generations of researchers (Vygotsky, Leontev, and Engeström) have seen the light of day. Smagorinsky (2011) laid out the original foundations of early generation activity theory. Today, development of activity theory is at the crossroads, momentarily tipping towards organizational consultancy in one vein of action research (Somekh & Nissen, 2011; Wells 2011) in concord with information science, systemic thinking, (Orland-Barak & Becher, 2011) digital communication, ethnography or psycholinguistics (Leitsch, 2011). Other contemporary approaches to analyzing narrowly defined and locally situated developmental activities include objectification related to HIV/AIDS (Marková, 2012) and bio-engineering (Nersessian, 2012).

Understanding human motivation is key to understanding activity theory as theory, be it by choice of action or by effect of motive, or development by collective input to perform in or analyzing object of activity. Roth and Lee (2007, p. 201) say the Russian word which translates *activity* carries with it aspects of meaning like *work, job, function* and *doing*. Kaptelinin and Nardi (2006, p. 60) say the concept of activity specifically suggests "a unit of subject-object interaction defined by the subject's motive." Chaiklin (2011, p. 141) clarifies a distinction of the concept *activity* which refers to "institutionalized practices of human life." Another related meaning ascribed to activity refers to "purposeful human transformation of nature." All the above definitions of activity cover explanatory principles for human behavior.

The contents of this book reflect ongoing development of theory and practice as suggested by cultural-historical activity theory (CHAT). General activity theorists argue that emphasis of research should be on mediated action in socio-cultural contexts. Their use of a generic method for doing so includes both historical and cultural

levels of analysis. For any definition of activity applies that research is grounded in everyday events, situations and activities. Likewise, crucial-central-developmental trajectories of phenomena like activity, awareness and personality emerge in joint (learning and developmental) activity between people. Reality and mind comes out as a co-constructed pair of "facts" supported by individual agents. A wide view on how to define activity embraces the emergent nature of mind and behavior, acknowledging the role of an interpretative framework influenced by transdisciplinary psychology, pedagogy, philosophy and sociology.

Concepts like awareness, action, agency, appropriation, object, objective, double stimulation and zone of proximal development relate to chapters directed towards the study of activity (systems), including concepts like artifact, tool and instrument plus multi-voicedness, contradictions and expansive cycles of work. Cole (1996) outlines a narrow analytical focus on the expansive meaning of artifact. His example is an indication of the depth and width of activity theory:

An artifact is an aspect of the material world that has been modified over the history of its incorporation in goal-directed human action. By virtue of the changes wrought in the process of their creation and use, artifacts are simultaneously ideal (conceptual) and material. (p. 117)

Co-ordinate evolution of activity, agency, mind and similar concepts has resulted in growth of studies covering individual achievement, shared activity, communication and societal development. The language we speak and the artifacts we use serve personal and shared purposes, they become tools and symbols for the development mind. Artifacts direct our inner attention and outer actions, supporting individual construction of "alternative worlds." The social worlds we produce, adapt to and participate in influence individual mind as we communicate, argue and persuade others. So do the social practices that past generations initiated and managed for our benefit.

A socio-cultural/cultural-historical approach to studying activity and mind suggests a paralell focus on the interrelatedness between individual and societal development. Social practices lead the way to continuous understanding of what it means to be human and to take action in collective activity. Provided we make room for addressing objects, qualities, people and objectives people continuously change. We also change the activities that we form and we are.

Thomas Hansson
Blekinge Institute of Technology, School of
Management (MAM), Sweden

REFERENCES

Bakhurst, D. (2009). Reflection on activity theory. *Educational Review, 61*(2), 197–210. doi:10.1080/00131910902846916

Barab, S., Dodge, T., Ingram-Goble, A., Pettyjohn, P., Peppler, K., Volk, C., & Solomou, M. (2010). Pedagogical dramas and transformational play: Narratively rich games for learning. *Mind, Culture, and Activity, 17*(3), 235–264. doi:10.1080/10749030903437228

Bedny, G. Z., & Harris, S. (2005). The systemic-structural theory of activity: Applications to the study of human work. *Mind, Culture, and Activity, 12*(2), 128–147. doi:10.1207/s15327884mca1202_4

Castells, M. (Ed.). (1999). *Critical education in the new information age.* Lanham, MD: Rowman & Littlefield Publishers Inc.

Chaiklin, S. (2011). Social scientific research and societal practice: Action research and cultural-historical research in methodological light from Kurt Lewin and Lev S. Vygotsky. *Mind, Culture, and Activity, 18*(2), 129–147. doi:10.1080/10749039.2010.513752

Clot, Y. (2009). Clinic of activity: The dialogue as instrument. In A. Sannino, H. Daniels, & K. Gutierrez (Eds.), *Learning and expanding with activity theory* (pp. 286–302). Cambridge, UK: Cambridge University Press. doi:10.1017/CBO9780511809989.019

Cole, M. (1996). *Cultural psychology: A once and future discipline.* London: The Belknap Press of Harvard University Press.

Cole, M. (2010). What's culture got to do with it? Educational research as a necessarily interdisciplinary enterprise. *Educational Researcher, 39*(6), 461–470. doi:10.3102/0013189X10380247

Ellis, V. (2011). Reenergising professional creativity from a CHAT perspective: Seeing knowledge and history in perspective. *Mind, Culture, and Activity, 18*(2), 181–193. doi:10.1080/10749039.2010.493595

Engeström, R. (2009b). Who is acting in an activity system? In A. Sannino, H. Daniels, & K. Gutierrez (Eds.), *Learning and expanding with activity theory.* Cambridge, UK: Cambridge University Press. doi:10.1017/CBO9780511809989.017

Engeström, Y. (1987). *Learning by expanding: An activity-theoretical approach to developmental research.* Helsinki: Orienta-Consultit.

Engeström, Y. (2008). *From teams to knots: Activity-theoretical studies of collaboration and learning at work.* Cambridge, UK: Cambridge University Press. doi:10.1017/CBO9780511619847

Engeström, Y. (2009a). The future of activity theory: a rough draft. In A. Sannino, H. Daniels, & K. Gutierrez (Eds.), *Learning and expanding with activity theory*. Cambridge, UK: Cambridge University Press. doi:10.1017/CBO9780511809989.020

Engeström, Y. (2010). *From teams to knots: Activity theoretical studies of collaboration and learning at work*. Cambridge, UK: Cambridge University Press.

Foot, K. (2002). Pursuing an evolving object: A case study in object formation and identification. *Mind, Culture, and Activity, 9*(2), 132–149. doi:10.1207/S15327884MCA0902_04

Freire, P. (1993). *Pedagogy of the city*. New York: Continuum.

Friesen, N. (2009). Discursive psychology and educational technology: Beyond the cognitive revolution. *Mind, Culture, and Activity, 16*(2), 130–144. doi:10.1080/10749030802707861

Hedegaard, M. (2012). Analyzing children's learning and development in everyday settings from a cultural-historical wholeness approach. *Mind, Culture, and Activity, 19*(2), 127–138. doi:10.1080/10749039.2012.665560

Hodkinsson, P., Biesta, G., & James, D. (2008). Understanding learning culturally: Overcoming the dualism between social and individual views of learning. *Vocations and Learning, 1*(1), 27–47. doi:10.1007/s12186-007-9001-y

Kaptelinin, V., & Nardi, B. (2006). *Acting with technology: Activity theory and interaction design*. Cambridge, MA: MIT Press.

Laclau, E. (1990). *New reflections on the revolution of our time*. London: Verso.

Latour, B. (1987). *Science in action*. Cambridge, MA: Harvard University Press.

Laurillard, D. (2002). *Rethinking university teaching. London*. Falmer: Routledge. doi:10.4324/9780203304846

Lee, Y.-J., & Roth, W.-M. (2008). How activity systems evolve: Making saving salmon in British Columbia. *Mind, Culture, and Activity, 15*(4), 296–321. doi:10.1080/10749030802391211

Leitsch, D. (2011). Vygotsky, consciousness, and the German psycholinguistic tradition. *Mind, Culture, and Activity, 18*(4), 305–318. doi:10.1080/10749031003713815

Leontev, A. (1977). Activity and consciousness. Moscow: Progress Publishers; Retrieved from http://www.marxists.org/archive/leontev/works/1977/leon1977.htm

Leontev, A. N., & Luria, A. R. (1968). The psychological ideas of L. S. Vygotsky. In B. B. Wolman (Ed.), *The historical roots of contemporary psychology* (pp. 338–367). New York: Harper & Row.

Marková, I. (2012). Objectification in common sense thinking. *Mind, Culture, and Activity, 19*(3), 207–221. doi:10.1080/10749039.2012.688178

Martin, D., & Peim, N. (2009). Critical perspectives on activity theory. *Educational Review, 61*(2), 131–138. doi:10.1080/00131910902844689

Nardi, B. (2007). Placeless organizations: Collaborating for transformation. *Mind, Culture, and Activity, 14*(1-2), 5–22. doi:10.1080/10749030701307663

Nersessian, N. (2012). Engineering concepts: The interplay between concept formation and modeling practices in bioengineering sciences. *Mind, Culture, and Activity, 19*(3), 222–239. doi:10.1080/10749039.2012.688232

Orland-Barak, L., & Becher, A. (2011). Cycles of action through systems of activity: Examining an action research model through the lens of activity theory. *Mind, Culture, and Activity, 18*(2), 115–128. doi:10.1080/10749039.2010.484099

Rasmussen, I., & Ludvigsen, S. (2009). The hedgehog and the fox: A discussion of the approaches to the analysis of ICT reforms in teacher education of Larry Cuban and Yrjö Engeström. *Mind, Culture, and Education, 16*(1), 83–104. doi:10.1080/10749030802477390

Rose, M. (2012). Rethinking remedial education and the academic-vocational divide. *Mind, Culture, and Activity, 19*(1), 1–16. doi:10.1080/10749039.2011.632053

Roth, M.-W., & Lee, Y.-J. (2007). Vygotsky's neglected leagcy: Cultural-historical activity theory. *Review of Educational Research, 2*(2), 186–232. doi:10.3102/0034654306298273

Rückheim, G. (2009). Digital technology and mediation: A challenge to activity theory. In A. Sannino, H. Daniels, & K. Guiterrez (Eds.), *Learning and expanding with activity theory* (pp. 88–111). Cambridge, UK: Cambridge University Press.

Russell, B. (1969). *On education.* London: Unwin Books.

Sannino, A., & Sutter, B. (2011). Cultural-historical activity theory and interventionist methodology: Classical legacy and contemporary developments. *Theory & Psychology, 21*(5), 557–570. doi:10.1177/0959354311414969

Senge, P. (1990). *The fifth discipline: The art and practice of the learning organization.* New York: Doubleday.

Shayer, M. (2003). Not just Piaget, not just Vygotsky, and certainly not Vygotsky as alternative to Piaget. *Learning and Instruction, 13*(5), 465–485. doi:10.1016/S0959-4752(03)00092-6

Smagorinsky, P. (2011). Vygotsky's stage theory: The psychology of art and the actor under the direction of perezhivanie. *Mind, Culture, and Activity, 18*(4), 319–341. doi:10.1080/1074903 9.2010.518300

Somekh, B., & Nissen, M. (2011). Cultural-historical activity theory and action research. *Mind, Culture, and Activity, 18*(2), 93–97. doi:1 0.1080/10749039.2010.523102

Stetsenko, A. (2005). Avtivity as object-related: Resolving the dichotomy of individual and collective planes of activity. *Mind, Culture, and Activity, 12*(1), 70–88. doi:10.1207/s15327884mca1201_6

Stetsenko, A., & Arievitch, I. (2004). The self in cultural-historical activity theory: Reclaiming the unity of social and individual dimensions of human development. *Theory & Psychology, 14*(4), 475–503. doi:10.1177/0959354304044921

Suchman, L. (2007). *Human-machine reconfigurations: Plans and situated actions.* Cambridge, UK: Cambridge University Press.

Svensson, L., Brulin, G., & Ellström, P.-E. (2002). Interaktiv forskning - För utveckling av teori och praktik. [Interactive research – Development of theory and practice]. (Ö Widegren, Ed.). Media-Tryck. Arbetsliv i omvandling.

Taleb, N. N. (2007). *The black swan: The impact of the highly improbable.* New York: Random House Publishing Group.

Vandebocoeur, J., & Collie, R. (2013). Locating social and emotional learning in schooled environments: A Vygotskian perspective on learning as unified. *Mind, Culture, and Activity, 20*(3), 201–225. doi:10.1080/10749039.2012.755205

Vygotsky, L. (1994). Imagination and the creativity of the adolescent. In R. van der Veer & J. Valsiner (Eds.), *The Vygotsky reader* (pp. 266–288). Oxford, UK: Blackwell.

Vygotsky, L. (1997). *Educational psychology.* Boca Raton, FL: St. Lucie Press.

Vygotsky, L. (2004). Imagination and creativity in childhood. *Journal of Russian & East European Psychology, 42*, 7–97.

Wells, G. (2011). Integrating CHAT and action research. *Mind, Culture, and Activity*, *18*(2), 161–180. doi:10.1080/10749039.2010.493594

Wenger, E. (1998). *Communities of practice: Learning, meaning, and identity*. Cambridge, UK: Cambridge University Press. doi:10.1017/CBO9780511803932

Wertsch, J. (1991). *Voices of the mind: A sociocultural approach to mediated action*. London: Harvester Wheatsheaf.

Wertsch, J. (1998). *Mind as action*. New York: Oxford University Press.

Worthen, H. (2008). Using activity theory to understand how people learn to negotiate the conditions of work. *Mind, Culture, and Activity*, *15*(4), 322–338. doi:10.1080/10749030802391385

Section 1
Information and Communication Technology

Chapter 1
Responsive Practices in Online Teacher Education

Thurídur Jóhannsdóttir
University of Iceland, Iceland

ABSTRACT

The chapter describes research on the development of teaching and learning in a distance teacher education programme in Iceland. The focus is on challenges that school-based student teachers faced in learning to become online students and the way in which their experience of teaching in schools contributed to the development of teaching and learning in the programme. Cultural-historical activity theory was used for analysing the development of individuals and activity systems as a dialectical process. The expansive learning theory directed the contradiction analysis to reveal tensions and challenges in the development of practice within the programme, as well as future developmental possibilities. Data includes interviews with school-based student teachers and observation of face-to-face sessions, as well as transcriptions of online courses. Results indicate that a combination of non-traditional student groups and new online tools called for changed practice in teacher education and that a new model of teaching and learning is emerging. In order to develop this model, schools and the teacher education faculty need to look at the education of student teachers as a shared responsibility and negotiate acceptable arrangements for the institutions involved.

INTRODUCTION

Teacher education for compulsory teachers was launched in a distance programme at the Iceland University of Education (IUE) in 1993. During the early years most student teachers held positions as uncertified teachers in rural districts where there was a shortage of certified teachers (Jónasson, 1996; 2001). This research was conducted some ten years after the programme´s inception when admission to the programme had been opened to all students who preferred the online distance model rather than the conventional campus based model. However, school-based student teachers still represented a substantial part of the student group and the study focused on them. Special attention was given to how they could draw on their experience as school teachers when participating in the programme as student teachers and the

DOI: 10.4018/978-1-4666-6603-0.ch001

way in which they contributed to development of teaching and learning within the programme.

In the middle of the first decade of the twenty first century distance students constituted up to half the number of students enrolled in the programme. Despite these notable changes in the student population there was little discussion on the implications these changes had for the teacher education, such as changes in curriculum or development of teaching and learning as well as development of the programme at a system level. The aim of the chapter is to provide an insight into learning and teaching in the programme, and how the practices developed.

- How do school-based student teachers learn to participate and function in the distance programme and how does it relate to development of teaching and learning in the programme?
- How is the development of the distance programme interrelated with distance student teachers' development as learners?
- What is the zone of proximal development for the distance teacher education programme?

DISTANCE TEACHER EDUCATION IN ICELAND

Lack of qualified teachers is a problem and alternative routes such as distance education have been explored to bring different populations into teacher education programmes, e.g. women in sparsely populated regions (Schwille & Dembélé, 2007). School-based student teachers have been given access to certification programmes where there is a shortage of qualified teachers and schools employ teachers without certification. This was the reason for the inception of distance teacher education in Iceland in 1993 when the Iceland University College of Education launched a full B.Ed. teacher education distance programme.

At the beginning the setup assumed that student teachers would gather on campus in Reykjavík several weeks a year during school holidays while the distance learning sessions consisted of self-study with support from lecturers via the Internet, mainly through text based email communication. Ten years after launching the distance programme the university had placed an increasing emphasis on the compatibility of online and on-campus programmes. Regardless if taken at a distance or conventionally on campus, the programme was offered to all applicants irrespective of residence. In 2004, however the percentage of distance students living in rural districts was 57 percent (Kennaraháskóli Íslands, 2005) and a survey from that year shows that 42 percent of distance student teachers were employed as teachers in schools (Björnsdóttir, 2009). Despite the altered admission guidelines, the programme still served rural communities and met the need for uncertified teachers to gain a professional degree.

During the years of fieldwork for this study in 2003-2006 it was assumed that it would take four years to finish the teacher education degree in the distance programme compared to three years in the conventional programme. However students often took longer to finish. In general each semester (fall August-December and spring January-May) included two one-week face-to-face sessions on campus, one at the start and another in the middle of the semester. The final exams could be taken on campus in Reykjavík as well as in schools and adult educational centres in the countryside. Distance student teachers were supposed to follow the same route as conventional on-campus students in practice teaching. They did three weeks in the first year, four weeks in the second year and five weeks in the third year. Rules on practice teaching expected school-based student teachers, in general, to do practice teaching in a different school than in the one in which they taught. However, exceptions were quite common and rules adapted to personal needs, such as family situations. With developments in information and communication technology online tools for use in distance education had become essential parts of the programme. The course management system in most distance courses at IUE in 2003-2006 was *WebCT*. However, lecturers could use other means for online communication. Free online tools such as text chat for instant messaging became available for internal student communication. Some teacher educators started to use audio files to deliver lectures.

THEORETICAL FRAMEWORK

Cultural-historical activity theory developed on the foundation of the theories of Vygotsky (1978) and Leontiev (1978) presuming that all phenomena should be studied as processes in motion driven forward by contradictions inherent in the unit being investigated (Blunden, 1997; Ilyenkov, 1977). The theory is appropriate for studying development and learning processes with an aim to investigate possibilities for the development of practice. The dialectical relationship of individuals and the activity in which they participate is central for investigating developmental processes, focusing attention on the way in which individuals use their agency to make sense of their participation in activities and in turn contribute to development. As an interpreter of the school of cultural-historical activity theory, Engeström (1987) put forward the expansive learning theory for application in research on collective learning and development of activity systems.

Expansive learning refers to processes in which an activity system, for example a work organization, resolves its pressing internal contradictions by constructing and implementing a qualitatively new way of functioning for itself (Engeström, 2007, p. 24).

Activity systems are constantly dealing with outside societal influences that have to be appropri-

ated and modified to internal factors in the relevant systems (Engeström, 1990; 2001). Contradictions act as driving forces for expansive learning when new or changed objects of activity are recognized and the need of the new object turns into a motive for meeting that need. In activity theory the object of activity is used for something at which an action is directed (Russian *predmet*) (Leontiev, 1981) (Leontiev, 1978, cited in Engeström & Sannino, 2010). Contradictions in activity theoretical terms are historically accumulating structural tensions that become noticeable in disturbances and innovative solutions (Engeström, 2005, p. 314). During the process of transformation people may find themselves in a *double bind* situation, meaning that they receive contradictory messages to which they are unable to react (Engeström, 1987). The *double bind* refers to tensions or disturbances caused by contradictions in the activity systems that have to be resolved to get the system going. Vygotsky developed the *functional method of double stimulation*, where a mediating tool is made available to the subject for mastering such situations (Vygotsky, 1978, p. 74) with the aim of enhancing agency and self-regulation of subjects. In a similar way Engeström suggests that the method Vygotsky developed through research on individuals can be applied to enhance agency in collective activities such as workplaces. He claims that by analysing tensions in activity systems and identifying their underlying contradictions it is possible to foresee emerging or possible development in collective human activities, i.e. the *zone of proximal development* for activity systems. Engeström (1987, p. 174) redefines Vygotsky's original concept suggesting it is "the distance between the present everyday actions of individuals and the historically new form of the societal activity that can be collectively generated as a solution to the double bind potentially embedded in the everyday actions"

The method of contradiction analysis is embedded in the expansive learning cycle (Engeström, 1999a; 1999b) which presupposes that four levels

Figure 1. The expansive learning cycle (Adapted from Engeström, 2001)

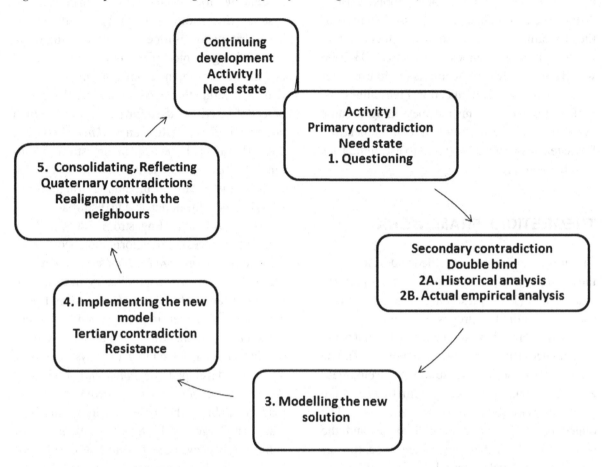

of contradictions may be detected. The cycle depicted in Figure 1 helps guiding formative interventions but has also been used for analysing learning processes as dialectical development of individuals and activity systems (Engeström, 2009a), and that is the way it is used in this study. The cycle presumes interrelationship of individual and systemic development and use of multilevel analysis distinguishing between individual and collective actions and system level changes. The model is appropriate for understanding development in activity systems and proposed as an analytical tool for identifying the *zone of proximal development* in studied activities. The analyses are supposed to generate insights in the form of concepts, visions, hypotheses and tools that may be used as a double stimulation by

people developing their practices in workplaces (Cole & Engeström, 2007). A second stimulation consists of something that supports practitioners in overcoming the double bind they might find themselves in when dealing with problems caused by contradictions in activities.

A first step in the expansive learning cycle is a need state (Figure 1) characterized by a pressing need for responding to the changed object. It is often manifested when individual practitioners start questioning the conventional practice in the activity. The need state of an activity system is reflected in conflicts between an ideal type of work and reality in practice (Pasanen, Toiviainen, Niemelä, & Engeström, 2005).

However, a pressure for developing of practice is usually initiated by secondary contradictions which manifest themselves in disturbances between e.g. changed tools and an old division of labour or changed objects and old tools or rules (Engeström, 1990). In this case people may experience a double bind situation which puts a pressure on them to search for solutions to overcome the troubles e.g. by developing new tools, reorganizing division of labour or revising the rules. Toiviainen (2003, p. 36) says individuals learn and develop as they face and resolve such contradictions.

The third step in the cycle consists of the formation of new models for enhanced practice based on re-thinking the object and motive of the activity. The new model of work is put in practice as a future oriented innovative solution to the problematic situation. In this study the emergence of a new model for teacher education in the distance programme is explored.

The fourth step harbors implementation of the new model which may cause tertiary contradictions to arise between new and old forms of practice, e.g. when practitioners resist reforms or there is resistance in the system where the originally troublesome activity continues as the general practice. The process of appropriation of novelties in an activity system causes imbalances and disturbances which have to be dealt with at collective and systemic levels. An expansive transformation is accomplished when the object and motive of the activity are reconceptualised to embrace a radically wider horizon of possibilities than in the previous mode to the activity. The last step in the expansive learning process contains evaluation and consolidation of the new form of practice.

A new way of functioning for one activity system may however initiate disturbances in neighbouring activity systems. This phenomenon calls for coordination of practices in interacting activities. Quaternary contradictions reveal tensions between the central activity and neighbouring activities. To solve these tensions the activities of the neighbouring systems have to tune their interactions at a systemic level. Resolution of contradictions opens up for qualitatively improved functioning activities consolidated in a new transformed practice. This is labelled Activity II in the cycle model (Figure 1). The new activity continues to develop by dealing with new contradictions deriving from on-going societal changes.

Studying contradictions systematically along the lines of expansive learning cycle enables for analysis of individual growth and collective development in the context of the subjects' activities. Analysis of student teachers learning to become online learners, as related to the development of the distance programme unveils the *zone of proximal development* for the programme.

DATA AND METHODS

The data for analysis are descriptions of the experiences of three school-based student teachers. The data was generated from interviews during ethnographic fieldwork. There is also transcription of three online courses in which they participated. The learning processes of these three distance students while becoming teachers in their local schools were examined in Jóhannsdóttir (2010b). Three schools regarded as representatives for typical schools in small fishing villages and towns along the Icelandic coastline were chosen as cases. In each of the schools one student teacher enrolled in the distance programme accepted to participate in the study. This author stayed in contact with them from two to three years for monitoring their experience in the schools as well as in the programme. Their pseudonyms are Lilith and Sarah and Sam. They had finished their first year in the programme when I first met them. In the part of the study presented here the focus was on their trajectories as school-based distance student teachers and programme participants.

In the spring of 2005 three courses in the programme were observed, both face-to-face sessions, and online sessions, as given on the courses' websites. When the courses were selected the criteria was that one of the three school-based student teachers, Lilith, Sarah or Sam, were enrolled and secondly that the courses were diverse in both content and setup. The first course, ethics, was a compulsory course, expected to be taken in the second year, in which Sam was enrolled with some 70 students. The second course was on arts and crafts, a part of the specialisation for arts and crafts teachers in which Sarah was enrolled with a group of 16 student teachers. The third course was on science and creative art in the lower primary school specialisation in which Lilith was enrolled in a class of around 50 student teachers.

Access to the online platforms permitted observation of transactions and communication between students and lecturers. When the courses finished the communications were printed out for further analysis. The data consisted of all entries on the discussion web and private mail between lecturers and students. Also included were assignments and directives from the lecturers and student teacher assignments shared online. The contribution of each student could be drawn both from online discussions in one of the analysed courses and from portfolio material.

Cultural-historical activity theory in general and the expansive learning theory in particular provided the lenses and tools through which this author made sense of the data. In the first phase the triangle model of the activity system (Engeström 1987) was used for analysing the transcripts of the courses and then the interview data on the experiences of the three students taking part in the research. The activity system of each online course was the unit of analysis, and focus was on student teacher actions on the course websites. The programme as experienced by each of the three student teachers was regarded as an activity system and student participation in the programme described from their perspective. Formulating the descriptions according to the structure of the triangle model opened up analysis of the interplay between the student teachers as subjects and the systemic perspective (Engeström & Sannino, 2010).

In the second phase expansive learning cycle was used for theoretical analysis of the learning trajectories of distance student teachers interacting with development of the distance programme. The aim of the analysis was to make sense of the situation by identifying events in the data which capture the experience of the student teachers when dealing with problems and challenging situations as participants in the distance programme. The analysis focused on student behaviors when encountering problematic situations and the way in which they overcame problems by drawing on resources offered in the activity system of the programme. Attention is drawn to which kind of resources they were able to use as double stimulation, and in turn how their improved participation contributed to development of a new model for practice in the programme. I analysed what constrained them in reacting to a problematic situation and also identified barriers that would need to be overcome for developing practice in the programme.

Activity theory suggests an alternative way of understanding generalization as theoretical assumptions that may be inferred from the empirical data (Picetti-Nascimento, 2014). Findings are expected to be presented in the form of concepts and hypothesis proposed for use in developmental work carried out by practitioners in workplaces where they are further developed and generalized (Engeström, 2009b). The hypothetical concepts are often depicted as intermediate concepts for indicating that they will be refined in practice where expansive concept formation is a collective endeavour. This implies that although the research questions relate to this particular programme the research approach supposes that the results and findings may be generalized for use in similar cases. Their generalizability is taken to be a "question of practical relevance for other activity systems facing similar contradictions in similar developmental phases" (Mäkitalo, 2005, p. 105), that is, if the findings may be used for supporting design of "locally appropriate new solutions" in other cases.

RESULTS

The interview data with student teachers as well as their contributions on their course websites were used for illuminating the experience of individual students' learning and development while enrolled in the programme. Sarah's narrative is an example of the students' experience in the programme. Identifying challenges and problems she encounters and the kind of support she uses for overcoming problems sheds ligth on her learning and development relative to the development of pracice in the teacher education programme (Figure 2).

Changed student groups and new online tools called for a changed practice between student teachers and teacher educators. Sarah felt that learning by participating in the discussion on *WebCT*, using the threaded discussion platform was a good way to deal with what the studies demanded.

I think it's best when we have to read and then submit input on WebCT. Like now in ethics, for example, we read a chapter and he puts forward a question and there is a kind of discussion around it (Interview, February 2004).

At the same time she felt it took her a lot of effort to compose and transmit her writings to the discussion panel.

Figure 2. Sarah's steps in learning to become a distance student in relation to programme development according to the expansive learning cycle

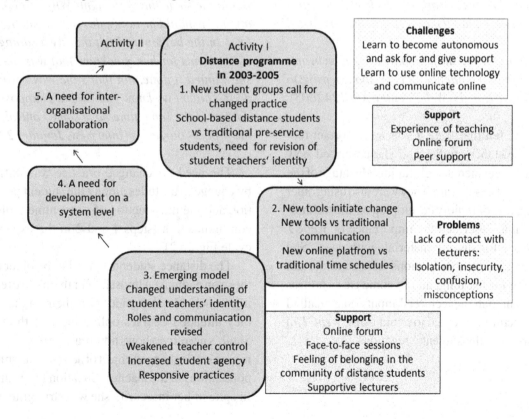

I find it extremely difficult to sit down and write. I write and then I erase it. I just find it difficult to put something in there (Interview, April 2005).

However, Sarah said she entered *WebCT* regularly and viewed what other students had sent and she was keen on praising their work. In another example she draws on her experience as a teacher when contributing with a relevant input into the discussion.

I think it is important that school teachers manage to present all assignments in diverse ways, using different teaching methods, because we are so extremely different. What suits me may not suit my best friend at all. One must be careful that the assignments don't take too long so the pupils don't lose interest in them.

I think subject integration is very interesting and all teachers should look into the possibilities of integrating different subjects. But then it's how to organize this sort of work, all teachers fight with a lack of time, right? If there is a will there is a way.

My opinion is that the national curriculum in arts and crafts is a guideline; it is far too extensive to be followed exactly (WebCT entry, April 24 2005).

Sarah felt that *WebCT* was an important tool for the distance studies and she described how teachers were increasingly taking advantage of the features of the software. They were also using other affordances of rapidly developing online technology. Sarah described the importance of *WebCT* as a place for sharing materials with peers. She also felt that the contributions were an important resource for learning, and in some cases no less important than the lecturers' inputs. She recalled when lecturers decided to avoid using *WebCT* in a course and the students' reactions.

Then we found it impossible not to have WebCT, where we could talk to each other, and we felt we needed to, you know (Interview, January 2006).

Sarah thought that sometimes it was not clear what students could expect from the lecturers. The lecturers' priorities decided how much freedom the students had to elaborate on the assignments. Uncertaininty about the lecturers' versus the students' role caused a confusing situation and insecurity. Sarah described how she experienced the situation when she thought that the teacher gave poor guidelines, but at the same time she was critical of her own reactions.

Last year you see it was quite clear how we should do the assignments, but still had some free choice, she wasn't saying put a full stop here and here, you know, but clear guidelines. And then this year it was remarkable how she was not nearly as clear. I thought it was really difficult because I didn't know exactly what she wanted us to do. But at the same time I thought: Why is it bothering me, I should be doing this for me and not for her? In the beginning I felt that I was doing the assignments for her, you know that was the way she wanted it done, not that's the way I want to do it. [Later] we know what we are supposed to do, but at the same time have some control over the process ourselves (Interview, January 2006).

The need for changed practice was initiated by change in attitudes among the student population and the introduction of new online tools for communication (steps 1 and 2 in the expansive cycle Figure 2).

The distance students tended to be older than those on campus. Almost half of them were teaching in schools alongside with their studies and they attended courses online most of the time. Sarah's narrative shows how practice developed in response to a changed object of activity (i.e. student population) in the teacher education programme. In spite of her insecurity she was struggling with her role as an agent and independent student, realizing that she should control her own learning. Her experience of teaching at school supported her efforts at gaining confidence in herself to contribute in online discussion. The habit of sharing products on the online platform made students aware that their solutions could be useful for their peer students. The school-based students often took on the role of connecting academic studies to practice in their schools, drawing on their experience of teaching and providing resources for other distance students by relating theories and practice and practice to theory.

Secondly the use of powerful online tools as mediators in teaching and learning initiated contradictions that students and lecturers noticed as tensions and problems. During that process different kinds of problems were identified, such as lack of contact with lecturers, feelings of isolation, insecurity, confusion and misconceptions. The online tools and methods were contradictory in that they initiated problems in teaching and learning practice. However, at the same time they supported developed practice by affording opportunities for discussion and collaboration and supporting students' participation in the programme. Students like Sarah, learned to communicate online and revise her understanding of what it meant to be an unconventional student. She learnt to become a distance student and contribute to the development of a new model of practice in the programme.

What supported the students in participating online was how they experienced peer support and a feeling of belonging in the community of distance students. They often helped out when there were technical problems or confusion on the organization of courses and by sharing experiences and feelings. They learned to ask for help and respond to other peoples' need for support in solving problems related to their situation as distance students. The online platform *WebCT* provided crucial support in overcoming the feeling of isolation in the distance programme. But the lack of lecturers' know-how in the use of

technology or their unwillingness to use it could be disturbing. When lecturers announced they would stay clear of *WebCT* or any other online platform for communication everything turned upside down among the distance students. The online technology was a tool that was expected to mediate teaching and learning and it was the most important tool for the functioning of the distance students.

Face-to-face meetings on campus supported the formation of a community during the first year of enrolment since it enabled distance students to get to know each other – a process which facilitated online communication. They were able to resolve frustrations that came up during the online sessions. Offensive irony and misunderstanding were much easier to sort out during face-to-face meetings. The feeling of belonging to the community of distance students supported learning and participation. However, the way in which the sessions on campus were planned mattered a lot. The students that participated in the study emphasized the importance of meeting in smaller groups, having an opportunity for an informal chat and time for personal bonding with peers. They felt that meeting the lecturers in class-size groups for personal contact with peers was more useful than sitting in big auditoriums listening to lectures. They wanted time and space for social practice and personal contact with peers and lecturers in order to get to know each other and form a community that could function online between the face-to-face sessions.

EMERGING PRACTICE BETWEEN STUDENTS AND LECTURERS

New online tools, in conjunction with revised pedagogical ideas had initiated changed practice and a new model for teaching and learning emerged in the programme (step 3 in the expansive learning cycle). Online discussion had become part of general practice in the programme and students in general expressed their pleasure with the online discussions. They felt it was of benefit to have an opportunity to develop their understanding in discussion with peers. However, the method gave rise to tensions and in the ethics course one student criticised discussion as a method for learning, questioning the value of peer contributions, as well as feeling that the lecturer should contribute and keep the discussion on track. This event captures the experience of this student in the programme and reveals the contradictions inherent in the situation.

The lecturer directed and motivated the discussion in the beginning by putting forward different questions to each group of students. Each student was supposed to contribute to the discussion about a defined pedagogical topic three times a week, drawing on readings from course literature. The teacher generally stayed clear of the discussion until the weekly discussion was closed. Then he gave a general response, reflecting on the discussion and taking examples from student contributions. He avoided to correct misunderstandings of particular students, but corrected students' understanding in general. However, one student complained in a private email to the teacher.

I think that this arrangement isn't working and I am not much of a better thinker after this assignment. In the first place we haven't received any criticism on our writing this term, which I feel is necessary to improve the writing. [...] I think that since our writing [on the discussion web] is part of the grade, you should plan it so that all students get a comment on their writing at least once (Student, April 18 2005).

The next day the same student sent another private email to the teacher, reflecting on the shortcomings of discussion as a method in online teaching and learning:

I also have opinions on what my peer students write and I think their contributions are of varying quality and often give reason for criticism. Your letters do not satisfy the need for personal criticism, though they do give us deeper insight into the subject each week, which is good. [...] The problems we are dealing with in the discussions are interesting but we tend to get stuck in discussion of a general kind. There I think you could interject with some comments to keep us on track, but then again you probably are given too little time for such activities (Student, April 19 2005).

By questioning the value of peer exchanges as well as the value of discussion as method the student points to a problem caused by contradictions between the ideal form of discussion as a method and the reality in practice. The ideal understanding of the method presumes that students are engaged and contribute to the discussion as autonomous individuals and the teacher's role is to guide the discussion, motivate and encourage students and correct misunderstandings. The general practice of lecturers, however, was to avoid interfering or contributing during student discussions. They preferred to provide general feedback when the time allocated for the relevant issue was up. Therefore students might be discussing for a week or more on their own without guidance or corrections of student's misconceptions.

In this case contradictions between new material and conceptual tools i.e. threaded online discussion and rules regulating lecturers' practice caused problems. The lecturers seemed to base the time they used for communication with students on schedules made for on-campus teaching, e.g. by entering once a week for round-up and feedback. Others lecturers adjusted their teaching time and mode to the new online practice. For example a lecturer in one of the courses entered the discussion board two or three times a day including holidays during her two-week module. Also instead of rounding up and responding generally to everybody she responded to the students individually with short comments. Her practice is identified as a precedent of emerging future practice in the programme. She changed her working schedule to overcome the contradictions inherent in the situation and met the need of the distance students thereby suppporting them in overcoming the feeling of isolation, insecurity and misconceptions.

The online forum was open at all hours while lecturers were only occasionally present. This arrangement resulted in weakened teacher presence and control in the official learning space. However, it was important that lecturers continued to serve in their roles as professional guides. On the other hand weak teacher control could be a challenge for the student teachers in their efforts at taking on autonomy and agency in their studies. This was a contradiction that students needed to overcome in their processes of learning to become distance students.

NEW AND OLD PRACTICES IN THE DEVELOPMENTAL PROCESS

Analysis according to the expansive learning cycle revealed a way in which the general practice within the distance programme developed in response to changes in the activity system of the programme, such as a changed student population and new tools and methods. The new model is described in step 3 (Figure 3).

Lecturers had revised their understanding of the object of the teacher education programme when student teachers had changed from pre-service on-campus students to in-service online students. Their revision affected teaching methods and the way in which they communicated with students. For students the changed understanding

Figure 3. The programme development according to the expansive learning cycle

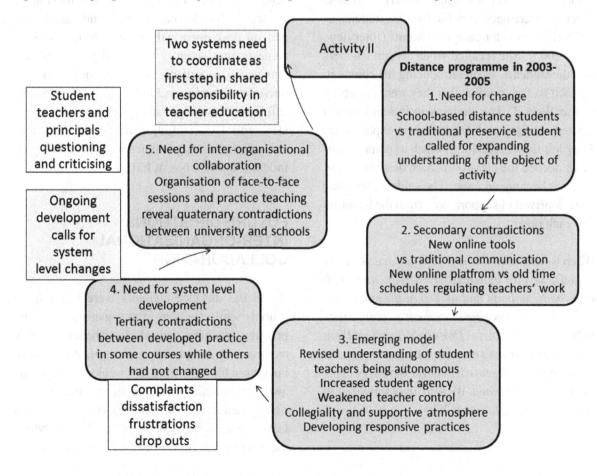

of themselves as distance student teachers in the programme had focused their attention on the mode of lecturer-student communication. Having accepted the obligations of being independent students they assumed that they had agency in their studies, they could be irritated and critical and did not accept strict control and authoritative directives from the lecturers.

The way lecturers addressed student teachers on the online platform was often a reason for tensions, disturbances, and hurt feelings among the distance students. The modes of communication depended on individual lecturers and made it difficult for students to realise what was acceptable conduct. They had to learn the limits between student agency and teacher control.

All three student teachers mentioned an event that captures how students experienced their situation. Lilith felt that the *WebCT* made it possibile to communicate, access and share materials. Theese functions were necessary for distance students as the classroom is for campus students (Interview, April 2005). She recalled when certain teachers told the students, when introducing the course in the face-to-face session, that they were not going to use *WebCT*. The students in the auditorium reacted strongly and demanded an explanation. They felt they needed it as much as campus students needed the classroom. Sam described how this fact became an issue. The students felt they were deprived of support, both from the lecturers and each other.

When we attended the later face-to-face session I talked to several students and it was the same with everybody, nobody had looked at the subject. It was just put off because there were no obligations to hand anything in. [...] We could have sent them email but we weren't working on any assignments or anything. They sent a letter every ten days, eight in all were distributed. We were only supposed to read (Interview, January 2005).

Assessment of the students' performance was based on a written final exam, which covered 100% of the grade for the course. Bit by bit the students decreased their activity and about one third of the students did not complete the course. According to Sam's explanantion this course deviated from the normal practice, where students were used to having obligations, including showing up online and participating in the community of distance students and teachers.

During processes of change old and new models of teaching and communication co-existed in the programme. This caused disturbances when individual lecturers acted as if everything was as it used to be. However, the majority of both students and lecturers acted according to changed ideas. This is symptomatic for tertiary contradictions arising when some practitioners have developed qualitatively better ways of functioning in an activity system while others lag behind (Figure 3, step 4). While the lecturers and students in general developed and practiced a new model, some of the lecturers were still planning their courses in accordance with the old model of university teaching and learning. Such situations call for acknowledgment of the changed practice at systemic level, and adjustment of rules and division of labour in accordance with the developing model (Figure 3, box at left).

FUTURE DIRECTIONS: INTER-ORGANISATIONAL COLLABORATION

When the distance students were teaching in schools while studying, the organisation of the practice teaching caused disturbances. Sam's experience portrays the problem. He had to leave his school for more than five weeks while he was away for practice teaching in another district. The situation in his school was vulnerable and a lack of qualified teachers was a problem which increased while he was away. Problems and disturbances manifested a pressing need for changes in how the school-based student teachers' practice teaching was organised. There was an obvious need for cooperation between the schools and the university programme.

Organisation of face-to-face sessions was another matter of concern for the school-based student teachers. It was disturbing for the pupils when the teachers left, especially at times when pupils were vulnerable, like at the beginning of the school year. The school-based student teachers called for their situation to be taken into account when face-to-face sessions were being planned. The principal in one of the schools pointed out that as student teachers they missed an important opportunity to learn from colleagues when they were away at a time when the school year was being planned and in its starting phase.

In both cases quaternary contradictions between schools and the programme as interacting activity systems were causing problems. The challenge was to develop an understanding of practice teaching as a shared object of the schools and the teacher training faculty (Figure 3, step 5 and the box above). Further development of the two interacting systems would need to assume inter-organisational collaboration including co-configuration of their activities at a collective system level (Engeström, 2004; 2007; Jóhannsdóttir, 2010a).

In negotiating shared objects in inter-organisational developmental work between activity systems Engeström et al. (1995, p. 333) point to the importance of identifying concrete problems, especially in the initial phases. In boundary work practice teaching and face-to-face sessions form a practical task suited for dealing with in the first phase of inter-organizational collaboration where rules on the organisation would be negotiated with the aim of overcoming tensions between the systems and developing practices. In this kind of work it is important to understand and actively coordinate multiple needs, and appreciate and actively overcome tensions in the interacting institutions (Engeström, 2007).

CONCLUSION

The chosen activity theoretical approach has opened up understanding of the learning and development between individual students and the programme design. The dialectical process has revealed future developmental possibilities. Analysis reveals how the student teachers develop as programme participants while at the same time contributing to an emerging new model of teaching and learning. Learning to function in the programme involves students who reconsider themselves as students and reassess the roles of students and lecturers. Online tools and methods afford the students opportunities for social practices in the form of dialogue and collaboration with their fellow students in support of their learning process. The students learn to participate online, cultivate modes of communication which relate to the revised understanding of themselves as unconventional students. The distance students' learning processes illustrate a journey alongside with the expansive learning cycle.

- Learning to function in the programme involved students reconsidering themselves as students and reassessing the roles of students and lecturers accordingly.
- The online tools and methods afforded the students opportunities for social practices in the form of dialogue and collaboration with their fellow students, supporting their learning.
- In order to be able to participate online, students learned to cultivate modes of communication which related to the revised understanding of the object of the programme activity.
- The distance students learned to use increased agency, which they gained with weakened teacher control, to take responsibility for their studies.

- The distance students learned to contribute to the online learning community and the programme development.

Another research question revolves around the way in which the development of the distance programme interrelates with distance student teachers' development as learners? According to Vygotsky (1978) individual development depends on participation in social life, and development of culture depends on individual creative contribution. The notion of an expansive learning cycle is built on this conceptualisation (Engeström, 1999a; 1999b). People enter an activity system and learn (internalize) by overcoming contradictions in developing their practice. The student teachers' learning processes reflect this cycle of internalization and externalization (Moran & John-Steiner, 2003). Having learned by internalizing their experience of culture and having developed skills and capacity the individual student teachers are ready to externalize by contributing their knowledge and skills to the development of the programme. Analysis of the student teachers' individual trajectories reveals an emerging model of teacher education.

- Changed understanding of distance student teachers identity, increased student agency (autonomy), teacher control replaced by teacher support.
- Role of students and lecturers being revised, changing the mode of student lecturer communication.
- Increased student collegiality, collaboration, asking for and receiving support from peers.
- Lecturers and students learning to respond to the needs of community members and developing responsive practice.

Focus of research has been on school-based student teachers. Analysis has revealed the zone of proximal development for further developing

that kind of a model for distance teacher education. The results show contradictions between school-practice and university practice indicating need for school-university collaboration. Problems and disturbances manifest a pressing need for changes in how the school-based student teachers' practice teaching is organised inferring a challenge to develop understanding of practice teaching as a shared object of the participating schools and the teacher education faculty. Organisation of face-to-face sessions colliding with beginning of the school year is another matter of concern as the student teachers missed an important opportunity to learn from colleagues when they were away at a time when the school year was being planned.

Student teachers' learning process, challenges and problems they faced and the kind of support that is useful in their circumstances have been clarified. Focus on the system level in the expansive learning cycle sheds light on how development comes to halt when neglected at collective or institutional level. Since the changes were not dealt with at a system level there were tensions and frustrations, e.g. when lecturers and student teachers failed to realise or accept demands for changed practice in the programme. For overcoming problems of this kind the teacher education department would have to accept and facilitate the changes at institutional level, for example, by changing rules and revising the way in which division of labour is defined.

The teacher education organisers did not acknowledge the importance of the situation of school-based student teachers in planning their activities. When access to the distance programme was opened for all to apply the focus on this group was diminished. The lack of a system level response to distance student teachers in general and school-based student teachers in particular, as a changed object of activity in teacher education, hinders development and causes disruptions. Analysis points to the need for acknowledging an emerging paradigm at an institutional level and adjusting rules and division of labour in accordance with the new model. In overcoming problems and developing practice the schools and the teacher education faculty at the university would need to look at the student teachers' education as a shared responsibility and negotiate for acceptable arrangements for both institutions involved.

REFERENCES

Björnsdóttir, A. (2009). Fjarnemar [Distance students]. University of Iceland.

Blunden, A. (1997). Vygotsky and the dialectical method. *Lev Vygotsky Archive*. Retrieved from 28/08/2006 http://www.marxists.org/archive/vygotsky/index.htm

Cole, M., & Engeström, Y. (2007). Cultural-historical approaches to designing for development. In J. Valsiner & A. Rosa (Eds.), The Cambridge Handbook of Sociocultural Psychology (pp. 484-507). Cambridge, UK: Cambridge University Press.

Engeström, Y. (1990). Developmental work research as activity theory in practice: Analyzing the work of general practitioners. In Y. Engeström (Ed.), Learning, Working and Imagining (pp. 69-106). Helsinki: Orienta-Konsultit OY.

Engeström, Y. (1999a). Activity theory and individual and social transformations. In Y. Engeström, R. Miettinen, & R.-L. Punamäki (Eds.), Perspectives on Activity Theory (pp. 19-38). Cambridge, UK: Cambridge University Press.

Engeström, Y. (1999b). Innovative learning in work teams: Analyzing cycles of knowledge creation in practice. In Y. Engeström, R. Miettinen, & R.-L. Punamäki (Eds.), Perspectives on activity theory (pp. 377-404). Cambridge, UK: Cambridge University Press.

Engeström, Y. (2001). Expansive learning at work: Toward an activity theoretical reconceptualization. *Journal of Education and Work*, *14*(1), 133–156. doi:10.1080/13639080020028747

Engeström, Y. (2004). New forms of learning in co-configuration work. *Journal of Workplace Learning*, *16*(2), 11–21. doi:10.1108/13665620410521477

Engeström, Y. (2005). *Developmental work research. Expanding activity theory in practice* (Vol. 12). Berlin: Lemanns Media.

Engeström, Y. (2007). Enriching the theory of expansive learning: Lessons from journeys toward coconfiguration. *Mind, Culture, and Activity*, *14*(1/2), 23–39. doi:10.1080/10749030701307689

Engeström, Y. (2009a). *Expansive concept formation at work*. CRADLE. Retrieved from http://www.helsinki.fi/behav/tiedepaiva/2009/CONCEPT%20FORMATION%20PLAN.pdf

Engeström, Y. (2009b). The future of activity theory: A rough draft. In A. Sannino, H. Daniels, & K. D. Gutiérrez (Eds.), Learning and expanding with activity theory (pp. 303-328). Cambridge, UK: Cambridge University Press.

Engeström, Y., Engeström, R., & Kärkkäinen, M. (1995). Polycontextuality and boundary crossing in expert cognition: Learning and problem solving in complex work activities. *Learning and Instruction*, *5*(4), 319–336. doi:10.1016/0959-4752(95)00021-6

Engeström, Y., & Sannino, A. (2010). Studies of expansive learning: Foundations, findings and future challenges. *Educational Research Review*, *5*(1), 1–24. doi:10.1016/j.edurev.2009.12.002

Ilyenkov, E. (1977). *Dialectical logic, essays on its history and theory* (H. C. Creighton, Trans.). Moscow: Progress.

Jóhannsdóttir, T. (2010a). Deviations from the conventional: Contradictions as sources of change in teacher education. In V. Ellis, A. Edwards, & P. Smagorinsky (Eds.), Cultural-historical pespectives on teacher education and development (pp. 163-279). London: Routledge.

Jóhannsdóttir, T. (2010b). *Teacher education and school-based distance learning: individual and systemic development in schools and a teacher education programme.* (PhD Doctoral thesis). University of Iceland. Retrieved from http://hdl.handle.net/1946/7119

Jónasson, J. (1996). *Spurningalisti nemenda 1996* [Questionnaire for students 1996]. Iceland University of Education. Reykjavík.

Jónasson, J. (2001). *On-line distance education – A feasible choice in teacher education in Iceland?* (Master of Philosophy Thesis). University of Strathclyde. Retrieved from https://notendur.hi.is/jonjonas/skrif/mphil/

Kennaraháskóli Íslands. (2005). *Kennaraháskóli Íslands, ársskýrsla 2004* [Iceland University of Education, yearly report 2004]. (S. Kaaber & H. Kristjánsdóttir, Eds.). Reykjavík: Kennaraháskóli Íslands.

Leontiev, A. N. (1978). *Activity, consciousness, and personality.* Prentice Hall. Retrieved from http://www.marxists.org/archive/leontev/works/1978/index.htm

Leontiev, A. N. (1981). *Problems of the development of the mind.* Moscow: Progress.

Mäkitalo, J. (2005). *Work-related well-being in the transformation of nursing home work.* (Doctoral dissertation). University of Oulu, Oulu, Finland. Retrieved from http://herkules.oulu.fi/isbn9514277678/isbn9514277678.pdf

Moran, S., & John-Steiner, V. (2003). Creativity in the making: Vygotsky's contemporary contribution to the dialectic of development and creativity. In R. K. Sawyer (Ed.), Creativity and development (pp. 61-90). Oxford, UK: Oxford University Press.

Schwille, J., & Dembélé, M. (2007). *Global perspectives on teacher learning: Improving policy and practice.* UNESCO: International Institute for Educational Planning. Retrieved from http://www.unesco.org/iiep/eng/publications/recent/rec7.htm

Vygotsky, L. S. (1978). *Mind in society. The development of higher psychological processes.* Cambridge, MA: Harvard University Press.

ADDITIONAL READING

Douglas, A. S. (2012). Creating expansive learning opportunities in schools: the role of school leaders in initial teacher education partnerships. *European Journal of Teacher Education*, 35(1), 3-15. Retrieved from 07/07/2013 doi: 10.1080/02619768.2011.633994

Edwards, A. (2010). How can Vygotsky and his legacy help us to understand and develop teacher education? V. Ellis, A. Edwards & P. Smagorinsky (Eds.). Cultural-historical perspectives on teacher education and development (63-77). London: Routledge.

Engeström, Y. (2009). From learning environments and implementation to activity systems and expansive learning. *Actio: An International Journal of Human Activity Theory*, 2, 17–33.

Engström, Y. (2011). Activity theory and learning at work. M. Malloch, L. Cairns, K. Evans & B. N. O'Connor (Eds.), The Sage handbook of workplace learning (74-89). London: Sage.

Jóhannsdóttir, T. (2013). 'What we wanted to do was to change the situation' Distance teacher education as stimulation for school development in Iceland. *Netla - Online Journal on Pedagogy and Education*. Retrieved from 16/04/2014 http://netla.hi.is/greinar/2013/ryn/010.pdf

Jóhannsdóttir, T., & Roth, W.-M. (in press). Experiencing (Pereživanie) as Developmental Category: Learning from a Fisherman who is Becoming (as) a Teacher-in a-Village-School. *Outlines. Critical Practice Studies*.

Nummijoki, J., & Engeštöm, Y. (2010). Towards co-configuration in home care of the elderly. Cultivating agency by designing and implementing the Mobility Agreement. H. Daniels, A. Edwards, Y. Engestrom, T. Gallagher & S. R. Ludvigsen (Eds.), Activity Theory in Practice. Promoting learning across boundaries and agencies. (49-71). New York: Routledge.

Roth, W.-M., & Jornet, A. (2014). Toward a Theory of Experience. *Science Education*, 98(1), 106-126. Retrieved from 06/07/2014 doi: 10.1002/sce.21085

Stetsenko, A. (2010). Teaching-learning and development as activist projects of historical Becoming: expanding Vygotsky's approach to pedagogy. *Pedagogies: An International Journal*, 5(1), 6-16. Retrieved from 07/07/2014 doi: 10.1080/15544800903406266

Stetsenko, A. (2013).The Challenge of Individuality in Cultural- Historical Activity Theory: "Collectividual" Dialectics from a Transformative Activist Stance. *Outlines. Critical Practice Studies*, 14(2), 7-28. Retrieved from 16/04/2014 http://ojs.statsbiblioteket.dk/index.php/outlines/article/view/9791

KEY TERMS AND DEFINITIONS

Contradictions: In activity theoretical terms are historically accumulating structural tensions that become noticeable in disturbances and innovative solutions. Contradictions act as driving forces for expansive learning.

Double Bind Situation: Refers to a situation people may find themselves in when dealing with transformations in activity system and they receive contradictory messages to which they are unable to react. However, tensions or disturbances caused by contradictions in an activity system that has to be resolved to get the system going.

Expansive Learning: According to Engeström's theory of expansive learning, is the kind of learning that is initiated when some individuals involved in collective activity begin to question existing practice, and develop new forms of the activity to overcome the contradictions causing the tensions in the current state of affairs. Expansive learning is conceptualised as stepwise expansion of the object of activity.

Expansive Learning Cycle: Is a model for guiding formative interventions. The model has also been used for analysing learning processes as dialectical development of individuals and activity systems. The cycle is appropriate for understanding development in activity systems and proposed as an analytical tool for identifying the *zone of proximal development* for activity systems.

Responsive Practice: Refers to an activity in which participants have developed a sense of collective subject by cultivating sensitivity to each other's needs and in turn construct practice that responds to these. In developing responsive practice it is important that participants develop shared understandings of the object of activity.

Second (or Double) Stimulation: Is something that supports practitioners in overcoming a double bind situation they might find themselves in when dealing with problems caused by contradictions in activity systems. Second stimulations may be in form of tools, signs, concepts, visions and hypotheses that support people in developing their practice.

Zone of Proximal Development for Activity Systems: Engeström redefined Vygotsky's original concept and suggested that it could be applied for analysing collective activity systems as well as individual development. According to Engeström (1987, p. 174), *zone of proximal development for activity systems* is "the distance between the present everyday actions of individuals and the historically new form of the societal activity that can be collectively generated as a solution to the double bind potentially embedded in the everyday actions".

Chapter 2
Young Learners:
Communication and Digital Tools

Fia Andersson
Uppsala University, Sweden

Stellan Sundh
Uppsala University, Sweden

ABSTRACT

This chapter describes a project aiming at investigating Swedish and Russian 12-year-old learners' use of ICT. They communicate in English on three shared blogs. Their exchanges and contributions are analyzed with a focus on mediating tools, modes of communication, and motives for collaboration. Ongoing activities are studied through classroom observations, interviews, and a research circle. Results show that ICT plays a vital role as a mediating tool and a motive for collaboration. Results indicate that Russian and Swedish learners manage to interact in authentic communication in English with the help of digital tools. Opportunities to explore a variety of digital tools resulted in new forms of representation. International collaboration through ICT indicates that conflicting issues and developmental opportunities may challenge the current education system.

INTRODUCTION

Today globalization plays a significant role in everyday life. People regularly meet cultures in geographically distant settings. Modern man is a partner in an international and multicultural community. We are exposed to media from a rich variety of sources and we are expected to contribute to a global community. ICT is supposed to bridge geographical distances and provide collaboration, transformation and learning in what Nardi calls "placeless organizations" (Nardi, 2007, p. 5).

There are ethical considerations about personal and private communication; e.g. is the use of ICT appropriate in young learners' communication in educational environments? We carried out a project in cooperation between Uppsala University Campus Gotland, schools in Gotland, Immanuel Kant Federal Baltic University in Russia and schools in the Kaliningrad region. Six classes were involved in the project and ongoing activities supplied data on three blogs.

DOI: 10.4018/978-1-4666-6603-0.ch002

BACKGROUND

Information and Communications Technology (ICT) provides opportunities for learners to document their learning processes in efficient and interactive ways. By using ICT learners provide accounts of their achievements at school. They share information with learners in geographically distant areas. The reported project investigates young learners' use of digital tools in international communication. English is the lingua franca in the Baltic region. It is taught and learnt as the first foreign language at school. Successful communication in English on ICT-platforms lies in reach owing to daily interaction and communication. Exchanges can be achieved without significant obstacles or geographical distances. Furthermore, English tends to be used in the learners' free time in ICT-contexts. Opportunities to use the English language outside class, described as Extramural English, correlate positively with the pupils' level of oral proficiency and the size of their vocabulary in a study among Swedish 16-year-olds (Sundqvist, 2009, p. 204). In successful teaching and learning, it is essential to develop the learners' awareness of progress, and encourage them to assess their interaction and production. Motivation is a challenge and a key word for the successful learner. It is necessary to motivate the learners to produce and interact in contexts which relate to their everyday lives. According to Gärdenfors (2010) the use of ICT can support motivation in informal as well as formal learning situations. Teaching and learning at ICT-platforms can be organized as assignments for individuals or groups of learners. Their learning process includes collecting material in portfolios where documents such as X-media productions illustrate progress. The learners' motivation for documentation can be strengthened if the material is published in social media, making communication real and authentic. Leffler and Lundberg (2012) claim that projects with a focus on increased cooperation with schools abroad, offer opportunities for increased meaningfulness,

connection with real life and motivation in the learners' language studies.

Curricula provide a framework and concrete guidelines for the teachers' work. There are several similarities in Russian and Swedish curricula, for example descriptions of learners' skills and their expected levels of proficiency. The difference lies in focus on interaction, strategies and confidence in the Swedish curriculum. In the Swedish curriculum there are descriptions at a general interactive and communicative level. The Russian curriculum contains detailed descriptions in terms of phonetics and structures. In the Swedish curriculum there are overall goals and guidelines and the use of ICT is directly addressed. Schools must ensure that pupils can use ICT in their search for knowledge and communication, creativity and learning but also to communicate in spoken and written English. An international perspective is emphasized in the Swedish curriculum and the learners should be able to understand their reality in a global context and prepare for a society with contacts across cultural and national borders (Skolverket, 2011). In the Russian curriculum a sociocultural component is emphasized where the learners have to know basic information about culture, traditions and aspects of modern life in English speaking countries. As regards stipulated goals of ICT in Russian schools, descriptions of student competence in the use of ICT is left outside the curriculum (Budarina, 2012). However, in both countries teachers should encourage the learners to develop interest in languages and culture.

THEORETICAL FRAMEWORK

The framework of activity theory, developed by Leontiev, and extended by Engeström focus on the relationship between human, the environment and activity plus needs and motives that lead to changes in an activity. Today variants of activity theory are used in a variety of disciplines, including education and cultural studies (Kaptelinin, 2013).

New phenomena such as digitalized offices and virtual classrooms are characterized by Engeström (2010, p. 199) as "fluid organizations". A similar concept like "placeless organizations" (Nardi, 2007) indicate that institutions control activities without the physical appearance of staff. However, there is a need to scrutinize what needs and motives drive the learners, and what the mediating tools are. It is central to activity theory to analyze the conflicting and challenging issues which occur during collaborative exchanges. Examples of these issues are caused by different curricula, working individually or in groups, technology needed and the way it is used to sustain and expand activities (Nardi, 2007, p. 20). Analysis focuses mainly on concepts, motives and needs but also on collaboration, mediating tools and language (Säljö, 2013; Wertsch, 1998).

Previous Research on ICT and Learning

Lave and Wenger (1991), Wenger (1998) and Säljö (2013) show that in teamwork, learners make use of their collective experiences. Learning together with more experienced peers has a positive influence on communication. Collaboration is central for learning processes in the tradition of Vygotskij to develop. Selander and Kress (2010) say learning equals meaning making through communication in multimodal media. The development of ICT and new digital tools implies that pupils become producers of information. Studying young learners' collaboration in ICT-mediated communication offers opportunities to learn if and how digital competences expand. The learning process then goes from the learner being a novice in contact with the tool, to naturalization where the mediating tool becomes transparent to the user. Säljö's (2013) model shows how learning to use mediating tools takes place in a process of four phases: 1/ initial examination where the user is dependent on external support; 2/ systematic examination with intensive use in specific practices, increas-

ing insight in the possibilities and limitations and reduced dependence on external support; 3/ the ability to explain the tool for a beginner and to appropriate, to master, mediating tools for certain purposes; 4/ naturalization where the mediating tool is transparent to the user (2013, p. 230).

Today most young learners have experiences in playing computer games. This is their entrance to the digital world and a platform for interest in digital tools like software programs, websites and blogs. The tools serve as content and as tools to create content e.g. on blogs. Gee (2007) discusses opportunities to learn by using mediating devices or any kind of tool or technology that people use to enhance performance beyond what could be done without the technology. He (2007, p. 104) argues that learning is mediated by "representations, technologies and other people, networked into knowledge systems" - and using a variety of tools. In collaboration, people interact and produce mutual knowledge and as Gee (2007, p. 89) claims: "people are smarter when they use smart tools" and they are even "smarter when they work in smart environments". Smart environments could be classroom situations where learners are offered equal opportunities to use digital tools for collaboration, communication and learning. In most parts of the world people claim that computer games is an "artifact" in young learners' lives. Gee (2006; 2008) and Shaffer (2006) discuss the potential of knowledge acquired when learning how to manage when playing games. How could people use such knowledge for various purposes? There is a growing interest in *serious games*. They are used for purposes other than entertainment and especially the use of games in education in order to improve learning, action and participation. A new world of digital resources including games complements and challenges traditional text-based information and similar learning materials. Gee (2008) and Shaffer (2006) suggest new media provide a sociocultural perspective on opportunities to learn. Kaptelinin and Nardi (2012) discuss technology affordances as possibilities for mediated human action and argue that there is a need to take a further step from (2012, p. 975) a "mediated action perspective on affordances which deliberately focuses on *individual* human action" to "extend the analysis to include mediated *collective* actions". This step, they claim, would be necessary since social and technological mediation are often inseparable.

Teaching and Learning of a Foreign Language

Learners are driven by communicative needs when they develop language proficiency and strive for further acquisition (Perdue, 2000, p. 301). But learners' communicative need can be further discussed; what are the learners' communicative needs? Ellis (1992) says first, the communicative need is a basic one which requires only formally simple resources. Second, there is an expressive need which requires more language skills for purposes of variety. Third, there is the learners' experience of a sociolinguistic need to consider. It makes them realize the need to use language in socially appropriate ways. These needs should be put in a context where the learners' activity and learning processes are seen in a relation to the children and the environment they are active in.

Besides these needs it is of interest to discuss social aspects and the learners' right to use their chosen variants for communication, i.e. the learner must start from a point where the language level he has achieved is a valid starting point without being corrected or monitored by a teacher (Tornberg, 2007). Learners are given the opportunity to use the foreign language and they learn for their communication to express opinions and views on topics that engage them. This kind of progressive thinking leads to an analytic discourse about ownership of language, about learners' ownership for communicative purposes and about influences of everyday life contexts. Ellis and Barkhuizen (2005, p. 9) claim such data provide material for investigating learners' competence in English.

The learners' language displayed on the blogs is spontaneous production. Their unplanned production implies that the contents was not scrutinized and/or corrected by a peer or teacher. It was produced spontaneously orally and/or in writing. On the other hand we may expect a certain degree of editing in written interaction. Chapelle (2007) says learners pay more attention to self-correction in written computer mediated communication compared to how they act in oral interaction. In this project communications can be expected to develop when the content in the communication changes from introductory presentations of the learners and their school, and supplies information on "advantages, benefits or rewards" other than the ones provided for a school context. This can be seen as a bridge to the children's vernacular culture and thereby encourage language learning (Gee, 2008).

The learner's mother tongue is essential in the analysis of the development of learner language proficiency because transfer from the mother tongue may be the reason for change in their functional approach (Ellis & Barkhuizen, 2005, p. 65; 119). In the present study we are eager to find non-standard features which are evident in all learners' production irrespective of their mother tongue and non-standard features which can be explained by interference of structures in the mother tongue. Estling Vannestål (2007) distinguishes between organizing of main clauses in simple sentences, compound sentences or main coordinated clauses and complex sentences consisting of main clauses which include one or more dependent clauses. She (2007, p. 75) says compound sentences are "typical of speech and young children's writing".

The Context of the Study

This project is an investigation of collaboration between Russian and Swedish young learners with ICT deployed as a mediating tool. We study the impact of technology on learning processes.

Analysis focuses on activities visible at blogs and in classrooms, i.e. actions when working with material for the blog. There are other contributions at the blogs and activities in the classrooms resulting from contributions. According to Kaptelinin (2013) activity theory is not to be used as a predictive model and "fed" with appropriate data. Instead the theory "aims to help researchers and practitioners to orientate themselves in complex real-life problems, identify key issues which need to be dealt with and direct the search for relevant evidence and suitable solutions". This is in line with the basic concepts of the research circle and crucial for the project (Andersson, 2007).

Authentic communication between learners of the same age at the blogs is supposed to be stimulating and encouraging for their learning. It is essential that the initiatives in their communication are taken by the learners at the blogs to lead them into collaboration, interaction and communication. ICT enhances oral communication and visual materials facilitate communication, particularly when the linguistic resources of English are limited. Additional means of communication other than written texts, such as visual material, show that young learners are authentically interested in sharing their experiences and finding out about others' lives and situations. At the end of the project when the evaluation is carried out the different educational contexts in the two countries are taken into account. The learners express their personal opinions on what they learned, and what was interesting and encouraging in the project.

The participating teachers met on a regular basis. Meetings with the Swedish teachers took place once a month. The research circle model was conducted in the Participatory Action Research-tradition (Reason & Bradbury, 2007). The research circle is an arena where researchers and practitioners meet using their respective knowledge and competence to jointly tackle practical and social science problems of mutual interest (Andersson, 2007). In the research circle experiences were discussed from ongoing activities in relation to the blogs. Planning of forthcoming activities was another characteristic activity. Teachers' input can be described as co-researchers. The Russian teachers were occasionally in contact with the lecturers at the university in Kaliningrad to discuss the project. A team of Swedish and Russian lecturers visited the Russian schools in December 2012 to evaluate and discuss the study. At the end of the second semester, the Swedish teachers and the Swedish researchers analyzed the project (Andersson & Sundh, 2013).

PURPOSE OF THE STUDY AND RESEARCH QUESTIONS

The purpose of the project is to study collaboration in interactive communication by young learners in Sweden and Russia when ICT is an integrated part of their learning process. Focus is on how young learners' activities at websites, in this case blogs, can be encouraged with the use of ICT. Documentation and communication at the blogs can be expected to change the context and situation of the learning processes by influencing the learners´ interest of using English and ICT; affecting activities across all school subjects, and, in addition, support inclusion of learners irrespective of previous knowledge or experience of digital tools. The purpose of the study is to find answers to how people use ICT as a mediating tool in communication and documentation; how people use ICT as a means for sharing produced material in collaboration between young learners in Sweden and Russia; what pedagogical implications, challenges and changes international collaboration on blogs lead to?

METHODS AND DATA

The participating schools were selected to represent primary schools in a typically Swedish and Russian environment. The schools and pupils were not randomly selected but the teachers of the classes at the schools were interested in participating in the study. The three schools on Gotland are minor schools in the countryside and the three Russian schools are larger than these Swedish partner schools. In the Kaliningrad region, two schools are situated in the countryside and one school in the city of Kaliningrad. All in all some 100 learners, aged 12, participated and the project was carried out between six classes. The Russian and Swedish learners were to communicate and use ICT and publish material at three different blogs and the teachers were to provide opportunities for communication between the learners. Each blog, and the learners participating and acting there, could in line with Lave and Wenger (1991), be understood as a *community of practitioners*. Emphasis was on the learners' collaboration in authentic communication with persons of their own age in another geographical region. The six classes collaborated in pairs at a shared blog and it was required that the communication was to be carried out between classes and not between individual learners. The idea behind the recommendation to work in groups was to provide support to all learners to participate in activities at the blogs and work collectively in the production and encourage inclusion. The activities at the blog were to take place during lessons as well as after school.

The first part of the collected data consists of contributions by the Russian and Swedish learners at the three blogs. The second part is the documentation from regular meetings in the research circles with Russian and Swedish teachers. The third part is material that includes answers in questionnaires and interviews completed by the learners and notes taken at school visits to the Swedish and Russian schools. Furthermore, the fourth part consists of the cultural aspects of education within a national

school system, both in Russia and in Sweden, and this information was provided in evaluations by teachers and university lecturers. The researchers took part of the blogs and gained knowledge about activities that went on in the classes. Evidently the data from classroom activities were limited and dependent on the teachers' observations and documentation, illuminated and discussed in the research circle. What is more, the blogs were public and thereby anyone could be acquainted with the content which implied that the learners had to be aware of ethical considerations of their contributions. The empirical data collected as described above was used in the analysis in the following way. Firstly, the learners' production was analyzed in terms of quantity and quality. In terms of quantity, the approach was an analysis of frequencies, occurrences, length of sentences and the number of words. In terms of quality, aspects considered were the degree of interaction, modes of communication, i.e. texts and visual material, and how they were combined, and finally the content in particular with regard to intercultural matters. These matters could be more abstract issues and include the learners' personal values and beliefs. Additionally, another issue was whether this cross-cultural communication between Russian and Swedish young people led to group discussions in the phase of production regarding what can, and ought to be published at a blog that is open for anyone to read. Secondly, the documentation from the meetings in the research circles formed the basis for the study of the on-going learning processes when the learners were active in communicating, collaborating and producing material. The focus was on sharing the teachers' strategies and experiences in inspiring and encouraging the learners in the collaboration. Evidently, pedagogical dilemmas were raised and strategies were scrutinized together. Thirdly, the learners' comments in questionnaires and in classroom meetings with interviews were analyzed, at least partly, in the framework of the research circle. Finally, the fourth part, namely the material regarding intercultural differences, were used in the continuous discussions in the research circles and was expected to be a prerequisite for a full understanding of Swedish and Russian circumstances at schools and thereby to create interest and analytical reflections so that the project with its aim could be completed. We can identify the following three phases in the analysis.

- Linguistic analyses and analyses of modes of learners' production, and
- Evaluations of the learners' responses in questionnaires and interviews, and
- Continuous analyses in discussions of the data collected in the research circles

The results in the section below are presented in the following way. Firstly the learners' contributions at the blogs are described. Secondly, an account is provided of these learners' activities in the production of these contributions. Thirdly, the results from the teachers' participation in the classroom and in the research circle are presented

ANALYSIS

The learners were active in their communication with their partner schools at the blogs. Their production and use of the English language was analyzed. Analysis of their exchanges includes the number of contributions at the websites, the number of words and the topics, defined as themes.

Collection of the data provides the researchers with samples of learner language usage. The sample can be described according to Ellis (2005, p. 23) as "naturally-occurring samples with no control and with primary attention to message content" and possibly include content of the learners' subjective theories (Grotjahn, 1991, p. 188) defined as "complex cognitive structures that are highly individual, relatively stable and relatively enduring, and that fulfill the tasks of explaining and predicting such human phenomena as action, reaction, thinking, emotion, and perception". Table 1 shows the learners' contributions on 585 occasions in English at the three blogs. The written contributions are more frequent than recordings of the learners' spoken English. There are ten times more written than oral entries and the total number is over 25 thousand words.

The themes identified in the contributions during the first semester were about personal identification, house and home, environment, daily life, free time and entertainment, travel, relations with other people, health and body care, education, shopping, food and drink, places, language and the weather. In the second semester there were some new themes added: traditions and celebrations, computer games, sports and holidays. Initially there were many individually written contributions but this feature slowly changed. Initially there was an element of conflict between working individually and working together in small groups but with the use of tools like cameras and ipads the need for collaboration was obvious.

Table 1. Number of Swedish and Russian learners' contributions at the websites September 2012 - May 2013

Websites	Written Contributions	Spoken Contributions
	Number of Contributions / Number of Words	Number of Contributions
kaliningradendre.se	277 / 15 617	19
kaliningradeskelhem.se	116 / 5 827	8
kaliningradsanda.se	145 / 3 705	20
Total	538 / 25 149	47

The linguistic analysis shows variation in the contributions in terms of range of vocabulary, idiomatic expressions, syntactic complexity and the language used in chats and blogs. Andersson and Sundh (2013) analyze the language in the contributions in detail. Examples of the learners' production are provided below. As regards the range of vocabulary, abstract nouns are of interest in contributions at the blog since they may correlate with a general range of vocabulary or indicate the degree of abstract thinking in the young learners' production (Sundh, 2003, p. 90). In what follows two nouns are used in an abstract meaning, namely *solution* and *heart*.

I also want to tell you how we do when we need help. We this in our school. You are trying to find a solution yourself if you do not we usually ask the friends for help before you going to teacher. (kaliningradeskelhem.se Oct 9)

I will tell you about Kafidralny cathedral, Kafidralny Cathedral stands in the heart of the city. Near the grave of Kant. (kaliningradendre.se Nov 28)

The learners' contributions were analyzed from the mode of communication. Different types and combinations of types of tools that were used at the blogs are: Text; Text with pictures; Text with animations; Recorded text; Recorded text with pictures; Recorded film; Recorded text with animations; Recorded and written text. Written contributions were by far more frequent than recordings of the learners' spoken English. The explanation of the high frequency of written contributions lies in the fact that these are the quickest ways when you want to send a message. You need time for planning and producing when you record a film or create animations. In spite of being more time-consuming we can find quite a few sequences where video cameras, iPads or mobile telephones are used for recordings. Some learners work out sequences where they add sound and music to make the movies. In these sequences there are indications that the learners enjoy working with material for the websites and an illustrative example is the application called the Voki, an avatar to whom you can give different shapes and voices. After recording a spoken message the voice can be changed so it will be the Voki who speaks to the audience. Using the avatar seemed to work as a strong motivating "gadget" for producing utterances, also among learners who were a bit quiet, shy and worried. The learners encouraged each other to communicate and participate at the websites in dialogues on familiar topics. The learners are interested in each other's contributions and inspire each other to try new tools, e.g. the use of the Voki in one school inspired other schools.

Following the learners' contributions on the websites, it is clear that the English language and the digital competences expanded. The learners learned from collective experiences and advanced peers. From a sociocultural perspective, the learners gradually learned by collaboration and interaction. This is clear from an initial examination where they depended on external support, over systematic examination with intensive use in specific practices and reduced dependence on external support. They improved their ability to explain the tool for a beginner and to appropriate mediating tools for specific purposes. Finally they acted in such a way that the mediating tool became transparent to the user (Säljö, 2013). In line with Vygotskij (1934/2001) and the theory of zone of proximal development (ZpD) learning processes in this project appear twice, first in a social dimension, between the learners as they collaborate in the creative process of formulating contributions together, and then in individual processes "inside" the learner (Vygotskij, 1978).

The learners' reactions and comments were collected, primarily from teachers' observations and in the learners' small exercises and exchanges with their teachers. More specific comments were gathered through a questionnaire and in interviews by the teachers and researchers. The learners mention main areas where they learned a great deal by collaborating at the blogs: the English language, cultural aspects through contacts with learners of the same age in Russia/Sweden, and, to work with a variety of digital tools. Another aspect mentioned was the importance of being encouraged by teachers and researchers.

The learners like to work at the blog because they have an opportunity to learn about daily life in Russia and in Sweden: "I think I have learned about pupils in Kaliningrad, how they are and how they work with their stuff". The Russian learners mentioned they learned about Swedish traditions and wanted to learn Swedish words. Swedish and Russian learners noticed that English was the first foreign language. One of them wrote: "We have about the same knowledge in English because we both have English as our first foreign language". Most of the learners wanted the project and collaboration through blogs to continue. The learners like to practice English at the blog due to authentic communication and genuine receivers. They find it useful and encouraging and they become brave in the course of the project. The following comments point to what most of the learners in both countries write and think.

I like to write and talk to them and probably they cannot so much English either or speak fluent.

You practice pronunciation and language when making movies and you practice spelling when you write.

I dare to speak and I write more and more fluent and it feels more natural to talk and write in English now.

Of course I dare to talk to them. It is not dangerous. They probably feel the same.

The learners provide aspects of learning of the English language as well and claim that their vocabulary, spelling and pronunciation improve during the project.

I like it very much because you learn so much more English.

I feel more confident when I am writing now.

I think I have learned more English than before we started the blog.

I have learned to write better in English and to spell better.

The learners seem to be aware that the use of ICT influences their proficiency to use the English language. In relation to digital tools we asked: "With what tools and in what way do you prefer to work at the blog?" and "What do think you learned using the blog"? The answers focus on what they learned using these digital tools, and obviously the English language is one aspect.

To write at the blog about yourself and make a Voki because then you can talk with your voice and tell something.

Record movies and embed them at the blog because then you are allowed to talk and write and that is the best because then you talk and use your body language.

To record when you are talking is what I like best.

Movies and, if it is possible, to record a dialogue (chat) and then we could have that dialogue at the blog.

I have learned to use the blog better and to make a Voki and I like the Vokis best because they are easy to make.

Making tutorials to other project schools is mentioned as engaging and useful. These tutorials informed on ethical regulations regarding e.g. what music, pictures and movies the learners were allowed to use at the blogs. Project participation means being active in collaborative work and contribute to the blogs. The learners express their experiences and feelings in the communication of the project: "I feel involved because I have written a lot on the blog and because I am involved in writing and talking to the others on the blog". Some learners claim they would have been more involved if their teacher had suggested topics to write about. Participation at the blogs seems to be encouraging and enjoyable and the groups of learners can be regarded as "communities of practitioners" (Lave & Wenger, 1991; Andreasen & Rasmussen, 2014). They take responsibility for writing, making movies or pictures etc., when contributing at the blogs. Although they are all active in different ways, some of them take the role of "legitimate peripheral participation" (1991), which, in this case means they are participating on ideas and design of the contributions without necessarily writing or talking in English. They learn from each other and work on contributions at the blogs providing opportunities for collaboration in groups and between novices and more advanced learners. The activity seems to stimulate inclusion of all learners. Social and technological "mediation" in different situations go hand in hand (Kaptelinin & Nardi, 2012). The learners claim they enjoy communicating with students in Kaliningrad and Gotland. One of the learners stated communication is at its best during dialogues at the blog: "because you cannot go there and meet them". Communication via comments, through videos and movies gives an "opportunity to find new friends and communicating at the blog is funnier than being pen pals". They like blogging in English and chatting on Skype is another favorite.

Teachers' Comments on Activities at Blogs and in Classrooms

The Swedish teachers met once a month in the research circle. They brought documentation from observations, experiences and dilemmas from activities in their classes to the meetings. Issues investigated by the group of researchers and teachers - and by the teachers and learners - grew out of matters of importance in everyday work in the classes. It is obvious that teaching and learning is a collaborative process, not only building on the teachers´ ideas but also on the learners´ ideas and experiences.

There are issues worth considering for successful work with learners at websites. The teachers claim that they meet technical problems with updating the websites. The absence of wireless internet connection is another obstacle since they have to move computers between classrooms. In some periods there are no responses, and the connection seems to be broken. This resulted in learners' losing interest in the blogs. Also, the learners were encouraged to be active at the blogs, but sometimes it was hard to find the available time. The teachers discussed how they could support activities at the blogs. Since the idea of the project was that the learners took the initiatives in the communication, it was crucial for the success to decide how to support without interfering in the learners' communication. In addition, to continue the communication successfully at the blogs, the teachers discussed appropriate requirements in terms of frequency and quantity of postings.

The learners' oral skill was worth taking into account since it is hard teaching and time-consuming for teachers and learners to practice and test it. The teachers discussed issues related to oral communication and production of films and podcasts. Production of oral contributions visible at the blogs was initially time-consuming. On the other hand, many oral activities took place in a context outside the formal classroom setting. Obviously the learners spontaneously used their language for communication in for instance Skype in the afternoons and evenings. It was considered important to include all learners in activities in relation to the blog. The teachers worked hard to include all learners in the project. Some of them had a hard time learning social interaction at school, in some cases due to a diagnosis of autism spectrum disorder.

Production at the blogs changed during the project. It became interactive with replies on the contributions and suggestions of new topics. The contributions and replies at the blogs were frequently read in class. In that way the learners found suitable themes for dialogues, such as traditions and holidays. This fact encouraged them to elaborate on the topics which would be unthinkable in a traditional classroom setting. Genuine responses and questions worked in favor of making the learners proceed in developing their topics in the dialogues.

The teachers reported that parents spontaneously mentioned the child's results in English and they saw participation in the project as a key issue. In addition, parents also said that they could see developments across subjects. The teachers heard comments like: "in the project there is a genuine receiver" and "this communication is real". In their opinion the learners with difficulties at school developed their language more than others and they seem to become confident in using English. The fact that teachers encouraged the learners to visit the blog once a week was also an influential factor that led them to show interest in each other with thoughts of future friendship.

Results show that producing and sharing produced material occurred quite often in the learners' spare time. Some of the learners were communicating with Kaliningrad in the evenings. The time difference was no obstacle. The project was a complement to conventional traditional teaching, where for instance more oral activities in English than is otherwise the case took place. Some learners made movies with real or disguised voices or they interacted on Skype. On Skype,

their activities could not be supervised or guided so they became independent participants in the communication. As a probable result of these conversations, teachers observed that the learners dared to act and also wanted to be recorded. The learners' ideas were realized - communicated and responded to at the blogs. The activities at the blogs made it possible for the learners to work individually and in groups with their communication. Their everyday life situations found their own voices. Initiatives were taken to produce tutorials for all the three blogs. The selection and choice of mediating tools was crucial.

The language production at the websites provided occasions for additional reviewing and checking by the learners' themselves. The learners saved their drafts of presentations and went back to study previous contributions at the websites. The learners asked how to write and spell and the teachers gave feedback which was perceived as a boost into their language proficiency in English. The contributions were even saved in "Learners' portfolios".

It was of great significance that there was a permitting attitude that gave the different schools and teachers' chances to work with the blogs in their own way. The teachers argue for deeper analyses whether the project benefits other knowledge and skills than just proficiency in English. Students claim that it is fun to participate in the project so evidently there is something amusing and stimulating in the activities but this experience needs to be scrutinized. The question is whether the communicative situation – and when perceived as authentic – is the useful aspect to work further with.

The teachers' motives to participate in the project can be summarized as follows. The project provides opportunities for young learners to practice English in collaboration with learners of the same age. English, being the first foreign language studied was now in a context for the learners where their linguistic limitations were not in focus. The learners' use of English was effective for their communicative purposes and this encouraged them further to produce longer and more elaborate contributions. Furthermore, this practice of English provided opportunities for the learners to learn more about ICT and digital tools while practicing English. Finally, the teachers state that this authentic communication with genuine receivers encouraged the collaboration at the blogs. This was highlighted as a core aspect since these learning situations can be difficult to arrange in traditional education. A driving force was also the teachers' interest in school life in Russia and Sweden respectively, since the countries are close geographically and have been in contact historically.

ICT is a useful tool which puts learners in an active role in international communication. The learners become independent in their language production but at the same time the activities imply both necessary cooperation in teams to solve both technical and linguistic difficulties, and inclusion of all learners in the processes providing a context where every learner can have a role to play. Working with ICT had pedagogical implications that influence the learners' activities across all subjects and not only in English and when working with the contributions at the blogs. The challenge of the project was to work in a cross-cultural context.

SOLUTIONS AND RECOMMENDATIONS

There are pedagogical implications of the study to consider. It was crucial that the learners were active at the blogs and made contributions and commented on others' contributions. The aspects influencing the learners' activities were identified and they were as follows. It was positive when the teachers encouraged their learners to be active at the blogs for instance when searching for and discovering uses of various digital tools, and furthermore by suggesting topics or linking the ordinary work at school, primarily in English, to

the topics at the blogs. On the other hand, these guidelines provided by the teachers which had the purpose to encourage the learners to be active in the discussions at the blogs could work in a contradictory way. In this way the teachers can become forces that take the initiative from the learners in their production and make them return to a school context. The learners could then leave their authentic communication and communicative motives and needs and consequently refrain from spontaneous communication (Chapelle, 2007; Ellis, 1992).

The learners' contributions turned out to show characteristics of authentic communication with genuine receivers. In addition, the learners experienced that their production was found by many visitors at the blogs from a good many countries. This was a surprise to the learners and to some of them it was encouraging. The language used was the learners' own property (Tornberg, 2007). The motive for being active at the blogs was the fact that they wanted to communicate with the use of ICT and have English as lingua franca (ELF) and at approximately the same level of proficiency. In these cross-cultural encounters with ELF, visual material facilitated interaction and understanding and ICT was the driving force for production in the communication at the blogs. Some of the learners developed their insights into efficient communication with the use of ICT and they discussed what modes and media to use in order to find a way to convey a message without misunderstandings. These discussions indicate an awareness of the receivers' chances to understand a contribution. This is evidently a social capacity, which they use hand-in-hand with different digital tools, and can be regarded to be in line with suggestions from Kaptelinin and Nardi (2012) saying that social and technological mediation often are inseparable.

The variation in length between the contributions and in combination with ICT implies either that the learners were at different stages in their learning or that they had different attitudes to contributing at the blogs. There is a tendency for longer contributions in the course of time and whether it is a matter of language proficiency or attitude remains unclear. Examples from one of the blogs show this difference in length.

My name is Amelia. I am a girl between 11 and 12 years. I go to Sanda school in grade 6. (Oct 3, kaliningradsanda.se)

I told my teacher about it and she said that we actually could start a server. Now I just want to know how many that play Minecraft and if someone volunteers to create a server and then we can go in and out on the server anytime we want! (March 6, kaliningradsanda.se).

The results of the analysis show that the average numbers of words in all contributions at the kaliningradsanda.com-blog is 31.4 words per contribution in September and 88.6 words per contribution in May. The average number of characters in all contributions and at the three blogs shows the same tendency: from 500 characters in September to 1500 characters in May. In addition, the Swedish learners were more productive than the Russian learners with 2/3 of the contributions being Swedish. The Swedish learners also commented on the absence of activities and responses by Russian learners.

The content in the production drifted away from a school context and came closer to the learners´ own culture and thereby their vernacular (Gee, 2008). As we have seen in the project, international communication in English at a blog stimulates intercultural awareness, cross-cultural communication and with contacts at an early age. This was seen when for instance the learners were interested in similarities and differences in schooling and life and to learn Swedish or Russian. To share different kinds of knowledge and experiences through digital tools and via social media, like in this project, is in line with the Swedish curriculum.

Working with the blogs also seems to provide collaboration between novices and more advanced learners, in the classrooms as well as with the partner school in Russia/Sweden, and it provides opportunities for inclusion of all learners in the activities. Although the learners were enthusiastic and active and used their different knowledge to enhance an appropriate communication, some of them took the role of "legitimate peripheral participation" which, according to Lave and Wenger (1991) means, that they were participating on ideas and design of the contributions but not necessarily writing or talking in English. This was more frequent in the beginning of the project when some of the learners were shy. The motive to collaborate might have been a bit vague for some learners in the beginning but when the contact between schools was established this seemed to have become clear.

Throughout the project, collaboration between the teachers increased and ICT in general became more widely used at the schools. Furthermore, the teachers became aware of the importance of time available to support and encourage production at the blogs although some production and communication also took place in the learners' spare time. They also noticed that the difference in time between Russia and Sweden was an obstacle for "in-real-time" communication.

Carrying on with the project in a long-term perspective seems easier when the head of the school gives substantial support to the project and when several teachers are involved. But on the other hand, one enthusiastic teacher can definitely be a prerequisite for the project but more teachers involved are to be preferred.

Computer games and other digital tools were experienced as an entrance to and a motive for learning more English. There is a new world of digital resources including games available, and according to Gee (2008) and Gärdenfors (2010) there are new opportunities to learn. This implies that computer games and other digital tools can complement, and challenge, traditional textbooks and other learning materials. It is timely to ponder on introducing computer games in English as a possible source for sharing and developing interests at a distance.

Teachers observed some cultural similarities and differences in their views on teaching and learning at school. They agreed on the significance of making the learners contribute to a great extent at the blogs but one observed difference was when comparing the curricula where it was clear that the Russian curriculum gives little time and space at school for the activities such as the ones in this project, which in a Russian context can be regarded as being extra-curricular.

FUTURE RESEARCH DIRECTIONS

For future research another study involving teachers in schools and researchers at universities would be valuable. The teachers could be asked to elaborate on collective writing, observations in classrooms and Skype-meetings for discussions and further analyses (Boellstorff, Nardi, Pearce & Taylor, 2013). According to Gee (2008) and Shaffer (2006), digital resources and games complement traditional textbooks and other learning materials. It would be interesting to explore and analyze new video-media in collaboration with teachers in schools and researchers at universities. Another suggestion would be to cooperate on the use of a common website for the involved teachers. Such a website could facilitate exchange of ideas on teachers' work including surveys, descriptions and evaluations of situations, the learners' skills, analyses and comparisons of teachers' work plus suggestions for new themes/topics at the website. Other examples are festivals and traditions, computer games and means of social media.

The research circle could prove to be a tool for sharing experiences in an international project. Participation can play a significant role in strengthening the individual teacher by challenging and innovating dialectic processes (Andersson, 2007; Reason & Bradbury, 2007).

Curricular differences at schools in the two countries provide possible explanations but research is needed before we can draw conclusions about the impact of cultural differences.

CONCLUSION

This study is based on project data collected in relation to activities at blogs and through observations by participating teachers. The project is multifaceted in terms of different categories of participants communicating in different ways; learners communicate, interact and share experiences; teachers organize, facilitate and encourage communication at the blogs; researchers meet participants and analyze activities and production of English. The blogs are public displays and anyone can become acquainted with the content. This implies that the learners have to be aware of the ethical considerations in their contributions.

The learners show interest in learning about the culture, values and language in Russia and Sweden respectively. Communication at the blogs creates new perspectives of the world and helps establish contacts for mutual understanding of different life styles. To share different kinds of knowledge and experiences through digital tools and via social media is in line with the Swedish curriculum. The project gives opportunities for people to learn about the circumstances, life and school among young people in the Baltic Sea region. Learning about situations in different parts of the world is important to avoid future misunderstandings and conflicts.

The learners of the project are offered a meaningful tool they learn from. Most of them are curious about ICT-tools and explore them on their own and in groups. They learn how to use these tools, and both learners and teachers realize that the teachers do not always have the knowledge of how to manage technical questions about ICT. In order to be successful in the learners' use of the blogs the learners need opportunities to communicate and interact in ways similar to the ones they find in current social media.

The project supplies the prerequisites for learners to take on responsibility for learning processes and influences on education. When analyzing the learners´ activities at the blogs from perspectives of language development, digital competences, inclusion and collaboration, we find that the time spent working with issues in relation to the blogs, was a time-saving business, providing opportunities; methods and didactical tools to contribute to inclusive education. Communication and documentation with digital tools work out well for inclusion of learners in the learning processes. From the teachers' perspective it would be of great value if two teachers at each school were involved in a similar project. That arrangement would enable for the parties to reflect on classroom and virtual activities.

Collaboration in communication by means of ICT is a challenge. Compared to educational traditions and routines, framed by cultural and historical aspects, where learning takes place inside the classroom, the use of ICT admits participation at a globalized arena without geographical boundaries, in "placeless organizations" (Nardi, 2007). Collaboration between Russian and Swedish learners and teachers could expand to schools around the Baltic Sea. The object for further studies in collaborative activities in an international perspective is *change of content* in classrooms and at school level. Nardi (2007) suggests collaboration, transformation and learning in placeless organizations as an ICT-theme for further study. In ICT-driven education the teachers' role changes towards less control of the content all in line with Engeström's (2010) concept of "fluid organizations."

REFERENCES

Andersson, F. (2007). *Att utmana erfarenheter: Kunskapsutveckling i en forskningscirkel.* (Doctoral thesis). Stockholm University, Stockholm, Sweden.

Andersson, F., & Sundh, S. (2013). *GOTKALC. COM: Young Learners on Gotland and in Kaliningrad in Communication in English with the Use of Digital Tools – the Pilot Study.* Visby: Gotland University.

Andreasen, K., & Rasmussen, P. (2014). Video mediated teaching and learning in Adult Education. In T. Hansson (Ed.), Contemporary Approaches to Activity Theory: Interdisciplinary Perspectives on Human Behavior. Hershey, PA: IGI Global.

Boellstorff, T., Nardi, B., Pearce, C., & Taylor, T. L. (2013). Words with Friends: Writing Collaboratively Online. *Interaction, 20*(5), 58–61. doi:10.1145/2501987

Chapelle, C. A. (2007). Technology and second language acquisition. *Annual Review of Applied Linguistics, 27,* 98–114. doi:10.1017/S0267190508070050

Ellis, R. (1992). Learning to communicate in the classroom. *Studies in Second Language Acquisition, 14*(1), 1–23. doi:10.1017/S0272263100010445

Ellis, R., & Barkhuizen, G. (2005). *Analysing Learner Language.* Oxford, UK: Oxford University Press.

Engeström, Y. (2010). *In From Teams to Knots Activity-Theoretical Studies of Collaboration and Learning at Work.* Cambridge Books Online. Retrieved from http://ebooks.cambridge.org

Estling Vannestål, M. (2007). *A University Grammar of English with a Swedish Perspective.* Lund: Studentlitteratur.

Gärdenfors, P. (2010). *Lusten att förstå: Om lärande på människans villkor*. Stockholm: Natur & Kultur.

Gee, J. P. (2006). Are Video Games Good for Learning? *Nordic Journal of Digital Literacy*, *1*(3), 172–183.

Gee, J. P. (2007). *What Video Games Have to Teach Us about Learning and Literacy*. New York: Palgrave/Macmillan.

Gee, J. P. (2008). A Sociocultural Perspective on Opportunity to Learn. In P. A. Moss, D. C. Pullin, J. P. Gee, E. H. Haertel, & L. J. Young (Eds.), Assessment, Equity, and Opportunity to Learn (pp. 76-108). Cambridge, UK: Cambridge University Press.

Grotjahn, R. (1991). The research programme subjective theories: A new approach in second language research. *Studies in Second Language Acquisition*, *13*(2), 187–214. doi:10.1017/S0272263100009943

Kaptelinin, V. (2013). Activity Theory. In *The Encyclopedia of Human-Computer Interaction* (2nd ed.). Aarhus, Denmark: The Interaction Design Foundation. Retrieved from http://www.interaction-design.org/encyclopedia/activity_theory.html

Kaptelinin, V., & Nardi, B. (2012). *Affordances in HCI: Toward a Mediated Action Perspective*. Paper presented at the Conference of CHI 2012. Austin, TX. doi:10.1145/2207676.2208541

Lave, J., & Wenger, E. (1991). *Situated learning: legitimate peripheral participation*. Cambridge, UK: Cambridge University Press. doi:10.1017/CBO9780511815355

Leffler, E., & Lundberg, G. (2012). Att vilja lära språk är entreprenöriellt lärande. *Lingua*, (2), 15–21.

Nardi, B. (2007). Placeless Organizations: Collaborating for Transformation. *Mind, Culture, and Activity*, *14*(1-2), 5–22. doi:10.1080/10749030701307663

Perdue, C. (2000). Organizing principles of learner varieties. *Studies in Second Language Acquisition*, *22*(3), 299–305. doi:10.1017/S0272263100003016

Reason, P., & Bradbury-Huan, H. (Eds.). (2007). Handbook of action research: Participative inquiry and practice. London: Sage Publications.

Säljö, R. (2013). *Lärande och kulturella redskap: om lärprocesser och det kollektiva minnet*. Lund: Studentliteratur.

Selander, S., & Kress, G. R. (2010). *Design för lärande. Ett multimodalt perspektiv*. Stockholm: Norstedts.

Shaffer, D. W. (2006). *How Computer games help children learn*. New York: Palgrave Macmillan. doi:10.1057/9780230601994

Skolverket. (2011). *Curriculum for the compulsory school, preschool class and the recreation center 2011*. Stockholm: Skolverket.

Sundh, S. (2003). *Swedish School Leavers' Oral Proficiency in English. In Acta Universitatis Upsaliensia 123*. Uppsala: Almqvist&Wiksell.

Sundqvist, P. (2009). *Extramural English Matters – Out-of-School English and Its Impact on Swedish Ninth Graders' Oral Proficiency and Vocabulary*. Karlstad: Karlstad University Studies.

Tornberg, U. (2007). Vem äger språkundervisningens språk?. In T. Englund (Ed.), Utbildning som kommunikation: Deliberativa samtal som möjlighet (pp. 361-379). Göteborg: Daidalos.

Vygotskij, L. (1978). *Mind in Society*. Cambridge, MA: Harvard University Press.

Vygotskij, L. (2001). *Tänkande och språk*. Göteborg: Daidalos. (Original work published 1934)

Wenger, E. (1998). *Communities of Practice: learning, meaning, and identity.* Cambridge, UK: Cambridge University Press. doi:10.1017/CBO9780511803932

Wertsch, J. V. (1998). *Mind as action.* New York: Oxford University Press.

ADDITIONAL READING

Aarsand, P. (2007). *Around the screen: Computer activities in children's everyday lives.* Linköping: Linköping University. Doctoral Thesis.

Aarsand, P. (2011). Barns spillning. Om digital spillkompetanse I ulika praksiser. In P-Aarsand (Ed.), Digitale medier i barns og unges hverdag. Norsk senter for barneforskning.

<ths>Åkerlund, D. (2013). Elever syns på nätet. Multimodala texter och autentiska mottagare. Åbo: Åbo Academy University Press. Doctoral thesis.</ths>

Åkerlund, D., Buskqvist, U., & Enochsson, A. (2010). *Learning design when the classroom goes online.* Paper presented at Designs for Learning 2010, Stockholm University, Stockholm, 2010, 17–19 March. Retrieved from 13/07/2009 http://publicering.se/dokument/Learning_design-On_line.pdf

Andersson, F. (2012). Att leda specialpedagogiska insatser. G. Berg, F. Sundh & C. Wede (Eds.). Lärare som ledare – i och utanför klassrummet (pp. 191-208). Lund: Studentlitteratur.

Bamford, A., & Wimmer, M. (2012). *The role of arts education in enhancing school attractiveness: A literature review* (EENC Paper, February 2012). Retrieved from 7/7/2013 http://cdc-ccd.org/IMG/pdf/school-attractiveness-paper-final-website.pdf

Barton, D., & Lee, C. (2013). *Language Online.* London: Routledge.

Council of Europe. (2012). *European Language Portfolio.* Retrieved from 07/07/2013 http://www.coe.int/t/DG4/Portfolio/?L=E&M=/main_pages/introduction.html

Engeström, Y. (2001). Expansive Learning at Work: Towards an activity theoretical reconceptualization. *Journal of Education and Work, 14*(1), 133–156. doi:10.1080/13639080020028747

Gee, J. P. (2008). Game-Like Learning: An Example of Situated Learning and Implications for Opportunity to Learn. P. A. Moss, D. C. Pullin, J. P. Gee, E. H. Haertel, & L. J. Young. Assessment, Equity, and Opportunity to Learn (pp. 200-221). Cambridge Books Online: Cambridge University Press.

Jansson, A. (2011). Becoming a Narrator: A Case Study in the Dynamics of Learning Based on the Theories/Methods of Vygotsky. *Mind, Culture, and Activity, 18*(1), 5–25. doi:10.1080/10749030903244210

Jansson, A. (2011). *"Nästan som en författare"-multimedialt berättande.* Stockholm: Stockholm University. Doctoral thesis.

Kjällander, S. (2011). *Designs for learning in an extended digital environment: Case studies of social interaction in the social science classroom.* Stockholm: Stockholm University, Department of Education. Doctoral thesis.

Koh, E., & Lim, J. (2012). Using online collaboration applications for group assignments: The interplay between design and human characteristics. *Computers & Education, 59*(2), 481–496. doi:10.1016/j.compedu.2012.02.002

Kress, G. R. (2010). *Multimodality: A social semiotic approach to contemporary communication.* London: Routledge.

Kuutti, K. (1996). Activity theory as a potential framework for human-interaction research. B. Nardi (Ed.), Context and Consciousness: Activity Theory and Human-Computer Interaction (pp. 7–44). Cambridge, MA: MIT Press.

Qvarsell, B. (1988). Children's Views on Computers: The Importance of Affordance. *Education and Computing*, *4*(3), 223–230. doi:10.1016/S0167-9287(88)80015-3

Rasmussen, T. (2007). *Two faces of the public sphere the functions of internet communication in public deliberation*. Retrieved from 5/7/2009 http://www.york.ac.uk/res/siru/dispo/abstract_rasmussen.htm

Sannino, A., Daniels, H., & Gutiérrez, K. D. (Eds.). (2012). *Learning and Expanding with Activity Theory*. Cambridge: Cambridge University Press.

Seidlhofer, B. (2011). *Understanding English as a Lingua Franca*. Oxford: Oxford University Press.

Selander, S. (2008). Designs of learning and the formation and transformation of knowledge in an era of globalization. *Studies in Philosophy and Education*, *27*(4), 267–281. doi:10.1007/s11217-007-9068-9

Selander, S., & Svärdemo-Åberg, E. (Eds.). (2009). *Didaktisk design i digital miljö – nya möjligheter för lärande*. Stockholm: Liber.

Sørby, M. (2008). Digital Competence – From Education Policy to Pedagogy: The Norwegian Context. In C. Lankshear & M. Knobel (Eds.), *Digital literacies: concepts, policies and practices* (pp. 119–150). New York: Peter Lang.

Sundin, O. (2012). Att hantera kunskap och information i den digitala samtiden. U. Carlsson & J. Johannisson (Eds.), *Läsarnas marknad, marknadens läsare: En forskningsantologi*. [Stockholm: Fritzes.]. *SOU*, *10*, 141–154.

Tsui, A. B. M., & Law, D. Y. K. (2007). Learning as boundary-crossing in school–university partnership. *Teaching and Teacher Education*, *23*(8), 1289–1301. doi:10.1016/j.tate.2006.06.003

Vettorel, P. (2013). English as a Lingua Franca in Wider Networking, Blogging Practices. *Journal of English as a Lingua Franca*, *2*(2), 147–173.

KEY TERMS AND DEFINITIONS

Authentic Communication: The emphasis is on the communicators' production and interaction. In contrast to traditional textbooks and other learning materials, the topics and modes of communication is what the communicator finds interesting and engaging.

Digital Tools: All sorts of tools used for documentation and communication where technology is the foundation, as for example internet, software programs, websites and blogs. The tools serve both as the content itself, and as a tool to create content such as contributions on blogs.

Genuine Receivers: In contrast to traditional classrooms conversations where you use English just to exercise the language, a genuine receiver is a person who you address in English because is it necessary to use that language while it is that language you have in common.

ICT: Information and Communications Technology (ICT) is often used as an extended synonym for information technology, but is a more specific term that stresses the role of unified communications.

Inclusion: is often used in relation to the concept "a school for all", meaning that all children, with or without a disability, should have the right to participate in education settings. Inclusion is often used in relation to Special Educational Needs and the focus should be on all pupils' rights to participate in the school community on the same terms and conditions.

Lingua Franca: is a language that is adopted as a common language between speakers whose native languages are different.

Multimodal: The concept is used in this text in a combination with literacy's or media. The term *multimodal literacy's* imply that children develop towards spoken, printed, visual and digital texts. These include, for example, listening to and using spoken language as they play, learning that printed language carries meanings, enjoying stories and rhymes, becoming familiar with literacy's that are valued by their own communities, learning about symbols and numeric sign systems, and learning to use and to navigate around the images, symbols, sounds, languages and layouts they encounter on digital screens.

Participatory Action Research (PAR): This research tradition emphasizes collective inquiry grounded in experience and seeks to understand the world by trying to change it, collaboratively and reflectively. Within a PAR-tradition questions and issues significant for those who participate as co-researchers are addressed. Three basic aspects should be integrated: *participation*, usually grown out of societal and democratic issues, *action* based on experience, and *research* aimed at trustworthiness and the growth of knowledge.

Research Circle: Following the tradition of Participatory Action Research, the research circle is often described as an arena where researchers and practitioners, as co-researchers, meet using their respective knowledge and competence to jointly tackle 'problems' of mutual interest (Andersson, 2007; Reason & Bradbury, 2007). The dialogue has a central position in the research circle and plays a significant role for both the individual's acquisition of knowledge and that of the group as a whole. Reciprocity and recognition of others as being equally valuable members of the research circle, and the recognition of one´s own experiences *vis à vis* the critical scrutiny of others, as well as change, challenge and empowerment, are essential notions. Knowledge acquired throughout the process in the research circle signifies that something new, something that hardly could have been formed solely through practice or through research, has been created.

Chapter 3
Learning in Video-Mediated Classes

Karen E. Andreasen
Aalborg University, Denmark

Palle Rasmussen
Aalborg University, Denmark

ABSTRACT

Modern technology and improved video technology have widened the possibilities of offering young people in peripheral regions of countries education, and in recent years, several innovation projects using video-mediated teaching have been implemented in Denmark and in the Nordic countries. In the Danish region, a comprehensive innovation project including video-mediated simultaneous teaching at two locations was implemented in 2008-2010 for students at a General Adult Education Centre. Drawing on Etienne Wenger's (2004) theory about learning and communities of practice and on theoretical perspectives from architecture on space and learning, the chapter discusses results from the dialogue research related to the project. Results indicate that video-mediated teaching has a significant impact on student participation and that it appears to be demanding for some students, especially students with social or academic problems.

INTRODUCTION

This chapter presents an analysis and discussion of results from a dialogical approach to research in an adult education project on video-mediated teaching and learning. Based on results from research in peripheral regions of Denmark and using Etienne Wenger's theory about learning in communities of practice, the chapter discusses potentials and challenges of video-mediated education as a context for studying student learning. Wenger's

theory represents one of the recent strands in sociocultural theories and activity theory.

During the 1980s, video technology began to reveal its potential in various educational purposes (Lawson et al., 2010), for example parallel teaching, which is video-mediated simultaneous teaching of classes of students at different locations. Teaching is usually conducted by one teacher at one of the locations and organized as either one-to-many or many-to-many settings (Lawson, 2010, p. 3). The teacher may alternate between

DOI: 10.4018/978-1-4666-6603-0.ch003

the rooms. The teacher may also be supplemented by an assistant in another room. The underlying premise is that it is economically viable to teach small classes and the described arrangement enables for teaching a class with few participants with a larger class (Andreasen & Rasmussen, 2013; Andreasen & Hviid, 2011; Gynther, 2009; Hedestig & Kaptelinin, 2005).

Interest in video-mediated teaching and learning has grown as a result of societal demands on educated labour and opportunities for lifelong learning. Several projects on video-mediated teaching in education have been carried out. However, video-mediated teaching remains at an early stage (Lawson, 2010, p. 307) as a research area. More specifically, research on the impact of contextual factors in student learning seems to be missing (Lawson, 2010, p. 295; Lögdlund, 2010). Complementary research on student identity and participation by and teaching of students with social and academic problems is needed (Lawson, 2010; Lögdlund, 2010). Our research specifically addresses contextual influences and provides analysis and discussion of results from dialogue research following one innovation project in peripheral regions of Denmark. The students are mainly young adults of which a majority has either social or academic problems, or both, and the project includes studies in several classes. Analysis focuses on student identities and participation.

BACKGROUND

From 2009-2011, VUC Northern Jutland carried out a large Danish innovation project with parallel teaching at General Adult Education Centres, i.e. video-mediated simultaneous teaching of two classes at two different locations (Andreasen & Rasmussen, 2013; Andreasen, 2012). General Adult Education (AVU) offers school subjects as single courses at 8th, 9th or 10th grade level to adults. The majority of the course participants have experienced difficulties in primary and lower secondary school (Danmarks Evalueringsinstitut, 2011; Katznelson, 2010; Pless & Hansen, 2010). The teaching is adapted to the students' backgrounds, for instance by matching assignments and academic level to the students' level of earlier schooling, and by allocating extensive time for individual guidance by teachers and professionals at the school. AVU is generally considered to be a success in ordinary classes, but without use of video technology (Katznelson et al. 2009; Katznelson et al. 2010). The majority of the course participants are young adults under 30. They have either dropped out of school without an exam or they would like to improve their results. A few students attend the course subject purely out of interest (Damvad, 2013; Danmarks Statistik, 2013). Course participants who live in peripheral areas may be unable to take courses in specific subjects. Also if there are just a few students, parallel video-based teaching will make simultaneous teaching of two groups possible, either in many-to-many settings or in few-to-many settings (Lawson, 2010). Experimental projects have been conducted in several locations and educational contexts, including other AVU centres (Andreasen & Hviid, 2011). However, conducting this type of teaching for precisely this group of students involves challenges for teachers and students. The students are young people, many of whom need professional or social support. They suffer from low self-esteem regarding their academic resources (Katznelson, 2010; Katznelson, 2009) due to negative experiences in terms of feeling accepted in these contexts. Reaching this group of young people with a teaching design that suits their special experiences and preconditions is important, as the video-mediated approach could help them gain access to further education.

MAIN FOCUS OF THE CHAPTER

The chapter focuses on the described problem and includes analysis and discussion of the special conditions for developing learning processes in the framework of video-mediated parallel teaching. Video-mediated parallel teaching differs in significant ways from teaching based on the physical presence of one class gathered at one local school. Application of video technology generates a characteristic context for social interaction in school classes (Jong, 2005; Stödberg & Orre, 2009). The design opens opportunities, but also limits and influences people's experience of, approach to and understanding of the teaching and learning activities and also of our human resources. While the physical space sets the frameworks for expression and communication, educational activities reflect different approaches to occupying these spaces; different ways to use the material frameworks through activities that facilitate interactions and social collaboration (Anastasiades et al. 2010). We have to approach video-mediated teaching as a framework for learning and also consider potentials, limitations and challenges of the technology (Christiansen & Gynther, 2010; Gynther, 2005; Hedestig & Kaptelinin, 2005).

Analysis with this aim in mind must address the physical-material side of teaching where interactions are framed by, for instance, possibilities and limitations of technology and the layout and physical character of the classrooms. We need to address how the physical environment is experienced and how it is taken into use by ways of organising teaching activities that allow social interaction, social relations, experiences and academic learning. The above suggests focus on results from dialogue research on parallel teaching in AVU classes VUC Northern Jutland. The discussion and analysis are based on Etienne Wenger's theory of learning in communities of practice. The theory provides a framework for analyzing the school class as a social context, participation and production of student identity. Video-mediated classrooms differ significantly on several aspects from common classrooms, and the material aspects of teaching and learning play an important role (Löglund, 2010). Wenger's theoretical perspective

enables elaboration of an integrating theory for understanding architecture and environment and also an extended analysis of the physical context of the video-mediated classroom.

THEORETICAL PERSPECTIVES

Wenger's theory offers a recent strand in sociocultural theory (Engeström et al. 1999, p. 12). Features of the theory are inspired by activity theory, specifically Vygotsky (Wenger, 2010, p. 164), e.g. the role of concepts such as "artefacts", "meaning" and "sense". According to Wenger (Wenger, 2010, p. 164): "Activity theory, sociocultural historical theory, and the CoPs model move beyond the emphasis on context to consideration of social and historical influences as critical mediators of the learning process". Other theories commonly used in discussions of e-learning include Bakhtins' theory on dialogue, Wertsch, Cole, Vygotsky and Leontjev, and specifically Engeströms' theory of expansive learning (Anastasiades et al., 2010; Sutherland, 2004, Hedestig & Kaptelinin 2005; Lawson, 2010).

Wenger's theoretical framework may include problems with video-mediated classes as contexts for school activities, student identity and participation. Engeström (2007) addresses some of these matters, but his main focus excludes definitions of "identity". Instead the theory refers to other theorists in such discussions. With a shared focus on dialogue, semiotic theories in Bakhtin and Wertsch are suitable for other things than analysing contextual influences (Engeström et al., 1999, p. 11). Wenger's (2004, p. 258) theory is characterised by extended theoretical perspectives and therefore we find it suitable for our analysis; e.g. for addressing the design of learning environments as "a systematic, planned and well thought out colonisation of time and space in the service of an enterprise". In addition, we include concepts and theory from architecture (Gammelby, 2012; Kirkeby, 2004; Kirkeby, Iversen &

Martinussen, 2009) to complement the analysis of video-mediated teaching as a context for learning with a focus on student identity and participation.

PARTICIPATION IN SCHOOL CONTEXTS

A school class of students is a group of people and also a context for social and academic learning. There are different ways of participation, different roles and identities among students. In his theory on learning in communities of practice, Etienne Wenger (2006a; 2004) discusses questions of how the communities we belong to form a framework for learning and the learning process. He (ibid.) emphasises that belonging to social communities gives activities meaning and, depending on affiliation and how we participate in the community, gives access to learning.

Wenger (2006b, p.1; 2010, p. 1) defines such communities as "groups of people who share a concern or a passion for something they do and learn how to do it better as they interact regularly". *Learning* consequently depends on *ways of participating* as well as making use of options to participate and becoming part of different forms of linguistic-symbolic and physical-interactive activities. Such processes include a socially oriented form of learning. They might refer to learning as the forming of identities, different ways of understanding ourselves and others, or to a more academic type of learning in the form of declarative-academic knowledge. These two forms of learning are each other's prerequisites (Wenger, 2004). At the same time, learning is connected with identities, with how we understand ourselves and others, which again affect how we participate in interactions.

Wenger (2006b, p. 1) further describes communities of practice as "formed by people who engage in a process of collective learning in a shared domain of human endeavour" and might for instance include "a *clique of pupils* defining their identity in the school". A school class might or might not be a community of practice in Wenger's sense, but each school class harbours different communities of practice, with some students belonging to none, one or several of them. Students who feel like outsiders are marginalised or even excluded from the school or class as well as from the communities with fellow students form in the specific class (Wenger, 2010). Experience with being an outsider in a school class is a severe problem in terms of participation and learning and also in a future perspective since it may influence student identities negatively (Wenger, 2010).

PARTICIPATION AND IDENTITIES

Wenger (2004, p.15) describes interplay between learning and identity as follows: "learning changes who we are and forms personal genesis stories in relation to our communities." It is important to include and discuss student identity in a context of teaching and learning. On the one hand the students' identities influence how they participate in school activities. On the other hand school classes form a significant context for their experiences, for their academic potential and for the production of identities. Such experiences may affect their choices for further education.

The physical, material and institutionalized contexts in which teaching takes place form the framework for interactions, create opportunities, limit them and thereby influence what can be termed as the social space, which is characterised by social interaction, belonging, relations, positions and identities, as well as various forms of participation. The design of the physical context contributes to experiences of participation and also facilitates participation. They enable, inhibit and limit active participation and push students into certain ways of participation. The material side of the learning context influences student opportunities to learn as well as their academic and social experiences. Specific examples related to the video-mediated parallel teaching include counselling situations where the student is located at a distance and asks questions to the teacher via video, which means that the entire class will be listening in. This situation is problematic in terms of participation; the student's positioning in relation to fellow students has consequences for the student's identity. Another example is problems with sound and image, which complicate and inhibit participation by online students. Ultimately a poor connection has an unfortunate impact on the role, position and identity of the participant.

Students in the AVU classes have different identities and self-understandings, a situation which affects how they see themselves and their opportunities in relation to school and education, to their fellow students and to the activities in which they participate. As discussed in social psychology, these issues are also connected to different roles and positions in communities, which relate to various degrees of participation and ways of participation (Gjøsund & Huseby 2010, p. 51). Wenger (2004, p.115) points to the fact that learning processes relate "to the defining of identities, determining who is who, who is good at what, who knows what".

General Adult Education (AVU) programmes stretch over a long period of time, and the distribution of student roles and positions vary across time (Wenger, 2002, p. 96). Depending on which challenges and tasks the group or team is working on and encounters during the work process, the same course participant could take on different positions and roles (Ibid.). Academic learning generally depends on the degree to which the individual student actively participates in the teaching activities and assume different active roles.

SPACES FOR LEARNING: REIFICATIONS AND ARTEFACTS

Wenger (2010, p. 2) addresses the physical environment. In a school classroom, furniture, decor

and architecture reflect or a reification of the "social history" (Lögdlund, 2010) of the school and of the school class. These material aspects of a specific contexts form participants' experiences of situations (Lögdlund, 2010; Wenger, 2004, p. 74ff). Depending on the students' individual experiences, the context indicates for each student a special kind of behaviour they can expect, including legitimate behaviour and distribution of roles.

As an area of scientific study, architecture deals with the design and arrangement of the physical or material room as well as its significance as a setting for interactions (Gammelby 2012 and Kirkeby, Gitz-Johansen & Kampmann 2004; Lögdlund, 2010). These theories provide perspectives on an extended analysis of parallel teaching as a context for learning, participation and production of identities. Kirkeby et al. address perspectives on what they call "IT-enriched spaces" (2009) with a focus on five exemplary or commonly encountered situations in teaching. Each of the five "spaces" set the stage for and support different types of activities. At the same time they reflect different expectations (Kirkeby et al 2009, p. 10ff); they are: *the instructive space*, which is characterised by a well-structured and teacher-led lesson. The participants solve tasks supported by the space; *the dialogue-based space*, where the participants cooperate and initiate their learning. Learning processes may be supported by IT; *the nomadic space* directed outwards to society and the surroundings which connects the school to these contexts; *the body active game room*, where you have an opportunity for "collaborative and kinaesthetic learning within a school context"; *the multi-facetted space*, which contains a great variation of activity choices and resources, which in turn allow several activities to take place at once.

Of these descriptions of the physical context, "the instructive space" and "the dialogue-based space" are relevant to our analysis. Kirkeby et al. (2004) and Kirkeby (2004) point to a series of dimensions in such activity-related spaces that are highly relevant for an in-depth analysis. In a further analysis of such spaces, Kirkeby et al. (ibid.) point to a dimension related to the creation of the atmosphere in a room, such as sound, smell, colour etc. They call this *the tuned space*. This perspective is relevant to our analysis. We include the above-mentioned perspectives in relation to student identity and participation.

THE EMPIRICAL STUDY

Ethnographic research aims at understanding and describing processes between people during different types of activities (Madsen, 2003, p. 22; Walford, 2008). The empirical methods utilised in this project include document studies, observations and qualitative interviews with course participants, teachers and project managers, as well as a qualitative questionnaire survey. Data collection lasted from spring 2011 to summer 2012. Observations were conducted on three parallel groups, and we visited classes and their parallel groups. Observations and interviews were conducted with two additional groups; only the main class was observed. The far away team closed down before completing direct observation. Individual qualitative interviews were conducted with ten course participants distributed between the groups. There was a group interview with five course participants from a single group. Individual qualitative interviews were conducted with six teachers and with the project manager. Interviews with a career advisor were also conducted.

ANALYSIS

Observations revealed two dominant learning spaces in terms of Kirkeby's (2004) categories. *The instructive space* comprises of lessons that are thoroughly structured and mainly teacher-led. Participants solve specific teacher-defined tasks and the physical space supports this process. The lesson design is either plenary teaching or task guidance. *The dialogue-based space* is reflected in situations where the participants stage their learning and learning activities. This type of learning space shows participants working together in groups on tasks and problem solving. The dialogue-based space uses video only for guidance and if the teacher is at the far end. This means that connected issues relate to guidance and guidance situations. On this background we focus on the instructive space in two dominant forms, one of which is guidance.

REIFICATION AND ARTEFACTS AT SCHOOL

The available spaces for teaching and learning are characterised by the staging of certain student and teacher identities via the mood and meanings reflected by the interior decor and architecture. From an analytical perspective it can be understood as reifications and artefacts related to the culture and history of the studied school. This fact held some problematic perspectives. With one exception the rooms used for the video-mediated classes were also used for everyday teaching at the VUC. The interior decor and equipment reflected this condition. As artefacts and as reifications of the school, the physical circumstances could be seen as the products and the mediators of the prevailing culture and activities of the system and culture which the students knew from primary school. Several students had negative experiences and memories from their time at school. This situation inspired scrutiny of the problem to provide students in peripheral areas with an opportunity to attend a positive class and a classroom environment.

Everything in the classroom was set up in a traditional fashion, only the video equipment stood out. Tables were set up in rows so the participants could face the teacher and the blackboard. Sometimes there was a whiteboard on the wall behind the teacher's platform. To accommodate the video equipment, lighting was dimmed when it was switched on. The colours of the walls and curtains were muted, white and dusty white, floors in greyish or brown-grey linoleum. On the walls were small cupboards or bookcases containing sheets of paper and a few books. Some rooms were decorated with cardboard panel illustrations from prior activities or teaching material. One room was used solely for parallel teaching. It was a small room and because of the restricted space all the tables were set up in two rows with a narrow passage between so that all participants could face the video screen.

The rooms corresponded to traditional classroom furnishings from elementary and middle schools - they could very well have been mistaken for such a classroom. The mood generated associations to the activities you would expect to take place in such surroundings as well as the type of behaviour that would be acceptable. They created associations like "instructive space", i.e. learning spaces characterised by teacher-led courses and plenary teaching (Kirkeby et al. 2004). The layout of the tables supported this conclusion suggesting a well-defined distribution of roles between students and teachers that in most people activate predetermined attitudes as to what would be happening. The furnishings encompassed recognisable elements that for some students generated a sense of ease and confidence. But as described, students at AVU often have negative recollections from their elementary and middle school days. For them the conditions may turn out to be problematic. The furnishings could bring back negative recollections and experiences and function as a staging of counterproductive identities, role distributions and behavioural patterns.

The aim of parallel teaching is to enable groups, often located in peripheral areas, to follow courses. Some of the far-end groups in our study were very small and over time many of them consisted of one or a couple of students. If there were several students left, they often sat apart, spread out in the room. To make it possible to view the entire group, the video equipment was installed high above them so that teacher and students watched the group from above in the image transmitted from the far end. As a result, the group appeared to be small. It was positioned as subordinate to the near-end group, which was always the larger of the two groups. Students in the far-end group spoke about the near-end group (mother-group) as the "real" group, suggesting they held an inferior position. The furnishings of the rooms and the video-based interaction may have contributed to and reinforced that impression among the students. Identity-related situations are of paramount importance, and the character and usage of the rooms affect how the students meet and understand the course, the activities, themselves and their co-students.

INTERACTION AND PARTICIPATION

Video equipment in classrooms expands the potential for interaction by giving the two groups an opportunity to be taught simultaneously. It also sets a framework for interaction with minor limitations. There are implications for formation of identity. The equipment is installed so that students and teachers can follow the image and the sound of communications, interactions in both classrooms as they interact. However, the technical equipment is sensitive to noise, which means that even very low noise appear as blaring and disturbing. This negative aspect of the technology influenced communications: "In a normal classroom you can talk to the person next to you but here it generates such noise that, what is he actually saying? You must keep very quiet" (Male student). The video equipment clearly set up a framework for the interaction between the two classrooms and for interaction in each classroom. The equipment supported teacher-led courses by providing an instructive space for interactions between teacher and students. The layout and positioning of chairs and tables also set focus on the teachers' performance.

In social science studies and history, dialogue and discussion are particularly important. The physical layout of the classroom could potentially encourage dialogue among participants. The conditions for video-mediated teaching imposed limitations that had a strong negative influence on teaching activities because focus was largely on internal communication. In comparison, mathematics is a subject with frequent switches back and forth between the teacher's presentation and individual work. Here the limitations of parallel teaching seemed to play a subordinate role except in situations involving individual guidance between the two classroom contexts. The ways the video equipment influenced the courses depended on the type of activities upon which they were based. In predominantly teacher-led courses their disturbing factors had little impact.

Parallel teaching is of little use in terms of potential for individual guidance of students in the far-end of the classroom. Students often need to see and follow the teacher's descriptions on a blackboard or a sheet of paper. The teacher also needs to see the students' written products. In such situations students positioned themselves in front of the camera and the guidance could take place directly while, for instance, a copybook could be presented to the teacher. All students at both locations could follow the exchange. The students' questions and problems became visible to and caught the attention of the entire group. Teachers and students were aware of the counterproductive aspect of this physical arrangement. Therefore the method was rarely employed. So the student would have to call the teacher or, if this was insufficient or for various reasons impossible, eventually abstain from asking. A female student describes the experience.

You don't really feel like doing it because he is on the screen up there and you can't hide and talk to him quietly since all the others in the class are there, so you don't really feel like talking to him if there is a problem or anything. Then it would

be an advantage if there were a loudspeaker or a microphone, so you could talk with him in that way, like it being more private and this you can't do this way.

On top of these limitations the teacher's concrete physical presence played an important role for some students. For instance, some students describe "feeling you get more help because he (the teacher) is right next to you rather than when he is at a different location" (male student). And it is "difficult to be in the group where the teacher is not present" (female student). The students had to work hard at attracting attention because the teacher divided his attention between the two classrooms. Here also, the physical presence would play a significant role. A male student describes how it feels being at the far-end of the classroom: "If you sit there totally stuck and he (the teacher) did not exactly observe it, then you just sat there gazing, so yes, this has been a challenge."

Interaction among the students as well as between students and teachers is essential if seen from a learning perspective. It was in many ways influenced by the video technology. The possibilities for internal discussion at each location were limited. Interaction between the two locations was also hampered for video and audio transmissions. A female student talks about the limitations of interaction, stressing the importance of body language.

It is also important to relate to this: Was he joking or did he really mean it? Sometimes a discussion can become a bit hectic (…) so I think it is important that the image, that's, like, where you can see if people are smiling or are winking. When you can't see how he reacts when he says it, then I often find it problematic because you don't know if people find what you are saying OK or they are joking.

Parallel teaching is demanding for students as the format requires individual work. This experience was accentuated by limitations and difficulties of the technical framework. For example, students needed to work individually when the technical equipment malfunctional. The teacher was prepared for such incidents and students were often informed about what they should work on. Some students seemed to adapt to these situations. They were able to act and work on the subject. However, for students in need of help and guidance or with special needs for contacting the teacher, it was hard to stay focused. In some cases, the students were unable to cope, even with telephone access to the teacher.

If you sit at a computer, you may listen to music from your ear-buds and then you don't hear what the teacher on the screen is explaining, and you know you are not going to get rebuked, you may also simply leave, naturally he (the teacher) will see that you leave, but he can't rebuke you for doing so. This is a bit difficult for me because I often pick the easy option of dashing away or listening to music pretending to work, it's easy if you are, like, a bit tired late in the day.

The students face special challenges and so do the teachers. They focus simultaneously on different aspects of teaching and learning. During courses when the teacher instructs two groups at the same time they had to be careful to let students from both rooms contribute to the discussions and ask questions. When preparing for their courses, the teachers needed documents for both groups, as well as a special set of tasks to be done in case of technical failure. They estimated that under such conditions they could only have one single lesson per day.

SOCIAL COMMUNITIES OF THE CLASS

"The social space" refers to student experiences of belonging to groups and also of building social relations and for participation. The social space refers to role distribution, identities and processes related to identity building. Each theme plays a role in terms of learning the subject matter.

Teaching is a framework for potential creation of social relations, but some real barriers appeared during parallel teaching classes. Due to the physical separation in two classrooms, contact between students from the parallel group were limited to the video conference. This drawback limited the experience of knowing each other internally in the groups. A female student explains that it was frustrating "to have class together with people that you neither know nor get to know". Others indicate that they would appreciate activities where the groups meet physically, especially to get to know each other. If "you could have activities together right from the outset, maybe you could mix the groups (…). Then you would get to know them".

However, small teaching groups had surprising potentials precisely in terms of creating a sense of belonging and relationship among the participants. This created a framework that in many ways appeared predictable and manageable. One female student put is like this: "When you are in a small group you get to know each other". She experienced this as a secure framework, a physical reality for students with special needs. The technology enabled for manageability and predictability in terms of whom they could expect to meet and what would happen.

I believe if you are only a few, you get closer to each other. We talked about it, if we were not quite sure about a point, we helped each other, and we used and supported each other. When working in groups we worked together. We talked about it and agreed upon how to proceed.

Another student from a small group also pointed out the positive potential for creating togetherness she had experienced in these circumstances. She referred to the opportunity to build friendships, for instance, where you chose to accompany each other to school: It "means (…) something that I have three friends that I accompany to school, with whom I talk a lot, so this is part of what inspires you to get up and go".

ROLES AND IDENTITIES

Interaction between people during parallel teaching was generally expected to play out as it normally does in elementary and middle schools, the type of interaction to which students have been socialised. It is a framework with clear distribution of roles. The teacher directs activities and the students perform according to the teacher's instructions and guidance. This role distribution was to a great extent supported by the furnishings of the room. Although somewhat exaggerated, the experience is described by a female student.

It has been a transgression for me, you feel you are under surveillance, I do not really understand it well when we are in the classroom (…) Suddenly the camera is on you, there is this sort of eye watching you, it's totally unpleasant, you really feel you are under surveillance, as if you were in the slammer, it is as if you're recorded on film, spied upon, it is all different when you sit in the same classroom. (…) you might as well sit at home and watch TV; you don't have the same contact to your teacher.

In terms of identity, cooperation with other students encompasses positive potentials that affect acquisition of subject matter knowledge. Cooperation offers a potential for belonging, feeling acknowledged by others and being part of the whole team. Trust in cooperation enables people to experience of and acquire knowledge by recognition. These aspects of learning are reflected in the students' descriptions of this type of activities. However, sometimes progress is complicated because the modes of communication are limited by the technology. Such problems affect communication negatively. One female

student says: "Working in groups is difficult because it's difficult to get through to the guy at the other end". Another student adds more details, describing how supervision by video makes her feel uncomfortable.

I don't know if I would call it embarrassing, but it's unpleasant when you know that everybody hears it (…) and sometimes you want the teacher to walk up to you, maybe the student sitting next to you hears it, but all of them don't. I've never asked a question in this way, I would like to have the teacher one-on-one, if not I'd rather skip it.

The same difficulties are described by another student.

You restrain yourself a bit, maybe it would be better if you knew them a bit more then you wouldn't feel so insecure.

The reason poor technology feels unpleasant is found in identity-related situations and positive experiences relate to how you feel, how people pay attention, who you are and what you say. The parallel teaching context helps people establish a modified framework for communication, which also plays a role for the student's capacity to preserve his identity.

SOLUTIONS AND RECOMMENDATIONS

First there is a need to differentiate between types of teaching situations: individualised teaching, plenary teaching, and cooperative learning in large or small groups as well as project work. Each situation is recognised for all kinds of teaching and holds opportunities and threats. Analysis focuses on types of teaching situations as contexts for participation, academic learning and production of identity. Options and limitations for active participation are discussed as are the problems they imply for social interaction, development of academic knowledge and identity. *Plenary teaching* supports active participation (Andreasen, 2012). There is an option for the students to "hide" and avoid pro-active participation. They may still acquire academic knowledge by observing and listening to discussions. The teacher influences heavily who is heard and who is neglected. Academically weak course participants avoid making a fuss about their anonymity. Simultaneously they have an opportunity to verify their identity and self-image. Conversely, taking on a passive role seems to have a confirming effect, while the opportunities to learn through active participation are reduced.

Collaborative activities and project work give many course participants the opportunity to contribute and participate actively. In parallel teaching, work in groups can have a lot to contribute as the activity supports development of academic knowledge. This is reflected in the course participants' descriptions of how group work is linked partly to experiencing oneself as part of a group where one is recognised and one's knowledge is acknowledged, and partly to the academic side of these processes. Group cooperation across contexts and localities is complicated because the technology affects communication negatively. One female participant explains: "In group work it is difficult, because it is difficult to get through to the guy on the other end".

Individualised teaching becomes a problem when participants communicate via video and when a course participant is at the far end and the teacher is at the near end of the classroom. The problems become evident when the teacher's guidance has to take place in a remote location where the teacher and course participant are situated at a distance. Their positioning exposes course participants who want to ask questions, as all course participants can follow the guidance dialogues on a large screen. Many students experience this as an uncomfortable display of their problems. One female course participant says: "I don't know if

I'd say it was embarrassing, but it is unpleasant when you know that everyone hears it".

FUTURE RESEARCH DIRECTIONS

Video-mediated teaching entails problems related to the participants' acquisition of academic knowledge, resources and experiences. On several points, there is a need for innovation in parallel teaching of the future. The layout and architecture of the spaces must be re-thought; an architecture that breaks with the dominant aspects of the traditional classroom must be developed that allows cooperation and discussions in teams, and students who need to consult the teacher should not be exposed to an entire group. Pedagogical aspects should be placed on collaborative working methods, on learning in cooperative relationships. The technology must facilitate for the participants to spend as little time as possible switching on or adapting to the systems. Course participants and teachers must re-think their roles. Course participants can become involved and understand themselves as "didactic designers", in the sense that they learn to organise their learning processes as formulated in relation to what is sometimes called 'didactics 2.0' (Christiansen & Gynter 2010).

CONCLUSION

If video-mediated teaching and learning is to function as a positive programme for young adults who study lower secondary school subjects, many elements need to be developed to match their resources and needs. Results from the project confirm that the didactics of video-mediated teaching has to be renewed, confirming results from other research in this field (Gynther, 2009). Modern educational systems are facing challenges in terms of providing citizens in all areas of countries with the necessary opportunities for education after primary school level. Parallel video-mediated teaching appears to be unexplored in relation to this problem both as a teaching practice and as a research area (Hampel & Stickler, 2012; Lawson et al., 2010). It holds important potentials to meet educational demands of society, but as our analysis shows it is also characterised by challenges and problems as a learning context. Specifically, problems arise in the teaching of students with academic problems and perhaps also low self-esteem concerning their academic potential. The problems are related to the more physical or technical limitations of the video technology, for instance in teaching situations with supervision or plenary teaching where active participation in discussions and interactions between students and also the emergence of communities of practices in the school class are influenced in problematic ways. The context may also affect student roles in the classroom and the production of identities as learners.

It is generally a form of teaching that places great demands on both participants and teachers. The teacher must stay updated on two locations at the same time, relate to everyone's needs, ensure that students can participate with questions and contribute to discussions whether they are in the near or the far location, ensure that teaching materials are accessible at both locations, etc. The students in the remote end must be able to work relatively independently in many situations. They must be energetic and clearly make themselves heard or demand attention when they have questions. Due to the technology, students must adapt to audio limitations and problems, just as they need to be highly disciplined during joint discussions so that everyone has the opportunity to contribute regardless of their location. To some extent, the form seems to pave the way for plenary teaching with strong learning control, but it is also strongly affected by the disadvantages of the technology.

The same applies to individual teaching based on video technology. Course participants at the remote location sometimes feel that possible academic weaknesses are put on display in an undesirable way. This can affect their identity formation and positioning in the community negatively. Collaborative activities are less affected by the limitations and frameworks of the technology and could also have potential to support the establishment of social relationships and community in the groups.

REFERENCES

Anastasiades, S. P., Filippousis, G., Karvunis, L., Siakas, S., Tomazinakis, A., Giza, P., & Mastoraki, H. (2010). Interactive Videoconferencing for collaborative learning at a distance in the school of 21st century: A case study in elementary schools in Greece. *Computers & Education, 54*(2), 321–339. doi:10.1016/j.compedu.2009.08.016

Andreasen, K. E. (2012). *VIU: Projekt VIrtuel Undervisning: Rapport fra følgeforskningen.* Aalborg Universitet: Institut for Læring og Filosofi.

Andreasen, K. E., & Hviid, M. K. (2011). *Evalueringsrapport: Projekt Parallel Pædagogik - Et udviklingsarbejde med VUC Sønderjylland og VUC Fyn & Fyns HF-kursus.* Aalborg Universitet og UC Syd.

Andreasen, K. E., & Rasmussen, P. (2013). Videomedieret parallelundervisning: Som rum for læring ved Almen Voksenuddannelse i udkantsområder. *Læring & Medier, 11*, 1–22.

Christensen, V. L., & Hansen, J. J. (2010). Innovativ læremiddelkultur. In K. Gynther (Ed.), Didaktik 2.0. Akademisk Forlag: København.

Christiansen, B. R., & Gynther, C. (2010). Didaktik 2.0 - didaktisk design for skolen i vidensamfundet. In K. Gynther (Ed.), Didaktik 2.0. Akademisk Forlag: København.

Damvad. (2013). *Nye udfordringer for VUC? Fokus på Almen Voksenuddannelse (AVU).* Lederforeningen for VUC og VUC Videnscenter.

Danmarks Evalueringsinstitut. (2011). *E-læring og blended learning på VEU-området. Undersøgelse af e-læring og blended learning på enkeltfag på VUC, VVU på erhvervsakademier og diplomuddannelser på professionshøjskoler.* Danmarks Evalueringsinstitut.

Danmarks Statistik. (2012). Forberedende voksenundervisning, almen voksenuddannelse og hf-enkeltfag mv. 2010/2011. *Nyt fra Danmarks Statistik, 122,* 9.

Danmarks Statistik. (2013). Kursister ved voksen- og efteruddannelse, VUC 2011/2012. *Nyt fra Danmarks Statistik, 71.*

Engeström, Y. (1999). Activity theory and individual and social transformation. In Y. Engeström, R. Meittinen, & R. Punamaki (Eds.), Perspectives on activity theory. Cambridge, UK: Cambridge University Press.

Engeström, Y. (2007). Enriching the Theory of Expansive Learning: Lessons from Journeys Toward Coconfiguration. *Mind, Culture, and Activity, 14*(1-2), 23–39. doi:10.1080/10749030701307689

Gammelby, M. (2012). *Plads til barndommen. En undersøgelse af sammenhænge mellem plads, rum og pædagogisk praksis i børnehaven. (Ph.d.-afhandling).* Aalborg Universitet, Institut for Læring og Filosofi.

Gjøsund, G., & Huseby, R. (2010). *Gruppe og samspil. 2. reviderede udgave.* København: Hans Reitzels forlag.

Gynther, C. (2005). *Blended learning: IT og læring I et teoretisk og praktisk perspektiv.* København: Unge Pædagoger.

Gynther, K. (2009). *Parallel undervisning – Videokonferencer i et remedierings- og re-didaktiseringsperspektiv.* Retrieved from http://ucsj.dk/fileadmin/user_upload/FU/IT_og_laering/Parllel_undervisning_og_videokonferencer.pdf

Hampel, R., & Stickler, U. (2012). The use of videoconferencing to support multimodal interaction in an online language classroom. *ReCALL, 24*(2), 116–137. doi:10.1017/S095834401200002X

Hedestig, U., & Kaptelinin, V. (2005). Facilitator's Roles in a Videoconference Learning. *Information Systems Frontiers, 7*(1), 71–83. doi:10.1007/s10796-005-5339-6

Hviid, M. K., Keller, H. D., Rasmussen, A., Rasmussen, P., & Thøgersen, U. (2008). *Kompetenceudvikling i udkantsområder: Almen og praksisnær kompetenceudvikling for voksne.* Aalborg: Aalborg Universitetsforlag.

Katznelson, N. et al. (2009). *Vejen mod de 95% (del I). En erfaringsopsamling fra projektet Ungdomsuddannelse til alle.* København: Danmarks Pædagogiske Universitetsskole. Kommunernes Landsforening. Undervisningsministeriet.

Katznelson, N. et al. (2010). *Vejen mod de 95% (del II). In Erfaringsopsamling fra projektet Ungdomsuddannelse til alle.* København: Danmarks Pædagogiske Universitetsskole. Kommunernes Landsforening. Undervisningsministeriet.

Kirkeby, I. M. (2004). *Skolen finder sted (Arbejdsrapport).* København: Statens Byggeforskningsinstitut.

Kirkeby, I. M., Gitz-Johansen, T., & Kampmann, J. (2004). Samspil mellem fysisk rum og hverdagsliv i skolen. In K. Larsen (Ed.), Arkitektur, krop og læring. København: Hans Reitzel.

Kirkeby, I. M., Iversen, O. S., & Martinussen, M. (2009). *Fremtidens hybride læringsrum. På vej mod en forståelsesramme for hvordan skolens it-berigede rum kan støtte arbejdsprocesser og skift mellem forskellige arbejdsprocesser.* Statens Byggeforskningsinstitut, Aalborg Universitet.

Lawson, T., Comber, C., Gage, J., & Cullum-Hanshaw, A. (2010). Images of the future for education? Videoconferencing: A literature review. *Technology, Pedagogy and Education*, *19*(3), 295–314. doi:10.1080/1475939X.2010.513761

Lawson, T., Comber, C., Gage, J., & Cullum-Hanshaw, A. (2010). Images of the future for education? Videoconferencing: A literature review. *Technology, Pedagogy and Education*, *19*(3), 295–314. doi:10.1080/1475939X.2010.513761

Lögdlund, U. (2010). Constructing learning spaces? Videoconferencing at local learning centres in Sweden. *Studies in Continuing Education*, *32*(3), 183–199. doi:10.1080/0158037X.2010.517993

Madsen, U. A. (2003). *Pædagogisk etnografi*. Aarhus: Forlaget Klim.

Pless, M., & Hansen, N.-H. M. (2010). HF på VUC – et andet valg. CeFU - Center for Ungdomsforskning: København.

Reiserer, M., Ertl, B., & Madl, H. (2002). Fostering collaborative knowledge construction in desktop video-conferencing: effects of content schemes and cooperation scripts in peer teaching settings. In *Proceedings of the Conference on Computer Support for Collaborative Learning: Foundations for a CSCL Community*. International Society of the Learning Sciences. doi:10.3115/1658616.1658670

Stödberg, U., & Orre, C. J. (2009). It's not all about video-conferencing. *Campus-Wide Information Systems*, *27*(3), 109–117. doi:10.1108/10650741011054410

Walden, R. (2009). The School of the Future: Conditions and Processes – Contributions of Architectural Psychology. In R. Walden (Ed.), Schools for the future: design proposals from architectural psychology. Hogrefe: Cambridge.

Walford, G. (2008). The Nature of educational ethnography. In G. Walford et al. (Eds.), How to do Educational Ethnography. The Tufnell Press.

Wenger, E. (2004). *Praksisfællesskaber*. København: Hans Reitzels Forlag.

Wenger, E. (2006a). Social læringsteori – Aktuelle temaer og udfordringer. In K. Illeris (Ed.), Læringsteorier: Seks aktuelle forståelser. Roskilde Universitetsforlag. Frederiksberg.

Wenger, E. (2006b). *Communities of practice. A brief Introduction*. Retrieved from http://wenger-trayner.com/wp-content/uploads/2012/01/06-Brief-introduction-to-communities-of-practice.pdf

Wenger, E. (2010). Communities of practice and social learning systems: The career of a concept. In C. Blackmore (Ed.), Social learning systems and communities of practice. Springer Verlag and The Open University.

Wenger, E., McDermott, R., & William Snyder, W. (2002). Cultivating Communities of Practice: A Guide to Managing Knowledge. Harvard Business Press.

ADDITIONAL READING

Allen, I. E., & Seaman, J. (2011). *Going the distance: Online education in the United States*. Wellesley: Babson Survey Research Group.

Anderson, T., & Dron, J. (2011). Three generations of distance education pedagogy. *International Review of Research in Open and Distance Learning*, *12*(3), 80–97.

Andersson, A. (2010). *Learning to learn in e-learning: Constructive practices for development. Örebro University, Swedish Business School at Örebro University*. Örebro University.

Andrews, T. (2002). *Using Videoconferencing for Teaching and Learning.* Teaching and Learning in Higher Education Series.

Bates, A. W., & Sangrà, A. (2011). *Managing technology in higher education: Strategies for transforming teaching and learning. San Franscisco.* Jossey-Bass/John Wiley & Co.

Birden, H., & Page, S. (2005). Teaching by video-conference: a commentary on best practice for rural education in health professions. *The International Electronic Journal of Rural and Remote Health Research, Education, Practice and Policy,* 5(356).

Garrison, D. R., & Vaughan, N. (2008). *Blended learning in higher education: Framework, principles, and guidelines.* San Francisco: John Wiley & Sons.

Granberg, C. (2011). *ICT and learning in teacher education. The social construction of pedagogical ICT discourse and design. Department of Applied Education/Interactive Media and Learning.* Umeå: University of Umeå.

Guri-Rosenblit, S. (2009). Challenges facing distance education in the 21st century: Policy and research implications. U. Bernath, A. Szücs, A. Tait, & M. Vidal (Ed.). Distance and e-learning in transition: Learning innovation, technology and social challenges. London: ISTE Ltd and John Wiley & Sons Inc. 5–21.

Halvorsen, B., Hansen, O.-J., & Tägtström, J. (2013). *Young people on the edge* (summary)

Kaptelinin, V. (2002). Social thinking reaches out to software practice: The challenge of bridging activity systems. Dittrich Y, Floyd C, Klischewski R. (Ed.). Social Thinking—Software Practice. Cambridge, MA, USA: The MIT Press, 45–68.

Keller, C. (2005). Virtual learning environments: Three implementation perspectives. *Learning, Media and Technology,* 30(3), 299–311. doi:10.1080/17439880500250527

Keller, C., & Cernerud, L. (2002). Students' perceptions of e-learning in university education. *Journal of Educational Media,* 27, 55–67.

Kirkeby, M. (2011). Architecture, pedagogy and children: The intersection between different action programs in school. Bengtson, J. (Ed.). Educational Dimensions of School Buildings. Peter Lang. Frankfurt am Main.

Labour market inclusion of vulnerable youths. Nordic Council of Ministers 2013. Denmark

Lave, J., & Wenger, E. (1991). *Situated learning: Legitimate peripheral participation.* Cambridge, U.K.: Cambridge Press. doi:10.1017/CBO9780511815355

Levinsen, K. (2011, April). Fluidity in the networked society: Self-initiated learning as a digital literacy competence. *Electronic Journal of E-Learning,* 9(1), 52–62.

Luck, J. (1999). *Teaching and Learning using Interacive Videoconferencing: Screen-based Classrooms Require the Development of New Ways of Working.* Rockhampton: Australian Association for Research in Education.

Luck, J. (2000). *Building a Learning community Using Interactive Videoconferencing.* Rockhampton: Central Queensland University.

Luck, J. (2003). Does geography shape the nature of an educational innovation. *Journal of Research in Rural Education,* 18(7), 152–158.

Säljö, R. (2010). Digital tools and challenges to institutional traditions of learning: Technologies, social memory and the performative nature of learning. *Journal of Computer Assisted Learning,* 26(1), 53–64. doi:10.1111/j.1365-2729.2009.00341.x

Salomon, G. (1992). What does the design of effective CSCL require and how do we study its effects? SIGCUE. *Outlook,* 21(3), 62–68.

Selwyn, N. (2011). Digitally distanced learning: A study of international distance learners' (non)use of technology. *Distance Education, 32*(1), 85–99. doi:10.1080/01587919.2011.565500

Selwyn, N. (2011). Will technology displace the school. N. Selwyn (Ed.). Education and technology. Key issues and debates. London: Continuum International Publishing Group. 139-161.

Wilson, G., & Stacey, E. (2004). Online interaction impacts on learning: Teaching the teachers to teach online. *Australasian Journal of Educational Technology, 20*(1), 33–48.

KEY TERMS AND DEFINITIONS

Adult Education Centre (VUC): Danish educational institutions' offering a number of different courses and educational programs at the ISCED 2 and ISCED 3 levels.

Communities of Practice: Wenger defines communities of practice as "groups of people who share a concern or a passion for something they do and learn how to do it better as they interact regularly" (Wenger, 2006b, p.1; Wenger, 2010, p. 1).

General Adult Education: General Adult Education (AVU) is a programme for adults to study general school subjects as single courses at a level corresponding to 8th, 9th or 10th grade in Danish 'Folkeskole' (primary and lower secondary school). Course participants who apply for these subjects have either not completed school with the exam in these subjects, or they would like to improve their results or attend the course subject purely out of interest.

Identity: Belonging to communities correspond with the creation, formation and "the defining of identities, determining who is who, who is good at what, who knows what" (Wenger, 2004, p. 115).

IT Didactics: Didactics of teaching in virtual environments, teaching being based on IT or integrating IT.

Parallel Teaching: Teaching of two physically separate school classes simultaneous using video.

Participation: Participation refers to processes of being engaged, active and involved in activities. Learning depends on our ways of participating in the communities to which we belong.

Roles: Belonging to social communities also includes different roles, which may be related to various degrees of participation and ways of participation.

Video-Mediated Teaching: Teaching mediated by the video media.

Chapter 4
Game Construction Activity in Higher Education

Hans Kyhlbäck
Blekinge Institute of Technology, Sweden

ABSTRACT

This activity theoretical discussion is based on experiences from teaching and learning in higher education (i.e. university students' activities in game construction). Learning by creating a new technical artefact is taken for granted. In higher education, the produced artefacts are the firsthand proof of students' work success. Sometimes, and prominently in game technology construction, such artefacts are further used and developed outside school. Digital games with an origin in higher education reach a level of maturity and technology utilization that goes beyond many student projects. The authors argue that successful making of artefacts is characterized by repeated and contextualized feedback, found as an intriguing interplay between activity systems in which the students participate. A driving force for students' efforts and achievements is found in a contradiction between school grade markings and becoming a professional producer of games.

INTRODUCTION

With a focus on the observation that some university students perform stunningly well and create impressive game artefacts in the course of their educational program, the aim of the study is to investigate how work proceeds. The involved teachers agree that the students do excellent work. This was the reason why I began to research the activity. Since the education programme has been around for only a short period of time, the results have not yet received much attention. Consequently there isn't much regular evidence

of the level of success, but for the results in this report that shortage isn't critical. The way the study program is designed and organised is non-conventional. In order to contextualize the case, the educational program at my home organization (Blekinge Institute of Technology, acronym: BTH), is partly presented on the university web page (February 2014):

Education to Master of Science in Game and Software Technology aims at students becoming proficient at applying the latest in Game, Visualization and Interaction Technology as

DOI: 10.4018/978-1-4666-6603-0.ch004

well as basic Computer Science Engineering and Software Technology. During the education students develop a number of demo applications that can be used in future employment applications. Students will also work in larger projects where they, together develop games. /.../ Upon graduation, students can work in game industry or development of other advanced software systems.

During their studies the students make "demo applications". They are considered to be valuable assets that go beyond the regular study program. Through the students' productive work, the education management promises a connection to working life outside school. In order to realize such a trajectory towards a professional status, the challenge for the school is to make and maintain higher technology education successful. Compared to traditional higher education, this project-based approach of BTH is different (Crawley et al., 2010; Markham, 2011). It is in line with an adaption to the need of game industry and students' professional engagement. At the same university information page, a former BTH student, now an esteemed businessman emphasises the close connection between the university and the game industry (my translation).

Our aim is to find the very best in all areas, and therefore it is a good thing that we can cooperate in the MSc program in Games and Software Technology, helping the students design their education. I am confident that through this partnership we will find many talented engineers. (Martin Walfisz, founder and former CEO of Massive Entertainment, February, 2014)

Massive Entertainment and Tarsier Studios are two successful examples of game producers initiated by students at BTH (Francke, 2014). With an un-critical view this seems as a happy path of coordination where the school produces highly educated and specialized professionals and the companies emerge and prosper by using former students' labour. The relation is however more complex than so. As a young and expanding branch, computer and video game production requires large investments in work hours and subsequently high salary costs. A major game company needs to work through a period of two or more years before there is a market response. There might be a pay-off in sales of the product or a disastrous failure. A new release of a software game is notorious risky, because even if the game is well done seen from a production perspective, the game might be a failure if it isn't well received as "amusing" or attractive in some way. Then the game players won't pay the license fee, and the game will fail to meet a required exchange value.

The rule for the game companies is harsh: make a success - or die. Since technical computer capabilities are growing and the share of people engaged in game playing is expanding, the game industry is exposed to outside forces of various kinds. As relatively early in its historical development this industry is a case in point illustrating a contradictory character of contemporary human work. High specialization of advanced computer technology and labour is required in game production. A Marxist analysis would characterize the game products, by two different but interrelated properties: exchange value determined by the market, and utility value appreciated by designated game players. According to Marx (1909), in capitalist production a contradiction between exchange and utility values is inherent in all products of labour. With such a view on human work in mind, the learning condition for a game engineering student is understood as determined by strongly related but opposed properties. Even if the students perceive of the new game they are making as amusing and rewarding, they know, in exchange its success or failure is judged on the market place.

It is only by being exchanged that the products of labour acquire, as values, one uniform social status, distinct from their varied forms of existence as objects of utility. This division of a product into a useful thing and a value becomes practically important only when exchange has acquired such an extension that useful articles are produced for the purpose of being exchanged, and their character as values has therefore to be taken into account, beforehand, during production. (p. 44)

Most future game products will be realized as commodities and a student's future work capacity will also be valued as a commodity on the labour market. Already at school, an unrest based on the contradiction between learning to produce something interesting and in making the usually school grades, strongly influence the life of the individual and the community of students (Nilsson & Wihlborg, 2011). This unrest is similar to other human work activities and the contradiction between utility and exchange value pertaining to it. To further aggravate this unrest, the thin line between success and failure of the game industry is a source of influence on higher education teaching and learning processes.

In order to grasp what successful game technology education is about, a simple first hand analysis provides an answer: the students remaining on a long term and demanding educational program, are relatively good because of the drop out selection and because they possess a genuine interest in what they do at school. Even if that pre-understanding were true, the entire story behind isn't clear. To find out, this case study takes a cultural historical activity theory (CHAT) approach in making analysis of observations and interviews (Engeström, 1987; Kuutti, 1995). The concept of contradiction is fundamental, and presumably suited to analysis of a case focused on learning and producing game artefacts. In order to guide the study, the overall question is: *how can it be that some students perform successfully?*

The visible and tangible result of students' productive work is remarkable. Involved teachers, with experiences from other study programs, maintain that a majority of those students, who keep up with planned course activities, are overall performing better than average. They fulfil curricular requirements and they also produce impressive game artefacts. Those students who complete their studies find attractive job positions to choose from when entering the world of professional life. Some top students actually take attractive job offerings even before the last terms of school is finished. So, an intuitive thought is that this education offers something of extraordinary value. An explanation reduced to a strong interest in solving technical problems doesn't seem to be satisfactory a satisfactory explanation. Consequently an initial assumption in the study was that the students, who learn how to construct games, are motivated and prepared for the tasks of game technology construction *because* they are qualified players of games. This chapter will explain if and why this assumption is correct.

With regular school assignments as a frame, the students are full time occupied in creating and constructing game artefacts. They are considered to be technicians, or more formally "game engineering students". So, they shall not be mistaken for game designers or professionals in equivalent work roles in the game producing industry. Another thing is that, within the limits of given courses, the students are free to choose the objects of their study and work efforts. They have much free space for their judgement and decision making. Assignments are seemingly well functioning in a number of projects resulting in game artefacts of various size and complexity. The study program manager comments on this, saying: "we don't start with [the usual] making another calculator, instead, the students start and make a little game, but it involves the same technological tasks".

A general observation is that the students don't just follow a straightforward syllabus sequence of doing A, B, C etc. On the contrary, much of their studies are up to themselves and their own decisions on a path becoming engineers for highly qualified positions. The overall learning goal is to appreciate and understand the combination of math, physics and programming. The teachers emphasize that this combination of subjects is necessary for successful achievements and completion of the study program. Mateas (2008) argue that procedural literacy is an ability to understand processes and writing computer code.

With appropriate programming, a computer can embody any conceivable process; code is the most versatile, general process language ever created. Hence, the craft skill of programming is a fundamental component of procedural literacy, though it is not the details of any particular programming language that matters, but rather the more general tropes and structures that cut across all languages. (p. 75)

In fact, the expressive power of computation lies precisely in the fact that, for any crazy contraption you can describe in detail, you can turn the computer into that contraption. (p. 82)

To master expressive computation, in making a computer game, the students have to integrate and use mathematics, physics and programming as the tools of a process. This is something we easily agree on to label procedural literacy. But what happens when the students create the game artefacts and their own learning? Obviously the students have an interest in developing the technology as such, but when we look closer to actions of calculations and writing computer code; Is the rewarding condition built on an universal human luck in putting things together and make them functional; What is a more complete picture; To what extent is human conduct a component in this complex activity? To understand what drives the students' efforts we need data produced from the activities in focus.

A fundamental tenet of CHAT is that human knowledge is embedded in culturally developed instruments, tools and signs; artefacts of which language represent the most advanced form. The human becomes more capable with help of those others, and expressed in the CHAT terminology: artefacts *mediate* human actions and operations played out in the world (Vygotsky, 1934/1987; Engeström, 1987). In order to fulfil human needs, mediated actions performed by a collective of people realize services and material production. Individuals are socialized through taking part in such coordinated change of the world. Through mediation the object of an activity is transformed into a wished for outcome, and the individuals internalize such an experience as an expansion of their personal capabilities.

The assumption about the students' capabilities generated by "a strong interest in solving technical problems" is however at risk to be explained from a singular individualistic perspective. One such assumption suggests that the student possesses extraordinary talents and what goes on is only a disciplined and structured learning of technological knowledge given at school. Further, a strong demand and obligation for the school to individually assess and grade the students' achievements emphasises skills isolated to the individual mind, something to be tested on regular examination events. But the CHAT approach provides a perspective sensitive for the interplay of individuals in a collective, in this case joint activity in development of new game technology solutions.

CHAT notions of contradictions, mediating artefacts and object oriented motive help counterbalancing an individualistic view on students' challenges and achievements. Contradictions are the driving forces of change and development. Everything, encompassing the natural and cultural world, has a potential of, and is more or less in a state of change. The cause of change is to be found in inner contradictions of anything, or to say an element that can be a natural thing, a culturally developed artefact or a social relation. But there are also contradictions between entities in the world, which in turn might affect the actual state of change and development. In the CHAT perspective human actions are motivated by activities. In a condensed format Kuutti (1996) explains with use of the term contradiction, the relation within and between activity systems:

Because activities are not isolated units but more like nodes in crossing hierarchies and networks, they are influenced by other activities and other changes in their environment. External influences change some elements of activities causing imbalances between them. Activity Theory uses the term contradiction indicating an unfit within elements, between them, between different activities or different development phases of a same activity. Contradictions manifest themselves as problems, ruptures, breakdowns, clashes, etc. Activity Theory sees contradictions as sources of development; real activities are practically always in the process of working through some of such contradictions. (p. 34)

The key thing is that the contradiction concept clarifies what moves on-going processes, and what makes human activities capable to transform the world. However, a contradiction does not tell by itself that it exists. A contradiction has to be explored by its manifestations in work and learning activities. Engeström and Sannino (2012) put it succinctly:

A crucial point is that contradictions cannot be observed directly; they can only be identified through their manifestations. This leads us to characterize four important types of discursive manifestations of contradictions. Taken together, these four kinds of manifestations " - dilemmas, conflicts, critical conflicts, and double binds - " may be used as a framework to analyze sequences of change efforts in organizations. (p. 369)

Contradictions are found in interpretations of interviews and participant observations of learning activities. A pure technological interest is initially assumed as being the dominant characteristic among the students, but what does the assumption imply? Can another side of the interest be revealed and what potential is there in the tensions in-between? What surrounding conditions with contradictory forces are the most important ones for the student's learning endeavour? Here it is assumed contradictions are at play and that a deep and diversified understanding can be gained with the CHAT framework providing a conceptual guidance.

So, looking closely at the data on game engineering students' learning activities is likely to tell a story about change and development. The relatively new and demanding study program builds on the combination of established engineering knowledge and rapidly changing computer hardware, of which the capacity of video equipment is expanding significantly over short time intervals. On a quest for understanding the students' achievements and the productive work they make, important drivers and interaction among key components can hopefully be revealed.

Next I explain the methodological approach. Then there is an account of results and a first level analysis of findings detailed with answers to questions: are the students also competent game players, and what are the objects of the students' activities? The third section provides a first level discussion about the revealed activities in the case. Finally there is a second level discussion about consequences for higher education and a conclusion contributing to higher education and answering to the question: how can it be that the students perform successfully?

METHODOLOGICAL APPROACH

The CHAT approach is recognized as a suitable method and theory in the field of Human Computer Interaction (Kuutti, 1996; Harrison et al, 2007). A CHAT study provides a journey on a quest for understanding, but probably not in finding a definite answer. CHAT is suitable for real life studies of human activities. Students' creation of game artefacts falls within the realms of such investigations. CHAT concepts of contradictions and mediation by tools and signs in human activities, is used as a research tool for maintaining focus on an interpretive treatment of the studied object. The contradiction concept helps to challenge a firsthand understanding in search for a more complete account. Data was gathered in several ways.

- Interviews with volunteer game constructors, four of them are students and three holds positions as teachers or highly qualified engineers. Interviews are performed with open-ended questions. They lasted for about 60 minutes/interview. Five of the interviews are audio recorded and partly transcribed, two are documented with paper and pen notes.
- Accounts from the construction of twelve completed game editors, produced by 66 students. The students' work is done during three editions of a 10-week half time course (Interface for Game Editor) in spring 2012, 2013 and 2014 respectively.
- Accounts from one student group in a 20-week full time course Large Game Project, preceded the Interface for Game Editor Course in winter 2013-2014.

Observations, talking and interviewing in the context of the students' work helped reveal the collective activity systems of which the students and teachers are participants. Further, in the analysis, the above mentioned and explained CHAT approach is applied. A manifestation of contradictions is the main guiding measure.

ARE THE GOOD STUDENTS JUST COMPETENT GAME PLAYERS?

One thing in common for the interviewed students and teachers is that before their studies they played computer and video games. But, their interest later changed into making actual contributions to games and the game playing communities they belonged to. To play games, and especially multiplayer games, entails that people connect and communicate through specialised forums. A play activity usually invites the player to create things and creatures, and furnish and populate the game. Changes in software and hardware are also discussed in parallel to playing the games. In particular, the young players who strive to be recognized as participants of specific forums and communities (Blogs) on the net discuss video cards of different make and versions in detail. What is possible with changed hardware, can the game mechanics become more smoothly and the rendering of visible objects improved? New challenges emerge in the discussions and in the individual's experiences. With their open attitude towards sharing experiences and possibility of manipulating and extending the games, a potential contribution is felt to be within reach. Some individuals find a way to realize a solution to a challenging technological problem in a game. Other students start their creative path in support of the community of players, e.g. setting up the technical infrastructure for sharing information about the game. Successful students have it all and before entering the higher education program they transform from game players to game constructors or game technicians because previous involvement in game design, construction and development.

When entering the five year study program "Degree of Master of Science in Engineering: Game and Software Engineering" the overall demand is to learn *procedural literacy*, a term Mateas (2008) argues for. Procedural literacy is needed as the foundation on the journey of becoming a fully competent game engineer. And that is enough to fuel a full time activity in participating in teaching and learning to master technological challenges. On the learning path, game playing games becomes less important. There are variations but all the interviewed students say playing the games isn't interesting.

Instead, they repeatedly say that the driving force is the challenge of solving a technological problem. The successful result, i.e. the solution, is often mentioned as "a component". This component will fit into a whole of a game and it is shared among the game community. After the satisfactory component is created, the student will take up another challenge and produce another game component. Such unrest seems common among those who create new things, see e.g. a conversation with M. Csikszentmihalyi, in Scherer (2002).

I was struck by how these artists would get completely lost in what they were doing for long periods of time. And yet, once they finished the canvas, they never looked at it again. (p. 15)

Similarly, for this case, to play a game is for those students not a lasting and "immersive experience", but to find a flow in contributions to the game constructs. The manager of the study program further confirms the change: "I have never heard any of the students say that they will go home and play a game". The interviewed teachers and students also pass on the same message: "we have the same attitude, we never play games, and the interesting thing is to solve technical problems". Consequently, the game engineering students cannot be regarded as players, or "users" of games, not even as players of the games they create.

WHAT ARE THE OBJECTS OF THE STUDENTS' ACTIVITIES?

In CHAT terminology the object of a human activity is anything emerging from a "free time" engagement to regular work activities. It is what motivates and coordinates human actions, and can be understood as a kind of "raw material" that is manipulated, maintained, transformed, expanded and turned into an outcome, which fulfils a need in the actual community. Here, the game engineering students put together mathematical and physical models and calculations. They convert them into executable computer code. The piece of code is written in a programming language (C++). For the skilled programmer, it is a human readable code entered into an editor which can be a simple one, or a fully fledge editor similar to a word processor. In next step a compiler, i.e. a specialised computer program reads the machine perspective of the same source code and transforms it into a machine code that the computer "understands" and can run. The interviewees refer to such a piece of product as a "component" or as a "branch", a concept for developed software, intended to exchange or complement/extend a part of a computer game.

The notion of object is central for the researcher functioning as a lens for observations in the world. In some activities it seems rather obvious what the object is. However, in other activities the object is not a straightforward thing to recognize. This problem is due to high specialisation and the fact that external observers, such as a researcher, are alien to what is going on and why things happen. Another difficulty of grasping the object is that the subjects often make rapid and frequent shifts of attention, and participation, between activities. In this case, the game technology development results in highly advanced artefacts created with the use of contemporary and new technologies. That is why the object of activities in focus is hard to grasp for the researcher. I will start analyzing one or in some instances of practice two fairly representative individual students, and later move on to a collective of students. Then I will present a first analysis version explaining what the object(s) are. Delimited to a single student, the analysis is captured in two phases of activity.

One activity focuses on creation of the game artefact (Table 1) and the other activity focuses on reflection (Table 2). An on-going shift between the two phases forms a recurring pattern, observed and reported in the game project courses. In Tables 1 and 2, the most essential CHAT concepts are listed in the leftmost column. They shall be taken as related, but actually as seen in Table 3, there are six related concepts or aspects. They make up a more complete picture of the activity system as a whole. I will supply further information about those aspects later (Engeström, 1987).

Table 1 shows contradictions and important aspects of the student's productive and creative work. During interviews they say "interest to solve technological problems" is the driving force for completion of school assignments and in making the game technology development. The term "component" is used as the thing a single student is assigned to take responsibility for during a longer period of time. A component shall be produced and finally meet requirements from the project's technical specification, of which constraints of computer memory use and performance are

Table 1. Activity with creational focus

CHAT Analysis Concepts	The Case: Game Technology Development	Contradictions at Play in the Case
Subject (of the Activity)	A student	The subject doesn't currently know how to use a mediating artefact, but in the phase of creational focus the contradiction is not dominant.
Mediating Artefacts (Instruments, Tools, Concepts, Signs)	Technology requirement specification, mathematical and physics models, programming language, computer source code, computer hardware (crucial such as the graphics card)	A partly problem solution (an artefact, e.g. a math /physics model) doesn't match the actual hardware specifications (especially problematic with many variants of graphics cards for PC). *Secondary contradiction*: a utilized computer routine (mediating artefact) doesn't match performance and memory constraints for the game component(s) at test (the object of activity).
Object (of the Activity)	Component (piece of runnable code) as the student(s) produce	The component transformation starts from given (although rapidly changing) available technology but needs to go through a creational step realizing an innovative new outcome. *Secondary contradiction* (the same described in the previous row).

Table 2. Activity of reflection focus

CHAT analysis concepts	The Case: Game Technology Development	Contradictions at Play in the Case
Subject (of the Activity)	A student	The subject doesn't currently know how to use a mediating artefact, the contradiction is dominant in this phase of reflection focus.
Mediating Artefacts (Instruments, Tools, Concepts, Signs)	School materials such as textbooks, technology manuals, tutorials and forum information on the net. Requirement specifications for the component (the piece of runnable code under development).	School textbooks and similar established knowledge doesn't match with current constraints of given new technology.
Object (of the Activity)	Technology requirement specification, mathematical and physics models, programming language, computer source code, computer hardware, computer science subjects.	The component construct doesn't fit with other components in the combined game problem solution. A math-physics-code combination for the component is too complex and out of scope of the student's current ability to deal with.

Table 3. Activity of coordination and fitting together of the game artefact

CHAT Analysis Concepts	The Case: Game Technology Development	Contradictions at Play in The Case
Subject	A student	The subject needs to adjust individual wish (of what to do) to the demand of creating the game as a whole.
Mediating Artefacts, Signs, Tools	Game technical specification, Criteria for performance and memory usage, game idea and story. Code and work standards, specific editors (e.g. Unity), programming libraries. Code base. Wiki and a blog.	Relying too much on given technologies (such as programming libraries) defer innovative solutions.
Object (of the Activity)	Components (or branches) put together as a whole game (or game editor).	The different components put together don't meet performance and memory constrains and the game doesn't meet expectations of novelty and innovation.
Rules	Keep updated with most recent information about new technology (especially graphic cards), share and take part of forum discussions on the net, honour those who contribute with novel problem solutions.	To solve a computer technology problem is the most amusing thing to be recognized for - not trying to make a complete game. Agile development method requires repeated periodic alignment and coordination of separate components under development.
Community	(4-8) game engineering students, (in Large Game Project course also: game programming and game design students), 2-4 teachers, forums and blogs on the net (the most comprehensive MobyGames at www.mobygames.com/).	Students emphasise specific component solutions, teachers emphasise curriculum requirements with a joint functional game solution.
Division of Labour	Lead and coordinate individual contributions for the resulting game artefact; creating components for core game engines, design the game idea and story, programming creatures and environment entities to complete the game.	To put forward an individual technical and innovative contribution over a disciplined coordination to the whole game artefact innovation.

fundamental. Those tasks involve making a mathematics model and often also a physics model for game entities' movements. The models are further transformed into programming source code, but this is not a simple straightforward work routine. Computer memory and performance constraints force the solution to be effective, which means it can be functional but not good enough since weaknesses become visible or not acceptable in another sense. A solution, or at least aspects of it, must be optimised. Often there is no given recipe to apply and achieve a solution matching the constraints. In a game development requirement the computer execution can be explicated, as no slower than "10 milliseconds per frame", of which a frame is a "round of the game" when movements and changes are updated.

The component will be functioning together with other components making the game dependent on all of its parts. The path of production is not like the assembly line. Instead the things fit together because they are given a new altered and transformed making up of transformed constructions. Either new or given, they are altered and transformed as the students make up creative constructions. Because of the novelty of working methods, work assessment repeatedly requires testing through execution of the code. Results from those operations challenge the demand of further optimization. Sometimes the results urge the students to question the chosen architectural foundation for the code. In the tests that the student performs, computer constraints are at play of which the potential of the graphics card is a dominant touchstone. Further, during the student's daily testing of a single component, the computer test environment is not the same as when all the parts are put together. So with relatively long intervals, complex testing must be done with several components working in cooperation. However, analysis in Table 1 opens up in detail to understanding the actual challenges.

The curriculum goals enumerate learning to use and reason about the mediating artefacts in Table 1. But beyond such knowledge, creational steps in the student's work are required. Then mathematics, physics and programming languages are used as productive means in making the components of game technology development. However, the student's interest must now and then be focused on the mediating artefacts as such. With fresh experiences from challenges the component work generates, another perspective on standard school subjects open up for the student. A reflective phase of a student's work is depicted in Table 2. The student focuses on the mediating artefacts, i.e. the established or given knowledge to be learnt and mastered.

A partial understanding of Table 1 and 2 suggests that a single student devotes time and effort to mainly two different phases of work. On a daily basis the students shift back and forth, and actually, the phases qualify for discerning two separate but connected activity systems. The first one for creating a component as part of a computer game, and the second one reflection for understanding and mastering the tools and supportive artefacts needed in the first activity system.

Thus at the centre of the study program, there exist in parallel one activity with an object that fits with the school curriculum and traditional labels of learning subjects such as a math, physics and fundamental computer knowledge. The other activity has an object with a tangible end, a more or less complete computer game. The combination realizes creative work that both the interrelated activity systems. Knowledge of the mediating artefacts is needed to construct the game, and the game as such shed light on learning and reflective tasks that fit into the school requirements.

Education is often more than a full time occupation. Creation of game, that is component production, is given priority on planned time. But the needs for reflection urge the student to interrupt and find some space, often beyond regular school time. During interviews, a student demonstrates a separate in-complete but useful game artefact that he uses for testing the given things which he picked up from text books. It is an action motivated by what is currently a challenge in the game creational activity and what he now needs to learn. The game engineering students individually often run parallel game constructs for the sole purpose of testing the things they pick up. In doing so, the student reflects and develops his or her own learning. In conclusion, the single student's work and interest is motivated by the challenging quests of making game components and solving a technical problem. In realizing the creative process, the students read and learn software engineering and computer science. But, in this case data suggest something more.

Neither the teachers nor the curriculum supply the interesting technology challenges as the object of learning. The study program is given the form of a number of regular courses with all the procedures of traditional curriculum knowledge to be learnt and examined. But the material objects they deal with are up to the students themselves to decide. They chose and make game artefacts at their own discretion. Their artefacts evolve throughout the courses and become complex constructs. In the end more or less complete games are realized. On the fourth year of studies the Large Game Project course integrates knowledge and experiences gained in previous courses. During a half year full time studies the students come together in project groups consisting of five to seven game engineering students and two to four game programming and/or technical artist students.

The *engineering students* are responsible for creating the game engines for mechanics, physics and graphics display. The *programming students* use and build on those engines, make contributions that furnish the game with characters and the environment that will become visible on the computer screen. The *technical artist students* are responsible for the game design, the game idea and story documented in a synopsis, which is further detailed into technical requirements. In another follow up study of a course in the fourth year, Interface for Game Editor Tools, the game engineering students work in project groups, but without regular participation of other categories of students. In the last course, which provides most of the data for our case, the students shift their focus towards the visible parts of a game. Still, the students are free to chose which game content to deal with, for example a follow up from their Large Game Project course or a new game created from scratch as the basis for their game editor application.

To explain a recurrent pattern in the study program at large, it is useful to pick up a concept of object orientation from regular computer science theory. Contemporary programming languages are dominantly considered as object oriented in a computer science sense, and clearly that object concept is not the same as in the CHAT terminology. Nevertheless, the idea behind such objects is that programming constructs shall be inspired by, and sometimes represent "the real world". That means according to the idea, all kind of existing, and imagined, things and thoughts in the world outside the computer. The programming language object, as realized in computer code, is a kind of smallest structural thing working together in a complete working computer program. It contains in itself *two essential aspects of computing*. Such an object is built on (1) carefully constrained and coherent pieces of data and (2) appropriate functions (sometimes called methods) that works upon and possibly change the values of that data. This means data hold values that can be stored but

also be retrieved, changed and again be stored, for example such an object might represent a house, a car, a person, a school, an event, whatever that is in some way sensible putting into machine code. The computer object understanding is useful in learning a programming language and it is also suitable as a metaphor for the smallest common dominator in computing. When a computer utilizes such objects, it works with thanks to the collaboration of objects in a context of other such computer objects. Is one of those two object aspects missing, there is not much computing to test and validate. So, a very appealing thing with the game engineering study program seems to be: the students chose the technology challenges themselves and they find solutions to the problems, solutions that are realized practically with the combination of meaningful data and functions that works upon it. Expressed with use of the above sketched computer object metaphor: the students create the objects with both data and functions working together in a very realistic way. But, as mentioned above, the hardware possibilities provide the actual ground and the constraints towards which the students work against.

Apparently the students work very much together in a number of project groups, of which each has, in CHAT terms, a game artefact as the object of their activity. The driving force denoted as "an interest to solve technological problems" is not something that exists in isolation and is alive only as an individual activity. In the following we will look closer at an expanded view on the game engineering program with use of three more CHAT concepts besides those already visible in Table 1 and 2. A computer game artefact in question is in the both studied courses something that requires several different components put together (Table 3). What unite them are technical dependencies dictated by the chosen architecture and the game design expressed in an idea and story. The unity of the components makes up a whole to be further elaborated by the project group's organisation. It follows a scrum agile development approach

(Schwaber, 2004), and in this case a "technical lead" role function as the coordinator of a collective will throughout the project and at regular scrum meetings. In the large project course a designated student holds this role, but in the game editor course the formal rules are vague. Initially the students collaboratively elaborated what partial contributions are needed to implement the design idea. Priority is given to components, all decided in joint sessions with attention to time constraints for the project. A teacher might intervene and help determine how much effort it will take to undertake certain tasks.

For an individual student there is a trade off in accepting what the project demands over a problem solution felt most attractive. Most likely there is a shared knowledge about the individual students' interests and current abilities, which seems to be fairly well respected in a division of different components to make. Up till now, the projects have been functioning and delivering much of the planned artefacts. Worth to mention is also that the students have high expectations on their own achievements, expectations that reach beyond the course tasks, since, as a student stated: there is high competition in the game industry. So, one need to be very alert on current knowledge about recent hardware and software releases relevant for the business, in order to keep up to the assumed standards. Although this view can be questioned, it is clearly an attitude among the students to act and behave in a professional way. An observed aspect of that is a high ability to both lead and participate in project meetings.

The project undertaking to make separate components, developed in different spaces of work, must in the end functioning together. Consequently the individual students must also function together. Usually the students are very capable of making a meeting productive in decisions about the joint plan. As an example from a seminar in the interface for game editors' course, the students should negotiate the object of their work. A game editor is a tool set that can be developed as an integral part of a digital game. It is used when setting up the "levels" (the playing ground/space) and for creating creatures and other items to populate the game. All the students discussed what to do and a necessary priority list. Initially there were ten tool labels for separate components at an overhead display, but finally the following four were given highest priority: Step in time, Click & Drag, Undo/Redo and Expanded camera controls.

A conclusion from the session is that the students act very respectfully towards each other and discuss all the candidate components. Although not very explicit, individual students had associations with one or two favourite tool labels, but in the end had to accept the joint decision. This they did very elegantly. A second conclusion is that the component labels were preliminary but working as terms in proximity to established labels used in other regular office oriented applications. The novelty of the components would qualify for new names and could in some cases be regarded as candidates for publications as specific patterns in computer interactive design. An ability to give new names and tell the story about the result of problem solving would of course be in line with an interest to gain recognition. That means recognition beyond the course assignments, and becoming a participant among those who are honoured for contributions to innovative computer problem solutions. Table 3 provides a perspective on the collective activity system of "coordination and fitting together of the separate components that realize the game artefact".

The CHAT perspective, and a first version analysis such as this, isn't satisfied with an explanation delimited to an individualistic view. Table 3 helps to see that a statement like "it takes a pure interest in technology" is a mere abstraction and not a sufficient explanation to why the students are productive and successful. The students for sure have a strong driving force in fitting things together and creating an innovation, which can be observed as a very common phenomenon. But in addition to the amusing thing, the students strive for and feel strongly a challenge to become recognized among those who are worth the honour as contributors of computer solutions. This details the explanation and it becomes clear that dealing with a distinct challenge, to solve a discrete computer technology problem is the rewarding thing. Such a contribution is feasible and can be expected to have a more sustained value compared to a risky quest for rewards associated with a whole game construct. In a longer time perspective developing a whole game might however become the really big thing, and actually that have happened. With roots in the BTH University two very recognized game industry businesses did start as students' creative technology construction (as mentioned above the examples of Massive Entertainment and Tarsier Studios). An individual game engineer, programmer, manager, artist, designer, will also be recognized in various ways of which a history record might be found in MobyGames, the oldest, largest and most accurate video game database for games of every platform spanning 1979-2014". But for an individual and more "average" student, the component scope seems still as the most realistic endeavour during the time at school.

So, what can be discerned as the object of the students' productive work? It seems as two objects are found in the first version analysis: Firstly the "Component (piece of usable code) the student(s) produce" which is undertaken by one, two or three students working together (Table 1). The outcome of their work is usable code intended as "tools" or "building blocks" to be used in the overall "coordination and fitting things together" activity system (Table 3). Secondly, the object is a game artefact put together with use of the components made in a number of associated activity systems. An elaborated analysis could make a complete picture of the first activity system in Table 1. The components are also intended for general use as small distinct computer solutions. Future research might discern and tell a more complete story

about the character of the associations between the first and the apparently more collective activity system. No doubt the first activity systems are likely to hold intriguing relations to communities mediated by the net and manifested as businesses in the established game industry as is reported here. Most likely, the first activity systems involve counterparts to the "Rules", "Community" and "Division of labor" parts given in Table 3.

Table 2 depicts a reflective activity system in which individual students turn their focus on given knowledge provided by schools, journals, internet media and computer manufactures. This can be considered as students' productive work even though only indirectly used for making tangible computer artefacts. This object is needed more obviously as a mediating tool in the systems depicted in Table 1 and 3. The outcome has also another sustainable value as an achieved ability which the individual student can carry on working with.

IDENTIFIED ACTIVITIES AND KINDS OF FEEDBACK

The assumption that a game developer is also a qualified player of the game in question is in this case false. They have dropped much of the interest they had as youngster to explore and master game playing. Instead, looking under the hood and testing expansion potentials of the code have become the new interest. Most likely their former experiences will hold a good deal when a game engineer is asked to explain what a particular game is about and how it works. But the point here is that in much of the game engineering students learning activities, there isn't much of a challenge provided as feedback from players of the actual games. The games are under construction most of the time and can't be fully tested as playable except at the very end of a project. The specific components made as tools and materials for a game, and as recognizable technical solutions, are nevertheless repeatedly tested. In the smaller activity system assessment and testing tools are made in order to get feedback on the question, e.g. if too much memory is used or if the execution time is too long in respect of the given constraints. A component is also tested with the other components, tests that generate valuable feedback for optimization and adjustment.

The qualitatively most valuable ground for feedback, and a finding of the case study, is made possible due to the game construction character in which both data and functions are available during learning activities. To be contrasted with other computing systems intended for use at banks, hospitals, companies and other large organisations - in a game all the content data that give character and abilities to the game creatures and environment, is within reach and often available for the students. Thus, a game realizes a complete system, or rather a complete domain, which fulfils the ideas in curricula for object-oriented computer learning. Consequently, the students and teachers don't need to simulate data that is mostly hidden and out of reach for the learners of software engineering and computing.

Another observation is that a student game construction project is possible to compare with other creative activities, for example making a theatre production. It involves tool production, a joint collective engagement and an outcome with innovative and imaginative qualities. To be immersed in, or become involved in a reflective process towards a theatre play, can be compared to what is going on in the students' game producing activities. So, the case study reveals students' productive work as instances of conceptualizing of model systems as "a set of constraints that allows for voluntary participation but also for rigorous analysis" (Cole, 1986, p. 31). Also, education in game technology can be compared to theatre production (Engeström & Kallinen, 1988). Who is the audience to judge over the moral and ethical value of game constructions as such, and give feedback on it, is an issue beside the immediate

focus of this study. But clearly, the way of organising game engineering education in a number of projects provides comprehensive context with a reasonable valid content. Such contexts offer an opportunity for the students to become deeply involved in technical development. Scholars of computer science might argue for rigorous standard courses, but Cooper and Cunningham (2010) address reasons for good connection with "real-world questions", that mean teaching computer science "in context":

In computer science, however, we often ask students to learn principles and processes with little context, or with contexts that have little meaning to them. /.../ Computer science would seem to want to connect to the real world, but computer science curriculum recommendations are silent about opportunity to do so, and most widely used texts do not seem to have much content addressing real-world questions. (p. 5)

Without doubt, making games involves a lot of feedback even if the real-world concern can be discussed. In this case, there is abundant feedback on computation and learning despite the fact that the engineering students are not the users of the games they make. We reveal a number of collaborating activity systems covering aspects of knowledge production beyond traditional curriculum assignments. Since the game artefacts contain relevant content during most of the time of development, it can be tested and it can feed back information on the activity. Such feedback informs about further optimization and improved construction of the component or about needed expansion of the students current knowledge. The coordination and fitting things together give feedback to the individual component focused activities. What is also found in the case is that there are connections to communities outside school containing feedback channels of considerable importance.

CONCLUSION

To provide an answer to the question why the students perform well, let's conclude that the everyday knowledge of the involved people of the case builds on a sincere interest and an ability to deal with a combination of mathematics, physics and computer code. Their interest is nurtured by a rewarding feeling of putting things together in an innovative creation. Another finding of this study is that a problem solution shall be challenging and possible to realize as something distinctly original: it is possible within the limits of study program to make a contribution which is valuable both inside and outside school. To be successful is difficult in isolation. A joint development project provides an important environment for productive innovative work. The ability to participate in communities that systematically organise highly advanced and specialized achievements is found in this case. To coordinate and negotiate with other people about why, what and when to find a technical solution is a skill required for becoming successful. In new game technology, it seems like suitable problems have to be solved. They are abundant and they lie within reach for a considerable number of interested students. A complete game is a complex and advanced artefact. It resembles much of needed technologies used in most other computer and software constructs. Furthermore, an advantageous circumstance is that the things that make up a game are potentially within access for the interested player - who eventually will become a game technology developer.

A project oriented approach combined with established and standardized curricula seem to have a vital impact on the students' ability to respond to a successful educational study program. In addition a student says:"at school we have access to the new versions of graphics cards. It is a good thing that the school offers a place and resources to try the new." There is also an interest in research that drives work with such a new hardware." The programming activities provide a specific opportunity for the students to operate at an arena of research and development. There is a potential to be considered and developed further in a school setting like this case. Fernández-Vara and Tan (2008) report about a similar but further developed approach.

By applying professional practices to a school project, we are also translating the social dynamics of the workplace, giving the students the opportunity to learn how to work professionally before they finish their studies. In a way /.../ we offer our students more room for experimenting with new methods that we would outside of academia. (p.32)

To realize the combination of productive learning in connection with professional game development outside school and offering a space for trying out new designs and solutions is a valuable contribution to successful education as well as an object for analysis and explanation to the students' success. The findings suggest there are consequences for higher education. With a project-based way of organizing education, the students are enabled to chose, negotiate and develop the object of their activities. This is a crucial precondition for the creation of novel game artefacts. Some of them are relevant contributions to the development of new technology. With an openness and readiness to deal with challenges, the students maintain connections to practices outside school. Furthermore, the project character of work and education seems to be an important feature for enabling creativity within the frames of regular computer sciences studies. As a fortunate combination, the project approach and the comprehensiveness of computer game artefacts allow the students to become professional subjects in practices similar to contemporary working life. The activity systems developed within the project-based education form contexts where feedback of various kinds is frequent, where creative work is welcome and recognized because of its intrinsic use value. Consequently, the educational program makes possible expansive learning (Engeström, 1987; Nilsson and Wihlborg, 2011) which means that people learn established knowledge and contribute to new game technology.

REFERENCES

Cole, M. (1986). Toward a cultural psychology of human activity systems. An interview. *Nordisk Pedagogik, 6*(1), 25–32.

Crawley, E., Malmqvist, J., Östlund, S., & Brodeur, D. (2010). *Rethinking engineering education: The CDIO approach*. Springer.

Engeström, Y. (1987). *Learning by expanding: An activity-theoretical approach to developmental research*. Helsinki: Orienta-Konsultit.

Engeström, Y., & Kallinen, T. (1988). Theatre as a Model System for Learning to Create. *The Quarterly Newsletter of the Laboratory of Comparative Human Cognition, 10*(2).

Engeström, Y., & Sannino, A. (2011). Discursive manifestations of contradictions in organizational change efforts. A methodological framework. *Journal of Organizational Change Management, 24*(3), 368–387. doi:10.1108/09534811111132758

Fernández-Vara, C., & Tan, P. (2008). The Game Studies Practicum: Applying Situated Learning to Teach Professional Practices. In *Proceedings of the 2008 Conference on Future Play: Research, Play, Share*. ACM. doi:10.1145/1496984.1496990

Francke, M.G. (2014). Ett högt spel. *Sydsvenskan* (sidor B4-B9), 2014-01-14.

Harrison, S., Tatar, D., & Sengers, P. (2007). The Three Paradigms of HCI. In *Proceedings of CHI 2007*. ACM.

Kuutti, K. (1996). Activity Theory as a potential framework for human-computer interaction research. In B. Nardi (Ed.), Context and Consciousness: Activity Theory and Human Computer Interaction. Cambridge, MA: MIT Press.

Markham, T. (2011). Project based learning: A bridge just far enough. Teacher Librarian (Vancouver), 39 (2), 38.

Marx, K. (1909). *Capital* (Vol. 1). London: William Glaisher.

Mateas, M. (2008). Procedural Literacy: Educating the New Media Practitioner. In Beyond Fun: Serious Games and Media. ETC Press.

Nilsson, M., & Wihlborg, M. (2011). Higher Education as Commodity or Space for Learning: Modelling contradictions in educational practices. *Power and Education, 3*(2), 104. doi:10.2304/power.2011.3.2.104

Scherer, M. (2002). Do Students Care About Learning? A Conversation with Mihaly Csikszentmihalyi. *Educational Leadership, 60*(1), 12-17.

Schwaber, K. (2004). *Agile Project Management with Scrum*. Microsoft Press.

Vygotsky, L. S. (1987). *Thinking and Speech. The collected works of L.S. Vygotsky* (R. W. Rieber & A. S. Carton, Eds.). New York, London: Plenum. (Original work published 1934)

ADDITIONAL READING

Bertelsen, O. W., & Bødker, S. (2002). Discontinuities. Floyd, C., Y. Dittrich, R. Klischewski (Eds.). Social thinking - Software Practice. MIT press, Cambridge, MA, 409-424.

Dawson, C. (2005). *Projects in Computing and Information Systems. A Student's Guide*. Pearson Edu Ltd.

Ehn, P. (1993). Scandinavian design: On participation and skill. Schuler, Douglas & Namioka (Eds.). Participatory design. Principles and practices. New Jersey, London: Lawrence Erlbaum.

Enerstvedt, R. Th. (1988). Pedagogy and the concept of activity. *Multidisciplinary Newsletter for Activity Theory*, 1(1/2), 6-13.

Engeström, Y. (1990). When is a tool? In *Twelve Studies in activity theory*. Helsinki: Orienta-Konsultit Oy.

Gargarian, G. (1996). The art of design. Y. Kafai & M. Resnick (Eds.), Constructionism in practice. Mahwah, New Jersey: Lawrence Erlbaum.

Gee, J. P., Hull, G., & Lankshear, C. (1996). *The new work order. Behind the language of the new capitalism*. Westview press.

Goodwin, S. (2005). *Cross-Plattform Game Programming*. Charles River Media.

Kaptelinin, V. (2002). Making use of social thinking: The challenge of bridging activity systems. Y. Dittrich, C. Floyd & R. Klischewski (Eds.), Social thinking – Software practice. MIT press, Cambridge, MA.

Keith, C. (2010). *Agile Game Development with Scrum*. Addison-Wesley.

Kyhlbäck, H., & Sutter, B. (2004). Who is involved in HCI design? An Activity-theoretical perspective. Proceedings of the third Nordic conference on human-computer interaction. ACM *International Conference Proceeding Series*, Vol. 82.

Lave, J., & Wenger, E. (1991). *Situated learning: legitimate peripheral participation*. Cambridge: Cambridge Univ. Press. doi:10.1017/CBO9780511815355

Leont'ev, A. N. (1978). *Activity, consciousness, and personality*. Englewood Cliffs, NJ: Prentice Hall.

Marx, K. (1845/1967). Theses on Feuerbach. E. Kamenka (Ed.), The Portable Marx. New York: Penguin Books.

McShaffry, M. (2009). *Game Coding. Complete* (3rd ed.). Charles River Media.

Nilsson, M. E. (2008). Digital Storytelling: A Multidimensional Tool in Education. T. Hansson (Ed.). Handbook of Research on Digital Information Technologies: Innovations, Methods, and Ethical Issues. IGI books.

Rabin, S. (2009). *Introduction to Game Development* (2nd ed.). Charles River Media.

Sutter, B. (1991). *Productive learning at University and college level? Department of Applied Psychology Reports, 40* (pp. 1–10). Sweden: University of Umeå.

Sutter, B. (2011). How to analyze and promote developmental activity research? *Theory & Psychology, 10/2011, 21*(5). Sage Publications.

Tidwell, J. (2010). *Designing Interfaces, Patterns for Effective Interaction Design*. O'Reilly Media.

Virkunen, J., Engeström, Y., Helle, M., Pihlaja, J., & Poikela, R. (1997). The Change Laboratory – a Tool for Transforming Work. T. Alasoini, M., Kyllöen, A. & Kasvio (Eds.). Workplace Innovations – Way of Promoting Competitiveness, Welfare and Employment. Ministry of Labour, Reports 3. Helsinki 1997.

Vygotsky, L. S. (1978). *Mind in society: the development of higher psychological processes*. Cambridge: Harvard University Press.

Wertsch, J. V. (1985). *Vygotsky and the Social Formation of the Mind*. Cambridge, MA: Harvard University Press.

Wihlidal, G. (2006). *Game Engine Toolset Development*. Course Technology PTR.

Winograd, T. (Ed.). (1996). *Bringing design to software*. NY, USA: ACM New York.

KEY TERMS AND DEFINITIONS

CHAT: Cultural-historical activity theory. Lev Vygotsky (1896-1934) and his colleagues A. R. Luria and A. N. Leont'ev formulated the concept of artefact-mediated and object-oriented action (Vygotsky, 1978, p. 40). A human individual never reacts directly (or merely with inborn reflects) to environment. The relationship between human agent and objects of environment is mediated by cultural means, tools and signs. Human action has a tripartite structure.

Contradiction: Opposed elements or forces within and between phenomena in the world.

Creative: Involving imagination in production of novel things and concepts.

Cultural-Historical Activity Theory: See the CHAT definition.

Game Construction: In realizing a game idea and story, designing and implementing mathematical and physics models in computer code.

Game Development: A systematic way of organizing work, involving phases of analysing requirements, designing and implementing computational components - for the purpose of making a complete digital game.

Game Technology Education: Higher education aiming at knowledge and skills in creating and making the core and fundamental building blocks required for an advanced digital video game.

Mediation: Human actions and operations realized with help of symbols, tools, language, i.e. actions mediated by all kind of artefacts.

Professional Practice: Established mode and way of work that is related to a profession.

Section 2
Education

Chapter 5
Collaborative Music Making and Artistic Agency

Karin Johansson
Lund University, Sweden

ABSTRACT

The focus of this chapter is on musical agency in professional contexts and in Higher Music Education (HME). What is musical agency? How can musical agency be investigated, promoted, and developed? Cultural-historical activity theory approaches hold a potential for exploring and answering such questions with a dialectical perspective on creativity. Three examples of interventionist studies from a one-to-one teaching situation, a professional improvisation project, and a student string quartet are given. They illustrate how individual musical acts influence and transform collective music making. Methodological conclusions are drawn and suggestions are made for the development of intervention studies of musical practice inspired by Change Laboratory methodology.

INTRODUCTION

The horizon against which this chapter should be seen is agency in professional music making and higher music education (HME) of classical musicians, that is, musicians educated to become professional practitioners in the field of Western art music. This is a dynamic cultural and socio-economic practice based on relationships to written scores, performance practices, audiences and societal institutions. The key context for educating musicians in this practice is the conservatoire tradition, where knowledge and experience of music as a craft and an art is held, transmitted and developed. In a system of mainly one-to-one tuition,

novices encounter and collaborate with masters for a number of years. Then they continue as masters in the field of music performance and production. This field holds the opposition between, on the one hand, carrying a wealth of tradition, and, on the other hand, aiming at creating something 'new'. Working as a musician is equally dependent on collective order and individual passion. Young people who enter the system and in due time become agents on the arena of music-making encounter an unclear future. What is the function and value of art music in society? What roles can be played by professional musicians of tomorrow? Will they be preservers of the conservatoire tradi-

DOI: 10.4018/978-1-4666-6603-0.ch005

tion, as a kind of museum wardens, or will they be renewals of high culture art music?

The overarching interest of this chapter might be framed as two questions that concern agency in contexts of professional music making and in HME: What is musical agency? How can musical agency be investigated, promoted and developed?

Based on my experience from previous studies, I believe that cultural-historical activity theory (CHAT) holds the potential for contributing both to the analysis of conditions for learning and creativity in music-making contexts and to the development of agency in music-making as a cultural practice. It might be argued that the concept of 'musical agency' can be formulated as learning outcomes, for example as students' ability to 'describe, analyze and interpret design, techniques and content autonomously as well as to reflect critically on his or her artistic approach' (Swedish Higher Education Ordinance). However, a focus on individual capacities is not enough. In activity theory, the concept of agency relates to the 'participants' ability and will to shape their activity systems' (Engeström & Sannino, 2010, p. 20). This quote points to how individual action and collective activity are always inextricably connected. Consequently, any object-oriented music-making situation may be studied as an activity system. Individual interpreting, improvising or composing are then seen as 'the tip of the iceberg representing individual and group actions embedded in a collective activity system' (Engeström, 2005, p. 61) rooted in structures of motives, rules and organization. Hence, musical agency is the capacity of individuals to act – in music, with music and through music – in music-making situations that contain certain rules for what is possible to know, learn and create in the context of power structures, labour distribution and socio-cultural patterns. On the one hand, individuals are offered differing degrees of epistemological and creative space (Krüger, 1998) and, on the other hand, they are influential and responsible as agents in the creation and maintenance of the activity *per se*. In

the context of a previous study, Johansson (2013a, p. 26) notes that "both in situations of education and performance, artistic work might be described as entering into a collective activity system, adapting to it and transforming it by expanding it into new zones of proximal development". The quote describes individual contribution to the collective activity system. As a complement to this view, Sannino (2013) points to how the individual gains agency and initiative when a personal need is attracted to and connected to a collective object. This dialectic relationship between individual action and collective activity is a stimulating factor in the forming of an artistic identity and profile. It indicates that 'musical agency' is never a solely individual asset, but is enacted in interaction with the collective goals of the activity.

Second, how can musical agency be investigated, promoted and developed? Theorizing a certain music-making situation as a cultural historical activity system is in itself one step in this direction. Thinking about musical learning and creative processes in this theoretical framework creates the possibility for studying artistic knowledge, creativity and aspects of musical identity as parts of a dynamic whole. A focus on musical agency provides the means for analyzing and understanding aspects of music making in ensembles as well as at individual levels as historically, structurally and inter-personally related. For example, a music student may experience dislike of and resistance towards learning and playing a certain repertoire piece. When seen as an aspect of musical agency, it is not enough to interpret such resistance as an individual problem. Even though the student might not be prepared to articulate it, playing the piece in question might mean accepting gender positions, power relations in tuition, or tacit aesthetical discourses. Difficult personal feelings need to be seen in relation to historical structures and object-relations at a collective level in the course of the training to become a professional musician.

As shown in research on the evaluation of courses in higher education (Nilsson, 2003), views on what constitutes the goal of a certain activity often differ substantially between teachers and students seen as groups, and possibly also inside these groups. Teachers, students and professional musicians may use activity systems on their own and in co-operation, for the understanding of power relations in existing contexts and as starting points for explorative endeavors. In the forthcoming examples, I show that already the formulation and discussion of a collectively shared object in music-making situations may have a radical and positive effect. This might seem simple but is connected to individual musicians' awareness of personal and collective history, traditions, skills and wishes in their practices. Consequently, the creation of expansive learning situations is facilitated. As pointed out by Peter Renshaw (2011), former Head of Research and Development at the Guildhall School of Music and Drama, musicians of today need to develop strategies and methods for life-long learning, which can be described as techniques for developing and rethinking agency. Education of musicians and music teachers of all genres rests upon the long-term study of musical craftsmanship and technique. This demands stamina, self-discipline and receptivity of the music students, as well as a willingness to incorporate traditional knowledge. Simultaneously, in the competitive and market-based cultural climate of today's musical culture, it is necessary to develop a strong and profiled artistic identity based on musical will-power and originality, aesthetic self-confidence and entrepreneurial abilities. Tensions often exist between the task of reproducing and continuing tradition, on the one hand, and individual artistic expression, on the other hand. Likewise, conflicts concerning musical identity, gender positions and economic status influence music making and learning. These complex issues

may be studied as inherent contradictions in the activity system of music production and can be explored not only as problems but as possibilities for development.

In recent projects (Johansson, 2012; 2013c; 2013d) I investigate approaches for interventionist studies of music making with inspiration from Change Laboratory methodology, as originally formulated by Engeström, Virkkunen, Helle, Pihlaja & Poikela (1996) and related formats such as the Clinic of Activity (Clot, 2009). As mentioned by Engeström et al (1996), the idea of formulating creative or educational art practices as laboratories is a familiar idea. Several researchers in HME have carried out developmental projects, for example, *Students' Ownership of Learning*, SOL, (Hultberg, 2010), *Teachers' Voices* (Johansson, 2013b) and *Innovative Conservatoire*, ICON (2013). These initiatives aim at articulating strategies and methods for learning and creating music in conservatoire settings that might be seen as 'artistic laboratories' (Smilde, 2008, p. 251). However, as yet there are no examples of attempts to develop and adapt the Change Laboratory method for artistic activities. Against this background, I will (i) give three examples from studies of musical practice made with inspiration from the Change Laboratory methodology, and (ii) discuss how they may contribute to creating tools and strategies for supporting learners in HME and professional musicians in transforming themselves as well as the collective activity in which they take part.

The examples are taken from a collaborative project of organ improvisation, from a study of vocal teaching in HME and from an interventionist study of a string quartet in a conservatoire. In the examples I explore the benefits of theorizing small musical ensembles as activity systems, pointing to important aspects that need to be taken into consideration when investigating music making.

ACTIVITY-THEORY, MUSIC EDUCATION, AND PERFORMANCE

Even though music making is a fruitful ground for investigating how artistic expression, creativity and learning relate to and interact with receptivity, tradition and reproduction, applications of activity theory in this area are still rare. A few projects in music education investigate, for example, the intensity of interaction in instrumental one-to-one lessons (Heikinheimo, 2009), peer collaboration in childrens' composing and arranging (Burnard & Younker, 2008), jazz student musicians' ways of practicing (Gravem Johansen, 2013) and the introduction of girls into the English cathedral system (Welch, 2007; 2011). As pointed out by Graham Welch (2007),

...there is much that can be gained by exploring the theory's key principles (the activity system as a unit of analysis, multi-voicedness, historicity, contradictions, expansive cycles) to generate a wider understanding of the relationships and contributions between top-down and bottom-up perspectives in an educational process related to music. (p. 33)

Knowledge of how to create and perform art music is often seen as residing with the individual, and the most common context for transmission of this knowledge is still the conservatoire tradition with its master-apprentice-like relationships. 'Outsiders' have normally no access to knowledge and in traditional scientific contexts, musical creativity is often seen as 'largely shrouded in mystery' (Juslin, 2001, p. 410). Such views result in a social marginalization of artistic activity and define it as a commodity in the area of entertainment and pastimes. However, a growing number of studies in the young discipline of artistic research (e.g. Frisk, 2008; Östersjö, 2008; Weman, 2008) show that processes of artistic expression, interpretation and knowledge creation may fruitfully be investigated and communicated from insiders' perspectives.

Research studies *in*, not *on*, musical practice are becoming frequent and lead to methodological development in collaborative projects where all participants take part in the design and analysis. For example, Hultberg (2005) develops formats for cooperation between musicians and a researcher acting as a privileged observer, and Östersjö (2008) describes the negotiations between interpreter and composer from his combined perspective as a musician and a researcher. In doing so, the practical work and musical interaction, as well as mainly unarticulated theoretical dimensions and structural relationships enacted by musicians in their practice become accessible for exploration and communication.

INTERVENTIONIST STUDIES OF MUSICAL PRACTICE

Many studies of music making can be compared to design experiments, in the sense that they aim at achieving effective instruction and acquisition of pre-defined learning contents more than 'an expansive transformation process led and owned by the practitioners' (Engeström, 2011, p. 9), which is the case in intervention studies and formative interventions. These start off from a contradictory object perceived by the participants. And they aspire at the collaborative reconceptualization and expansion of this object. It might be argued that effective learning, for example the internalization of an established canon of repertoire, is always crucial for any musician who wants to be a successful professional artist; classical music making is as much a craft as it is an art. However, this view is not in any way opposed to a focus on participants' musical agency, which relies on integrating as well as transforming the musical culture. As in all artistic work, musical agency is dependent on a combination of learning and creative abilities – of internalization and externalization. In any activity, there are at least two levels of dialectical relationships, connected to the reproduction and transformation of culture: (i) the dialectical relationship between individual action and collective activity, and, (ii) the dialectical relationship between internalization and externalization. While educational research often emphasizes internalization, the theory of expansive learning (Engeström, 1987; 2005) forms the background to Change Laboratory methodology. It points to an essential feature of contemporary activities, i.e. the object of the activity has to be created at the same time as it is learned, and is under constant reconsideration and negotiation. The blurring of the line between internalization and externalization has always been central to creative artistic work, at least for the individual and independent artist. Artists constantly create – and learn – previously unknown and new modes of expression, new forms of performance and new ways of presenting artistic knowledge. As noted by Teräs (2007, p. 62), the Change Laboratory method has been developed as a tool for working-life situations in which the old is no longer good enough, but the new has not yet been discovered. While individual artists usually have such tools at their disposal as a natural part of their creative work, educational and ensemble situations rarely allow all participants to take part in the creation and development of a common object. Due to traditionally hierarchical structures in the training of musicians and in professional ensembles, participants sometimes lack the power to influence their activity from the inside. In the end, the results may be individual loss of motivation as well as collective artistic stagnation. The Change Laboratory methodology provides the means for accessing complex questions of motivation, artistic goals and quality in ways that are beneficial for individual musicians and for music as a cultural practice.

Change Laboratory developmental research grew out of a need for new modes of dialectics between (i) close embeddedness and reflective distance; (ii) practice-driven redesign and idea-driven construction of visions; (iii) long, medium and short cycles of innovation and change; and,

(iv) tools of daily work and tools of analysis and design (Engeström et al, 1996, p. 11). In my studies of music-making, this structure corresponds to the following needs: (i) developing critical creativity, which means training to use reflection from both inside (reflection-in-action) and outside (reflection-on-action) perspectives, (ii) developing awareness of the relationship between aspects of art and craft in music making, (iii) developing ability to take responsibility for and exert influence upon short-time individual goals as well as the collective, long-term objective, and, (iv) developing ability to set individual music making in an ensemble into contexts, concerning instrumental affordances, hierarchical structures and conditions for creativity. Altogether, the list of tasks should be seen in the light of a need for new perspectives on musicianship from educators, institutions and musicians alike.

THE TERM *CONTRADICTIONS* IN STUDIES OF MUSICAL PRACTICE

A crucial and rewarding part of interventionist studies of music is to investigate how inherent, historically generated and systematic contradictions challenge agents in a system with seemingly incompatible tensions, but also to study how these contradictions provide the energy for innovations and development. The concept of contradictions originates in Hegel's philosophy as developed by Marx and Engels. Contradictions also relate to the Russian philosopher Evald Ilyenkov (2010) and to proponents of activity theory as represented by Yrjö Engeström and the Centre for Research on Activity, Development and Learning (CRADLE). Contradictions in CHAT are usually described at four analytical levels, which relate to the system of music production as follows:

- The contradiction between use value and exchange value is a fundamental and omnipresent one, to which all others in a capitalistic society relate. Classical music as an overarching societal object in itself holds this contradiction: on the one hand, it is constructed as a non-profit, high-culture path to understanding knowledge with the aim of estimating 'l'art pour l'art', and on the other hand it is a commodity for leisurely entertainment and relaxation. Art music is a publicly funded and regulated activity as well as a free market. Every specific music-making situation therefore represents a point of interaction between different kinds of agents, often with contradictory interests.

- Contradictions appear between nodes (Engeström & Sannino, 2010) in Engeström's activity triangle. They become visible when new tools or rules are introduced. A present-day example shows that introduction of documented bachelor and master theses in the higher education of fine and performing arts has caused a lively debate on whether verbal, critical reflection should have a place in the education of artists. So far, the situation has resulted in a number of creative initiatives that remain to be evaluated.
- Contradictions between old and new forms of the activity may be exemplified by new conditions encountering musicians as performers, with new ways of interacting with audiences.
- Contradictions between activity systems are manifested in public musical life, where music producers like symphony orchestras, record companies and the Church often have other goals than educational institutions.

These are a few examples of possible contradictions at an arena where musicians as practitioners, teachers and lifelong learners find themselves in their professional lives. Apart from describing different kinds of tensions, the layers of contra-

dictions also picture stages, or steps, in a typical process of change where new structures appear. This can fruitfully be studied by a focus on disturbances, which are defined as 'deviations from the normal scripted course of events in the work process, interpreted as symptoms of manifestations of inner contradictions of the activity system in question' (Engeström & Sannino, 2011, p. 372). An illustrative example of such a process is the creation of the bourgeois organ concert in the 17th century, which actually came about as a result of the Reformation and the ban on organ music in the liturgy in parts of Europe (Snyder, 2007). This 'revolution' created an arena for hitherto unknown forms of music making, with new aesthetic values and new roles for the listening audience.

In sum, the concept of contradictions is a valuable theoretical tool for exploring various forms of musical practice. Studies of contradictions may shed light on the flow between individual and collective levels of knowledge and experience.

THE TERM *SCRIPT* IN STUDIES OF MUSICAL PRACTICE

With the aim of investigating agency by focusing on epistemological and creative space in music-making (Krüger, 1998; Johansson, 2012) – that is, on what is possible to know, learn and create considering the given power structures and socio-cultural patterns – I have found the notion of the 'script' applicable. The term originates in cognitive psychology where it describes sequential schemes for actions at individual level. When used in activity-theoretical contexts it refers to collective, historically evolving and mostly tacit regulations for procedures of learning. In the third example focus is on the musical and social interaction in a string quartet rather than on intra-psychological processes of individual members. Engeström (1992) characterizes a script as a tool turned into a rule and states that scripts

...regulate standard procedures in repeatedly occurring cultural situations. Although the script may be available in a quite explicit form (e.g. as a written formula or rule), the participants in a scripted event are seldom aware of the script they are following. (p. 79)

This view is often relevant in music making situations. For example, speaking of artistic work in a string quartet Waterman (2003, p. 124) states that interpretative work is often not spelled out in detail but "may well be realized holistically and without over-tedious analytical discussion". Musicians who are encultured in similar practices quickly adapt to existing scripts in new situations and do not need explicit rule descriptions in order to understand what is going on. They bring script knowledge with them. This is an unproblematic situation as long as the scripts coincide. However, the scripts may become what Teräs (2007) in a study of intercultural learning among Finnish immigrants calls 'shadow scripts':

A shadow script is a script that people learn through their enculturation process and which becomes part of their intercultural encountering. On the other hand, all the scripts we learn through experience and participation in different cultural practices are potential shadow scripts. However in intracultural situations we usually know the unspoken scripts, take them for granted, and follow them, and the shadow script does not cause disturbances. In all situations there are potential shadows, but they only become visible in certain circumstances – when the sun is shining. Thus, a shadow requires the existence of light for it to become visible. (p. 97)

When one script dominates the scene others will function as disturbances - but they also provide developmental energy. The point of formulating an artistic version of the Change Laboratory method is to capture this developmental energy by creating boundary zones – what Gutierrez et al (1999) call

a Third space – (Teräs, 2007, p. 31), where scripts and shadow scripts may be articulated, analyzed and changed. Concerning HME activities like instrumental tuition, Heikinheimo (2009) remarks that interaction in one-to-one lessons seldom enters expansive cycles precisely because of the strength of the script in the conservatoire tradition. In the context of instrumental music tuition the script usually means that the teacher is also the master in a master-apprentice relationship that is still the most common in the conservatoire tradition. The master holds the initiative, asks questions and gives advice and criticism. The position offered to the student/apprentice is that of a learner without much knowledge but with a need to learn (Jahreie & Ottesen, 2010). At the same time, this situation relates to the overarching script of HME, formulated as a tacit agreement that students desire and accept a period of subordination, after which they want to and are expected to break away from dependence (Ljungar Chapelon, 2008). Corresponding scripts exist in professional musical practice but are not easily accessed. As underlined by Hultberg (2010), low levels of awareness and reflection upon structural tensions result in a restricted degree of agency for all parties involved, and a focus upon scripts in ensembles might be a first step towards investigating how people construct common objects in music making.

In the following, I present three of my previous research studies with relevance for the investigation of musical agency. The first two examples are described in detail elsewhere (Johansson, 2008; Johansson, 2013c; Johansson, 2013d).

INTERVENTIONIST STUDIES OF MUSICAL PRACTICE

Exploring musical agency is the cornerstone of this chapter. The theme will be illustrated in three examples taken from studies of one-to-one instrumental tuition, professional organ improvisation and repertoire playing in a string quartet.

When stepping into such music making contexts, individual musicians accept conventional roles and interactional structures for their participation. They contribute with craftsmanship, expertise and experience to a common goal; here represented by the production of musical learning, explorations of improvisations and collective interpretations. Although fairly small in size, the constellations in the examples form collective activity systems where people are involved in expansive learning processes. They share a common object and engage in division of labour and rules of the activity. The examples embody several of the characteristic features of Western musical culture and illustrate aspects that are relevant for interventionist studies of similar socio-cultural practices. They also describe experiments with the methodological rules for 'interventions that open up the zone of proximal development of the activity system' (Engeström, 2009, p. 327). The method for doing so is to follow the object, give the object a voice and expand the object.

INTERPERSONAL ASPECTS OF MUSICAL AGENCY

All activities present participants with a framework that regulates their epistemological and creative space. The degree of musical agency in a certain music-making context is related to how agents conceive of and utilize this space with its possibilities and limitations. In a first example of one-to-one vocal tuition, the project had the purpose of uncovering and verbalizing obstacles and options for students' independent learning. It was carried out as a longitudinal case study during a complete academic year. Two undergraduate vocal students and their teacher participated. With a design as a cycle of expansive learning, the teacher and the students questioned and investigated their practice with me in the role of researcher. I conducted interviews, made video recordings and stimulated recall sessions, and led focus group discussions. In

my role as an intervening, participating observer I put probing questions based on my familiarity with the studied practice. Besides being a researcher, I am also a conservatoire-trained organist, a professional musician and previously an instrumental teacher in the academy.

A remarkable observation at the initial stage of the study was that the common object actually proved to be missing. This result confirms Daniel's (2008) observation that asking fundamental and seemingly simple questions about the object of a certain activity constitutes "a very powerful first step in the identification of systemic contradictions" (p. 137). The sheer attempt to define the common object revealed to the participants as well as to me, the researcher, that the parties were unaware of what they were trying to achieve. The initial interviews and practice sessions showed that the students seriously resisted what they believed to be the goal of the tuition, that is, to become solo singers. However, their expectations did not correspond to explicit statements in steering documents, course descriptions or curricula. Neither did the teacher articulate this as an objective. The teacher and the students had completely opposite views on goals, methods and knowledge development. Their objectives and attitudes to musical practice differ completely. The teacher holds that the goal is to become a solo singer but the students think that the goal is to sing but not becoming a solo singer. The teacher thinks that singing is a craft for everyone but the students believe that singing is a gift and impossible to learn. Finally, the teacher thinks that as a consequence the students should work hard but the students conclude that they should not practice.

This finding might seem to be a difficult starting point for a collaborative project, but already the formulation of the contradictory object provided the teacher and the students with motivation for extensive reflective work. They verbalized and examined positive insights as well as experiences of tensions and difficulties – that is, manifestations of contradictions - during vocal lessons, performances and exams. Problems were unearthed and discussed but were not necessarily solved during the school year. The teacher described this process of articulating obstacles, confronting obstacles and transforming obstacles into options as a 'creative dialogue'. This format made it possible for the participants to verbalize their experiences and share inside perspectives on musical learning. Our work resulted in repeated self-confrontations and in an expanded and shared object: at the end of the study the students were - somewhat surprisingly - active as solo singers in professional contexts. They saw themselves as singers, although in other ways than their teacher had anticipated. Their initial refusal to imitate and identify with the teacher may be seen as an aspect of agency; at the outset they had no means for formulating alternative opinions on the activity and the only possible action was to resist. Their resistance initially functioned as an obstacle for the development of their vocal and artistic skills but transformed into a tool for shedding light on crucial issues that otherwise would have remained unarticulated. It became a success story. The students could then independently utilize the knowledge offered to them by their teacher. Suggestions for changes in the institutional practice of one-to-one vocal teaching were produced, such as the introduction of video recordings of all exams. These were implemented and are currently being evaluated.

Although planned to systematically proceed through a Change Laboratory process, this study made a halt at the crucial step of defining a common object. However, the result in terms of musical agency development for the participants was significant, mainly because of their commitment to follow the object. This ambition was in turn facilitated by the fact that I as an insider/researcher could recognize and discern subject-specific details in the participants' interaction. These were then fed back into the group. Our collaborative process of investigating the activity created a Third space where suggestions for new

scripts could be explored and the shadow script of instrumental tuition questioned. In this, often tacit, script, instrumental teachers expect their students to be and become creative and independent agents of art while at the same time adhering to tradition. The education of classical musicians therefore holds specific tensions between tradition and independence, craftsmanship and artistry, reproduction and innovation. Studies point to how the one-to-one teaching situation itself and the teaching strategies that are used are often counter-productive to the aim of developing agency (Gaunt, 2008; Johansson, 2013b). In the context of this project, the answer to the question 'What is musical agency?' would be that it is an aspect of life-long learning that needs to be recognized already during early stages of training. Today's music students require tools for rephrasing their definitions of what it means to be a successful musician (Bennett, 2008) and continuously identifying their needs for competence development (Smilde, 2008) throughout their careers. Laboratory settings as in this project may enable the establishment of creative Third-space dialogues that promote musical agency by acknowledging the existence of contradictory objects.

INTRAMUSICAL ASPECTS OF MUSICAL AGENCY

Musical agency has an intra-musical dimension that concerns the development and expansion of expressive and creative spaces in musical action. The following example of organ improvisation focuses on this aspect. Organ playing contains a paradoxical contradiction: Organists improvise mainly as soloists and have the acoustical power over large soundscapes, in massive buildings and in front of large audiences. A main focus in their profession is to create music that suits the situation. At the same time they are not expected to be individual and personal as musicians but to subordinate themselves to a collective ritual. In playing, they act as co-creators of a structure where the musician is expected to improvise in dialogue with the congregation and the ritual rather than to express individual musical ideas. Due to this fact, it can be difficult to discern what individual musical agency is and how people experience it. The artistic research project *Rethinking and revisiting organ improvisation* (Johansson, 2013d) aimed at investigating musical language(s) and creative strategies situated in dialectical relationships between the individual and the collective, and between internalization of existing culture and externalization of art. It included five participants and the present author as performers during six sets of workshops and concerts in Scandinavia. As a theory-based project, we began by exchanging experiences in sessions where the whole group revisited previous findings (Johansson, 2008). These pointed to how the meaning and function of improvisation differ between two activity systems - the liturgy and the concert – with differing socio-historical and musical structures.

The ambition of the project was to access layers of musical inspiration and expression. We did so by *investigating innovative ways of playing*. We did so by *stimulating ways of listening* detached from ritual function, and we did so by deploying *experiencing ways of interacting* that stood free from musical habit. The project was experimental in the sense that in our laboratory situations we established rules that prompted us to question and challenge the current activity. Workshops and concerts were conceived of as experimental spaces where we worked with detailed plans for decontextualizing individual habits, conventions and regulating structures. With a collaborative approach to conducting and analyzing the study, we created a Third space with a script for rethinking and revisiting our practices. This script rested on our ability to create and deliver performances. Neither the format nor the content was pre-planned. It might be described in terms of a) maintaining a structural flexibility in the concert format by re-

fraining from planning and practicing, b) expanding the scope for individual artistic expression by avoiding traditional musical styles or genres, and c) destabilizing our habitual positions as soloist musicians by creating frameworks that require intense listening and interaction.

Succeeding analyses show that we failed to follow this script, at least at the beginning. The initial concerts were successful with respect to producing good music but we did not interact, listen or expand the scope for expression. All players presented themselves in music convincingly but avoided risk-taking. In fact, we followed a shadow script with one, very strong rule: in concerts, musicians must convince the audience of their competence. Displaying uncertainty and lack of direction is a taboo. However, in the process of delivering the six concerts, this objective gradually changed. We failed to leave the concert formats and content open but our attempts resulted in unfamiliar situations. These situations caused collective frustration and insecurity concerning turn taking, formats and interaction but also forced us to listen in new ways. Even though they were unpleasant at the time and experienced as artistic failures in actual performance they were, surprisingly enough, evaluated as producing especially good music by all players when we analyzed the recordings. Our unwilling withdrawal from the habitual, caused by a destabilization of 'normal' procedures, opened up for musical boundary crossing and for expanding the object. Clarifying and formulating a script for our collective activity had precisely the effect mentioned by Teräs (2007): it shed light on the shadow script and made us aware of the influence it exerted on us. Furthermore, it provided the musical inspiration and courage needed for daring us to deviate from the script. Expanding our creative space meant that we all had to step out of our artistic comfort zones. Consequently, a result of the project is the realization that emotional distress in performance can be a signpost of imminent artistic border crossing. Enduring this kind of anxiety and insecurity then becomes an important ingredient in promoting musical agency. It can also be seen as a matter of how the rules of the script are transformed into tools.

INTRAPERSONAL ASPECTS OF MUSICAL AGENCY

One important component of musical agency is the construction of a subjective need for music as the central driving force and motivating factor in an activity. This is featured in an example of a string quartet at an academy of music. The members were all music students at bachelor and master university programs. Playing in a student string quartet with the relative absence of a teacher and comparative equality of the participating musicians represents an intermediary state between training and professional life. Students encounter a socio-culturally established format for musicmaking in which they may explore the complexity of musical interaction and the scope for individual initiative (Davidson & Good, 2002). In this way, the quartet functions as one culturally constructed body. At the same time it constitutes a unique set-up of musical personalities. This particular quartet existed for several years and had a well working internal communication. They did not have a clearly defined problem at the onset of the project, which is usually the starting point for a Change Laboratory study. However, the members were motivated to engage in analytical work and the study was carried out as a longitudinal investigation of the string quartet in educational, rehearsing and performing situations during the academic year of 2013-2014. I conducted individual interviews with each member. I also observed and recorded nine performances during rehearsals, lessons, exams and concerts. The material was used as mirror data in a concluding group interview with feedback and reflections on the individual interviews.

Historically, the string quartet has been an all-male, hierarchically ruled activity (Potter, 2003). The script for a working string quartet has remained roughly the same since the days of Haydn's quartets at the end of the 18th century. The crucial characteristics are that a) musicians act as tools for realizing the composer's intentions, thereby maintaining the hierarchy between composer and performer, b) players are positioned in roles that structure their scope of expression and influence (Murnighan, 1991), c) in rehearsals the first violinist leads the activity with the relative silence of other players, and d) performances are mainly given in traditional formats.

As expected, the mirror material points to how the musicians step into and identify with conventional roles in the rehearsals. These confirm and reproduce the string quartet script: the first violinist has a leading and pedagogical role and the second violinist discusses details while the viola player and the cellist are verbally withdrawn. The musicians are comfortable in these positions and well aware of the consequences of adhering to and deviating from the script. They describe themselves as free to relate in constructive ways to historical conventions. In the individual interviews, all players emphasize how important the personal need is as a motivation for playing.

I want to do music, and I couldn't do anything else. The feeling of getting to play music that you like is so wonderful, even if no one is listening.

Music is such a big part of my everyday life – I'm addicted, and I have to practise. That's not always fun, but it's always so positive to see that things happen. It's the most natural means of expression for me and I'm always keen on doing all kinds of strange things.

Very early on, I knew that I wanted to become a musician and I first played the violin. But then one day I got to try the viola and I found it amazing, a fantastic instrument.

The physical feeling of playing and practising is something you miss as soon as you don't do it. It's extremely addictive, but not in a bad way.

The quotes illustrate that personal motivation and passionate engagement with music is a natural part of what it means to be a musician. However, the same quotes also suggest a complicated picture. As mentioned, the learning and creative environment of the conservatoire tradition presents students and teachers with a challenge that all musicians are familiar with but seldom articulate in structural terms: The demand for simultaneous subordination and independence in ways that often seem to be incompatible.

In terms of the principle of double stimulation (Vygotsky, 1978), this dilemma may be seen as the first stimuli. Successful learning and development requires, on the one hand, incorporation and preservation of the tradition, adoration of masters and honoring craftsmanship through long years of practicing and fine-tuning instrumental skills. On the other hand, a fundamental aspect of becoming a musician is the development of musical originality, artistic experimentation and a sense of ownership. The findings in the string quartet project suggest that students in higher music education can be described as carrying out double stimulation experiments (Vygotsky, 1978; Engeström, 2007). The first stimulus is the contradictory situation inherent in the learning situation. The second stimulus is their motivation; the conception of an individual addiction to playing and a strong personal relationship to the instrument functions as a psychological tool for handling and successfully transcending the double-bind situation where simultaneous subordination and independence is required.

This explains the common proneness of agents in HME to describe their learning and developmental trajectories, including personal issues, conflicts and problems as individual feats

(Gaunt, 2008; Johansson, 2012). Contextualizing personal experience and relating it to political, aesthetical and hierarchical structures would threaten the conception of individual passion as the main driving force and necessitate taking standpoints that might be counterproductive to a successful career. At the same time, focus on individual factors as the only explanation for both success and shortcomings may render the individual vulnerable, especially in times of adversity. Throughout their training and professional lives, musicians have the opportunity to test and improve the reliability of their motivation and driving force, and to investigate how their jobs relate to collective objects in established musical life. Becoming a professional musician might also be described as a process through a number of critical transitions going from an objectless need state to the discovery of an object that is societal relevant (Sannino, 2013). Taking part in history-making through artistic initiative, desire and choice – that is, connecting a personal need to a collective object – means gaining agency and initiative. In line with this contribution, an important part of promoting musical agency is to enhance the awareness of how personal motivation and collective objects interrelate. One of the aims of conducting intervention studies adapted to contexts of artistic creativity and learning is to make such processes of knowledge building in the conservatoire tradition visible, accessible and discussable.

INTERVENTIONIST METHODOLOGY AND MUSICAL PRACTICE

These interventionist studies exemplify methodological aspects related to research into musical practice. They cover (i) the researcher's position and double role, and (ii) the role and function of theoretical input.

THE RESEARCHER'S POSITION AND DOUBLE ROLE

There is the researcher's position and double role to consider in developmental work designed as Change Laboratories. As noted in other studies of HME (Gaunt, 2008), it is beneficial, even necessary, to be an insider in order to conduct research in the conservatoire tradition. Consequently, the researcher's position is far from neutral or detached. Being simultaneously the researcher and an insider in the system under investigation presents specific advantages and difficulties. One of them is that the researcher might be the former teacher or a fellow musician of the participants. This complex position can be somewhat uncomfortable. Still, a number of studies in this area suggest that it is difficult to access valuable data unless you are an insider. In the studies presented here, this was my position. For the last twenty-five years, I have worked as a musician, an organ teacher in HME, and a researcher, in various combinations. This places me both on the inside and on the outside of the culture that I am studying. I am inevitably a part of it, but in the process I have gained knowledge about my pre-understanding of the studied phenomenon.

In the first and third examples, I took on the role of participating observer. Twenty years ago, I was a student at the same programme as the students in the first example, I taught one of their main instruments and I am acquainted with the conditions for their future musical occupations. In the individual interviews with the students I recognized their experiences of complications concerning identifying with the role as a singer. Discussions about these matters made a deep dialogue possible. Our conversations illustrate how familiarity with the studied culture is important for gaining access, trust and extended knowledge. At the same time, I need to continuously balance sensitive situations that may appear and to be aware of an ethical responsibility towards the students-musicians.

In the second example, I combined my role as a researcher with that of a performer and workshop participant. This position can be emotionally and intellectually exhausting but is a crucial characteristic of successful artistic research projects. The ability to switch between mental and emotional positions is a central aspect of professional musicianship and a technique internalized in the musician's mindset as a psychological tool for evaluation, re-creation and re-thinking of ongoing artistic processes. Switching between roles includes knowing how to shift between closeness and distance both to the music in question and to oneself as a performer. Extending this function to include having a research position is a gradual change more than a qualitative shift. This capacity can be communicated for further development in a special way by artistic research projects, since musicians conducting artistic research develop and transfer their knowledge about these processes into a context where it is made accessible to the collective of other musicians, artistic researchers and researchers from other disciplines. This is a valuable methodological contribution to further development of artistic research projects. Interventionist studies of professional music making and HME need to take into account the significance and influence of the researcher being simultaneously a participant in the investigated practice. This may require re-design in the set up of the group and the planning of the study, for example, providing time and space for shifting perspectives.

THE ROLE AND FUNCTION OF THEORETICAL INPUT

For the researcher there is the role and function of theoretical input into practice based studies of musical activity to consider. In line with Change Laboratory methodology, the intention behind these studies was to introduce the theoretical tools of activity theory as a second stimulus to the players. The intention was to conceptualize and explore the flow between individual and collective levels of knowledge and experience. However, as shown in the first example, and as noted by Daniels (2008), a surprising first finding in intervention studies is often that participants are neither aware of nor able to articulate what their object of the activity is, while the definition of the object in activity theoretical terms may be very close at hand for the researcher.

In the second example the participants read my thesis on organ improvisation (Johansson, 2008), in which they all took part, in order to become informed of activity-theoretical ways of thinking. In the third example, the activity system together with applications and exemplifications from other music-related studies were introduced at the second group meeting. In both these cases, relating participants' individual music making to collective systems and theoretical structures resulted in resistance towards making these connections. My conclusion is that in contexts like this, that so heavily rely on individual passion, effort and motivation as tools for handling the double-bind situation, theory needs to be introduced progressively and carefully. The risk of constructing polarization between - presumably - individual needs on the one hand and collective demands on the other hand may then be avoided. This finding confirmed my impression from previous projects, namely that a theoretical conceptualization of the activity might at first discourage rather than encourage the participants to expand their thinking of their practice. However, the participants' initial resistance or incomprehension can have many reasons and is not necessarily to be interpreted as static attitudes but as a pedagogical and methodological challenge. A facilitating factor is often the presence, or appearance, of a serious problem. In such cases, all participants are motivated to open up for 'outside' tools. When things work smoothly, however, tolerance is low for disturbing factors that threaten to push people out of their comfort zones. For instance, the study in the third example began at a point when the

participants were content and happy with the object of playing music and not inclined to talk about difficulties. In this situation, it would have been a top-down procedure and ethically problematic for the researcher to impose a picture of historical contradictions on the students. Consequently, the dialogue started from the question of 'why is this working so well' rather than 'what do we need to change'. In line with the recommendations to "follow the object, give the objects a voice, expand the object" (Engeström, 2009, p. 327), we started by digging into what kind of an object 'playing music' can be. This gave the project an open, explorative character. In conclusion, the absence of a problem may be seen as a resource for development.

FUTURE RESEARCH DIRECTIONS

As a consequence of intervention studies, emotionally difficult and artistically challenging situations may appear during music making or teaching and learning of music. Such situations present risks of conflict and even failure. However, if/when endured and collectively articulated, they also present students, teachers and musicians with tools for musical expansion by reinforced agency. One suggestion for future research is to investigate the so called 'dark sides' of creativity (Cropley, 2010) and the outskirts of creative comfort zones. Another aim for future research is to describe working methods for musical boundary crossing.

CONCLUSION

Musical agency can be investigated and promoted at interrelational, intramusical and on intrapersonal levels in interventionist studies inspired by Change Laboratory methodology. The profiled music making situations may in themselves be seen as laboratories in the sense that they 'naturally' enact a kind of learning processes, albeit most often without an external analytical perspective. When they become research situations through the intervention of researchers, or the conversion of a musician into a researcher, another level of analysis is introduced. The activity theoretical approach makes it possible to use the tension between subordination and artistic independence as an outspoken first stimulus, for investigating relationships between internalization, externalization and transformation. Analyses of contradictions may serve the purpose of articulating tacit dimensions of artistic music making, inspire and support the questioning of established norms, reaching out towards new modes of expression and examining alternative ways of knowing.

REFERENCES

Bennett, D. (2008). *Understanding the classical music profession: The past, the present and strategies for the future.* Farnham, UK: Ashgate.

Burnard, P., & Younker, B. A. (2008). Investigating children's musical interactions within the activities systems of group composing and arranging: An application of Engestrom's Activity Theory. *International Journal of Educational Research, 47*(1), 60–74. doi:10.1016/j.ijer.2007.11.001

Clot, Y. (2009). Clinic of activity: the dialogue as instrument. In A. Sannino, H. Daniels, & K. D. Gutiérrez (Eds.), Learning and expanding with activity theory (pp. 286-302). Cambridge, UK: Cambridge University Press.

Cropley, A. J. (2010). The dark side of creativity: what is it? In D. H. Cropley, A. J. Cropley, J. C. Kaufman, & M. A. Runco (Eds.), The dark side of creativity (pp. 1-14). Cambridge, UK: Cambridge University Press. doi:10.1017/CBO9780511761225

Daniels, H. (2008). *Vygotsky and research.* London: Routledge.

Davidson, J. W., & Good, J. M. M. (2002). Social and musical co-ordination between members of a string quartet: An exploratory study. *Psychology of Music, 30*(2), 186–201. doi:10.1177/0305735602302005

Engeström, Y. (1987). *Learning by expanding.* Helsinki: Orienta-Konsultit Oy.

Engeström, Y. (1992). *Interactive expertise studies in distributed working intelligence. Research Bulletin No. 83.* Helsinki: University of Helsinki, Department of education.

Engeström, Y. (2005). *Developmental work research: Expanding activity theory in practice.* Berlin: Lehmanns Media.

Engeström, Y. (2007). Putting Vygotsky to work: the Change Laboratory as an application of double stimulation. In H. Daniels, M. Cole, & J. Wertsch (Eds.), The Cambridge companion to Vygotsky (pp. 363-382). Cambridge, UK: Cambridge University Press.

Engeström, Y. (2009). The future of activity theory: A rough draft. In A. Sannino, H. Daniels, & K. Gutierrez (Eds.), Learning and expanding with activity theory (pp. 303-328). Cambridge, UK: Cambridge University Press.

Engeström, Y. (2011). From design experiments to formative interventions. *Theory & Psychology*, 1–31.

Engeström, Y., & Sannino, A. (2010). Studies of expansive learning: Foundations, findings and future challenges. *Educational Research Review, 5*(1), 1–24. doi:10.1016/j.edurev.2009.12.002

Engeström, Y., & Sannino, A. (2011). Discursive manifestations of contradictions in organizational change efforts. A methodological framework. *Journal of Organizational Change Management, 24*(3), 368–387. doi:10.1108/09534811111132758

Engeström, Y., Virkkunen, J., Helle, M., Pihlaja, J., & Poikela, R. (1996). The change laboratory as a tool for transforming work. *Lifelong Learning in Europe, 2*, 10–17.

Frisk, H. (2008). *Improvisation, computers, and interaction: rethinking human-computer interaction through music.* Malmö Academy of Music, Lund University.

Gaunt, H. (2008). One-to-one tuition in a conservatoire: The perceptions of instrumental and vocal teachers. *Psychology of Music, 36*(2), 215–245. doi:10.1177/0305735607080827

Gravem Johansen, G. (2013). *Å øve på improvisasjon: Ein kvalitativ studie av øvepraksisar hos jazzstudentar, med fokus på utvikling av imporivsasjonskompetanse* [To practise improvisation: A qualitative study of practising practices among jazz students, with a particular focus on the development of improvisation competence]. Oslo: Norges Musikkhøgskole.

Heikinheimo, T. (2009). *Intensity of interaction in instrumental music lessons.* Helsinki: Sibelius Academy.

Hultberg, C. (2005). Practitioners and researchers in cooperation – method development for qualitative practice-related studies. *Music Education Research, 7*(2), 211–224. doi:10.1080/14613800500169449

Hultberg, C. (2010). *Vem äger lärandet?* [Students' ownership of learning]. Stockholm: Myndigheten för nätverk och samarbete inom högre utbildning.

Ilyenkov, E. V. (2010). *Dialectical logic. Essays on its history and theory.* Delhi: Aakar Books.

Jahreie, C. F., & Ottesen, E. (2010). Learning to become a teacher: Participation across spheres for learning. In V. Ellis, A. Edwards, & P. Smagorinsky (Eds.), Cultural-historical perspectives on teacher education and development (pp. 131-145). London: Routledge.

Johansson, K. (2008). *Organ improvisation - activity, action and rhetorical practice.* Malmö: Lund University.

Johansson, K. (2012). Experts, entrepreneurs and competence nomads: The skills paradox in higher music education. *Music Education Research, 14*(1), 47–64. doi:10.1080/14613808.2012.657167

Johansson, K. (2013a). Musical creativity and learning across the individual and the collective. In A. Sannino & V. Ellis (Eds.), Learning and collective creativity: Activity-theoretical and sociocultural studies (pp. 23-39). London: Routledge.

Johansson, K. (2013b). *Walking together with music: Teachers' voices on the joys and challenges of Higher Music Education.* Malmö: Malmö Academy of Music.

Johansson, K. (2013c). Undergraduate students' ownership of musical learning: Obstacles and options in one-to-one teaching. *British Journal of Music Education, 30*(2), 277–295. doi:10.1017/S0265051713000120

Johansson, K. (2013d). (Re)thinking organ improvisation: Revisiting musical practice. In H. Frisk & S. Östersjö (Eds.), (re)thinking improvisation: artistic explorations and conceptual writing. Malmö: Malmö Academy of Music.

Juslin, P. (2001). Communication of emotion in music performance. In P. Juslin & J. A. Sloboda (Eds.), Music and emotion. Oxford, UK: Oxford University Press.

Krüger, T. (1998). Teacher practice, pedagogical discourse and the construction of knowledge: Two case studies of teachers at work. Bergen University College.

Ljungar-Chapelon, A. (2008). *Le respect de la tradition Om den franska flöjtkonsten: Dess lärande, hantverk och estetik i ett hermeneutiskt perspektiv.* Malmö: Lund University.

Nilsson, K. A. (2003). Enklare och nyttigare? Om metodiken för ämnes- och programutvärderingar [On methods for evaluating courses and programmes]. *National Agency for Higher Education Report, 2003*, 17.

Östersjö, S. (2008). *Shut up 'n' play! Negotiating the musical work*. Malmö: Lund University.

Potter, T. (2003). From chamber to concert hall. R. Stowell (Ed.), The Cambridge companion to the string quartet (pp. 41-59). Cambridge, UK: Cambridge University Press.

Renshaw, P. (2011). Working together. An enquiry into creative collaborative learning across the Barbican–Guildhall Campus. London: Barbican Centre and Guildhall School of Music and Drama.

Sannino, A. (2013). Critical transitions in the pursuit of a professional object: Simone de Beauvoir's expansive journey to become a writer. In V. Ellis & A. Sannino (Eds.), Learning and collective creativity: Activity-theoretical and sociocultural studies. London: Routledge.

Smilde, R. (2008). Lifelong learners in music; research into musicians' biographical learning. *International Journal of Community Music, 1*(2), 243–252. doi:10.1386/ijcm.1.2.243_1

Snyder, K. (2007). *Dietrich Buxtehude. Organist in Lübeck*. Rochester, NY: University of Rochester Press.

Swedish Higher Education Ordinance. (n.d.). Learning outcomes and terms for qualifications in the fine, applied and performing arts. Author.

Teräs, M. (2007). *Intercultural learning and hybridity in the culture laboratory*. Helsinki: University of Helsinki.

Vygotsky, L. (1978). *Mind in society*. Cambridge, MA: Harvard University Press.

Waterman, D. (2003). Playing quartets: A view from the inside. In R. Stowell (Ed.), The Cambridge companion to the string quartet (pp. 97-126). Cambridge, UK: Cambridge University Press.

Welch, G. F. (2007). Addressing the multifaceted nature of music education: An activity theory research perspective. *Research Studies in Music Education, 28*(1), 23–37. doi:10.1177/1321103X070280010203

Welch, G. F. (2011). Culture and gender in a cathedral music context: An activity theory exploration. In M. S. Barrett (Ed.), A cultural psychology of music education (pp. 225-258). Oxford, UK: Oxford University Press.

Weman, L. (2008). "...världens skridskotystnad före Bach" historiskt informerad uppförandepraxis ur ett kontextuellt musikontologiskt perspektiv, belyst genom en fallstudie av Sonat i E-dur, BWV 1035, av J S Bach. Luleå tekniska universitet, Luleå.

ADDITIONAL READING

Attali, J. (2011). *Noise. The political economy of music*. Minneapolis, London: University of Minnesota Press.

Barrett, F. J. (1998). Creativity and improvisation in jazz and organizations. *Organization Science, 9*(5), 605–622. doi:10.1287/orsc.9.5.605

Bennett, D. (2007). Utopia for music performance graduates. Is it achievable, and how should it be defined? *British Journal of Music Education, 24*(2), 179–189. doi:10.1017/S0265051707007383

Black, S. (2008). Creativity and learning jazz: The practice of listening. *Mind, Culture, and Activity, 15*(4), 279–295. doi:10.1080/10749030802391039

Borgdorff, H. (2011). The production of knowledge in artistic research. M. Biggs & H. Karlsson (Eds.), The Routledge companion to research in the arts (pp. 44-63). London: Routledge.

Chanan, M. (1994). *Musica practica. The social practice of Western music from Gregorian chant ot postmodernism*. London, New York: Verso.

Coessens, K., Crispin, D., & Douglas, A. (2009). *The artistic turn. A manifesto*. Ghent: Orpheus Institute.

Cook, N., & Everist, M. (Eds.). (1999). *Rethinking music*. Oxford: Oxford University Press.

del Rio, P., & Álvarez, A. (2007). Inside and outside the zone of proximal development: an ecofunctional reading of Vygotsky. H. Daniels, M. Cole & J. Wertsch (Eds.), The Cambridge Companion to Vygotsky (pp. 276-306). Cambridge: Cambridge University Press.

Dyndahl, P. (Ed.). (2013). *Intersections and interplays: Contributions to the cultural study of music in performance, education, and society*. Malmö: Malmö Academy of Music.

Edström, A.-M. (2008). *Learning in visual art practice. (PhD)*. Lund: Lund University.

Ellis, V. (2010). Studying the process of change. The double stimulation strategy in teacher education research. V. Ellis, A. Edwards & P. Smagorinsky (Eds.), Cultural-historical perspectives on teacher education and development. (pp. 95-114). London: Routledge.

Goehr, L. (1992). *The imaginary museum of musical works*. London, New York: Oxford University Press.

Johansson, K. (2012). Organ improvisation: Edition, extemporization, expansion, and instant composition. D. J. Hargreaves, D. E. Miell & R. A. R. MacDonald (Eds.), Musical imaginations. Multidisciplinary perspectives on creativity, performance, and perception (220-232). Oxford: Oxford University Press.

Jörgensen, H. (2009). *Research into higher music education. An overview from a quality improvement perspective*. Oslo: Novus Press.

Moran, S., & John-Steiner, V. (2003). Creativity in the making: Vygotsky's contemporary contribution to the dialectic of development and creativity. R. K. Sawyer (Ed.), Creativity and development (61-90). Oxford: Oxford University Press.

Murphy, E., & Rodriguez-Manzanares, M. A. (2008). Using activity theory and its principle of contradictions to guide research in educational technology. *Australasian Journal of Educational Technology, 24*(4), 442–457.

Nerland, M. (2007). One-to-one teaching as cultural practice: Two case studies from an academy of music. *Music Education Research, 9*(3), 399–416. doi:10.1080/14613800701587761

Peruski, L. (2003). *Contradictions, disturbances and transformations: An activity theoretical analysis of three faculty members' experience with designing and teaching online courses. (PhD)*. Ann Arbor: Michigan State University.

Presland, C. (2005). Conservatoire student and instrumental professor: The student perspective on a complex relationship. *British Journal of Music Education, 22*(3), 237–248. doi:10.1017/S0265051705006558

Prichard, C. (2002). Creative selves? Critically reading 'creativity' in management discourse. *Creativity and Innovation Management, 11*(4), 265–276. doi:10.1111/1467-8691.00258

Roth, W.-M., & Radford, L. (2010). Re/thinking the zone of proximal development (symmetrically). *Mind, Culture, and Activity, 17*(4), 299–307. doi:10.1080/10749031003775038

Rowe, V. C. (2009). Using video-stimulated recall as a basis for interviews: Some experiences from the field. *Music Education Research, 11*(4), 425–437. doi:10.1080/14613800903390766

Sannino, A. (2011). Activity theory as an activist and interventionist theory. *Theory & Psychology, 21*(5), 571–598. doi:10.1177/0959354311417485

Sawyer, R. K. (2003). *Group creativity. Music, theater, collaboration.* New York: Psychology Press.

Sawyer, R. K. (2008). How creative contributions emerge over the lifespan. *Mind, Culture, and Activity, 15*(3), 263–265. doi:10.1080/10749030802186793

Seltzer, K., & Bentley, T. (1999). *The creative age. Knowledge and skills for the new economy.* London: Demos.

Shepherd, J. (1991). *Music as social text.* Cambridge: Polity Press.

Small, C. (1998). *Musicking. The meanings of performing and listening.* Hanover, London: University Press of New England.

Smith, R. (2006). Epistemological agency in the workplace. *Journal of Workplace Learning, 18*(3), 157–170. doi:10.1108/13665620610654586

Toulmin, S. (1999). Knowledge as shared procedures. Y. Engeström, Miettinen, R. & Punamäki, R-L-. (Ed.), Perspectives on Activity Theory (53-64). Cambridge: Cambridge University Press.

Victor, K. (2005). The object of activity: Making sense of the sense-maker. *Mind, Culture, and Activity, 12*(1), 4–18. doi:10.1207/s15327884mca1201_2

KEY TERMS AND DEFINITIONS

Cultural Historical Activity Theory: A theory of human development that sees human societies and their individual members as mutually constitutive. Personal development is shaped by the process of enculturation and individuals' thoughts and deeds serve to maintain or to alter the cultural milieu. At the heart of CHAT is therefore a tension between education as enculturation and education for autonomy and originality.

Higher Music Education (HME): Education concerned with training musicians for the first, second and third cycle qualifications in the fine, applied and performing arts (Bachelor, Master, Licentiate and Doctor). In this chapter HME relates to the training of professional musicians at Bachelor and Master level.

Intervention Studies: Or formative interventions, have the aim of increasing participants' possibility to shape and influence the activity systems of which they take part.

Musical Agency: A person's space and opportunity for learning and creating music in a certain context of music making. This might be any kind of teaching situation, practice session or performance where musicians express and develop musical ideas and artistic standpoints.

Musical Practice: Music making as a practice in contexts of education as well as performance. Thus, a musical practice might be one-to-one teaching in a conservatoire, the work of a freelancing string quartet or the regular state-financed playing in a symphony orchestra.

Chapter 6
Vocational Learning Mediated by Constructive Competition

Charlotte Jonasson
Aarhus University, Denmark

ABSTRACT

Competition among students has been found to support motivation, learning, and knowledge if interrelated with collaboration. In this chapter, it is argued that the development of constructive competition is closely related to competitive intentions and material resources. Drawing on activity theory, learning is understood as materially mediated activity in a collective cultural setting and involving transformation of novel concepts and objects. The presented findings in this chapter are based on a field study, where students and teachers participate in activities of vocational learning and preparing for apprenticeship. The findings show that the students' competitive intentions for achieving recognition of their cooking skills mediate engagement and vocational learning for students at risk of dropping out. Findings further suggest that the students' participation in and conceptualization of vocational activities are materially mediated through competitive actions and deployed artifacts like "timing" and use of food ingredients. A central conclusion presented in the chapter is that it is important to take into account the particular competitive intentions and the related mediating artifacts of constructive competition, through which student engagement and learning is developed.

INTRODUCTION

There is competition in many arenas, in the family, at school, at the workplace and in sport activities (Fülöp, 2004). Competition can be defined in terms of individuals or groups pursuing exclusive goals (Deutsch, 2000; Wittchen, Krimmel, Kohler, & Hertel, 2013). Interpersonal competition has been conceptualized in distinct ways (Brown, Cron, & Slocum, 1998; Murayama & Elliot,

2012): First, competition is defined in terms of a characteristic trait of the person in terms of a dispositional preference to compete with others. Second, competition is defined in terms of perceived environmental competitiveness, and third, in it is defined as structural competition representing an actual situation in which two or more people strive for a mutually exclusive achievement and outcome. In particular the latter two understandings of competition are important

DOI: 10.4018/978-1-4666-6603-0.ch006

for investigating an educational context and activity, to which competitive interactions pertain as well as the achievement of results among e.g. competing students (Murayama & Elliot, 2012).

Research on student performance covers aspects of competition among students, often defined as negative or destructive competition in working toward competitive goals involving self-protective strategies leading to poor achievement. (Johnson & Johnson, 1994; Kohn, 1986). Other studies and meta-analysis suggest that there is a positive relation between competition and student performance (Johnson & Johnson, 1989; Murayama & Elliot, 2012). Competition has also been considered the negative opposite of collaboration in that competition may be arranged in ways that hinder each other's performance and encourage some people to gain success at other peoples' expense (Kohn, 1986). Collaboration, on the other hand, has been argued to be fundamental to contributing to development of critical thinking, engagement in creativity and willingness to take on other peoples' well-being (Dillenbourg, Baker, Blaye, & O'Malley, 1996; Mercer, 2005). However, other research argues that competition works in complex ways, where competition and collaboration are interrelated concepts and processes (e.g. Fülöp, 2004). In this vein of research, a few studies focus on what is defined as constructive competition (Fülöp, 1999, 2004; Sheridan & Williams, 2006), i.e. a social and cultural phenomenon that enhances peoples' ambitions and learning potential clarifying that combined competition and collaboration is a multidimensional educational phenomenon that motivates people for learning (Williams & Sheridan, 2010). The studies are conducted in different educational settings, where children, adolescents and teachers act in competitive situations and take on board a socially mediated learning perspective on the process. Moreover, the studies emphasize that collaborative and competitive processes are interrelated, each being a requisite of the other. One example of the interrelationship is a description of

how students were found to not only want to win but want to spur one another forward and during this process in order to develop reciprocal guidance and to deepen each other's knowledge of new areas and contexts (Sheridan & Williams, 2011).

Williams and Sheridan (2010) and Sheridan and Williams (2006) call for attention to studies of the conditions for constructive interrelated competitive and collaborative patterns in schools, and how this focus affect students' interaction and learning. In one of their studies (Williams & Sheridan, 2010) they show that three conditions are needed for constructive competition and collaborative learning. The first condition is positive attitudes where values and ways of acting among teachers and pupils involve efforts to include competition as a potentially constructive input to collaboration. The second condition applies for organizational characteristics and covers an open climate with mutual encouragement to do well. It also includes friendships and room for collaboration intertwined with competitive wants of achievement as good as that of peers. The third condition relates to learning, where learning needs to be regarded as meaningful, interesting and challenging. All three conditions cover important influences on learning processes. They are argued to motivate people to learn and to support development of constructive competition. Fülöp (2002; 2004) identifies the characteristics of competing people finding that the particular goals of competition are central criteria for constructive competition to develop. She emphasizes that competition is a goal oriented behavior and that the goal or intention of competition is not merely winning but also improvement or gaining knowledge. Competing individuals may adopt multiple goals of knowing and learning along with ways or strategies for accomplishing such goals (Fülöp, 2002). Moreover, Fülöp (2004) argues that in relation to the intentions of competition, explicit criteria of evaluation of the reached competitive intention must be accounted for if constructive competition is to develop. These findings are further supported in a meta-analysis of relations between competition and student achievement. Murayama and Elliot (2012) argue that positive relations are mediated by the goals of performance, which the competing persons hold. Yet in relation to this result, further research should provide clarity in terms of the specific interactions of context and people, and their various goals (Hansson 2014), that may relate to the development of constructive competition (Johnson & Johnson, 2012).

Knowledge may be needed of how, in a specific context, constructive competition is interdependently connected to particular and potentially diverse goals of or intentions of competition and ways of accomplishing such competitive intentions as part of particular contexts. Furthermore, the criteria of evaluation need to be studied in terms of how the criteria relates to development of constructive competition. In this regard, there may be a need for debating how particular intentions or goals of competition may be recognized and by whom. Furthermore, Fülöp (2004, p. 133) suggests that particular resources and their potential scarcity means that a competitive process can take various forms, all depending on the nature of resources. Various resources in the competitive context are important for constructive competition that leads to learning. While such conditions related to the goals of competition have been suggested, it has been difficult to study the conditions under which competition is constructive (Fülöp, 2004; Williams & Sheridan, 2010). Attention should be brought to explanations of how particular competitive goals or intentions are pursued and potentially afforded in terms of e.g. social or material resources forming the central criteria for development of constructive competition.

In terms of the school context, prior studies focus on academic courses in primary or secondary school. Yet, in regard to the interrelatedness of collaboration and competition and the various goals and resources of competition, another school context may support novel findings. Vocational Danish schools have recently initiated reforms aiming at student engagement and learning. This effort is due to dropout problems and a societal lack of faith in the vocational schools, e.g. as reflected in the decline of student entrances (Jonasson, 2013b). In recent years, vocational schools have made efforts to emphasize their orientation and ideals of being a 'World Class Education' by e.g. participating in and hosting World Skills competitions for students in a wide range of vocational professions. Yet, in everyday school life school-based vocational training orients towards preparing the students for competitive and collaborative aspects of working life; especially aspects related to particular goals and materials in a future vocational activity. Therefore, a study conducted at a Danish vocational school is suitable for providing insight into how aspects of competition develop as part of everyday school life activity and related to efforts at enhancing student engagement and learning for future apprenticeship (Jonasson, 2013c).

PURPOSE OF THE STUDY

Based on these prior studies of constructive competition between students in school, there is a need for exploring what intentions the students' competitive actions are oriented towards and how their actions afford students' learning and engagement. Knowledge is also needed about how constructive competitive actions mediate in terms of particular socio-material resources and contextual conditions: How is student learning and engagement in a vocational school afforded by competitive intentions and related use of socio-material resources?

OBJECT OF ACTIVITY AND MEDIATING ARTIFACTS

Cultural-historical activity theory (CHAT) is the chosen analytical framework for studying processes of student learning mediated by competitive intentions. Proponents of activity theory argue that learning evolves through the activities that people engage in. Moreover, activity theory centralizes the goals and intentions of learners in a larger community as mediating learning outcomes (Engeström, 1987). Activity theory centralizes the object of activity as the focus of achievement (Cole & Engeström, 1993; Engeström, 2001).

In regard to vocational education, the object of activity can be specified in terms of vocational learning. In this regard, Lindberg (2003b) has conceptualized 'vocational knowing', where, according to the teachers, experience of working with the content of the particular vocation, such as methods, techniques, planning and preparing for the vocation are the central objects of the activity. Following such a perspective, vocational activities refer to a cultural-historically transformed, distributed and evolving complex structure of mediated and collective human agency motivated by a collective concern for developing vocational skills, knowledge and ways of doing things (Engeström, 1999; Roth & Lee, 2007). In terms of the object of activity, Hedegaard (2005) states that people are involved in activities containing as it were particular intentions of learning, which, according to Hedegaard (2005, p.192) are: "the goal-directedness of the person's daily activities and describe the person's will in specific situations". This is relevant in terms of the aim of this study to research the competitive intentions and the way these intentions afford students' engagement in their development of vocational knowing. Pertaining also to such learning intentions, Gutierrez and Larson (1995) show how teachers' authoritative scripts and instructional intentions collide with students' counter-scripts and learning intentions. The students' counter-scripts deserve special attention.

These counter scripts, however, are neither necessarily harmonious nor overlapping. The emergence of this less apparent counter script reveals the inherently multi-voiced and dialogic nature of any classroom. (Gutierrez & Larson, 1995, p. 447)

Gutierrez and Larson (1995) argue that while counter-scripts may have little influence on the teacher's script, 'third spaces' of bridging such diverse intentions in their teaching-learning processes are developed (Engeström, Rantavuori, & Kerosuo, 2013). Development of 'third space' was studied by observing the 'competing discourses (Gutierrez & Larson, 1995, p. 452) of the classroom, which are continuously negotiated between student and teacher.

Taking on a socio-cultural perspective, learning involves interactions and negotiations between newcomers and experts in an activity system (Lave, 2011; Mäkitalo, 2012; Wertsch, 2007). In this regard social interaction comprises of collaborative actions and acts of competition. The newcomers may compete with each other in order to reach particular goals (Williams & Sheridan, 2010). People learn to compete constructively by interacting with others holding different ways of thinking as important resources of learning (Säljö, 1991). Furthermore, the learning outcomes of competitive actions may be subjected to evaluations through ongoing interactions and negotiations. Such opportunities may further the conditions for development of novel concepts and objects of the activity system (Mäkitalo & Säljö, 2009). Competitive actions may produce expansive cycles of learning in terms of transformation of the concepts and objects of the activity system (Engeström, 1987; 2001).

While studies of counter-scripts and learning intentions have had the teacher-student relations as primary focus, collisions may occur between the students' diverging learning intentions. Also, competing discourses may influence the students' learning. In this regard, competition may comprise that the particular intentions of competition involve understandings of outcomes, accomplishments, or loss that can be evaluated as good or less good, influencing persons' participation in the activities. In turn, such evaluations of competitive activities can become central resources for developing the goals or intentions of the competitive activities. One goal may be to go beyond one's own expected or recognized potentials, with or without the support of others (Sheridan & Williams, 2011).

Taking on an cultural historical activity theoretical perspective, learning is socially and materially mediated and situated in a cultural setting involving appropriation of mediating cultural resources such as language, which is a constitutive means in human activity (Mäkitalo, 2012; Säljö, 1991). Yet, while much attention has been paid to natural languages as ideational and material resources (Volosinov 1973), attention has also been paid to other central artifacts or material tools intertwined with social action and meaning, shaping and reflecting outcomes of learning (Engeström, 1999; Roth & Lee, 2007). Holland and Cole (1995) argue:

To be sure, artifacts have a necessary material aspect and they are manufactured or produced in the sense that they are created in the process of goal directed human actions. But they are ideal in that their material form has been shaped by their participation in the interactions of which they were previously a part and which they mediate in the present. (p. 476)

In this vein of argument Roth and Lee (2007) state that the act of using a particular artifact is relevant for understanding learning as a mediated process. From an anthropological perspective, Ingold (2010) emphasizes the 'thinginess' of materials in movement such as brick and mortar in house construction, which the builders give form as part of their shared activities. Central to such trajectories of movement cover what people do with the materials such as in this case the cook in relation the ingredients of a meal. In practice, Ingold (2010, p. 96) says people and material should be understood as "trajectories of movement, responding to one another in counterpoint, alternately as melody and refrain". The iteration of

people's skilled practice involves ongoing correction in the form-giving of the material, artifacts and environment (Ingold, 2006). This skilled practice can be understood as processes of learning and becoming, where the students gradually become full practitioners through their participation in and form-giving of the environment (Jonasson, 2013a; Lave, 2012; Lindberg, 2003a). In this regard, the form-giving cooking practices at a vocational school, which the students participate in, call for attention to the potential practiced trajectories of movements of persons and materials as part of their vocational engagement and becoming prepared for apprenticeship.

In regard to form-giving activities the question is whether trajectories of form-giving develop in different (competing) ways and how to understand them as processes of learning in terms of developing new concepts for their collective activities. In this chapter I am preoccupied with clarifying how competition between people may intertwine with (competing) trajectories of form-giving; this is a new focus compared to prior research.

An Ethnographic Approach to Studying Vocational Activity

Based on the research objective guiding this study, a suitable school context was needed to collect the data. The researcher was granted relatively extensive access to perform fieldwork at a Danish vocational school over a period of one year and for one to five days a week. The Danish VET upper secondary educational system consists of alternating programs in which students shift between periods of apprenticeship at a company and periods of attendance at a vocational school. Much attention is directed towards connecting school and workplace learning. Before entering the main course, where apprenticeship is initiated, the students complete a basic course at a vocational school. The vocational school in which the research was carried out was located in a medium-sized Danish provincial town.

The unit of analysis (Säljö, 2009) pertaining to the present chapter is based on the researcher's participant observation and interviews at a basic course in culinary education. Focus is on learning activities involving student competition and mediating artefacts. This study is part of a larger project carried out in three basic courses at the school, which has an overall focus on retention processes and student engagement. The vocational students in this basic course were considered to be the less engaged students. They belong to the vast group of students considered to be at-risk of dropping out (Jonasson, 2013c). The students' ages ranged from 17 to 52 years. Many of them had experiences with unskilled labour - some even at restaurants and hotels. A substantial part of the lessons were conducted as school-based vocational training taking place in the school kitchens and restaurant involving interaction between students and teachers.

Data Collection and Analysis

The aim of the research is to explore the students and teachers' shared activities pertaining to completing a basic course at a Danish vocational school. For pursuing this purpose, an ethnographic field study was chosen as an appropriate method. The ethnographic field study is suited to studying interactional processes in which notions and categories are shared, negotiated, changed or transformed between people (Hammersley & Atkinson, 1997; Walford, 2009). The main data sources consist of participant observation, semi-structured interviews and school documents. When using participant observation, the researcher ideally develops an ability to recognize and understand the social organisation of interaction (Putney & Frank, 2008; Spradley, 1980). In addition to taking notes on participant observations, numerous informal conversations with students and teachers

were written down and used (Sanjek, 1990). Data from semi-structured interviews (Bernard, 1995) with students, teachers and school managers were used. The interviews were conducted in Danish and translated into English.

Analysis started early during fieldwork, in accordance with Spradley's (1980) ethnographic circle of data collection, analysis and theorizing. Analysis of the data involved an iterative process in which potential openness to theories and ideas are used to inform data. Eventually the data is used to change ideas and theoretical concepts (Hammersley & Atkinson, 1997). Prior studies and perceptions of student competition and activity theoretical concepts of learning and mediating material resources informed the selection and analysis of the intrinsic, and out-standing, thematic case narratives on how student learning is afforded through competitive activities (Braun & Clarke, 2006). Data triangulation of various data from interviews and observations was used (Hammersley & Atkinson, 1997) in an effort to obtain a deep understanding and to create 'thick descriptions' of central themes (Geertz, 1973). Analysis was supported by the qualitative data analysis program QSR NVivo 9, which was used to code and sort out the data according to central themes related to the purpose of research (Miles & Huberman, 1994). The findings evolving through the analysis are presented in the succeeding narratives.

LEARNING, COMPETITIVE INTENTIONS AND MEDIATING ARTIFACTS

The empirical findings of this study pertain to how constructive competition is afforded by recognized outcomes of the intentions of learning, and the socio-material resources functioning as conditioning constructive or destructive competition related to particular learning intentions of becoming recognized as skilled in cooking.

Improving Vocational Skills by Competing for Recognition

The students would often emphasize aspects of competition with themselves and with the other students related to two interrelated aims. The students shared an overall aim of their engagement and participation of improving their vocational skills in terms of becoming capable of cooking good food that was being recognized as tasteful by their fellow students, teachers or customers from their spare time work (Jonasson, 2012). This overall purpose was expressed in terms of the students' competing for recognition by their teacher or fellow students as a sign of mastering their vocational practices. One expression of the ongoing competitive activities for recognition was the students' request to get grades on their food. There were always some students who would openly ask if they could get grades for today's lesson and dishes. Sometimes the teacher would agree to this but at other times s/he would argue that this was not about getting the good grades but about working well with dedication on the given assignments. However, when asking a group of students why grades were important a student commented like this.

Well it is important for me to do good, I want to know whether my food is good or not and also, well, I guess it makes us a bit more eager, you know, like if my mates get [grade] 10 I want at least the same cause I cook better food [laughing].

An ongoing competition between the groups of students was expressed in terms of grades. They gave the students something to strive for; an extra inducement to working hard on their assignments and not to let other students surpass them. Competition among the students also meant that even though the teachers did not give them grades for all their assignments, the students would pay much attention to how their group as well as the other groups did in the tastings and oral evalua-

tions made by the teacher. Afterwards they often discussed what worked well and what was not highly praised.

On one occasion one of the students expressed dissatisfaction with his group not getting good grades or judgments by the teacher on their latest assignments. Rather, their group was scolded for not showing engagement in the assignments, not paying attention to the recipes and generally choosing the easiest preparing method of garnitures. Instead they spent time outside school smoking and making fun in the vegetable storage room, where there was less teacher attention. However, the open negative reviews of the group's cooking bothered Mark who during the afterwards dish washing said: "Well at my work [in a kitchen] I can make much better food than this. I just think this is too easy, you know not much to do and then we start fooling around".

The next class of students knew that they were going to make pot roast. This time Mark showed up with a recipe on stuffed tomatoes. His group spent most of their time in the kitchen and only once did one of the group members leave to have a cigarette. On two occasions the group went into a heated discussion of when the roast was done and whether another group member had put too much salt in the sauce. The first student showed the others what to do regarding the stuffed tomatoes. He carefully read the recipe and refused to use a couple of tomatoes that were cracked while scraping out the seeds. At several occasions the other students passed by the tomatoes and tasted the filling. When arranging the plates the first student made sure that the tomatoes were garnished with parsley and only the best servings of roast and sauce were allowed on the plates. During the teachers' assessment of the food the following information was shared.

Teacher: See, the filling is just perfectly firm and not squishy at all. Mark, how the hell did you just all of a sudden come up with such a thing?

Mark: What do you mean, I am always this pre-pared [the other students and the teacher laughed], nah, I asked my mom for this recipe because she always makes them for special occasions and stuff and I thought they fitted this roast perfectly.

Teacher: Well then, praise to your mom and you.

Before cleaning away their dishes, the group spent time taking pictures of their food displays. In terms of gaining the other students' and teachers' recognition for the quality of the food, competition was sometimes formalized in terms of the main course with the students' highly engaged participation in national school vocational competitions. Yet, lack of informal recognition also brought about a heated discussion – even when lacking recognition was the display of some sort of a joke. This was the case when one of the groups gained positive comments and praise from their teacher on their preparing of sauce. When commenting on their well-recognized sauce, two of the group members exchanged opinions:

Dennis: Yeah, you see, I simply just know how to nail a sauce so that it tastes like you have never had it before.

Mona: That is damn well a lie. You know that I was the one who made that sauce, not you.

Dennis: Relax, Mona, I'm just teasing, I know you made that sauce, but still, I make a bloody good sauce and better meat balls than you do.

The girl laughed and hit Dennis on the shoulder, but a couple of days later, when it was actually the making of meat balls on the program, the girl, who worked with one of the other girls made sure she was primarily in charge of cooking meat balls. Some of the students had during the teacher's instructions moaned that they all knew how to cook meat balls, nothing special about that. However, the teacher said: 'Well, pay attention to the surface. Are

meat balls supposed to be triangular shaped? – not really but it is necessary to ensure that the meat balls are crisp all over and not just on two sides then forgetting the remaining sides'. Afterwards, Mona worked particularly hard on the meat balls. First, she carefully added salt to the ground meat arguing that this would release the elasticity of the meat and took care not to make the minced meat firm. She then proceeded to make a couple of small try-out meat balls to adjust the taste and temperature of the pan and after this added some pepper and turned down the heat. She attended to turning the meat balls as to leave a crisp surface all over the meat balls. After having completed a pan of meat balls she said to me: "I know Dennis is just having his fun and that's you know just fine with me, but he is damn well not going to take the honor of my work, that pisses me off. Taste this one [meat ball], that's better than what he's cooking over there". The crisp surface and a soft texture was particular acknowledged by her teacher during assessment of the food.

These examples show how competitive aspects may involve frustration and joy and above all an eagerness to prove oneself through dedication to work. The students shared competitive intentions of cooking food that was recognized by the teacher or other students as good. To reach this goal of recognition of their cooking, the students engaged in improving their vocational knowing in terms of efforts to form and serve novel dishes or develop skilled techniques. The students' goal to compete for recognition was related to aspects of collaboration, which can be seen in the way the students were constantly encouraged to improve their work by fellow students and teachers' critique and challenges of their cooking. The students' competitive intention of reaching recognition for cooking good food is closely related to the students' development of constructive competition comprising vocational engagement and learning. In the following analysis, the material affordances for such constructive competition are outlined.

Competing Action and Timing as a Mediating Resource for Vocational Skills

The classes in the kitchen involved particular aspects of competition against time and timing the cooking activities. The traditional arrangement seemed to call for particular socio-material resources and conditions of cooking and learning to cook. One teacher explained the situation.

In the kitchen it is really a matter of timing, I mean you can't just prepare the main course and then 'oups' I forgot to start on the dessert. So when we make the students not just have all the time in the world it is not only because we need to have the kitchen cleaned and all before we go; they have to get to know the pressure when they start in a kitchen.

From time to time the teachers at the culinary course would organize lessons where the students should prepare and present particular dishes within a certain amount of time. The students who often worked in small groups would be given approximately one and a half hour to prepare the dishes. Then the groups would present the food to the teacher with an interval of approximately five minutes. Then it was time to clean up in the kitchen.

The time for presenting the food was often scheduled at the black board. Sometimes the teacher just wrote the groups up. At other times the students could choose among the different times. Some of the groups would take one of the first times arguing that they would then have time to clean the kitchen and go for an early smoke before the next classes. However, other groups held other priorities. One group debated like this about which time to choose: "We can't make it for the first couple of presentations. Well, then let's take one of the last then we also have time to check out the other's dishes". This group had, when the first groups started to present, already prepared most of

their food and started to join the teacher and the students already finished in the teacher's tasting of the presented food. At one such occasion the teacher commented on a group's presentation of the food on plates. They were cold, and this was one of the reasons why the sauce had started to solidify on the surface: "Sorry guys, but I do not want to eat this – that's not appetizing and not what you expect as a customer". The teacher questioned whether they had kept the sauce warm for exactly the right time and doubted if the other parts of the dish were also done and in the right time for their serving. One of the student groups, which had not yet presented their food, overheard this assessment. They went down to put their plates in the oven and kept an eye on the heating sauce letting it simmer just up to the moment where serving time was up.

One of the groups often scheduled themselves as the first to present seemed to put an honor in working fast and in a structured way. They would always have their work station well equipped having, before the class began, prepared their knives, their cloths and having turned on the gas for the stove. They would quickly run through the today's assignment and recipes. Then they would divide the parts between the members of the group. They were often the first group to enter the vegetable storage room, thereby ensuring fresh vegetables and being the first to select the best pieces of meat and, later on, a space to use the best oven. Their speedy timing would also give other students opportunities of learning, e.g. when some of the other groups passed by they could observe how they handled difficult parts and methods. One such example was the group being the first to part a chicken in the prescribed eight pieces and adding the right amount of corn starch on a proper non-boiling temperature to their fruit porridge. The other students afterward returned to their work station and tried to replicate what they had observed. The teachers would often recommend the students to do so.

At these occasions the fast working group would seldom openly reveal their choice of methods and one time, when they had refused to answer direct questions from some of the other students about how long time their chocolate mousse needed to sit in the fridge in order to become firm, one of the group members said to the researcher: "did you see it, I think it is so annoying they always come by and think that we will just help them out because they don't pay attention and get started". However, being the first group at sometimes seemed to cause missed opportunities of improving their work methods. On some occasions, the fast working group would present first and miss out on opportunities to check out the other groups' work processes. This was the case when the teacher spent some time with one of the groups, explaining that their black-spotted schnitzels may have turned out better had they used cleared butter for their frying pan – a method which they had been instructed to carry out during another cooking lesson. The students in this and other listening groups applied this in their assignment. Yet, this piece of advice was too late for the fast working group having already applied non-cleared butter; this also being commented on when they presented their food to the teacher: "ah, as you can see you didn't succeed with the frying. It's black here and there [pointing], that doesn't look good. Perhaps you fried it too hard". However, the non-cleared butter was not mentioned as a suggestion, perhaps since the students didn't know this could be relevant and the teacher thought they had cleared the butter like all the rest of the groups. The fast working group would at later classes spent some time interacting with the other students in order to observe and discuss particular difficult procedures; perhaps having experienced the importance of taking time to not only compete on time and efficiency but also collaborate on their efforts to improve their cooking skills.

The findings show how the particular competitive intention of cooking food implied the students' learning of skilled interaction and use of particular socio-material resources or conditions inherent to cooking and handling of delicate ingredients and methods. The students seemed to develop competing approaches to reach their shared goal of cooking that was recognized as tasty, timely and nicely presented. Where some students emphasized development of skilled attention to working independently, fast and time-efficient other students emphasized taking the time to learn and experience their own and other's handling of delicate ingredients and timing. Through an interweaving of their competing approaches to reach recognition the students learned about the interrelated resources and conditions of the timing in handling ingredients and methods, the timing of their cooking adjusted to the scarce time allowed by customers waiting in the restaurant and the timing of learning cooking methods by checking out each other's work and gaining pieces of advice that applied to the precise cooking activities. However, it was rather difficult for the students to integrate the socio-material resources of timing. In particular, the students who failed to challenge themselves and others experienced that collaboration and mutual attention were important to sustain internal competition. Instead they turned to protectionism. Learning the importance of paying attention to other students' handling of socio-material resources in the kitchen became a central outcome of the ongoing competition as well as collaboration with others.

SOLUTIONS AND RECOMMENDATIONS

The empirical findings show that development of constructive competition is interdependent of how particular intentions of learning develop. In relation to prior research on constructive competition, which has shown the conditions under which attitudinal, organizational and meaning-related conditions for constructive competition develop, this study shows how constructive competition is afforded by particular socio-material resources connected to particular intentions of learning.

With regard to previous studies of conditions for constructive competition (Fülöp, 2004; Williams & Sheridan, 2010), this study emphasizes the need for paying attention to what is the exact purpose of the students' competition. In this case, the students' shared intention is to be able to cook what is recognized by fellow students, teachers, and potentially future customers, as good food. The centrality of competition involves students competing with themselves and with others. They may, in friendly and serious ways challenge their teachers or peers' recognition of the outcome of the intentions of learning. Lacking recognition may involve competitive processes, where the students wish to prove themselves and they become engaged in doing so. Constructive competition leading to engagement may be informed by particular intentions of learning, where competition involves striving for particular recognized outcomes of the intentions of learning. Collaborative aspects of competition (Fülöp 2004; Sheridan & Williams, 2006) may involve being each other's critiques regarding reaching the intentions of competition.

While due attention has been paid to competition conditioned by people's interaction and collaboration (Fülöp 2004; Johnson & Johnson 1994), these findings show that constructive competition is conditioned by particular artifacts or material resources of design efforts at learning (Ingold, 2006; 2010). This conclusion corresponds with activity theoretical notions of material resources mediating persons' learning (Yrjö Engeström, 1999; Holland & Cole, 1995; Roth & Lee, 2007). One aspect of the students' competitiveness were related to timing of the material 'thinginess' (Ingold, 2006; 2010) of food ingredients. In regard to the cooking methods needed to succeed in the cooking assignments, timing also played a role in regard to groups

competing with one self and others to be fast, on time, or even first with their food.

In regard to prior studies of the goals of competition (Sheridan & Williams, 2011), the findings show that attention is needed to how competing approaches for reaching the students' shared goals of competition may develop and influence vocational teaching and learning. The students compete in order to excel in and being recognized for cooking good food. Yet it seemed that learning to cook could turn out in various or even competing ways as trajectories of movement (Ingold, 2010). As the findings show, and in accordance with Gutierrez and Larson's (1995) studies, competition involves 'counter scripts' or counter-learning intentions of on the one hand keeping to yourself, to your methods and your procedures if you aim at working fast and efficiently. On the other hand competition involves counter scripts of taking time to observe other's cooking and adjust and refine cooking methods living up to the purposes of the vocational school of taking time to gain experiences with procedures. Both form-giving learning intentions were recognized as important by the teachers. Both approaches seem to enable for the students to become skilled in cooking. In some cases interaction between competing form-giving approaches lead to looming contradictions. When they became open conflicts, they related to some of the students' experiences of the socio-material challenges of competing against time in such a manner as to overlook the collaborative and potentially time-consuming potentials of sharing cooking methods and learning by paying attention to other groups' try-outs. In the cases where collaboration and attention to activities in other groups were beside the point in the students' form-giving procedures, the competitive goals of recognition were not related to the development of vocational learning. Nonetheless, the students' form-giving of delicate ingredients as part of cooking of food was closely connected to the students' enhanced engagement in constructive and competitive processes. The findings suggest that connections between collaborative aspects and competitive aspects are important to enhance as integrated part of the students' form-giving and learning activities. An important condition of the learning situation and part of the tradition of cooking learning activity was the organization of students in teams. This may be related to the students' various development of counter learning intentions and thus influence the connections between collaborative and competitive aspects. Yet, this needs to be further investigated in future studies of both team-based and individual-based traditions of vocational activities.

The students' pursuit of competing learning intentions and form-giving goals afforded learning in terms of being able to handle difficult methods, giving room to collaborative ways of improving cooking skills and to widen the students' perspectives into 'third space', bridging middle grounds (Gutierrez & Larson, 1995) on how to pursue their intentions of becoming skilled in cooking.

FUTURE RESEARCH DIRECTIONS

This study investigates how, as part of vocational activities, students' goals to compete relate to their development of student engagement and learning. Future studies may further investigate, whether competitive goals of recognition may also lead to negative forms of competition. A future study could also involve the position of the teacher and how this is related to the development of constructive competition. Further knowledge of how distinctions between constructive competition and destructive competition as resources for learning are developed is in demand. Generalization of the results of this study to other educational contexts, suggests that a point of departure may be to define the specific intentions and mediating artifacts of competition pertaining to such contexts.

CONCLUSION

Competition among students is potentially constructive for learning and engagement. The present chapter investigates how such constructive competition is afforded. The findings show that constructive and destructive competitive processes were afforded by the particular intentions of competing to cook good food. Such attempts were structured by particular socio-material resources and competitively developed skills of timing. A focus on how constructive student competition is afforded by the socio-material resources of particular intentions adds to studies of student competition with a primary focus on the values, interactions and social organization that form conditions for student competition.

REFERENCES

Bernard, R. H. (1995). *Research methods in anthropology: Qualitative and quantitative approaches*. Thousand Oaks, CA: Sage.

Braun, V., & Clarke, V. (2006). Using thematic analysis in psychology. *Qualitative Research in Psychology, 3*(2), 77–101. doi:10.1191/1478088706qp063oa

Brown, S. P., Cron, W. L., & Slocum, J. W. (1998). Effects of traint competitiveness and perceived intraorganizational competition on sales-person goal setting and performance. *Journal of Marketing, 62*(4), 88–98. doi:10.2307/1252289

Cole, M., & Engeström, Y. (1993). A cultural historical approach to distributed cognition. In G. Salomon (Ed.), *Distributed cognitions: Psychological and educational considerations* (pp. 1–46). Cambridge, UK: Cambridge University Press.

Deutsch, M. (2000). Cooperation and competition. In M. Deutsch & P. Coleman (Eds.), *The handbook of conflict resolution: Theory and practicee* (pp. 21–40). San Francisco: Jossey-Basss.

Dillenbourg, P., Baker, M., Blaye, A., & O'Malley, C. (1996). The evolution of reserarch on collaborative learning. In P. Reimann & H. Spada (Eds.), *Learning in humans and machines* (pp. 189–205). Oxford, UK: Elsevier.

Engeström, Y. (1987). *Learning by Expanding: An Activity-Theoretical Approach to Developmental Research*. Helsinki: Orienta-Konsultit.

Engeström, Y. (1999). Activity theory and individual and social transformation. In Y. Engeström, R. Miettinen, & R. L. Punamäki (Eds.), *Perspectives on Activity Theory* (pp. 19–38). Cambridge, UK: Cambridge University Press. doi:10.1017/CBO9780511812774.003

Engeström, Y. (2001). Expansive learning at work: Toward an activity theoretical reconceptualization. *Journal of Education and Work, 14*(1), 133–156. doi:10.1080/13639080020028747

Engeström, Y., Rantavuori, J., & Kerosuo, H. (2013). Expansive learning in a library: Actions, cycles and deviations from instructional intentions. *Vocations and Learning, 6*(1), 81–106. doi:10.1007/s12186-012-9089-6

Fülöp, M. (1999). Students' perception of the role of competition in their respectivwe contries: Hungary, Japan, and the USA. In A. Ross (Ed.), *Young citizens in Europe* (pp. 95–219). London: University of North London.

Fülöp, M. (2002). *Competition in educational settings*. Paper presented at the Faculty of Education, University of Ljubljana. Ljubljana, Slovenia.

Fülöp, M. (2004). Competition as a culturally constructed concept. In C. Baillie, E. Dunn, & Y. Zheng (Eds.), *Travelling facts: The social construction, distribution, and accumulation of knowledge* (pp. 124–128). Frankfurt, Germany: Campus Verlag.

Geertz, C. (1973). *The interpretation of cultures: selected essays*. New York: Basic Books.

Gutierrez, K., & Larson, J. (1995). Script, counterscript, and underlife in the classroom: James Brown versus Brown v. Board of Education. *Harvard Educational Review, 65*(3), 445–471.

Hammersley, M., & Atkinson, P. (1997). *Ethnography: Principles in practice*. London: Routledge.

Hansson, T. (2014). Modeling and analyzing contextual influences. In T. Hansson (Ed.), *Contemporary Approaches to Activity Theory. Interdisciplinary Perspectives on Human Behavior*. Hershey, PA: IGI Global.

Hedegaard, M. (2005). Strategies for dealing with conflicts in value positions between home and school: Influences on ehtnic minority students' development of motives and identity. *Culture and Psychology, 11*(2), 187–205. doi:10.1177/1354067X05052351

Holland, D., & Cole, M. (1995). Between discourse and schema: Reformulating a cultural-historical approach to culture and mind. *Anthropology & Education Quarterly, 26*(4), 475–489. doi:10.1525/aeq.1995.26.4.05x1065y

Ingold, T. (2006). Walking the plank: meditations on a process of skill. In J. R. Dakers (Ed.), *Defining technological literacy: Towards an epistemological framework* (pp. 65–80). New York: Palgrave Macmillan.

Ingold, T. (2010). The textility of making. *Cambridge Journal of Economics, 34*(1), 91–102. doi:10.1093/cje/bep042

Johnson, D. W., & Johnson, R. T. (1989). *Cooperation and competition: Theory and research*. Edina, MN: Interaction.

Johnson, D. W., & Johnson, R. T. (1994). Learning together and alone: cooperative, competitive and individualistic learning. Needham Heights, MA: Allyn and Bacon.

Johnson, D. W., Johnson, R. T., & Roseth, C. J. (2012). Competition and performance: More facts, more understanding? Comment on Murayama and Ellion (2012). *Psychological Bulletin, 138*(6), 1071–1078. doi:10.1037/a0029454 PMID:23088571

Jonasson, C. (2012). Teachers and students' divergent perceptions of student engagement: Recognition of school or workplace goals. *British Journal of Sociology of Education, 33*(5), 723–741. doi:10.1080/01425692.2012.674811

Jonasson, C. (2013a). Defining boundaries between school and work: teachers and students' attribution of quality to school-based vocational training. *Journal of Education and Work,* 1-21.

Jonasson, C. (2013b). *Trust in vocational schools?* Paper presented at the JVET 10th International Conference 2013. Oxford, UK.

Jonasson, C. (2013c). Why stay in school: Student retention processes in vocational schools. Germany Scholars' Press.

Kohn, A. (1986). *No contest: The case against competition.* Boston, MA: Houghton-Mifflin Company.

Lave, J. (2011). *Apprenticeship in critical ethnographic practice.* Chicago: Chicago University Press. doi:10.7208/chicago/9780226470733.001.0001

Lave, J. (2012). Changing practice. *Mind, Culture, and Activity, 16*(2), 156–171. doi:10.1080/10749039.2012.666317

Lindberg, V. (2003a). Learning practices in vocational education. *Scandinavian Journal of Educational Research, 47*(2), 157–179. doi:10.1080/00313830308611

Lindberg, V. (2003b). Vocational knowing and the content in vocational education. *International Journal of Training Research, 1*(2), 40–61. doi:10.5172/ijtr.1.2.40

Mäkitalo, Å. (2012). Professional learning and the materiality of social practice. *Journal of Education and Work, 25*(1), 59–78. doi:10.1080/13639080.2012.644905

Mäkitalo, A., & Säljö, R. (2009). Contextualizing social dilemmas in institutional practices: Negotiating objects of activity in labour market organizations. In A. Sannino, H. Daniels, & K. Gutierrez (Eds.), *Learning and expanding with activity theory* (pp. 112–128). New York: Cambridge University Press. doi:10.1017/CBO9780511809989.008

Mercer, N. (2005). Sociocultural discourse analysis: Analysing classroom talk as a social mdoe of thinking. *Journal of Applied Linguistics, 1*(2), 137–168. doi:10.1558/japl.2004.1.2.137

Miles, M., & Huberman, M. A. (1994). *Qualitative Data Analysis.* London: Sage.

Murayama, K., & Elliot, A. J. (2012). The competition-performance relation: A meta-analytic review and test of the opposing processes model of competion and performance. *Psychological Bulletin, 138*(6), 1035–1070. doi:10.1037/a0028324 PMID:23088570

Putney, L. G., & Frank, C. R. (2008). Looking through ethnographic eyes at classrooms acting as cultures. *Ethnography and Education, 3*(2), 211–228. doi:10.1080/17457820802062482

Roth, W.-M., & Lee, Y.-J. (2007). 'Vygotsky's neglected legacy': Cultural-historical activity theory. *Review of Educational Research, 77*(2), 186–232. doi:10.3102/0034654306298273

Säljö, R. (1991). Learning and mediation: Fitting reality into a table. *Learning and Instruction, 1*(3), 261–272. doi:10.1016/0959-4752(91)90007-U

Säljö, R. (2009). Learning, theories of learning, and units of analysis in research. *Educational Psychologist, 44*(3), 202–208. doi:10.1080/00461520903029030

Sanjek, R. (1990). *Fieldnotes: The Makings of Anthropology. Uthaca.* Cornell University Press.

Sheridan, S., & Williams, P. (2006). Constructive competition in preschool. *Journal of Early Childhood Research, 4*(3), 291–310. doi:10.1177/1476718X06067581

Sheridan, S., & Williams, P. (2011). Developing individual goals, shared goals, and the goals of others: Dimensions of constructive competition in learning contexts. *Scandinavian Journal of Educational Research, 55*(2), 145–164. doi:10.1 080/00313831.2011.554694

Spradley, J. P. (1980). *Participant observation.* New York: Holt Rinehart and Winston.

Walford, G. (2009). For ethnography. *Ethnography and Education, 4*(3), 271–282. doi:10.1080/17457820903170093

Wertsch, J. (2007). Mediation. In H. Daniels, M. Cole, & J. Wertsch (Eds.), *The Cambridge Companion to Vygotsky* (pp. 178–192). Cambridge, UK: Cambridge University Press. doi:10.1017/CCOL0521831040.008

Williams, P., & Sheridan, S. (2010). Conditions for collaborative learning and constructive competition in school. *Educational Research, 52*(4), 335–350. doi:10.1080/00131881.2010.524748

Wittchen, M., Krimmel, A., Kohler, M., & Hertel, G. (2013). The two sides of competition: Competition-induced effort and affect during intergroup versus interindividual competition. *British Journal of Psychology, 104*(3), 320–338. doi:10.1111/j.2044-8295.2012.02123.x PMID:23848384

ADDITIONAL READING

Akkerman, S. F., & Bakker, A. (2011). Boundary crossing and boundary objects. *Review of Educational Research, 81*(2), 132–169. doi:10.3102/0034654311404435

Berner, B. (2010). Crossing boundaries and maintaining differences between school and industry: Forms of boundary-work in Swedish vocational education. *Journal of Education and Work, 23*(1), 27–42. doi:10.1080/13639080903461865

Bowker, G. C., & Star, S. L. (1999). *Sorting things out - classification and its consequenses.* London: MIT Press.

Chaiklin, S., & Lave, J. (1996). *Understanding Practice: Perspectives on Activity and Context.* New York: Cambridge University Press.

Daniels, H. (2011). Analysing trajectories of professional learning in changing workplaces. *Culture and Psychology, 17*(3), 359–377. doi:10.1177/1354067X11408137

Dreier, O. (2009). Persons in structures of social practice. *Theory & Psychology, 19*(2), 193–212. doi:10.1177/0959354309103539

Engeström, Y. (1987) .*Learning by expanding: An activity theoretical approach to developmental research,* Helsinkin: Orienta-Konsultit Oy.

Engeström, Y., Engeström, R., & Kärkkäinen, M. (1995). Polycontextuality and boundary crossing in expert cognition: Learning and problem solving in complex work activities. *Learning and Instruction, 5*(4), 319–336. doi:10.1016/0959-4752(95)00021-6

Fenwick, T., & Edwards, R. (2010). *Actor-network theory in education.* London: Routledge.

Gutierrez, K. (Ed.). (2009). *Learning and expanding with activity theory.* New York: Cambridge University Press.

Ingold, T. (1993). Technology, language, intelligence: A reconsideration of basic concepts. In T. R. Gibson & T. Ingold (Eds.), *Tools, language and cognition in human evolution.* Cambridge: Cambridge University Press.

Ingold, T. (2001). From the transmission of representations to the education of attention. In H. Whitehouse (Ed.), *The debated mind: Evolutionary psychology versus ethnography.* Oxford: Berg.

Konkola, R., Toumi-Gröhn, T., Lambert, P., & Ludvigsen, S. (2007). Promoting learning and transfer between school and workplace. *Journal of Education and Work, 20*(3), 211–228. doi:10.1080/13639080701464483

Lave, J. (1988). *Cognition in practice.* Cambridge: Cambridge University Press. doi:10.1017/CBO9780511609268

Lave, J. (1990). The culture of acquisition and the practice of understanding. In J-W Stigler. R.A. Shweder & G. Herdt. (Eds.). Cultural Psychology (pp. 259-286). Cambridge, UK: Cambridge University Press. doi:10.1017/CBO9781139173728.010

Lave, J. (1996). The practice of learning. In S. Chaiklin & J. Lave (Eds.), *Understanding practice, perspectives on activity and context* (pp. 3–32). Cambridge, UK: Cambridge University Press.

Mäkitalo, Å. (2003). Accounting Practices as Situated Knowing: Dilemmas and Dynamics in Institutional Categorization. *Discourse Studies, 5,* 495–516. doi:10.1177/14614456030054003

Mäkitalo, Å., & Säljö, R. (2002). Talk in institutional context and institutional context in talk: Categories as situated practices. *Text, 22*(1), 57–82. doi:10.1515/text.2002.005

Nielsen, K. (2006). Learning to do things with things: Apprenticeship in bakery as economy and social practice. In A. Costall & O. Dreier (Eds.), *Doing things with things: The design and use of everyday objects* (pp. 209–224). UK: Ashgate Publishing Limited.

Toumi-Gröhn, T., & Engeström, Y. (2003). *Between school and work: New perspectives on transfer and boundary-crossing.* Oxford: Pergamon.

Wertsch, J. (1985). *Vygotsky and the social formation of mind.* Cambridge, MA: Cambridge University Press.

Willis, P. (1981). Cultural production is different from cultural reproduction is different from social reproduction is different from reproduction. *Interchange, 12*(2-3), 48–67. doi:10.1007/BF01192107

KEY TERMS AND DEFINITIONS

Constructive Competition: Means competition between persons as a social and cultural phenomenon that enhances persons' ambitions and learning and as a multidimensional educational phenomenon that motivates people in learning situations.

Counter-Scripts: The term refers to contradictory learning intentions between e.g. the students' counter-scripts going against the teachers' more authoritative scripts. Competition may involve such counter-scripts and lead to conflicts of form-giving the materials and gaining recognition.

Form-Giving Trajectories of Movements: An expression which means the iteration of practice involving ongoing correction in the form-giving, joined forces of practitioner and material.

Learning Intentions: Refers to the goal-directedness, will or pursuit of particular goals in persons' daily activities.

Mediating Artifacts: Are cultural artifacts having both material and ideal aspects and mediating subject-object relations.

Vocational Activities: The expression covers cultural-historical transformed, distributed and evolving complex structures of mediated and collective human agency motivated by a collective concern for developing vocational skills, knowledge, and ways of doing things.

Vocational Learning: From a socio-cultural perspective, learning involves interactions and negotiations between newcomers and old-timers in an activity system. In regard to a specific vocation, the students gradually become full practitioners through their participation in the vocational activities.

Chapter 7
Project–Based Instruction in Teaching Chinese as a Foreign Language

Juanjuan Zhao
University of Cincinnati, USA

ABSTRACT

In this chapter, Cultural Historical Activity Theory (CHAT) is used as a framework to examine Project-Based Instruction (PBI) in a Chinese foreign language classroom at a U.S. high school. The implementation of PBI arose from an action research project that resulted from a teacher's perceived need to improve students' engagement, cultural knowledge, and communicative language skills. Data collected include interviews, surveys, classroom observations, teacher reflective journals, and student projects. Data is first analyzed thematically and then reframed from the perspective of CHAT. Findings reveal that PBI motivated students in learning, enhanced cultural understanding, and improved their language skills. Despite the positive evaluation of PBI, there are contradictions within the activity reported such as the tool of language as a barrier. Students wanted to keep traditional learning activity and PBI. Furthermore, analysis of the findings suggest that CHAT is a suitable framework for educational research.

INTRODUCTION

Project-based instruction (PBI) is a teaching and learning method that uses authentic, complex and real life projects to motivate learning and socialize students through a series of individual or group activities (Beckett, 1999; 2006). These activities generally include the steps of selecting project topics, designing project activities, researching and gathering information, developing products, and oral or written reporting (Hedge, 2002).

Completion of such activities integrates various skills ranging from basic information processing to project producing that mirrors real-life tasks. Students may find these tasks motivating, empowering or challenging yet helpful in their aspiration to obtain learning autonomy and boost confidence (Stoller, 1997).

The approach has been widely employed in English as second and foreign language education and numerous studies have reported positive outcomes of it. The benefits include authenticity of students' experiences and the language they

DOI: 10.4018/978-1-4666-6603-0.ch007

are exposed to (Ke, 2010), enhanced motivation, engagement and the joy of learning (Lee, 2002), promotion of communicative competence (Wu & Meng, 2010), improved language skills (Levine, 2004), cross-cultural knowledge (Abrams, 2002; Bateman, 2002), simultaneous language learning, content knowledge and skills (Beckett & Slater, 2005), and increased learning autonomy and independence (Coleman, 1992). In addition, the favor toward PBI is due to its distinguishing features of a student negotiated-curriculum (Doherty & Eyring, 2006) in which learning is student centered with the teacher playing the role of a facilitator (McDonell, 1992). However, despite the popularity and benefits of PBI for teaching and learning English as second and foreign language, little research has examined the effectiveness of the approach in teaching and learning Chinese as a foreign language (CFL).

Meanwhile, interest and enrolment in learning Chinese as one of the critical languages in the U.S. have surged as American economic ties to China deepen (Zhao & Huang, 2010). As a result, an increasing number of native Chinese speakers who were previously educated outside U.S. came to teach Chinese in U.S. (Lin, 2009). These teachers are great sources of knowledge to students in terms of their combined linguistic competence and cultural knowledge. However, concerns have been raised towards their lacking of training and understanding of US education in general and pedagogy in particular. Such shortcomings may affect students learning outcomes negatively (Schrier, 1993). This is so because these teachers act out an education system that demonstrates a teacher-centered and exam oriented method. American education, on the other hand, is student-centered in which the teacher act as a facilitator for the students' learning. It focuses on establishing an engaging learning environment where teachers are able to work collaboratively with the students (Haley & Ferro, 2011). As a result, native Chinese speakers are criticized for their traditional grammar translation approach to teaching and learning. They are also criticized for a teacher-centered environment that fails to address the needs and expectations of learners in K-12 contexts, i.e. in primary and secondary education (Chu, 1990). Under this circumstance, it becomes imperative for researchers and educators to look at pedagogies and strategies that practitioners can adopt to meet the learning needs and interests of students and also sustain the growing interest and development of CFL (Wang, 2007). For this study PBI is defined as a student-motivational approach implemented in a CFL setting to address the demand.

Following a classroom-based action research approach, the teacher researcher implemented PBI as an intervention and examined its effectiveness in teaching CFL at a U.S. high school. This study aims at exploring students' and the teacher's perceptions and experiences of PBI from the lens of cultural historical activity theory (CHAT) in the dynamics of classroom settings. The chapter purports to be pragmatic and theoretical, linking theory with practice by providing practitioners with a tool for researching their classrooms, showing the feasibility of using PBI in teaching Chinese as a foreign language, and demonstrating the contribution of CHAT in interpreting students' and their teacher's experiences.

PREVIOUS RESEARCH

In order to obtain an overview of the foci and trends of studies on CFL, this author reviewed literature on CFL mainly for English native speakers in North America published from 1999 to present. The literature review includes search for K-12 settings and higher education in databases such as *Education Full Text, Education Research Complete, and Arts & Humanities Citations* Index as well as library search for books, theses and dissertations. The following key words were used to identify relevant literature: Chinese as a foreign language, teaching Chinese, Chinese language, Chinese instruction, and learning Chinese.

In addition, literature was also found based on the *Bibliography of Research on Chinese Language Education* (1999-2008) published by the University of British Columbia and in journals including *Foreign Language Annals; Journal of the Chinese Language Teachers Association; Journal of Chinese Linguistics; Canadian Modern Language Review; Modern Language Journal; System; Linguistics and Education; Journal of Pragmatics; Language Policy; Language Teaching Research; Language Assessment Quarterly; Language Learning & Technology; and Language, Culture & Curriculum.* As a result, a total number of 339 relevant publications were found. Abstracts of articles, theses and dissertations, and introductions in books were reviewed and classified into ten major categories (Table 1). Categorization was based on subject descriptions provided by the journals, databases as well as keywords in the articles.

This systematic search reveals a limited number of studies that explored CFL pedagogy, a few addressed the teachers' and the students' voices, and none of them focused on project-based CFL instruction. For example, among the 339 publications on CFL, almost half of them were linguistics-oriented focusing on general linguistics, psycholinguistics, comparative and historical linguistics. The second highest percentage of the literature fell into second language acquisition including studies and discussions about inter language, language transfer, sequences of acquisition, learning processes and strategies of specific language skills (e.g. vocabulary, tone and pragmatic competence). Compared to linguistics research, studies that explored the practical aspects of language education, especially the approaches and methods employed in teaching and learning of Chinese languages, were hard to find. For example, only a few studies investigated computer assisted learn-

Table 1. Focus areas of CFL research

Categories	Subcategories	Number of Publications (N= 339)	Percentage
Linguistics-Oriented	General Linguistics	96	42.1%
	Psycholinguistics	33	
	Historical Linguistics	4	
	Comparative Linguistics	10	
Second Language Acquisition	Second Language Acquisition	57	16.8%
Language Teaching	Educational Technology	33	19.7%
	Teaching Strategies & Pedagogies	17	
	Teaching of specific skills	17	
CFL Issues and Perspectives	CFL Issues and Perspectives	24	7.1%
Textbook/Curriculum Development	Textbook/curriculum Development	13	3.8%
Teacher and Students Perspectives	Student Voices	7	3.3%
	Teacher Voices	4	
Report of Programme	Report of Programme	8	2.4%
Language Assessment	Language Assessment	7	2.1%
Teacher Education & Development	Teacher Education & Development	6	1.8%
Others	Language for Specific Purposes	2	0.9%
	Parent Perceptions	1	

ing activities (Zhang, 2004), corrective feedback (An, 2006; Wen, 1999); task-based instruction (Lai, Zhao & Wang, 2011), form-based instruction (Jin, 2005) and learner-as-ethnographer approach (Lu, 2012). There was a low amount of articles discussing teaching of specific language skills such as reading and writing, or examining application of technologies in classrooms. None of them specifically studied project-based instruction (PBI). As noted earlier, Chinese language teaching is criticized for a grammar translation approach that emphasizes classical Chinese texts for academics. Furthermore, the teacher-centered environment does not adequately address the needs of learners in K-12 contexts. Thus a PBI-model that highlights student-centered learning and collaboration between teachers and students is highly desirable. Additionally, only a few studies explored the perspectives of teachers and students towards their teaching and learning experiences with issues, challenges, and successes (Duff & Li, 2004). Such studies could potentially provide valuable information for CFL studies in general and CFL professionals in particular.

THEORETICAL FRAMEWORK

Action research (AR) is a practitioner research approach for teacher practitioners to gain a deep understanding of students' learning as well as to improve students' learning outcomes and their own teaching practices (Suter, 2006; Nolen & Putten, 2007). Researchers usually examine the problems bewildering them and discover needs and opportunities for subsequent interventions through careful and systematic analysis of the studied situation (Mertler & Charles, 2008). Advantages of involving classroom practitioners in AR have been widely reported. For example, classroom-based AR aims at addressing particular problems and find out solutions to issues in a specific teaching or learning situation (Edge, 2001; Wallace, 1998). Teachers are researchers in their classrooms oper-

ating through systematic and documented inquiry of particular aspect of learning and teaching. Thus they can gain a deep understanding of learning activities in a classroom and use that knowledge to increase student learning as well as their teaching practices (Chamot, Barnhardt & Dirstine, 1998). As a practitioner research approach, it provides a way to bridge the gap between academic research and practical classroom applications (McNiff & Whitehead, 2006).

A substantial body of literature has documented application of AR in English language teaching and learning (Burns, 1999, 2005; Borg, 2003). As Burns (2005) summarized, the use of AR in English language teaching covers teacher education, classroom-based AR by practitioners, collaborative AR in educational programs, and AR by teacher educators. However, the literature review of studies in CFL revealed a gap in the use of AR in all areas. There was only one classroom-based research found, a dissertation study in which the instructor investigated the implementation and feasibility of learners-as-ethnographers approach in achieving intercultural learning among American students learning Chinese as a foreign language (Lu, 2012). Thus this study addresses gaps in the literature by implementing PBI in CFL instruction, examining the students' and the teacher's experiences of PBI, and using language teacher research for evaluating development of the students' learning and the teacher's teaching practice.

In order to investigate students' experiences with PBI and the dynamics of classroom project activities, the author employed Cultural Historical Activity Theory (CHAT) as a theoretical framework. CHAT (Engeström, 1999) focuses on providing a holistic view of an activity system that represents a complex reality beyond one single actor's individual actions. Its purpose is to capture the complexity of reality of human behavior by focusing on the studied phenomenon, the individual subject and the context rather than studying an issue or a subject independently. Activity as the chosen unit of analysis is defined as a specific choice that engages human agency with "definite needs, motives, tasks, and goals as its contents" (Davydov, 1999, p. 50). Unlike most events in nature that involve direct action between a subject and on an object, activity in CHAT mediates the use of culturally established instruments such as language, artifacts and procedures. There are several key components of an activity (Figure 1). Subjects are actors engaged in the activities (can be a person or a group), acting upon an object with predetermined goals, using tools (artifacts or concepts) in the course of carrying out the activity. Objects exist in two forms, either as material entity or as an objective or image of goal (Roth & Lee, 2007). Accomplishment of a goal, engages a collective effort of actors who contribute by sharing divided labour and providing contributions, as well as the compliance of rules and regulations guiding execution of activity in the system. The activity is embedded in a community, which makes up part of the social cultural context. Instruments, rules, community, and division of labour reciprocally influence the achievement of the object. CHAT is a method and a theory for studying entities embedded in an environment. Figure 1 denotes components and relations.

Influenced by classical German philosophy ranging from Kant to Hegel, Marxism and psychological work of Vygotsky (Engeström, 1999), activity theory has undergone three generations. The first generation draws heavily from Vygotsky's concept of mediation, that is, human interaction with the outside world through artifacts with primary focuses on individuals (Roth & Lee, 2007). Leontev and Luria develop Vygotsky's work by adding social, cultural and historical dimensions to it (Eliam, 2003; Stesenko, 2003) and making activity the unit of analysis. Eventually Engeström (1999) expanded activity systems to include networks of interacting systems, the conflicting nature of social practice, multiple perspectives, historical background of a social structure, and transitions and reorganizations within and between activity systems. This outline of crucial activity theoretical aspects of human behavior is known as third generation activity theory or CHAT.

Figure 1. Activity system (Engeström, 1987, p. 78)

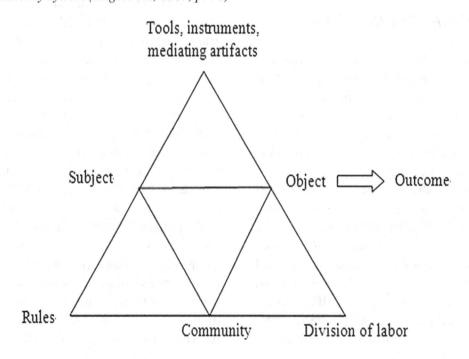

Activity systems are interconnected and part of a network of activity systems that comprise larger activity systems. The focus on interactions among systems and the elements within a system gives rise to the possibility of studying contradictions and tensions among and within main and supporting systems. This feature of third generation CHAT allows researchers to identify aspects of the systems that form coherent and contradictory qualities. Activity systems are multi-voiced. There are multiple participants playing multiple roles. Participants bring with them multiple points of view deriving from differing histories, traditions, motives and interests. Noting the presence of multiple perspectives indicates the importance of supplying collective contributions of singular subjects in activity systems. Multi-voicedness on the other hand, multiplies in networks of interacting activity systems. Such multi-voicedness can become a source of conflict, causing imbalances to appear in the system and demanding actions of negotiation between the subjects. Activity systems are historically constituted. This means that any phenomenon has to be studied and understood against its socially and culturally embedded historical context. Tensions and problems within a system can generate disturbances reaching a point when a new element has to be brought in from outside, causing reorganization of the activity.

In this study, the third generation of CHAT illustrates project activities by application of basic elements of activity systems such as subjects, mediated tools, rules, community, division of labour and objects. This study also employs the key features of third-generation CHAT to supports the analysis of students' experience of PBI-learning as well as the teacher's experience in the process. Using CHAT as a framework for analyzing and interpreting research helps the researcher capture the complexity of project activities by including roles of students and teachers in the process, the impact of tools and artifacts and the relations among each entity in the PBI activity and beyond.

COLLECTING AND ANALYZING DATA

The school is an urban high school in Cincinnati, Ohio, U.S.A. with around 700 enrolments, among which the majority are African-American students. It is a school focusing on science, technology, engineering and mathematics (STEM). It emphasizes development of student skills in the fields of STEM as a way to help them succeed in the 21st century. Chinese was introduced as a new program in 2011. There were two Chinese classes. One class had taken Chinese for one academic year and the other class had taken Chinese for half an academic year at the time when data collection ended. Classes were held in a computer lab where each student had access to a computer for carrying out assignments and project tasks. A total of eighteen students participated in PBI as part of their coursework. Ten of them agreed to be interviewed and surveyed. Findings of the two groups were reported together because they shared similar experiences of PBI.

Following a classroom-based AR approach, the teacher researcher implemented an intervention using PBI in Chinese language classroom. The purpose was to improve students' learning outcomes. The cycle of practitioner research used in the PBI-approach was based on Baskerville and Wood-Harper's (1996) steps for doing action research. They consist of diagnosing, action planning, action taking, evaluating and specifying learning. During the first stage, the teacher-researcher identified learning problems among students, e.g. focusing on students who failed to actively participate in classroom activities or being late for submission of assignments submission. During the second stage, the teacher planned PBI as an intervention with the purpose of improving students learning outcomes. During the third stage, the teacher implemented PBI. During the fourth stage, the teacher evaluated progress by gathering data that would help analysis of interventions' effects. During the fifth stage, teacher researcher specified learning based on the collected data and shared knowledge for future teaching and learning activities and research interventions.

Data collected for this study included projects, teacher observations, teacher reflective journals, students' project diaries, surveys and interviews with students. During the projects, the teacher kept a reflective journal and took notes. They included description of the classroom setting, project activities, interactions between the teacher and the students related to project tasks, and the teacher's experience with PBI. Project diaries are summarization tasks that ask students to record their linguistic achievement, content and skills learnt from a project (Beckett & Slater, 2005). The diaries were handed over to students for self-assessment after a project was finished. At the end of the term, an electronic survey was distributed to each student for feedback on PBI. Interviews were conducted in the last two weeks before the semester ended. Interviews were semi-structured and each of which lasted for about half an hour. Among the ten students who agreed to participate in the study, nine interviews and surveys were collected. Missing data consisted of one student from the lower level class who did not show up for the interview and one student from the higher level class who did not turn in her survey.

This study took a cultural historical activity theory perspective, congruent with AR which is defined as a transformative methodology (Somekh, 2005). Just like AR, CHAT considers an activity in its dynamic form by taking into account tensions and contradictions as well as transformation. With this in mind, the collected data were analyzed following a two-stage approach. During the first stage, interview transcripts and the qualitative survey were analyzed using interpretive analysis (Hatch, 2002) through open coding and domain analysis (Spradley, 1980). The purpose was to find themes and patterns in the data. Interpretive analysis was also applied in analyzing the other types of data. This type of inductive analysis of the data allows researchers

to construct meaning from data and make sense of the social phenomenon which is being studied (Hatch, 2002). The second stage of analysis was to reframe the theme and patterns identified from a CHAT perspective. Basic components and key features of CHAT were applied in further examination of the data. In addition to its alignment with AR, another rationale for the use of CHAT in data analysis is its ability or organizing, sorting and clarifying a complex phenomenon found in activity (Nussbaumer, 2011). As a descriptive tool, CHAT provided perspectives to examine relationships as well as environments that influence teaching-learning activities and has the capacity to reveal points of intervention and indirect relationships (Daniel, 2004). Adopting CHAT for data analysis provided the teacher researcher with a holistic and a detailed view of students' learning through PBI in classroom settings.

FINDINGS AND DICUSSION

Results of the students' evaluations of PBI activity are based on interviews, surveys, project diaries and project products. They are also based on the teacher' observations and experiences recorded in a reflective journal. These perceptions are examined and categorized according to basic components and key principles of CHAT, resulting in five themes: positive PBI activity, balancing of PBI and conventional teaching and learning activity, contradictions in PBI activity, transitions and reorganizations to PBI activity, and finally expansive learning-ways for a better PBI activity.

Positive PBI Activity

The object of the PBI activity is defined as the goal of taking Chinese classes, i.e. acquisition of Chinese language and culture based on students' responses in the interview and the survey. The student participants say that PBI enhances their learning of Chinese culture, improves their language skills and motivates learning. These positively stated outcomes of PBI suggest that the method is a beneficial approach for learning Chinese.

Most of the students said that doing projects improved their understanding of Chinese culture. They wanted to learn about Chinese culture. The result is consistent with the literature on benefits of PBI in helping students gain cross-cultural knowledge (Abrams, 2002; Bateman, 2002; Gu, 2002; Wu & Meng, 2010). Students liked to participate in the PBI project because they "learned a lot more about the Chinese culture" and "a lot of things that I didn't know about China". In doing a project about high-school life in China, one student found that Chinese students had a tight study schedule and little time for play. Through the project activities, not only she was able to see how high school students in China spend their time on study, but by comparing the two different education systems, she was motivated to learn in school. She also expressed her desire to learn more about Chinese and the culture.

Henry (1994) divided projects into structured, semi-structured, and unstructured designs. In structured projects, a teacher determines and specifies the topic, materials, and the presentation, with the purpose of training students how to do project work. Semi-structured projects are defined and organized by students and the teacher equally. In unstructured projects, activities are decided and organized by the students alone. In this study, each student participated in a total of five projects among which three are semi-structured, one structured and one unstructured. Students reported that projects of all types improved their language skills, including listening, speaking, reading and writing. Participation also improved their character writing and recognition abilities. One student said that through PBI she learned "about the Chinese culture and new words, sentence structures, characters and much more". Many students stated that they liked projects about ordering food in a Chinese restaurant and finding

a Chinese name for themselves. Not only did they learn new words and characters, but also used the language for communication. This speaks to the previous finding about about PBI's benefits in improving target language skills (Gardner, 1995; Fragoulis, 2009; Hilton-Jones, 1988).

Rules refer to the school requirements and specific language class rules that the students need to follow. Students' interview responses demonstrated their comparison of behaviors in relation with classroom rules in two different settings that represent conventional schooling and PBI. In the conventional learning activity, in addition to lectures and classroom activities, students devoted most of their time to working on individual assignments following the same format every day. They expressed sentiments of boredom as a result of the repetitive format of the teacher's arrangements. Some of them also felt there were too many assignments and all they wanted to do was to finish the assignments. So in the end they did not think that they have gained much knowledge from doing the assignments. Some students revealed that in the traditional teaching and learning activity, they misbehaved in class due to lack of engagement and motivation in learning. For example, three students said they talked to each other in class when they were not supposed to do so. They also browsed websites irrelevant to the lessons when they got tired of work. The following interview excerpt from a student explains:

I guess it's the format of every week. You do this thing, this thing on this day. I mean, it gets old, you get tired of it and you wish you don't want to do it anymore. I think that's why I start to talk more because of the same thing. It wasn't anything new.

In contrast, the students stated that PBI was a fun learning experience. The design gave them a break and an opportunity to relax from doing repetitive assignments. Also according to the students, PBI was a fun method because it connected to students' learning interests. A majority of the interviewed students rated a project on Chinese names as their favourite activity because whilst completing the task they were able to find an individual Chinese name for themselves and learned the characters of their names. A project on ordering food in a Chinese restaurant was also rated high. Students said that they liked Chinese food and going to Chinese restaurants. Doing the project help them learn how to order food. Projects engaged and motivated them to learn because during the process they explored and practiced things for everyday use. For example, one student put it in this way:

I think learning different ways to say and look at type of objects we use every day is important in doing a project.

For food, there are all kinds of different food. It is just fun to learn different stuff.

Furthermore, some students believed that project activities connected to their interest by providing space to express their personality. One student said that she liked creative projects that let her put her personality into the activity. She enjoyed designing, drawing, and coloring projects, as well as writing characters on her project products. By enabling such expressions, PBI engaged and motivated students to learning, thus solving the disciplinary issues in conventional teaching and learning activity.

Balancing PBI with Conventional Learning Activity

Reported outcomes of PBI show how students perceived PBI differently from activities in the compulsory mainstream schooling. Students characterized PBI as more fun, creative, diverse, relaxed and supportive of their understanding of Chinese culture and language learning. They referred to conventional arrangements for teach-

ing and learning as boring and less supportive of student learning interests and goals. Apparently, they preferred PBI to conventional learning activity. However, none of the students wanted to learn only through PBI in spite the benefits they articulated. Instead, they wanted to "keep the assignments" and "switch to projects for a change". They enjoyed balancing between traditional ways of teaching and learning and PBI. Through lessons and assignments they learned Chinese with regard to vocabulary, sentence structures and grammar rules, obtaining a good understanding of the language. Through projects, they learned about Chinese culture, new words and expressions for daily use. They also benefited from the opportunity to practice their language skills. It seems that the students are clear about what each learning activity brings to them. Despite the various benefits of participating in PBI, participation in and by itself does not "teach" basic language knowledge such as vocabulary, sentence structures and grammar rules as effectively as lectures do. Beckett (2005) and Eyring (1989) discovered that although most of the students demonstrated enthusiasm working on projects and enjoyed the process, some of them perceived PBI negatively, feeling that it did not provide space for them to learn basic linguistics knowledge. Instead, they preferred the conventional way of learning that focused on linguistic content, particularly vocabulary and grammar.

According to Beckett & Slater (2005), one explanation to the above is that students are unaware of learning that takes place in project activities. As students are used to following traditional ways of teaching and learning during which teachers teach what they need to learn, they find it hard to be confident and comfortable with the potential for learning in PBI. Another reason is due to the students' fear of autonomy and power as it appears in a student-centered learning approach. Because PBI involves students actively participating in research, gathering and analyzing data, they experience new demands for self-control, autonomy and responsibility for their learning process. By keeping up numerous learning activities, students acquire flexibility and ability to choose between a variety of designs for teaching and learning. Another explanation for some students' choices of keeping two learning approaches is that PBI provides more opportunities for students to practice the language that they find challenging. Students' preference for keeping conventional teaching and learning and PBI activity is a theme that demands for further investigation.

Contradictions in PBI Activity

Activity theory suggests that we study contradictions, dilemmas or dissonances between and among the components of the system. Subjects in PBI are mainly students who explore possibilities for self-control over their learning process, especially in unstructured projects designed by students themselves. Throughout the project activities, the teacher facilitated students' learning, providing guidance and keeping students focused on project tasks. However, based on the teacher observations, at the beginning of project activities, students experienced a hard time accepting the role of the teacher-facilitator rather than teacher-knowledge provider. When they encountered problems in projects, students often resorted to the teacher in their search for answers. One of the most frequent questions students asked was: "what is ##?" and "how do you say ## in Chinese?" These questions appeared when they came across new words or language they had learned but forgot. Yet now they were supposed to find out the expressions by themselves. PBI was but one of several teaching and learning activities in the class, so students had to shift between PBI activity system and traditional learning systems. As a result of switching back and forth, they sometimes became confused about the roles of the teacher-"is s/he a facilitator or a knowledge giver?" Previous studies also suggest that students had difficulty in accepting the teacher's new role. But they gradually got used

to it and eventually they took responsibility of their learning in PBI (Fragoulis, 2009; Gu, 2002).

In PBI, the major difficulty with projects encountered by students was how to overcome language issues. The constructs of the language and characters which can be considered as tools in PBI, were perceived by the learners as the greatest barrier to their learning outcomes. Students expressed in the interview that they really liked participation in projects, but doing projects in Chinese was a challenging task. Chinese sentence structure, character recognition and writing were frequently reported to be difficult tasks, especially for students at a high level of proficiency who were required to use Chinese often during the projects. All four of the students from the higher level of class stated that learning sentence structures and characters were challenging. One student said: "It's kind of hard for me to do projects because I don't get the sentence structures. Every time I work with something, it stays in my head". Other students felt it was difficult to put words in the right order because they found themselves first thinking in English and then translating ideas into Chinese. Two out of five students from the lower level class mentioned characters as barriers and one thinks it is sentence structures. As a consequence, the structure of the sentences was far from appropriate.

PBI was reported positively by students because of its authenticity of learning experiences and the language students are exposed to and use (Ke, 2010; Stoller, 2006) as well as the opportunity for students to think in target language (Beckett, 2005). In this study, most of the students indicated that it was challenging to use and think in Chinese to do projects, but they also pointed out that hard work resulted in valuable learning for them. Students emphasized the importance of tool skills (language proficiency) in a successful completion of a project. To help students adapt to project activities, future practitioners of PBI should consider teaching vocabulary and sentence structures of the projects. Teachers should ensure that students learn the prerequisites of language learning before they start a new project (Roblyer, Edwards, & Havriluk, 1997).

Objects refer to project activities such as selecting a topic, searching for information and writing a report. In comparison to unstructured projects organized by the students, they believed that structured projects designed by the teacher were more difficult. They liked projects designed and organized by them because they could explore things they were interested in and experience flexibility by doing the projects in their own way. The excerpt from one student in the interview puts it clearly:

I like the one assigned by ourselves. Because sometimes the projects that are assigned by the teacher could be kind of difficult even it is stuff we've already done. But getting the information needed and putting them to the PowerPoint is what is hard because we are used to doing our own assignments, making it in our own way and researching for information.

On the other hand, students admitted that selecting and designing their projects probably would not support the operations that help learning the language they need to learn. They can easily go off track when the teacher's guidance is missing. Structured, assigned and designed projects, however, teaches students knowledge they should know even though the tasks are challenging. Similar to their comments to contradictions between tool and outcome, they say projects assigned by the teacher are 'difficult but have a potential for learning'. They would like to do projects designed by themselves and by their teacher. In a way their preference illustrates an attitude towards balancing learning autonomy and teacher guidance. It further implies that teacher practitioners should incorporate both structured learning activities and unstructured activities, so that the students can acquire and practice new knowledge more effectively.

Transitions and Reorganizations

Tensions within the conventional learning activity system led to the adoption of PBI as a new approach. As noted earlier, some students misbehaved in class due to lack of motivation for learning emerging from repetitive assignments. If analyzed from a CHAT perspective, there was a harmful tension between tools and rules. Rules refer to refer to classroom norms and rules for student behaviours. Tools are the assignments that students were asked to complete as a way to practice and learn the language. The teacher discovered the mismatch between tools and rules, but the differences later on accelerated to tensions within subjects generating contradictions between the teacher and her students. The teacher reflected on the matter in her journal, recording that students browsed websites irrelevant to the lessons in class. They talked to each other when the teacher was lecturing and played online games or listened to music during assignments despite the teacher's warnings. From a multi-voiced perspective, this imbalance arises from the differences between the teacher and the students in terms of motives and beliefs. Chinese was an elective course that most of the students took with explorative expectations in mind. The teacher however initially overlooked students' intentions and put strong efforts on helping the students practicing the language with intensive assignments which could demotivate the students. This may result into misbehaviours of some students. In dealing with classroom management, the teacher felt frustrated as it overtook her role as instructor. According to CHAT's emphasis on social and cultural context, the teacher's educational and cultural background could shed light on her frustration. The teacher was mostly educated in a Confucian culture in which teachers are the evident authority with absolute and supreme respect from the students (Shi, 2006). The reverence with which a teacher is held is reflected in sayings such as "being a teacher for one day entitles one to a lifelong respect from the student that befits his father" (Hu, 2002, p. 98). The Confucian culture emphasizes respect for, obedience to and duty to the parents. This cultural description implies the authoritative role of a teacher. In such a culture, students are expected to behave with respect and politeness to a teacher. Cultural differences explain the struggles the teacher went through in experiencing lack of respect and the urge to earn respect from the students.

Additionally, there was the tension between the teacher (subject) and her school community. When students misbehaved, the teacher could report it to school (community) for help. She could also manage and solve problems on her own by talking to students or changing her teaching strategies so as to improve the relationship. Based on the teacher's reflective journal, it revealed that she would rather handle problems by herself. Reporting it to the school board would only result in isolation of the students in an alternative learning centre. Such a solution could not improve the establishment of a good relationship with the students. So instead of relying on the school community, the teacher attempted to manage issues of discipline by herself.

Contradictions also appeared between mediating tools and learning object/outcomes, a finding which has been suggested earlier in "balancing PBI with traditional learning activity". Students stated that the way they learned Chinese in conventional learning activity could not sustain their interests or meet their goals of learning to speak the language and understand the culture. The teacher found a similar problem, alerting her to the fact that the mediating tools did not meet her teaching goals. She noticed that students spent most of their time on computers attempting to finish their assignments, but they lacked opportunities to speak the language. Learning materials like e-textbooks and assignments focused on testing their memory for vocabulary and grammar rules. They failed to provide students with space to actively use the language or explore the culture. As such, the teaching tools were ineffective for building students' language communicative competence and cultural knowledge. From the teacher's perspective, all the components of a conventional learning activity system did not work out well for the parties. Tensions and imbalances within the teaching and learning activity caused the teacher to reflect and adjust her teaching approach by introducing PBI as a stimulus, a new tool to the system. Therefore implementation of PBI is a process of double stimulation in which the problematic situations within the traditional learning activity become first stimulus, urging the teacher to introduce PBI as the second stimulus (Engeström, 2007).

SOLUTIONS AND RECOMMENDATIONS

Studied contradictions and reorganizations demonstrate a process of internalization and externalization, which refer to subject(s)' understanding of contextual structures and processes in "organizing of external stimuli and using them to accomplish objective" (Leontev, 1981, p. 183). Externalization happens when participation in an activity causes individuals to transform their internal thought process. And these internal constructions result in individuals who shape the activity in which are engaged. The process begins with an exclusive emphasis on internalization, but when the disruptions and contradictions of the activity become challenging, internalization takes for the form of critical self-reflection and externalization in the subjects as their search for possible solutions increase (Engeström, 1999). Along with the process comes expansive learning (Engeström, et al, 2002, p. 216), that is, "learning what is not yet there by means of actions of questioning, modeling, and experimentation". In this sense, the diagnosis of classroom problems, planning and implementing of PBI to the classroom includes a cycle of expansive learning. There is yet another learning cycle foreseen if contradictions within a PBI activity are handled constructively.

Students suggested ways to improve PBI activity, one of which was to develop the students' language skills. Such efforts include learning of sentence structures and practicing Chinese characters in order to address the language difficulties that the students encountered in doing projects. While practicing their target language in a PBI project, the students noticed weakness in conducting dialogues, in their ability to write and memorize characters. So they wanted to learn about sentence structures and expressions, as well as words for daily use (Hilton-Hones, 1988).

I want to learn more about the sentence structures and the characters. I know the pinyin, but I need to learn more characters because if I go to China, there is no pinyin. So we need to learn a lot of characters so we can actually read it and use it.

In addition, the interviewed students reported that familiarity with vocabulary used for project tasks influence their PBI experience. It would appear less challenging for them if lessons and projects focused on the same language and information that they learned. Put differently, projects should be based on the content and words the students learn during lessons. Students also described the importance of availability of resources and of searching and collecting relevant information in the successful completion of projects. A few students said that it was hard to find information for their choice of topics. Some of them had to change their project topics due to limited information. They decided on certain projects when they knew that they could gather the information needed. Students hoped that the teacher was aware of the resources at hand when they design new projects. For example, one student experienced difficulty in finding the relevant information for his project.

I want to compare what Chinese people do in China and what we do. I want to see what the differences are and what would be the same. I

then switched it into just like Chinese traditions because I could not find specific things that most of Chinese people do every day. It is hard to find information.

Suggestions to improve PBI activities require further action from the students and the teacher. They also draw implications to teacher practitioner for future implementation and design of PBI in Chinese language teaching. Students in this study point out their needs for improvement of teaching and learning about sentence structure, character writing and recognition. This should draw teachers' attention to their teaching content and strategies to help students develop relevant linguistic abilities and knowledge required for carrying out project tasks. Future teacher practitioners also need to pay attention to students' knowledge and familiarity of vocabulary in designing projects as well as the availability of resources.

FUTURE RESEARCH DIRECTIONS

Students' and the teacher's experiences and perceptions of PBI demonstrate that the deployed "method" is a feasible and effective teaching and learning activity for learning Chinese as a foreign language. Findings of the study prove that PBI defined as a student-centered approach motivates and engages students in learning. PBI is a feasible teaching approach for Chinese language teachers to adopt in their teaching practice. Teachers seeking for a less teacher-centered approach in meeting students' needs and expectations will find PBI beneficial. However, this study is limited due to its nature of classroom-based case study. Care should be taken about how to apply these findings to other contexts. Future studies can investigate PBI in CFL classrooms or schools with different ethnic populations. Perhaps more broadly speaking, and as Beckett (2002, p. 64) suggests, research studies are needed to "examine implementation of project-based instruction at various levels of

L2 instruction in different contexts". This is true, especially with the case of CFL, as the interest and numbers of non-Chinese learners studying Chinese is a growing world-wide phenomenon (Wang & Higgins, 2008).

CONCLUSION

The findings of this study show that PBI motivates students' learning, improves their language skills and enhances their cultural knowledge. PBI provides students with opportunities to use the language instead of solely relying on language input that emphasizes memorization of the words and language constructs. Students perceived PBI to be more beneficial and supportive of their learning, at least in comparison with traditional lectures and activities. However, students did not think that PBI should replace traditional classroom activity, instead they sought for a balance between learning activity systems. They wanted to learn the basic linguistic knowledge from lectures and practice language as well as explore the Chinese culture with PBI. CHAT analysis reveals contradictions within PBI activity. For example, the language (characters and sentence structures) and computers were tools for helping students work on projects in PBI activity. At times those tools could become barriers to learning. In addition, students were reluctant to accept the role of the teacher as a facilitator in PBI, at least at the beginning of the project works. They had a hard time dealing with the shifting roles in two learning activity systems. These contradictions, especially tools functioning as barriers, point to a need for the students and the teacher to address such issues and make PBI a better learning experience.

More importantly, our findings demonstrated the contribution of CHAT in providing a unique perspective to understand students' and teachers' perceptions and experiences of PBI. It helped categorize complex learning phenomena, drew on aspects of an activity, and considered interac-

tions and contradictions between individual and contextual factors. In the current study, inductive analysis summarized the students' and the teacher's perceptions of PBI into binary perceptions of PBI in terms of benefits and difficulties. CHAT provided the author with a lens to examine types of benefits and difficulties. The author was able to find out how the PBI project design and implementation benefited and hindered students' learning. This aspect was achieved by breaking them down into various facets of an activity. Therefore future CHAT researchers may see the importance of paying explicit attention to the multiple facets that constitute the activity system, in order to construct and describe a profound understanding of the studied topic.

This study also adds to teacher research by demonstrating how classroom research enables the teacher to become a researcher and practitioner. Conducing classroom-based research helps the teacher reflect on her teaching, particularly with respect to pedagogies and instruction strategies. The teacher of this study felt confident with the implementation of PBI and her competence to deliver instruction in general. PBI helps the teacher understand the importance of teaching activity as part of the students' learning experience and for improving the teacher-student relationship. It broadens the teacher's repertoire by allowing her to try out new strategies and approaches in her teaching practice. The research experience with PBI helps the teacher become a better and more experienced teacher than she would otherwise be.

Methodologically, this study displays compatibility between CHAT and action research. The teacher practitioner diagnosed issues in her class, implemented PBI, and evaluated applications by following an action research procedure. Then she used CHAT to explore the meanings of preceding actions. Application of CHAT and action research connects a theoretical lens with practice. In addition, CHAT as a theoretical framework, works perfectly with action research methodology. The combination fully explains the action research cycle by analysis of tensions and transformations. This conclusion is grounded on the fact that both strands recognize and reflect the dynamic movement and conflicting nature of reality.

REFERENCES

Abrams, Z. I. (2002). Surfing to cross-cultural awareness: Using internet-mediated projects to explore cultural stereotypes. *Foreign Language Annals*, *35*(2), 141–153. doi:10.1111/j.1944-9720.2002.tb03151.x

An, K. (2006). An investigation of error correction in the zone of proximal development: Oral interaction with beginning learners of Chinese as a foreign language. *Dissertation Abstracts International. A, The Humanities and Social Sciences*, *67*(6), 2026–2027.

Baskerville, R. L., & Wood-Harper, A. T. (1996). A Critical Perspective on Action Research as a Method for Information Systems Research. *Journal of Information Technology*, *3*(11), 235–246. doi:10.1080/026839696345289

Bateman, B. (2002). Promoting openness toward culture learning: Ethnographic interviews for students of Spanish. *Modern Language Journal*, *86*(3), 318–331. doi:10.1111/1540-4781.00152

Beckett, G. H. (1999). *Project-based instruction in a Canadian school's ESL classes: Goals and evaluations*. (Unpublished doctoral dissertation). University of British Columbia, Canada.

Beckett, G. H. (2002). Teacher and student evaluations of project-based instruction. *TESL Canada Journal*, *19*(2), 52–66.

Beckett, G. H. (2005). Academic language and literacy socialization of secondary school Chinese immigrant students: Practices and perspectives. *Journal of Asian Pacific Communication*, *15*(1), 191–206. doi:10.1075/japc.15.1.12bec

Beckett, G. H. (2006). Beyond second language acquisition: Secondary school ESL teacher goals and actions for project-based instruction. In G. H. Beckett & P. Miller (Eds.), Project-based second and foreign language education: Past, present, and future (pp. 55-70). Greenwich, CT: Information Age Publishing, Inc.

Beckett, G. H., & Slater, T. (2005). The Project Framework: A tool for language and content integration. *The English Language Teaching Journal*, *59*(2), 108–116. doi:10.1093/eltj/cci024

Bibliography of Research on Chinese Language. (2008). *Education University of British Columbia Center for Research in Chinese Language and Literacy Education*. Retrieved from http://crclle.lled.educ.ubc.ca/bibliography.html

Borg, S. (2003). Teacher cognition in language teaching: A review of research on what language teachers think, know, believe and do. *Language Teaching*, *36*(2), 81–109. doi:10.1017/S0261444803001903

Burns, A. (1999). *Collaborative action research for English language teachers*. Cambridge, UK: Cambridge University Press.

Burns, A. (2005). Action research: An evolving paradigm? *Language Teaching*, *38*(02), 57–74. doi:10.1017/S0261444805002661

Chamot, A., Barnhardt, S., & Dirstine, S. (1998). *Conducting action research in the foreign language classroom*. Washington, DC: National Capital Language Resource Center.

Chu, C. (1990). Semantics and discourse in Chinese language instruction. *Journal of the Chinese Language Teachers'. Association*, *25*, 15–29.

Chu, C. (1990). Semantics and discourse in Chinese language instruction. *Journal of the Chinese Language Teachers'. Association*, *25*, 15–29.

Chu, M. (1990). Teaching Chinese as a functional language. *Journal of the Chinese Language Teachers Association, 25,* 93–96.

Coleman, J. A. (1992). Project-based learning, transferable skills, information technology and video. *Language Learning Journal, 5*(1), 35–37. doi:10.1080/09571739285200121

Daniels, H. (2004). Activity theory, discourse and Bernstein. *Educational Review, 56*(2), 121–123. doi:10.1080/0031910410001693218

Davydov, V. V. (1999). The content and unsolved problems of activity theory. In Y. Engeström, R. Miettinen, & R.-L. Punamaki (Eds.), Perspectives on activity theory. New York: Cambridge University Press.

Doherty, D., & Eyring, J. (2006). Instructor Experience with Project work in the Adult ESL classroom: A Case Study. In Project-Based Second and Foreign Language education: Past, present, and future. Greenwich, CT: Information Age Publishing.

Edge, J. (Ed.). (2001). *Action research. Case studies in TESOL practice.* Alexandria, VA: TESOL.

Eliam, G. (2003). The philosophical foundations of Alexander R. Luria's neuropsychology. *Science in Context, 16,* 551–577. PMID:15025065

Engeström, Y. (1999). Activity Theory and individual and social transformation. In Y. Engeström, R. Miettinen, & R. L. Punamäki (Eds.), Perspectives on Activity Theory (Learning in Doing: Social, Cognitive and Computational Perspectives). Cambridge, UK: Cambridge University Press.

Engeström, Y. (2007). Enriching the theory of expansive learning: Lessons from journeys toward coconfiguration. *Mind, Culture, and Activity, 14*(1-2), 23–39. doi:10.1080/10749030701307689

Engeström, Y., Engeström, R., & Suntio, A. (2002). Can a school community learn to master its own future? An activity-theoretical study of expansive learning among middle school teachers. In G. Wells & G. Claxton (Eds.), Learning for Life in the 21st Century: Sociocultural perspectives on the future of education. Oxford, UK: Blackwell.

Eyring, J. L. (1989). *Teacher experience and student responses in ESL project work instruction: A case study.* (Unpublished doctoral dissertation). University of California Los Angeles, Los Angeles, CA.

Eyring, J. L. (1997). *Is Project Work Worth It?.* Distributed by ERIC Clearinghouse.

Fragoulis, L. (2009). Project-Based Learning in the Teaching of English as A Foreign Language in Greek Primary Schools: From Theory to Practice. *English Language Teaching, 2*(3), 113–119.

Gardner, D. (1995). Student produced video documentary provides a real reason for using the target language. *Language Learning Journal, 12*(1), 54–56. doi:10.1080/09571739585200451

Gu, P. (2002). Effects of project-based CALL on Chinese EFL learners. *Asian Journal of English Language Teaching, 12,* 195–210.

Hatch, J. A. (2002). *Doing qualitative research in education settings.* Albany, NY: SUNY.

Hedge, T. (2002). *Teaching and learning in the language classroom.* Oxford, UK: OUP.

Henry, J. (1994). *Teaching through projects. Open and distance learning series.* London: Kogan Page.

Hilton-Jones, U. (1988). *Project-based learning for foreign students in an English-speaking environment* (Report No. FL017682). Washington, DC: US Department of Education.

Hu, G. (2002). Potential cultural resistance to pedagogical imports: The case of communicative language teaching in China. *Language, Culture and Curriculum*, *15*(2), 93–195. doi:10.1080/07908310208666636

Jin, H. G. (2005). Form-focused instruction and second language learning: Some pedagogical considerations and teaching techniques. *Journal of Chinese Language Teaching Association*, *40*(2), 43–66.

Ke, L. (2010). Project-based College English: An Approach to Teaching Non-English Majors. Chinese. *Journal of Applied Linguistics*, *33*(4), 99–112.

Lai, C., Zhao, Y., & Wang, J. (2011). Task-Based Language Teaching in Online Ab Initio Foreign Language Classrooms. *Modern Language Journal*, 9581–103.

Lee, I. (2002). Project work made easy in the English classroom. *Canadian Modern Language Review*, *59*, 282–290. doi:10.3138/cmlr.59.2.282

Leontev, A. N. (1981). *Problems of the development of the mind*. Moscow: Progress Publisher.

Levine, G. S. (2004). Global simulation: A student-centered, task-based format for intermediate foreign language courses. *Foreign Language Annals*, *37*(1), 26–36. doi:10.1111/j.1944-9720.2004.tb02170.x

Lin, C. T. (2009). *Chinese Guest Teacher Program*. Paper presented at New York College Board. New York, NY.

Lu, M. (2012). *Using the learners-as-ethnographers approach to enhance intercultural learning among American college students learning Chinese as a foreign language* (dissertation). Retrieved from http://search.proquest.com/docview/1038368174?accountid=2909. (1038368174).

McDonell, W. (1992). The role of teacher in the cooperative learning classroom. In C. Kessler (Ed.), Cooperative Language Learning: A Teacher's Resources Book. Englewood Cliffs, NJ: Prentice Hall Regents.

McGroarty, M. (1989). The benefits of cooperative learning arrangements in second language instruction. *Journal of the National Association for Bilingual Education*, *13*, 127–143.

McNiff, J., & Whitehead, J. (2006). *All You Need To Know About Action Research*. London: SAGE Publications.

Mertler, C. A., & Charles, C. M. (2008). *Introduction to educational research*. Boston: Allyn & Bacon.

Nolen, A. L., & Putten, J. V. (2007). Action research in education: Addressing gaps in ethical principles and practices. *Educational Researcher*, *36*(7), 401–407. doi:10.3102/0013189X07309629

Nussbaumer, D. (2012). An overview of cultural historical activity theory (CHAT) use in classroom research 2000 to 2009. *Educational Review*, *64*(1), 37–55. doi:10.1080/00131911.2011.553947

Roblyer, M. D., Edwards, J., & Havriluk, M. A. (1997). *Integrating educational technology into teaching*. Upper Saddle River, NJ: Prentice-Hall.

Roth, W.-M., & Lee, Y.-J. (2007). Vygotsky's Neglected Legacy: Cultural-Historical Activity Theory. *Review of Educational Research*, *77*(2), 186–232. doi:10.3102/0034654306298273

Schrier, L. L. (1993). Prospects for the professionalization of foreign language teaching. In *Developing language teachers for a changing world*. Lincolnwood, IL: National Textbook.

Shi, L. (2006). The successors to Confucianism or a new generation? A questionnaire study on Chinese students' culture of learning English. *Language, Culture and Curriculum*, *19*(1), 122–147. doi:10.1080/07908310608668758

Stesenko, A. (2003). Alexander Luria and the cultural historical activity theory: Pieces for the history of an outstanding collaborative project in psychology. *Mind, Culture, and Activity*, *10*(1), 93–97. doi:10.1207/S15327884MCA1001_10

Stoller, F. (2006). Establishing a theoretical foundation for project-based learning in second and foreign language contexts. In G. H. Beckett & P. C. Miller (Eds.), Project-Based Second and Foreign Language education: Past, present, and future (pp. 19-40). Greenwich, CT: Information Age Publishing.

Stoller, F. L. (1997). Project work: A means to promote language content. *English Teaching Forum*, *35*(4), 2-9.

Suter, W. N. (2006). *Introduction to educational research: A critical thinking approach*. Thousand Oaks, CA: Sage.

Wallace, M. (1991). *Training foreign language teachers*. Cambridge, UK: Cambridge University Press.

Wang, L., & Higgins, L. T. (2008). Mandarin teaching in the UK in 2007: A brief report of teachers' and learners' views. *Language Learning Journal*, *36*(1), 91–96. doi:10.1080/09571730801988504

Wang, S. C. (2007). Building societal capital, Chinese in the US. *Language Policy*, *6*(1), 27–52. doi:10.1007/s10993-006-9043-2

Wen, X. (2009). Teaching listening and speaking: An interactive approach. In M. E. Everson & Y. Xiao (Eds.), Teaching Chinese as a Foreign Language. Boston: Cheng & Tsui.

Wu, S., & Meng, L. (2010). The integration of inter-culture education into intensive reading teaching for English majors through Project-based Learning. *US-China Foreign Language*, *8*(9), 26–37.

Zhang, L. (2004). Stepping carefully into designing computer-assisted learning activities. *Journal of Chinese Language Teaching Association*, *39*(2), 35–48.

Zhao, H., & Huang, J. (2010). China's Policy of Chinese as a Foreign Language and the Use of Overseas Confucius Institutes. *Educational Research for Policy and Practice*, *9*(2), 127–142. doi:10.1007/s10671-009-9078-1

ADDITIONAL READING

Brown, A. (2009). Students' and teachers' perceptions of effective foreign language teaching: A comparison of ideals. *Modern Language Journal*, *93*(1), 46–60. doi:10.1111/j.1540-4781.2009.00827.x

Burton, J. (1997). Sustaining Language Teachers as Researchers of Their Own Practice. *Canadian Modern Language Review*, *54*(1), 84–109. doi:10.3138/cmlr.54.1.84

Dick, B. (2002). Postgraduate programs using action research. *The Learning Organization*, *9*(4), 159–170. doi:10.1108/09696470210428886

Duff, P. (2008). Issues in Chinese language teaching and teacher development. P. Duff, & P. Lester (Eds.). *Issues in Chinese Language Education and Teacher Development*. Selected Papers from the Shanghai Symposium, 5-48.

Dunn, A. H. (2011). Global village versus culture shock: The recruitment and preparation of international teachers for U.S. urban schools. *Urban Education*, *46*(6), 1379–1410. doi:10.1177/0042085911413152

Engeström, Y. (2001). Making expansive decisions: An activity theoretical study of practitioners building collaborative medical care for children. K. M. Allwood & M. Selart (Eds.), Creative decision making in the social world. Amsterdam: Kluwer.

Fox, R., & Diaz-Greenberg, R. (2006). Culture, Multiculturalism, and foreign/world language standards in U.S. teacher preparation programs: Towards a discourse of dissonance. *European Journal of Teacher Education, 29*(3), 401–422. doi:10.1080/02619760600795270

Haley, M., & Ferro, M. S. (2011). Understanding the Perceptions of Arabic and Chinese Teachers Toward Transitioning into U.S. Schools. *Foreign Language Annals, 44*(2), 289–307. doi:10.1111/j.1944-9720.2011.01136.x

Haley, M. H., Midgely, A., Ortiz, J., Romano, T., Ashworth, L., & Seewald, A. (2005). Teacher Action Research in Foreign Language Classrooms: Four Teachers Tell Their Stories. *Current Issues in Education, 8*(12). Retrieved from 17/05/2007 http://cie.ed.asu.edu/volume8/number12/

Horwitz, E. K. (2005). Classroom Management for Teachers of Japanese and Other Foreign Languages. *Foreign Language Annals, 38*(1), 56–64. doi:10.1111/j.1944-9720.2005.tb02453.x

Hutchison, C. B. (2005). *Teaching in America: A Cross-Cultural Guide for International Teachers and Their Employers.* Dordrecht, Netherlands: Springer.

Linnell, J. D. (2001). Chinese as a second/foreign language teaching and research: Changing classroom contexts and teacher choices. *Language Teaching Research, 5*(1), 54–81.

Noffke, S. E., & Somekh, B. (Eds.). (2009). *The Sage Handbook of Educational Action Research.* Los Angeles, London: Sage Publications.

Nunan, D. (1989). *Understanding language classrooms: a guide for teacher-initiated action.* New York: Prentice Hall.

Shoring, N. (1995). Project work: Why should you include it in your teaching program? *Australian Science Teachers Journal, 41*(3), 28–29.

Somekh, B., & Nissen, M. (2011). Cultural-Historical Activity Theory and Action Research. Introduction to Special Issue. *Mind, Culture, and Activity, 18*(2), 93–97. doi:10.1080/10749039.2010.523102

Sowa, P. (2009). Understanding our learners and developing reflective practice: Conducting action research with English language learners. *Teaching and Teacher Education, 25*(8), 1026–1032. doi:10.1016/j.tate.2009.04.008

Stoecker, R. (2005). *Research Methods for Community Change: A Project-Based Approach.* London: Sage Publications.

Stuart, K. (2012). Narratives and activity theory as reflective tools in action research. *Educational Action Research, 20*(3), 439–453. doi:10.1080/09650792.2012.697663

Wang, S. C. (2012). Sustaining the Rapidly Expanding Chinese Language Field. *Journal of the Chinese Language Teachers Association, 47*(3), 19–41.

Weiss, T., & Feldman, A. (2010). Understanding change in teachers' ways of being through collaborative action research: A cultural–historical activity theory analysis. *Educational Action Research, 18*(1), 29–55. doi:10.1080/09650790903484517

William, R. P., & Barbara, M. (1999). Observing classroom processes in project-based learning using multimedia: A tool for evaluators. *The Secretary's Conference on Educational Technology.*

Zhang, G. X., & Li, L. M. (2010). Chinese language teaching in the UK: Present and future. *Language Learning Journal, 38*(1), 87–97. doi:10.1080/09571731003620689

KEY TERMS AND DEFINITIONS

Chinese as a Foreign/Second Language: The situation that Chinese is not the native language or official language used in people's daily lives. It is a subjects taught at school or learned by personal preference. Chinese as a foreign language (CFL) is different from Chinese defined as a second language (CSL). The latter represents the context where Chinese is a means of communication used in people's daily lives.

Classroom-Based Action Research: A type of educational action research in which practicing teachers act as researchers in the classroom. Through systematic and reflective inquiry, teacher researchers aim at addressing problems and finding solutions to issues of a particular aspect of teaching and learning.

Contradictions in PBI Activity: Within the PBI activity system, there are negative experiences of and contradictions between components in the learning activity. For example, there are hidden dilemmas between projects assigned by the teacher and designed by students (contradiction between subject and object), confusion about the teacher's role as facilitator and knowledge-provider (contradiction between subjects and division of labor), and difficulty with language (contradiction between tool and outcome).

Conventional/Traditional Learning Activity: The teaching and learning situation before adoption of PBI is a learning activity system in which lectures and assignments are the main teaching methods/tools. This activity system co-exists with PBI activity when the latter was applied.

Critical Languages: Refers to less commonly taught languages such as Arabic, Chinese, Japanese, Korean and Russian.

Language Flagship: A U.S. national language program that offers, supports and funds language education from Kindergarten to higher education. Flagship languages include critical languages such as Arabic, Chinese, Hindi and Urdu, Korean, Persian, Portuguese, Russian, Swahili and Turkish.

Project-Based Instruction: A student-centered method for socializing students into language learning through projects. PBI activity is a term for representing PBI as a teaching and learning activity system that includes the basics of activity system such as subject, object, outcome, tools and other key characteristics of CHAT.

Chapter 8
Outdoor Science in Teacher Education

Oleg Popov
Umeå University, Sweden

ABSTRACT

This chapter is an account of the development of prospective teachers' competence to conduct outdoor science education. At the Department of Science and Mathematics Education, the students participate in outdoor education courses. They also plan, manage, and evaluate outdoor lessons designed as assignments in science education, participation in school practice, and summer courses. Many student teachers evaluate and analyse the pedagogical aspects of outdoor science when they carry out research projects in schools for their graduation thesis work. In order to understand the activity of science teaching and learning outdoors, a qualitative study was conducted. It was based on interviews with teacher educators and included studies of students' examination papers. A Cultural Historical Activity Theory (CHAT) lens was applied to the study. The theoretical framework helped to identify the prospective teachers' abilities and skills to design, implement, and evaluate tasks related to the professional competence of delivering outdoor science activities.

INTRODUCTION

Teaching and learning outdoors has a long educational history. Traditionally, the main forms of such outdoor activities are associated with fieldwork and outdoor educational visits, particularly in relation to the biological and geo-sciences (Dillon et al., 2006). The potential of natural settings and open air environments for science teaching has been actively explored by researchers and teacher educators around the world. For a review of the literature see Dillon et al. (2006) and

Tilling and Dillon (2007). Some educators have even expressed the conviction that "the future of school science lies outdoors" (Slingsby, 2006, p. 51). However, while there is a broad agreement that field studies are a laudable and form a necessary part of science education, Tilling and Dillon (2007) suggest that there is a decline in outdoor educational activities. Science studies in many schools and teacher education institutions are almost exclusively limited to indoor activities.

The situation can be partly explained by science teachers' low interest in organising outdoor lessons. This came as a consequence of their

DOI: 10.4018/978-1-4666-6603-0.ch008

poorly developed pedagogical competence to conduct educational work outside the classroom. The situation is likely to become even worse if teacher education does not prepare prospective teachers for such work, as is often the case. Traditionally, science teachers are trained to teach in the classroom, in the computer room or in the laboratory. It is logical to assume that transfer of teaching from indoors to outdoors activities can be a problem. These issues need further investigation. What can be learned from teacher education institutions that systematically try to develop outdoor teaching competence?

In order for the reader to understand the findings presented in this chapter, we need to say some words about the current situation with regard to science teacher education. The situation at our university reflects the dynamics of the situation at national and global level. Over the last decade experienced science teacher educators have noticed a decrease in the preparedness, interest and motivation to study science by the students enrolling on the courses for prospective primary and secondary school teachers. This lack of interest has led to a reduction in the breadth and depth of content and methods of science given in teacher education. When students are offered elective courses in science they tend to avoid choosing them. However, outdoor education courses go against this trend. They still attract many applicants in spite of the heavy weight of science. The department has a long tradition of training prospective teachers in outdoor pedagogy. Outdoor studies are conducted in different forms and on different occasions, such as science course assignments, school practice, diploma work projects, activities with school children visiting the university campus, and on master degree courses. Usually, outdoor educational experiences receive very positive participant evaluations. Student teachers learn to recognize learning opportunities in the world around them. They learn to discover science as a means to explain natural phenomena while being in the natural environment.

Teachers' ability to teach constitutes the core of their professional competence. In this study we began by conceptualizing teacher competence. We used a definition developed by Döhrmann, Kaiser and Blömeke (2012) in a Teacher Education and Development Study in Mathematics (TEDS-M). Then we expanded on their project. They suggested that professional competence includes cognitive as well as affective-motivational aspects. Cognitive abilities are founded on a combination of subject knowledge and pedagogical knowledge. Affective-motivational characteristics include professional beliefs, motivation and meta-cognitive abilities such as self-regulation. We felt that practical ability or embodied knowledge of practical outdoor experiences should be added to the classification offered by Döhrmann, et al. (2012) particularly for a description of science teachers' professional competence. In order to illustrate this contention, we would like to ask the reader to consider the case of boarding a canoe for a study trip on a lake. Motivation and theoretical knowledge are important, but the practical experience of keeping balance when stepping into the canoe will be decisive for initiating this activity without getting wet. Practical ability is usually meaningful and of course strongly context-bound.

This chapter aims to explore some aspects of prospective science teachers' professional competence that could with advantage be developed in an outdoor context. The role of context in science education is increasingly attracting the attention of researchers. This is reflected in recent academic publications (Lee, Wu, Tsai, 2013; Hansson, 2015). Nonetheless, the use of an outdoor context for training prospective science teachers remains an area with potential for further educational research and development of pedagogical practice.

Situated outdoor science teaching can be investigated with advantage through the theoretical lens of Cultural Historical Activity Theory (CHAT). This theoretical approach has been found to be productive since many outdoor educational projects deploy the principles and theoretical constructs of CHAT in the design, implementation and discussion of outdoor practices. The potential of CHAT for developing science education has recently been explored by several researchers (Giest & Lompscher, 2003, Roth, Lee & Hsu, 2009). Application of CHAT also helped us make some pedagogical deliberations about the particularities of teaching and learning in an outdoor context.

THEORETICAL FRAMEWORK

Cultural Historical Activity Theory is particularly concerned with the understanding of different kinds of human activity and the effects of proactively changing the context of activity in order to transform practice (Roth et al, 2009). In this study we focus on developing an understanding of how different aspects of prospective science teachers' competence could be constructed in an outdoor context. The importance of context operating as an active component of the learning process that interplays with learner's and teacher's activities was suggested by Vygotsky (1978). Following his line of thought, we focused on developing our understanding of how to study the laws and properties of nature in natural settings. Also, the context of active social interactions can strengthen prospective science teachers' professional competence. Undoubtedly, the main challenge of the teaching profession is to teach students how to learn, or in Cultural Historical Activity Theory terms, to organise productive learning activities in school.

According to Leont'ev (1981), the first and most fundamental form of human activity is external, practical, collaborative activity that is internalised later in human thought. Another fundamental claim of CHAT is that human activity can be understood only if we take into consideration the mediating artefacts (technical and cognitive tools) that mediate any activity (Leont'ev, 1981). In outdoor science teaching, investigation techniques or skills of scientific inquiry are artefacts of particular significance. They include observing, measuring, classifying, hypothesizing, etc. Important technical and cognitive tools are also different kinds of models.

CHAT suggests that the development of generic cognitive skills can be stimulated by properly organized learning activities. Kinard and Kozulin (2008, p. 25) say: "The learning activity includes *orientation* in the presented material, *transformation* of the presented material into a *problem*, *planning* the problem-solving process, *reflection* on chosen strategy and problem-solving means, as well as *self-evaluation*". When doing outdoor science, the content of learning is the acquisition of knowledge (embodied in learning objects) about properties and laws of nature. According to CHAT, the goals and motives of learning are considered the key components of learning activities. Leont'ev (1981) emphasised that the motive of learning determines the sense of the concrete learning activity. In general, learning activity is about learning to learn (Claxton, 2002) which is decisive in modern society (Friedman, 2007). In teacher education, the goal of learning activity is moreover about learning to teach, i.e. to develop teachers' professional competence. In our case, this ambition includes introducing student teachers to the experiences and intellectual challenges of outdoor learning and reflection on how to organise similar activities with their classes of students in the future.

As a unit of analysis in this study, we chose an activity oriented to developing prospective teachers' outdoor science education competence. We intend to develop the students' ability to conduct science studies in an outdoor context. Structurally, outdoor learning activities consist of *goal oriented actions* for solving particular tasks related to learning in an outdoor context.

METHODS

A qualitative study was carried out at Umeå University in 2013. The data collection was organized through an analysis of ten students' research project reports carried out at the Department of Science and Mathematics Education. It also included semi-structured interviews with five teacher educators. Convenience sampling was used in the selection of informants and data. Analysis of the student teachers' reports gave insight into the students' visions and the practice of the outdoor lesson designs. We learnt about the students' perceptions of the particularities of working in an outdoor educational context. All the student reports had been defended at the department over the last ten years. Our interviews focused on prospective teachers' learning and their learning to teach outdoors.

All of the teacher educators interviewed have been teaching outdoor courses for several years. They have also served as supervisors of the analyzed student teacher projects. The language of the interviews was Swedish. The interviews lasted from 45 to 60 minutes, they were tape-recorded and later some transcripts were translated into English. Validation of the interviews was carried out through follow-up discussions with the interviewees.

In the process of data analysis, the findings were thematically grouped and summarized. Quotations were used to exemplify the character of each group. In this way, categories of responses were generated. The results of the study are presented in a rather aggregated form with regard to sources of information, e.g. we avoid articulating which group of informants highlighted a particular theme. On the one hand this is done because students' projects are usually developed in tight collaboration with supervisors and therefore based on shared ideas. On the other hand, students often refer to and reflect on their own experiences of attending teacher education courses in their examination project reports.

The theoretical framework also contributed to the identification of themes during the process of data analysis. CHAT methodology highlights the role of contextual factors and mediating tools in the process of the realization of specific tasks. A review of current CHAT literature helped to achieve an understanding of the issues discussed in this chapter, such as empowerment of student teachers learning how to teach in complex and changing outdoor environment.

LEARNING TO TEACH SCIENCE OUTDOORS

We attempt to provide an analysis of findings concerning prospective teachers' learning to work with science outdoors. Different pedagogical considerations arose from the data collected in the light of a Cultural Historical Activity Theory perspective. Four headings relate to the conceptual issues of competence, context, learning activity and mediation.

Expanding a Zone of Teacher Competence Construction

Initial teacher education provides a variety of learning opportunities for construction of professional competence. An outdoor context could potentially be an optimal zone for learning, but unfortunately it is also a most challenging zone. Not only does new knowledge come true there, but previously acquired knowledge is also challenged by practical applications. Outdoor practical activities were reported to provide an opportunity for prospective teachers to make sense of their prior scientific knowledge acquired through formal and informal education.

In general, one of the fundamental features of teachers' professional competence is considered to be the ability to relate subject knowledge to knowledge associated with practical pedagogy. In order to clarify enhancement of students learning,

Lucas (2007) with reference to Bernstein talks about this as a problem of "recontextualization". His outline suggests that decontextualized academic subject knowledge needs to be related to the context-bound experiential knowledge that learners bring to the scene. The latter includes what in science education is called everyday knowledge or learners' pre-conceptions. Issues related to methods for connecting theoretical (decontextualized) knowledge to practical (context-bound) knowledge in outdoor education was discussed in several student projects.

Furthermore, the interviewed teacher educators reflected on the decrease in space and time for laboratory practice available for prospective science teachers. There is a tendency for practical work in sciences to become infrequent and to be used mainly to illustrate previously leaned theories. The real nature of experiment as a source of scientific knowledge and provider of significant evidence about the veracity of scientific assumptions has become obscured. In that sense, science-directed practical activities outdoors can elucidate different aspects of the nature of science. Such perceptions are important to consider for a competent science teacher. This issue will be discussed in detail.

In the courses which contain an outdoor component, prospective teachers had the possibility to experience the learning potential that exists within and between contexts. They could learn to expand their pedagogical repertoire by contrasting and comparing contextual influences on their learning, development and competence. Teacher educators and colleagues in the study group possessed and exercised a broad collective expertise of acting in a variety of contexts. Students' reflections on the multiple pedagogical opportunities provided by varying contextual conditions allowed them to see the potential for expanding their professional competence. Here some features of teacher competence were related to contextual changes. It is a relevant question to ask how an outdoor context can help expand the teachers' zone of professional development.

Contextual Influences

Changing the educational context from indoors to outdoors activities can lead to new patterns of social relations among the students and between the teacher and the students. These affective changes were identified in many school projects. Learners could show new aspects of their personality during outdoor activities. Outdoor behaviours were in contrast to their usual behaviour shown in the classroom. These changes were rather complex and apparently they depended on many factors. It is worth mentioning that the outdoor context challenged the prospective teachers to learn to manage dynamic group relationships and gender roles in different age groups. They also became aware of the development of emotional, behavioural, social and other non-cognitive competencies, all of which are important for successful science education.

The entire pedagogical process is influenced by changes in the learning environment. Both categories of informants reflected on the importance for learners to develop the *competences of seeing and foreseeing contextual influences*. These are related, for example, to consideration of the structure and properties of context and the complexity of the phenomena embedded in it. The absence of 'walls and a roof' to frame learning changes the 'initial and boundary conditions' for solving the pedagogical tasks posed by the teacher. Different kinds of *uncertainty* characterise the open-air learning environment. We could distinguish reflection about the presence of fuzzy uncertainty as it appears in facts, assumptions and descriptions of natural objects or phenomena. We could also distinguish stochastic uncertainty as it appears in the occurrence of phenomena and their repeatability. Teacher educators and student teachers reported both of these as valid influences in/on an outdoor context. The teacher educators also mentioned effects of *transferability* – what is learned out of the classroom is easier to apply for the learners in an out-of-school context.

Another important component of outdoor education competence could be called the *ability to respond to the context*. Students teachers learn to know themselves through the new context. They gain confidence to find, design and manage outdoors practical activities for different weather conditions. However, it takes time "for experience to reach the head", as one teacher educator formulated it, meaning such a basic thing as to learn to dress properly in order to avoid freezing, making routine controls of equipment in advance, etc. These routines are important aspects of building the prospective teachers' professional competence.

Outdoor science activities were reported to demand the use of cooperative learning. Many of them proved to be too complex to be dealt with individually. Collective activities in turn foster communication, group discussions and decision-making. The power of collaboration proves itself by empowering individual student learning. However, participation in collective activities allows for individual assessment demanded by the teacher education curriculum. Conducting individual monitoring of progress, diagnostics and final outdoor assessments was reported as a demanding task by the teacher educators. One way of carrying out individual assessment in the studied reports was to have certain students closely monitored throughout each session and to register the students' summative reflections at the end of each outdoor session.

Informants have also drawn our attention to other challenges in the outdoor context. Normally, people are used to being outdoors, mainly for recreation, sports and leisure. But they rarely go outdoors for learning. Therefore, they have to learn to learn outdoors. To a certain degree this also concerns the necessary schooling-in phase for prospective teachers when they start their outdoor courses. Placement of learning activities in a new context demands a new kind of orientation from the teachers. Learners have to learn to consider the outdoors as an educational environment.

Findings show that organization and structuring of outdoor teaching and learning demands implementation of rather advanced organisational and leadership skills. The informants also mentioned that in order to design outdoor science education activities, they would have to manage and coordinate interplay between *narrow-local micro-*, *intermediate meso-* and *comprehensive global-macro* levels of context:

- Learning environment, individual teacher, student group, actual space, time and tasks
- Institutional policy, leadership, curriculum and culture
- Supra-institutional, national socio-cultural and politico-economical frames.

The teacher educators and the student teachers in their rapports expressed concerns that educational authorities at meso- and macro-levels provide less active support for outdoor education than they did ten years ago. This support was more obvious in the previous curriculum for schools and teacher education. The student teachers' reports show that the local school context, traditions and culture strongly influence the organisation of outdoor science studies. They discourage or encourage the teachers' initiatives in conducting outdoor projects. The student teachers also reflected on the relationship between the local and global context. They raised concerns about the importance of knowing and using the social, cultural and historical dimensions of the local context and the necessity of critically connecting it to the global context, in particular if regarded from a scientific-ecological perspective.

Identifying and Delimitating the Object of a Learning Activity

The informants underlined that science content teaching outdoors is often a more pedagogically demanding job than is traditional indoors education. Natural phenomena and objects in real life contexts seldom provide obvious "hints" or explicit suggestions concerning what and how to study.

At least if compared with rather obvious-transparent support offered by a laboratory setting. Laboratory environment is designed for science exercises and provides many explicit and implicit suggestions about science principles that can be discovered and studied there. In contrast to indoor settings, clear instructions and teacher guidance are often needed in the process of identifying *learning objects* (science content) outdoors. Studying science outdoors demands the consistent elimination of "noise" in the form of insignificant or disturbing features. What constitutes "noise" in any particular case? What should be taken out of consideration in order to build a model that helps to understand a phenomenon? In order to answer these questions learners need carefully designed "scaffolding" to assist the development of their scientific reasoning and Modeling skills.

Consider the case of a warm air balloon. Mechanical, thermal and chemical effects have very complex interplay there. Depending on the aim of study certain features become more important than others. So, the student teachers learn to "eliminate noise" from the complex reality of outdoors in order to formulate "solvable problems". They develop *problem-construction competency* by learning to build and study models of physical reality. Using CHAT terminology we can also say that they learn to identify the *content* of the learning activity.

Informants noted that planning the study of a phenomenon, such as resistance of air, could often be more difficult than planning measurement of an object, such as for example the weight of a stone. The task of selecting what property to measure is normally more explicit in the study of the object like a stone than it is in the study of a phenomenon like resistance of air. An appropriate model needs to be created to reflect the phenomenon being studied. To do so, the students have to be able to handle a variety of cognitive artefacts and Modelling tools. They also need to develop

an ability to stay committed to solving a task for a longer period of time. The extended time span proved to be problematic for some students.

Prospective teachers have to be prepared to work with authentic problems that arise in everyday life. In the students' research projects (Sverin, 2011) several types of authentic problems were explored. There were tasks without a single right answer - open ended problems. There were tasks varying with changing environmental circumstances, for example depending on weather conditions. And there were tasks that demanded preliminary agreement about what is to be found out or measured. Sverin (2011, p. 52) found that at an initial phase of working with authentic tasks "the students had difficulties to formulate solvable problems, because they were used to working with closed, end-of-chapter problems with given answers. They did not perform any preparatory work at home to be able to identify and formulate solvable problems." Criteria for framing authentic problems were discussed before classes and lectures as well as a choice of criteria for identifying what accounts for an acceptable answer. Nevertheless, high school students needed close guidance when working with authentic tasks and elements of scientific inquiry in order to succeed.

It is relevant to highlight findings about making and overcoming mistakes. Usually, outdoor tasks allow several correct solutions. Outdoor tasks provide an opportunity to investigate and practice genuine scientific inquiry. The students learn to try out ideas, make mistakes and learn to accept that mistakes are a natural part of the learning process. Also included in the process is systematic reflection and self-evaluation. Probing plausible suggestions, eventually making mistakes and overcoming them, which are typical features of any scientific activity, become a natural part of learning that prospective teachers learn to deal with and value.

Student teachers had to learn to learn outdoors pedagogy and to develop competence to teach others to learn in an outdoor context. In most of the outdoor courses they practiced the design of school-oriented learning tasks. The tasks included leading their future students in different search directions, formulating "solvable" problems, finding out alternative solutions, discussing and choosing the most appropriate tasks for provoking deep discussions.

New Tools and New Roles for the Tools That Mediate Learning

People use a variety of mediating artefacts that shape the ways they think and act. They are physical instruments as well as symbolic and cognitive meaning-making tools. Regardless if taken together or individually they mediate investigations, reflective actions and communication. Glasgow, Cheyne and Yerrick (2010, p. 48) describe mediated processes of inquiry in science: "Scientists use their background knowledge of principles, concepts and theories, along with scientific process skills, to construct explanations for natural phenomena to allow them to understand the natural world." Mental and manipulative skills serve as important tools in the culture of understanding and advancing science. These are investigation techniques, science process skills and generic tools of scientific inquiry. This section of the chapter provides illustrations based on collected data, describing how physical and mental artefacts adapted for outdoors in science education could be used.

As a means to stimulate learning in their school projects, the student teachers used physical artefacts of large dimensions such as cable drums, cars and barrels. The saying that "size matters" proved to be legitimate starting point especially when learners have the possibility to explore physical phenomena outside their classroom walls. For example, for the study of torque in the physics course the following investigation with a sewing spool is usually suggested: "If the thread leaves the spool from the bottom of the axle when gently pulled, would the spool move forward or backward?" This experiment, when adapted to the outdoor environment using a rope and a large sized cable drum, gave an informative visual effect and provoked active discussions.

Disposable materials such as soft drink plastic bottles have been widely used as tools for science teaching around the world. Launching a water-rocket is probably one of the most popular science education activities conducted outdoors. The Internet and Google search engine offers millions of hits if you search "water rocket". Even primary school students can change different parameters prior to launching a rocket. They cover e.g. the proportion of water and air in the bottle. They have excellent opportunities to influence and observe plastic bottle rocket's flying capacity.

Several prospective teachers have reflected on and designed projects based on an experiential learning approach. They explore how outdoor learning can be assisted by direct bodily contact with surrounding natural objects. For example, feeling the force of air-resistance through an open car window gives first-hand experience and facilitates understanding of the physical properties of air. The human body itself becomes a tool of learning and remembering. People use different properties and parts of the human body for practical estimations and measurements. Historically, such knowledge has developed in different cultures when the need arose to know distances, compare and observe changes. However, human bodies as data collecting devices have limitations in a variety of ways. As an example, inaccuracies in measuring the speed of sound propagation, by seeing a flash and hearing the sound of a distant explosion, depend on individual reaction times. To gain personal experience of what it means to take exact measurements was found to be of great methodological value for the students.

As mentioned, science process skills such as measurements and estimations are important mediating artefacts of science learning activities. Conducting a measurement task outdoors can be more demanding than when it is conducted indoors. Consequently the studied informants elaborated extensively on this issue. Changes in environmental conditions like wind, humidity and sunshine influences the precision of measurements and make the reproducibility of experimental conditions and results far more problematic than if conducted in a corresponding laboratory setting. The outdoor context provides rich opportunity for reflection on precision, error and uncertainty in taking measurements. The importance of considering uncertainties becomes apparent and visible if conducted in such circumstances. Braund and Reiss (2006, p. 218) state that science out-of-classroom provides the possibility to introduce the 'messiness of science' through authentic practical work. When different groups of students measure the same object using the same method or different methods and get varying results – there is an opportunity to discuss general principles of taking measurements in science.

Generic skills of estimations are very important in the practice of science. This was underlined by famous scientists like Richard Feynman (Gleick 1992). When conducting outdoor experiments students had to choose apparatus and measuring devices with an appropriate scale. Therefore, the need arises to plan and think ahead of time and estimate what values and magnitudes can be expected to be measured in an experiment. It is only then that the students will have an opportunity to note whether their choices and predictions corresponded to reality. They may also discuss the nature of any discrepancies noticed. So, taking measurements outdoors present practical and intellectual challenges to the students. Finding an attractive way to teach precision and errors in measurements has always been a challenge for science educators but work in outdoor settings provides an opportunity to analyze and discuss these issues.

Time to learn is an important pedagogical tool. Observations, experiments and investigations in an outdoor environment often demand a special kind of studies. This quality supplies a potential pedagogical advantage but also an administrative challenge. The teacher educators considered the extended time of students' engagement in learning activities as a positive factor –"learning takes time!" However, they also recognized potential difficulties in making the necessary class-schedule arrangements in schools that require administrative support.

CONCLUSION

Modern society demands citizens with the ability to learn how to learn (Claxton, 2002). According to Friedman (2007) this contention implies several mental operations and practical abilities.

… to constantly absorb, and teach yourself, new ways of doing old thing or new ways of doing new things. […] it is not only what you know but how you learn that will set you apart. Because what you know today will be out-of-date sooner than you think. (p. 309)

From a CHAT perspective the need to learn-to-learn suggests that school systems, head teachers and teachers should focus on the systematic formation of learning activities that enable students to learn independently and efficiently (Giest & Lompscher, 2003). The uncertainty and complexity of the context shaping science learning outdoors is of course a model of the real life uncertainties and complexities that students have to learn to deal with. The ability to adjust pedagogical actions to "fluid" learning contexts is an important feature of teachers' competence. In the same way that there cannot be a universal size of clothing for all children there is no universal teaching method that suits all learners all the time. It is however possible to consider the rationale of transferring science learning outdoors as a Modelling process that assist prospective teachers in their attempts at developing the ability to adjust their actions to a new or changing learning environment. Our findings show that learning activities outdoors provide rich and relevant experience corresponding to the demands of complex modern life with many in-built uncertainties. The OECD Core Competencies Framework defines personal attributes and skills enabling delivery of a role/job in a modern workplace. They develop in outdoor science education and they constitute an important part of teachers' professional competence:

- *Flexible thinking* involves the ability to adapt to a variety of situations, individuals or groups effectively.
- *Analytical thinking* is the ability to identify patterns between situations that are not obviously related and to identify key or underlying issues in complex situations.
- *Drafting Skills* is based on the ability to communicate respectfully ideas and often technical information in writing to ensure that information and messages are understood and have the desired impact.
- *Teamwork and team leadership* implies working cooperatively with others, be a part of a team, and assume the role of leader of a team.
- *Achievement focus* means generating results by assuming responsibility for one's performance and the correctness of one's interventions, recognising opportunities and acting efficiently, at the appropriate moment and within the given deadlines.

The student teachers' projects organised in schools covered the use of different mediating artefacts, investigative techniques, science process skills and generic tools of scientific inquiry. Such artefacts are important tools for managing outdoor science as well as for developing the learners' mental tools for future needs. The student teachers realized the important role played by the context in studying nature directly in natural settings. Their projects allowed for studying practical activities with a joint collaborative enactment of a shared goal.

Arguments about the importance of expanding science education to include outdoor settings always balanced the request for *complementarity* of indoor and outdoor teaching approaches. This combination allows discovery of different aspects of the students' learning potential and provides them with rich learning opportunities. Teaching science outdoors develops the learner's abilities to observe, ask, presume, verify and conduct a critical analysis of data. These skills of critical thinking are important in many professional activities, including student teachers' and teacher students' lessons. However, learners need guidance and collaboration in acquiring investigative techniques and critical thinking skills. The teacher can guide the students' work by suggesting learning tasks and monitoring the inquiry process based on their background and capabilities (Popov & Tevel, 2007). The complexity of real world situations demands that the teacher takes on the role of a researcher and partner for the students rather than a possessor of the right answers.

The natural environment provides genuine opportunities for meaningful learning based on a combination of minds-on and hands-on activities, but it also requires additional preparation and carefully designed pre-, in- and post-field work to make outdoor learning activities productive. In Claxton's (2002, p. 29) words: "environments 'afford' resources, but these resources do not become functional aids to intelligent learning unless they are perceived as such by the learner." Kinard and Kozulin (2007) describe elements that constitute the core of learning activity: analysis of the task, planning of action, and reflection. They define reflection as a "trademark" of an approach focusing on development of learning to learn. The teacher educators of this study agreed with this, one of them saying: "Activity without reflection is meaningless, reflection without activity is empty. They should be in symbiosis. We always give feedback on students' reflections. This is a constitutive part of our profession."

In summarizing the findings, one can add that outdoor activities can generate a feeling of empowerment in prospective science teachers, providing confidence and understanding of science processes when working in the expanded learning context. They develop the ability to use a broad range of mediating artefacts of learning and an open-minded approach to the study of natural objects and phenomena. Group work, team building, collective learning and the context of active social interactions proved to be a solid basis for outdoor education.

The primary distinguishing characteristic of the learning activity is that its main expected outcome is development of the subject of the activity – the learner. Outdoor science broadens learning opportunities and provides individual learning challenges for every student. Outdoor science also constitutes a zone for developing teacher professional competence. A teacher with the confidence to work in an outdoor context succeeds in organising meaningful science learning activities. This is a finding which lies in line with how CHAT conceives of a teacher. del Rio and Álvares (2002, p. 72) say s/he is an: "architect of meaning" who is capable of "bringing together physical and mental action, affectively as well as intellectually charged, and socially as well as instrumentally mediated". We hope that the pedagogical aspects of outdoor educational work presented in this chapter can lead to the further empirical and theoretical development of science teachers' professional competence.

REFERENCES

Braund, M., & Reiss, M. (2006). Validity and worth in the science curriculum: Learning school science outside the laboratory. *Curriculum Journal, 17*(3), 213–228. doi:10.1080/09585170600909662

Claxton, G. (2002). Education for the learning age: a sociocultural approach to learning to learn. In G. Wells & C. Claxton (Eds.), Learning for Life in the 21st Century: Sociocultural Perspectives on the Future of Education. Blackwell Publishing.

Davydov, V. V. (1990). Types of Generalisation in Instruction. In Soviet studies in mathematics education (Vol. 2). Reston, VA: National Council of Teachers of Mathematics.

del Rio, P., & Álvares, A. (2002). From activity to directivity: the question of involvement in education. In G. Wells & C. Claxton (Eds.), *Learning for Life in the 21st Century. Sociocultural Perspectives on the Future of Education* (pp. 59–72). Oxford, UK: Blackwell Publishing. doi:10.1002/9780470753545.ch5

Dillon, J., Rickinson, M., Teamey, K., Morris, M., Choi, M. Y., Sanders, D., & Benefield, P. (2006). The value of outdoor learning: Evidence from research in the UK and elsewhere. *The School Science Review, 87*(320), 107.

Döhrmann, M., Kaiser, G., & Blömeke, S. (2012). The conceptualisation of mathematics competencies in the international teacher education study TEDS-M. *ZDM Mathematics Education, 44*(3), 325–340. doi:10.1007/s11858-012-0432-z

Forsgren, T., & Johansson, R. (2004). *Fysikundervisning utomhus. (Unpublished undergraduate thesis).* Umeå University, Umeå, Sweden.

Foster, S. (1989). Streetwise physics. *The School Science Review, 70*(254), 15–17.

Friedman, T. (2007). *The World is Flat: A Brief History of the Twenty-first Century.* New York, NY: Farrar, Straus and Giroux.

Giest, H., & Lompscher, J. (2003). Formation of learning activity and theoretical thinking in science teaching. In A. Kozulin, B. Gindis, V. S. Ageyev, & S. M. Miller (Eds.), Vygotsky's Educational Theory in Cultural Context. Cambridge, UK: Cambridge University Press.

Glasgow, N. A., Cheyne, M., & Yerrick, R. K. (2010). *What Successful Science Teachers Do: 75 Research-Based Strategies*. Thousand Oaks, CA: Corwin Press Inc.

Gleick, J. (1992). *Genius: The Life and Science of Richard Feynman*. New York, NY: Pantheon Books.

Hansson, T. (2014). Modeling and analyzing contextual influences. In T. Hansson (Ed.), Contemporary Approaches to Activity Theory: Interdisciplinary Perspectives on Human Behavior. Hershey, PA: IGI Global.

Kinard, J., & Kozulin, A. (2008). *Rigorous Mathematical Thinking: Conceptual Formation in the Mathematics Classroom*. Cambridge, UK: Cambridge University Press. doi:10.1017/CBO9780511814655

Lee, M.-H., Wu, Y.-T., & Tsai, C.-C. (2013). Research trends in science education from 2003 to 2007: A content analysis of publications in selected journals. *International Journal of Science Education*, *31*(15), 1999–2020. doi:10.1080/09500690802314876

Leont'ev, A. N. (1981). The problem of activity in psychology. In J.Wertsch (Ed.), The Concept of Activity in Soviet Psychology (pp. 7-71). New York, NY: M.E. Sharpe Inc.

Lucas, N. (2007). Rethinking initial teacher education for further education teachers: From standards-led to a knowledge-based approach. *Teaching Education*, *18*(2), 93–106. doi:10.1080/10476210701325077

Markström, P., & Cedergren, A. (2005). *Praktisk fysik i grundskolans tidigare år. (Unpublished undergraduate thesis)*. Umeå University, Umeå, Sweden.

Nilsson, P., Pendril, A.-M., & Pettersson, H. (2006). Learning physics with the body. In R. Janiuk & E. Samonek-Miciuk (Eds.), Science and Technology Education of a Diverse World: Dilemmas, Needs and Partnerships. Lublin, Poland: Marie Curie-Sklodowska University Press.

OECD Competency Framework. (n.d.). Retrieved February 25, 2014, from http://www.oecd.org/careers/oecd%20level%201_v1.pdf

Popov, O., & Tevel, I. (2007). Developing prospective physics teachers' skill of independent experimental work using outdoors approach. *Baltic Journal of Science Education*, *6*(1), 47–57.

Roth, W.-M., Lee, Y.-J., & Hsu, P.-L. (2009). A tool for changing the world: Possibilities of cultural-historical activity theory to reinvigorate science education. *Studies in Science Education*, *45*(2), 131–167. doi:10.1080/03057260903142269

Slingsby. (2006). The future of school science lies outdoors. *Journal of Biological Education*, *40*(2), 51-52.

Stetsenko, A. (2005). Activity as object-related: Resolving the dichotomy of individual and collective planes of activity. *Mind, Culture, and Activity*, *12*(1), 70–88. doi:10.1207/s15327884mca1201_6

Sverin, T. (2011). *Open-ended problems in physics: Upper secondary technical program students' ways of approaching outdoor physics problems* (Student research paper). Umeå Universitet.

Tilling, S., & Dillon, J. (2007). *Initial Teacher Education and the Outdoor Classroom: Standards for the Future: A Report on the Training of Pre-Service Teachers to Support the Development of Outdoor Teaching in Secondary Science Education. Field Studies Council*. Association for Science Education.

Vygotsky, L. S. (1978). *Mind and Society*. Cambridge, MA: Harvard University Press.

ADDITIONAL READING

Arievitch, I. M., & Haenen, P. P. (2010). Connecting Sociocultural theory and educational practice: Galperin's approach. *Educational Psychologist, 40*(3), 155–165. doi:10.1207/s15326985ep4003_2

Chaiklin, S., & Hedegaard, M. (2013). *Cultural-historical Theory and Educational Practice: Some Radical-local Considerations*. Nuances: estudos sobre Educação, Presidente Prudente, SP, v. 24, n. 1, p. 30-44, Retrieved June 6, 2014, from http://revista.fct.unesp.br/index.php/Nuances/article/viewFile/2151/chaiklin

Cole, M., & Engeström, Y. (2007). Cultural-historical approaches to designing for development. J. Valsiner, A. Rosa (Eds.) The Cambridge Handbook of Sociocultural Psychology. Cambridge university press.

Davydov, V. V. (1999). What is real learning activity? M. Hedegaard, J. Lompscher, (Eds.). Learning Activity and Development. Aarhus, Denmark: Aarhus University Press, 123-138.

Davydov, V. V. (2008). *Problems of Developmental Instruction: A Theoretical and Experimental Psychological Study*. Hauppauge, NY: Nova Science. (Original work published 1986)

Engeström, Y., & Miettinen, R. (1999). Activity Theory a well-kept secret. Y. Engeström, R. Miettinen & R. L. Punamäki (Eds.). Perspectives on Activity Theory. (1-16). USA: Cambridge University Press.

Friedman, T. L. (2007). *The World is Flat: A Brief History of the Twenty-frist Century*. USA: Farrar, Straus and Giroux.

Garner, R. (1990). When children and adults do not use learning strategies: Towards a theory of settings. *Review of Educational Research, 60*(4), 517–529. doi:10.3102/00346543060004517

Hattie, J., Marsh, H. W., Neill, J. T., & Richards, G. E. (1997). Adventure Education and Outward Bound: Out-of-class experiences that have a lasting effect. *Review of Educational Research, 67*(1), 43–87. doi:10.3102/00346543067001043

Kaptelinin, V., & Nardi, B. A. (2006). *Acting with Technology: Activity Theory and Interaction Design*. USA: MIT Press.

Kozulin, A. (2003). Psychological tools and mediated learning. A. Kozulin, B. Gindis, V. S. Ageyev & S. M. Miller (Eds.). Vygotsky's Educational Theory in Cultural Context (15-38). USA: Cambridge University Press.

Lompscher, J. (1999). Learning activity and its formation: ascending from the abstract to the concrete. M. Hedegaard, & J. Lompscher, (Eds.). Learning Activity and Development. Aarhus, Denmark: Aarhus University Press, 139-166.

Martin, P. (2008). Teacher qualification guidelines, ecological literacy and outdoor education. Australian. *Journal of Outdoor Education, 2*(2), 32–38. http://www.latrobe.edu.au/education/downloads/martin_p_Ecologicla-literacy-and-OE.pdf Retrieved June 6, 2013

Minner, D. D., Levy, A. J., & Century, J. (2010). Inquiry-based science instruction – what is it and does it matter? Results from a research synthesis years 1984 to 2002. *Journal of Research in Science Teaching, 47*(4), 474–496. doi:10.1002/tea.20347

Neill, J. T. (2008). *Enhancing Life Effectiveness: The Impacts of Outdoor Education Programs. University of Western Sydney*. Retrieved from 06/06/2013 http://www.ervaringsleren-nederland.nl/documents/experiental%20learning%20NEILL%202008.pdf

Peck, C. A., Gallucci, C., Sloan, T., & Lippincott, A. (2009). Organizational learning and program renewal in teaching education: A socio-cultural theory of learning, innovation and change. *Educational Research Review*, 4(1), 16–25. doi:10.1016/j.edurev.2008.06.001

Popov, O. (2006). Developing outdoor activities and a website as resources to stimulate learning physics in teacher education. *Journal of Physics Teacher Education Online*, 3(3), 18–24.

Popov, O., & Engh, R. (2013). *Exploring pedagogical potential of outdoor context in teaching physics for prospective primary and secondary school teachers*. Paper presented at International Conference of the Outdoor Learning Environment. 3-8 February 2013, Weizmann Institute of Science, Israel.

Steele, A. (2011). Beyond contradiction: Exploring the work of secondary science teachers as they embed environmental education in curricula. *International Journal of Environmental and Science Education*, 6(1), 1–22.

Stetsenko, A., & Arievitch, I. M. (2004). The self in Cultural-Historical Activity Theory: Reclaiming the Unity of social and individual dimensions of human development. *Theory & Psychology*, 14(4), 475–503. doi:10.1177/0959354304044921

Talyzina, N. F. (1988). The modern state of the activity theory of learning. M. Hildebrand-Nilshon & G. Ruckriem. (Eds.) *Proceedings of the 1st International Congress on Activity Theory*. Berlin, 1986, 1, 219 – 227.

van Parreren, C. (1986). Development through instruction. E. Bol, J.P.P. Haenen & M.A. Wolters (Eds.). *Education for Cognitive Development*. Proceedings of the Third International Symposium of Activity Theory. Den Haag: SVO/SOO, 38 – 46.

Wells, G. (2003). Inquiry as an orientation for learning, teaching and teacher education. G. Wells & C. Claxton (Eds.). Learning for Life in the 21st Century. Sociocultural Perspectives on the Future of Education. Blackwell Publishing. Oxford. 197-210.

Wertsch, J. V. (1991). *Voices of the Mind. A Sociocultural Approach to Mediated Action*. Cambridge, Massachusetts: Harvard University Press.

Zuckerman, G. (2004). Development of reflection through learning activity. *European Journal of Psychology of Education*, 19(1), 9–18. doi:10.1007/BF03173234

KEY TERMS AND DEFINITIONS

Competence: The ability of a person to reach specific achievements in order to be considered successful in the corresponding community of practice. It consists of cognitive, interactive, affective and practical capabilities and also attitudes and values, which are required for carrying out tasks and solving problems.

Cultural Historical Activity Theory: A theory of human development that sees human societies and their individual members as mutually constitutive. Personal development is shaped by the process of enculturation and individuals' thoughts and deeds serve to maintain or to alter the cultural milieu. At the heart of CHAT is therefore a tension between education as enculturation and education for autonomy and originality.

Learning Activity: An activity that has learning as a goal and also attached to the concept is an expected outcome. Learning activity involves transformation of the material by learners. The concept implies that new knowledge develops, involving appropriation of generalised ways of acting.

Mediating Artefacts: The tools that people use and that shape the ways they think and act. These could be physical objects as well as symbolic and cognitive meaning-making tools that mediate communication and reflective actions.

Outdoor Context: Out-of-classroom open-air environments where natural and social dimensions are intertwined.

Outdoor Science Education Competence: An expression of the ability to teach and facilitate science learning in an outdoor context. Valued by different educational actors, experience of practical outdoor activities is essential in this respect.

Prospective Teachers: Are student teachers enrolled in a teacher education program for primary and secondary school.

Chapter 9
Creative Musical Practice in an Educational Context

Anna Linge
Kristianstad University College, Sweden

ABSTRACT

This chapter is based on the author's doctoral thesis. She provides an account of a project on creativity in music education, more specifically a musical classroom for developing creativity. The aim of the study is to find examples or mechanisms of creative pedagogy. This study complements the current tradition for studying methods in teaching and learning music. Creative, prescriptive, and communicative designs of teaching and learning interact during sessions of music making. The empirical findings enable a discussion of the conditions that define creative music making as art and/or play as a socio-cultural activity.

INTRODUCTION

My interest in research on creative education is based on personal experiences as a music teacher - that is, through education and practice. I started investigating music making practices by considering why and how creativity and motivation took place in teaching and learning of music. According to Craft (2003), education should plan for creative activity to take place (Linge, 2013). In current organization of teaching, teachers can be very creative during the planning phase, far more so than during application and/or evaluation. Education should support creative thinking and skilled performance, for example by means of border-line crossing exercises and surprising activities. Schools are supposed to foster *creative*

ability by means of risk-taking, collective intelligence, fantasy and cooperation (Hargreaves, 2004; Robinson, 2010). Creativity can be found at many levels of educational practices, fulfilling several functions. The fact that schools prepare students for creativity later in life shows the need to define types and levels of creativity.

The term *mini-c*, where the 'c' stands for creativity, is connected to creative ability in students that develop socio-culturally at school. In contrast, the term *Pro-C* defines creativity which develops through practice-oriented environments. Valuable contributions to participatory learning happen outside schools (Kaufman & Beghetto, 2009). *Creative competency* defined as expertise at many levels under labels such as *little-c* and *Big-C* (Kupferberg, 2003; Welch, 1998). The col-

DOI: 10.4018/978-1-4666-6603-0.ch009

lective historical development of music education differs from the development of *creative ability* in the professional artist. Individual perception of the mission of an activity and the situated context influence the development of creative activity.

BACKGROUND

Music education focuses on dealing with efficient methods as means to achieve fixed moral ends and technical skills. For a long time musical literacy was considered a measure of how to interpret the concept of musical works of art correctly (Goer, 1992; Green, 1997; Small, 1998; Wolf, 1987). This stand meant that musical activity developed from being a basic social skill to becoming an object of art expressed through the musical text or sheet music. The current shift into post-modernity or *pre-modernity* means that functions that used to hold modernity together erodes and fall to pieces (Carr, 2006). In music education, the shift could become fruitful because people emphasize and adopt a genuinely natural attitude towards musical interaction. For example, Green (2008) and Regelski (2007) found such development in traditional African music making (Kwami, 2001; Westerlund, 2002). Green (2008) found sociologically relevant informal learning processes going on and expanding musical acculturation outside school.

It is reasonable for music education to encourage creative 'knowledge-in-action' (Elliot, 1995) and defining music as activity-based *musicing* (Small, 1998). This would be a wise move for students, musicians, audience or staff in any interactive context. The role of the teacher will shift from transmission of knowledge to *flexibility and creativity*. For this to happen, musical practices must find ways to stimulate reflection bacause only then teachers can become aware of things they need to change. But even so, music educators catch sight of things they consider relevant in relation to their perceived mission. They see how teaching fills a social function and also satisfies needs like

creativity and flexibility. Practice-related problem solving innovation requires new ways of thinking and acting (Regelski & Gates, 1999; Popov, 2014). One way to deal with challenges is to reflect on relations between developmentyal practices and theoretical development. Reconciling qualities and relations between practice and theory, however, is a classic problem frequently discussed in the educational literature. Finding the form of meeting in music making could benefit from reflection on both. Practices developed through an advanced course provide an opportunity to develop teaching and learning processes that will eventually strengthen existing experience and development of the students' autonomy. Ax and Ponte (2008) say: "The environment gives form to the teacher to develop skills towards a profile of routine or improvisation. The complexity of the task and the need of change make more use for flexibility and improvisation." Through critical reflection, teachers challenge the taken-for-granted way of doing things, providing access to their professionalism as teachers and musicians.

A relevant objective for research is to explore phases in music educational practice that make the creative teaching didactically explicit. This is a combined effort at understanding the music teachers' knowledge and validating this author's ability to make correct observations. Clarity of approach is crucial because music education suffers from a sad history of regarding music making as a stabilizing cultural transmission and conservation of a limited number of qualities (Jorgensen, 2003). Critical music teacher researchers like Regelski (2009) deplore the fact that people consider music education to be an independently valuable activity. It is important to see that individual music teachers are unaware of how their curricula is rooted in collective practices. Music education as a social phenomenon is just as often separated from the surrounding context. Therefore it is important to understand how music defined as both a phenomenon and an activity flourishes in many social practices. Music education serves different cultures included in larger practices (Regelski, 2009). Also, the post modern musical landscape is chancing and hence supports a flexile pedagogy.

The Swedish society of musical culture has supported The great tradition which historically consists of classical Western music. jazz, folk music and popular music have moved towards a common center and tody those genres are included in higher music education. New media have made a major impact on the music repertoire. The traditional relationship between the musical master and the apprentice may now well be nothing more than a recording on the Internet (Lundberg et al, 2000; Georgii-Hemming & Kvarnhall, 2011).

TEACHING AND LEARNING MUSIC: PROCESS OR PRODUCT?

There are traditional problems and choices in aesthetic and musical learning, e.g. every teacher must choose and focus on the product or process in crative teaching and learning. From a socio-cultural point of view, the activity around an object or artefact is crucial for communication, learning and development. Also in pragmatism and in Dewey's work called *Art as Experience* (1934), the value of the art lies in the quality of the experiment surrounding the object, here termed the process. In pedagogy the musical artefact or object has been regarded as a culturally valuable item which people reproduce in a complicated creative learning process. The choice between focusing on reproducing the product and exploring it through a creative process in teaching music separates schools of *formalism* from schools of *praxialism*. Seen from a formalist view, Reimer (2003) believes that music defined as form or product should focus on musical instruction. That would be a way to add valuable qualities add achieve cultural stability. Even more so focusing on the quality of form can contribute to cultural change. Praxialism (Elliot, 1995) emphasizes the authentic music-making process, defining it as a

way to construct musical knowledge. In contrast to this view, Reimer (2003) believes that musical processes and musical products form interdependent units of analysis. Westerlund (2002), though, reminds us to take into account claims of power that shape musical production and education, driving musical products and processes in specific directions.

According to Kratus (1990), musical creativity is an exclusive product of its creator, whereas the creative process and the creative product are independent units of analysis which change with instruction, objective and people. The participatory activity of music making offers many options. Creative processes evolve between teacher and students, and also between the students themselves, and the artefact created in school - as re-interpretations of previous work. Evaluation of the music making process is based on how the students perform and complete their assignments rather than if they have been creative enough. Another way to look at music education, also related to process and product, is to recognize what motivates people to learn to play in socio-cultural settings as opposed to formally arranged musical activity.

FORMAL AND INFORMAL LEARNING

People who learn to play music are motivated by socio-culturally situated and instrinsically motivating factors. Can teaching and learning at school make musical activity as motivating as among peers and other significant musical practitioners, masters and role models? In music education, Folkestad (2008) diuscusses the difference between informal and formal teaching and learning of musical ability. Clarifying relations between natural settings and school settings is a task for educational praxis to discuss. Because musical activity is a diverse global phenomenon, analysis should provide relevant and consistent conclusions about how we understand the subject of teaching and learning. Green (2008) has taken this assignment onboard and developed informal methods of supporting formal teaching and learning. Development of pedagogical praxis includes provision of help, support and scaffolding, but only when absolutely necessary. Students work the same way as popular musicians would do: collaborating, supporting and helping one another and promoting a creative atmosphere. But Green's (ibid) invisible teaching method has met with criticism. For example, informal learning could mean that the activity is teacher-led. At other times teaching and learning is a formal activity, regardless if the students are working independently or with a teacher. Formal and informal teaching and learning is a continuum variously positioned between poles. Informal learning focuses on the act of *playing* and formal learning focuses on *how* people play music. Informal methods of musical creation outside or inside school take on more or less formalized shapes, all depending on whether the environment focuses on *how to* play or on the *activity of playing* (Allsup, 2008; Folkestad, 2006, 2008; Saar, 1999). Another way to separate musical education from education in other subjects suggests that in order to develop expert knowledge, the teacher can expand assimilated day-to-day knowledge with the help of formal learning methods (North, 2008). In teaching a creative ability like music making, teachers and students must be able to switch between formal and informal practices (of teaching and learning) because creativity is dependent on knowing technically *how* to *play* as well as mastering the informal activity of *playing*.

ANALYTICAL CONCEPTS FOR STUDYING ACTIVITY

Activity theory is a suitable method and a theoretical perspective for examining musical teaching and learning. Activity theory originates from Georg W. F. Hegel (1770-1831) and Karl Marx (1818-1883).

They claimed that life is in constant transformation. For Marx the process is based on a materialistic view of the world. Knutagård (2003) says Marx regarded the object (alternatively artefact) of an activity as the central criterion for collective and individual coperation, and this point was further developed in the socio-cultural school or theory. Lev Vygotsky (1895-1934), Alexei Leontev (1903-1979), and Alexander Luria (1902-1977) represent the Russian socio-cultural theoretical school. According to theory, people live and act in a variety of contexts.

Individuals experience of difficulties that affect the socio-cultural structures as (historically) defined phenomena. Communication in contexts, via activity systems, and in practice fields involves the use of objects, utensils and various symbol systems. An object, such as the meaning of a term, appears accordingly to the activity surrounding it. Activity systems evolve over time and bears evidence of a specifically developed use of a tool based on historical roots (Cole & Wertsch, 1996). Engeström (1999) argues that contemporary Vygotskian research fails to sufficient attention to the historical process in the individual agents mind and the specific context. The historical perspective is lost in Vygotsky's texts because they were written under the Marxist-Leninist view of history and time. This problem causes a lack of understanding for the differences between practices and cultures of historical development. According to Engeström (ibid.) people wrongly believe that all cognitive systems, symbols and tools are equivalent. What constitutes a learner's development, learning and understanding of content is a generalized process with historical and cultural significance. Activities that develop in individual practices form a basis for development of appropriate tools. Any collective activity system must cover for analysis from individual and historical perspectives. Engeström (1999) says Vygotsky saw the use of artefacts as functionally separate from how we react to other humans. By acquiring specific tools, the ability to think develops. Engeström (ibid.) claims that socio-cultural research is chiefly concerned with the internalization of already given cultural tools as opposed to such tools that children to create themselves.

Engeström (1999) divides the learning process into stages of *internalization* and *creative externalization*. Internalization is the phase in which an individual learns the rules and routines of work through social participation. The creative externalizing phase describes learning resulting in a capacity for self-reflection (Johansson, 2014). When a student or a person learns to play a musical instrument, informally or formally, he or she takes part of the collective wisdom and knowledge that has developed (with) the artefact. In this case the very process has becom what Engeström (1987) calls a *conceptual tool*. Knowledge mediates between generations, and continues within the individual's thought, mind, and lifetime (Säljö, 2000; Wertsch, 1998). Cole and Engeström (1993) describe elementary cognitive processes taking place inside the individual; although higher cognitive functions require socio-cultural stimulation, thinking is a socially transmitted skill. Cole and Engeström (ibid) argue that conceptual tools and symbols are cultural artefacts, inspiring, actualizing and supporting processes going outwards and inwards, i.e., between people interpersonal and inside people's heads intrapersonal operations. Because the tools or artefacts have cultural significance, Engeström (1999) considers them to be socially organized behaviors of an activity. As such they are crucial for learning processes and outcomes. In such sought after settings, educators practice cultural transmission or conduct cultural creative exploration, to practice and achieve both results (Cole & Engeström, 1993). Mediation of conceptual tools can result in what Wertsch (1998) terms *mastery*, *i.e.* a result of learning which is distant from personal adaption and cultural innovation. Learning which expands the learners' previous expectations is called *appropriation* (ibid). Musical patterns, symbols or tools have

significance for humans only if situated in a socio-cultural context. The small child learns to recognize culturally specific phrasing and similar musical elements. And from an early age the child develops pictorial representations of what he or she perceives of as musical quality (Sloboda, 2005).

Tools for Studying Music

This section describes how Vygotsky's (1925/1971) theory of inner images interacts with cognition and the ability to influence man's choice between options. Vygotsky (ibid.) emphasizes the importance of creative arts for intellectual selection and growth. The function of art conveying emotions is valuable to human development and cognition. According to Vygotsky, an object of art must contain qualities that have potential to transform and generalize a personal experience with other people's experiences in the same cultural environment. Vygotsky's concept of quality requires common rules of interpretation for studying any context. Hence, the criticism which Vygotsky's conception of qualitative art encounters claims that cultural canons are problematic. In line with socio-cultural theory, production and understanding of art as well as perceptions of quality are contextually embedded (Smagorinsky, 2011). Vygotsky's term *perezhivanie* describes how emotional experiences in art frame identity and cognition. The emotions that the context evokes provide a deepening of cognitions. This crucial process is also present in everyday thinking between citizens. Vygotsky (1925/1971) criticizes over-reliance on reason and rationality on the grounds that creative arts reinforce emotions, alter human potentials for learning, create balance between man and environment and they organize people's socio-cultural behaviour, personality-wise and neuro-psychologically. Vygotsky (1995) discusses how everything created is represented as well in our imaginations as in the world because imagination breeds on external needs. The product of imagination becomes part of reality and the surrounding culture. In this way, man reproduces culture by innovative actions. These creative actions relate to our ability to adapt to conditions and circumstances, a vital characteristic of what it means to be human. Vygotsky (ibid) believes that our creative ability is the ground for artistic, technical and scientific creation. All inventions are preceded by perception and past experience. Man has an ability to draw on previous experiences, a need for imagination and creativity often has its origin in collective activity. Imagination helps the brain go beyond lived experiences. The relationship between fantasy and a reality represents a higher form of thinking. Imagination broadens experience and people gain experiences based on imagination. Through internal images, man portrays music, visual stimulations and literary works of art. Vygotsky (ibid) differentiates between affection and association. Affections are connections in loose form, and associations make up intellectually perceived impressions reflecting similarity of thoughts and objects. To Vygotsky, music is affection and affections help people choose between options. This broadening and deepening of emotions and its artistic transformation forms a psychological basis for defining music as an art form. Vygotsky (1995) says music gives form to feeling and extends it. Experiences of various musical forms resemble experiences of the world, and the feelings and past experiences related to music turn into an internalizing process. What is perceived of as straightforward impressions in the sensory world is given great importance in the emotional world if conveyed as music. Vygotsky claims that creative ability is based on the senses in a procedure he terms *dissociation and association,* concepts that resemble convergent and divergent thinking. Dissociation processes fragment reality of one or few aspects of what the brain is looking for. This feature is important in art and science. Association is the subsequent remaking of the dissociated item. Everything is related to the need to adapt to an environment where different needs arise. Here

Vygotsky stresses the need to stimulate thinking in pictures and analogous thinking emerging from past experience. If a person is restricted in development of imagination, this can have a serious impact on his or her creative ability. To create something without an external model presupposes a strong ability to imagine how things should, could and/or would appear. Imagination is plastic when it is based on external appearances. It is emotionally laden inside the subject's head when based on inner expression. The teenager is balancing between functions of imagination, impression and externalization. To train people's imagination is important for human development and behaviour (ibid).

Problem Description and Purpose of the Study; Performance and Creativity

In socio-cultural theory, the creative process and activity around social objects or physical materials are significant for learning. Musical education focusing on the product as well as the creative process stresses the role of instruction for balancing between performance and creativity. Educational performativity aims at preparing the students to act and play according to a specific musical role which is culturally defined and traditionally transferred between master and apprentice. Performance is connected to teaching that nurtures a given musical role. Such teaching and learning aim at generating uniformity of the musical product (Brinkman, 2010). The tradition of transmission between teacher and students consequently requires variation with a transformative, creative socio-cultural pedagogy where emotions facilitate cognition and result in knowledge, an outcome which strengthens students' self-confidence and appropriation. It is important that the teacher is willing to balance the teaching of performance against/with inspiring creativity, the acknowledged skill of a professional teacher (Burnard & White, 2008). Hence music pedagogy from a societal perspective develops either through a controlled and creative focus (Hargreaves & North, 1997) or through contradictions between performativity and creativity (Burnard & White, 2008). It is important to construct an educational environment that results in creative habits and abilities because the arrangement provides the student as performer with the skill to switch between performativity and creativity when necessary (Burnard & White, 2008; Kratus, 1990).

Project Description and Method

Linge (2013) builds a methodical framework on critical realism (Danermark, 2003; Sayer, 1992). According to critical realism, social science research should search for understanding that goes beyond the obvious and connect observations to a firm theoretical foundation. Understanding a phenomenon like creative music education is always coincidental, as are the underlying mechanisms that connect at various times within cultural structures of the studied phenomenon. Here, these structures offer instructional choices or other cultural factors that influence musical education. They are often hidden from casual observation, and they become discernable through the researcher's use of analytical tools. The purpose of my studies is to find out what chatracterizes creative music education? There are research questions attached to the purpose of the study: What mechanisms contribute to authentic problem solving in musical pedagogical practice; What mechanisms combine to form a technical internalization with transformative learning; What mechanisms combine external and internal motivations for a creative musical education?

On three occasions a group of a total of five music-teacher colleagues met for group interviews discussing creative musical learning. At the first meeting, five music teachers attended during a one-hour call. At the second meeting, five music teachers attended during an hour of group interviews, and at the third meeting two

music teachers attended during a one-hour call. Two musical ensemble classes with musical direction at two Swedish upper high schools were observed. Students were completing their third year in different educational programs. Both groups are representative of a "normal" sample. The first musical ensemble class was observed on nine occasions, totalling 30 hours. The second musical ensemble class was observed on seven occasions, totalling 12 hours. Categorization of observations into mechanisms is primarily inductive, inspired by Glaser (1978; 2010), where the researcher creates distance through conceptualization. *Inductive* classroom observations form a conceptual basis for an observation schedule, looking for creative events in the classroom proceedings that will fit into the schedule. Inductive group interviews ensued by questions based on previous interviews. The approach is *abductive*, according to critical realism; that is, what appears from a research point of view should be seen in a new theoretical context, using selected theory. The last analytical phase is *retroduction,* describing the mechanisms that enable for creative music education (Danermark, 2003).

RESULTS OF THE STUDY

Results describe what music teachers identify as creative phases in their classroom praxis. Direct researcher observations of creative learning in musical ensemble practice complement the teachers' views. The students act as collaborators in the creative classroom, negotiating and renegotiating how to perform at an upcoming concert. Renegotiating a situation in a meaningful way equals intelligent reasoning, according to Dewey (Westerlund, 2002). During the process, teachers should encourage students' personal choices and decisions. Dewey distinguishes between primary and secondary reflective experience, firstly as inductive and secondly as deductive practice. The inductive phase is triggered by a problem or violation of a previous experience. The deductive phase describes a proposed solution. The overall problem solving process relates to the particular individual problem at hand without reference to rules or principles. Deductive analysis can only be understood after testing conclusions in a new context. The teacher's task is to organize a stimulating environment for musical experimentation. Reflection occurs both in the performer's head and during creative practices (Westerlund, 2002). By using theoretical guidance from creativity research of problem solving, flow, play and games, interview data and observation notes are analysed and discussed. Theories of activity, reflection and problem solving help studying and understanding creative aspects of music education. In order to develop a creative ability, students need an opportunity, for example, to participate in musical activity and solve musical problems. Such practices help the students' develop ownership of knowledge, process and result - in this case by means of a transformative teaching method (Blair, 2009). According to Weisberg (1993), problem solving is a natural process based on the daily encounters and problems people face and overcome. Problem solving activity characterizes people's ability to adapt to the environment (Popper, 1999). Learning by problem-solving is a wise way to go. Problem-solving makes creative adjustment of established knowledge possible and feasible, i.e. to change or enhance the tradition in a personal way. Caillois (2001), Csikszentmihalyi (2006) and Huizinga (1945) suggest analytical theories and concepts which relate to musical activity and support the making of a creative learning environment.

Problem Solving Musical Practice

An authentic learning environment for problem-solving is reflected in this author's observations of the students' engagement. As they are learning (about) music, the students favour certain role models but the teachers' feedback is also important. Recorded artists that the students use as examples for musical activity serve as pedagogical role models. They make up the starting points for dealing with collective problem solving processes. The activity was recorded in the observations and it was also based on students' selected list of Spotify favourites. The students negotiate their musical knowledge with current understanding of the characteristics of musical elements and how they should be performed. There is adjustment to the original tune going on when the students' performance help creating a similar sound as heard on the recording. Students learn to compromise among the options, and compromising is an important factor in problem-solving learning. Find excerpts from observations of student behaviour in a musical ensemble.

'Do not listen to me; the bass drum should be in the back beat!' 'What about the key?' The teacher helps to tune the instruments properly. Guitarists sit closer together. 'Should we skip to be at the back beat?' 'No, I think we'll make it. We play again after the break.'

The teacher is one of many educators who demonstrate a solution. Yet emphasis is on the students trying to solve their problems. A teacher explains the situation.

Often they can. They are so good, they will find out themselves. It's perfect; I do not need to do anything. Sometimes it's boring, when it stands still. Then there's nothing happening. Then you tell them. And it may well be a bit of it; they're working that way in the ensemble.

The students' efforts are creative and their results have an unpredictable character. Analysis of what produces a creative music education shows that authentic learning is based on everyday knowledge. This fact needs to be taken into account so that efforts at teaching and learning incorporate types of unpredictability (Weisberg, 1993). Not knowing the outcome in advance is an important aspect of the activity to develop because properly executed it generates a sense of creativity so that learning becomes challenging and motivating (Abbott 2004; Weisberg 1993). The teacher refers to himself as a musician:

In case you talk about creativity as a form of self-esteem, so it is not quite certain that it is always there. I mean, sometimes it has the fixed routines if you sit and will play music, and I know well not always, although I think it's fun to play so I might not always be in this creative state when I play. You go on automatic, you know, almost ... if I know the end result, then it might affect the feeling of creativity.

Student Preferences and Choice

Creative teaching develops the ability to identify problems and to deal with different solutions through a negotiating approach. Properties such as collective intelligence and interpersonal skills prepare students for the future (Hargreaves, 2004; Robinson, 2011).The teachers explain the importance of engaging students in many contexts, whether they get to choose the music they play or organize concerts and gigs. One teacher explains why creativity is often found in students' choices.

When you feel at home in one piece, it feels like it is only then that one can begin to work creatively [...] and make informed choices. [...] The creativity is maybe, maybe some choice; as to make informed choices.

This quote suggests that teaching and learning is culturally relevant for the students. Being able to choose is a motivating factor, if choices were related to individual skills. Feelings are imbued in what is to be learned and the possibility of students making personal choices creates the necessary balance in the problem-solving process (Csikszentmihalyi, 2006).

Students learn to check the process by asking questions and eventually allocating responsibility to one another. In this way, they regulate the process efficiently with the time they have available. The teacher-led part of the process becomes beneficial in interaction with the students' drive. If the teacher directs the students' focus to a problem during the ongoing process s/he will distract them with his or her personal goals. Find a quote from observations of the activity in the pupils' musical ensemble.

The teacher notices that the song is too fast and pays attention to the students. 'Is it not too fast?' The teacher demonstrates on his instrument how fast the song is possible to perform. Students: 'Honestly, this really needs practicing. This song has not been a priority at all!' Teacher: 'We take another four minutes!'

Flow, Group-Flow, Play, and Games

Flow theory shows, in a similar way as in problem-solving, that challenge and motivation can bring balance and flow. Being in the flow means that musical learning by developmental work processes come easily and quickly; a sense in the actors that time and space disappears. Flow is autotelic, that is, it finds is purpose and existence within itself (Csikszentmihalyi, 2006). My observations suggest that the students assess and confirm each other's effort with looks, words and smiles.

The concentration is ceaseless in students. They are reflected in the response of each other and remind each other to assume the right attitude. The solo singer or choir sings at the heart, which seems to be a desirable role for most people. Students ask and discipline each other by the question: 'Are you in control?' After every break that naturally takes place the students are even more motivated. They have developed a strong team spirit. Active listening means no problem to do many things at the same time as looking at your smart-phone, in the mirror, dancing, hugging, and combing hair.

Flow requires frames and a visible target for the activity (Abbot 2004, Weisberg 1993). Sawyer (2003; 2007) sees musical creativity as a collective process, and he explores how this develops with jazz musicians, how they create group-flow based on the participants being equal and mastering the fundamental skills of the genre (Sawyer, 2003).

Music provides energy and helps students to focus. It's a bit messy and the classroom is reorganized constantly. But students do not lose their commitment. On the Internet students find the text and tablature for the songs. They are also looking at the text or listening to the vocal harmonies on their mobile phones. In an ongoing negotiation, the students reconcile their opinions. They ask each other for advice, but not on the most efficient way. 'We do not care if this goes wrong, here we go!' They are coaching each other to cope with the technical problems that arise, such as how to widen the throat when singing: 'Imagine you want drink a glass of water, or swallow a cucumber.'

Huizinga (1945) clarifies that music is like other cultural games, competitive and outside the mainstream, and as such it is autotelic. Huizinga relates how musicians have traditionally had a low societal status, but contests and competition between musicians have always attracted public interest. Musical play is, by its autotelic function, like a state of flow. Caillois (2001) argues that some games are explorative rather than competitive. A game is a cultural creation and it brings about cultural renewal about, in a process which influences behaviour in society. 'As-if' games, and how they relate to musicians being able to enter an imaginary world, are suited to explaining the creative musical classroom. Musical activity connects how the students exploit cultural roles that, in turn, help them prepare for an upcoming concert by pretending it is actually happening,

play-acting the event and then enacting it as an 'as-if' function.

When the new song is introduced, it increases commitment and the teacher helps to identify the different parts of the song. The new song gives some students a dreamy gaze. They are negotiating about who will play and sing and teacher assigns roles. They also discuss whether they will have time to learn any new song in relation to the time available.

A teacher explains that students often experience music as fun, provided they do so voluntarily. This sense of volunteering and self-control is a mechanism behind creative involvement. It is an autotelic function, related to functions of playfulness and play. The students use a variety of gestures and media as their ideal means for developing their multimodal skills, without losing focus (Selander & Kress, 2010) on the main activity. They use simultaneous communication, which means that they synchronize their objectives, actions and movements.

Two keyboards stand next to one another. One of the players synchronizes their play with an eye towards the more advanced classmate. A girl is taking notes and observing the great chain of events in the classroom. After the song she asks the other, 'Did I count wrong? Shall we halve the interlude?' The teacher gives an assessment: 'It's quite monotonic, that song, so you may wonder how you will keep it interesting.' The girl in charge of the song gives a suggestion: 'We run it again and we go with more energy; it will get better!' They start playing the song, and also singing girls are now more focused on harmonizing their voices.

In a creative learning environment it is important that the teacher lets the students suggest the content of the lesson plan. This is especially crucial when the contents and design of a lesson fail to attract or engage student interest.

'I would like you to teach me that,' or 'Do you know how to do it?' There are those times I find it fun and inspirational. Then you try to make a context in which these things can be used. [...] Then maybe you try your way so that they will discover how we should go on. Then I'll come with suggestions. Then we might have made a little song with some riffs that both are involved in!

The teacher's and the student's roles can turn into an experiment that supports the students' motivation. The teachers' learning process can result in imitation learning, as Popper notes (1999). Creativity starts from a familiarity with the functioning of tools or cultural artefacts at hand. In this case the tools fulfil the teacher's purpose of balancing between the students' initiative and the teacher's mediation of how to perform the game. The teacher can reinforce the students' knowledge and skills when needed (North, 2008).

There are many ways to stimulate creativity. Being able to find technical difficulties in one musical piece is one option (Blair, 2009). Practicing directly on the instrument is another way to become inspired, as one teacher remarks. Another option is to refrain from practicing for a period of time so that mastering the technique eventually falls into place.

Often when you're doing something, and then let it go for a while, so the subconscious takes over, it will continue after all. And that is, it is a kind of creativity that you are not aware of. And so all of a sudden, for example, if I write a text, and it is not really working, so next time you pick up the pen so there it is.

The students are easily affected by one another's creativity. The teachers may encourage endurance in the students completion of tasks, an objective which will eventually inspire creative skills (Brinkman, 2010). A teacher may also show something inspiring to the students. By trying out new things their motivation grows, even when they

break away from familiar teaching styles. They do so even when they are influenced by their initiative to create music. A teacher retells the students' story about how they found new ways to practice the musical ensemble.

It may well be the case that when you break the usual frame, the standard framework as they always have. It is the same with the musical ensemble. [...] Some have said that when we have the ensemble we are late, we're tired, and we do nothing. So we gathered here at the holidays and played. We had decided it ourselves and we played really well and everyone was really good and everyone did their best. They broke the conventional teaching frame then. We stand there as a teacher and we're going blah, blah, blah. They do it themselves because they themselves choose.

Finally, observations show that if the teacher stands in the centre of the teaching process, the students' focus can fade away. The teacher needs to be available and be invited in by the students without disturbing their creative learning process. The teacher is playing with the students. They comment appreciatively on the teacher's play (Green, 2008): 'Are you going to put your fine ...' The teacher tests various comp variants for the rhythm section. 'Oh, how beautiful it sounds!' The teacher shows different models and sound. 'Hey! No synthesizers!' Everyone laughs. The teacher is part of the playful action. Students would like to continue to repeat the process after class.

PEDAGOGICAL STRUCTURES

Pedagogical structures change and stimulate a creative music education. A creative process sometimes contributes to knowledge building. In this section I examine the teacher's role as an intermediary and a stimulus to student-centred problem-solving. I also examine the tools to be internalized (Wertsch, 1998). The student role in creative learning involves *learning to ask questions and engageing in their learning process.* Initially the students imitate the music. Eventually they transform the music, making it their own by negotiating performance with each another. Their interest in the task is an importing motivating factor (Csikszentmihalyi 2006). This process is in many ways *collective.* The educator shares most of the responsibility with the students. The teacher's choice results in a free-floating cooperative environment where students dare to *try new solutions and are willing to take risks.* As in any school subject, the teacher's role in music education is to *provide feedback* (Blair, 2009; Karlsson, 2008). Alternatively the teacher can entice the students and become *a role model,* inspiring the students to try and *construct a pattern* for others to control and transform (Nielsen, 2000). It is important that the teacher eventually hands over responsibility to the students (Blair, 2009). When the teacher puts himself at the centre of things results relate to him and what he does. Yet *the teacher can only concentrate on the task at hand.* The teacher's task is to *organize teaching and learning activities* so that the students' suggestions lead to new learning.

Practicing and internalization is crucial to student learning. The tools for enhancing musical knowledge are appropriated in a multimodal fashion, e.g. when the students utilize the multitude of resources the classroom designs supply. There are musical instruments, computers, cell phones and the like. Outcomes of the creative process depend on the tool used, but students suffering from communicative pedagogy become less creative than others (Tarufi, 2006). A teacher discusses the problem of "right-and-wrong" pedagogy.

Well, it is so because they think it's right or it's wrong. It's ... several things that are right! So it is black or white as well. There are many, who want to have, 'but how do we put it? [chord on a piano]. They come and ask, again and again. And it´s like ... well, I do not know ... they get stuck in the mind-set. It is as it should be so.

The teachers discuss previous teaching experiences. Some of the students bring up the subject in a musical ensemble class. Their experiences are based on communicative pedagogy in a municipal music school.

I also notice on the ensemble, that you can have a really good student coming and puts the notes perfectly on his sax, cello or whatever it is. But once you get there that you should create something yourself, in some eight bars there, 'makes one there 'and so on, so ...Then they become totally confused and says, 'What shall I do, say what I shall do! While someone else, perhaps a guitarist runs a little fills. 'Yes, drrrrr'. Instead of daring to fail, be creative, to invent.

But they have never done it

No, I know. Except those who played a little freely, maybe played in the big band and got a solo, or stuff like that. [...] That's it, we're trying to get them to work more creatively in ensemble form. It is this they learn from each other, I think.

Problems with communicative pedagogy can result in counter creative musical expressions. The teachers stress the importance of *variation and that varying learning between performance art and creativity* provides the sought varied musical competency (Burnard & White, 2008). The teacher's organization of teaching and learning indicates that students *have a goal* that they will try to achieve. The ambition to succeed will help the students form a creative environment which resembles an informal working life setting (Dewey, 1910). When students control their influences on learning, they create *a real problem.* In addition, a cooperative learning movement between teacher and student can arise during which *increased motivation* increases teacher knowledge and support student learning (Bruner, 2006).

SOLUTIONS AND RECOMMENDATIONS

This study contributes to music education, more specifically to research on creativity in shared music making activity. There are discernible phases in the studied activity and there are specific mechanisms that characterize creativity in music education. New structures and rules see the light of day. They suggest that students re-create the previous rules of the pedagogical game. They include two major themes: *making something your own* and *making your own, that is, autonomous learning and your own creation*. This result imbues a spirit of day-to-day learning, where problem-solving activities motivate and make possible creative abilities based on students' commitment to learning (about) music making.

Creative learning as expressed through research is an educational goal aiming at teacher preparations for autonomous and transformative learning in music education. The theory of creative music education – as developed in this chapter – serves as model for schools that will make the educational context motivating and engaging for the students. Several mechanisms in the present study serve as didactic factors to account for during preparation, management and evaluation of teaching and learning directed towards development of creativity. For the benefit of music pedagogy praxis, the suggested mechanisms will help making creative music teaching and learning explicit, for example by making explicit the role of scaffolding. The mechanisms were analysed by socio-cultural and activity theory and the concept of *perezhivanie*. The first mechanisms are related to *authentic problems* in teaching and learning. Here students find educational problems and they learn how to manage various options as solutions. Teachers must engage students in different parts of the learning-process so that teaching may become culturally relevant for the students. The potential of music (making) to engage emotions increases student motivation because at their age they experiment with cultural identities and musical roles. According to Vygotsky, cultural context and emotions form a basis for cognitive process to develop into higher mental functions. An authentic problem is cultural-historically relevant. The teacher can develop it if emotions were deployed as a tool for guiding perception and cognition. The concept of *perezhivanie* shows that musical engagement synchronizes and situates students in a cultural context inside and outside school. Musical engagement grows if the students may imitate music of their own choice. The musical product that the students imitate interacts with the musical process. The teachers' and students' different roles are experimented with in order to help the parties guide and share musical experiences. Other mechanisms involve *internalization and transformative learning*. Cognition and emotion clearly interact in the appropriation of musical instruments, an act and an ambition which requires a balance of technical skill and musical decision making. Then creativity and learning can become autonomous. Practicing an instrument facilitates transformative learning if conducted and executed in a playful form. Further mechanisms address how *internal and external motivation* combines in creative musical teaching and learning. Students 'infect' each other with motivation by moving from inner to external motivation and then back to inner motivation. As external motivation, students remind each other to stick with their goal and commitment to the task. Their learning goal is the upcoming concert. It forms a comprehensive framework for their shared activity. Situated learning defined as a framework for creativity interacts with emotions and expectations that govern the students' attention. To keep activity and motivation going, frames of teaching designs change according to students' and teachers' needs. Understanding describing and challenging the role of the teacher serve as a framework for altering the teacher's role from being at the centre of pupils' attention to being at hand. This change leads to the continuous student interest in the task. The changing role of the teacher is always based on professional and informed pedagogical choices.

FUTURE RESEARCH DIRECTIONS

Development of phases of education is needed. Music making is a challenging subject containing many elements, e.g. abstract literary knowledge, technical skill, cooperation, perception and so forth. The subject of stimulating music (making) in schools provides us with a model of how knowledge takes physical, cognitive and intermediary forms. My suggestion for further study covers knowledge about how different forms of knowledge interact in the subject of music. And also to study what kind of creative knowledge music develops, all of course relative to schooling, tuition and curricula. The space for the arts at school is at risk, but it could become a springboard for expanding research on creativity in relation to society's need for globalization, innovation and sustainability.

CONCLUSION

In the act of delivering formal musical teaching and learning teachers strive towards becoming creative. They apply strategies that support students' commitment and motivation. Creative activities build on playfulness and engagement, often self-driven by the students and at times supported by a teacher or a team of teachers. The students appropriate musical artefacts by transformative education. Eventually, learning objects become autonomous, i.e. the students' motivation develop a basis for effective learning (*perezhivanie*). A creative problem to explore the world of music arises out of something familiar, provided od course it is transmitted from others as conceptual tools or via personal experience. Learning from problem solving is motivating and ensures quality of education and learning, making new knowledge

culturally relevant and renewing. Striving for balance between teaching for performance and teaching for creativity makes teaching and learning an interesting and unpredictable activity, even in relation to a demanding curriculum. Teaching is a practical skill and the teacher must be able to switch focus between product and process. In the course of time the students' exploration of musical skills and knowledge turns into creative habits. But creative teaching and learning need variation and planning. Then conceptual tools can be mastered and appropriated in ways that encourage and motivate music students' creative ability and personal growth.

REFERENCES

Abbott, A. D. (2004). *Methods of Discovery: Heuristics for the Social Science*. New York: Norton.

Allsup, R. E. (2008). Creating an educational framework for popular music in public schools: Anticipating the second-wave. *Visions of Research in Music Education, 12*(1-2).

Ax, J., & Ponte, P. (2008). *Critiquing Praxis: Conceptual and Empirical Trends in the Teaching Profession*. Rotterdam: Sense.

Blair, D. V. (2009). Stepping aside: Teaching in a student-centered music classroom. *Music Educators Journal, 95*(3), 42–45. doi:10.1177/0027432108330760

Brinkman, D. J. (2010). Teaching creatively and teaching for creativity. *Arts Education Policy Review, 111*(2), 48–50. doi:10.1080/10632910903455785

Bruner, J. S. (2006). *In Search of Pedagogy: The Selected Works of Jerome Bruner*. London: Routledge.

Burnard, P., & White, J. (2008). Creativity and performativity: Counterpoints in British and Australian education. *British Educational Research Journal*, *34*(5), 667–682. doi:10.1080/01411920802224238

Caillois, R. (2001). *Man, Play and Games*. Wantage: University of Illinois Press.

Carr, W. (2006). Philosophy, methodology and action research. *Journal of Philosophy of Education*, *40*(4), 421–435. doi:10.1111/j.1467-9752.2006.00517.x

Cole, M., & Engeström, Y. (1993). A cultural-historical approach to distributed cognition. In G. Salomon (Ed.), Distributed Cognitions: Psychological and Educational Considerations. Cambridge, UK: Cambridge University Press.

Cole, M., & Wertsch, J. V. (1996). Beyond the individual-social antimony in discussions of Piaget and Vygotsky. *Human Development*, *39*(5), 250–256. doi:10.1159/000278475

Craft, A. (2003). The limits to creativity in education: Dilemmas for educator. *British Journal of Educational Studies*, *51*(2), 113–127. doi:10.1111/1467-8527.t01-1-00229

Csikszentmihalyii, M. (2006). *Flow: Den optimala upplevelsens psykologi*. Stockholm: Natur och kultur.

Danermark, B. (2003). *Att förklara samhället*. Lund: Studentlitteratur.

Dewey; J. (1910). *How we think*. London: D.C. heat and company.

Dewey, J. (1934). *Art as experience*. New York: Minton, Balch & Company.

Elliot, D. J. (1995). *Music matters: A new philosophy of music education*. New York: Oxford University Press.

Engeström, Y. (1987). *Learning by expanding: an activity-theoretical approach to development research. (Dissertation)*. Helsinki: University Helsinki.

Engeström, Y. (1999). Activity theory and individual and social transformation. In Y. Engeström, R. Mittinen, & R.L. Punamäki (Eds.), Perspective on activity theory. Cambridge, UK: Cambridge University Press.

Folkestad, G. (2006). Formal and informal learning situations or practices vs formal and informal ways of learning. *British Journal of Music Education*, *22*(2), 135–145. doi:10.1017/S0265051706006887

Folkestad, G. (2008). Review article. *Music Education Research*, *10*(4), 499–503. doi:10.1080/14613800802547755

Georgii-Hemming, E., & Kvarnhall, V. (2011). YouTube som musikalisk erfarenhet. In C. Ericsson & M. Lindgren (Eds.), Perspektiv på populärmusik och skola. Lund: Studentlitteratur.

Glaser, B. G. (1978). *Theoretical sensitivity: Advances in methodology of grounded theory*. Mill Valley, CA: Sociology Press.

Glaser, B. G. (2010). *Att göra grundad teori: problem, frågor och diskussion*. Mill Valley, CA: Sociology Press.

Goehr, L. (1992). *The imaginary museum of musical works: An essay in the philosophy of music*. Oxford, UK: Clarendon.

Green, L. (1997). *Music, gender, education*. Cambridge, UK: Cambridge Univ. Press. doi:10.1017/CBO9780511585456

Green, L. (2008). *Music, informal learning and the school: A new classroom pedagogy*. Aldershot, UK: Ashgate.

Hargreaves, A. (2004). *Läraren i kunskapssamhället: I osäkerhetens tidevarv*. Lund: Studentlitteratur.

Hargreaves, D. J., & North, A. C. (n.d.). *The Social Psychology of Music*. Oxford, UK: Oxford University Press.

Huizinga, J. (1945). *Den lekande människan*. Stockholm: Natur och kultur.

Johansson, K. (2014). Collaborative music making and artistic agency. In T. Hansson (Ed.), Contemporary Approaches to Activity Theory: Interdisciplinary Perspectives on Human Behavior. Hershey, PA: IGI Global.

Jorgensen, E. R. (2003). *Transforming music education*. Bloomington, IN: Indiana Univ. Press.

Karlsson, J. (2008). *A novel approach to teaching emotional expression in music performance*. Uppsala: Acta Universitatis Upsaliensis.

Kaufman, J. C., & Beghetto, R. A. (2009). Beyond big and little: The four c model of creativity. *Review of General Psychology, 13*(1), 1–12. doi:10.1037/a0013688

Knutagård, H. (2002). *Introduktion till verksamhetsteori*. Lund: Studentlitteratur.

Kratus, J. (1990). Structuring the music curriculum for creative learning. *Music Educators Journal, 79*(9), 33–37. doi:10.2307/3401075

Kupferberg, F. (2003). Kritik, tilpasning, autencitet og kommunikation. Kreativitetsregimer i moderniteten. *Dansk Sociologi, 14*(3), 43–62.

Kwami, R. M. (2001). Music Education in and for a pluralist society. In C. Plummeridgc & C. Philpott (Eds.), Issues in music teaching. London: RoutledgeFalmer.

Linge, A. (2013). *Svängrum: För en kreativ musikpedagogik*. (Dissertation). Malmö: Malmö högskola.

Lundberg, D., Malm, K., & Ronström, O. (2000). *Musik, medier, mångkultur: Förändringar i svenska musiklandskap*. Hedemora: Gidlund.

Lurija, A. R. (1979). *The making of mind: a personal account of Soviet psychology*. Cambridge, MA: Harvard U.P.

Lurija, A. R. (1981). *Language and cognition*. Washington, DC: Winston.

Nielsen, K. (2000). Musikalisk mästarlära. In K. Nielsen & S. Kvale (Eds.), Mästarlära: Lärande som social praxis. Lund: Studentlitteratur.

North, A. C. (2008). *The social and applied psychology of music*. New York: Oxford University Press. doi:10.1093/acprof:oso/9780198567424.001.0001

Popov, O. (2014). Outdoor science in teacher education. In T. Hansson (Ed.), Contemporary Approaches to Activity Theory: Interdisciplinary Perspectives on Human Behavior. Hershey, PA: IGI Global.

Popper, K. R. (1999). *All life is problem solving*. London: Routledge.

Regelski, T. A. (2007). Music Education: What is the 'value added' for self and society?. In B. Stålhammar (Ed.), Music and human beings: Music and identity. Örebro: Örebro Universitet.

Regelski, T. A., & Gates, T. (2009). Preface and introduction. In T. A. Regelski & T. Gates (Eds.), Music education for changing times: Guiding visions for practice. Dordrecht, The Netherlands: Springer.

Reimer, B. (2003). *A philosophy of music education: Advancing the vision*. Upper Saddle River, NJ: Prentice Hall.

Robinson, K. (2011). *Out of our minds*. Chichester, UK: Capstone.

Saar, T. (1999). *Musikens dimensioner: En studie av unga musikers lärande.* (Dissertation). Göteborg: Göteborgs Universitet.

Säljö, R. (2000). *Lärande i praktiken: ett sociokulturellt perspektiv.* Stockholm: Prisma.

Sawyer, R. K. (2003). *Group creativity: Music, theater, collaboration.* Mahwah, NJ: Erlbaum.

Sawyer, R. K. (2007). *Group genius: the creative power of collaboration.* New York: Basic Books.

Sayer, A. (1992). *Method in social science: A realist approach.* London: Routledge.

Selander, S., & Kress, G. R. (2010). *Design för lärande: Ett multimodalt perspektiv.* Stockholm: Norstedts.

Sloboda, J. A. (2005). *Exploring the musical mind: Cognition, emotion, ability, function.* Oxford, UK: Oxford University Press.

Smagorinsky, P. (2011). Vygotsky's stage theory: The psychology of art and the actor under the direction of Perezhivaine. *Mind, Culture, and Activity, 18*(4), 319–341. doi:10.1080/1074903 9.2010.518300

Small, C. (1998). *Musicking: The meanings of performing and listening.* Hanover, NH: Univ. Press.

Tarufi, J. (2006). Processes and teaching strategies in musical improvisation with children. In I. Deliége & G. A. Wiggings (Eds.), Musical creativity: Multidisciplinary research in theory and practice. Hove, UK: Psychology Press.

Vygotsky, L. S. (1995). *Fantasi och kreativitet i barndomen.* Göteborg: Daidalos.

Vygotsky, L. S. (2001). *Tänkande och språk.* Göteborg: Daidalos.

Weisberg, R. W. (1993). *Creativity: Beyond the myth of genius.* New York: Freeman.

Welch, G. F. (1998). Early childhood musical development. *Research Studies in Music Education, 11*(1), 27–41. doi:10.1177/1321103X9801100104

Wertsch, J. V. (1998). *Mind as action.* New York: Oxford University Press.

Westerlund, H. (2002). *Bridging experience, action, and culture in music education.* Helsinki: Sibelius Academy.

Wolff, J. (1987). Foreword: The Ideology of Autonomous Art. In R. Leppert & S. McClary (Eds.), Music and Society: The Politics of Composition, Performance and Reception. Cambridge, UK: Cambridge University Press.

ADDITIONAL READING

Bergman, Å.(2009). *Växa upp med musik: ungdomars musikanvändande i skolan och på fritiden.* Diss: Göteborg: Göteborgs universitet.

DeNora, T. (2000). *Music in everyday life.* Cambridge: Cambridge University Press. doi:10.1017/CBO9780511489433

Green, L. (2001). *How popular musicians learn: A way ahead for music education.* Aldershot: Ashgate.

Nilsson, B. (2002). *'Jag kan göra hundra låtar': barns musikskapande med digitala verktyg.* Malmö: Musikhögskolan.

Strandberg, T. (2007). *Varde ljud!: om skapande I skolans musikpedagogik efter 1945.* Diss. Umeå Universitet.

Zimmerman Nilsson, M.-H. (2009). *Musiklärares val av undervisningsinnehåll: en studie i ensemble och gehörs-och musiklära inom gymnasieskolan.* Diss. Göteborgs Universitet.

KEY TERMS AND DEFINITIONS

Informal Musical Learning: Musical learning that takes place outside school, but also a way of teaching music in schools that has students learning from peers and master-apprentice learning as a model. The focus lies in the activity of *playing*.

Formal Musical Learning: Learning in a school context but also musical learning outside school that is culturally formalized. The focus lies in *how* music is played.

Flow: A psychological condition when people experience time and place disappearing and are fully engaged in performing a task.

Performance: Maintenance of cultural roles and collective identities, that is, musical roles in traditional performing and ensembles.

Product and Process: The musical product can be sheet-music to interpret or re-create but also a creative outcome of a musical activity or process.

Svängrum: A pedagogical room where transmission of musical tradition is varied with musical exploration for creative music education.

Section 3
Work Practice

Chapter 10
Micro–Analysis of Concepts for Developing Networking in Social Work

Laura Seppänen
Finnish Institute of Occupational Health, Finland

Laure Kloetzer
CNAM, France

ABSTRACT

Inter-institutional or inter-functional network collaboration at work increasingly provides new challenges for professionals. A developmental network intervention based on the approach of Developmental Work Research was conducted in the field of Social Services for Divorced Families. The objective was to examine cross-functional limitations through joint reflection of examples of clients' trajectories and to discuss possibilities for developing client-oriented network collaboration between services. With the help of interlocutory analysis, the professional concepts in use were tracked in sequences of intervention discussions. The analysis reveals how "hybrid concepts," defined as concepts in use in the professional environment and re-used as intervention tools by the researchers, could support joint reflection by the professionals on the current limits of their collaboration. It also reveals how "professional concepts" may serve as resources to mediate client-services' and service-service relations. Finally, conditions and challenges for designing activity theory-based interventions for promoting client-oriented network collaborations are sketched.

INTRODUCTION

While network collaboration is an increasing trend in work life, there is demand for developmental interventions for networking and boundary crossing purposes. The original interventionist versions based on Developmental Work Research

(DWR) (Engeström, 1987) such as the Change Laboratory (Virkkunen & Newnham 2013) were not designed to tackle the complex setting of multiple collaborating activities. Applications have later been developed for networking or boundary crossing purposes between activities (Engeström & Kerosuo, 2007; Kerosuo 2006;

DOI: 10.4018/978-1-4666-6603-0.ch010

Ruotsala 2014; Seppänen et al. 2009; Toiviainen et al., 2009). The combination of the creation of solutions and their dissemination can be enhanced if an intervention is carried out by a network of actors and organizations (Bodrožić 2008), or by establishing pluralist communities of inquiry (Lorino, Tricard & Clot, 2011).

The context of this chapter is a short two-workshop intervention carried out in order to promote client-oriented network collaboration between distinct professional functional units in social work. The empirical case comes from the field of Social Services for Divorced Families (SSDF) in Finnish social work services, which are facing pressures to change both in funding and service quality. Improving collaboration between specialized services is envisioned as a way to overcome current limitations. The case study involved three municipal functional units of social affairs, Family Counseling (FC), Family Law Issues (FLI) and Child Protection (CP), consisting of professionals with different backgrounds, goals and functions, but all supporting or dealing with the same clients.

This paper is the result of long-running collaboration between two groups working with and on developmental methodologies at work: the Finnish Developmental Work Research team (DWR) and the French Activity Clinic team. Cross discussions on theoretical and methodological frameworks and on results have been going on for ten years in different settings, including symposia in international conferences and a special issue on Dialogue and Interaction in Developmental Methodologies (Kloetzer & Seppänen, 2014).

The goal of this paper is to push this collaboration one step further by conducting a joint analysis of data collected during a Change Workshop intervention. This paper therefore joins one internal researcher (the first author) who directed and conducted the intervention process in a DWR tradition from beginning to end, and one external researcher (the second author) from the Activity Clinic tradition, also experienced in developmental interventions and the analysis of dialogues in developmental interventions, who followed and commented on this intervention process. The two researchers engaged collaboratively in a detailed analysis of selected data, which will be presented in this paper. The investigation of the intervention data combines DWR with interlocutory analysis, as developed by the French group of the Activity Clinic (Kostulski & Kloetzer, 2014).

In the first part of this chapter, we present the need for increased networking and the case studied, i.e. the municipal organization of social work with divorced families. We then describe the developmental intervention carried out in SSDF. We particularly explain the design and use of one method, using hybrid concepts of 'worry' and 'green areas'. In the second part, entitled Mediations in cross-functional social work, we interpret and analyze in detail one episode of the intervention discussion in which the mentioned 'method of worries' was used. The findings show the professional concepts that were uncovered by this developmental method. Although the professional concepts found were efficient mediations between each service and their clients, cross-institutional mediations to support the inter-functional collaboration of professionals were lacking in the episode analyzed. We describe the critical findings concerning the difficulty of professional concepts to mediate cross-functional collaboration, as well as their potential for cross-functional mediation. In the third and last part of the paper, we sketch and discuss ideas and challenges for designing and facilitating developmental, activity theory-based interventions for promoting cross-institutional or cross-functional, client-oriented collaborations. Moreover, we reflect upon the benefits of the joint analysis which used resources of both DWR and interlocutory analysis. Questions for future research will be posed at the end.

NETWORKING SERVICES AND THE INTERVENTION

Networking or other relatively open organizational constellations of organizing work is an increasing trend in work (Boltanski & Chiapello, 2005; Head, 2008). Networks are conceptualized in different ways depending on the discipline or research tradition. Here, we apply an object-oriented approach to networking: collaboration is directed towards a shared object and production of use value, in which the common interest is found through complementary capabilities (Miettinen et al., 2008, p. 7). The notion of the object, following Leont'ev (1978) within activity-theory approaches, means something both given and constructed. In the constructed capacity, the object gains motivating force that gives shape and direction to activity. The object-oriented nature of networking is particularly salient in public and public-related services, where multiple different specialized service providers have the same clients. For instance, patients can receive care for different diseases in many hospitals and health centers. Efficiency in pursuing one's professional goals here is not independent of what others do for this client. Therefore, improving services may require understanding the whole path of the client through distinct institutional units. In this context, meeting the needs of clients more comprehensively requires different actors to evaluate their existing service practices together and reflect on the needs of their shared clients. This inter-professional reflection process may help them gain a new understanding of their services, as well as modify the services themselves or create new ones. Assumedly, this can be promoted by developmental interventions.

Sectorized services try to govern the complexity of client situations by dividing it into parts, and by trying to govern each part by one specialized function. But the everyday issues of people and families can seldom be clearly separated from one another (Seikkula & Arnkil, 2005). Specialization, while improving the means to deal with specific problems, also produces communication and consistency problems. Our assumption, based on the object-oriented conceptualization of the network, is that cross-institutional or cross-functional collaboration can be enhanced by extending practitioners' understanding of clients' needs and trajectories. This is the approach in the research project on service networks in which SSDF is one of five investigated service networks (Seppänen et al., 2012). Service users are referred to in many ways – as stakeholders, citizens, consumers, co-producers, customers, clients, or captives (Jung, 2010). Here, we choose to use client as a general term.

Service providers' relations with their clients are an essential part of their work. Our understanding of the service-client relation is directed by the activity-theoretical notion of the object that motivates activities and which connects concrete activities to societal needs. We deal here with two trends of client orientation and networking, which are often supposed to be interrelated: overcoming fragmentation requires crossing sectored and organizational boundaries through collaboration; client orientation is seen as helping productivity and enabling a better response to clients' evolving needs (Virtanen et al., 2011).

In this study, the central partners in the SSDF network are Family Counseling (FC), Family Law Issues (FLI) and Child Protection (CP). When parents divorce and obtain joint custody, the municipal unit of FLI often helps them make a contract on the different matters concerning their children, and verifies it. Meetings between children and the parent with whom the children do not live is part of the contract. If parents are not able to agree, the issues are solved in the magistrate's court. CP gets involved when concern or 'worry' for the child arises, caused by, for example, difficulties in care and upbringing, violence, drug use or other crises. Divorced families can turn to FC, which helps in questions related to the upbringing of children and adolescents, and in problematic or crisis family situations. The need to study and develop these

Table 1. Features of the network in social services for divorced families (Seppänen, Cerf & Toiviainen, 2013)

Feature	SSDF
Clients	Divorced families with children who have long-term relations with various social and legal services
Clients' agency	Parents have ownership of their own matters throughout the trajectory, except when they take a matter to court.
Societal interests embedded in the clients	Overall well-being of families, children's rights.
Service actors in the network	In municipal social services: Family Legal Issues, Child Protection and Family Counseling. Outside municipal social department: Child psychiatry clinics, magistrate's courts, schools, health care, police, etc.
Network features	Flat (no clear hierarchy between the three municipal social services). Inter-unit collaboration is case-by case.

service functions' mutual network collaboration came partly from municipal decision-makers and funders; partly from practitioners who articulated, in different ways, the need for more collaboration (Seppänen, Cerf & Toiviainen, 2013); and partly from the project's researchers.

Unfortunately, a divorced family case may be prolonged if parents use children against each other in their quarrel, or if parents bring, sometimes repeatedly, their disputes to the magistrate's court, which complicates the matter by creating further mistrust. These cases are difficult for service professionals and affect their well-being. If the parents have joint custody of the children, then the contract has to articulate the when and how the parent with whom the children do not live can meet their children. The strategy of these social services, both locally and nationally (Ministry of Social Affairs and Health 2010) is to develop more preventive and anticipatory service practices. This is a complicated matter because the number of clients in difficult situations is increasing. Table 1 condenses the main features of SSDF clients and the network. Although the separate functional units of SSDF are institutionalized, its network collaboration is not.

Our data are extracted from a workshop in which practitioners from these three social services came together to examine and reflect on a complex service trajectory of a client family undergoing a prolonged divorce, involving a child. All units had

participated in the process. One episode from this workshop has been selected, in which a method, inspired by Vygotsky's (1978) method of dual stimulation, was used to uncover tensions and mediations between the social service functions and between a client family and the services. The concept of 'worries', which has a long history in the domain of social work in Finland (Seikkula et al. 2003), was used as an intervention tool. Next, we turn to the method of intervention.

DESIGNING THE METHOD OF INTERVENTION

Networking is not only challenging for service practitioners; it also sets new demands for researchers carrying out developmental interventions. Network participants in an intervention do not necessarily share the common history of one workplace. Thus we cannot assume that they share the same language or professional concepts. This in turn makes participants' understanding of both the client and their possible mutual collaboration more diverse and multi-voiced. The boundary crossing needed in network constellations can be understood as an extension and a reconceptualization of the boundaries of the objects of the interlinked activities, in a way that connects them as parts of a broader, partly shared object that the two activities jointly carry out (Virkkunen &

Newnham, 2013, p. 190). In normal work activities, the same material object, taken here as the client's trajectory, is conceptualized in different ways without paying attention to interdependencies between these objects. In a developmental network intervention, the first stimuli are the problematic situations that are related to ruptures and disturbances in the coordination of the separate objects of the activities (Virkkunen & Newnham, 2013). We assumed that the disturbances experienced by clients in their service trajectories would make disturbances and interdependencies between objects observable.

Therefore, we collected 'mirror data' from clients and interviewed several parents. We were unable to interview the children due to research ethical reasons. The interviewees were purposefully selected from among prolonged divorced family cases in which it seemed that the clients were not being helped by the services. This may be why the interviewed clients were critical of the social services they had used (Schaupp et al. 2013, 12). The criticality of the interviews regarding the services made the stories very challenging mirror data. The stories created a strong confrontation, but the participants were skilled in handling resistance, opposition and critique in their work.

The basis for the investigation is the activity-theoretical notion of mediation, in which means of mediation can be tools, instruments or sign systems. Activity exists only as mediated and gives meaning to the tools and signs (Vygotsky, 1978; Lektorsky 2009, p. 84). We examine how professional concepts may or may not operate as symbolic resources for cross-functional collaboration. We focus on mediation in client understanding (in the client-services relation), and in mutual collaboration and the division of labor between service providers (in the service-service relation). Our method follows the Vygotskian principle of double stimulation in which excerpts from parents' interviews form the first stimulus and are expected to produce emotional confrontation. The researchers' questions, focusing on the 'worry',

are the second stimulus - a possible mediating artifact that participants may use when making sense of the first stimulus.

The objective of the designed method was to discover when client-service spaces signal the need for service actions, and to uncover the 'green areas' that need a new kind of collaboration. By identifying worries as signs for services to act, the method aimed to help collaboration by supporting the sharing of experiences, views and professional concepts. Simultaneously, this would enhance collective reflection on and the evaluation of the responsibilities of each function in providing the required services. By confronting the different points of view of others, one can learn to understand more about one's own perspective (Seikkula & Arnkil, 2005, p. 34).

In developmental interventions, it is important to find such concepts that can mediate between researcher-interventionists' aims and professionals' work activities. The following concepts, used first by the professionals and later used as tools of intervention by researchers, were thought to help this mediation.

HYBRID CONCEPTS DEPLOYED AS INTERVENTION TOOLS

Worry is a word regularly used by social services, concerning children and adolescents in particular. Dialogical methods such as 'Taking up one's worries' (Eriksson & Arnkil 2009) 'the zones of subjective worry' or Anticipation Dialogues (Seikkula et al. 2003) have been proposed in the R&D of Finnish social services. The principle is that instead of diagnosing and explaining the problem to the client and asking them to change their activity, the professional tells the client their own worry, and asks the client to help diminish this (sharing worries). This changes the relation and opens a dialogue about the matter rather than narrowing it down through a closed definition. Mirja Satka (2010) says:

The zones of worry express through words the intuitive feeling and moral reasoning experienced by a practitioner in relation to a client's life situation and the possibilities of the service system to help them: the concept of worry, built on activity theory, is linked above all with the professional relation. The tacit professional knowledge regarding the encounter (with the client) is articulated and made visible in a way that enables oral expression of the worry regarding the child's situation from the perspective of different professions. It is a question of important feedback method for the service system, focusing on the relation between operational resources and local context. (translation LS, italics original). (p. 190)

Although the methods proposed by Arnkil and his colleagues were not standard practices in the local social services concerned here, they may nonetheless have influenced how the concept of 'worry' is used in professional discourse which, in Vygotskian terms, can be considered a hybrid between scientific and everyday concepts.

The concept of worry has been used in combination with the notion of 'grey areas' – if a professional feels that their own actions to support the child or family are insufficient and do not know if anyone else has control of the situation either, but still feels that reporting the situation to CP would be a too stringent move, then the professional is in the grey zone of worry (Arnkil, Eriksson & Saikku, 1998). The concept of *green areas* in turn comes from a previous discussion in the steering group of our study, in which the common notion of 'grey areas', meaning not falling into responsibility of any of the service providers, was renamed as 'green areas'. As one workshop participant claimed, the grey zone implies: this is not my business, while the green zone means: how can I help you in this matter? Green instead of grey

Figure 1. Subjects responsible for the 'worry' in five short stories about a child's situation in the service trajectory of a divorced family. Examined by workshop participants and marked X.

	1	2	3	4	5
Child Protection	X	X	X		X
Family Counseling	X		X		X
Family Law Issues					X
Mother/ Father	X	X	X	X	X
Others, eg Child Psychiatry Clinic			X		

views the zones as possibilities for collaboration rather than as problems. Part of the concepts and expressions used in the second workshop were taken from the discussion of the first workshop. For instance, the complex service situation was called a *jungle* or a *mess*. Clients were seen to be in both *justice and helping systems* within these social services (Excerpt 1). Justice machinery here refers mostly to the magistrate's court, but also to FLI, who partly implement the tasks required by the courts. The concepts of justice and helping systems were later used in the second workshop (Figure1).

Excerpt 1. Family Counseling practitioner: Somehow, as in the fathers' story, when there were no other means, they ended up in this justice machinery, and then they get stuck there as victims of some sort... it is difficult to see what this all started from. In a way, the helping system is outside of this [justice machinery]. The justice machinery makes it go round and you follow its rules. You have to react at the right moment and if you can't react in a way that means you can hold on to your rights to see the child, it's a horrible sort of, it sounds like a game you can't steer. You are just a pawn. Of course, the helping system is somehow outside all this. Or, if these two worked together, would that be the solution? (First SSDF workshop 12.6.2012)

THE WORKSHOPS IN SSDF

The theme of the first workshop was *how services face the crises of the divorced parents*. Based on parts of father's and mother's interviews as first stimuli, two groups of participants investigated the instances in which the family's matter was taken to magistrate's court: what the parents' objectives and instruments were in these situations, and how they seemed to justify their actions. After this, each function presented its own service activity to the other participants, using the model of an activity system (Engeström, 1987) as a second stimulus. In the end, discussion was stimulated by the question 'What practices could be developed to enhance clients' positive agency and the network collaboration of the services'?

The second workshop examined *the service process from the perspective of the family's child*, and the kind of worries the situations experienced by the child caused different service providers. Our episode and analysis comes from this phase, and the design and use of the intervention method involved in this first phase are described in more detail in the following two subsections. In the second phase, the aim was to discuss the direction in which client-oriented networking could be developed. It included a great deal of developmental talk such as questions, change intentions and developmental evaluation of the service system and helped participants, in a beneficial way, to focus on the relation between the central questions concerning clients and the forms of collaboration between services. Thirdly, the final aim was to collect and discuss ideas on how to proceed with developing collaboration. Thirteen and 11 participants from SSDF took part in the first and the second workshop, respectively. They were facilitated by two researchers. Next, we describe the use of the first phase's method.

USE OF THE METHOD

In the first phase of the second workshop, five small stories from the parents' interviews dealing with a child, a girl of 10 years, were delivered on paper to the participants as first stimuli. They were also given a map, a second stimulus, of the complex trajectory of this family on which the five stories were temporally located. The stories were first discussed by the whole group, and then cross-functional pairs of two professionals analyzed one story through the following questions: what kind of trouble did the child seem to have in the story, and whose worry is or should this trouble be? Later, the findings and ideas of the pairs were collectively discussed, and those people, to whom the worry belonged, i.e. service providers, parents or others, were depicted in a table by a facilitating researcher, as expressed in the discussion (Figure 1).

The stories and the method made the professionals express their own practices and clarify their rationales to the group. The discussion was supported by a table (Figure 1). In practice, this materialized as the concept of 'green areas'. After all the stories were discussed, the researcher asked, while pointing to the table (Figure 1): Can we see any green zones here? Here, the table (Figure 1) served as a second stimulus. The concept of worry, the table and the concept of green zones formed the methodical skeleton of moving from the clients' situation, to services, and then to network collaboration. Below, we turn to the analysis of a discussion episode around one of the five stories called: The child running away. We introduce the methodology of interlocutory analysis, as well as the way in which professional concepts were used in this analysis.

MEDIATIONS IN CROSS-FUNCTIONAL SOCIAL WORK

Analyzing dialogue in developmental interventions is a backdoor to understanding transformation, development of the activity and building of new shared objects of discussion, thought and activity (Kloetzer & Seppänen, 2014). Analysis of the SSDF episode here is conducted through the construction of the interlocutory architecture of the sequence. Interlocutory Logic (Trognon & Kostulski, 1996) is a theory based on the formal properties of speech acts (Austin, 1962; Searle & Vanderveken, 1985), which analyzes interlocution (the linguistic part of the interaction) as an architecture emerging through the conversational progression at the utterance level, i.e. on how utterances are connected one to the others.

In the version of Interlocutory Logic developed in the Activity Clinic perspective (Kostulski, 2011), the researchers identify the architecture of the discussion step by step, considering how the local organization of utterances may change the meaning of the activity of discussion that it realizes. This interlocutory analysis is dynamic, it tracks the evolution of the structure and meaning of the discussion by a careful analysis of the connections of speech acts through their formal properties at the micro-level, and therefore highlights for example how the symbolic mediations are used by the practitioners as argumentative tools in the discussion process. It therefore allows us to track not only the professional concepts used in this context, but also how they are used and with which effects. The close analysis of the progression of speech acts at the utterance level (more precisely, in between utterances) makes the emerging structure of the discussion visible, with its turn points, dead ends and turnarounds.

PROFESSIONAL CONCEPTS AS ANALYTICAL TOOLS

Professional concepts are everyday concepts (Vygotsky, 1978) that are mastered in a professional activity by its practitioners and potentially transmitted, and in this movement displaced, refined and improved through training, mentoring or everyday practice (Kloetzer, 2012). These professional concepts play a critical role in the activity: they support understanding of what is going on in professional situations, as well as decision-making in real-work process, communication and coordination at the workplace. Research on understanding of these concepts focused on vocational training. In that context, they have been called "pragmatic concepts", defined as "schematic and operative representations, elaborated through and for action, produced by a collective and historical process, and mainly transmitted through experience and companionship" (Samurçay & Rogalski,

1992). The strength of pragmatic concepts comes from their multi-functionality. They are double-sided: one side is turned towards real time action, i.e. diagnosing the situation according to specific objectives; the other side is turned towards the cognition, the organization of the representations (Vidal-Gomel & Rogalski, 2007). They are at the same time dynamic, operational representations of the work, reducing the complexity of the situation to its most significant variables for action, and long-term organizers of representations, integrating new observations into a consistent "conceptual structure" (Pastré, 1999; 2005) of the situation. Stabilized professional activities have a well-established set of professional concepts, whereas emerging activities produce a lot of new professional concepts. However, in all professional activities, even the most stable ones, these professional concepts get transformed and change as the activity itself, and the workers, evolve. Professional concepts have been the focus of investigation in former research. Here we use them as analytical tools and track their development in the dialogue through interlocutory analysis.

THE STORY OF THE RUNAWAY CHILD: WHOSE WORRY?

The following story was examined using the above method. It was about a girl who was visiting her father at his home, as stated in the legally confirmed contract. Both parents and the child were clients of FC, which, as was routine, were investigating the child-mother and child-father interactions. Suddenly, the child ran away from her father back to her mother. That evening the father had an appointment with Family Counseling for the analysis of the interaction between himself and his daughter. Because the child had run away, the mother, rather than the father, brought the child to the appointment. There was an open conflict between the two parents. The father would have liked the child to go back to his home because it was his legal meeting time, as stated in the contract. The mother, however, thought that the child should be with her because she had just run away from her father. In this situation, the parents 'threw the ball' to the FC therapists, who decided in favor of the father, in line with the contract. The mother's story also expresses other concerns, such as the child having to confront the social authorities and the father alone. As an example of this, she claimed that the girl had told her: "they (the authorities) cannot understand that my father is bad because he talks so nicely to them".

The data episode concerning the participants' joint examination of this story is particularly interesting because here, the method did not seem to work in the way the researchers expected. Despite the evident distress of the child, in this instance, according to the data, none these service functions expressed a need to take action. The discussion was difficult and even the hybrid concept of 'worry' was criticized. We chose this episode precisely because of its difficulty. By analyzing it we may better understand the conditions and limitations of both the method and cross-function mediation in SSDF. We would like to emphasize, however, that the analysis of this episode does not do justice to the whole intervention, which was generally fruitful in terms of developmental ideas and possibilities (Seppänen, Cerf & Toiviainen, 2013). The multi-layered story, as told by the mother in the interview, was not easy to understand. The FC therapists present in the workshop remembered this situation and had to explain it to the other participants. Below, we first outline the episode that shows and interprets interesting excerpts from the perspective of hybrid and professional concepts. Then we turn to the micro-analysis of hybrid and professional concept use. The discussion emphasized that it had been a confusing situation for the child. From the perspective of FC, the worry was about how to support the father so that the child does not feel the need to run away from him. However, the parents wanting FC to decide where the child should go was an unexpected and unwanted problem for FC.

Excerpt 2. Three periods (...) mean a silence, possibly indicating hesitation.

Researcher 1: This worry actually came very physically to FC, if we think about whose worry it should be, do you think it belongs to FC?

Family Counseling Therapist 1: Well let's say that it came, considerably, to be our worry. But it was not a worry according to the original plan. The appointments were for quite another purpose.

Researcher1: Yes, so this worry should not... in your opinion, belong to FC, or?

Family Counseling Therapist 1: Well at least it didn't... yes, it shouldn't, it didn't promote the process we were carrying out [with the family].

The head of FLI drew attention to what the girl, according to the mother's reported speech, had said. Her worry was, above all, whether the girl feels that nobody believes her.

Excerpt 3. Family Legal Issues 3: I'm thinking about what the child said, although it was the mother who said it: "they cannot understand that my father is bad because he talks so nicely to them", and if the child thinks like this, does it mean that she also feels that nobody... believes what she says because (...)

Family Legal Issues 3: the father can talk so nicely. This is quite important, if a child says this, what is... the story behind this?

Family Legal Issues 1: I think that this is quite typical of what parents say about each other when they can speak, well, then the authorities believe them.

Family Legal Issues3: Yes, exactly.

Family Legal Issues1: It is very common, almost in every case.

Family Legal Issues3: Yes indeed.

The original idea of the girl possibly feeling that nobody believes her turns into a question of mistrust between the parents in dispute, which in turn seems to affect how social workers trust what parents say. Tolerating the distrust between the parents is an important mediator and psychological tool for social practitioners working with parents in a prolonged divorce. Here, it is anchored as a common feature of their work, and is not questioned. Simultaneously, this excerpt also shows how the child's issue becomes silenced under the loud dispute of the parents. The point raised by the head of FLI (3) remains an observation in the discussion, and does not lead to any action. Next there was a lengthy discussion about the possible role of FLI in the story. The child running away violated both the father's right to meet the child and the contract. The FC therapist, hesitating, sketched 'the violation of the contract' as the worry, questioning who the actors of this worry are.

Excerpt 4. Family Legal Issues 2: I was thinking about our... role here. That this should be our worry, as in the violation of the contract, somehow I can't see that.

Family Counseling Therapist 1: Yes, it was only kind of... I said this was not a worry that really belonged to Family legal issues, but in a way... that... the worry that exists here is that the validated contract did not, in fact, function in any way. So, I don't know whose worry it is but the contract was violated in practice. So is the contract wrong, or somehow unsuitable, or was there some other reason why it did not function, but that it was... the situation showed this.

The conflict here was between the contract as a legal device and the actions of the family, when the "contract was violated". FLI representatives responded that, basically, as long as the parents themselves do not come to them and ask for help, i.e., give them an assignment, FLI is not able to act. They need *the request* from the parents.

Excerpt 5. Family Legal Issues 3: Well maybe the worry is challenging here...

NGO researcher: Yes it is.

Family Legal Issues 3:... in different functions because I don't really, I'll try to understand the previous idea (Family Legal Issues2)... the clients come to us with their worry, so if these parents had come, or one of them, had taken the initiative, then they would have come to us with their worry which was this dysfunctional contract, but now they didn't... we can't act if we are not asked to do so.

NGO researcher: No (inaudible)

Then, another therapist from FC questioned the concept of worry, because it assumes a problem before acting.

Excerpt 6. Family Counseling Therapist 4: Well, what is this about, I wonder about the word worry. There's a problem with the word worry. The worry is a kind of motor that makes people act. If you are not worried there is nothing. You want to act, so is worry really a suitable word here? It is problematic because you should make people worried in order to be involved in the activity. When you read this story, the mother's or father's worry...

The researcher then asked what would be a better word, stating that the concept of worry belongs to 'helping rhetoric' and may exclude the justice system involved. A CP worker supported the FC therapist:

Excerpt 7. Child Protection 2: I think, if I can continue, even if you don't have a concrete request to do something, but...what even child protection doesn't do, but some perspective of expertise to a... situation. When you don't know everything, and this is so sectorized, so... I somehow [think that], through this networking we get [more expertise], that this expert can say something about this matter that I can't. It doesn't have to be a worry yet, but a weak signal (laugh). Or something, what words do we use nowadays?

A new professional concept, a weak signal, was proposed here. Even though there is no request yet, the service network may bring expertise and support for individual practitioners, also in cases of 'weak signals' where there is no worry yet. This discussion did not continue, because the researcher asked again about CP's role in this story. The two colleagues from CP answered this in general terms, which made clear that this case of a child running away did not fulfill their criteria for action. Then, the researcher concluded: "It seems that, when talking about requests, in this case, there is no one to take responsibility for them". This is seen in the column number four (Figure 2) where no worries (X) are marked in the rows of the three service functions. Then, the discussion turned to the next story.

MICRO-ANALYSIS OF THE EPISODE

In this sub-section, we analyze both the hybrid and professional mediating concepts as they appear in the discussion of the episode. The professionals' concepts are present in the professionals' talk and mediate their everyday activity (here the concept of "interaction"), whereas hybrid concepts are taken from the professionals' talk and literature on social services and the ideas of the researchers (in the intervention, the concept of "worry"). When reflecting on the story, we are interested in how these concepts operated. The concept of 'worry' mediated the relations of FC with their clients by observing the child's confusion, supporting the father in spending time with his child, and concerning about the violation of the contract. The 'worry' did not match FLI's framework for action. Worry is interestingly re-interpreted in two ways: first, for FLI, a worry comes only after a parent's worry has created a *request* for FLI to act. This idea anchors (Marková 2000) the story in the existing framework of FLI, showing a condition and a rule for their action. The second interpretation is that proposed by the CP worker, the concept of a *weak signal* instead of a worry. Two ideas may be behind this: First, a strategic need for more anticipative and preventive services, where 'a weak signal' implies something, whereas a worry means that a problem has already occurred. The 'traffic light framework', popular in social services (Seppänen 2009), may exemplify this. Green stands for normal, yellow for risky situations, and red is when a problem already exists. In this sense, the concept of a weak signal may have been a new framing, or objectification in Marková's (2000) terms, that goes further than the assumption that first there needs to be a

worry or a problem. A weak signal can indeed be a promising professional concept, but it was not elaborated on here and cannot yet give criteria for services on when or how to act. Second, going from worries to weak signals may indicate a move from focusing on negative problems to looking at the positive germs or possibilities at hand. On the basis of the overall workshop discussion of 3.5 hours, both these ideas are plausible. The main professional concepts used in our episode can be seen in Table 2.

What does our analysis tell about needs for action and inter-functional collaboration in this service network? One striking result when we look at the right hand column (Table 2) is that all these professionals' concepts enable the practitioners from different functions to mediate their relationships with some aspects of divorced families, but not to their colleagues from different functions. In this confrontation with the data and following discussion, the professionals and researchers discuss the case using professional concepts to support their analysis and argumentation, but they do not manage to create efficient cross-functional concepts for the future cases. The professional concepts serve as mediations within a service,

Table 2. Professional concepts in the data

Professional Concept	Unit or Function	Used in Relation to...That is, What Does this Professional Concept Reveal About the Client-Object and the Services
Interaction, interaction prob-lem	FC	Part of the quality of child-mother or child-father relations.
Investigation	FC	Investigation of interactions (above) are carried out to enable planning of therapies or other FC support.
FC visit	FC	Investigations are carried out during family members' visits to FC.
Meeting	FC	In joint custody, children have a right to regularly meet both parents.
Meeting contract	FC, (FLI)	Meetings are agreed in the contract made in the divorce. FLI support parents in making the contract and legally confirm it.
Assignment	FLI	A parent or both parents contact FLI about the contract, which creates an assignment for FLI. Otherwise FLI does not act.
Running away	(CP)	A child, expressing something by running away. Serious cases of running away belong to the tasks of CP, but not the case in Story 4.
Weak signal	At least CP, maybe shared?	Network collaboration may bring new expertise to actors by revealing weak signals.

but do not manage to cross the boundaries, even in the discussion, as client-driven collaboration may require. *Running away*, as it appeared concretely in the story and Figure 2, did not come to lead any of these functions to service action. *Weak signal* as discussed above emerged as a new promising concept.

However, the professional concept of "meeting contract" appears to function in a cross-functional way. It derives from the professional concept of meeting, used by FC to describe the problem in the case. It is first mentioned by FC with the form "meeting contract" ("a meeting contract which does not come true as it was agreed") after a question of the researchers regarding whose worry the case is, and later generalized with the term "contract" ("a worry that exists here is that a contract made and validated in fact did not come true in any way", then qualified as "wrong contract"), also in an attempt to make sense of the case with the concept and tab of "worries" offered by the researchers as second stimulus in the situation. The concept of "contract" is used by workers from a different background (FLI) in an attempt at understanding the legal status. "Is it a contract or a decision?" is a question which led to the interesting answer "it is a worry under elaboration". The term is then recoined as "unworkable contract" by the people from FC. In the discussion, the concept of "contract" does not serve as a cross-functional mediating tool. However, the emerging notion of "unworkable contract" may be efficient as a cross-functional concept.

DISCUSSION

The workshop helped the professionals articulate and share differing practices. Its discussion was very rich in developmental talk (Seppänen, Cerf and Toiviainen 2013). Perhaps the most important outcomes were the ideas on how to further develop the collaborative services, such as learning more about networking methods, using the clients'

natural networks and support persons more, and better identification of divorce cases at risk of crisis. Later, in an SSDF project meeting, there were general motivation and plans to experiment with these ideas. Moreover, these workshops yielded reflection on and questioning of some established institutional practices between FC and Child Therapy Clinics, which have been examined elsewhere (Seppänen, Cerf & Toiviainen 2013; Heikkilä 2014). Within these longer timeframes of the workshop and the research project, the meaning of the analyzed episode above was essentially to make visible, through the interlocutory analysis of hybrid and professional concepts, the diversity and multi-voicedness of these social services. Next, these findings are discussed in terms of professional concepts and their capacity to mediate.

Professional Concepts and Mediation in SSDF

One interesting finding is that the professional concepts tracked in this sequence serve as functional, and not inter-functional, mediations. They are used by professionals from one profile and cannot cross the borders of different functions. None of them, after being used by one professional, is re-used in the discussion between professionals. They do not enable to connect talks of different professionals, nor their concerns or work objects. These professional concepts may serve within an institutionalized sector to think and coordinate action, but they do not manage -at least in this sequence- to serve as cross-functional psychological tools to help the professionals from different functions reflect on a shared case, and coordinate further joint action. The professional concepts mentioned in this sequence all relate the services to their client (service-client relation), but none of them connects the services together (service-service relation). The analysis of this sequence highlights first, the lack of cross-functional mediations which could support the professionals in optimizing and coordinating their joint, networked, activity. As stated above, the most promising professional concept which appears to function in a slightly cross-functional way is the professional concept of "meeting contract". Conceptualizing the contract as a practice which links the making the contract with putting it into practice could have developmental potential for collaboration in social work (Poikela, 2010). It is hypothesized that some professional concepts may serve as germs for enhancing cross-functional mediations as they appear to be stronger than others for mediating the functional relations. This leads the discussion to developmental questions of enhancing network collaboration.

How to Develop Cross-Functional Mediation

The methods of intervention, as they are both designed and used, substantially impact on the intervention outcomes. According to Engeström & Sannino (2012) we need to look at instruction and learning as dialectically intertwined. The prescribed and planned process which the instructor is trying to implement must be compared and contrasted with the actual process performed by the learners. The two will never fully coincide. The gap, struggle, negotiation and occasional merger between the two need to be taken as key resources for understanding the processes of learning as processes of formation of agency" (Engeström & Sannino, 2012, p. 46). The meaning-generating effect of diversity, prevalent in networks, cannot always be presupposed. In inter-cultural or inter-professional collaboration, it should be encouraged that the other participants and their arguments be taken as strange and new, because in this way, meaning and concept formation can be generated by actively working on diversity (Akkerman et al., 2006). Following this, the aim of the method design and use in our episode was to make diversity visible by examining the boundaries of worry and the division of labor between functional units. The first stimulus was stories

concerning the child. They were already mediated by the parents' interpretations and therefore they made up complicated mirror data. The concreteness of the stories was their developmental strength. The second stimulus was the concept of worry, which was initially thought to be a shared concept among professionals. The analysis of the sequence reveals that it is not the case. "Worries" appeared to be ambiguous stimuli, triggering attempts by the professionals to make sense of them in different contexts. Its ambiguity may originate from its transition from the informal use of the professionals to its (perhaps semi-formal, if considered from the participants' view) use in the intervention, i.e. its hybrid nature. However, this ambiguity was not problematic for the goals of the workshop, which were to support collective thinking and elaboration. Ambiguous as it may be, the concept of worry triggered discussions among professionals in which they expressed different views and perspectives on the case. We would even argue that this ambiguity, combined with the formal exercise of filling a table with crosses to identify worries, which was pursued energetically by the researchers, contributed to the ability of the professionals to elaborate from their professional perspectives on the problematic case. Ambiguity can be an important feature of second stimuli applied in developmental network interventions. In this sense, the concept of worry perfectly played its role to support collective elaboration in dialogue.

BENEFITS OF JOINT ANALYSIS

The DWR-informed and Activity Clinic-informed interlocutory joint analysis in this chapter has been beneficial at least in two respects. First, our findings suggest that multi-voicedness may be an underused resource in practical developmental interventions following DWR. In the SSDF case, this means that it is useful for professionals to know and understand the differing professional concepts of other functions. Multi-voicedness is both inter-individual and intra-individual, because one person may go through various perspectives or voices during her activity (Kloetzer, 2008). This is important because the motivation and questioning, also in the collective discussion, can be enhanced by the multiple voices or double binds experienced by individuals. Second, the analysis has revealed how professional concepts may change their function when they are taken into use by interventionists. Worry and green areas are examples of how their purposeful use in the intervention transforms them from professional to hybrid concepts. The nature of professional concepts is situational and action-bound.

FUTURE RESEARCH DIRECTIONS

This particular episode was chosen because, initially, it was hypothesized that strong institutionalized and stabilized professional concepts may, besides enable, also limit professionals from seeing things (such as weak signals) that can be relevant or essential in a long run. The findings concerning the concept of running away of the child partly support this hypothesis. But the outcome of the episode (Figure 1) may also be seen as handing the responsibility over to the parents, an important aspect in client orientation, suggesting that sometimes it is wise for the services not to act. Also, as shown in the excerpt 3, children's matters may be observed but do not necessarily lead to service actions. The boundary between services acting or not acting needs to be investigated further. Also, an interplay between 'justice and helping systems', as proposed by one professional, could be an important research topic, because the justice system seems to affect the social services more than the analysis here has been able to show. However we might find traces of this in the weight given to the concept of "meeting contract" among the

professionals. The SSDF intervention of this chapter followed the principles of DWR. Collaboration between DWR and Activity Clinic approaches came later during the phase of data analysis. Their joint application in designing and implementing developmental interventions would help better understand their similarities and differences, and extend the instrumentality or other resources in understanding and enhancing mediations.

CONCLUSION

We approached the question of how to develop inter-functional network collaboration from the perspective of analyzing professional concepts in a developmental intervention following the principles of Developmental Work Research. An episode in which professionals from three functions of social services for divorced families made sense of and reflected on a service situation of a client was analyzed. The various contexts of the episode were described. One interesting finding is that the professional concepts tracked in this sequence serve as functional and not inter-functional mediations, and could not cross the borders of different functions. It is hypothesized that some professional concepts may serve as germs for enhancing cross-functional mediations as they appear to be stronger than others for mediating the functional relations. Based on the findings, questions of developing cross-functional collaboration were discussed. The concept of worry was used as a second stimulus in the intervention. "Worries" appeared to be ambiguous stimuli, triggering attempts by the professionals to make sense of them in different contexts. It is argued that this ambiguity, combined with a formal visual exercise, contributed to the ability of the professionals to elaborate from their professional perspectives on the problematic case.

REFERENCES

Akkerman, S., Admiraal, W., Simons, R. J., & Niessen, T. (2006). Considering diversity: Multivoicedness in international academic collaboration. *Culture and Psychology*, *12*(4), 461–485. doi:10.1177/1354067X06069947

Arnkil, T. E., Eriksson, E. & Saikku, P. (1998). Huolen harmaa vyöhyke. [The grey zone of the worry, in Finnish]. *Dialogi, 1998*(7), 8-11.

Austin, J. L. (1962). *How to do things with words.* Oxford University Press.

Bodrožić, Z. (2008). *Post-industrial intervention. An activity-theoretical expedition tracing the proximal development of forms of conducting interventions.* Helsinki: University of Helsinki, Department of Education.

Boltanski, L., & Chiapello, E. (2005). *The new spirit of capitalism.* London: Verso.

Engeström, Y. (1987). *Learning by expanding. An activity-theoretical approach to developmental research.* Helsinki: Orienta-Konsultit.

Engeström, Y., & Kerosuo, H. (2007). From workplace learning to inter-organizational learning and back: The contribution of activity theory. *Journal of Workplace Learning*, *19*(6), 336–342. doi:10.1108/13665620710777084

Engeström, Y., & Sannino, A. (2012). Whatever happened to process theories of learning? *Learning. Culture and Social Interaction*, *1*(1), 45–56. doi:10.1016/j.lcsi.2012.03.002

Eriksson, E., & Arnkil, T. E. (2009). *Taking up one's worries.* National Institute for Health and Welfare.

Head, B. W. (2008). Assessing network-based collaborations. Effectiveness for whom? *Public Management Review*, *10*(6), 733–749. doi:10.1080/14719030802423087

Heikkilä, H. (forthcoming in 2014). *The dialectics between transformative agency and work-related well-being in network activity*. Manuscript under elaboration.

Jung, T. (2010). Citizens, co-producers, customers, clients, captives? A critical review of consumerism and public services. *Public Management Review*, *12*(3), 439–446. doi:10.1080/14719031003787940

Kerosuo, H. (2006). *Boundaries in action. An activity-theoretical study of development, learning and change in health care for patients with multiple and chronic illnesses.* University of Helsinki.

Kloetzer, L. (2008). *Analyse de l'homélie de la messe dominicale: Langage et conflits de métier dans l'activité des prêtres: La part de Dieu, la part de l'homme.* (Doctoral thesis in Psychology). CNAM, Paris, France.

Kloetzer, L. (2012). Development of professional concepts through work analysis: Tech Diving under the loop of Activity Clinic. *Mind, Culture, and Activity*, *20*(4), 318–337. doi:10.1080/1074 9039.2012.688087

Kloetzer, L., & Seppänen, L. (2014). Dialogues and interactions as "the nursery for change". *Outlines - Critical Practice Studies, 15*(2), 1-4.

Kostulski, K. (2011). Formes et fonctions psychologiques des réalisations langagières: Vers une psychologie concrète du langage. In Note de synthèse en vue de l'obtention de l'Habilitation à Diriger des Recherches. Université de Paris 8.

Kostulski, K., & Kloetzer, L. (2014). Controversy as a Developmental Tool in Cross-Self Confrontation. *Outlines: Critical Practice Studies*, *15*(2), 54–73.

Lektorsky, V. A. (2009). Mediation as a means of collective activity. In A. Sannino, H. Daniels, & K. Gutiérrez (Eds.), *Learning and expanding with activity theory.* Cambridge, UK: Cambridge University Press. doi:10.1017/CBO9780511809989.006

Leont'ev, A. N. (1978). *Activity, consciousness, and personality*. Englewood Cliffs, NJ: Prentice-Hall.

Lorino, P., Tricard, B., & Clot, Y. (2011). Research methods for non-representational approaches to organizational complexity: The dialogical mediated inquiry. *Organization Studies*, *32*(6), 769–801. doi:10.1177/0170840611410807

Marková, I. (2000). Amédée and how to get rid of it: Social representations from a dialogical perspective. *Culture and Psychology*, *6*(4), 419–460. doi:10.1177/1354067X0064002

Miettinen, R., Toikka, K., Tuunainen, J., Freeman, S., Lehenkari, J., Leminen, J., & Siltala, J. (2008). *Informaatiotekninen kumous, innovaatiopolitiikka ja luottamus* (Vol. 234/2008. sivu 3, 9.6.2008). Helsinki: Tekesin katsaus 234/2008.

Ministry of Social Affairs and Health. (2010). *Socially sustainable Finland 2020*. Strategy for social and health policy, Ministry of Social Affairs and Health. Retrieved from http://www.stm.fi/c/document_library/get_file?folderId=2765155&name=DLFE-15321.pdf

Niskala, A. (2010). Mallinnus sosiaalityön kehittämisen välineenä [Modeling as a tool in developing social work, in Finnish]. Asiakkuus sosiaalityössä. Gaudeamus Helsinki University Press.

Pastré, P. (1999). La conseptualisation dans l'action: Bilan et nouvelles perspectives. *Education Permanente*, *139*(2), 13–35.

Pastré, P. (2005) Analyse d'un apprentissage sur simulateur: de jeunes ingénieursaux prises avec la conduit d'une central nucléare. In Apprendre par la simulation. Toulouse: Octarés.

Poikela, R. (2010). *Asiakassuunnitelma asiakaslähtöistä auttamista tavoitteellistamassa.* [From a client plan to user perspective in multiprofessional social work. A method of emerging object with multiple voices. In Finnish, abstract in English]. Valtiotieteellinen tiedekunta. Helsinki, Helsingin yliopisto. Väitöskirja.

Ruotsala, R. (2014). Developing a tool for cross-functional collaboration: The trajectory of an annual clock. *Outlines. Critical Practice Studies*, *15*(2), 31–53.

Samurçay, R., & Rogalski, R. (1992). Formation aux activités de gestion d'environnements dynamiques: Concepts et methods. *Activités (Vitry-sur-Seine)*, *8*(2), 4–31.

Satka, M. (2010). Varhainen puuttuminen ja sosiaalityö. In M. Laitinen & A. Pohjola (Eds.), *Asiakkuus sosiaalityössä* (pp. 181–276). Helsinki: Gaudeamus Helsinki University Press.

Schaupp, M., Seppänen, L., Korpelainen, E., Kira, M., & Toiviainen, H. (2013). *Yhdessä vihreälle alueelle. Kohaus-hankkeen raportti eroperheiden palveluverkostosta. Julkaisematon raportti*. Helsinki: Työterveyslaitos.

Searle, J. R., & Vanderveken, D. (1985). *Foundations of illocutionary logic*. Cambridge, UK: Cambridge University Press.

Seikkula, J., & Arnkil, T. E. (2005). *Dialoginen verkostotyö*. Tammi.

Seikkula, J., Arnkil, T. E., & Eriksson, E. (2003). Postmodern society and social networks: Open and anticipation dialogues in network meetings. *Family Process*, *42*(2), 185–203. doi:10.1111/j.1545-5300.2003.42201.x PMID:12879593

Seppänen, L. (2009). Kuvia ja näkökulmia perheneuvolatyön lähikehitykseen. *KONSEPTI - Toimintakonseptin Uudistajien Verkkolehti*, *5*(2). Retrieved from www.muutoslaboratorio.fi

Seppänen, L., Ala-Laurinaho, A., Launis, K., & Schaupp, M. (August 2009). *Representing changes in work in and for developmental interventions*. Paper presented at the 17th World Congress on Ergonomics: Changes, Challenges and Opportunities. Beijing, China.

Seppänen, L., Cerf, M., & Toiviainen, H. (2013). *Multi-voiced customer understanding in the zone of proximal development of public service networks*. Paper presented at the EGOS 2013 Conference. New York, NY.

Seppänen, L., Schaupp, M., Toiviainen, H., Ala-Laurinaho, A., Heikkilä, H., Kira, M., et al. (2012). *Palveluverkostojen asiakasymmärryksen tutkimuslähtökohtia: Konseptimuutosten haasteet ja työhyvinvointi* Retrieved from https://helda.helsinki.fi/handle/10138/32393

Toiviainen, H., Kerosuo, H., & Syrjälä, T. (2009). "Development Radar": The co-configuration of a tool in a learning network. *Journal of Workplace Learning*, *21*(7), 509–524. doi:10.1108/13665620910985513

Trognon, A., & Kostulski, K. (1999). Éléments d'une théorie sociocognitive de l'interaction conversationnelle. *Psychologie Française*, *44*(4), 307–318.

Vidal-Gomel, C., & Rogalski, J. (2007). La conceptualization et la place des concepts pragmatiques dans l'activité professionnelle et le developpement des compétences. *Activités (Vitry-sur-Seine)*, *4*(1), 49–84.

Virkkunen, J., & Newnham, D. S. (2013). *The Change Laboratory. A tool for collaborative development of work and education*. Rotterdam: Sense Publishers.

Virtanen, P., Suoheimo, M., Lamminmäki, S., Ahonen, P., & Suokas, M. (2011). *Matkaopas asiakaslähtöisten sosiaali- ja terveyspalvelujen kehittämiseen*. Helsinki: Tekesin katsaus 281/2011.

Vygotsky, L. S. (1978). *Mind in society: The psychology of higher mental functions*. Cambridge, MA: Harvard University Press.

ADDITIONAL READING

Clot, Y. (2009). Clinic of activity: the dialogue as an instrument. A. Sannino, H. Daniels & K. Gutiérrez (Eds.) Learning and expanding with activity theory. (286-302). Cambrigde: Cambridge University Press.

Clot, Y., & Kostulski, K. (2011). Intervening for transforming: The horizon of action in the Clinic of Activity. *Theory & Psychology*, *21*(5), 681–696. doi:10.1177/0959354311419253

Edwards, A. (2010). *Being an expert professional practitioner: The relational turn in expertise*. Dordrecht: Springer. doi:10.1007/978-90-481-3969-9

Edwards, A., Daniels, H., Gallagher, T., Leadbetter, J., & Warmington, P. (2009). *Improving inter-professional collaborations. Multi-agency working for children's wellbeing*. Routledge.

Engeström, Y. (2007). Putting Vygotsky to work: the Change Laboratory as an application of Double Stimulation. H. Daniels, M. Cole & J. W. Wertsch (Eds.), The Cambridge Companion to Vygotsky (363-382): Cambridge University Press.

Engeström, Y. (2011). From design experiments to formative interventions. *Theory & Psychology*, *21*(5), 598–628. doi:10.1177/0959354311419252

Engeström, Y., & Sannino, A. (2012). Concept formation in the wild. *Mind, Culture, and Activity*, *19*(3), 201–2012. doi:10.1080/10749039.2012.690813

Greeno, J. G. (2012). Concepts in activities and discourses. *Mind, Culture, and Activity*, *19*(3), 310–313. doi:10.1080/10749039.2012.691934

Hall, R., & Horn, I. S. (2012). Talk and conceptual change at work: Adequate representation and epistemic stance in a comparative analysis of statistical consulting and teacher workgroups. *Mind, Culture, and Activity*, *19*(3), 240–258. doi:10.1080/10749039.2012.688233

Pereira-Querol, M. A., Seppänen, L., & Virkkunen, J. (2014). Exploring the developmental possibilities of environmental activities: On-farm biogas production. *Environmental Science & Policy*, *37*, 134–141. doi:10.1016/j.envsci.2013.09.010

Virkkunen, J., & Ristimäki, P. (2012). Double stimulation in strategic concept formation: An activity-theoretical analysis of business planning in a small technology firm. *Mind, Culture, and Activity*, *19*(3), 273–286. doi:10.1080/10749039.2012.688234

Wertsch, J. V. (2007). Mediation. H. Daniels, M. Cole & J. Wertsch (Eds.), The Cambridge Companion to Vygotsky (178-192): Cambridge University Press.

KEY TERMS AND DEFINITIONS

Developmental Intervention: Purposeful action by a human agent to support the redirection of ongoing change. The interventionist comes between an actor's actions so that the activity finds a new direction. (Virkkunen & Newnham 2013).

Developmental Work Research (DWR): An interventionist research approach, developed originally in Finland during 1980s and 1990s. Being mainly based on works of L. S. Vygotsky, A. N. Leont'ev and Y.Engeström. DWR applies a dialectical view of development. Some of its key principles are crystallized in a model of an activity system and a cycle of expansive learning (Engeström 1987).

Dual Stimulation: Vygotsky's method in which a person is given a task to be accomplished, and a neutral object is made available for her which s/he can use in accomplishing the task (Engeström 2007).

First Stimulus: A task given to an individual or group to be accomplished in dual stimulation. In developmental interventions the first stimulus can be videotaped, textual or audio taped material from participants' own work in the task of re-interpreting it. In Developmental Work Research the first stimulus is often called mirror data.

Mediation: Instead of acting in a direct, unmediated way in the social and physical world, our contact with the world is indirect, mediated by signs and tools e.g. professional concepts. Mediation builds a link between individuals' mental processes and social historical processes (Wertsch 2007).

Networking: As a third alternative besides hierarchy and markets for organizing activities, networking is seen as an increasing trend in work that has potential in solving problems related to, for example, quality of services or efficiency. In this chapter, networking is conceptualized as inter-functional or inter-institutional collaboration towards a shared object such as customers.

Professional Concept: Concepts that are mastered in a professional activity by its practitioners and potentially transmitted and refined through training, mentoring or practice (Kloetzer 2012).

Second Stimulus: A neutral object or sign that is made available to participants in accomplishing a task in a developmental intervention. It is important that the second stimulus is explicitly fulfilled by the participants with specific contents that correspond to their assessment of the situation in order to have personal sense for them (Engeström 2007).

Chapter 11
Explorative Actions in Search for a New Logic of Business Activity

Päivi Ristimäki
University of Helsinki, Finland

ABSTRACT

This chapter analyzes a Finnish ICT firm's explorative actions after the firm's predominant business logic based on technological product development had come to the end of its lifecycle. The explorative actions are seen here both as a means of learning to break out from the historically formed work routines and as a means for inventing a new ground for business logic. For this study, an analytical model was created for depicting explorative actions in the ICT firm's marketing. The analysis of engendered explorative actions during the period of three years shows how new modes of interacting with the customers contributed to the managements' strategic reorientation. The explorative actions intertwined aspects of exploration and exploitation in a dialectical unity of opposites. The study also highlights the role of everyday experience of problems and the role of intellectual understanding of an aggravating contradiction in activity as stimuli to take explorative actions.

ORGANIZATIONAL BACKGROUND

This is a study of a small-sized and semi-independent Finnish ICT firm (labeled hereafter FICT). The business activity of the firm emerged some thirty years ago with an invention of a new software application (later in the text 'basic product'). In 1996, FICT was incorporated to become a daughter firm of an internationally operating ICT company. The vision of the firm was to innovate within new emerging technologies. However, product development in neither the internet nor mobile technology succeeded financially well enough. Therefore, in 2005 the parent company split the FICT's business activity into three small business firms. The main part of product development was now in the hands of the parent company. Since then, FICT's business was again based on the basic product. At this point, an internal developmental project was introduced in FICT to solve practical challenges of upgrading the basic product. Six months later, this developmental activity in the firm turned to

DOI: 10.4018/978-1-4666-6603-0.ch011

the management team´s strategic planning activity to appraise business sustainability. The outcome of these developmental efforts materialized in two respects. First, to upgrade the product a list of improvements for work practices was produced. A series of workshops were organized to collectively interpret and prioritize what needed to be improved. Additionally, the management team created a suggestion for alternative strategic options (termed as alternative business models) in order for the board of directors to gain mandate for new business openings (Virkkunen & Ristimäki, 2012). The FICT´s management team expected to create a partner network and gain growth as a dealer of technology-related services of partner firms. However, as this study indicates, more developmental actions were needed to interpret and trace a sustainable and adaptable solution for business activity.

INTRODUCTION

The era of information and communication technology embodies techno-socio-economic transformation processes triggered by profound technological innovations. Perez (2002; 2005) portrays technological revolutions as surges of development in two phases. In the first, the installation phase, new potentials for productive activity are created through the evolution of applications of the inventions. The groundbreaking product development in this phase is supported by financial investors expecting high revenues by taking high risks. According to Perez (2014, p. 7), "technology-push" characterizes the mode of development in that period. After the bubble of overinvestment in the new technologies bursts out in a financial crisis, a new period starts in which the development is based more on "demand-pull" and broad deployment of the new technologies in all areas of the society. The deployment phase of the information and communication technological surge has been characterized by the development

of dedicated, industry-oriented applications and the production of comprehensive ICT architectures providing largely shared, dynamic and networked ICT ecologies and enabling new service concepts (Prahalad & Krishnan 2008; Perez 2014). Cusumano, Suarez & Kahl (2008) have described the spreading of the use of new information and communication technologies with the help of a business lifecycle model. According to them, business activities are predominantly engaged in products through new technological innovations. Experimentation in the markets with various product concepts leads to a standard solution and turns the focus on competition and cost efficiency in the production of the standard solution. After the broad use of the standard product, the focus of competition moves on technology-related services and the support of the implementation and use of technological applications.

Cusumano (2004, p. 5-7) states that in this phase a firm has to tackle simultaneously both the requirements of software as an expanding and integrating technology and the requirements of the competed business of its use. This can be interpreted to indicate that in the lifecycle of the markets of new technology two profound expansions in the object of the business activity take place: one from product development to mastering also the production and distribution of the product and another from that further to mastering also the use contexts of the new technology. These expansions and the changes in the market conditions of new technology-related businesses call for major changes in the logic and model of the business of the firms whose activity depends on new technologies.

According to March (1991), there is a trade-off in business strategy between exploitation of existing and exploration of new resources and knowhow. Exploitation means extending the limits of the prevailing activity by choosing from existing alternatives or by creating new options on the basis of the prevailing premises. Exploration means breaking away from the predominant activity and searching for options outside its boundaries. March claims that exploration and exploitation are two alternative modes of using resources that has to be balanced in business activity. Lately however, Lavie, Stettner & Tushman (2010, p. 113) have pointed out that exploitation and exploration are not dichotomous options but that both exist in varying degrees in business transformations. Much of the research on exploration and exploitation in business development has focused on the forms of achieving the balance March (1991) calls for through creating "adaptive or ambidextrous organizations" (Raisch, Birkenshaw, Probst, & Tushmann, 2009; Smith & Lewis, 2011).

In light of Perez's (2002) theory of technology surges and Cusumano, Suarez & Kahl's (2008) theory of lifecycles of technology- related businesses, one can expect that the need and possibilities for exploration and exploitation do not remain the same but each phase in the lifecycle represents a different set of knowhow and resources to be exploited and new areas to be explored; first the needs and combinations of product features, then the principles of production and distribution, and finally the expansion of business through the development of related services. This corresponds with the view of the evolutionary character and particularity of each business change process that Stacey (1995) and McGrath (2010) highlight. Exploration and exploitation can thus be seen as interacting aspects and moments in the movement into a higher form of the business activity through simultaneous destruction and preservation. Exploration involves the bringing of the already existing to an unknown terrain and reinterpreting it by assessing what needs to be preserved and what should be destroyed (Virkkunen & Virkki, 2014).

The Cultural Historical Activity Theory provides a dialectical approach to analyze the systemic structure and transformation of an activity. This theory highlights subject-object interaction as the central feature of the activities of living beings. The specific characteristic of human activity is that this interaction is culturally mediated through

historically evolved tools including concepts and signs that function as intellectual tools and tools of psychological and social regulation, rules and forms of division of labor. The theory conceptualizes the transformation of an activity as a process of re-mediation, that is, as a process of replacing some existing mediators with new ones. This process comprises simultaneous exploitation of some aspects of existing mediators, abandonment of some of them and exploration and implementation of new ones (Engeström 1987; Virkkunen 2007). According to Leont'ev (1978, p. 58-69), the object of a collective activity, what it transforms and to what it is transformed through the activity, is the distinguishing characteristic of an activity and its true motive, but does not determine directly the nature of the involved individuals' actions that are mediated through the division of labor, available instruments, and rules of the activity (Engeström 1987, p. 78) Leont'ev (1978) characterizes three dialectically interdependent systemic levels which can be identified in human activity.

Thus, in the general flow of activity that makes up the higher, psychologically mediated aspects of human life, our analysis distinguishes, first, separate (particular) activities, using their energizing motives as the criterion. Second, we distinguish actions – the processes subordinated to conscious goals. Finally, we distinguish the operation, which depends directly on conditions under which a concrete goal is attained. These units of human activity form its macrostructure. An important feature of the analysis that leads to distinguishing these units is that it does not rely on separating living activity into elements. Rather, it reveals the inner relations that characterize activity. (p. 64-65)

In the analysis of this study the difference and dialectical relation of short-term, goal-directed actions and more durable object-oriented activity is central. In this study a search for a new business logic is analyzed by focusing on explorative actions taken in the context of the prevailing business activity in which, however, an expansion of the object and purpose of the business activity is reached.

FOCUS OF THE CHAPTER

The study focuses on FICT's management's new marketing actions in customer interface after the parent company had reduced FICT's business to comprise the selling of the basic product and FICT had made the initial developmental efforts to stabilize business. During three years' time several new products, new tools, methods and work patterns for meeting customer needs were introduced in order to find opportunities to secure the sustainability and growth of FICT's business. The firm's marketing events formed a platform for the interaction with its customers and to launch new products. After a marketing event the management started customer-based sales activities the outcomes of which were then reflected in the meetings of FICT's new management team. The perceptions of materialized outcomes of the marketing and sales actions had an impact on the following actions taken in customer interface. Thus FICT's marketing comprised chains of interdependent actions related to the exploration of untapped possibilities. The purpose of the study is to trace how the actions of exploration in the customer interface served the management team's learning, strategic reorientation, and search for a new logic for FICT's business. The following two sections present the longitudinal data and the method of analysis used in the study.

MANAGEMENT EFFORTS AT TRANSFORMING FICT'S BUSINESS ACTIVITY

The study concerns assessment meetings of three marketing events that FICT's management team

organized in intervals of one and a half years during 2007-2010. Before the marketing events, new network partners with promising service-based technology products were traced and products to be sold were selected and commercialized, and the events were planned and promoted. In the events the sales of new products was initiated. Afterwards the management team in FICT assessed the outcome of the launch of the new products and product features. The management team planned the following phase and steps in marketing and sales on the basis of their interpretation of the success of the realized actions.

In the analysis of the successive marketing events, a model of a cycle of development was created to depict the connections of each explorative action to other actions in the chain of FICT's marketing and to the responses of the customers. The analytical model and the study of connected marketing events enabled to depict the function of each explorative action in the cyclically proceeding learning process that comprised the internalization of new ideas and instruments of marketing and the externalization of new business ideas in new patterns of work in customer interface. This interplay between retooling and re-objectification of activity in the phases of the three cycles of explorative actions is illustrated in Figure 1.

In the cycle, indications represent symptoms of deteriorating efficacy of the firm's modes of business actions which, therefore, needed to be assessed and remodeled. The cycle starts from complications in the realization of the FICT management team's plans. These were based on indirect indications of the effects of the previous actions on customer reactions and triggered the management to refine and redirect their marketing strategy. As new actions were taken in the next marketing event on the basis of the refined strategy, the response from customers provided direct indications of the effects of the actions in the form of customers' new demands concerning products and service processes. The previous indirect indications were therefore intensified

Figure 1. The model used in the analysis of the management's explorative actions

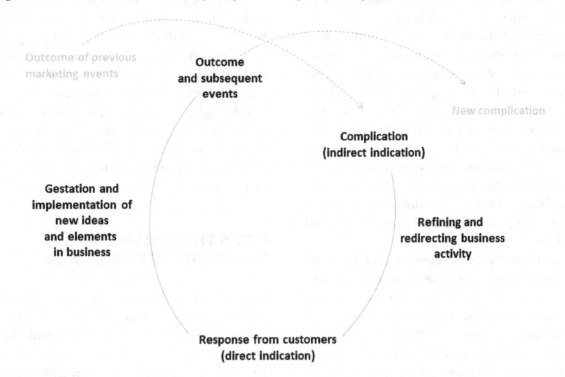

by direct indications of customer reactions. This triggered a search for new ideas and elements in business activity to satisfy the expectations of customers. Many of the discovered ideas were then piloted in the sales actions after the marketing event. The outcomes of the remodeled business activity then triggered new complications when the realization of the new ideas did not lead to positive customer response.

COLLECTION AND ANALYSIS OF LONGITUDINAL DATA

The data consist of transcribed recordings of the management team's discussions in three team meetings. The meetings were held to follow the on-going marketing actions and to configure and guide the subsequent sales and promotion actions. The three marketing events were differed from each other in a way that mirrored the intensity

and nature of the on-going change in the business. The change of the business situation was also reflected in the quality of the conversations in management team meetings. The first piece of data was collected in May 2007 in a meeting of FICT´s service director and product director who evaluated an annual marketing event that for several years had been organized with the same concept called "Spring Cruise". The second piece of data originates from a managerial meeting in November 2008. This meeting was arranged in the midst of a series of events under the title of "FICT Road Show". The series of marketing events lasted from autumn 2008 until the beginning of year 2009 and was targeted mainly for new potential customers. During FICT Road Show sales personnel and other members of the staff travelled around Finland to promote FICT as a product dealer. The third piece of analyzed data was collected in a meeting of FICT directors and the marketing manager in May 2010 right after the remodeled event for key account customers called "Expert Days" had been organized. The researcher of the study participated in each of these management meetings as an interventionist that partly observed and partly facilitated the conversation. For the completion of data analysis, secondary data was required mainly to identify and interpret the outcome of each marketing event and business activity. Primary and secondary data comprise a qualitative, ethnographic data material from FICT´s business activity within five years. The data consist of transcriptions of the total of 75 hours. The primary data of the study is depicted in Table 1.

In the analysis, the content and specific nature of each meeting was first determined. Thereafter, the findings of the secondary, supporting pieces of data derived from events outside the meeting were linked to the discussions in the meetings in order to interpret the changes in the business situation of the firm. In this phase a preliminary analysis of the explorative actions and the analytical model was created on the basis of the analysis of the themes in the management team's discussions. In

the following sections of this study the analysis of the data is elaborated. First, a short history of FICT's marketing is provided portraying the essential marketing events and their outcomes. Thereafter a closer analysis is presented of the explorative actions with the help of the analytical model (Figure 1.). This is depicted in a table to display both the vertical and horizontal movement in explorative actions. Finally, the findings of the analysis and the conclusions of the study are presented.

FICT´S THREE MARKETING EVENTS BETWEEN 2007-2010

In 2005 FICT, the former producer of a groundbreaking technology was turning into a product dealer with high profitability but with limited financial resources and limited resources for product development. The service director emphasized the first phases of the change as follows.

Table 1. The data corpus of the study

Marketing Event	Date	Primary Data for Analysis	Length of the Data
FICT Spring Cruise	May 2007	Meeting of FICT´s Product Director and Service Director on 18th May 2007, i.e. within a couple of days after FICT Spring Cruise. The purpose of the meeting was to evaluate the status of business from the perspective of FICT´s service-based product which promoted for customers at the workshops of the event.	2:12:15
FICT Road Show	September 2008 - February 2009	New business development team´s "business snapshot" meeting on 19th November 2008. The participants of the snapshot meeting are CEO, Sales Director, Product Director and Marketing Manager. In the meeting the participants informed each other, made new plans and decisions regarding FICT´s business actions for the near future. The meeting took place in the midst of a series of FICT Road Show.	1:13:20
FICT Expert Days	May 2010	An assessment meeting of Expert Days on 18th May 2010 was participated by CEO, Sales Director, Product Director and Marketing Manager. In the meeting the participants reflected the renewed concept for marketing events and brainstormed business opportunities.	1:54:48

...earlier when we sold "the basic product" we offered only product technology and the customer was obliged to find elsewhere "an essential component in technology" in order to be able to use the product. In practice, we offered only 1/3 of the whole. Now, the starting point is that we will offer a turnkey solution...

The marketing event in May 2007 was the first opportunity to present the new FICT to the customers.

Marketing Events I: FICT Spring Cruise 2007

FICT Spring Cruise was an annually organized two-day cruise trip for ICT managers and decision makers in FICT´s customer organizations. The main emphasis in the Spring Cruise had always been to support customer relationships when launching new technology products and features in the products. Under the changed circumstances FICT wanted to stress the new potential in business activity and to promote two technology-related service products which during the event were displayed as separately available add-on services. During the first day of the Spring Cruise event the management team of FICT introduced emerging technological trends and the overall development of information and communication technology from its own business perspective. During the second day, product presentations were given for the representatives of the customers in optional workshops. Practical organization of the event followed the model of earlier Spring Cruise events. However, a customer need came up which indicated that more clarifications were needed for service products. Therefore it also turned out that there is a need for distinct documentation and standardization of new service products and turnkey solutions. Thus in the assessment meeting the product director and the service director discussed the specification of the service products, the turnkey solutions and the pricing system. The service director was concerned with possible misinterpretations of the customers, because he had realized that customers interpreted identical documents differently.

When dealing with the sales offer with customer X (during the Cruise) it turned out how little the customer understands about the document. It is only a sales offer... In practice, it is almost identical with the offer for another customer.

Hence the product director and service director concluded that neither was the documentation of product and production processes sufficient nor had they been internally discussed enough with employees of different functions in the firm. They discovered a risk of misunderstanding due to deficient documents, sales offers, and pricing principles. This observation led to two developmental ideas. The first idea was that customer relations should comprise more elements of counselling and collaboration. Secondly, there was a need for collaboration and information sharing was needed between different functions within the firm. Later it was realized that the expectations of the management team to rapidly increase revenue with new products and a turnkey solution were not met with subsequent sales actions. The new technology-related service products did not offer a sufficient basis for business growth. Therefore a year later, FICT decided to initiate a new internal project called New Business Development. It focused on finding new product partners and more products to be provided by FICT. The management team speculated also about the sufficiency of the existing customer base and the potential for growth within it and decided to search for new prospects outside the existing customer segments of public sector organizations and medium-sized private companies. Therefore a new form of marketing event was created to present FICT to private sector organizations as an experienced and service-oriented partner.

Marketing Event II: FICT Road Show 2008 – 2009

FICT Road Show was arranged between September 2008 and February 2009 as a series of marketing events in several localities in Finland. For the audience of the events the earlier promoted service products were not introduced as topic any longer. The management team had made new partner contracts and in consequence wanted to raise the service products of the new partners to key promotional elements of the events. Therefore during the events the participating staff of FICT acted in a supportive role and let representatives of their partnering firms speak for themselves and for their products. Moreover, the management team had made new arrangements and a new organization to reinforce customer support. Some of the experts in the service team were promoted to technical managers in order to work more intensively in customer interface and counsel them in technical issues. The technical managers were also expected to discover new customer needs and product priorities. Therefore their participation in marketing events was vital. Until then, it had become evident that the basic product was reaching the end of its life-cycle as a stand-alone software system. Therefore the new service products that were highlighted at the customer encounters had been selected carefully. However, the introduced new products were in fact just new features in 'the basic product' that the management team expected to prolong the basic product´s life span and give the firm more time to find a new permanent solution for saving their business. Therefore the purpose of FICT Road Show was both to increase the number of customer and sales contacts and to search for potential products outside the area of the existing software applications. Furthermore, FICT's management wanted to create a new business image according to the revised logic of the business. In the midst of the series of marketing events a snapshot meeting of New Business Development Group was carried out to evaluate the state-of-affairs in business. The management team´s perception of how to approach the customers was crystallized in the following words of the CEO who emphasized "a push type of interaction":

Our experiences from last spring show that it is hard for our customers to accept that we ask around how they should be served. On the contrary, we have to have our own story to tell them and sell it to them.

As the first impressions of the marketing events were encouraging, the atmosphere of the meeting was positive as the expressions of the directors revealed:

Act A raises our profile.

Product P will surely create demand.

... by doing Z we will build a new image.

However, keeping a good profitability was more and more based on cutting down the costs rather than on increases in sales. Therefore, the management team also wanted to systematize and organize the follow up of sales. The service director had particularly highlighted the need for predictability and proactivity in business. FICT Road Show was a heavy investment in the search for new elements for the business. The management team expected the customer base to grow and generate sales to pay back the costs of the events in a short run. However, many of the participants at the events were existing customers and a quick response was hard to gain under the conditions of the recently started financial regression. In addition at the end of year 2009 FICT lost one of its biggest customers. This loss was a major turning point in FICT´s business. Later the management team reported that from autumn 2009 on the business was "very silent". These experiences led the FICT´s management team to turn business focus back on the existing customers. The resources of all employees were required for the salvation of the firm. This demanded even more work than previously and led to the following changes. The management team harnessed the service team to search for new ideas at each and every encounter with the customers. A new documentary tool was created for the service employees and it was anticipated to create more collaborative and future oriented working patterns with the customers. The tool was supposed to assist the service employees to identify the customer's unfilled needs. The service team was a trustworthy daily link between FICT and its customers. Many customers had been loyal to the FICT's 'basic product' because it was considered a stable and reliable software system that was well supported by the service team. Moreover, the customers were satisfied with the personal customer care they gained from the service team. For these reasons FICT's management team decided to renew the earlier Spring Cruise and a new type of an event was organized for customers' technical contact persons.

Marketing Event III: Expert Days 2010

During 2010 FICT still had more than 100 organizations as their regular customers who were paying for licenses of 'the basic product'. However, the customer base was clearly shrinking and it was obvious that the business based on product sales of the basic product was losing grounds. A true standpoint for the marketing event called Expert Days were the existing customer organizations and their specific needs and interests which the personnel working on a daily basis with customers had specifically scanned before the event. Due to the effects, the event was more properly coordinated with partnering companies and included product integration based product development. The purpose of the event was to sustain prevailing customer satisfaction at high level and to advance sales by assisting in the purchasing process of customers. The product presentations

were organized as "hands-on workshops" to ease customer perception of the new features and service products and thereby to fasten the decision-making of customers. Now the business activity of FICT was clearly in a double bind situation between 'preserving a product-based logic' and 'orientation towards a new service-based logic'. Critique towards the firm's own business activity was raised in the conversation of the management team. In the following excerpt the sales director expresses the contradictory situation in the business filtered from the experiences at encounters with customers.

The customers have to make double estimations if they will buy from us. The first reason is always the price, of course. The other reason is also a significant matter for them. It deals with the connectivity of our 'basic product' to their systems. Customers have to think also the life cycle of our product and our business. Because, .. in this case... they are not necessarily buying a product with a normal life cycle. Our customers understand that this collaboration may not last more than three years, for example. If an expensive system is in question, it is a big deal for them. Of course we can try to solve the challenges by offering some solutions to prolong the life cycle...

It was obvious that FICT could no longer operate at its "comfort zone" as the CEO had described their position and behavior during previous years. Because of the good business profitability, marks of change had not triggered actions of changing the business logic, but now the loss of customers turned the profitability down and the need for new solutions was experienced more acutely. During the assessment meeting of Expert Days, the service director had launched the idea of 'customer clinics' as a form of special treatment for individual customer. This idea inspired the sales director to model an expansive solution for the crisis of their business activity.

Here I see a connection to service business ... in the future a customer could outsource their infrastructural development for us, expect us to make suggestions on how to develop it, what hardware would be needed, what type of virus defence system should be acquired, and which supplier could be used ... this type of services would bring us consultative elements ... from our perspective this would mean that we also have to start discussions with IT directors about our role for their business if we could have a consultative role related to their business, if we could take care of their infrastructures.

This new logic of business activity was, however, never materialized. The changes aggravated into a double-bind situation too late. During that time there were some twenty employees left in FICT, which means only about five per cent from the number of employees FICT had had when the business was prospering. A few months later the parent company made a decision to merge FICT´s business activity with the company´s local office in Finland. Thus the parent company no longer trusted the ability of FICT to create new business or remain profitable. The business related to the 'basic product' continued under the supervision of a department of the parent firm's local office in addition to its other software solutions that were supposed to replace FICT´s 'basic product' in the course of time.

EXPLORATIVE ACTIONS IN THE THREE MARKETING EVENTS

The marketing events analyzed in this study constituted the core of FICT´s marketing and sales activity. The data shows that each marketing event was organized on the basis of different goal and had a different focus. These events formed, however, a consistent series of actions taken to sustain and to grow the business. In the progression from one marketing event to the other both

an aggravation of inner contradiction and an intensification of explorative actions can be traced. The inner contradiction escalated in the course of successive, expanding complications influenced by customers´ demands and by evolving software markets and competition. In addition, the emerging financial crisis in global economy retarded customer procurements. The intensification of explorative actions was related to the richness of the search efforts for a new business solution.

In 2007 during the organization of "Spring Cruise" the need had manifested in FICT to productize technology-based add-on services, standardize production processes and develop collaborative practices. Only the complication related to the awareness that 'the basic product' was reaching the end of its life-cycle indicated the need for more efforts to accelerate the business activity. In 2008 when the series of "FICT Road Show" was launched, a new perspective had been identified to extend the business activity with opportunities that new products and new partners as well as a new image and new customers were expected to offer. FICT Road Show was built on traditional ideology of mass marketing and transaction-based sales and became too massive investment related to its outcome in approaching and reaching new grounds for business activity. As efforts for finding a new productive business solution failed, the management team gradually set out to emphasize the response from customers in the development of the business activity. Finally, when the FICT´s management team faced the complication of losing customers, the business activity was in a double bind situation between the mechanisms that preserved the product-based logic and the shifting object of activity related to the need to develop customer-oriented and service-based business logic. Therefore the focus of business actions in FICT was turned to tapping the potentiality of existing customers. Expert Days was an event organized to meet the needs of fewer, yet reliable and loyal clients. In the following table the steps

Table 2. Explorative actions in the marketing activity of FICT

Explorative Actions	2007-2008	2008-2009	2009-2010
Complication	A need to launch add-on service products and a turnkey solution of the basic product	Basic product reaching the end of its lifecycle	Increasing loss of customers and turnover
Refinement in business logic	Specification and documentation of existing products and production processes	Expanding business offering and building new business image by tracing new partners, products and customers	Focusing on existing customers and their needs Integrating firm´s internal and external actions
Response from customers	Customers´ problems to interpret FICT´s new type of offer	FICT do not attract new customers	Need to solve customers´ ICT infrastructure related challenges
Gestation of new elements for business logic	Customer counselling Development of internal information sharing	Harnessing all employees to search for new products and services that attract and satisfy customers	From product provider to system consulting partner
Outcome and following events	Sales of new products failed	New product repertoire and new integrative service products found	Parent company´s decision to merge FICT´s business with its local office.

of explorative actions are condensed depicting a learning process in FICT.

The study of explorative action brings out a system of interlocked experiential and evolutionary phases and their outcomes in FICT´s business activity. The nature of the learning process of the management team constituted of a pendulum of explorative actions which variedly stressed prevailing elements or introduced new elements in business activity which became maintained, elaborated or renounced. Thus explorative actions can´t be characterized as purely explorative or purely exploitative. The learning process intertwined both stretching of the limits and trespassing of the boundaries of the prevailing activity and created a zone of relative continuity of the business activity in FICT until the purposeful intervention of the parent company. The findings of the study show that the explorative actions were needed to reinforce the activity of planning and strategic visioning which were the initial developmental efforts in the firm. The analysis explicates that explorative actions were the most essential constituents in generating the transition from defending the prevailing territory of the highly product-orientated activity to the perception of business

logic outside the consonance with the past. Thus a strategically vital process of learning embedded in explorative actions reoriented the management team from treating customers as receivers of new technology or a source of business to perceiving them as potential partners and participants in the search of the service-based logic. The change in FICT´s directors´ perception of their customers follows Normann´s (2001, p. 15-25) illustration of strategic paradigms in production which depicts an evolving relation between the logic of a production system and a perceived view of customers. The evolution of the strategic paradigm also converges with management team´s conception of the products which expanded from technological merchandises to solutions for providing value for the customers´ technological infrastructures. Furthermore, the directors' interpretation of the meaning and the specific substance of services became more distinct and applicable in the modeling of FICT´s own production system. In the light of the traditional technology-based orientation in business activity services are seen, firstly, as products providing additional features to actual technological product offering and, secondly, as a support in the use of technology (Virkkunen,

Pihlaja & Ristimäki 2010, p. 73-74). Now, the idea of services as knowledge intensive commodity and a saleable expertise was identified as a potential core of business activity. However, the parent company decision to integrate the FICT´s business activity with the business of their local daughter company in Finland prevented FICT from implementing new, relevant ideas that would have changed the logic of business activity.

CONCLUSION

In this study the explorative actions were analyzed that were taken in three marketing events of a Finnish ICT firm in order to find new logic for business activity. The explorative actions triggered the management team to attempt a strategic reorientation of FICT towards a new logic of business. The perception of the prevailing reality of the product-based logic of the firm was related to the "culturally given" principles as generalized recipes in FICT´s business activity manifesting the reproduction of the cultural schemas of "technology push" logic. As Sewell (1996, p. 842) points out, the cultural schemas give the subjects the motivation and the shared meanings in a collective activity. According to Giddens (1984, p. 64) there is a human need for "ontological security" that leads the subject to maintain the known world and reproduce the prevailing structures. The interpretation of an alternative reality of a service-based logic challenged the existing nature of the business activity of FICT as a result of the explorative actions taken within the prevailing activity. Customer encounters in the explorative actions brought up both limitations in the current business and possibilities for a different form of business. In their study of automation of production processes von Hippel and Tyre (1995) found that most of the developmental problems to be tackled under uncharted circumstances cannot be anticipated "by an office desk" and that relevant problematization can only take place in practical

encounters. Recently also researchers of business strategy have highlighted the dynamic nature of the formation of a new business logic and the key role of experiential learning in it (McGrath, 2010; Sosna, Trevinyo-Rodríguez & Velamuri, 2010; Baden-Fuller & Haefliger, 2013). Experiential practices can, however, consist of different types of actions. In FICT the explorative actions realized a kind of "trial-and-error" learning that lacked a strong motive because of the lack of a clear vision of the object of the future activity–such an object, the idea of ICT infrastructure service, only emerged in a late phase. Hatchuel (2001, 266) calls this type of explorative actions of "rehearsal activity" as learning devices that are *not to be designed to test a solution... but that are designed to learn about what has to be learned or could be learned."* Thus the knowledge needed for questioning the firm´s current practices could only be obtained through open explorative actions that are neither tied firmly to the current thinking or to a specific hypothesis of the future. Only the aggravation of an inner, systemic contradiction within the activity can trigger such an open search process. This can, however, be supported through a systematic analysis of the history of the activity and the evolution of inner contradictions in it. Sannino (2014) has applied the metaphor of warping to describe the genesis of agentive action for change. Warping consists of throwing the kedge anchor and, once it has settled on the ground, pulling it for moving the vessel toward the desired direction. The actions of throwing the kedge in the attempt to find a suitable ground are search actions. Only when the kedge is hooked to the ground the crew gains control of the situation and is able to pull the vessel out of the stall. These are taking-over actions when the vessel is still in the troubled area, but the crew is able to maneuver it. Breaking-out actions occur when the vessel is moved away from the problem area. The FICT management's explorative actions can be understood as the kind of search actions of 'throwing a kedge' which Sannino (2014) describes. The management team's 'kedge' of the explorative marketing actions did not settle on a new ground to enable the management to gain control of the business situation and to take the breaking out actions to move the business away from the troubled area.

REFERENCES

Baden-Fuller, C., & Haefliger, S. (2013). Business models and technology innovation. *Long Range Planning*, 46(6), 419–426. doi:10.1016/j. lrp.2013.08.023

Brown, R. (1992). Managing the "S" curve in innovation. *Journal of Business and Industrial Marketing*, 7(3), 41–52. doi:10.1108/08858629210035418

Cusumano, M. (2004). *The business of software: What every manager, programmer, and entrepreneur must know to thrive and survive in good times and bad*. New York: Free Press.

Cusumano, M., Suarez, F. F., & Kahl, S. (2008). *Product, process and service: A new industry lifecycle model* (MIT Working Paper). Retrieved May 5, 2014, from http://web.mit.edu/sis07/cusumano.pdf

Engeström, Y. (1987). *Learning by expanding: An activity-theoretical approach to developmental research*. Helsinki: Orienta-Konsultit.

Giddens, A. (1984). *The constitution of society*. Cambridge, MA: Polity.

Hatchuel, A. (2001). Towards design theory and expandable rationality: The unfinished program of Herbert Simon. *Journal of Management and Governance*, 5(3/4), 260–273. doi:10.1023/A:1014044305704

Lavie, D., Stettner, U., & Tushman, M. L. (2010). Exploration and exploitation within and across organizations. *The Academy of Management Annals*, 4(1), 109–155. doi:10.1080/19416521003691287

Leont'ev, A. N. (1978). *Activity, consciousness, and personality*. Englewood Cliffs, NJ: Prentice-Hall.

March, J. (1991). Exploration and exploitation in organizational learning. *Organization Science*, 2(1), 71–87. doi:10.1287/orsc.2.1.71

McGrath, R. G. (2010). Business models: A discovery driven approach. *Long Range Planning*, 43(2-3), 247–261. doi:10.1016/j.lrp.2009.07.005

Normann, R. (2001). *Reframing business: When the map changes the landscape*. Chichester, UK: John Wiley & Sons. Ltd.

Ollman, B. (2003). *Dance of the dialects: Steps in Marx's method*. Champaign, IL: University of Illinois Press.

Perez, C. (2002). *Technological revolutions and financial Capital: The dynamics of bubbles and golden ages*. Cheltenham, UK: Edward Elgar Publishing Limited. doi:10.4337/9781781005323

Perez, C. (2005). *Respecialization and the deployment of the ICT paradigm: An essay on the present challenges of globalization*. Paper for the IPTS FISTERA Project, Nov 2005. Retrieved May 6, 2014, from http://www.carlotaperez.org/papers/PEREZ_Respecialisation_and_ICTparadigm.pdf

Perez, C. (2014). *Green and socially equitable direction for ICT paradigm*. Working Paper 2014-01. Globelics, working paper series. The global network for economics of learning, innovation, and competence building systems. Chris Freeman Memorial Lecture GLOBELICS 2012. Hangzhou, P.R. China. Rev. March 2014. Retrieved May 7, 2014 from http://www.globelics.org/wp-content/uploads/2014/04/wpg1401.pdf

Prahalad, C. K., & Krishnan, M. S. (2008). *The new age of innovation: Driving co-created value through global networks*. New York: The McGraw-Hill Companies Inc.

Raisch, S., Birkinshaw, J., Probst, G., & Tushmann, M. L. (2009). Organizational ambideterity: Balancing exploitation and exploration for sustained performance. *Organization Science*, *20*(4), 685–695. doi:10.1287/orsc.1090.0428

Sannino, A. (2014). *Double stimulation as anchoring forward: The unity of conceptualization and agentive action*. Paper presented in the 11th International Congress on the Learning Sciences. Boulder, CO.

Sewell, W. Jr. (1996). Historical events as transformation of structures: Inventing revolution at the Bastille. *Theory and Society*, *25*(6), 841–881. doi:10.1007/BF00159818

Smith, W. K., & Lewis, M. W. (2011). Towards a theory of paradox: A dynamic equilibrium model of organizing. *Academy of Management Review*, *32*(2), 381–403. doi:10.5465/AMR.2011.59330958

Sosna, M., Trevinyo-Rodríguez, R. N., & Velamuri, S. R. (2010). Business model innovation through trial-and-error learning: The Naturhouse case. *Long Range Planning*, *43*(2-3), 383–407. doi:10.1016/j.lrp.2010.02.003

Stacey, R. D. (1995). The science of complexity: An alternative perspective for strategic change processes. *Strategic Management Journal*, *6*(6), 477–495. doi:10.1002/smj.4250160606

van de Ven, A. (1992). Suggestion for studying strategy process: A research note. *Strategic Management Journal*, *13*(S1), 169–188. doi:10.1002/smj.4250131013

Vargo, S. L., & Lusch, R. F. (2008). From goods to service(s): Divergences and convergences of logics. *Industrial Marketing Management*, *37*(3), 254–259. doi:10.1016/j.indmarman.2007.07.004

Virkkunen, J. (2007). Collaborative development of a new concept for an activity. *@ctivités, 4*(2), 158-164.

Virkkunen, J., Pihlaja, J., & Ristimäki, P. (2010). Tuotteesta palveluun – Liiketoiminnan kehityksen epäjatkuvuuden hallinta ohjelmistoyrityksessä. In Hyötyläinen & Nuutinen (Eds.), Mahdollisuuksien kenttä: Palveluliiketoiminta ja vuorovaikutteinen johtaminen (pp. 72-88). Helsinki: Teknologiainfo Teknova Oy.

Virkkunen, J., & Ristimäki, P. (2012). Double stimulation in strategic concept formation: An activity-theoretical analysis of business planning in a small technology firm. *Mind, Culture, and Activity*, *19*(3), 273–286. doi:10.1080/10749039.2012.688234

Virkkunen, J. & Virkki, M. (2014, in process). *Transformative organizational learning as a process of ascending from the abstract to the concrete: The creation of the business model for Kemira Grow How*. Academic Press.

von Hippel, E., & Tyre, M. J. (1995). How learning by doing is done: Problem identification in novel process equipment. *Research Policy*, *24*(1), 1–12. doi:10.1016/0048-7333(93)00747-H

ADDITIONAL READING

Bateson, G. (1972). *Steps in an ecology of mind*. New York: Ballantine.

Blunden, A. (2009). An interdisciplinary concept of activity. *Outline*, *1*, 1–26.

Burgelman, R. (1991). Intraorganizational ecology of strategy making and organizational adaptation: Theory and field research. *Organization Science*, *2*(3), 239–262. doi:10.1287/orsc.2.3.239

Cussins, A. (1992). Content, embodiment and objectivity: The theory of cognitive trails. *Mind*, *101*(404), 651–688. doi:10.1093/mind/101.404.651

Cusumano, M. (2010). *Staying power: Six enduring principles for managing. Strategy & innovation in an uncertain world*. Oxford: Oxford University Press.

Cusumano, M. (2010). Technology strategy and management: The evolution of platform thinking. *Communication of the ACM, 53*(1), 32-34. Retrieved from 10/05/2014 http://www.lingnan.net/mba/back/edit/uploadfile/20120927142825285.pdf

Drucker, P. F. (2008). *The age of discontinuity: Guidelines to our changing society*. New Jersey: Trasaction Publishers.

Engeström, Y. (2001). Expansive learning at work: Toward an activity theoretical reconceptualization. *Journal of Education and Work, 14*(1), 133–156. doi:10.1080/13639080020028747

Engeström, Y. (2011). From design experiments to formative interventions. *Theory & Psychology, 21*(5), 598–628. doi:10.1177/0959354311419252

Engeström, Y., Pasanen, A., Toiviainen, H., & Haavisto, V. (2005). Expansive learning as collaborative concept formation at work. K. Yamazumi, Y. Engeström, & H. Daniels (Eds.), New learning challenges: Going beyond the industrial age system of school and work (pp. 47–77). Osaka: Kansai University Press.

Engeström, Y., & Sannino, A. (2010). Studies of expansive learning: Foundations, findings and future challenges. *Educational Research Review, 5*(1), 1–24. doi:10.1016/j.edurev.2009.12.002

Kim, W. C., & Maubourgne, R. (2005). *Blue ocean strategy: How to create uncontested market space and make the competition irrelevant*. Boston: Harvard Business School Press.

Levinthal, D., & March, J. G. (1981). A model of adaptive organizational search. *Journal of Economic Behavior & Organization, 2*(4), 307–333. doi:10.1016/0167-2681(81)90012-3

Mintzberg, H. (1978). Patterns in strategy formation. *Management Science, 24*(9), 934–948. doi:10.1287/mnsc.24.9.934

Nelson, R., & Winter, S. (1982). *An evolutionary theory of economic change*. Cambridge: Harvard University Press.

Normann, R. (1977). *Management for growth*. Chichester: John Wiley & Sons Ltd.

Normann, R., & Ramírez, R. (1998). *Designing interactive strategy: From value chain to value constellation*. Chichester: John Wiley & Sons Ltd.

Orlikowski, W. J. (1996). Improvising organizational transformation over time: A situated change perspective. *Information Systems Research, 7*(1), 63–92. doi:10.1287/isre.7.1.63

Pereira Querol, M. A., Seppänen, L., & Virkkunen, J. (2014). Exploring the developmental possibilities of environmental activities: On-farm biogas production. *Environmental Science & Policy, 37*(March), 134–141. doi:10.1016/j.envsci.2013.09.010

Pettigrew, A. M. (1990). Longitudinal field research on change: Theory and practice. *Organization Science, 1*(3), 267–292. doi:10.1287/orsc.1.3.267

Pettigrew, A. M. (2000). Linking change processes to outcomes. In M. Beer & N. Nohia (Eds.), *Breaking the Code of Change*. Boston: Harvard Business School Press.

Pihlaja, J. (2005). *Learning in and for production: An activity-theoretical study of the historical development of distributed systems of generalization. Department of Education, University of Helsinki*. Helsinki: Helsinki University Press.

Raisch, S., & Birkinshaw, J. (2008). Organizational ambidexterity: Antecedents, outcomes, and moderators. *Journal of Management, 34*(3), 375–409. doi:10.1177/0149206308316058

Stacey, R. D. (2010). *Complexity and organizational reality: Uncertainty and the need to rethink management after the collapse of investment capital*. Oxon: Routledge.

van Mierlo, B., Leeuwis, C., Smits, R., & Woolthuis, R. K. (2010). Learning towards system innovation: Evaluating a systemic instrument. *Technological Forecasting and Social Change*, *77*(2), 318–334. doi:10.1016/j.techfore.2009.08.004

Vygotsky, L. S. (1978). *Mind in society: The psychology of higher mental functions*. Cambridge: Harvard Business Press.

KEY TERMS AND DEFINITIONS

Business Lifecycle: Business-related or industry-level theories and models of lifecycle highlight sequence of stages in business development and progression of business in a prefigured order. Thus the business activity of an enterprise or the industry proceed along a lifecycle which follows stages from embryo to maturity leading either to an end of the business or to a new business entry. Each phase in business lifecycle embeds rules and logic featuring the particular period in business activity. (van de Ven 1992; Cusumano, Suarez & Kahl 2008). One of the models of business lifecycle of technology firms is depicted as "S" curve which refers to intensity in the evolution of business. An emergent technology takes time, requires financial resources and knowhow without gaining revenue. The exquisite growth begins when technology as an innovative product enters the "unconquered" market and meets the needs of customers. When achieving its limits under circumstances of competition a business reaches the stage of maturity (Brown 1992; Cusumano, Suarez & Kahl 2008).

Business Logic: A production activity embeds cultural-historically formed methods of practices and use of tools, signs and language that are shared by a collective system of actors. Business logic qualifies the nature of the production system. From activity theoretical perspective business logic is related to the notion of activity concept that characterized the systemic relation and interdependence of the object, tools and principles of activity such as rules and the forms in division of labor (Virkkunen 2007). A change in the dominant logic of production is evidenced to progress from mass production-based to information and communication technology-based principles (Perez 2002). Vargo & Lusch (2008) portrays this change at a micro-level as a transition from goods-dominant logic to service-dominant logic.

Dialectics (in Research): "… understanding anything in our everyday experience requires the we know something about how it arouse and developed and how it fits into the larger context or system of which it is a part. … After all, few would deny that everything in the world is changing and interacting at some pace and in one way or another, that history and systemic connections belong to the real world. The difficulty has always been how to think adequately about them, how not to distort them, and how to give them the attention and the weight that they deserve. Dialectics is an attempt to resolve this difficulty by expanding our notion of anything to include, as aspects of what it is, both the process by which it has become that and the broader interactive context in which it is found. Only then does the study of anything involve one immediately with the study of its history and encompassing system." (Ollman, 2003, p. 13.)

Explorative Actions: From activity theoretical perspective explorative actions can be seen as a means of learning to break out from the historically formed prevailing work routines and inventing new opportunities in an organizational transformation. A dialectical unity of opposite aspects of exploration is embodied in actions for extending the limits of the prevailing activity and breaking away from the predominant activity.

Thus, both explorative and exploitative actions are intertwined in explorative actions.

ICT Era: Techno-economic paradigm / long-term technological revolution of about 60-70 years generate economic and social changes with clusters of new, dynamic technologies, infrastructures and industries. Perez (2002) claims that the developmental surge of information and communication technology started in 1971 with the launch of Intel's microprocessors. There are two different periods of developmental activity in ICT era. The period of technology installation initiates a technological revolution followed by technology deployment of its use. An on-going turning point in ICT era is supposed to shift the focus of technology development and the principles of "technology push" to "demand pull" and full deployment of user-oriented technology applications. (Perez, 2002).

Mediation: A new constituent i.e. a new instrument is inserted into interaction between subject and the object that then creates a new relation between them and, thereby, remediates activity. The intersection of a new constituent reveals divergent qualities in activity and mediates renewal of the systemic structure in activity (Virkkunen & Virkki, 2014). The mediation of the second order stimulus brings forth the disharmonious demands between object of the existing, direct world and the remediated object of a new world. The contradiction revealed by mediation then triggers development of historically formed activity system.

Systemic Levels of Activity: Following Vygotsky's conception of external, instrumental and interactive activity as a generator of internal psychological processes, Leontjev (1978, p. 58-69) characterizes activity with a hierarchical structure following Vygotsky's conception of external, instrumental and interactive activity as a generator of internal psychological processes. His conceptualization of hierarchy of activity brings out the mediating interdependence between the true motive (i.e. object) of durable collective activity vis-à-vis individual goals and conditions of daily actions and operations more sensitive to alteration.

Chapter 12
Networking around Supervisors in an Industrial Corporation

Riikka Ruotsala
Finnish Institute of Occupational Health, Finland

ABSTRACT

This chapter presents a network-level developmental intervention conducted in an industrial corporation. It focuses on production supervisors' changing work and follows how practitioners from the organizational support functions of human resources, occupational safety, and occupational health services build collaboration with supervisors. The notion of "client understanding" provides a starting point for the study: in order to serve supervisors, the support functions need to understand the challenges in the supervisors' operational environment. Results show that attaining client understanding requires, firstly, joint analysis of the sources of the problems and, secondly, the adaptation of dynamic and systemic explanations for them. The study describes the process of how client understanding, in the form of making generalizations, expands during the intervention. The findings have practical relevance for evaluating and developing collaborative practices in networked multi-activity settings.

INTRODUCTION

In the emerging era of co-configurative work (Victor & Boynton, 1998), organizations are increasingly coupled with their clients in collaborative endeavours to produce products and services together. This means that work is performed, managed and developed in increasingly complex and continually transforming network constellations. There is a growing need to understand dynamic inter-relations and complexities in organizational settings. Many organization studies have approached the issue from the

managerial perspective: integrative thinking, dynamic problem-solving, decision-making, and managing contradictory tensions are considered to be managers' core tasks (Sterman, 2001; Keating, Kauffmann & Dryer, 2001; Smith, Binns & Tushman, 2010). However, in modern networked work, the ability to see, envision and construct the "whole picture" cannot be left to managers alone; this requires the creation of collaborative work practices within and between organisations. This challenges practitioners to cross boundaries, to build relational agency (Edwards, 2009) and to understand how their work activities form a com-

DOI: 10.4018/978-1-4666-6603-0.ch012

prehensive, unified whole. In activity theoretical terms, this means an object-oriented approach to networks: grasping how the coupled activity systems (Engeström, 1987) work together and determining the network's shared object of activity.

This chapter explores the issue of network collaboration from the client perspective. We draw particular attention to the challenges in client-service provider collaboration. *Clients* are comprehended here as the networks' (partially) shared object of activity – something that compels the involved parties, that is, the *service providers* to form networks and to collaborate in novel ways. We argue that building successful, comprehensive services in networks is far more easily said than done. This is due to fragmented service production, which derives from a long tradition of the professional specialization and functional division of labour. Fragmented services may cause 'grey zones', overlapping work, and simply result in missing the complete needs of the client. Be the client a patient with multiple illnesses (Kerosuo, 2006), a divorced family, or a prisoner (Seppänen, Toiviainen & Kira, 2014; Seppänen & Kloetzer, 2014), many individual and societal aspects create the need for the development of more integrated network collaboration. This study focuses on a support service network within an industrial corporation. The production supervisors within one of the corporation's production units are viewed here as internal clients. They form an intersecting point in the collaboration for practitioners from the organizational functions of human resources, occupational safety and occupational health services in the area of well-being promotion. The study presents a Developmental Work Research (DWR) based intervention (Engeström et al., 1996; Virkkunen & Newnham, 2013), in which the practitioners from the above mentioned service functions wanted to learn to better support supervisors in carrying out well-being related strategies and procedures in their daily work on the shop floor. The practitioners' interest in examining

their collaboration with the production supervisors stemmed from a recent corporate acquisition, in which the production unit became a part of the corporation. The intention of the intervention was to 'put supervisors in the centre' and view the ongoing changes and transforming practices from a wider, cross-functional perspective. We examine how the support functions reframed their services and built up collaboration during the intervention process.

The study leans on the notion of *client understanding,* which is defined as the service providers' conceptualization of the relationship between clients and services. It includes, firstly, the identification of the client's current and forthcoming problems, and secondly, the recognition of how they relate to the services provided (Seppänen et al., 2014). In this study this required, for example, reviewing the mixture of the function-specific tools and procedures assigned to the supervisors. For example, the role of the human resource function is to be the supervisors' partner in managing personnel issues and providing procedures to support them in implementing focal practices such as performance appraisals and personnel surveys. The occupational safety function, on the other hand, provides tools and models to ensure a safe work environment and safe work processes. The tools for this include, for example, risk assessments, incident reporting, and accident investigations. Occupational health services' collaboration with the organization supports prevention enacted by the law, in the form of health assessments and workplace health surveys. First, it was important to gain information on how these tools responded to the needs of the supervisors (client-service relation). In the light of this information, the support functions could better co-ordinate their activities and develop collaborative practices (service provider-service provider relation). This way, the notion of client understanding encompasses the idea of transformational, dynamic activities as inter-related and networked systems. In this study, client understanding is comprehended as a form of system understanding, which in the third generation activity theory (Engeström, 2009; Kerosuo, 2006; Toiviainen et al., 2009) refers to seeing beyond one's own activity system and depicting the (partially) shared object of work at the network level. In this chapter, we examine how client understanding – as a way of making generalizations in a collective problem-solving process – evolves and changes during a developmental intervention. More specifically, what kind of problems, explanations and solutions do the practitioners from the service functions provide while analysing supervisors' work and how does the way of explaining them change during the intervention?

LOGICS BEHIND GENERALIZATIONS

Why we are interested in analysing the way in which generalizations are made when studying client understanding? We propose that the way the service providers describe and conceptualize clients' problems also addresses the range of possible solutions. We are particularly interested in analysing the explanations behind the problems. We argue that the expansion of client understanding requires adopting system-level explanations, i.e., recognising the dynamic links between different activities. In the following, we determine the criteria against which the system-level statements and the way of making qualitatively different kinds of generalizations can be reflected. For this purpose we introduce a central activity theoretical principle of ascending from the abstract to the concrete. In addition, we shed light on three different ontological views behind the reasoning: the metaphysics of properties, the metaphysics of relations, and dialectics.

As in the third generation activity theory studies and interventions (Engeström, 2009; Seppänen & Kloetzer, 2014), this study also examines a group of interconnected activity systems that cross

organizational and professional boundaries. In developmental interventions, this means that the degree of system analysis becomes more complex to manage: handling the wholeness of activity systems' dynamically evolving developmental trajectories becomes more difficult. The question arises as to how the participants who primarily pay attention to the everyday disturbances within their own activity systems find a motive to go beyond 'their own agenda' and reconceptualise change in a wider context, more systemically. In DWR interventions, a resolution for evolving tensions and contradictions is found through the collective process of expansive learning. The process comprises seven specific learning actions which construct an ideal-typical form of expansive learning cycle (Engeström, 2001; 2011). The learning actions include questioning, analysing and modelling the model, examining it, implementing it, evaluating the process and consolidating the outcomes. The aim of these actions is to generate a collective process of concept formation, that is, to ascend from the abstract to the concrete (Davydov, 1990). The method requires contemplating the underlying difference between the notions of 'abstract' and 'concrete'. Here, abstract refers to empirical concepts that describe and separate objects and phenomena into classes by comparing their external qualities. This means that empirical concepts are perceived as detached from the concrete whole, from their functional and historical interconnections, and remain static. Concrete, on the contrary, relates to theoretical thinking and concepts which provide access to dynamic understanding of a whole, that is, the changing, developing and inter-acting objects and phenomena that form a system (1990, p. 19-20; 118-120). Based on the dialectical idea, the principle of ascending from the abstract to the concrete enables the creation of a new *theoretical* idea or concept that leads to a qualitatively novel pattern of activity. This is achieved by capturing an abstract, the modest possible explanatory model of the system relations – a germ cell – which is then gradually enhanced and tested in practice. (Davydov 1990; Engeström, 1987; Engeström & Sannino, 2010).

In this study, we trace system relations as a form of client understanding by focusing on the ways in which practitioners from the service functions make generalizations. Particular attention is paid to finding indications of evolving theoretical concepts and systemic ways of explaining and solving the problems. To add more analytical power to the analysis, we apply Charles Tolman's (1981) considerations on the different historically evolved ontology behind scientific reasoning. He distinguishes between the metaphysics of properties, the metaphysics of relations, and dialectics. First, the metaphysics of properties dates back to the early phases of modern science, when explanations for phenomena were sought from the inherent qualities attached to objects (empirical concepts). Studying distinct properties did not, however, explain how the relations between objects emerge. This led to an influential leap forward in science, as relationships between independent and dependent variables began to form the hard core of research activity. This logic refers to the metaphysics of relations. As rationalized by Tolman (1981), the major limitation in this ontology; i.e. the metaphysics of properties and the metaphysics of relations, is that taken together they do not explain change and development. They do not reach system understanding in explaining phenomena.

Dialectics and the notion of 'concreteness' come to the fore once more; "The concrete understanding of a thing is an understanding of it in its interconnections and movements. To extract a thing from its interconnections is to abstract it" (1981, p. 42).

Tolman's arguments on different explanatory rationales can be applied when analysing the way in which generalizations are made in the collective problem-solving process. Schaupp (2011) used Tolman's three ontological categories in her DWR intervention study which examined the qualitative change in human resource developers' conceptualizations of a road-building organization's learning challenges in capability building. In her study, the proportion of the dialectical-orientated problem statements and suggestions for solutions in discussions increased notably towards the end of the intervention. She concluded that the shift towards more systemic and dialectical thinking regarding the object of capability building was a result of providing more complex models and real-life cases during the developmental intervention. For complementary analyses on empirical and theoretical generalization see Virkkunen & Ristimäki (2012) and Virkkunen et al. (2012). In accordance with Schaupp's methods of analysis, we propose the following markers for evaluating the emergence of client understanding and the way of making generalizations in the practitioners' discussions (Table 1).

Table 1. Proposed markers for analysing explanation modes

Ontological Categories (Tolman, 1981)	Analytical Principles of Problem Statements and Suggestions (Schaupp, 2011)	Markers for Analysing Explanation Modes in this Study
Metaphysics of properties	A single quality or a stand-alone phenomenon of a thing	An attributed single characteristic, a stereotyped expression, or a static quality (abstract, empirical generalization)
Metaphysics of relations	Related things or the relationship alone	Referring to linear cause and effect relationships
Dialectics	A reference to a historical change in the internal relations or temporal development of the system as a whole	Explaining dynamics and 'wholeness', wider timeframe for development

INTERVENTION DESIGN AND DATA

Next, we briefly introduce the intervention design and the starting point for the intervention. We also depict the process of data analysis. The data analysis consisted of two phases. First, we analysed the contents of the selected topic-related discussions. We depict how we traced client understanding in the practitioners' proposed problem statements, the explanation modes and solutions ideas. The second phase in the analysis focused on tool mediation. We examined the interventionist- and practitioner-initiated models and concepts that mediated the discussions. This allowed us to more precisely reflect on the influence that the models and concepts may have had on the emergence of client understanding (Seppänen & Kloetzer, 2014).

Context of the Intervention

This one-and-a-half year intervention takes changes in production supervisors' work as a 'window' to examining the transformations in a manufacturing facility located in Finland. The data, which consisted of, for example, interviews and a developmental intervention, were collected in a post-acquisition transition phase, during which the factory was adjusting to being a business unit of a global corporation. The production was typical manufacturing shift work in which the workers and the supervisors had a clear division on labour. The core of production supervisors' work was to organise and supervise workers' daily work on the shop floor. The organizational change situation combined with simultaneously growing economic pressures had resulted in many renewals of organizational procedures. The practitioners from the support functions of the organization – that is from human resources, occupational safety and occupational health services – wanted to obtain information on how the transforming practices may have added confusion to supervisors' work. The focus was particularly on supervisors' self-perceived well-being at work

and on how they promoted workers' well-being, that is, how supervisors carried out well-being related strategies and procedures in their daily work. As in the notion of client understanding (Seppänen et al., 2014), supervisors are viewed here as shared clients of the above-mentioned in-house support services. The working hypothesis for the intervention was that in order to serve supervisors better, the practitioners in support functions need to understand both the current and evolving challenges in supervisors' operational environments. The intervention consisted of eight *planning meetings* and three *workshop sessions*. Planning meetings were a forum for a steering group to jointly discuss the progression of the study and prepare the implementation of the workshop sessions. The steering group consisted of the three researcher-interventionists and the practitioners of the organizational support functions. The amount of participants attending the planning meetings varied from three to seven. The three workshop sessions formed the core of the intervention. In workshop sessions, four production supervisors and two of their superiors modelled their changing work and collaboration with the practitioners from the support services. The three researcher-interventionists facilitated both the planning meetings and the workshop sessions.

Methods for Tracing Client Understanding

The data analysed in this study is delimited to seven intervention planning meetings. One planning meeting, second in order, was excluded from the data analysis since the contents overlapped to a great extent with the first the meeting. This was due to its introductory nature, caused by reforming the group of participants. The dynamics of the planning meeting discussions were typically as follows: the interventionists initiated questions and provided models or representations in a hypothetical form, on which the practitioners commented and provided different perspectives. The practitioners were quite freely allowed to dominate the discussions. Overall, the discussions were lively, forward driven and dialogue based. For the purpose of data analysis, the planning meetings were divided into *Pre, During* and *Forward* categories. The first three meetings, which were held before the joint workshops, formed the 'Pre' category. The following two planning meetings, which were temporally closely linked to the workshops, were named the 'During' category. The orientation of the 'Forward' category, which included the two last meetings, focused on future collaboration and the evaluation of the intervention. This three-fold categorization is used throughout the following data analysis. As the first step of the analysis, the transcribed data was organized into topic-related episodes on the grounds of the discussion contents. The topic-related episodes consisted of speech turns, the number of which typically varied from 20 to 50. As the interest of this analysis lies in shedding light on client understanding, the episodes, which covered supervisory work and/or its relations to support functions, were selected for the analysis. In total, 90 topic-related episodes, including 375 speech turns, were examined. The discussions were analytical in nature; the practitioners interpreted problems and underlying causes from various perspectives, that is, the discussions formed a collective problem-solving process. The typical structure of the discussions may be depicted in two ways: as a chain of *proposed problem – explanation$_{1-n}$ – focused problem* or a chain of *proposed problem – explanation – solution idea*. On the basis of these elements, the detailed data analysis focused on:

Problem statements: The detailed problem statement analysis was conducted with the help of the activity system model (Engeström, 1987). The problem statements were coded in conjunction with the elements of the supervisors' activity system; subject, object, tool, rules, community and division of labour. As the proposed problems were rich and nuanced, the contents were further coded into subcategories. In the case where a

proposed problem dealt with relations between support services and supervisors, the problem was coded either as between two activity systems or alternatively as a network of interacting activity systems.

Explanation modes: The iterative rounds of analysing different causes behind the problems generated three ontologically different categories of explanations; attributing individual characteristics, referring to structural and causal relationships, and giving dynamic and systemic explanations. The focus was on determining the markers according to which generalizations were made regarding the underlying causes. The markers were modified and complemented in relation to the central literature references (Davydov 1990; Tolman 1981; Schaupp, 2011, see Table 1).

Solution ideas: The generated solution ideas were analysed according to their contents and the level of agentive action; resisting interventionists or management, explicating new possibilities or potentials in the activity, envisioning new patterns or models of the activity, committing to concrete actions aimed at changing the activity, and taking consequential actions to change the activity (Engeström, 2011; Sannino, 2008; Haapasaari et al., 2014; Heikkilä & Seppänen, 2014).

Interventionists' Toolbox

The second phase of the data analysis concentrated on tool mediation. DWR provides broad theoretical angles and a powerful practical toolbox for system level analysis. One method used to facilitate expansive learning actions leans on Vygotsky's (1978) principle of double stimulation. It is based on the creative interplay between first and second stimuli. The first stimulus refers to a problematic task at hand to which an assisting instrument, for instance an illustrated model or a concept, is offered as a second stimulus. The purpose of the second stimulus is to function as a psychological tool in widening the sphere of problem-solving, and to provide access to solutions that would otherwise remain hidden. In this intervention, the shared problem of interest was the supervisors' changing work, which required reframing of the collaborative practices between the support services and supervisors accordingly. For the second stimuli, the interventionists offered multiple illustrations, models and concepts to facilitate a more systemic view of solving the existing tensions within the network. As a final step of the data analysis, the second stimuli were traced and analysed to evaluate their influence on the emergence of client understanding. Altogether the interventionists introduced a total of 14 mediating concepts and tools. The interventionist-initiated system models included different kinds of illustrations of coupled activity systems or continuums of their inter-related developmental trajectories. Typical examples were also analytical models for evaluating function-specific procedures and tools. Some of the models were applied through the intervention process. We also examined what kind of second stimuli the practitioners themselves initiated. This is important to distinguish, since it is common that participants replace and combine offered models with their own conceptualizations (Engeström & Sannino, 2010, p. 15), which can also be interpreted as an indication of participants' enhanced agency. An example of the practitioner-initiated concept was an annual clock which is discussed later in detail.

EXPANSION OF CLIENT UNDERSTANDING

In this section we present the results on how client understanding – as a way of making generalizations in a collective problem-solving process – evolved and changed during the intervention. We first present how the practitioners depicted the challenges in supervisors' work. Second, we focus on the explanation modes and, third, we depict the solution ideas for future network collaboration. Last, we discuss the role of tool mediation, that

is, what concepts and tools had an influence on the expansion of client understanding.

Analysing the Sphere of Problems

The starting point of the analysis was to focus on problem statements in which the practitioners analysed actual and evolving problems in supervisors' work (the first step in attaining client understanding). In addition, the analysis aimed to examine how the ways of describing the problems changed during the intervention. The content areas of the identified problems covered various issues at the different levels of activities. Primarily, attention was directed towards the supervisors' activity system. Secondly, the challenges were identified in the collaboration practices between a service function and supervisors' activity. Thirdly, some difficulties were more widely recognized at the network level; problems seemed to arise from more complex interrelations between the service functions, and further, in their relation to the supervisors' activity. The majority of the problem statements, 83% (n=353), dealt with supervisors' activity systems, 6% of statements were at the inter-activity level and 11% were at the network level. The excerpt below presents an example of this kind of the network level statement. The practitioner reflects on how the support functions could genuinely help the supervisors. He believes that the challenges in supervisors' work may be caused by the support functions' top-down communication and fragmented functional division of labour:

Practitioner 1 (Planning meeting II): "Little by little, I'm beginning to understand this issue... We look at supervisors and ask them about the problems caused by unclear, clear and heavy communication from the support functions. In what way do we complicate their work? My crystal ball tells me that the actions we're now moving towards might not exist in the supervisors' field of activity. We might come to a conclusion that it is the support functions who have to sit down and start to think about how we could communicate, serve, help... To sincerely be there to support supervisors instead of pushing our own agenda on them. So, how we can genuinely help supervisors? I don't know if this is just me, but..."

Our main interest rested in the potential variation in the practitioners' problem statements during the intervention. Table 2 shows variation which appears from the use of levels of activities and temporal categories of Pre, During and Forward. They are coded with the help of elements in the activity system (Engeström, 1987), i.e. subject, object, tools, rules, community and division of labour. In the case where a proposed problem dealt with relations between support services and supervisors, the problem was generally coded to the class of community. Table 2 assembles the three main problem areas in each temporal category.

As can be perceived from Table 2, the core of the problem analysis – supervisors' object of activity – was the most central issue throughout the intervention. In each category, approximately half of the statements were related to this. In the 'Pre' category, making use of standardized function-specific tools was regarded as a challenge. Also, subject-related issues such as supervisors' leadership skills were mentioned. In the 'During' category, rules and the division of labour were observed as the other main problem areas. However, a shift towards a more systemic view of analysing problems can be distinguished in the 'Forward' category. During the last two meetings, almost a third (28%) of the problem statements

were directed towards community; either the inter-relations between a service function and supervisors, or the wider, combined network relations between the service functions and the supervisors. An indication of expanded client understanding was also found within the statements concerning supervisors' objects of work. Towards the end of the intervention, the problem statements covered a more comprehensive view of supervisors' work. At the beginning, the issues concentrated more on problematizing how supervisors perform single tasks, but at the end, the concerns focused on how supervisors can manage the whole range of their changing work in relation to the changes simultaneously taking place in other actors' work.

Providing Explanations

As regards the analysis of practitioners' interpretations of the causes behind the recognized problems, the focus was on how the way of making generalizations changed during the intervention. On the basis of the iterative rounds of the data analysis, we can distinguish three explanation modes based on different logics of reasoning; attributing individual characteristics, referring to structural and causal relationships, and giving dynamic, systemic explanations. The differences between the groups are based on Tolman's (1981) ontological categories and Schaupp's (2011) analytical principles, presented in Table 1. The distribution of the explanation modes and their change during the intervention is represented in Figure 1. The first mode of *attributing individual characteristics* explains that the challenges stem mainly from the

Table 2. Changes in problem statements

Pre	During	Forward
38% Object of activity	56% Object of activity	46% Object of activity
22% Tools	13% Rules	14% Community: Service function and supervisor relation
13% Subject	12% Division of labour	14% Community: Network of service functions and supervisors

supervisors' nature of work and capabilities in general. This explanation mode was typical at the beginning of the intervention, particularly when rationalizing mismatches between the supervisors' different objects of activity. For instance, the gap of moving from the traditional-fashioned machine/production-based management style towards the more worker-centred coaching approach was in this mode explained by supervisors' preference for maintaining old routines. The weight of this explanation mode diminished considerably after the practitioners analysed changing work together with the supervisors in the workshops sessions. At the beginning, over one third (39.5%) of all explanations belonged to this group, whereas at the end, the proportion was only one fifth (20.3%) of the explanations (Figure 1). This implies that the multi-voiced interaction with the supervisors and the power of real cases that supervisors brought into the discussions provided new perspectives to the practitioners' about the actual and evolving challenges in supervisors' work.

The second, and the most dominating explanation mode, was *referring to structural and causal relationships*. Approximately half of the explanations fell into this category, regardless of the temporal phase of the intervention (Figure 1). In this group, the problems were explained by straightforward cause-effect relationships, which were typically related to structural and organizational factors. For instance, supervisors' successful implementation of a coaching-based way of leading workers was now seen as impossible due to the operational fact that one supervisor had far too many subordinates

Practitioner 2 (Planning meeting III): "And of course one issue, when we consider supervisors' roles in promoting well-being at work, is that of course everyone is responsible for their own well-being [...] Does one supervisor have too many subordinates to realistically be able to do his job? Because some supervisors have lots of subordinates. So, frankly speaking, there is no

Figure 1. Distribution of explanation modes during the intervention

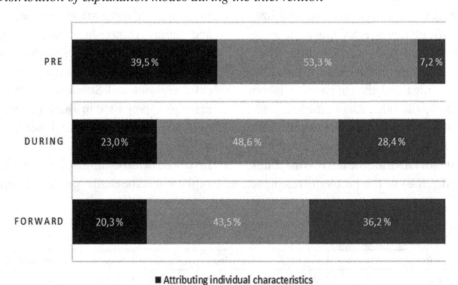

- Attributing individual characteristics
- Referring to structural and causal relationships
- Giving dynamic and systemic explanations

way he can be aware of everything they do, or handle, for example, two rounds of performance appraisals a year..."

Practitioner 3: "These are exactly the kind of big questions, when we discuss supervisors' own well-being at work and estimate their level of requirements. So, what can we realistically do? These are the areas in which resources are being reduced and tightened all the time."

Similarly, inconsistencies in newly-launched, harmonized function-specific tools and practices transformed organizational decision-making procedures, and – more abstractly – the specific nature of production work was claimed to cause struggles in supervisors' daily routines. As reported above, regarding the problem statement analysis, the sphere of the identified problems expanded to the inter-activity and network level towards the end of the intervention. An emerging issue of relevance was how supervisors manage to keep pace with the whole variety of changing practices. Respectively, the scope of explanations widened to the level of dynamic interrelations between the different organizational functions. In this third explanation mode, *giving dynamic and systemic explanations*, the way of explaining the problems transformed from attributing single features or causal-linear factors to considering the sum of the functions' interwoven but often asynchronous developmental paths that pulled in different directions. The proportion of this systemic explanation mode increased from 7.2% to 36.2% (Figure 1). In the following excerpt, the organization's changes and intermixing management models were seen to cause problems in supervisors' work:

Practitioner 1 (planning meeting V): "In my opinion, the whole issue culminates in the fact that the whole organization is still in a transition phase, where different kinds of management cultures and models are mixed. So, we have nice visions of how to operate according to leadership ideas but, at

the same time, substance management is cast in concrete. So, different management models are at odds with each other, contradict each other, and the issues only become real when they reach the supervisor's desk. And in general, I see it as a problem that groups do not know what their responsibilities are. [...] I think this is the issue that comes to the supervisor's desk. He has to combine all these models."

Practitioner 4: "It sort of realizes there at his desk."

Next, we take a look at what kinds of solution ideas the practitioners attached to these proposed problems and explanation modes.

Proposed Solution Ideas

The idea of DWR interventions is to jointly generate a new model – a solution – of a qualitatively new kind of activity. What kind of solution ideas did the practitioners' analysis generate in this particular intervention? The total amount of proposed ideas and innovations remained relatively low during the whole intervention. The quality of the proposals is, however, more interesting. During the intervention, the solution ideas included introducing a leadership training module, modification of function-specific tools and procedures, reframing supervisors' roles and job descriptions, and adjustments in the line organization's division of labour. These development ideas remained, however, at the general level and kept returning to the discussions during the course of the intervention. The notions can be considered non-expansive, since they did not go beyond talk of generating actions, nor did they break away from the existing functional boundaries. As regards the different layers of agentive action (Engeström, 2011), they did not pass the envisioning phase. Interestingly, one exception among the solution ideas led to committing to concrete actions at the network level. In the second planning meeting, the practitioners initiated the concept of an annual clock. This is a co-ordinating tool, which is typically used in organizations – in graphic or written form – to help in the planning, scheduling and managing of specific operations that take place within the period of one year. It emerged in the intervention as the practitioners' attempt to synchronize the overlapping and inconsistent well-being-related practices assigned to supervisors. The annual clock was developed as an expansive mini-cycle (Engeström, Kerosuo & Rantavuori, 2013) of its own, as the reciprocal co-emergence of depicting problems, giving explanations and providing solutions. The developing trajectory of the annual clock is reported in more detail elsewhere (Ruotsala, 2014).

SOLUTIONS AND RECOMMENDATIONS

On the basis of our findings about mediating concepts and tools we can conclude that there was a clear shift towards more systemic client understanding, that is, viewing the sources and the solutions of supervisors' evolving needs through more dynamic and inter-related connections. The shift could be traced from the change in how the practitioners made generalizations. Two specific remarks on how the practitioners used specific vocabulary to depict system complexities during this intervention can be presented. First, the frequency of the practitioners' phrase of 'management of the whole' increased towards the end of the intervention. It was referred to on many occasions to depict the dynamic and systemic state of affairs in the network. Although the explanatory power of the concept remained at quite a general level, its increased use indicated expanded client understanding. Secondly, the example of the annual clock depicts how a theoretical concept (Davydov, 1990) was created collectively. The idea of the annual clock grew through multifaceted conceptualizations; first it had the status of

a conceptual object, then an illustrated model and tool, and finally it was depicted as a potential collaborative evaluation practice, defining how collaboration could be developed within the network in the future (Ruotsala, 2014). In this sense, the annual clock provided a germ cell-like idea of expanding the network's object of activity. What factors contributed to these shifts in client understanding? The annual clock also sheds light on this question by bringing out the nature of successful second stimuli. The concept, and later in an illustrated model and demonstrated tool, of the annual clock was the practitioner-initiated second stimulus. It was the only mediating means that enhanced collective agency among the practitioners during the intervention process. Even if the other interventionist-initiated models were good, they did not reach the same level of agency by committed actions at expanding the activity (Engeström, 2011). This finding emphasizes the importance of the practitioner-initiated mediating means which enable to cross functional boundaries.

FUTURE RESEARCH DIRECTIONS

As systemic interconnectedness constantly increases in the modern way of organizing work, tensions and disturbances reside in between networked activities. This growing complexity challenges existing intervention methods. Even though DWR interventions have strong theoretical foundations that also provide a set of helpful practical tools, interventionists face numerous new methodological and practical challenges when they enter the complex terrain of network intervention. More research on successful intervention methods in network settings is needed. Furthermore, as developmental interventions typically provide only a limited snapshot of complex change situations, there is a need for more knowledge on post-intervention consequences (Kajamaa, Kerosuo & Engeström, 2008). Follow-up and evaluation studies of DWR interventions would provide important insights into their strengths and weaknesses in conjunction with increasingly dynamic work settings. Another line of research is transformative agency (Engeström, 2011; Haapasaari et al., 2014; Heikkilä & Seppänen, 2014); how collective agency emerges and where it leads. Also, accumulating research on how expansive learning cycles develop in network interventions would progress the study of learning in multi-activity settings (Toiviainen, 2003; Toiviainen & Kerosuo, 2013).

CONCLUSION

This study focused on a support service network within an industrial corporation. It examined how practitioners from organizational functions of human resources, and occupational safety and occupational health services reframed their services in relation to supervisors' changing work during a developmental intervention. An explicitly shared point of departure for the intervention was the notion of client understanding, which depicted the need to develop network collaboration: to better serve supervisors, the support functions need to understand the challenges in the supervisors' operational environments. The research interest was to trace evolving client understanding from the practitioners' discussions in planning meetings. The analysis focused on how the way of making generalizations in a collective problem-solving process changed during the intervention. Detailed data analysis scrutinized problem statements, explanation modes and solution ideas that covered supervisory work and/or its relations to support functions. The findings revealed a shift towards viewing supervisors' work in more dynamic and systemic inter-relations during the intervention. The shift could be seen in, for instance, how problems were analysed. Towards the end of the intervention, the problems were seen to derive from the interwoven development logics between the organizational functions, which sometimes pulled

in different directions. Hand in hand with the transforming problem depiction, the explanations related to underlying causes and factors behind the problems expanded. The way of explaining the problems transformed from attributing single features or causal-linear factors to giving more systemic explanations. Based on the determined analytical markers, this qualitative transformation was grounded on the ontological level, as the explanation mode moved from the metaphysics of properties and relations towards dialectics (Tolman, 1981; Schaupp, 2011). The proposed solution ideas were analysed in relation to the different levels of agentive actions (Engeström, 2011). The majority of envisioned solutions remained at a general level and did not generate agency among the participants. An exception was a collectively conceptualized and illustrated tool, an annual clock, which enhanced agency by committing and taking consequential actions to expand network collaboration (Ruotsala, 2014). The annual clock was modelled as a shared and regular evaluation practice between the support functions and the supervisors. In this sense, it provided a germ cell-like idea of expanding the network's object of activity. Expanded client understanding must be assessed in relation to the mediating models and concepts (second stimuli) that were offered and initiated during the intervention. Among the multiple models, the practitioner-initiated annual clock was the most important mediating artefact. This implies that building common ground for network collaboration requires the creation of shared mediating means to grasp the object. Although the annual clock seemed to deliver the expectation with regard to widening the understanding of supervisors' work and expanding the potential for network collaboration, it only carries potential before it is grounded in real practice. Schaupp (2011, p. 222) points out that even though new, more dynamic and systemic understanding is attained in relation to the object of activity, the activity may not expand if it collides with old organizational practices, for instance, a stiff functional division of labour. The findings imply that there are no shortcuts to build successful network collaboration. Networks remain merely meaningless structures if their essence is not processed, that is, a shared object of activity. The notion of client understanding could help service networks identify 'grey zones' and urge them to develop new collaborative practices together with their clients. In this study, commitment to joint learning processes was required, which enabled to ascend from the abstract to the concrete. In resolving complex learning challenges, there are no easy ways out.

REFERENCES

Davydov, V. V. (1990). *Types of generalization in instruction: Logical and psychological problems in the structuring of school curricula*. Reston, VA: National Council of Teachers of Mathematics.

Edwards, A. (2009). From the systemic to the relational: relational agency and activity theory. In A. Sannino, H. Daniels, & K. Gutiérrez (Eds.), Learning and expanding with activity theory (pp. 197-211). Cambridge, UK: Cambridge University Press.

Engeström, Y. (1987). *Learning by expanding: An activity-theoretical approach to developmental research*. Helsinki: Orienta-Konsultit.

Engeström, Y. (2001). Expansive learning at work: Toward an activity theoretical reconceptualization. *Journal of Education and Work, 14*(1), 133–156. doi:10.1080/13639080020028747

Engeström, Y. (2009). The future of activity theory: a rough draft. In A. Sannino, H. Daniels, & C. Gutierrez (Eds.), Learning and expanding with activity theory (pp. 303-328). Cambridge, UK: Cambridge University Press.

Engeström, Y. (2011). From design experiments to formative interventions. *Theory & Psychology, 21*(5), 598–628. doi:10.1177/0959354311419252

Engeström, Y., Rantavuori, J., & Kerosuo, H. (2013). Expansive learning in a library: Actions, cycles and deviations from instructional intentions. *Vocations and Learning, 6*(1), 81–106. doi:10.1007/s12186-012-9089-6

Engeström, Y., & Sannino, A. (2010). Studies of expansive learning: Foundations, findings and future challenges. *Educational Research Review, 5*(1), 1–24. doi:10.1016/j.edurev.2009.12.002

Engeström, Y., Virkkunen, J., Helle, M., Pihlaja, J., & Poikela, R. (1996). The change laboratory as a tool for transforming work. *Lifelong Learning in Europe, 1*(2), 10–17.

Haapasaari, A., Engeström, Y., & Kerosuo, H. (2014). The emergence of learners' transformative agency in a change laboratory intervention. *Journal of Education and Work*, 1–31. doi:10.1080/13639080.2014.900168

Heikkilä, H., & Seppänen, L. (2014) Examining developmental dialogue: the emergence of transformative agency. *Outlines – Critical Practice Studies, 15*(2), 5-30.

Il'enkov, E. V. (1977). *Dialectical logic: Essays in its history and theory*. Moscow: Progress.

Kajamaa, A., Kerosuo, H., & Engeström, Y. (2008). Työelämän kehittämisprojektien seuraamusten jäljillä - Uusi näkökulma arviointitutkimukseen. *Hallinnon Tutkimus, 26*(4), 61-79.

Keating, C. B., Kauffmann, P., & Dryer, D. (2001). A framework for systemic analysis of complex issues. *Journal of Management Development, 20*(9), 772–784. doi:10.1108/02621710110405479

Kerosuo, H. (2006). *Boundaries in action: An activity-theoretical study of development, learning and change in health care for patients with multiple and chronic illnesses*. Helsinki: University of Helsinki, Department of Education.

Ruotsala, R. (2014). Developing a tool for cross-functional collaboration: the trajectory of an annual clock. *Outlines – Critical Practice Studies*, *15*(2), 31-53.

Sannino, A. (2008). From talk to action: Experiencing interlocution in developmental interventions. *Mind, Culture, and Activity*, *15*(3), 234–257. doi:10.1080/10749030802186769

Schaupp, M. (2011). From function-based development practices to collaborative capability building: an intervention to extend practitioners' ideas. In R.F. Poell & M. van Woerkom (Eds.), Supporting Workplace Learning: Towards Evidence-based Practice (pp. 205-224). Dordrecht, The Netherlands: Springer.

Seppänen, L., & Kloetzer, L. (2014). A microanalysis of professional and hybrid concepts in social work: How to develop mediations for networking? In T. Hansson (Ed.), Contemporary Approaches to Activity Theory: Interdisciplinary Perspectives on Human Behavior. Hershey, PA: IGI Global.

Seppänen, L., Toiviainen, H., & Kira, M. (2014). Palveluverkostojen asiakasymmärrys muutoksessa. In T. Pakarinen & T. Mäki (Eds.), *Henkilöstöjohtaminen kurkiauran kärkeen: Uudistumisen sykettä palveluihin* (pp. 135-150). Helsinki: Edita.

Smith, W. K., Binns, A., & Tushman, M. L. (2010). Complex business models: Managing strategic paradoxes simultaneously. *Long Range Planning*, *43*(2-3), 448–461. doi:10.1016/j.lrp.2009.12.003

Sterman, J. D. (2001). System dynamics modeling: Tools for learning in a complex world. *California Management Review*, *43*(4), 8–25. doi:10.2307/41166098

Toiviainen, H. (2003). *Learning across levels: Challenges of collaboration in a small-firm network*. Helsinki: University of Helsinki.

Toiviainen, H., & Kerosuo, H. (2013). Development curriculum for knowledge-based organizations: Lessons from a learning network. *International Journal of Knowledge-Based Organizations*, *3*(4), 1–18. doi:10.4018/ijkbo.2013070101

Toiviainen, H., Kerosuo, H., & Syrjälä, T. (2009). "Development Radar": The co-configuration of a tool in a learning network. *Journal of Workplace Learning*, *21*(7), 509–524. doi:10.1108/13665620910985513

Tolman, C. (1981). The metaphysics of relations in Klaus Riegel's "Dialectics" of human development. *Human Development*, *24*(1), 33–51. doi:10.1159/000272623

Victor, B., & Boynton, A. C. (1998). *Invented here: Maximizing your organization's internal growth and profitability*. Boston, MA: Harvard Business School Press.

Virkkunen, J., Newnham, D., Nleya, P., & Engeström, R. (2012). Breaking the vicious circle of categorizing students in school. *Learning Culture and Social Interaction*, *66*(3-4), 183–192. doi:10.1016/j.lcsi.2012.08.003

Virkkunen, J., & Newnham, D. S. (2013). *The Change Laboratory. A tool for collaborative development of work and education*. Rotterdam: Sense Publishers.

Virkkunen, J., & Ristimäki, P. (2012). Double stimulation in strategic concept formation: An activity-theoretical analysis of business planning in a small technology firm. *Mind, Culture, and Activity*, *19*(3), 273–286. doi:10.1080/10749039.2012.688234

Vygotsky, L. S. (1978). *Mind in society: The psychology of higher mental functions*. Cambridge, MA: Harvard University Press.

ADDITIONAL READING

Béguin, P., & Rabardel, P. (2000). Designing for instrument-mediated activity. *Scandinavian Journal of Information Systems, 12*, 173–190.

Bodrožić, Z. (2008). *Post-industrial intervention. An activity-theoretical expedition tracing the proximal development of forms of conducting interventions*. Helsinki: University of Helsinki, Department of Education.

Engeström, Y., & Kerosuo, H. (2007). From workplace learning to inter-organizational learning and back: The contribution of activity theory. *Journal of Workplace Learning, 19*(6), 336–342. doi:10.1108/13665620710777084

Engeström, Y., Nummijoki, J., & Sannino, A. (2012). Embodied germ cell at work: Building an expansive concept of physical mobility in home care. *Mind, Culture, and Activity, 19*(3), 287–309. doi:10.1080/10749039.2012.688177

Engeström, Y., Pasanen, A., Toiviainen, H., & Haavisto, V. (2005). Expansive learning as collaborative concept formation at work. In K. Yamazumi, Y. Engeström, & H. Daniels (Eds.), *New learning challenges: Going beyond the industrial age system of school and work*. Osaka, Japan: Kansai University Press.

Engeström, Y., & Sannino, A. (2012). Concept formation in wild. *Mind, Culture, and Activity, 19*(3), 201–206. doi:10.1080/10749039.2012.690813

Head, B. W. (2008). Assessing network-based collaborations. Effectiveness for whom? *Public Management Review, 10*(6), 733–749. doi:10.1080/14719030802423087

Launis, K., & Pihlaja, J. (2007). Changes in production concepts emphasize problems in work-related well-being. *Safety Science, 45*(5), 603–619. doi:10.1016/j.ssci.2007.01.006

Leadbetter, J. (2004). The role of mediating artefacts in the work of educational psychologists during consultative conversations in schools. *Educational Review, 56*(2), 133–145. doi:10.1080/0031910410001693227

Lektorsky, V. A. (2009). Mediation as a means of collective activity. In A. Sannino, H. Daniels, & K. Gutiérrez (Eds.), *Learning and expanding with activity theory* (pp. 75–87). Cambridge, UK: Cambridge University Press.

Leont'ev, A. N. (1978). *Activity, consciousness, and personality*. Englewood Cliffs, NJ: Prentice-Hall.

Nicolini, D., Mengis, J., & Swan, J. (2012). Understanding the role of objects in cross-disciplinary collaboration. *Organization Science, 23*(3), 612–629. doi:10.1287/orsc.1110.0664

Roth, W.-M., & Lee, Y.-J. (2007). "Vygotsky's neglected legacy": Cultural activity theory. *Review of Educational Research, 77*(2), 186–232. doi:10.3102/0034654306298273

Star, S. L., & Griesemer, J. R. (1989). Institutional ecology, "translations" and boundary objects: Amateurs and professionals in Berkeley's Museum of Vertebrate Zoology, 1907-39. *Social Studies of Science, 19*(3), 387–420. doi:10.1177/030631289019003001

Teräs, M. (2007). *Intercultural learning and hybridity in the Culture Laboratory*. Helsinki: University of Helsinki, Department of Education.

Virkkunen, J. (2004). Developmental interventions in work activities: an activity theoretical interpretation. In T. Kontinen (Ed.), *Development intervention: Actor and activity perspectives* (pp. 37–66). Helsinki: Center for Activity Theory and Developmental Work Research and Institute for Development Studies, University of Helsinki.

KEY TERMS AND DEFINITIONS

Annual Clock: A coordinating tool, which is typically used in organizations, in graphic or written form, to help in the planning, scheduling and managing of specific operations that take place within the period of one year.

Ascending from the Abstract to the Concrete: The principle underlies a collective process of concept formation that aims to create a new theoretical idea or concept that leads to a qualitatively novel pattern of activity. This is achieved by capturing an abstract, the modest possible explanatory model of the system relations – a germ cell – which is then gradually enhanced and tested in practice. Abstract refers to empirical concepts that describe and separate objects and phenomena into classes by comparing their external qualities. Concrete, on the contrary, relates to theoretical thinking and concepts which provide access to the dynamic understanding of a whole.

Client Understanding: This notion is defined as the service providers' conceptualization of the relationship between clients and services. It includes, firstly, the identification of the client's current and forthcoming problems, and secondly, the recognition of how they relate to the services provided (Seppänen et al., 2014).

Developmental Work Research (DWR) Intervention: A formative intervention that is typically conducted in and between activity systems facing major changes in their activities. Intervention is based on the theory of expansive learning and it pursues expanded activity, collective concept formation and emerging agency.

Dialectics: Activity theory's origins of system thinking lie in understanding dialectics (Il'enkov, 1977). Dialectics refers to the philosophy of internal relations. According to dialectic-theoretical thinking, contradictions are the source of systemic change and development. The power of contradictions originates from the struggle of opposites, which generates movement (Tolman, 1981).

Double Stimulation: Vygotsky's (1978) principle of double stimulation is based on the creative interplay between first and second stimuli. The first stimulus refers to a problematic task at hand to which an assisting instrument, for instance an illustrated model or a concept, is offered as a second stimulus.

Metaphysics of Properties: This ontological view of the metaphysics of properties dates back to the early phases of modern science when explanations for phenomena were sought from the inherent qualities attached to objects (Tolman, 1981).

Metaphysics of Relations: This ontological view of the metaphysics of relations refers to the logic of explaining relationships between independent and dependent variables (Tolman, 1981).

Chapter 13
Interventions for Learning at Global Workplaces

Hanna Toiviainen
University of Helsinki, Finland

ABSTRACT

This chapter discusses the need for rethinking cultural differences when designing and implementing learning interventions at global workplaces. Selected concepts of cultural-historical activity theory and anthropological and philosophical studies of globalization are included. Empirical data from a learning intervention directed towards a globally distributed design engineering project is analyzed. The purpose is to find intermediate concepts weaving together abstractions of culture and development with immediate observations of cultural differences. Conclusions drawn from intermediate notions imply that spontaneous presumptions about cultural differences and the developmental potential of an activity may distance the actors in global units from the object of collaborative production. Participants may become alienated from their true motive for working. In the design of future learning interventions in globalizing work, sociocultural embeddedness and universality of human activity make up the challenging starting points.

INTRODUCTION

Understanding cultural differences is important in a global world, but the way researchers approach such differences needs to be reconsidered. Several decades back cultural psychologists and anthropologists argued against "the deficit hypothesis" (Cole & Bruner, 1971). This hypothesis referred to the assumption that a community under conditions of poverty, typically among minority ethnic groups, is a disorganized community, which expresses itself in various forms of deficit regarding parental attention and school performance. In contrast, stated Cole and Bruner (ibid., p. 874), attention should be directed towards "the range of capacities readily manifested in different groups and then to inquire whether the range is adequate to the individual's needs in various cultural settings". Cultural *difference* rather than deprivation is at stake when an individual faces demands to perform in a manner which is inconsistent with past cultural experiences, summarize Cole and Bruner (ibid.).

In the past decades, cultural differences and cultural diversity were mainly discussed in the context of inequality in multi-cultural societies.

DOI: 10.4018/978-1-4666-6603-0.ch013

In the age of globalization, the differences that people face at multicultural workplaces have increased. Due to the mobility and distribution of work, defining cultural difference in terms of group membership seems inadequate and far too general. Still, nation-based characteristics dominate the extant business management literature (Hofstede, 1984; Deresky, 2011; Moran, Harris, & Moran, 2011). Furthermore, such an approach appeals to a practitioner's mind as an obvious explanation of cross-cultural issues. Understanding national characteristics may prove to be helpful in everyday encounters, but does such an understanding of differences enhance learning?

In order to develop learning interventions in global work practices, researchers should begin by going beyond the obvious focus on national characteristics. The cultural-historical activity theory represents a productive critical approach suited to tackling cultural issues involved in workplace learning. For an activity-theorist researcher, a promising way to go beyond obvious assumptions is to follow a concrete societal activity in transformation. The findings of a reported pilot project implementing global design engineering in a Finnish international company will be used to carry the storyline of this presentation.

This chapter reflects on the possibilities of extending learning interventions developed in and for local- and nation-based contexts to global cross-cultural workplaces. I address my main concerns of understanding cultural difference, development, and learning needs in global work. I do so by combining and discussing analytical activity-theoretical and anthropological concepts. The combination of interpretative resources links my analysis to the long tradition of cultural-historical activity theory research, which has substantially drawn from anthropological methods and approaches for investigating human communities (Engeström & Middleton, 1996; Yanow, 2000).

A general understanding of cultural differences in terms of space and location will first be problematized in the light of literature and empirical findings. Secondly, I provide some empirical evidence on the meaning of global and globalizing work practices for those employees who have to manage cultural difference in distributed work. Thirdly, I discuss the possibilities of global workplace learning interventions and present data from a concrete case. In the experiment reported, the purpose of the cross-cultural learning intervention was to expand the given perspective on cultural difference by directing attention to the shared object of activity. The previous literature and the empirical findings from the author's research case will alternate throughout the chapter. After a discussion of the future research directions, the chapter closes with a summary of the findings and the conceptual perspectives offered by cultural-historical activity theory as a tool for dealing with cultural differences during workplace learning.

DENATURALIZING CULTURAL DIFFERENCES

Anthropologists Akhil Gupta and James Ferguson (1992, p.7), note that "the fiction of cultures as discrete, object-like phenomena occupying discrete spaces becomes implausible for those who inhabit the borderlands". They are migrant workers, nomads, members of the transnational business and professional elite. Other people cross national-cultural borders more or less permanently. They are immigrants, refugees, exiles and expatriates. Gupta and Ferguson problematize the relationship between physical space and culture. They challenge two naturalisms, the ethnological habit of taking the association of a culturally unitary group and "its" territory as natural, and the national habit of taking the association of citizens of states and their territories as natural (Gupta & Ferguson, 1992, p. 11). Anthropologists need to question a pre-given world of separate and discrete "peoples and cultures," and see instead a difference-producing set of relations in historical process (Gupta & Ferguson, 1992, p. 16). The authors' (ibid.) discuss the *deterritorialized age* with a reference to neither the Internet nor the current trend of digitalization of work. Nevertheless, a perceptive analysis of the times still holds good.

An anthropology whose objects are no longer conceived as automatically and naturally anchored in space will need to pay particular attention to the way spaces and places are made, imagined, contested, and enforced. In this sense, it is no paradox to say that questions of space and place are, in this deterritorialized age, more central to anthropological representation than ever. (p. 17; 18)

Naturalization of culture and space is a form of cultural essentialism that the feminist philosopher Uma Narayan (1998, p. 88) criticizes. She points out that discursive reiteration of "essential differences" between cultures (Western/Non-Western, Ours/Others') forms senses of cultural identity prescribing them to groups of people who inhabit these discursive contexts. Even cultural relativism, as an obvious alternative, often seems to promote scripts of cultural difference that, says Narayan, set up sharp binaries between "Western" and "Non-western" cultures failing to ". . . reveal both sides of the binary to be, in large measure, *totalizing idealizations*, whose imaginary status has been concealed by a colonial and postcolonial history of ideological deployments of this binary" (Narayan, 1998, p. 101, italics in original). Rather than rejecting the existence of cultural differences, Narayan (ibid., p. 102) recommends taking into account the multiplicity of real differences in values, interests, and worldviews that traverse contemporary national and transnational contexts. This multiplicity of real differences is outside the immediate focus of her discussion and, therefore, not further elaborated by her. For me, her conception refers to and calls for intermediary concepts and findings between direct observations and the cultural idiosyncrasies on which we base our interpretations of cultural differences.

A simplistic example would be that we observe a business meeting with long pauses between turn-takings by participants. As this meeting is chaired by a Finnish team and as we know that Finns are said to tolerate silence in social situations beyond the average, at least if compared to European neighbors, our interpretation of communication may get stuck on this superficial notion, therefore failing for the analyst to see that the topic of the meeting is tricky requiring reading, thoughtfulness and reflection. Tolerance to silence in a certain culture may be a valid notion but there is a risk that this notion reinforces rather general cultural and potentially misleading interpretations. Another example comes from research (Toiviainen, Lallimo, & Hong, 2012) conducted at an established Finnish technology engineering and consulting company. The company piloted the first project in which some of the essential parts of the design were distributed across the company's units in Finland and China. The company sent senior experts, i.e. Finnish expatriates, to the developing engineering unit in China. They were supposed to apply the same practice of local presence to the *design engineering phase* as the company had traditionally done in the *building phase* when running local projects at the building sites all over the world. However, the delegation of design activity to a global network was problematic, as the tradition of the co-location of the design team was strong with an emphasis on an intense face-to-face interaction with the project taskforce. For example, the senior manager and country coordinator in China talked about previous experiences as a manager of another Asian office:

As a rule, the more distributed the project, the more it is at risk of failure. So when we got a big project, we used to rent a new floor, locate the whole project group there separated from others, and force our subcontractors to bring their designers there. Even if some of the guys had idle time, we rather let him/her hang around than be allowed to go back to other jobs in another office.

This was what we learned to do. However, time has passed and I guess this model will not work in future, but there is an extremely big step to be taken by the company in terms of training, people, and recruitment in order to operate in networks. (Excerpt from group interview data)

This kind of strong and naturalized co-location was unlikely in a globally distributed project. To bridge the gap in the distributed pilot project, the task force in Finland invited three designers from the Chinese unit to the headquarters in Finland. The purpose was to let them adjust to the company's established design practices and learn to use tools and systems. The Chinese engineers stayed in Finland for three months working with the project coordinators in the area of mechanical engineering. Toiviainen, Lallimo, & Hong (2012) have labeled this example of cross-cultural exchange an expansive learning effort in global work. Unfortunately, the effort to integrate the new designers to the local community was less successful than meant. During the exchange period, for instance, the project coordinators realized that the visitors refrained from initiating discussions about design issues with the coordinators. The coordinators later on explained this reluctance by referring to cultural assumptions, such as the fear of losing face, becoming the source of problems, or being used to working under hierarchical management. On the other hand, the expatriates operating in China pointed out that the individualistic Finnish working culture must have been a shock to the visitors. This is what an expatriate manager concluded.

So the basic knowledge and the basic lessons should be given here [in China], and only after that should they go [to an exchange period]. When they go there as newcomers and don't know anything and haven't worked in any of the firm's offices, people there can easily say that these guys don't understand. (Excerpt from group interview data)

Here denaturalization takes place by seeing the Chinese engineers as newcomers in the company, rather than as the representatives of a foreign culture. We avoided mentioning the unsuccessful exchange period in the interviews with the Chinese engineers. This is how a previous visitor addressed learning based on his experiences during the project.

So I think between projects if we can have several meetings, in different places where engineers sit together discuss problems or questions [that would be very helpful]. It is impossible to do in office, but we can do it through the Internet or a conference call, or even better with a video conference call. It does not need to take place often; in three or five sessions, people can get to know each other and their area. The advantages are, first, that we can see the people with whom we are working and possibly make a new friend, then we may solve challenges together or find answers for each other. We might also unify our engineering practices; lastly, individuals can contact each other more by mail or Skype when they have questions and they will know [who to contact and] who can help them. This is very good way to improve [the company and the quality of our work products]. It can also help us understand more about our system. (Excerpt from e-mail message)

We do not need to know that the writer is a Chinese young engineer in order to understand the insightful contents of his message. But we need that background knowledge in order to realize the learning potential of the newcomers entering a global network. Some of the Finnish coordinators actually realized this potential during the pilot project. This young engineer was assigned a coordination task across the Finnish-Chinese units in the project that followed. To summarize, denaturalization of cultural differences means distancing from the notions of obvious differences in terms of nationality, location and space. Instead, researchers as well as the studied people start to pay attention to the multiplicity of differences in interests, worldviews and learning possibilities that traverse national and transnational contexts. In the studied case, denaturalization took place both when people were giving up the historically deeply-rooted ideal of co-location of the design team and were seeing the distant designers as newcomers rather than as representatives of foreign culture. The actions of denaturalization were instrumental in helping the project coordinators realize the learning potential of the new global actors in the design project.

DEVELOPMENTAL VISIONS OF GLOBAL WORK PRACTICES

Cultural differences include the unavoidable question of development and social progress that cultural-historically oriented researchers face when traversing various cultural contexts. Michael Cole (2005) argues that we need to address this question in order to examine issues that specify the impact of schooling on development. He points to the fact that Wertsch, del Rio, and Alvarez (1995) explicitly rejected the use of the term 'cultural-historical,' which for them was associated with the Marxist idea that cross-cultural variations are really cross-historical, with modern technological society as the highest rung (so far) on the ladder of history. Cole himself does not follow this line of argument, but forewarns that the topic is treacherous, a viewpoint with which it is easy to agree. At the same time, we must realize that in the ten years since he described the "Modern technological society," it has become even more diverse and geographically dispersed and the problems of its poor sustainability have multiplied on a global scale. Recent titles on web pages, "How Chinese Innovation is Changing Green Technology" and "China–Green Technology Leader: Has the Future Arrived?" reflect this change. The demand for cross-cultural development, however, also concerns the "developed"

party. When companies expand their global activities, they need to change. On a local level, changes open up alternative directions to cope with transformation and still maintain the meaningfulness of work. On the other hand, we know that the local agency is constrained by the definition of strategy, and in the pilot case, it seemed to imply that the global distribution of the design work was to be carried out quite separate from the concerns of the implementers. In the pilot project analyzed in the previous section, the experienced task force team members in Finland clearly saw their own future threatened. By listening to their concerns expressed in a group interview, we envisioned three alternative developmental directions of change, which we discussed with them in a feedback meeting organized by the project manager. The first concern, *the end of work*, presented the employees' worry about continuation of expert work in the headquarters in Finland. The second concern, *distant communication and workload*, expressed resistance towards the increasing task load of networking, and the third concern, *new project organization for networking*, formulated a need to reorganize work so as to manage global networks. All three concerns reflected how employees thought at the beginning of the first networked design project. The new networking model related to a real business deal; it had to be implemented "on-line" shaped as a demanding customer project. Implementation of the model was not preceded by a planning and simulation phase to test working across distant offices. Data is provided by the task force members during a group interview.

The End of Work

Task force members discussed the first vision of future work at the beginning of the global design project. A commonly shared concern was that the expertise of previous engineers would be transferred to the new global engineers, which would mean an end to their jobs. The task force members commented:

This works as long as someone is in charge of an activity, but in the long run, the expertise will disappear, design experience will not accumulate in this firm, and there will be no advisers. It will be the end of the whole job.

In the future, the machines will be built for China and the Chinese will design them. What will our future task be?

We have to make ourselves indispensable; we shouldn't give all our knowledge to them.

We have to find something we can use to secure our own position.

The engineers' worry of losing work, of course, reflected development in the global labor markets and was warranted in that context. The risk of losing one's own knowledge and skills when transmitting them to novices, however, offers an adverse starting point for learning. Neither is there a learning theory to support the risk. Rather, this type of knowledge-transfer dilemma is acknowledged by evolutionary business research showing that threats, mistrust and opportunistic behavior in an initial phase of inter-organizational relationships prevent collaboration and learning (Dodgson, 1993; Inkpen & Currall, 2004).

Distant Communication and Workload

The second vision of the global pilot project emerged from the immediate experiences of the senior engineers. The time-consuming control function of the project coordinators was disturbing. They had difficulty in using e-mail as the main channel of communication. The existing tools in the network for engineering design, communication and instruction attached to the project were

inappropriate. This was something that the task force members commented on.

Networking increases the total workload; when done in China and [City in Central Finland] someone has to be tied to control, keep watch, and be in charge of quality.

Our concern is whether they in China know the tool and will design in the same way. Written instructions are required.

Design-area coordinators send a lot of communications to China, but the situation is quite desperate to try to write and provide an explanation for every step by e-mail.

There is so much to discuss through e-mail that you don't have time to orientate yourself to any other tasks.

It would be much easier for me to work with the people I know; I know what they can stand and that the department [is near and can be contacted]. I get no surplus value from working with some remote workgroup.

Another tool-related aspect that characterized this vision was that skillful use of the company-specific tools required local participation and long-term experience. According to the task force members:

Mastering the tools is one aspect, but real mastery requires many years' experience to be able to do this work.

So much experience, knowledge, and insight are incorporated in the tool, that it cannot be learnt anywhere but in [this company].

Regarding the learning option and direction for the task force, this view shows an effort to master new distributed work and expresses the need to re-tool and re-mediate globalizing activity (Miettinen, 2006). The fact that new tools were neither available nor created during the hectic project problematized expansive learning spanning to future projects and sustained the idealization of the locally organized design work.

New Project Organization for Networking

The third vision is based on an articulated need for an organization-level change and a changed relationship between the project coordinators and the global team members. In contrast to the pessimistic vision 1, the senior engineers saw that their role would change and new tasks and roles would have to be created in the global network. In contrast to vision 2, they admitted that adhering to control and to the ideal of local teams would not be an option in the future. The expansive potential of the task force's learning was in seeing the project activity in the new context of a global network. The limiting factor may come from seeing the change as organizational. Subjects, tools, the division of labor and the community will change, whereas the object of activity, design of technical solutions for industrial sites, will remain the same as long as there will be demand on the capabilities achieved in the company's history. Of course, it may not be true and may be observed by looking at their web site to see how the business concept is presented today compared with the presentation five or ten years ago. The task force members envisioned:

Globalization requires us to recruit new people to take care of these links and communication. We haven't found new models of activity, yet; they have to be created.

When we start to work in a network, the whole project organization should be renewed.

The mutual relations of the design units will change; the [headquarters] will remain a relatively

small actor while [other units] will grow. Actors and teams will change.

We don't need a coordinator here anymore; we rather need a coordinator out in the world.

There has to be our coordinators who teach the Chinese designers our ways of working. It is different work than what they [coordinators] are used to do locally [at building sites].

The analysis of the developmental visions of global work practices highlights that major transformations of work create open-ended courses of action for the workers. Whether the optional developmental directions turn to real alternatives depends on workers' cultural resources to broaden their views of work. Organizational and managerial volition is needed to consider the alternative paths leading to global activity and to give support to workers' change agency. Freeland (1997, p. 135) says, "[C]ultural templates may shape actors' understanding of the world and the options available to them, but there is always a certain openness to those understandings – they are the subject of struggle, negotiation, and strategic manipulation rather than unthinking reproduction." The openness of understandings creates fertile ground for learning interventions, but what are the conditions of learning and agency in global workplaces?

CROSS-CULTURAL INTERVENTION FOR LEARNING

In the preceding section, I analyzed some experienced actors' developmental visions in an internationally established company going through phases of globalization. A new unit of less experienced actors is, of course, an important target of development in itself, but the participants involved should be seen as developmentally active and agentive from the beginning. My final argument is that this calls for interventions in workplace learning and raises ethical issues about the potential of interventions. We may question "the Nordic perspective" (the topic of the Nordic ISCAR conference 2013) and whether it translates to workplace practices on a global level. The growing global uniformity in education has been criticized for legitimizing the actions of rich over poor nations and ensuring the hegemony of global elites (Spring, 2008, p. 352). In the research on workplace learning, "Globalization dominance and loss of cultural relevance" is one of the trends, according to Cairns and Malloch (2011). Spring (2008, p. 340) remarks that in adult education "global discourses on education and knowledge economy changed the earlier humanist vision of lifelong learning to one focused on the ability of workers to adapt to a changing world of work".

"Have we witnessed a veritable decolonization, or are we simply ensconced in a more sophisticated process of recolonization?" ask Carr and Thésée (2012, p. 15) in their book *Decolonizing Philosophies of Education*. From this vantage point, Nordic countries with a non-colonial history and a long history of democratic labor market relations are drawing attention when educational models are searched worldwide for elementary, vocational and now eventually for workplace learning. Tuomo Alasoini characterizes the "Finnish model for workplace development"(as represented by the TYKES program under his leadership) in terms of the synergic advancement of productivity and the quality of working life, cooperation between management and staff in augmenting of the local learning process, interaction between researchers and consultants, and a wide coverage by sector (Alasoini, 2009, pp. 178;179). The Finnish strategy is process (vs. product) oriented, as development projects rely strongly on collaborative local processes and direct staff participation. Fostering cooperation between universities, consultants, and workplaces is an explicit aim (Alasoini, 2009; Gruber & Harteis, 2011). Bjørn Gustavsen (2007) notes that learning oriented forms of work organization are more widely applied in the Scandinavian

countries than is generally the case in European countries. He characterizes the "Scandinavian model" (Finland included) in the word "trust." This is a general cultural assumption that cannot be directly applied as an explanation of observed behavior, as was critically remarked in the first part of this paper. Gustavsen (ibid.) uses his notion to identify the preconditions and circumstances of learning at work. Trust can be used to create different forms of cooperative organization and to meet different challenges, but: "[T]here is only one basic condition that all forms [of cooperative organization] have to meet: all actors must have a certain degree of freedom in their work role, otherwise trust is not possible" (ibid., p. 668).

INTERVENTION IN ACTION

I conclude from the previous that the interventions for workplace learning are a political issue in a post-colonial, globalizing world. Michael Cole and Yrjö Engeström (2007) in their article *Cultural-Historical Approaches to Designing for Development* discuss the sustainability of the CHAT-based (Cultural-Historical Activity Theory based) formative interventions and point out that challenges arise from the problematic conditions that the interventions were designed to address, such as poor education and difficulties in the organization of work. Another source of challenges is the "resistance that arises when their [interventions'] success come into conflict with the large social conditions that underlie the social problems they were designed to transcend" (ibid., p. 504). Interventions are a form of critical theorizing revealing that the modern industrialized bureaucratized societies systematically undermine the values they espouse, such as educational equality, Cole and Engeström claim. The CHAT-based interventions show societies that there is a way of realizing the values and solving the problems, but they often lack political will to do so, summarize Cole and Engeström (2007). Political challenges are involved in new intercultural formative interventions, such as the implementation of the series of Change Laboratories for facilitating expansive school transformation in Botswana (R. Engeström et al. 2014). The analysis reveals the necessity of addressing multiple interrelated levels of development ranging from teachers' local practices to national education and further to global discussion. The case in question is a path-breaking example of innovative learning interventions designed in and by networks of global research partnership (Virkkunen & Newnham, 2013).

In the before-mentioned pilot project of global engineering design, we wanted to examine the potential of cross-cultural workplace learning intervention. A two-day workshop was organized in the Chinese office to gather data on the perspectives of this new global unit. Based on activity theory the focus of the methods was on the object of activity, in this case, on the project

implemented to design an industrial mill for a customer. The Chinese engineers working in this project reflected on their experiences. Most of the designers were young employees capable of communicating in English and acting as translators for their non-English-speaking peers. In a small-group assignment, each group was asked to fill in a problem-solution-log by formulating two problems that they had faced during the pilot project (Toiviainen et al., 2012). One of the problem cases described is displayed in Figure 1: "Doing the work without knowledge of why we are doing it – Not solved yet – Organize visits to the sites or built-up [--] mills."

According to an activity-theoretical interpretation, asking *why* and *where-to* questions represents a high level of conceptual thinking and should therefore be addressed in workplace learning and even in the design of technological support (Engeström, 2007). The suggestion given

Figure 1. Problem-solution log used in the Chinese design office

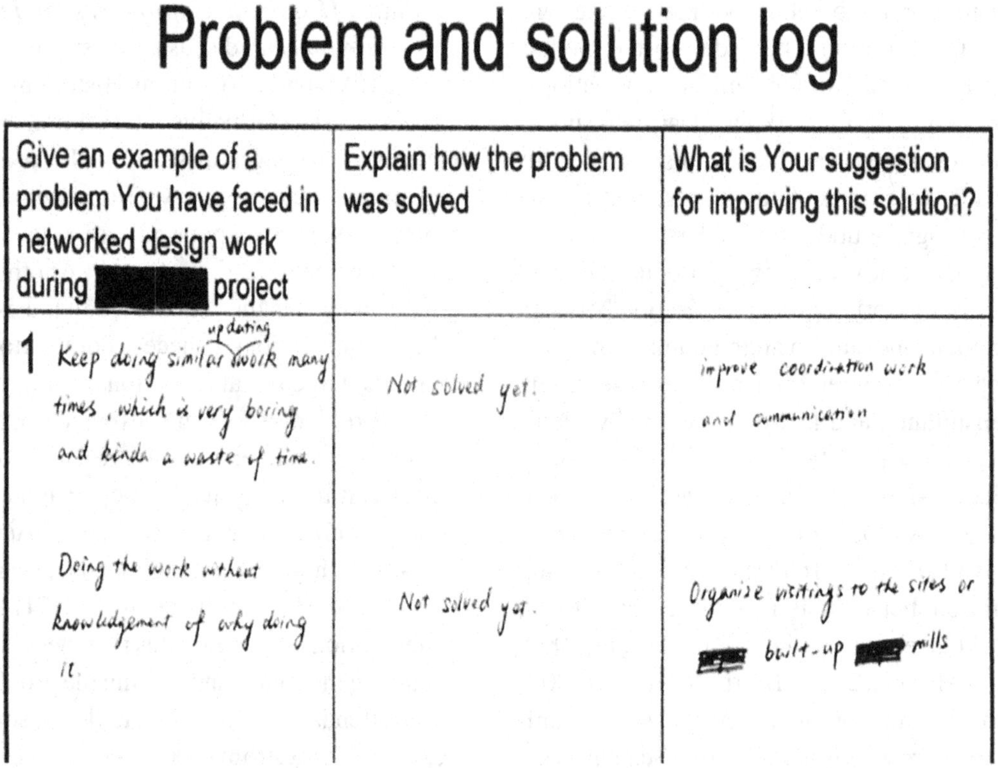

Problem and solution log

Give an example of a problem You have faced in networked design work during ███ project	Explain how the problem was solved	What is Your suggestion for improving this solution?
1 Keep doing similar work many times, which is very boring and kinda a waste of time. (updating)	Not solved yet.	improve coordination work and communication
Doing the work without knowledgement of why doing it.	Not solved yet.	Organize visitings to the sites or ███ built-up ███ mills

in the example is at the same time practical and theoretically sound – "organize visits to the sites or built-up mills." The Why-question occurs in a network of complex interrelated activities that distance the actors from the object of activity. Cultural differences may be involved, recalling the Finnish coordinators' notion of the Chinese engineering practice. They pointed out that the emphasis is on the building site activities. Designing takes place partly on the spot in contrast to the Finnish way of spending hours and hours at the office preplanning and planning before approaching the site.

FUTURE RESEARCH DIRECTIONS

Cultural-historical activity theory-based research on learning in globalization is in its early stages. Anh and Marginson (2013) introduce the Vygotskian sociocultural theory modified for settings in which educational practices have global, national, and local ("glonacal") dimensions. They highlight two Vygotskian principles, the genetic method and mediation by artifacts that, when revisited, have much to offer even to the investigation of current global phenomena in education.

But if Vygotsky was less than fully open to the possibilities of subjects in space and the multiple glonacal dimensions, he was insightful about subjects in time, ranging from the ecological domain to the domain of day-to-day life. In principle, his insights into the communicative formation of mentality, and the use of artifacts to shape human development and social relations–infused by a critical dialectical method with roots in Hegel and Marx–should be as useful in investigating cross-border effects in education as in investigating localized schooling. (p. 149)

Articulation of global, national, and local dimensions represents these authors' effort to conceptualize human actions and conditions of

learning breaking the local and national boundaries. In the empirical case study on a cohort of Vietnamese pre-service teachers, they show that the global elements in the teachers' ontogenetic domain (the individual lifespan) were mediated in their day-to-day micro genetic domain (immediate events) (Anh & Marginson, 2013, p. 157). The interplay of global and local and the meaning of national identities or territorial boundaries become ever more contested when analyzing cross-cultural communities and translocality (Greiner & Sakdapolrak, 2013). Takahashi and Hirai (2010) criticize such cross-cultural research that is prone to find differences among cultures and to explain the diversities with the ecocultural knowledge already at hand. They state:

We believe that it is time for cross-cultural studies to embrace the fact, or at least the hypothesis, of human universality. If we neglect the universals among humans, we shall surely fail to grasp substantial roles of ecocultural factors in human development. (p. 363)

This is in line with the discussion of this paper. It highlights that while much is owed to cross-cultural studies for understanding how deeply human development is embedded in sociocultural context, this understanding should also account for concepts and approaches discussing "biological heritage and human nature fostered in the universal human environment" (Takahashi & Hirai, 2010, p. 363). For the future of cultural-historical activity theory, this represents an exciting task to both revisit its methodological foundations and create new vocabulary for properly addressing learning embedded in the cultural dimensions of globalization.

CONCLUSION

This author's (Toiviainen et al., 2012) experimental learning interventions to globalizing work practices gave impetus to revisit cultural differences and to analyze the possibilities of development in this specific context. The presentation joined the discussion of focal concepts carried out in the cultural-historical activity theory through recent decades (Cole & Bruner, 1971; Cole & Engeström, 2007). The case of implementing globally distributed design engineering in a Finnish international company provided empirical data for the discussion.

Anthropologists and philosophers have problematized the relationship between space and culture and a pre-existing world of separate and discrete "peoples and cultures." To go beyond the naturalisms and idealizations involved, researchers should analyze the difference-producing set of relations as they emerge and evolve in historical processes. In doing so, intermediate concepts and notions are needed to weave together the abstractions of culture and development, on the one hand, and the immediate observations of cultural differences and learning in every-day activities, on the other. The intermediate level notions produced through this analysis are summarized.

First, it is not uncommon that the problems of cross-cultural communication are explained in terms of cultural idiosyncrasies, such as "being used to hierarchical management." This may block an active search for ways to share the practices across cultures and places orienting themselves to the same object of activity. In the case study reported in this article, treating the globally distributed actors as newcomers helped the project coordinators realize the learning potential in them during the pilot engineering design project.

Secondly, the expansion of activity to a global network is a dramatic change of many uncertainties compared with the traditional locally organized work. The meaningfulness of work is at stake. Existing participants in the midst of such a process may try to maintain control by idealizing the local practice. Expansive learning potential resides in seeing the profound changes not only in overall organization of work, but also even in the object of activity when it becomes distributed, virtual, and increasingly multicultural.

Thirdly, global organizations have presented cross-cultural training programs based on universal compliance norms equally set for all members. To what extent do they represent learning interventions open to cultural variety encouraging the activeness and agency of the learners? Agency and freedom to act make learning interventions a political issue at globalizing workplaces. In the case of global engineering design, the participation in a complex distributed network caused a situation, in which the object of activity was hidden from the learners. The learning intervention experiment enabled the formulation of a 'why' question articulating the 'not-solved-yet' lack of sense and meaning.

The intermediate notions implicate that when seemingly self-evident cultural differences and the possibilities of development remain "unreflected" the actors in global units are at risk of being distanced from the object of collaborative production and alienated from their true motive for working. At worst, cross-cultural training enforces cultural idiosyncrasies and the adaptation to an object of activity as if it were historically unchanging. An activity-theoretical approach may help in recognizing learning potential in global newcomers–the potential easily hiding behind cultural differences.

REFERENCES

Alasoini, T. (2009). Alternative Paths for Working Life Reform? A Comparison of European and East Asian Development Strategies. *International Journal of Action Research, 5*(2), 155–183.

Anh, D. T. K., & Marginson, S. (2013). Global learning through the lens of Vygotskian sociocultural theory. *Critical Studies in Education, 54*(2), 143–159. doi:10.1080/17508487.2012.722557

Cairns, L., & Malloch, M. (2011). Theories of work, place and learning: New directions. In M. Malloch, L. Cairns, K. Evans, & B. N. O'Connor (Eds.), The SAGE Handbook of Workplace Learning (pp. 3-16). London: Sage Publications Ltd.

Carr, P. R., & Thésée, G. (2012). Discursive epistemologies by, for and about the de-colonizing project. In A. A. Abdi (Ed.), Decolonizing Philosophies of Education (pp. 15–28). Rotterdam: Sense Publishers. doi:10.1007/978-94-6091-687-8_2

Cole, M. (2005). Cross-Cultural and Historical Perspectives on the Developmental Consequences of Education. *Human Development*, *48*(4), 195–216. doi:10.1159/000086855

Cole, M., & Bruner, J. S. (1971). Cultural differences and inferences about psychological processes. *The American Psychologist*, *26*(10), 867–876. doi:10.1037/h0032240

Cole, M., & Engeström, Y. (2007). Cultural-Historical Approaches to Designing for Development. In J. Valsiner, & A. Rosa (Eds.), The Cambridge handbook of sociocultural psychology (pp. 484-507). Cambridge, UK: Cambridge University Press.

Deresky, H. (2011). *International management. Managing across borders and cultures: Text and cases* (7th ed.). Boston, MA: Pearson.

Dodgson, M. (1993). Learning, Trust, and Technological Collaboration. *Human Relations*, *46*(1), 77–95. doi:10.1177/001872679304600106

Engeström, R., Batane, T., Hakkarainen, K., Newnham, D. S., Nleya, P., Senteni, A., & Sinko, M. (2014). Reflections on the use of DWR in intercultural collaboration. *Mind, Culture, and Activity*, *21*(2), 129–147. doi:10.1080/10749039.2013.879185

Engeström, Y. (2007). Enriching the Theory of Expansive Learning: Lessons from journeys toward coconfiguration. *Mind, Culture, and Activity*, *14*(1-2), 23–39. doi:10.1080/10749030701307689

Engeström, Y., & Middleton, D. (Eds.). (1996). *Cognition and Communication at Work*. Cambridge, UK: Cambridge University Press. doi:10.1017/CBO9781139174077

Freeland, R. F. (1997). Culture and Volition in Organizational Decision-Making. Review Essay. *Qualitative Sociology*, *20*(1), 127–137. doi:10.1023/A:1024772516671

Greiner, C., & Sakdapolrak, P. (2013). Translocality: Concepts, Applications and Emerging Research Perspectives. *Geography Compass*, *7*(5), 373–384. doi:10.1111/gec3.12048

Gruber, H., & Harteis, C. (2011). Researching Workplace Learning in Europe. In M. Malloch, L. Cairns, K. Evans, & B. N. O'Connor (Eds.), The SAGE Handbook of Workplace Learning (pp. 224-235). London: Sage Publications Ltd.

Gupta, A., & Ferguson, J. (1992). Beyond "Culture": Space, Identity, and the Politics of Difference. *Cultural Anthropology*, *7*(1), 6–23. doi:10.1525/can.1992.7.1.02a00020

Gustavsen, B. (2007). Work Organization and 'the Scandinavian Model'. *Economic and Industrial Democracy*, *28*(4), 650–671. doi:10.1177/0143831X07082218

Hofstede, G. (1984). *Culture's Consequences: International Differences in Work-Related Values (Abridged edition)*. London: SAGE.

Inkpen, A., & Currall, S. (2004). The Coevolution of Trust, Control, and Learning in Joint Ventures. *Organization Science*, *15*(5), 586–599. doi:10.1287/orsc.1040.0079

Miettinen, R. (2006). The Sources of Novelty: A Cultural and Systemic View of Distributed Creativity. *Creativity and Innovation Management*, *15*(2), 173–181. doi:10.1111/j.1467-8691.2006.00381.x

Moran, R. T., Harris, P. R., & Moran, S. V. (2011). *Managing Cultural Differences: Global Leadership Strategies for Cross-cultural Business Success* (8th ed.). Burlington, MA: Elsevier/Butterworth-Heinemann.

Narayan, U. (1998). Essence of Culture and a Sense of History: A Feminist Critique of Cultural Essentialism. *Hypatia*, *13*(2), 86–106. doi:10.1111/j.1527-2001.1998.tb01227.x

Spring, J. (2008). Research on Globalization and Education. *Review of Educational Research*, *78*(2), 330–363. doi:10.3102/0034654308317846

Takahashi, K., & Hirai, M. (2010). Toward a New Stage of Cross-Cultural Studies: Ordinary People in Individual by Culture Interactions: Essay Review of Women and Family in Contemporary Japan by Susan D. Holloway. *Human Development*, *53*(6), 361–365. doi:10.1159/000321890

Toiviainen, H., Lallimo, J., & Hong, J. (2012). Emergent learning practices in globalizing work – The case of a Finnish-Chinese project in a Finnish technology consulting firm. *Journal of Workplace Learning*, *24*(7/8), 509–527. doi:10.1108/13665621211261016

Virkkunen, J., & Newnham, D. S. (2013). *The Change Laboratory: A Tool for Collaborative Development of Work and Education*. Rotterdam: Springer. doi:10.1007/978-94-6209-326-3

Wertsch, J. V., del Rio, P., & Alvarez, A. (1995). *Sociocultural Studies of Mind*. Cambridge University Press. doi:10.1017/CBO9781139174299

Yanow, D. (2000). Seeing organizational learning: A 'cultural' view. *Organization*, *7*(2), 247–269. doi:10.1177/135050840072003

ADDITIONAL READING

Cole, M. (1998). Can cultural psychology help us think about diversity? *Mind, Culture, and Activity*, *5*(4), 291–304. doi:10.1207/s15327884mca0504_4

Engeström, Y. (2008/2010). *From Teams to Knots: Activity-Theoretical Studies of Collaboration and Learning at Work*. Cambridge University Press. doi:10.1017/CBO9780511619847

Engeström, Y. (2011). From design experiments to formative interventions. *Theory & Psychology*, *21*(5), 598–628. doi:10.1177/0959354311419252

Gutiérrez, K. D. (2008). Developing a sociocritical literacy in the Third Space. *Reading Research Quarterly*, *43*(2), 148–164. doi:10.1598/RRQ.43.2.3

Kaptelinin, V., & Nardi, B. (2012). Activity Theory in HCI: Fundamentals and Reflections. *Synthesis Lectures on Human-Centered Informatics*, *5*(1), 1–105. doi:10.2200/S00413ED1V01Y201203HCI013

Kerosuo, H., Toiviainen, H., & Syrjälä, T. (2011). Co-configuration and learning in and for networks—The case of Forum of In-house Development in South Savo. In T. Alasoini, M. Lahtonen, N. Rouhiainen, C. Sweins, K. Hulkko-Nyman, & T. Spangar (Eds.), Linking Theory and Practice – Learning Networks at the Service of Workplace Innovation (pp. 162-182). Helsinki: Tekes.

Kitayama, S., & Cohen, D. (2007). *Handbook of Cultural Psychology*. New York: Guilford Press.

Lewis, R. (1997). An activity theory framework to explore distributed communities. *Journal of Computer Assisted Learning*, *13*(4), 210–218. doi:10.1046/j.1365-2729.1997.00023.x

Sharples, M., Taylor, J., & Vavoula, G. (2007). A Theory of Learning for the Mobile Age. In R. Andrews & C. Haythornthwaite (Eds.), *The Sage Handbook of Elearning Research* (pp. 221–247). London: Sage.

Toiviainen, H., & Kerosuo, H. (2013). Development Curriculum for Knowledge-Based Organizations: Lessons from a Learning Network. *International Journal of Knowledge-Based Organizations*, *3*(3), 1–18. doi:10.4018/ijkbo.2013070101

KEY TERMS AND DEFINITIONS

CHAT-Based Formative Interventions: Developmental and learning interventions aimed at changing the societal practices locally and globally. Interventions are a form of critical theorizing supporting agency for realizing the values and solving the problems of communities.

Cultural Essentialism: This philosophy leads to discursive reiteration of "essential differences" between cultures presenting differences as pregiven that the discourses of difference merely describe rather than help construct.

Deficit Hypothesis: An assumption, according to which a community under conditions of poverty expresses itself in various forms of deficit. Cultural psychologists in the 1970s argued against this hypothesis and suggested instead the concept of cultural difference that reflects individual's past cultural experience.

Expansive Learning Efforts in Global Work: Participants' collaborative creation and implementation of new tools and practices aimed at improving the mastery of the global and distributed work.

Globalization of Education and Learning: The growing global uniformity in education has raised fear of losing cultural relevance and the humanist vision of lifelong learning.

Glonacal: A heuristic concept drawing on the Vygotskian sociocultural theory by modifying it for settings in which educational practices have global, national and local ("glonacal") dimensions.

Hypothesis of Human Universality: This assumption takes a critical stance to such kind of cross-cultural research that is prone to find differences among cultures and to explain the diversities with the ecocultural knowledge already at hand (cf. cultural essentialism).

Naturalization of Space and Culture: The ethnological habit of taking the association of a culturally unitary group and "its" territory as natural, which anthropologists have questioned.

Newcomers of a Learning Community: Newcomer-perspective denaturalizes the pre-given "cultural differences," emphasizes newcomers' learning potential and the whole community's learning by questioning the taken-for-granted practices and tools.

Problem-Solution-Log: A simple fill-in tool developed by interventionists in order to encourage participants to analyze the problems faced, the solutions created, and further development ideas during a globally networked project.

Scandinavian Model of Workplace Learning: Learning oriented forms of work organization are claimed to be characteristic of Scandinavian countries captured in a keyword "trust".

Section 4
Methodology

Chapter 14
Subject Matter Analysis in Physical Education

Carolina Picchetti Nascimento
University of São Paulo, Brazil

ABSTRACT

Educational research grounded in the theoretical perspective of developmental teaching can provide some ideas, challenges, and proposals to be discussed. From a developmental perspective, the fundamental content of teaching and learning covers the theoretical concepts of each school subject. Through the area of physical education, the author discusses the process for identifying and systematizing the theoretical concepts that organize school subjects. This discussion is proposed from the point of view of its philosophical foundations in dialectical materialism and from concrete possibilities and challenges in educational research. Through analysis and systematization of the essential and necessary relations that organize physical education and by an attempt at making these relations concrete, the author highlights the value and challenges that arise during a process of a subject matter analysis in educational research.

INTRODUCTION

A developmental teaching tradition in educational practice conceptualizes and proposes theoretical concepts as the main content of teaching and learning aiming at students' development of theoretical thinking (Davydov, 1990). In this tradition, a theoretical concept means a system of the essential and necessary relations that constitute and organize a phenomenon, which differs from a definition or from an empirical concept. A general orientation for working with theoretical concepts in teaching and learning is present both in Davydov's ideas (1990; 1983) of developmental teaching and in

Vygotsky's ideas (2009) of scientific concepts. For instance, Davydov (1990, p. 299) synthesizes that a theoretical concept is a means for "mentally reproducing or constructing an object's essence. Having a concept of an object means mastering a general method of constructing it, a knowledge of its origin". To act with the ideas of developmental teaching in current teaching and learning processes it is important to understand the theoretical and philosophical principles that support the perspective. However, it is equally important to produce and discuss concrete examples that people use in their attempts at dealing with those ideas. One can find some of these concrete examples in Davydov

DOI: 10.4018/978-1-4666-6603-0.ch014

(1990; 1983), Hedegard (1990), Chaiklin (1999), Lompsher (1999), Hedegaard and Chaiklin (2005). Nevertheless, the specific task of identifying the conceptual relations in a given subject matter and designing learning tasks through them seems to be an exception rather than a focus in educational research within a cultural historical tradition. The task of identifying and systematizing the essential relations of a school subject is different from accomplishing a developmental teaching. Nonetheless, this action is the very and substantial basis for it. In this chapter I defend the idea that one of the general objectives in educational research grounded in a developmental teaching tradition relates to the identification and systematization of the essential and necessary relations that organize a school subject. The purpose of this chapter is to discuss educational research by means of a concrete attempt at working with subject matter analysis in physical education. I introduce some general problems related to the process of analysing physical education as a pedagogical practice. For doing this analysis I highlight the value of the concept of *activity*. Through the exposition of the process for identifying the essential relations in *physical education* and through the concrete challenges that arise during this analysis, I discuss the idea of subject matter analysis as a general objective in educational research directed to contribute to a developmental teaching approach in teaching and learning processes.

BACKGROUND

Physical education is a school discipline that traditionally deals with a particular set of human activity whether it is named Physical Culture activities, Sport activities or Athletic activities. Besides the matter about which term would be best suited for referring to those phenomena, a theoretical use of the term activity in those expressions can contribute to an understanding of the educational role of the respective discipline. To concentrate on the discussion of the theoretical meaning of the term activity, I will use the expression physical education activities, as a general reference to the different manifestations related to a voluntary and non-utilitarian bodily action like Game, Dance, Gymnastic, Combat Games, Athletics and Swimming. From a theoretical perspective physical education activities must be understood, first and foremost, as a product of societal practice. These activities embody societal needs, objects and goals, historically produced in a field of voluntary and non-utilitarian bodily actions. In this sense, physical education activities can be understood as being connected to and arising from other kinds of human activities, namely: play and art. On this topic, Elkonin (1998) outlines the developmental process of bodily actions.

It seems to us that the most likely course of development progresses from dramatic play to athletic play, rather than vice versa. The rules of human interaction leading to real world success, reinforced an infinite number of times through real group activities, are gradually isolated. Their representations outside actual utilitarian situations become the content of athletic games. (p.19)

With this understanding in mind, one can say that the methodological key for identifying and systematizing the essential and necessary relations that constitute and organize physical education activities is the analysis of the human relations embodied in these activities. Through the analysis of these relations one can identify the *objects* of physical education activities. The term "object" has an everyday meaning related to a physical, sensorial and material object, a thing. However, for a cultural historical tradition (Marx, 2004; 2007; 1996 and Leontiev, 1983; 1979) the term *object* refers mainly to the relations that *motivate* and organize one's action, representing the general content of a person's action. Leontiev (1983, p. 68) says: "a constituting characteristic of an activity is its object-relatedness. Properly, the concept of its object (Gegenstand) is already implicitly contained in the very concept of activity". The object of an activity refers to a historical and societal materiality; it refers to the *ideal* content of human relations (Ilyenkov, 1977). The object of an activity will always embody a certain synthesis of human capacities and modes of actions developed by mankind. This is an example of what Vygotski (1995) named as cultural means or cultural signs. This conceptualization also holds true for the analysis of physical education activities. Game, Dance, Gymnastic, Swimming and all kinds of the particular activities in physical education are organized by specific *objects*. This is why identifying human relations embodied in these objects represents the methodological key for elaborating a theoretical understanding of physical education activities. Through this, one can go beyond the procedure of identifying the external characterizing features of these activities, such as being competitive, requiring physical effort, displaying motor ability or promoting health.

Leontiev (1983, p. 68) argues for unity between object and subject in activity theory. An activity is, at the same time, a) *the structure* or *the substance of an activity*, "in its independent existence as subordinating to itself and transforming the activity of the subject". It is also b) the *subject's action in this structure*, "an image of the object [...] an activity of the subject". An activity, therefore, is first of all a product of a collective subject acting in some societal conditions: i.e. a product of societal practice. The essential relations for producing and reproducing this activity are synthesized in its *object*. At the same time, an activity is the very actualization of this objet through an individual. An individual acts in an activity which structure exists as an independent thing from himself, as a product of societal practice. By acting in this activity and reproducing its object the individual allows the actualization of the activity in current reality and for himself. Because of this mutual and concrete relation in an activity, one can find a mutual and concrete relation between the con-

cepts of object and motive in Leontiev's theory (1983). From the point of view of the activity of the subject the *object* of this activity can become his *motive*. According to Leontiev (1983, p. 83) "For the terminology proposed by me the object of an activity is its real motive". In synthesis, an *activity* exists simultaneously as a product of societal practice which is embodied in the *objects* of the activity and as the subject's activity or the individual's actions for reproducing the objects of an activity. Both dimensions exist only in this mutual and permanent relationship to each other, and they are separable just through our thoughts, as a tool for analysing human activities.

In order to be able to act and to reproduce the structure of an activity a person does not necessarily have to understand the essential relations that organize the activity. But if one wants to *intentionally* reproduce and improve an activity, an ambition which is particularly important in teaching and learning, one has to understand the essential and necessary relations that constitute and organize an activity structure. This holds true for Physics, Literature, Biology, Social Science or Physical Education. A conceptualization of these essential and necessary relations means elaborating a *theoretical concept* for those activities. In this sense, the *concept* of physical education activity should explain the system of the essential and necessary relations that constitute and organize activities in the field of voluntary and non-utilitarian bodily actions. Considering the general aim of pedagogical activity as it is understood in cultural historical theory, the concept of physical education activity should contribute to individual's development of theoretical thinking. For this, a proposal of a conceptualization of physical education has to explain the *process* through which the essential and general relations that organize these activities come true in many particular forms of physical education activities, such as: games, dance, combat games, athletics contest, swimming and circus.

CONCEPTUAL FRAMEWORK

Before analysing how these general statements were elaborated in our research in the area of Physical Education, it seems important to make a brief introduction of some key concepts involved in a subject matter analysis, namely the concepts of *essence*, *abstract* and *concrete*. Within a cultural historical perspective the *essence* of a phenomenon is related to a certain set of relations that is *necessary* for the very existence of the phenomenon under consideration. Davydov (1990) and Ilyenkov (2008) quote Spinoza's example about the essential relations for the concept of circumference.

If we define a circle as a figure in which "all straight lines drawn from the center to the circumference are equal, everyone can see that such a definition does not in the least explain the essence of a circle, but solely one of its properties". According to the correct mode of definition, a circle is "the figure described by any line whereof one end is fixed and the other free". This definition, indicating the mode of the origin of a thing and a comprehension of the "proximate cause", and thereby containing a mode of its mental reconstruction, enables one to deduce all the other properties of it, including the one pointed out above (Ilyenkov, 2008, p. 21).

A concept of a circumference should indicate the general mode of action to produce a circumference, as a synthesis of the essential and necessary relations of this phenomenon. Therefore, it represents the relations that allow one to mentally reconstruct the phenomenon as well as to explain the different forms or characteristics that may arise from it. Although Spinoza's math example is adequate for expressing the concept of essence, when one is referring to a phenomenon that has a societal and historical nature, as in physical education activities, the problem of the meaning of "essence" must be explained beyond this example.

The essence of a human activity is not an eternal attribute of a phenomenon, something that has always existed and will always exist as such. It is rather the opposite, an essence is a set of objective relations, socially and historically constructed through human practice. The essence of a human activity refers to human relations that became essential through societal practice (Davydov, 1990; Marx & Engels, 2007; Ilyenkov, 2008). The essence of physical education activities was not present in all societies and through all the times of human history. The ancient Greeks, with its Athletics events related to recreating gods' capacities in the individuals (Hawhee, 2004), the Aztecs, with sacrificial ball games (Wilkerson, 1991) and contemporary society, mainly with Sports (Guttman, 1978) produced different kinds of activities regarding bodily actions. Each one of them embodied different societal relations regarding human action to the world, to others and to oneself. The fact that the Aztecs played with balls is not enough to make a parallel line connecting this action with our current forms of ball games activities. Maybe it is enough to remember that the Aztecs ball games were a part of a sacrificial activity with religious, political and economic purposes that motivated the existence of such actions. Hawhee (2004, p. 6) says, "whereas these days athletics might function as a metaphor for politics, education, or, in the most clichéd way, for life, I am suggesting that for the ancients [Greeks], athletics were, at times, all these things together".

In this sense, no matter how similar a picture of these ancient ball games and our current ball games is, they were produced by specific societal relations. Each one produced and embodied different essential relations in their objects. This is why taking some elements that compose physical education activities, such as bodily movement, physical effort etc. is neither enough nor adequate for understanding physical education activities as concrete forms of human activity. The importance of understanding the essential relations of an activity is that just with them and through them one is able to understand a given phenomenon in its concreteness. The concrete and the abstract have, also, a specific conceptualization within the cultural historical tradition, quite opposite from their daily notions. For this last one, concrete refers to the sensory dimension of a phenomenon whereas abstract refers to a verbalization of some features of this phenomenon.

Within a dialectical and materialist tradition the concrete means the multiple and diverse forms of reality. Marx (2011, p. 54) says: "The concrete is concrete because it is the concentration of many determinations, hence unity of the diverse". But as such, the concrete is not immediately available for us. Immediatly, the concrete can be grasped only in its appearance, in its empirical forms of existence, for example as a sensory representation. As this whole or unity of different and diverse relations, the concrete has to appear as a product of thinking: a product of a theoretical analysis of reality. To reconstitute the reality in our thought, in its multiple and diverse forms, it is necessary to grasp the different moments of this phenomenon, which is only possible through mediation of abstractions. An abstraction acts as a means to achieve the phenomenon in its concrete form, i.e. in its different, multiple forms. An abstraction, within this theoretical approach refers to a substantial abstraction (Ilyenkov, 2008; Davydov, 1990) or, more exactly, to the essential and necessary relations in a phenomenon. In my understanding these substantial abstractions can be conceptualized as being the germ-cell (Marx, 1996) or the unity of analysis (Vigotski, 2009).

Therefore, in this theoretical perspective, neither can the concrete be reduced to the sensory aspect of reality, like bodily movement and physical effort, nor can the abstract be reduced to any empirical feature depicted from a phenomenon and simply transformed in words, like health, competition and pleasure. Although bodily movement stands out as the immediate starting point

in an analysis of physical education activities it is far from the starting point for this analysis. This starting point in a theoretical analysis is on the essential and necessary relations identified in the phenomenon. It is through these relations that people can engage in the process of ascending from the abstract to the concrete (Ilyenkov, 2008; Davydov, 1990). The movement from abstract to concrete is at the same time an expression of the process of a theoretical analysis and an expression of the main outcome of such analysis.

PROBLEM STATEMENT AND PURPOSE OF THE STUDY

Considering these introductory concepts related to a process of a subject matter analysis, we can approach the discussion about the "how" regarding this task of making a theoretical analysis in the area of Physical Education. In order to accomplish a theoretical analysis of physical education activities one has to identify the substantial abstractions that contain the essential relations developed and materialized in these activities through societal practice. These essential relations assume different concrete forms of manifestations like e.g. football, rugby, swimming, running, tag games, tug of war, ballet and acrobatic gymnastic. Explaining the process through which the essential relations are concretized in each particular activity is a means to systematize the basis of the fundamental content of one's action in reproducing physical education activities. The purpose of the next part of this chapter is to explain the content of these substantial abstractions of physical education activities as well as the process through which the analysis of these activities were achieved. This exposition will allow us to discuss general aspects of a theoretical analysis of subject matters directed to contribute for student's development of theoretical thinking in teaching and learning processes.

ANALYSIS OF PHYSICAL EDUCATION ACTIVITIES

To propose a theoretical concept for physical education activities it seems that we should begin by analyzing those concrete forms of activities that are usually taught in Physical Education: e.g. Games, Combat Games, Dance, Athletics and Gymnastic. But in this case one should ask: what is being considered as concrete in these activities? Are these subjects considered as concrete by those attributes that we see, we play and, eventually that we transform into words to describe the features of those activities? Is concrete the sensory and empirical forms of these activities? And finally, at the beginning of our study do we know what dance, game or athletics are as concrete phenomena? Do we really know them as a synthesis of relations so that we can begin the analysis of physical education activities directly from these forms? If the answer to this question is "no, we do not know yet what these activities are as concrete phenomena" this would be Hegel's (1966) respose.

If anyone, impatient of the consideration of the abstract beginning, should demand that we begin, not with the Beginning, but directly with the matter itself, the answer is that the matter is just this empty Being: it is in the course of the Science that we are to discover what the matter is; the Science must not, therefore, presuppose this as known. (p. 87)

The empirical and sensory forms of physical education activities constitutes an integral part of the analysis. However, if one starts the analysis from the empirical and sensory abstractions probably the result would be produced through depicting different features from the manifestations such as bodily movement, physical capacities, coordination, health, pleasure, victory etc. considering them as the final result of the analysis. And in this case, the concreteness of physical education activities would be reduced to these multiple features systematized as a collection of definitions. This is why the starting point for a theoretical analysis is not on the sensory concrete, although this sensory and empirical concrete is a first starting point for the analysis. Therefore, an abstraction – in the sense explained here – is a first product of the investigation. Nevertheless, this first product is the fundamental condition for engaging in a theoretical analysis, which makes true the affirmation that the starting point in a subject matter analysis is the essential relations that organize the phenomenon under study. Although this affirmation can be logically accepted it has to be explained. Let's start by paraphrasing Hegel: "If anyone, impatient of the consideration of the abstract beginning, should demand that we begin, not with the abstractions of physical education activities, but directly with its sensory material forms like game, dance etc., the answer is that these forms are just this empty Being: it is in the course of a theoretical analysis of them that we are to discover what physical education activities (game, dance, athletic etc.) are as concrete forms of this reality". Starting from the essential relations of physical education activities involves not mainly the proposal of a definition or a name for these substantial abstractions, but the explanation of the relations inside these abstract relations. It is only through these abstractions that one is able to reconstitute the process of becoming of these essential relations, i.e. its internal relations, and into its different and multiple forms of existence. At the beginning, these relations are represented as abstractions of the phenomenon that one wants to reproduce in its concreteness. For elaborating these substantial abstractions one has to analyse concrete manifestations of physical education activities. The analysis of particular manifestations is not a task related to compare different manifestations to each other trying to depict what seems to be important or common to all of them neither a moment for applying previous abstractions depicted from empirical manifestations.

When one is analysing a concrete manifestation of physical education, e.g. a tag game or a statue play, the task has to do with the analysis of the internal dynamic of this particular manifestation under analysis, its fundamental moments and processes. This requires an analytical action directed towards intentionally provoking changes in the phenomenon: replacing rules, objectives, conditions etc. Through this procedure, one could follow the process of development of these concrete manifestations in their fundamental moments and characteristics, from their simplest forms of existence to their most developed forms. This methodological requirement for a theoretical analysis is the condition for identifying the substantial abstractions of these activities. This general principle is synthetized in the idea that the essential relation is achieved, says Ilyenkov (2008, p. 81): "by a thorough analysis of the particular rather than an act of abstraction from the particular". To engage in this kind of analysis one has to study those particular manifestations of physical education activities in which the essential relations are (Kopnin, 1978, p.184-185): "sufficiently developed and not covered by causalities that have not a direct relation with it". This general principle from Kopnin (ibid.) is also synthetized in Marx's (2011, p. 58) famous sentence "human anatomy contains the key to the anatomy of the ape". Some forms of play, for instance tag game, hide and seek, tug of war etc. are particular and concrete forms of manifestation of the essential relations of physical education activities. But this does not mean that these concrete activities are adequate cases for the task of identifying the substantial abstractions of Physical Education. This is so because in these concrete forms of activities the essential relations of physical education may appear as hidden relations, poorly developed or even inaccessible if it is still not known which relations are these. Therefore, it is necessary to analyse those particular activities that already manifest the most developed forms of existence of these essential relations of physical education. This

is the case of Dance as a form of Art and Game as a form of Sport. Once the essential relations of the phenomenon are identified and systematized in a concept, one can return to those simplest cases of the phenomenon (as the aforementioned forms of play) to analyse them in their process of development. This is particularly important and relevant for the process of exposition of the results achieved. Now, the researcher can make the reverse path of the investigation, starting the exposition from the simplest forms heading towards the most developed ones.

Essential Relations in Physical Education

Let's start the exposition of the essential relations of physical education by introducing a distinction between bodily action and bodily movement. An action is at the same time an intentional action, directed toward a goal and an operational action, achieved under certain conditions (Leontiev, 1983). In bodily actions this operational dimension is on bodily movement. The movement of jumping, for example, is directed to a generic goal of overcoming forces of gravity through bodily impulse, either vertically or longitudinally. But this generic goal for a jumping movement does not produce a direct meaning in human activity neither produces the activity itself. A movement of jumping can be directed to produce, for instance, a choreographic form in a ballet play, a mark in a high jump competition or an oppositional action in a volleyball game. Although the ballet, the high jump and the volleyball game use a same bodily movement, the motives and goals that organize each activity transform in a decisive way the very existence of a jump movement. These general motives and subsequently, the general objects of physical education activities are named in our analysis as *the creation of an artistic image with bodily actions*, *the mastery of one's own bodily action* and *the controlling of other's bodily action*. These are the essential and abstract relations of

Figure 1. A proposal of a theoretical model for physical education activities

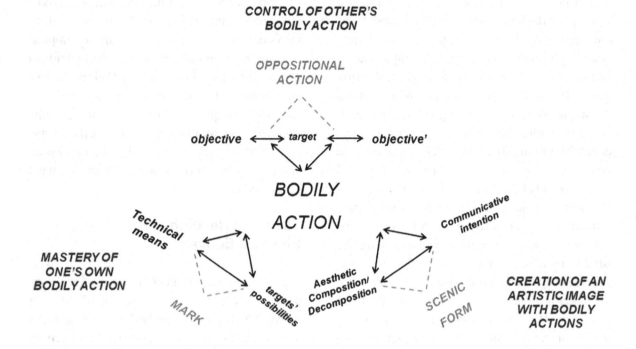

physical education activities. As such, they represent the starting point for a subject matter analysis. Figure 1 depicts a theoretical model developed as a synthesis of the essential and necessary relations of physical education activities.

According to Davydov (1990), a theoretical model is a means of synthetizing the essential relations found out in a phenomenon, the "relations inside the relations".

Models are a form of scientific abstraction of a particular kind, in which the essential relationships of an object which are delineated are reinforced in visually perceptible and represented connections and relationships of material or symbolic elements. This is a distinctive unity of the individual and the general, in which the features of a general, essential nature come into the foreground (p. 261).

Located in the centre of Figure 1 is bodily action, the first element of the model. As any kind of action (Leontiev, 1983; Berstein, 1996),

a bodily action is directed towards obtaining a goal and it is organized by a motive: the creation of an artistic image, the mastery of bodily action and the controlling of other's bodily action. This is why bodily action is presented in the centre of the model with the necessary connections to one of the general and essential objects that organizes, stimulates and creates a bodily action. The model systematizes the internal and essential relations of each of the three objects of physical education activities. The creation of an artistic image is produced through the relations between a communicative intention and the processes of composition and decomposition of bodily actions in space, time and force, both directed to produce a scenic form. The mastery of one's action is produced through the mutual relations between technical means and a range of possible targets, both directed to produce a mark as a reference for one's maximum possibility for a specific bodily action. The controlling of other's actions is produced through the specific interrelation between oppositional objectives directed towards a same target and producing oppositional actions among bodily actions. The model in Figure 1 depicts and systematizes the essential and necessary relations that one has to involve and reproduce in actions when the agent is dealing with the structure of concrete activities such as football game, hopscotch play, 100 meters sprint running, ballet play and tag game, whether one is teaching whether one is learning these activities. However, the explanation of the relations synthetized on the model is only achieved through concrete cases. Before advancing to this concrete analysis, let's make a brief terminological discussion about the names of the three essential relations of physical education.

When physical education relations are named as being the creation of an artistic image, the mastery of one's own action and the controlling of other's action, one could consider that it would be better to name them as Dance, Athletics and Game, respectively. After all, when the relation of controlling of other's action is proposed aren't we talking about games, in which there is an internal opposition between goals and among the players? When the relation of mastery of one's own action is proposed aren't we talking about athletics contests, in which the subject has to be maximally aware of his bodily movement possibilities? And, finally, when the relation of the creation of an artistic image is proposed aren't we talking about dance, in which the subjects have to create choreographies with their bodies? On the one hand, any name could be used for those three relations synthetized in the model, but the most important thing to consider is the meaning or the concept that one is attributing to them (Vigotski, 2009). Therefore, in principle, one could name these relations with those very well-known names in Physical Education, i.e. Dance, Athletics and Game. But, on the other hand, by doing so one will have to deal with the meanings that already exist inside those terms. Someone could ask, for instance, about other forms of physical educa-

tion activities like swimming, circus, gymnastic, wrestling etc. wondering if they are names of other general relations of physical education, once Game, Dance and Athletics were presented as general relations of them. The argument is that words-notions like game, dance, athletics, wrestling, swimming etc. represent a sensory and empirical existence of physical education activities, that is, they represent empirical conceptualizations constructed through the external features that one sees, plays and describes in the activities. Moreover, each one of these activities represents particular cases of physical education activities. They are particular syntheses of the internal and essential abstractions of physical education, rather general relations of it. This is why the essential relations of physical education will be named with the terms introduced before: the creation of an image, the mastery of one's own action and the controlling of other's action. The terms Game, Dance, Athletics etc. will be used for expressing particular forms through which essential relations take form in current society. This means that for explaining physical education activities in their concreteness one has to explain both: the internal and necessary relations in each one of the substantial abstractions of physical education activities and the process through which these essential relations are manifested in different forms of activities as Game, Combat game, Dance, Athletics, Circus etc.

A concrete activity embedded as it were in the concept of Leontiev (1983) is always a system of objects. Nevertheless, a concrete activity possesses one of these objects as the core of its system. When an object occupies the centre of a particular activity it modifies the other objects that compose the system making them subordinated to its internal relations. Because of this, one can talk about activities of physical education that possess the controlling of other's action as the core relation of its particular structure, for instance Game and Combat game. Others that possess the mastery of one's own action as this core, for instance Gymnastic and Athletics, while others possess the creation of an artistic image as their main relations, for instance Dance, Mime and Circus. Despite having a particular relation as its core, a concrete activity of physical education will always constitute a particular system of those essential relations or objects. Understanding these mutual relations is fundamental for understanding physical education activities in their concreteness. This is why a theoretical conceptualization does not fit the purpose of classifying a phenomenon. The purpose is to understand how to act with those relations in concrete activities and how to explain process from these abstractions to particular activities understood in their concreteness. The next section of this chapter contains a discussion of two examples of particular activities in physical education. One of them relates to Dance and the other with Games in an attempt at presenting the essential and abstract relations of physical education in their movement to a concrete analysis of the activities.

ANALYSING CASES OF PHYSICAL EDUCATION

Sometimes, the elements that compose an activity, grasped in a direct way and only in their empirical features, are taken as an expression of the activity itself. This is the case of conceptualizing physical education activities through definitions as movement, physical effort, dexterity and so forth. Based on this understanding, an activity could be defined by its concreteness without the need of making such a complicated analysis as a subject matter analysis seems to be. In the next section I will present concrete examples from the area of physical education about the value of engaging in such "complicated analysis" when one wants to work in the perspective of a developmental teaching and learning at school.

Dance

As many terms used in daily life the term "Dance" has an empirical meaning that is justified in its use in everyday situations. From a daily point of view dance refers to any situation that involves bodily movement performed with music and being expressive. Therefore, any individual's movement with the background of music would be named as dance. This is so because the criterion for defining what dance is or is not is given by those elements that appear to us in most examples of dance activities, notably: music, coordinated movement and expressive movement. This empirical meaning of the term dance is not a problem for its use in these daily situations. But it becomes a problem when it is used in this everyday meaning in physical education teaching situations or in educational research. From a theoretical point of view the concept of dance activity refers to a particular form of activity in which the creation of an artistic image with bodily actions occupies the core of its structure. Therefore, conceptualization of dance has to be elaborated through the essential relations that take part of it and not through a synthesis of its different elements. This last point seems to be particularly important for a process of a subject matter analysis because it allows us to highlight differences between an analysis through elements from an analysis through the essential relations of the phenomenon. For discussion, an interesting example can be provided by the different school dances labelled as modern dance in the middle of 1950'. These schools were an attempt at breaking up the aesthetic and technical patterns proposed and imposed by classical ballet as the only truth in dance. Some of these schools claimed a need to consider any place, e.g. public squares, gymnasiums, regular rooms etc. as valid for dance presentations. They were trying to break up the hegemony of the stage as the only acceptable space for dance presentations. Other schools claimed a break with movement technique imposed by classical ballet. They proposed the need to use daily and "natural" movements instead of artificially composed gestures. These different dance schools emphasized that in principle any element could be used as an element for creating dance. There would not be an *a priori* in dance when one talks about its different kinds of elements. A particular dance may have or not have music, have or not have speeches during the presentation, have or not have logical ideas for communicating, have or not have a stage, have or not have a specific technique, have or not have beauty in movements. And if all these things may or may not take part in a particular dance is because they are precisely their elements. Any element of dance appears in a particular dance first as a product of its main object, that is the "creation of an artistic image with bodily actions" in which the general and essential relations are the relations among a communicative idea and the processes of composition and decomposition of bodily actions in shape, space, force and time. These are the necessary relations that one has to act for reproducing the object. After this first determination an element can determine the concrete content and form of a particular dance activity.

What is the importance of this understanding of dance activity for pedagogical practice in Physical Education? Let's analyse a concrete learning task that aims at promoting student's relation to dance activity: a statue play. The goals in this form of the statue play are: a) dancing through the space with the background of music; b) when the music stops perform a statue with the body. The structure of this play proposes two actions to be performed. The first one refers to perform bodily movements according to the characteristics of the music: strong, smooth, fast, slow etc. The second action refers to creating different static positions with bodily actions to represent a certain form or figure (a statue). In appearance, this play would be an adequate form for student's relations to dance and mime activities, for the play proposes to dance and to mime. Creating an artistic image with bodily action refers to reconstitute the form

of things through manipulating bodily actions in space, time and force in its connections with a certain communicative intention. To artistically represent a certain thing through bodily actions the individual has to realize its artistic possibilities, which means "to disrupt the natural relationship of the elements in which they were perceived" (Vigotsy, 2004, p. 21). One has do compose and decompose this "thing" in such a way that he is not reproducing the object itself, but rather creating another object: an artistic object. In this specific statue play it is not necessary to create a scenic form with bodily actions to take part in and to reproduce the structure of this particular form of activity. One can simply move/not move to accomplish the play's goals. It is not necessary to intentionally reproduce the form of the music or to represent the shapes of a figure with bodily actions. In this specific play the music exists mainly as a sign to orient the subjects to accomplish the goals of moving while there is music and stop moving when there is no music. Despite the declarative approach to dance and mime the real object that organizes the structure of this concrete statue play refers to mastering the contrast between dynamic movements and static movements. The climax of the play and, therefore, its central and effective content lies in mastering the relation between static and dynamic movements. Music becomes a support or a sign either to move or to stop moving. This content refers to the structural dimension of the activity (Leontiev, 1983, p. 68) "in its independence existence as subordinating to itself and transforming the activity of the subject". A professional ballet dancer acting in this same statue play would probably perform the most developed forms of the creation of an artistic image with bodily actions, because this relation already exists for him as his activity. But for those who did not appropriate the activity, this form of the statue play does not allow the individual's relation to the creation of an artistic image with bodily actions. In this particular statue play the relation of creating an artistic image does not occupy the core of its structure; it does not exist as a necessary relation to be reproduced through one's activity. The object that occupies the core of this specific form of the statue play is mastering one's own action in relation to the contrast dynamic and static movements.

For a pedagogical reproduction of an activity that has as its core object the creation of an artistic image with bodily actions (e.g. dance, mime and circus) one has to organize concrete forms of manifestation in which acting with the process of creating artistic images emerge as an essential relation to be performed by an individual's activity. The statue play has to be transformed in the direction of requiring the individual to act in the process of composition and decomposition of bodily action in space, time and force related to a certain communicative intentionality. Understanding the essential relations that constitute a given activity is fundamental to knowing which relations one should engage with in order to reproduce the objects of an activity. If dance is understood as an arithmetic sum of elements e.g. music + coordinated movement + costumes, a learning task will probably focus on organizing children's relation to these elements as the necessary actions for reproducing dance activity. If Dance is understood as a particular product of creating an artistic image with bodily actions, a learning task would focus on organizing processes of composition and decomposition of bodily actions according to a communicative intention. Those would be the necessary actions for developing the students' relation to dance, mime or circus.

Game

The same discussion about essential relations and elements applies for game activity. Competition and victory seem to be the defining features of game activity. However, considering the previous discussion about an analysis through elements and through relations we could ask whether "competition" represents an essential relation in game or

one of its elements or moments. For introducing this discussion in the analysis of game activity a particular game named as "the conquest of the ball" will be analysed. In this game, the initial objective is to catch a ball that is separated by an equal distance from two players disputing the game. The player who gets the ball first achieves the objective of the game. The players share a same objective of reaching the ball. Their objectives are concurrent for they are directed to a same target, but they are not opposite to each other: an objective is not presented as an oppositional objective of the other. Because of this, the action of a player cannot interfere on the other player's action. The game does not propose the objective of preventing the other to achieve the ball. Each player has to deal just with his own goal: achieving the ball, which means that the opposition existent in this game is related mainly or just to the result. This particular form of dispute in which the players are acting at the same time and toward a same target, gives rise to a particular kind of interference on player's actions. But this interference is not structurally determinant for the existence of the particular dynamic of the game. Rather, this particular kind of interference arises in any activity organized as competition. The singular presence of the other can cause interference in one's action. But as such, this general type of interference is not the direct content of any of the players' action in an activity.

What is really under dispute is the players' capacity to reach the target, their capacity to master their own actions regarding speed. It is possible to withdraw from this competitive situation and in doing so highlight the fundamental objective of the game: to reach as fast as possible the place where the ball is. Therefore, besides the dispute situation the core relation that one has to deal with in this concrete game is to achieve a better mark for oneself. The motive that organizes this activity is the mastery of one's own action. To allow for the emergence of the controlling of other's action as the core object of this particular game it would be necessary modify its initial conditions, directing them towards the mutual oppositional objectives in the game. If the game proposes the objective of achieving the ball and bringing it to his own field it has to propose an objective directly opposite to this one, i.e. preventing the other player from bringing the ball to his field. This opposition could be manifested as a general opposition between modes of attack and defence. With the introduction of oppositional objectives the main content of the game changes substantially. Reaching the ball first or fast is no longer the determinant condition for achieving the game's objective, because a player can catch the ball and be immediately caught by the other, which leads him to not accomplish the game's goal. Therefore, the dispute or competition is no longer related just to the final result (i.e. reaching a place first), but it is in the very process for achieving this result. It is necessary to anticipate, act and control the other player's action, whether for catching the ball in an appropriate moment or hindering the other from catching the ball at an appropriate moment. This is true whether focus is on escaping with the ball or hindering the other from escaping with the ball. Bodily actions become internally opposite to each other in the sense that one action just exists as such because of the existence of the other action opposed to it. The interference among actions is no longer occasional, secondary or directed only toward the result. The interference becomes a proper opposition. Now the essential and necessary actions that emerge from the game have to do with acting in relation to oppositional objectives directed to a same target, both to prevent other's actions and to avoid the prevention of the other against my actions. In this particular game of the conquest of the ball to prevent the other to achieve his objective the player has to touch the other's shoulder (the same procedure as in a tag game). The existence of these relations as the core relations of an activity gives rise to a particular characteristic of game activity: the need of perceiving a game situation beyond what is immediately and visually given.

Any situation in a game requires an anticipated action from the players. It requires realizing what this situation is likely to be compared to what it already is. The game has a double existence, in the players mind as they are planning what the game could be or should be in order to overcome the other's opposition, and in actual reality as the players's actions that were possible to be performed. Acting in the structural relations of the object of controlling other's action is oriented to the future status of the game: to what it can become according to individuals' possibilities to transform the game conditions. This in-built tension among oppositional objectives directed towards a similar target and with it the need of anticipating the other player's action in order to control it lies at the heart of game activity like football, rugby, volleyball etc. and also at the core of combat games activity like wrestling, judo, fencing etc. Therefore, these are the central relations with which one has to act for reproducing the structure of particular forms of Game activities.

DISCUSSION

A subject matter analysis is directed to systematize the internal and essential relations of a given phenomenon. As any theoretical analysis a subject matter analysis is done through the investigation of the development of a phenomenon, that is through historical analysis in the sense conceptualized by Vygotski (1995) and Ilyenkov (2008). The peculiarity of a subject matter analysis, however, is that it is organically connected to the general motive of pedagogical activity: to contribute to students' theoretical thinking. Systematizing the essential relations in a given area is a means for proposing which relations one should necessarily act for reproducing the object of an activity. Identification of the essential relations in a given subject area and within educational purposes was a basic and fundamental problem in Davydov's theory of developmental teaching. Davidov (1988) produced a comprehensive theoretical analysis in math and outlined an analysis of essential relations in Russian language and in arts. Despite being the very and fundamental basis for teaching, none of these analyses represents a ready-made content for it. We can say the same thing regarding our essential and abstract relations in Physical Education: none of them can be directly applied in teaching and learning processes. The fact that a subject-matter analysis does not produce direct content for teaching and learning seems to reinforce the widespread idea in educational research about the need for taking content knowledge and pedagogy together. Shulman (1987) named this urge as pedagogical content knowledge. However, Siedentop (2002, p. 368) argues "it is equally clear that to do so requires that the parameters of the content knowledge domain be identified". Indeed, a subject matter analysis – in the sense proposed in this chapter – is not a direct content that one is able to apply in teaching. However, the contradiction between a subject matter analysis and the actual teaching and learning process is not on the apparent opposition between academic knowledge and pedagogical content knowledge. Within a developmental perspective, both in a subject matter analysis and in teaching and learning processes knowledge has to exist as theoretical knowledge. However, while in a subject matter analysis theoretical knowledge can appear mainly in its general dimension, in teaching and learning the theoretical knowledge has to appear as actualized in a particular phenomenon, and mainly in particular learning tasks. This polarization among the general and the particular dimensions of knowledge is the real opposition between subject matter analysis and teaching and learning processes. Therefore the character of the opposition is the ultimate reason why the product of subject matter analysis does not provide a direct content for teaching. But once we are assuming that a subject matter analysis does not result in a direct content for teaching and learning, it becomes important to justify the need of such analysis for schooling processes. In

order to be able to respond to such a challenge one has to answer two other questions. The first question is related to the understating or conceptualization of educational process, through which one can answer the ultimate pedagogical "why-question" regarding the task of making a subject matter analysis: whether the task of identifying the essential relations in an area is determinant for schooling process or not. Once one understands, with Davydov's position in mind, that this is the fundamental content for individual development of a theoretical relation to the world, a subject-matter analysis becomes a tool and a need for supporting the teaching and learning process, even though it is only able to present this fundamental content in its general dimension. The second question to be answered is related to a practical task about whether a given area possesses a systematization of its essential relations. When one starts to seek an answer for this question in a specific subject matter, one does not normally find these conceptual relations systematized. Usually, systematization of knowledge in textbooks, syllabus and even in academic texts expresses an empirical dimension of the phenomenon. However, if in a given field we were able to find a systematization that reflects the theoretical relations in the area it would not be necessary to add an extra effort in the analytical process. In this case subject matter analysis would be done and therefore relatively finished. Although a subject matter analysis can always be improved in some extension, when the area succeeds to identify and systematize its essential relations the researcher problem moves from the systematization of these relations to the understanding about how to accomplish them in the teaching and learning process. Sometimes these two research problems come close in research. Nevertheless, they may also appear separated, as in the case of research directly oriented to accomplish a subject matter analysis like in this chapter.

Understanding the conceptual relations in a given subject area provides a fundamental beginning for producing or designing a developmental teaching. Designing a learning task means working with a concrete activity, whether in Physics, Biology, Social Science or Physical Education. Understanding the structural relations of these activities is the fundamental basis for designing a learning task in pedagogical activity. This is the main purpose of a subject matter analysis. However, a subject matter analysis produces systematization of the essential relations in a phenomenon in its general dimension. This is why a subject matter is not a ready-made content for teaching. In teaching and learning process these essential relations will never appear as such, in this pure form, as a pure general solution. Rather, they appear actualized in concrete cases: as a particular synthesis of those general relations of the phenomenon and their singular features. Considering this analysis, the essential relations of physical education activities are the relations abstracted from its multiple and diverse forms of existence. Although the essential relations have an objective existence in reality – as ideal forms of human relations (Ilyenkov, 2008) – they do not exist in this pure form as abstractions. When one is teaching a physical education activity like for example a game, the agent is not dealing with game in general or with the relation of controlling other's bodily action in this abstract form. Rather, he deals with a concrete and particular activity like a tag game, catching the flag, dodge ball, football etc. with its multiple and diverse relations. But without understanding the mediation of those abstract relations the concreteness of these phenomena cannot be understood. In this sense, one could consider that achieving these abstractions is the main product of a theoretical analysis of a subject matter. In the case of physical education, focus is on the abstract relations of creating an artistic image with bodily actions, controlling of other's bodily action and mastering one's own bodily action. Nevertheless, if the abstractions were the fundamental product of a subject matter analysis this product would come close to a definition of physical education activities and,

therefore, it would be distant from the intention of producing a theoretical proposition of it. Even though these abstractions are essential, they are still abstractions of physical education activities and they become concrete just through the analysis of particular cases of the phenomenon. Therefore, the main product of a subject matter analysis is on the process of moving from the essential abstractions to the concreteness of a particular phenomenon. In this analysis of physical education the product is on the movement from the abstract relations of creating an artistic image and controlling of other's action to Dance and Game analysis, respectively, here portrayed as attempts to move from abstract to concrete (Ilyenkov, 2008).

A theoretical subject matter analysis is directed to elaborate a general mode of action for analysing particular cases through identified and systematized essential abstractions. This general mode of action allows analysis of any particular case of the phenomenon, as a particular synthesis of the general and the singular dimensions of it. Even so, no matter how concrete this analysis is (i.e. how one succeeds in synthetizing the multiple relations of a phenomenon), the result of the analysis will never be a direct thing to apply for teaching and learning. For accomplishing teaching and learning one has to make a similar movement of analysis by focusing on a/ the singular features of the concrete phenomenon to be worked out, e.g. a particular case or phenomenon; b/ the particularities of designing learning tasks and didactic procedures; c/ the contributions of this phenomenon for student's development of theoretical thinking.

In order to accomplish a concrete learning task in a process of teaching "Collective Games", it would be necessary a/ to make a concrete analysis of a specific game (capture the flag), producing a synthesis about how the "controlling of other's actions" is concretely related to the singularities of this game: its internal dynamic of attack and defence; its set of rules; the processes of perception and analysis of game situations; the strategic knowledge available; the dexterity and/or physical capacities required etc. It would be necessary b/ to analyse the concrete conditions for teaching (different grades, material conditions, methodological procedures etc.) Finally, it would be necessary c/ to analyse the concrete relations of an individual to the game structure, for instance deciding on the direction toward victory or toward the object of controlling other's action as his very and fundamental motive for acting. Although these concrete tasks of analysis can still be considered as a part of a subject matter analysis they represent another field of investigation in educational research, related mainly to the determination of teaching contents and strategic learning actions and of the specific contributions of physical education activities to students' development of higher psychological functions.

For this, a subject matter analysis is simultaneously connected to the actualization of teaching and learning process in concrete situations and independent from it. It is connected to it because a subject-matter analysis proposes the essential relations that one has to act for reproducing the structure of a given activity. This is the fundamental content of one's action for reproducing the activity. Understanding the essential relations that constitute a given activity is fundamental for knowing which relations one should engage for intentionally reproducing the activity as his own activity. Besides, a subject matter analysis proposes a general mode of action for analysing the particular cases of a phenomenon, concretizing the abstract relations. At the same time, a subject matter analysis is independent from teaching and learning process because it is not the end point for designing learning tasks. One still has to deal with the particularities of schooling practice as defined by syllabus content and goals through different grades, material conditions for teaching, methodological procedures etc.

Although there is no cause-effect relation between a subject matter analysis and the designing of teaching and learning process, there exists a

"predominant moment" (Luckacs (1979) in this relation. The product of a subject matter analysis sets the basis for acting in relation to achieving the required mediations for designing concrete learning tasks for children. A subject matter analysis will always be a kind of an "abstraction" for pedagogical activity. But if we succeeded to determine these abstractions in their essential relations, we would be able to systematize the necessary abstractions for accomplishing a developmental teaching in pedagogical activity. And through these abstractions a whole new research process would be related to concretize the essential and necessary relations of a phenomenon in actual learning activity.

CONCLUSION

Explaining physical education activities through a theoretical analysis was a means for achieving the main goal of this chapter. I discussed the conceptual framework and some concrete challenges that arise in the process of a subject matter analysis, highlithing its value for educational research based on a developmental teaching tradition. It is important to understand the general principles related to a theoretical analysis within a cultural historical perspective, for instance, the concept of essence, the movement from abstract to the concrete, the idea of a historical analysis and the role of a theoretical concept. However, when one analyses these concepts through concrete examples he can appreciate some possibilities, limits and challenges related to acting with these concepts and making them alive in a research. In this sense, a concrete explanation of a specific attempt at making a subject matter analysis can contribute to move forward the general principles related to a developmental teaching tradition in cultural historical theory. Educational research cannot be reduced to an investigation of the essential relations of subject matter. Nevertheless, the claim is that one cannot improve teachers training, classroom organization and didactics content without a comprehensive understanding of the essential relations that organize the area. This is so because these essential relations are the ones with which one should engage for reproducing the structure of an activity in teaching and learning process. A subject matter analysis has the potential to produce a theoretical analysis for a specific human activity in the context of achieving educational purposes. Sharing concrete attempts at making these analyses contributes to the process of actualizing the ideas of a developmental teaching in pedagogical activity.

REFERENCES

Chaiklin, S. (1999). Developmental teaching in upper-secondary school. In Learning activity and development (pp. 187-210). Aarhus University Press.

Davidov, V. V. (1988). *La enseñanza escolar y el desarrollo psíquico: investigación teórica y experimental.* Moscú: Editorial Progreso.

Davydov, V. (1990). *Types of generalization in instruction: logical and psychological problems in the structuring of school curricula. (Soviet studies in mathematics education* (J. Kilpatrick, Ed.). Reston, VA: National Council of Teachers of Mathematics.

Elkonim, D. B. (1998). *Psicologia do Jogo.* São Paulo: Martins Fontes.

Guttmann, A. (1978). *From ritual to record: The nature of modern sports.* New York: Columbia University Press.

Hawhee, D. (2004). *Bodily arts: Rhetoric and athletics in ancient Greece.* Austin, TX: University of Texas Press.

Hedegaard, M. (1990). The zone of proximal development as basis for instruction. In L. C. Moll (Ed.), Vygotsky and education: Instructional implications and applications of sociohistorical psychology. Cambridge, UK: Cambridge University press.

Hedegaard, M., & Chaiklin, S. (2005). *Radical-local teaching and learning: A cultural historical approach.* Aarhus: Aarhus University Press.

Hegel, G. W. F. (1996). *Science of Logic.* Allen & Unwin.

Ilyenkov, E. V. (1977). *The concept of the Ideal.* Retrieved from http://www.marxists.org/archive/ilyenkov/works/ideal/ideal.htm

Ilyenkov, E. V. (2008). *The dialectics of the abstract and the concrete in Marx's Capital.* Delhi: AAKAR books.

Kopnin, P. V. (1978). *A dialética como lógica e teoria do conhecimento.* Rio de Janeiro: Civilização Brasileira.

Kosik, K. (1976). *Dialética do Concreto.* Rio de Janeiro: Paz e Terra.

Leontiev, A. (1983). *Actividad, Consciencia y Personalidad.* Havana: Pueblo y Educación.

Lompsher, J. (1999). Learning activity and its formation: Ascending from the abstract to the concrete. In M. Hedegaard & J. Lompscher (Eds.), Learning activity and development. Aarhus, Denmark: Aarhus University Press.

Lukács, G. (1979). *Ontologia do Ser Social: Os princípios ontológicos fundamentais de Marx.* São Paulo: Livraria Editora Ciências Humanas.

Marx, K. (1996). *O Capital* (Vol. 1). São Paulo: Nova Cultura.

Marx, K. (2011). *Grudrisse: Manuscritos econômicos de 1857-1858; esboços da crítica da economia política.* São Paulo: Boitempo.

Marx, K., & Engels, F. (2007). *A ideologia alemã*. São Paulo: Boitempo.

Shulman, L. S. (1987). Knowledge and teaching: Foundations of new reform. *Harvard Educational Review, 57*, 1–22.

Siedentop, D. (2002). Content Knowledge for physical education. *Journal of Teaching in Physical Education, 21*, 368–377.

Vigotski, L. S. (2001). *Psicologia da Arte*. São Paulo: Martins Fontes.

Vigotski, L. S. (2009). *A construção do pensamento e da linguagem*. São Paulo: Martins Fontes.

Vigotsky, L. S. (2004). *Imaginación y creación en la edad infantil*. Havana: Pueblo y Educación.

Vygotski, L. S. (1995). *Obras Escogidas* (3 vols.). Madri: Visor.

Wilkerson, S. J. (1991) And then they were sacrificed: the ritual ballgame of Northeastern Mesoamerica through time and space. In The Mesoamerican Ballgame. Tucson, AZ: University of Arizona Press.

ADDITIONAL READING

Bernstein, N. A. (1996). On Dexterity and its development. M. L. Latash & M. T. Turvey (Eds.). Dexterity and its development. Erlbaum Associates.

Bourcier, P. (2001). *História da dança no ocidente*. São Paulo: Martins Fontes.

Chaiklin, S. (2002). Developmental teaching in secondary schools. G. Wells & G. Claxton, (Eds.). Learning for life in the 21st century. Oxford: Blackwell, 167-180.

Chaiklin, S. (2006). Reflections on the future development of developmental teaching research. H. Giest (Ed.). Erinnergun für die Zukunft – Pädagogische Psychologie in der DDR. Berlin: Lehmanns Media.

Chaiklin, S. (2012). Dialectics, politics and contemporary cultural-historical research, exemplified through Marx and Vygotsky. H. R. J. Daniels, (Ed.). Vygotsky and Sociology. London: Routledge, 24-43.

Davidov, V. V. (1982). *Tipos de generalización en la enseñanza*. Havana: Pueblo y Educación.

Davidov, V. V. (1988). *La enseñanza escolar y el desarrollo psíquico: investigación teórica y experimental*. Moscú: Editorial Progreso.

Davydov, V. V. (1998). The concept of developmental teaching. *Journal of Russian & East European Psychology, 36*(4), 11–36. doi:10.2753/RPO1061-0405360411

Davydov, V. V. (1999). What is real learning activity? M. Hedegaard & J. Lompsher, (Eds.). Learning activity and development. Aarhus: Aarhus University Press.

Debord, G. (1997). *A sociedade do espetáculo: comentários sobre a sociedade do espetáculo*. Rio de Janeiro: Editora Contraponto.

Dunning, E. (1999). *Sport matters: Sociological Studies of Sport, Violence, and Civilization*. London: Routledge.

Engels, F. (2004). Sobre o papel do trabalho na transformação do macaco em homem. In *Antunes, Ricardo. A dialética do trabalho: escritos de Marx e Engels*. São Paulo: Expressão Popular.

Engeström, Y. (1996). Non scolae sed vitae discimus: como superar a encapsulação da aprendizagem escolar. In H. Daniels (Ed.), *Uma introdução a Vygotsky*. São Paulo: Edições Loyola.

Kaptelinin, V. (2005). The object of activity: Making sense of the sense maker. *Mind, Culture, and Activity*, *12*(1), 4–18. doi:10.1207/s15327884mca1201_2

Kozulin, A. (1986). The concepto f activity in soviety psychology: Vygotsky, his disciples and critics. *The American Psychologist*, *41*(3), 264–274. doi:10.1037/0003-066X.41.3.264

Leontiev, A. N. (1978). *O desenvolvimento do Psiquismo*. Lisboa: Livros Horizontes.

Lompscher, J. (1999). Motivation and activity. *European Journal of Psychology of Education*, *14*(1), 11–22. doi:10.1007/BF03173108

Oliveira, B. A. (2005). A dialética do singular-particular-universal. A. A. Abrantes, N. R. Silva, & S. T. F. Martins (Eds.). Método histórico-social na psicologia social. Petrópolis, RJ: Vozes.

Rubtsov, V. (1996). A atividade de aprendizado e os problemas referentes à formação do pensamento teórico dos escolares. C. Garnier et al. (Eds.). Após Vygotsky e Piaget: perspectiva social e construtivista. Escola russa e ocidental. Tradução Eunice Gruman. Porto Alegre: Artes Médicas.

Siendentop, D. (2002). Content knowledge for physical education. *Journal of Teaching in Physical Education*, *21*, 368–377.

Speak, M. (1999). Recreation and sport in Ancient China: Primitive society to AD960. J. Riordan & R. Jones, (Eds.). Sport and Physical Education in China. London: Spon Press.

Vigotski, L. S. (2004). *Teoria e Método em Psicologia*. São Paulo: Martins Fontes.

Vygotski, L. S. (1996). *Obras Escogidas*. Tomo IV. Madri: Visor.

Vygotski, L. S. (1997). *Obras Escogidas*. Tomo I. Madri: Visor.

Vygotsky, L. S. (2009). *A transformação socialista do homem*. In: URSS: Varnitso, 1930. Tradução Marxists Internet Archive, english version, Nilson Dória, 2004. Disponível em: http://www.marxists.org/portugues/vygotsky/1930/mes/transformacao.htm. Acesso em: 22 de Abril de 2009.

Zaporozhets, A. V. (1987). Estudio Psicologico del desarrollo de la motricidad en el niño preescolar. V. Davidov & M. Shuare (Eds.). La psicología evolutiva y pedagógica en la URSS: antología. Moscou: Editorial Progreso.

Zinckenko, V. P. (2006). La psicologia socio-cultural y la teoria de la actividad: revisón y proyección hacia el futuro. J. V. Wertsch, P. Del Rio & A. Álvarez (Eds.). La mente sociocultural. Aproximaciones teóricas y aplicadas. Madrid: Fundación Infancia y aprendizaje.

KEY TERMS AND DEFINITIONS

Abstraction: The essential and necessary relations in a phenomenon separated from its multiple forms of manifestations and existence.

Activity: For Leontiev an activity is a set of actions organized and stimulated by a motive. An activity is defined by its object. An activity is understood both as a collective product of societal practice (in its independent existence) and as an activity of the subject (the individual acting in an activity).

Concept or Theoretical Concept: A system of the *essential* and *necessary* relations that constitute and organize a phenomenon.

Concrete: The phenomenon understood in its multiple and diverse forms as a synthesis of a theoretical analysis of it.

Essential Relations: A set of *objective relations* socially and historically constructed through human practice. The "essence" of a human activity refers to the human relations that *became essential* ones in a certain historical condition.

Model: A model is a way to visually reinforce the essential relations identified in a phenomenon in its multiple connections.

Object: What *motivates* and organizes one's action in an activity. It embodies specific modes of action and the essential relations of an activity in its general and particular dimensions.

Societal Practice: Human being's actions, both practical and subjective, elaborated under specific historical conditions. Societal practice produces human activities in a certain historical time.

Subject Matter Analysis: A subject matter analysis is a theoretical analysis directed to identify the essential relations that organizes a given area to be taught in teaching and learning processes. A subject matter analysis aims to systematize a general mode of action for analysing any particular manifestation of the phenomenon and through this determine contents and learning strategies.

Theoretical Analysis: The analysis directed to reproduce the movement from the abstract to the concrete in a given phenomenon. It deals both with the identification of the essential abstractions and with the actualization of them in concrete and particular cases of the phenomenon.

Chapter 15
Modeling and Analyzing Contextual Influences

Thomas Hansson
Blekinge Institute of Technology, School of Management (MAM), Sweden

ABSTRACT

Working practices rather than purpose or instrumentation defines workplaces as individually motivated or systems controlled units of analysis. In this chapter, analysis of religious work in spiritual organizations covers interview data on employees' experiences of their organizations. Methodological consideration applies for comparison between concepts, models, and theories. Results on religious workplace characteristics emerge from applied activity theory and a model of literary analysis. Religious people perceive and conceive of their workplaces as self-controlled, purpose-driven, administratively structured, and multi-faceted environments. As their words come out during interviews, the data they supply differs from their perceived workplace impressions. Deployed activity and literary theory plus empirical data make up the means for analyzing the impact of setting, purpose, individual action, and collective activity.

BACKGROUND

Contemporary workplaces thrive on shared discourses, language in action and situated practices. Natural language is the primary means for establishing, upholding and developing relations between thought and language, form and contents, structure and meaning plus object and objective. A comprehensive display of relations between thought-language-action-activity is crucial to understanding human behavior. In narrowing down on relevant issues for activity theoretical research, Daniels and Edwards (2004) plus Martin and Peim (2009) suggest focus on (a) rela-tions between individual acts and organizational practices plus (b) exploration of ambivalence over conceptualizations of agent (who), action (how, fast, carefully, honestly) and agency (how, by what means). As a result of studies into the interrelatedness between language and action, Enerstvedt (1971, p. 53) says "social action has-contains-reflects linguistic structure". With the exploration of relations between social action, shared acts and natural language follow that singular human acts go beyond and produce natural language. On the other hand, natural language is a personal (autonomous) construct *and* collectively accepted (social) convention. What remains is that

DOI: 10.4018/978-1-4666-6603-0.ch015

natural languages are functional instruments for defining the limits and impact of singular (speech) acts. By studying people's work life experiences influenced by cultural characteristics and operating on routines, beliefs and environments I explore the dynamics of verbal communication as well as the contents of religious work. Analyzing organizational routines and problem solving among employees in religious settings (= i.e. the physical space that somebody occupies) forms a challenge, regardless if the object of study are religious or secular environments. Enerstvedt (1977, p. 61) characterizes religious discourse by claiming that believers reflect their "*concrete experience of the world*" (italics in original), e.g. "harmony" between religious purpose and social control. Also, employees' reflection on workplace experiences are hidden from direct scrutiny. For employees in a spiritual organization, fellow citizens expect a specific code of conduct and a given role related to a religious mission. Engeström (1987) suggests rules and regulations, community plus division of labor for analysis of such an environment. What remains to cover for a study of religious behavior is application of an analytical "filter" that helps research describe how people experience of their job settings (management, task and working routine) and their objectives (future oriented aspiration).

PROBLEM STATEMENT AND PURPOSE

There are degrees of impact emerging from/exercised on relations between context, objective and activity. The researched issue is to decide on the degree to which e.g. division of labor and rules and regulations influence people's perceptions of the main activity. Do analytical concepts and models do so to a different degree than do public objectives and private goals? Another purpose of the study is to sort out the impact of individual and collective influences on behavior among reli-

gious people, be it by physical setting or abstract objective. In doing so the explanatory power of Engeström's (1987) theory and Burke's (1970) typology of constituents of human motivation and behavior are applied to empirical interview data. There is, however, an important note on approaches to analyzing and understanding human behavior, for example as in this study during interviews or on people's jobs. Burke's use of the concept *Purpose* is near-synonymous with everyday words like *aim, target* and *objective*. However they differ from Engeström's (1987) use of the analytical concepts *Object/Objective* (Foot, 2002). Leontev (2002) defines Object/Gegenstand as a tangible and an intangible object, a material "thing" *and* a psychological Purpose/Objective, especially so in relation to the concept of activity (Stetsenko, 2005). So Gegenstand/Objective exists in relation to other things – as a physical object towards which people exercise direct action. The conceptual pair is also an ideal abstraction, a reasonable purpose, a motivational target towards which people aspire. According to Leontev (2002, p. 56) the ideal Purpose/Gegenstand of e.g. religious activity "defines and changes the subject's activity." (transl. by this author) The ideal Purpose/Gegenstand of the activity is a product of reflective thought which emerges as a result of the subjects' participation in a shared activity. Put differently, reflection is a dialectic process through which the material world influences personality, and the subject in turn influences the world by his actions. In order to pursue the given double objective, i.e. to characterize religious activity and to assess the validity of interview data, I have conducted a study on missionary work among US and Swedish missionaries in Norway, Latvia and Sweden respectively. The research questions cover aspects of: Who is the agent, how does s/he act, what is a "religious" action, what are the relations between setting and purpose? This study also turned out as an attempt at researching the validity of interview data.

PREVIOUS RESEARCH

People have a natural feel for aspects of self-controlled agency and evolving collective work. For example, Vygotsky (1987) emphasizes the impact of agency and cooperation for the development of activity systems. Kaptelinin & Nardi (2006, p. 11) outlines agency versus structure, saying: "activity theory has always had a strong notion of the individual, while at the same time understanding and emphasizing the importance of a socio-cultural matrix within which individuals develop." In a different but related line of research, Latour (2000) suggests that a relevant theme for research is to identify and explain the impact-function-meaning of personal initiative (Agency) versus environmentally controlled necessity (Scene). On this note, Asplund (1980) refers to *actus* in e.g. a religious agent completing assignments by compassionate, helpful and patient behavior. *Status* on the other hand, refers to systemic efficiency of performance defined by social roles. In this study US-teachers, US-missionaries and Swedish clergymen report their work experiences – be it by individually mediating input, by organizational adaptation or by the format of the interview.

Finding a relevant unit of research, knowledge object or purpose of a study is an easy job provided that the researcher focuses on one aspect of a studied phenomenon only. For Dewey (1910) the singular how-question suffices for securing a meaningful focus. However, Dewey refrains from explaining how *how* understood as "method" differs from *how* meaning "by what quality" and/or "by what artifact". Also, it is a complex task for the researcher (Jackson, 2012) to narrow down an empirical study on the "why-reason and how-method of thinking". This fact applies, of course, for any researchable context. Janzen et al., (2011) present parameters deployed for identifying influences on human behavior. Their "quantum approach" consists of several how- and what-questions: How does learning occur; How does transfer of knowledge occur; How should instruction be structured to facilitate learning. Then follows: What factors influence learning; What is the role of memory; What types of learning are best explained; What is the relevance to instructional design. Janzen's et al. how- and what-questions seem intuitively relevant, but they are far from sufficient instruments for describing, analyzing and understanding the behavior, attitude and purpose people display during interviews and at spiritual workplaces.

From a complementary perspective of motivational grammar, Burke (1970) – an influential literary critic – analyzes question words, verbal action and the book of Genesis (Rueckert, 1963). On the significance of the choice of scientific concepts Burke (1962, p. 23) says: "If you reduce the terms to any one of them, you will find them branching out again,; for no one of them is enough." Wertsch (1998, p. 12) refers to Burke's pentad of question words, describing their complementary construct as a heuristic for analyzing and understanding motivation Objective/Gegenstand in mediated/mediating action. As opposed to Burke, proponents of the first CHAT-generation emphasize the significance of mediated action between object and people. In a review of general activity theory, Bakhurst (2009, p. 200) holds that second generation CHAT-proponents emphasize why-Purpose as a crucial influence to analyzing and explaining how people (re-)construct a Scene for sharing and eventually understanding their siutated experiences, be it as expressed during interviews or as impressions of their jobs.

Individual and Contextual Impact

Most social scientists would agree on two main influences on human behavior, i.e. individual initiative (motivation) and environmental affordances. They also argue, however, that individual agency needs to be complemented by collective (objects of) activity controlling individual motivation and collective objectives. On the issue of complementary input to a theoretical model of contextual influences and affordances, some social science researchers say that e.g. other people, organization of work and artifacts form significant parts of the environment. Taken together, universally adaptable activity theoretical concepts (Hansson 2014), models and designs of method and theory defined as a comprehensive analytical instrument, enables for researchers to design adaptable theoretical constructs of neither individual nor environment influences, but forming adaptable-flexible theoretical constructs of a shared activity. They contain common activity theoretical qualities which enable for the analyst to relate motivation in man to natural affordances. Another argument for choosing general activity theory in social science research is that the approach enables for the researcher to overcome critical analytical steps of research on qualitative data. Activity theory offers a combined holistic design for managing an interventionist method aiming at production and/or collecting of data, change of routines and analysis of data.

Modeling Behavior

Using literature as a basis for understanding human psychology is a popular choice. For example, Vygotsky's research started in linguistics and literature. In analyzing literary quality in drama, poetry and fiction by question words related to activity systems, settings and objectives, Burke (1962), a contemporary literary critic, expands research by a compound of "descriptors". Goffman (1959) supplies a similar dramaturgical perspective on human behavior. Burke's descriptors, however, respond to questions by implementation of ASAAP-words like act (how), scene (where), agent (who), agency (by what artifacts) and purpose (why). Interpreting interview data by analysis of religious employees' answers to ASAAP-questions about workplace dynamics primarily involves all the above qualifying constituents, especially Purpose (why). This is so because the why-purpose of a religious act/activity is given, obvious, self-evident for the studied context, to save people. Analysis

of how religious people perceive of themselves and their workplaces is a matter of understanding how ASAAP-descriptors combine and function. Dickinson (2009, p. 126) says: "The five elements go beyond naming who, what, when, where and why." In this study Burke's parameters make up a framework for generating comprehensive understanding of people's workplace experiences. Gutierrez (2007) notices affinity between Engeström´s (1987) "triangular model" and Burke's "grammar of motives". By connecting second generation CHAT with a grammar of motives, the compatibility of approaches becomes a resourse operating between nodes in a triangular model and analytical ASAAP-descriptors. So, there is isomorphism between Engeström's (1987) choice of analytical concepts like Subject, Object, Objective primarily deployed for describing agency in activity systems and Burke's (1962) necessary/sufficient categories/elements (Hansson 2014) employed for understanding literary drama as social construction among people. Key words like Agent, Agency and Purpose help carrying out literary analysis and interpreting people's workplace experiences. It matters little if analysis is about stage acting in a play or reported workplace behavior. Burke's framework covers combinations of Scene, Agent and Act; i.e. dynamics between setting, people and behavior. Adding to the potential for analyzing the dynamics of human behavior, Asplund (1980, p. 154; 159) argues that there is a centre of gravity on Scene (i.e. work experiences vs. interview data) in Burke's construct, saying there are dynamic relationships to explore by means of the formula Act + Agent = (defines) Scene = (produces) Act + Agent. Issues of Purpose is left out of Asplund's discussion. In this study the searchlight is on issues of consistency within and between Engeström's (1987, p. 78) sub-triangles (production, consumption, distribution, exchange) and Burke´s ASAAP-descriptors. The former model is theoretically relevant and the latter becomes verifiable by empirical data on two related but differents Scenes; one portraying religious canvassing and the other covering interviews between Pedagogy students and religious missionaries.

Continuity, routines, stability, structure and flow characterize people's appreciation of the ways of the world. However, in times of disruptive change rare moments of luck or disaster strike. Such in-built positive or negative *deviation* from the natural-normal stream of life complements the underlying assumption of Engeström's (1987) concept of *natural contradiction* which assumedly characterizes an overwhelming number of life events at work and during interviews equally. Burke's (1962) ASAAP-model covers analysis of recurring situations and behaviors. The idea of an unexpected rare situation, moment, activity or phenomenon covers, in chronological order, life on Earth, Jesus Christ, Krakatau volcano explosion, Holocaust genocide and attack on Twin Towers. In-built and irregular deviation from socially-constructed norms and natural dialectical contradictions characterizes human constructions of what life on earth is or what it should be about. In order to be able to form a theory on normal but rare deviation rather than natural contradiction going beyond a theory of organizational control - as pre-supposed by Engeström (1987) - dialogue appears as a developmental concept for analyzing what happens to extraction and presentation of data during interviews. The interview is a pre-staged deviation enacted on a public scene. Such semi-structured exchanges differ from informal communicative exchanges, meetings and encounters. Find Burke's (1962) literary ASAAP- (Act, Scene, Agent, Agency, Purpose) dimensions of human behavior illustrated in a model designed for analyzing *in-built deviation* and *everyday routines* – here defined as natural contradictions. Also find concepts originating from Engeström's triangular model of activity theory, deployed for analyzing mainstream procedures, behaviors and activities by *natural contradiction*. The model for analyzing rare and regular activity in Figure 1 is a tool for understanding religious respondents'

work place experiences and testing the validity of interview data.

Figure 1 clarifies levels of analysis for the intertwined character of (A-B) on individual agency and collective activity. The model outlines (A-C) relations between *in-built deviation* and *natural contradiction* at levels of individual action, enabling for methodological consideration about the character of data extracted from interviews that are supposed to illustrate genuine workplace experiences. Finally, (A/B-C/D) taken together illustrate complementary methods of analysis separating between logical comprehensive-systemic *analysis* and one-off mediating *creativity* (Vygotsky, 1994; Johansson 2014; Linge, 2014).

Searching and Finding

During a course in pedagogy, a group of university students collected data on workplace characteristics. They did so without reference to e.g. individual initiative, organizational support, administrative demand or available resources. Analysis of the religious respondents' answers uncovers perceptions of setting, people and behavior. The studied religious people provide data by answering questions about a space/place location (where), colleagues (who), individual acts (how) and means (how). They provide data for interpreting the dynamics of Engeström's (1987, p. 78) triangular model, in particular enabling for a study of interrelationships between nodes in the Small Scene interview setting defined by a Production sub-triangle of Subject-Instrument-Object/ Objective. Big Scene workplace related triangles consist of analytical concepts for Consumption (Subject-Object-Community), Exchange (Subject-Rules-Community) and Distribution (Object-Division of Labor-Community). Taken together, Small and Big Scene relations reveal how dynamics between setting, colleagues and acts affect religious people's job experiences. Outlining a method for analyzing how people perceive of their jobs is a seemingly straightforward task

Figure 1. Modeling behavior in contexts of investigation (A-B) and justification (C-D)

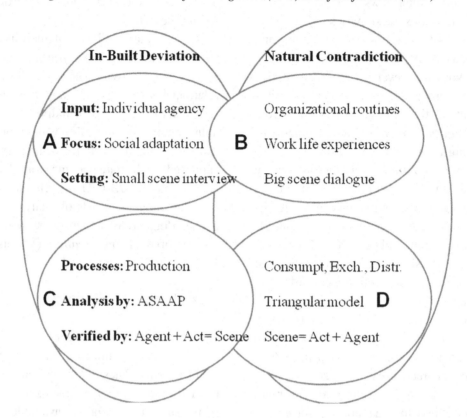

- ask the subjects and you will learn. However, such endeavors involve analysis of psychological processes. First of all, the familiarity of the concept of workplace characteristics is deceptive. Second, the very concept needs defining. "How did you manage, operate, control, cope and learn to do it" etc. are everyday questions, begging for a narrow description of the agent's input, performance and outcome. But in defining "doing something" the analyst usually provides an outline of a comprehensive scene by describing-explaining how an agent performs an act. Adverbs like *swiftly, carelessly* or *diligently* indicate the quality of such operations. In defining "doing something" the analyst provides an outline by describing-explaining how an agent acts by mediating physical, mental or linguistic artifacts. During such work the analyst looks for *action verbs* like *manage* a meeting, *operate* a machine, *control* a lever, *cope* with resistance, *learn* the Bible or *do* homework.

There is a need for a model for qualifying personally motivated/motivating influences characterized as an Agent who Acts on a motive (Objective/Gegenstand) with a Purpose in mind and influencing Small Scene production triangle in a number of ways. The analyst also needs a systemic prerequisite characterized as Big Scene workplace impressions influencing Agent to perform contextualized Acts. The first part of Burke's formula (Agent + Act = Scene) matches analysis of religious workplace dynamics by means of individual acts. They relate to Engeström's sub-triangles Production and Exchange. The second part of the formula (Scene = Act + Agent) covers systemic-organizational influences deployed as matching (sub-triangles of) Distribution, Exchange and Consumption. The respondents' answers enable for analysis of a multitude of initiatives, references, meanings and reflections. On the one hand concepts like

Scene-where; Agent-who, Act-how and Agency-how are clear. On the other hand their meaning is "transcendental" and subject to interpretation. Furthering the relatedness between activity theory and ASAAP-descriptors, Burke (1962, p. 317) says human thought materializes as linguistic categories: "Instead of calling them necessary 'forms of experience', however, we should call them necessary 'forms of talk about experience'." His suggestion also applies for the deployed ASAAP-descriptors. Their multiple meaning make up a precondition for studying higher mental functions, individual learning and collective development. So everyday use of language claims distinctive functions of how to experience of the workplace. Taken together, Burke's and Engeström's line of reasoning forms a prerequisite for analyzing interview data on religious workplaces.

RESULT

This is an account of the balancing of students' questions about Scene and Purpose versus the respondents' appreciation of dynamics between Act, Scene, Agent, Agency. The context of investigation covers religious organizations saving people in US-Norwegian, US-Latvian and Swedish-Swedish cultures. A group of Swedish pedagogy students completed a basic level (30 hp) course in pedagogy in 2010. Their objective was to explore what and how people learn at work. They contacted respondents, formed questions, conducted interviews and wrote a report on workplace learning. Their focus was on employees in religious positions, jobs and workplaces. Missionary respondents in Norway, Latvia and Sweden agreed to participate. The students' interview questions cover colleagues (who), performance (how), purpose (why) and workplace (where) characteristics, partly overlapping Burke's (1970) question words. In studying the respondents' workplace experiences I have opted for answers to questions on Scene and Objective. The reason is that learning about religious respondents' experiences of (Scene) forms a necessary component for understanding elements like Act or Agent. By asking "How can you tell if something is wrong in your classroom?" you expect an answer on (Scene). So you do in responses to the question "Have you been offered any kind of leadership or in-service training?" or "What is leadership like at your workplace?" and "How do you notice when something is wrong in the classroom?" However, the respondents' answers frequently allows for classifications involving two or more defining (ASAAP) characteristics. Such frequently expressed relationships appear between e.g. (Small) Scene-Agent or Agent-Act (Asplund, 1980), i.e. distributions enabling for analysis of the systemic and context-related (Big Scene) dynamics of Production, Consumption, Distribution and Exchange sub-triangles (Engeström, 1987).

Teaching and Learning on a Big and a Small Scene

US-teachers in Norway portray their school as a place in need of attentive leaders with a fair amount of structure, individualism and self-control. There is a sense of humanitarian consideration, reflection and empathy in the respondets rather than in descriptions of what they do or aim at doing. Some of them display a mix of teacher competence defined as an ability to (Act) by using a toolbox of educational gadgets. One respondent, however, ranks action and reflection over personal ability, and shortcomings in the setting. Yet another respondent defines fostering (Purpose) by means of contextualized tasks in a traditional classroom. Find examples of combined influences on the respondents, as reported during the interviews.

- **Agent-Scene:** "I've told other teachers that it's not wrong to steal someone else's good idea." "If you see some other teacher doing a technique: why not learn from someone who does something well?"

- **Agent-Agency:** "You notice when things are not working through trial and error. When it doesn't work, I try again, some different way." Or I may just repeat that lab and omit certain parts of it, or tweak it."
- **Scene-Agent-Agency:** "After a while you learn to see what will work for you."
- **Agent-Act-Agency:** "I don't really journal… I talk to colleagues a lot …" but also "A lot of times, what I've learned has come through failures and then feedback from other people –and not positive feedback."
- **Scene-Agent-Scene:** "Some of it I learned from my teacher's education." and "In school I was mostly bored and it's just so awful to see kids when they're bored."

On stressing the importance of individual action, the US-teachers say: "When you've noticed the things you need to learn a lot of it seemed to have happened the first few years". There is good person-environment (P-E) fit, due to exchange initiated by subjects who study and learn from clear rules. On the theme of collective Big Scene activity they say: "I took a course … at the University of Wisconsin… I don't know if I've read too many books on instruction". By taking an academic course the religious teacher covers for organizational demands rather than for satisfying personal needs. Informal learning seems to be a first priority. Production of and participation in courses generate dynamics, but there is little indication of rules and routines relative to past generations of people (exchange), community (consumption) or division of labor (distribution). This is an example of self-centered input by Agency firstly and Big Scene influences secondly.

Missionary Work on a Small Scene

Student questions for US-missionaries saving Latvian citizens have a focus on the main activity of saving people by talking to them and elaborating on actors, behavior, setting, tools and goals.

Contrary to the students' motive for interviewing, the contents carries with it a specific purpose to the Big Scene: "Have you been offered any kind of leadership or in-service training course?", "Could you imagine yourself in a similar position?" and "In that case, how will you try to realize your ambition?" Other student questions reflect the overall objective (Purpose) of religious work, "Would that be advisable in any way from a missionary point of view?" There is a complex counter-factual question combining Agency-Act-Scene: "If you ran your organization as a company and tried to make a profit, would that require additional information just to make money?" Answers to the questions describe the respondents' mission from a self-centered position, i.e. they relate to personal development and competence to deliver God's words. But during interviews with the students the respondents portray themselves as humble servants sticking to organizational career paths, following rank and holding low career expectations. Their ambition is to help others by christening them. Just like US-teachers in Norway they consider themselves to be spiritual agents of stability rather than revolutionary change. One of them describes life as an arena for saving others. Another respondent is all about believing in God while yet another one talks about self and an explicit purpose to follow the Book of Mormon.

- **Purpose-Scene:** "The very purpose is to help us develop and become something other than believers when we are here." "I have other purposes in my life." Of course, all young men have the opportunity to work as missionaries. This is something you like to be a part of." "Life on earth gives an opportunity to develop."
- **Agent-Purpose:** "I have no plans to advance in the hierarchy – or whatever you choose to call it. I have no ambitions to become a Prophet." "We all want to change and become like Jesus Christ, simply to become a good human being. This has noth-

ing to do with getting a position with sta-tus. It is not a primary personal objective."

- **Scene-Agent-Purpose:** "In-service train-ing is for my personal development and as part of a life project, a greater plan, to start over and to begin a new life."

With reference to Big Scene Agency the US-missionaries say: "In everything we do we try to learn, Sunday school, clergymen meetings, with families". The quote illustrates a purpose-ful subject operating on measures for production and exchange of knowledge (informal and formal learning) saying: "We study the scriptures for four years." They study, reflect and learn by adhering to the rules and regulations of their belief. This is an explicit mention of the purpose of their activity. There is compatibility between personal need and organizational resources. "It was my calling so I gladly accepted the terms and it's the same for all young men". Professional development happens by rituals, calling, faith and belief in the sub-triangle of exchange. They say: "I took in-service courses or seminars when I was younger; one between ages 12 and 18 and another between 8 and 30". The quote signifies production of knowledge without explicit mention of purpose or character of neces-sary or sufficient components in the sub-triangle Production. "I have attended one of those very valuable, inspiring, powerful and idea-producing meetings". The last example contains production and exchange of knowledge between religious people, enabled by means of specific agency. "For example, when I became a teacher I was asked to accept that post." Focus is on the rules of the community (Scene) supplying the means for helping individual functioning (production) by personal initiative to deliver services (exchange) and knowledge to the community. Then follows a reference to the physical setting: "I learn at the institute in town, twice a week." On the one hand, the agent's personal need, motivation and objective are hidden from study. On the other hand, organi-zational arrangements are based on administrative

demands and resources for generating (production) rather than sharing (exchange) knowledge. As a way of promoting collective activity a Mormon respondent says: "We are regularly encouraged to apply for participation in leadership courses". Demands for in-service leadership training seem to function as an organizational pillar, an expression of the organization's authoritative prerequisites.

Religious Administration on a Big Scene

Student questions for clergymen in a Swedish congregation have a focus on the Big Scene: "What are the characteristics of leadership on your job?" There are questions where Act is combined with Small Scene: "What would you change on your job if you had the opportunity?" Taken together the questions suggest a balanced approach characterized by even weight on Small and Big Scene, because the respondents' answers cover where (setting), how (method/means) and what (contents) of their work. The students' questions probe into Acts on religious Scenes. There are few questions on Purpose, possibly because the student-interviewers are aware of the why-purpose of spiritual activity (salvation, christening, ethics). They know about the impact of charismatic leadership (Agent) and they are fa-miliar with the functioning of mediating (Wertsch, 1998) artifacts like The Bible, traditions, rules of conduct, other people etc. The students' questions elicit valid responses which further construction of a comprehensive picture of spiritual work. The Swedish clergymen respond to questions on workplace characteristics defined by Agent-Act or Scene-Agent dimensions.

- **Scene:** "Of course I try to find a hands-on training program in my vicarage and my home organization offers specific courses and formal education about services, fu-nerals and administrative routines." "All clergymen attend a variety of in-service courses throughout their careers and they choose a course they are interested in."

- **Agent:** "I have wanted to become a clergyman ever since I was a kid." "I had to study on my own, think things through, study and so on."
- **Act-Purpose:** "He does not mix with the details of the things I do but he defines my tasks and expects me to carry them out on my own."
- **Agent-Act:** "Studying religion was great fun."
- **Agency-Act:** "And I think it is a good idea to educate oneself, not believing you know everything."
- **Agent-Act-Purpose:** "Yes, I study and learn an academic Master course 120hp in pedagogical leadership. And I do it all for myself."

In an indication of individual action relative to their calling the Swedish clergymen say: "We regularly meet and try to find the time to discuss theological questions". The quote is about exchange of information in a closed group. There is nothing to do with personal initiative, rules, regulations or other people, i.e. merely collective internal (re)production of truths. Another example, "I have attended many spiritual health courses, conversational therapy and so on." is about information (exchange) in a familiar and close religious group. In describing collective activity the respondents say: "We have divided labor so that I can work as district visitor and deal with adult issues". This culturally impregnated collective of people is an example of an anonymous agent/subject without indication of the finer details of the setting. Focus is on exchange and distribution between community and church by division of professional labor. One of them says: "Now I face a real challenge: performing a burial and it feels hard, how can I carry it out properly?" Focus is on public performance in a conservative community by division of labor plus rules and

regulations of the Big Scene setting related to hands on religious services.

Summary of Reported and Experienced Influences

One half of the analysis is on here-and-now influences on human interaction. The A-C- side of Figure 1 covers *in-built deviation* with a focus on Agent + Act= Scene. Socio-cultural Small Scene influences cause interviewees to respond by delivering "distorted" data, primarily because the setting enables the Agents to construct socially acknowledged rather than "true" (speech) Acts. Another half of the analysis is on there-and-then qualities of their workplace memories. The B-D-side of Figure 1 covers interviewee reports structured by their *natural contradictions*. Workplace experiences are inside the interviewees heads and their constructions, representations and adaptations of workplace experiences fail any attempt at reconstruction by Big Scene= Act + Agent. In spite of people's innate ability to construct reality by relating theses to antitheses and forming an idea of an experienced phenomenon based on natural contradictions, extraction of Big Scene Agent and Act qualities remain "closed" from analysis. They are merely memories inside the religious respondents' heads. As a consequence of this line of analyzing the data, there is individual action to *report* in the "close" interview setting and there is collective activity to *interpret* in "expansive" workplace settings. Interview data on person-centered (Agency) covers Small Scene Agent/Act classifications. Analysis suggest they illustrate the Big Scene dynamics of Engeström's (1987) sub-triangle on Production by Subject-Instrument-Object and Exchange by Subject-Community-Rules and Regulations.

1. Action verbs (Act) like *notice, learn, happen, do, learn, study, accept, study, attend, accept, learn, meet* and *discuss* suggest personal action-agency. The respondents' answers

assist Big Scene nodes in sub-triangles of Production by Subject-Instrument-Object and Exchange by Subject-Community-Rules and Regulations.

2. Action verbs like *study, apply, work, perform* and *carry out* relate to situated demands and personal ability on a Small interview Scene. In spite of the fact that the students' questions elicit answers on workplace experiences, action verbs play a minor part compared analysis of relations within and between Consumption- and Distribution sub-triangles.

3. References to question words *where (University of Wisconsin), who (we)* and *what (books; division of labor, performing rites)* indicate a Big Scene focus on the workplace.

The preceding quotes on Scene/Agent describe a basis for analyzing the dynamics of Engeström's (1987) sub-triangles on Consumption by Subject-Community-Object and on Distribution by Object-Community-Division of labor.

INTERPRETING THE RESULT

Martin & Peim (2009) say research benefits from studies of relations between individual acts and organizational practices. In analyzing the descriptive power of a combined Engeström/Burke approach to understanding dynamics between individual acts and shared activities by Scene and Purpose (= object of activity) there are some conclusions to draw (Miettinen 2005). First there is dynamics at work within and between activity systems and sub-systems. Second, there is a Small Scene perspective on individual tasks as experienced during interviews. Third, there is a Big Scene perspective on religious workplace activities defined by the characteristics of the setting and awareness of personal and professional objectives. In answering Martin and Peim's (2009) suggestion for further research on ambivalences over

conceptualizations of agent (who), action (how) and agency (how), one finding of this study relates to the close interview setting operating by/operating on the respondents responses. Data supplied by Mormon missionaries reflect the experienced reality of a close dialogical context shared with students during the interviews. On the issue of individual action and social practices Säljö (1997) comments on this fact suggesting (Säljö, 2001, p. 111) it is reasonable to: "talk about the ability to master certain types of skills and discourses under the premises offered by a certain type of institutional practices." The Mormon respondents prioritize impressions generated by the Small Scene interview. They combine concrete situated influences (Enerstvedt, 1977) to their data rather than – as US-teachers and Swedish clergymen do – reflect on de-contextualized Big Scene workplace experiences and characteristics. Small Scene analysis refers to a sub-triangle on relations between Subject-Instrument-Object and describing Production of interactions, information and knowledge. Another Small Scene sub-triangle contains relations between Subject-Community-Rules and regulations describing Exchange of information, knowledge and experience. Several religious employees respond to the students' questions by promoting Production and Exchange of knowledge. By being self-sufficient agents and meeting with their peers they foster each other by adhering to institutional rules. The dynamics between sub-triangles of Production and Exchange make up the staging of workplace experiences. The religious respondents form a legion of missionaries by applying/repeating individual acts relative to a shared Purpose. They move and communicate in closed groups, learning with, by and from colleagues. This study verifies to an alleged rather than proven fact that during interviewing the interviewer and the interviewee equally fall victims to here-and-now influences of human interaction. Such influences blind the subjects to the fact that during interviews they are actually exploring their social relation rather than searching and/or providing an account of the characteristics of their workplace. Due to the fact that people alternate between roles of interviewer and interviewees another complication apperas in the search for valid interpretation of interview data. "Social coloring" of the interviewees working life impressions appear because of their inablility to separate between their professioonal roles as respondents (in one kind of interview) *and* missionaries who attract potential believers and future members of religious communities (in a different kind of interview).

CONCLUSION

The respondents describe missionary work in concrete terms, just like they would if they were to compare the interview situation with familiar settings they encounter when they interpret the Book of Mormon, save people or preach God's words. However, interview data reflect a striking difference between the researcher's ambition to gather valid data and the respondents' preference for adapting to the dialogical two-person-format of the interview. Orchestration of Engeströms sub-triangles, Burke's motivational grammar and Martin and Peim's (2009) suggestion for further research resulted in analysis of data generated in close interviewer-interviewee setting. The respondents' pieces of information illustrate the subjects' interactions influenced by Small Scene agency. Analysis also covers the respondents' reports on Big Scene organizational structures by supplying detailed information on job-related tasks. In analyzing religious workplace experiences, the respondents refrain from highlighting the meditational means (Agency) as well as the overall activity (Big Scene). On the other hand they employ implicit Purpose and explicit Small Scene references as they report self-controlled Agent-Act-Agency influences on the quality of Production and Exchange during missionary work. This result is in line with Bakhurst's (2009)

definition of individual motive or collective objective (Gegenstand) as a behavioral principle for practitioners and followers of activity theory.

REFERENCES

Asplund, J. (1980). *Socialpsykologiska studier* [socio-psychological studies]. Stockholm: Awe/Glebers.

Bakhurst, D. (2009). Reflection on activity theory. *Educational Review, 61*(2), 197–210. doi:10.1080/00131910902846916

Burke, K. (1962). *A Grammar of Motives and A Rhetoric of Motives*. New York.

Burke, K. (1970). *The Rhetoric of Religion: Studies in Logology*. London: University of California Press.

Daniels, H., & Edwards, A. (Eds.). (2004). Sociocultural and activity theory in educational research. *Educational Review, 56*(2).

Dewey, J. (1910). *How we Think*. Boston: Heath and Company. doi:10.1037/10903-000

Dickinson, E. (2009). The Montana-meth project: Applying Burke's dramatistic pentad to a persuasive anti-drug media campaign. *Communication Teacher, 23*(3), 126–131. doi:10.1080/17404620902974824

Enerstvedt, R. (1971). *Vetenskap som pedagogic: En analys av vetenskapens medel och mål.* [Science and pedagogy: Analysis of means and ends in science]. Verdandi debatt.

Enerstvedt, R. (1977). *Mennesket i et fylogenetisk og ontogenetisk perspektiv* [Human beings in a phylogenetic and ontogenetic perspective]. Oslo: Forlaget Ny Dag.

Engeström, Y. (1987). *Learning by expanding: An activity-theoretical approach to developmental research*. Helsinki: Orienta-Konsultit.

Foot, K. A. (2002). Pursuing an Evolving Object: A Case Study in Object Formation and Identification. *Mind, Culture, and Activity, 9*(2), 132–149. doi:10.1207/S15327884MCA0902_04

Goffman, E. (1959). *The Presentation of Self in Everyday Life*. Anchor Books.

Gutierréz, K. (2007). Commentary. In C. Lewis, P. Enciso, & E. Moje (Eds.), Reframing Socioclultural Research on Literacy: Identity, Agency and Power. Routledge.

Hansson, T. (2014). Social science universals. In T. Issa, P. Isaias, & P. Kommers (Eds.), Multicultural Awareness and Technology in Higher Education: Global Perspectives. Hershey, PA: IGI-Global.

Jackson, P. (2012). How we think we think. *Teachers College Record, 114*(2). Retrieved from http://www.tcrecord.org

Janzen, K., Perry, B., & Edwards, M. (2011). Aligning the quantum perspective of learning to instructional design: Exploring the seven definite questions. *International Review of Research in Open and Distance Learning, 12*(7).

Kaptelinin, V., & Nardi, B. (2006). *Acting with Technology: Activity Theory and Interaction Design*. Cambridge, MA: The MIT Press.

Latour, B. (2000). When things strike back: A possible contribution of science studies to the social sciences. *The British Journal of Sociology, 51*(1), 107–123. doi:10.1080/000713100358453

Leontev, A. N. (2002). *Virksomhed, bevisthed og personlighed* [Activity, Consciousness and Personality]. København: Hans Reizels Forlag.

Martin, D., & Peim, N. (2009). Critical perspectives on activity theory. *Educational Review, 61*(2), 131–138. doi:10.1080/00131910902844689

Miettinen, R. (2005). Object activity and individual motivation. *Mind, Culture, and Activity, 12*(1), 52–69. doi:10.1207/s15327884mca1201_5

Rueckert, W. H. (1963). *Kenneth Burke and the Drama of Human Relations*. Minneapolis, MN: Academic Press.

Säljö, R. (1997). Talk as data and practice – a critical look at phenomenographical inquiry and the appeal to experience. *Higher Education Research & Development, 16*(2), 173–190. doi:10.1080/0729436970160205

Säljö, R. (2001). The individual in social practices. *Nordisk Pedagogik, 21*(2), 108–116.

Stetsenko, A. (2005). Activity as object-oriented: Resolving the dichotomy of individual and collective planes of activity. *Mind, Culture, and Activity, 12*(1), 70–88. doi:10.1207/s15327884mca1201_6

Vygotsky, L. (1987). Thinking and speech. In R. W. Rieber & A. S. Carton (Eds.), The collected works of L. S. Vygotsky: The fundamentals of defectology. New York: Plenum.

Vygotsky, L. (1994). Imagination and the creativity of the adolescent. In R. van der Veer & J. Valsiner (Eds.), The Vygotsky Reader. Oxford, UK: Blackwell.

Wertsch, J. (1998). *Mind as Action*. New York: OUP.

ADDITIONAL READING

Avis, J. (2009). Transformation or transformism: Engeström's version of activity theory. *Educational Review, 61*(2), 151–165. doi:10.1080/00131910902844754

Bedny, G., & Harris, S. R. (2005). The systemic-structural theory of activity: Applications to the study of human work. *Mind, Culture, and Activity, 12*(2), 128–147. doi:10.1207/s15327884mca1202_4

Billett, S. (2006). Relational interdependence between social and individual agency in work and working life. *Mind, Culture, and Activity*, *13*(1), 53–69. doi:10.1207/s15327884mca1301_5

Blunden, A. (2009). An interdisciplinary concept of activity. *Outlines (Copenhagen)*, *1*, 1–26.

Cole, M. (2010). What's culture got to do with it? Educational research as a necessary interdisciplinary enterprise. *Educational Researcher*, *39*(6), 461–470. doi:10.3102/0013189X10380247

Ellis, V. (2011). Re-energizing professional ceativity from a CHAT perspective: Seeing knowledge and history bin practice. *Mind, Culture, and Activity*, *18*(2), 181–193. doi:10.1080/1074903 9.2010.493595

Engeström, Y. (2008). Enriching activity theory without shortcuts. *Interacting with Computers*, *20*(2), 256–259. doi:10.1016/j.intcom.2007.07.003

Engeström, Y., & Sannino, A. (2010). Studies of expansive learning: Foundations, findings and future challenges. *Educational Research Review*, *5*(1), 1–24. doi:10.1016/j.edurev.2009.12.002

Gredler, M. (2007). Of cabbages and kings: Concepts and inferences curiously attributed to Lev Vygotsky. *Review of Educational Research*, *77*(2), 233–238. doi:10.3102/0034654306298270

Holt, R. (2008). Using activity theory to understand entrepreneurial opportunity. *Mind, Culture, and Activity*, *15*, 52–70.

Kaptelinin, V. (2005). The object of activity: Making sense of the sense-maker. *Mind, Culture, and Activity*, *12*(1), 4–18. doi:10.1207/s15327884mca1201_2

Miettinen, R. (2006). Epistemology of transformative material activity: John Dewey's pragmatism and cultural historical activity theory. *Journal for the Theory of Social Behaviour*, *36*(4), 389–408. doi:10.1111/j.1468-5914.2006.00316.x

Nardi, B. (2005). Objects of desire: Power and passion in collaborative activity. *Mind, Culture, and Activity*, *12*(1), 37–51. doi:10.1207/s15327884mca1201_4

Smagorinsky, P. (2011). Vygotsky's stage theory: The psychology of art and the actor under the direction of *Perezhivaine. Mind, Culture, and Activity*, *18*(4), 319–341. doi:10.1080/1074903 9.2010.518300

Tappan, M. (2006). Moral functioning as mediated action. *Journal of Moral Education*, *35*(1), 1–18. doi:10.1080/03057240500495203

Vygotsky, L. (1934/1962). *Thinking and Speaking*. Transcribed by A Blaunden. Retrieved April 15, 2014from http://www.marxists.org/archive/vygotsky/works/words/

KEY TERMS AND DEFINITIONS

Act: An star performs (acts) in a show. It could also be a formal and official record of something.

Agency: Is the faculty of exerting instrumental power, describing the state of being in action.

Agent: An agent is somebody with the power to act. Action and agency are closely related terms.

Contradiction: Meaning that a proposition that is false for all values of its natural variables.

Deviation: A deviating act includes anumber of things; leaving the trodden path; a wandering from the (common) way; variation from the agreed way, breaking an established rule, departure from the right course or from the path of duty. Deviation could also mean transgression, an act of sin, an error or an offense.

Fylogenesis: Birth and development of a collective of human organisms, the human race.

Modeling: Learning a new skill by copying other people. This is the art of sculpting something specific from raw material and create a representation of something.

Ontogenesis: Birth and development of an individual human organism.

Purpose: An intention to reach a desired result; near-synonymous words are aim, goal, objective and target.

Scene: This is the geographical location of an event that attracts the bystanders'/viewers' attention.

Chapter 16
Creativity in Education:
Play and Exploratory Learning

Beth Ferholt
Brooklyn College, City University of New York, USA

Anders Jansson
Jönköping University, Sweden & Stockholm University, Sweden

Monica Nilsson
Jönköping University, Sweden

Karin Alnervik
Jönköping University, Sweden

ABSTRACT

The goal of this chapter is to respond to the scarcity of literature on creativity that is relevant both to CHAT and in the field of education. The authors explore Vygotsky's writings on creativity, imagination, art, and play in relation to three Swedish preschool projects that practice a pedagogy of exploratory learning. Also included are discussions of imagination versus realistic thinking, syncretism in children's creative work, and play as a creative activity. Because this study was a formative intervention, the pedagogy of exploratory learning became significant in the analysis. The bulk of the chapter consists of thick descriptions of the projects and discussion of aspects of creativity as they appear in the projects. The data was collected by teachers and a research team that consisted of the authors of this chapter. Data collection in the three projects took place before the intervention took place, during the initial phases of the intervention, and after the intervention had become an annual theme for the preschools. The research was initially guided solely by a cultural historical understanding of creativity, while the analysis brought CHAT into dialogue with postmodern writings that are related to exploratory learning.

INTRODUCTION

Creativity is central to L. S. Vygotsky's understanding of human development "in all of its expressions encompassing processes of being, doing and knowing" (Stetsenko, 2014, p. 183). Broadly, creativity is inherently a unique form of change

and Vygotsky's theoretical framework requires genetic analysis precisely because the historical conditions which shape us and which we shape through creative activity are – also inherently – constantly changing. More specifically, Vygotsky (2004) argues that we are all creative and that we are creative throughout the lifespan:

DOI: 10.4018/978-1-4666-6603-0.ch016

There is a widespread opinion that creativity is the province of a select few ... This is not true. If we understand creativity in its true psychological sense as the creation of something new, then this implies that creation is the province of everyone to one degree or another; that it is a normal and constant companion in childhood. (p. 33)

However, creativity does not hold a prominent place in second or even third generation cultural historical activity theory (CHAT) within the field of education. This is the case despite Vera John-Steiner and colleagues' (John-Steiner, 2000; Connery et al., 2010) important work on creativity, and Yrjö Engeström's (1987) work on creativity at an institutional level, i.e. expansive learning. CHAT that concerns itself with education has focused on appropriation of tools, tool or sign mediation and the zone of proximal development (see for example Säljö, 2010). This work has particularly addressed cognitive and constructionist approaches to learning. We address this lacuna within CHAT within the field of education by using CHAT to analyze children's creativity in play and learning in three preschool projects.

The projects took place at preschools that practice *exploratory learning*, an approach that is inspired by the pedagogy developed in the preschools of Reggio Emilia. The notion of exploratory learning, based on Reggio Emilia's pedagogical practice, has been discussed by many pedagogues and educational researchers, among them Gunilla Dahlberg and Hillevi Lentz Taguchi of Sweden. A major source of inspiration for Dahlberg and Taguchi has been the work of the French philosophers Gilles Deleuze and Félix Guattari. Exploratory learning emphasizes children's creative exploration by means of multiple interacting aesthetic means, called the "hundred languages" of children.

Through our own research, the preschools to which we refer, above, have recently incorporated, and in doing so recreated, a CHAT-based approach to play called *playworlds*. In playworlds play is understood to be the primary form of early childhood imagination, and therefore closely related to creativity. Our shift towards a focus on creativity within CHAT that concerns itself with education is, therefore, in dialogue with postmodern approaches to learning. In such a dialogue Vygotsky's work on imagination, creativity and play constitute an important interlocutor.

The three preschool projects that we will discuss came to our attention during a research project in which we engineered a meeting between the Vygotskian play pedagogy of Gunilla Lindqvist (1995), *the creative pedagogy of play*, which we have come to call playworlds (Marjanovic-Shane, et al., 2011), and the pedagogical approach of exploratory learning. Our understanding of the preschools' projects is shaped by their positions within this research project. The first of these projects took place before playworlds was introduced to the preschools and the second took place during the initial phases of this project. The third project took place when playworld had been chosen by the preschools as their new annual theme.

We begin with a discussion of Vygotsky's theory of creativity. We then present playworlds and exploratory learning, and describe the above-mentioned research project. The bulk of the chapter is a discussion of aspects of creativity as they become evident in the three preschool projects. This discussion is guided by our cultural historical theoretical understanding of creativity, based in turn on the work of Vygotsky. One key objective is to introduce and explore concepts in Vygotsky's writings on creativity, specifically: imagination versus realistic thinking; syncretism in children's creative work; and children's play as a form of creative imagination that, in relation to adults' forms of creative imagining, lacks *only* in experience.

VYGOTSKY'S THEORY OF IMAGINATION AND CREATIVITY

In "Imagination and Creativity in Childhood" (2004, p. 2) Vygotsky begins by defining the creative act as "(a)ny activity that gives rise to something new." To hone this definition he makes a distinction between a "reproductive" activity in which "nothing new is created," but, instead, there is "a repetition of something that already exists," and a "combinatorial or creative activity" in which one is "not merely recovering the traces of stimulation that reached my brain in the past." (2004, p. 3) In creative activity, Vygotsky (ibid., p. 4) writes: "I never actually saw this remote past, or this future; however, I still have my own idea, image, or picture of what they were or will be like." Vygotsky's (2004) basic distinction explains why anyone who is engaged in creative activity, including children, produces something novel:

If human activity were limited to reproduction of the old, then the human being would be a creature oriented only to the past and would only be able to adapt to the future to the extent that it reproduced the past. It is precisely human creative activity that makes the human being a creature oriented toward the future, creating the future and thus altering his own present. (p. 3)

Vygotsky (2004, p. 6) explicitly argues that all humans, including children, are creative: "If we understand creativity in this way, it is easy to see that the creative processes are already fully manifest in earliest childhood." Furthermore, he (ibid., p. 6) writes that, "we can identify creative processes in children ... especially in their play." For Vygotsky a child's play is not just a reproduction of what she experienced, but is a creative revision of her impressions. Play is embodied imagination and creativity.

Vygotsky (2004, p. 12) describes the creative developmental process by sketching four basic ways that fantasy is associated with reality: (1) Anything that your imagination creates is always based on elements from reality - from your past experiences. (2) The second type of link is made possible through one's own experience and imagination of someone else's experience, for example through stories. (3) Emotions that arise in reality affect the imagination, but imagination also affects emotions. (4) Fantasy can become reality. This occurs when a given material form is crystallized imagination coming back to reality, and is therefore a new active force with the potential to change reality: "It is this probability to combine elements to produce a structure, to combine the old in new ways, that is the basis of creativity." Vygotsky further describes the imaginary process as a process of interpretations with complexes of transformations, distinctions, regroupings, densification, shrinkages and exaggerations.

In play the child combines impressions and uses them to construct a new imaginary reality to suit her own needs and desires. The creation of this imaginary situation is the first step in the child's emancipation from the constraints of the situation, writes Vygotsky, and this step is made possible when play dominates over objects and actions. In contrast to the child's previous *exploration*, when object dominated over meaning, in play meaning dominates over the object, such that a wooden stick becomes a horse. The stick functioning as a "pivot" becomes a bridge between the "here and now" and the "possible otherwise."

In the process of giving things and acts meanings other than those that they have outside of play, the child develops symbolic language and abstract thinking. Abstract thinking is a prerequisite for play but also develops in play. Vygotsky writes (1978, p. 104): "In a development perspective, the creation of an imaginary situation is considered as means to develop abstract thinking."

PLAYWORLDS AND EXPLORATORY LEARNING

As stated above, this research project was designed in such a way that it would bring a central component of Lindqvist's (1995) play pedagogy, the *playworld* activity, to three Swedish preschools. The preschools were inspired by the preschool pedagogy developed in the internationally known municipal preschools of Reggio Emilia. The goal of the project was to bring a current approach to playworlds into interaction with the pedagogy of exploratory learning that was being practiced in the preschools. We wanted to explore the relationship between playworlds and exploratory learning, and also the relationship between play and learning.

Playworlds

In Lindqvist's (1995) playworld activities within her creative pedagogy of play, interaction between adults and children is structured around a piece of literature or a work of art. Adults and children work together to "bring the literature to life" (ibid., p. 72) through drama and play. The participants assume roles based on characters from a work of literature, and make use of the intrinsic dynamism between world, action and character in drama and play. Through joint scripted and improvisational acting, and set design, the children and the adults transform their classroom into a world inspired by a book. Lindqvist (1995, 2001) provides rich and concrete examples of playworlds.

Contrasts between the formation of playworlds in Sweden, Finland and the U.S. allows us to isolate three conditions that we believe are essential in the creation of the shared responsibility for directing the adult-child joint play that is at the heart of playworlds (Ferholt & Lecusay, 2010). First, adults in a playworld enter fully into children's play by taking on play roles, putting on costumes and entering character. In doing so they are required to partially step outside of their role as teacher and join the children in the role of fellow actor. Second, the children as well as the adults co-construct the environment in which play takes place. The children do not play in an environment that has been designed for them by adults alone. Third, Lindqvist's pedagogy grounds play in works of children's literature that address epistemological and ethical dilemmas of great interest to people in a variety of life stages. Because of this the teacher is personally invested in the topics, and therefore in the process and the outcomes of a playworld. The teacher is at least as interested in play as a tool for furthering the children's and his or her own understanding of a topic, such as "fear," as he or she is interested in furthering the child's development. Furthermore, these dilemmas are such that it is the combination of different perspectives, rather than skills or experience that come with age, which produces solutions, e.g. What is real? What to do if someone you love is doing something harmful to themselves and others? What does one do in the face of conflicting options? (Hakkarainen, unpublished manuscript).

It is because, as Vygotsky argues, children's play is a form of creative imagination that only lacks, in relation to adults' forms of creative imagining, experience, that the above conditions are possible. And it is these three conditions that allow adults in playworlds to learn from the creative imaging of children. The children who join with adults in playworlds lack in experience, but they are expert players.

Exploratory Learning and Pedagogy of Listening

Exploratory learning and the accompanying pedagogy of listening are also based on a perception of the child as creative. This approach originates from the municipal preschools of Reggio Emilia, as mentioned above, and from the founding father of these preschools, Loris Malaguzzi (Dahlberg, et al., 2007). Malaguzzi considered the preschool to be a multicultural arena or a "town square." He conceived of the preschool as a player in a democratic society where activity is created and shaped through dialogue between citizens. However, Malaguzzi is perhaps best known through his poem, *A Child has a Hundred Languages*, which explains that spoken and written "languages" are just two of the many ways that children express themselves and make sense of the world. Other "languages" include dancing, drawing, singing, painting, sculpting, etc., i.e. aesthetic forms of different kinds.

In Sweden, in exploratory learning the child is considered to be a culture and knowledge creator through these hundred languages (Dahlberg & Lenz Taguchi, 1994). Furthermore, children develop theories and hypotheses about the world that should be considered as possible as those of adults (Lentz Taguchi, 2009). It is because of these considerations that teachers working within this preschool practice often ask the children about their ideas and understandings.

Also central to exploratory learning is that the environment and the materials available for aesthetical expressions are considered to be a "third pedagogue," signifying their importance in the children's creative explorations. Olsson (2009) writes that in exploratory learning it is important that the environment and the materials make it possible for children and pedagogues to formulate problems and questions that they will explore, rather than supporting a search for correct answers and solutions. The materials are thought of as tools that give children an opportunity to be creative as they explore their thoughts and hypotheses about the world.

In the municipal preschools of Reggio Emilia and in the preschools of this project, a space called an *atelier*, conceived of as a place of research, invention and exploration, and an *atelierista*, a "teacher" with an arts background, support the above-described processes of exploration and listening. It is through the atelier and the atelierista

that the hundred languages are integrated into the preschools. In the preschools of this study there are both an atelierista for visual arts and an atelierista for music, drama, dance / movement and rhythm.

A final important concept in this pedagogy is *documentation*, as exploratory learning is focused on open-ended learning and intense child involvement (Alnervik, 2013). Pedagogical documentation is used to guide a project's direction based on what teachers perceive to be the children's meaning making processes. These processes are revisited through documents by children and pedagogues. The observations and documentations of children's creativity and expressions then become shared stories for reflections that become the basis for children's and adults' future meaning making processes. When documentations are reflected upon they become pedagogical documentation.

The Reggio Emilia approach and exploratory learning have primarily been conceptualized and discussed in Sweden from a variety of postmodern perspectives (Dahlberg, et al., 2007; Elfström, 2013). Lentz Taguchi (2010) discusses and analyzes exploratory learning projects using Barad's (2007) concept of intra-activity, focusing on potentiality in learning in the intersection between agents of different kinds: humans, material objects and discourses. A recurring metaphor in postmodern writings is the "Rhizome" and *rhizomatic learning*. This is a philosophical concept from Deleuze and Guattari (1987). It describes learning as anything but a linear and goal directed activity. A component of rhizomatic learning is *"lines of flight,"* which imply a state of detachment and "inbetweenness," i.e. a positive force happening when an event takes a leap away from a habitual act (Lentz Taguchi, 2010). From a CHAT perspective it is interesting to note that Engeström (2007) compares Deleuze & Guattari's concept of rhizome with the concept of *mycorrhizae*, highlighting the horizontal and multidirectional connections in human lives in contrast to the dominant vertical, tree-like images of hierarchy.

THE RESEARCH PROJECT

In exploratory learning play is often seen as an expression of a traditional Fröbel-inspired pre-school didactics that is based on a view of the child as "nature" (Dahlberg & Lentz Taguchi, 1994). Play is also sometimes spoken of as "playful learning," which is a resource in exploration. Our research project was conceived from a playworld perspective, which understands play to be crucial in children's exploration of the world and themselves. However, our project was designed to take place across the differences, both practical and theoretical, between playworlds and exploratory learning.

Exploration of the differences and similarities between playworlds and exploratory learning was a great part of the inspiration for the research project. We hoped to "play with" the contradiction that arises when one appreciates both the value of children's creativity – their ability to produce new insights, which may be of value to people of all ages – and the need of adults to enculturate children if our species is to survive. The project was also designed to contribute to a preschool didactics inspired both by CHAT and by postmodern theory and practice, while bridging the duality between the two. Our research team hypothesized that playworlds might form a bridge between exploratory learning and free play, i.e., the traditional way of understanding play in preschools, which implies children playing without participating teachers at times which are sandwiched in between structured pedagogical activities such as "circle time."

We consider our methodological approach to be what Engeström (2008) calls a formative intervention. According to Engeström, Vytgotsky's methodological principle of double stimulation leads to a concept of formative interventions. Engeström (2008, p. 15) describes formative interventions by contrasting them with "the linear interventions advocated ... by the literature on design experiments:"

- The subjects construct a novel solution or novel concept, the contents of which are not known ahead of time to the researchers.
- The contents and course of the intervention are subject to negotiation and the shape of the intervention is eventually up to the subjects.
- The aim is to generate intermediate concepts and solutions that can be used in other settings as tools in the design of locally appropriate new solutions.

Lindqvist's playworld research, U.S. playworld reasearch and current Swedish playworld research can all be described as formative interventions. Lindqvist (1995) did not use the term formative intervention, but she related her research methodology to double stimulation and to didactic experiments.

This research project was both the context in which we brought CHAT and postmodern *pedagogies* into dialogue concerning creativity, and the medium through which we collected the data we present, below. We will now discuss the three projects that showcase aspects of creativity, and discuss these three projects in terms of a cultural historical theoretical understanding of creativity.

The First Case: Imagination and Realistic Thinking

Exploratory learning projects take as their starting point phenomena that are often found in nature, such as light and sound, and also phenomena such as symbols or communication. In this way, unlike playworlds, they are in obvious accord with the Swedish curriculum (Skolverket, 2010), which emphasizes subject areas such as math, science, technology and language. An international trend stresses the importance of early childhood education as means of increasing a country's international "competitiveness" (Vallberg-Roth, 2014). All preschools, therefore, have to relate their projects and pedagogical work to such subject areas. In opposition to what is prevalent in the resulting literature – contemporary discussion of the relationship between play and learning (Pramling Samuelsson, 2003; Fleer, 2011) – we take as a point of departure that subjects such as math, etc., as well as play, require both imagination and what Vygotsky calls "realistic thinking." In analyzing and reflecting upon this first project we work from Vygotsky's (2004) claim concerning imagination and realistic thinking:

... the two processes (imaginary and realistic thinking) develop as a unity. There is no essential independence of the two developmental processes. Moreover, by observing the forms of imagination that are linked with creativity, that is, the forms of imagination that are directed toward reality, we find that the boundary between realistic thinking and imagination is erased. Imagination is a necessary, integral aspect of realistic thinking. (p. 349)

Vygotsky states that the processes of imagination and of realistic thinking develop as a unity. According to Vygotsky, imagination is the basis for all creative activity. Vygotsky's position can be observed particularly well in play, but, as stated above, we theorize that imagination and realistic thinking are significant in both play and exploratory learning, and also that imagination can be observed in exploratory learning. This implies that the often taken-for-granted assumption, that play engages imagination while learning engages realistic thinking about facts, is problematic.

The question we ask in this section is: What does the interplay between imagination and realistic thinking look like in children's theorizing in this particular project? More specifically, the description below highlights ways in which elements of the teachers' experiences of the project at the start of the project allow them to imagine the next steps in the project. The following description of the project shows that very few of the project activities actually repeat pre-existing knowledge or pre-existing methods of exploration.

We also emphasize in the description below just how the children and their teachers, a class of five-year-old children and their three teachers, work together in this project. They imagine possible scientific theories and methods based on prior experiences within the project. They imagine and re-imagine their own and others' experiences through many media (languages) and through many revisits/re-presentations of collective and individual experiences. They show emotional engagement that drives their imaginative processes, and imaginative processes that drive their emotional engagement. Finally, they create theories of space and sound that may be scientifically sound, and which shape adult and child participants' understandings of the relationship between space and sound, and between our senses. This process is discussed in terms of rhizomatic learning, as mentioned above.

The following description of the project is based solely on the teachers' pedagogical documentation. The preschool pedagogista, who is also an author of this paper, presented the succeeding documentation to the three "outsider" researchers in our team when we began preparations for the project. The project was initially named "Children's Relationship to Place." Math, science and sustainability were meant to be the designated content areas.

The teachers first chose a place for exploration on a near-by university campus that had interested the children the previous year. The children enjoyed the campus courtyard and a metal table with metal figurines attached to it. They also enjoyed a tunnel, which they passed through to reach the campus. They would call "ho ho!" as they passed through this tunnel, in order to create an echo, and in this way this project became a project about space and sound.

The project started in August and in October the teachers reformulated the aim of their upcoming project with these words: "Right now it's working with the questions that the children are trying to understand about sound: How is sound made?; How to make sounds in different ways?; How does it sound when different materials interact?; How to create different rhythms and tempo?; When you use the body as a tool, how does it sound and how does that sound change?" The teachers reflected on and developed suggestions for how to organize environments, materials and activities in order to explore these questions with the children. They suggested a reorganization of a "sound corner" and provided materials for sound creation and for symbolizing sounds as signs. For example, they provided long strips of paper as sound tracks

Figure 1. Long strips of paper, which were sound tracks, here with staffs printed on them for the musical notes

and added long staffs on some of these papers for musical notes (Figure 1).

We would like to point out that reproduction or the repetition of something that already exists is made very difficult to achieve from the very beginning of this project. The teachers' suggestions match the children' questions in their variety of type, scope and levels of abstraction, such that it would be nearly impossible to state an objective for the project that related to more than one or two of the questions or suggestions. The teachers appear to be following the children's opening of the project to numerous possibilities, instead of narrowing down the project to known outcomes at the start.

The decision concerning the materials was an instant success. The teachers reflected: "Here the children explore the new staffs. It is the first time we see that they use printed notes with the other materials." What the children are doing at this point in the project is laying out material for making noises, improvised instruments made of small pieces of metal, etc., on the same long strips of paper with staffs printed on them – and on which they have written notations representing sounds. Then the teachers and the children decide to bring their sound making tools and symbols/ signs, i.e. their staffs and all written and materials/ instruments they have put on their staffs, to their Place to play the concert and explore the sounds. On the way to the Place they pass through the tunnel. One of the teachers asks the children if they want to try to play the concert in the tunnel and reminds them that they often explore the sound of their voices in the tunnel.

Teacher: *Where in the tunnel should we play our concert?*
Child 1: *In the middle, this – (She looks up at a lamp that sits on the wall.)*
Child 2: *This is not the middle!*
Teacher: *How will we know where the middle is?*

Child 1: *It takes more time to run here than there (she points to the two possible directions to run).*

One child moves the basket with the tools towards the middle of the tunnel. Another child runs both ways and compares the distances. They agree on a place in the middle of the tunnel and they start picking up their sound creation tools. They help each other to read the sound signs so that every sound is in the right order. When they are ready the concert begins. Then they talk together about how the sounds sounded in the tunnel. They think it sounded 'like *little* sounds and *quiet* sounds.'

The children then continue on their trip with their teachers and arrive at their Place, where they set up for their concert again. Getting everything in place and in the right order requires planning and negotiation. They play their concert again and compare the results with the concert in the tunnel in these words:

Teacher: *Did you hear any difference from when we played in the tunnel?*
Child 1: *Here on the site, it sounds lower.*
Child 2: *It also echos.*
Teacher: *Why does it echo?*
Child 3: *It is dark and the ceiling, which makes it sound more in the tunnel.*

The children further explore by experimenting in various ways. When at the table with the figures, one child immediately starts to drum on the figurines. Another child picks up chestnuts that she has in her pocket. She hands them to the figurines and accidentally drops one. There is a new noise when the nut bounces between the figurines. Children and teachers crawl under the table to listen to this sound being repeated. A third child thinks it sounds like bells that play. The teacher produces a roll of wire that she has in her pocket and begins to test how it sounds on the different figurines. Two children are immediately

eager to try themselves. The teacher asks: "Why does it sound different?" A child says "They're bigger and smaller," pointing to the bowls with figures inside.

The teachers reflect on this event, saying: "Children use different scientific theories, for instance that it is dark in the tunnel and that this is why the tunnel makes it sound strongly." The teachers discover children's theories about sound, light, distance, echoes and air. During the many trips to the Place many dialogues involve traces of scientific reasoning that are intertwined with imagination and everyday experiences. For instance, the children discover that when they beat a drum quietly they hear no echo:

Teacher: *Why does the silent sound not echo?*
Child 1: *Because the sound does not reach the air.*
Child 2: *The air feels when it will echo. Then it responds back! The quiet sounds do not echo.*

One child has a theory about why it echoes in the tunnel but not outside: "The air will go out right away." Then teachers challenge the children with questions.

Teacher: *The sound is invisible but if the sound had a color, where do you think you would see that it went?*
Child 1: *It stays on the ground.*
Child 2: *First down and then up (pointing to the drum and then up in the air).*
Child 3: *The wind goes back and forth (pointing to something bouncing around the place), the sound comes along. The wind catches the sounds. I think it goes there (pointing at the figure).*
Teacher: *Let us try to listen there.*

Here we interrupt the narration of the project, offering an analytic point that might complement the overarching analysis above. At this moment the teachers recognize the children's theories as possible and valid, exactly at the moment in which the children create theories of space and sound. This process shapes adult and child participants' understandings of the relationship between space and sound and the relationship between the senses. This is, therefore, a moment when fantasy becomes reality in the creative cycle.

After many trips to the Place and many concerts, redesign of the sound corner in the classroom and sign making of sounds, the group starts to explore if they can turn the sound concert into a dance. The teachers ask the children: "What would the different dance steps/movements look like?" In this new sub-project the children start to create steps for the sounds that the symbols represent. One of the teachers challenges the children to carry on in silence, as it seems there is a rhythm of a dance in this first exercise. The teachers reflect that it seems so easy for the children to find movements based on the symbols and that the steps and the communication between the participants in the dance enables them to create their dance. The children repeat the steps and movements in order to remember what they had decided upon. Later a teacher asks: "Shall we have music?" A child responds, "Yes, it will be easier to remember everything. We'll have quiet/slow music."

Although many exploratory learning projects in preschools could be used to demonstrate a CHAT understanding of creativity, the rhizomatic features of this particular project help us to illustrate the dialogue we are creating between CHAT and postmodern theories of learning concerning creativity. The objective of the project was to focus on issues of sustainability, math and science. The project achieved this objective, but process took the shape of a meandering (of lines of flights), where goals and means were intertwined. This particular project did not illustrate a straightforward goal rational activity, but, rather, processes of imagination and realistic thinking developing as a unity. The children built their hypotheses, theories and understandings on both experiences and imagination.

The Second Case: Play, Narration, and Animation

The second project that we will discuss and analyze is an animated film project that was carried out by children and teachers, but supported by the preschools' visual atelierista. The project was anchored in the preschool's overarching language project for the academic year and the objective was to embrace various subprojects on children's sign making in the hundred languages or hundred semiotic modes. The teachers formulated the purpose of this project in this way: "Together with the children, try to understand how stories build up through play." The teachers' interest in relationships between narrative and play meant that they related the language project of their current year to emerging discussions of play and playworlds, the project which would officially begin in the upcoming academic year.

In describing this second project we highlight the occurrence of what Vygotsky calls syncretism in children's creative work. This CHAT concept is seldom discussed in the field of education. Vygotsky argues that children's creative work in a variety of art forms is syncretic, that is, interrelated in several ways.

Firstly, individual types of art have a general character:

We have already stated that the primary form of creative works by children is syncretic, that is, involving creation in which individual types of art are still not separated or specialized (Vygotsky, 2004 p. 67, italic added).

Second, Vygotsky claims a broader syncretism:

But children show even broader syncretism, uniting different modes of art in one single artistic endeavor. The child composes and acts out what he is saying... The child draws and at the same time talks about what he is drawing. The child dramatizes and composes the speeches for his characters (Vygotsky, 2004 p. 67, italic added).

When Vygotsky discusses children's creative work he underscores the close relationships of children's dramatic work and play. In reasoning about creativity and art Vygotsky states:

This syncretism points to the common root that unites all the different branches of children's art. This common root is the child's play, which serves as the preparatory stage for his artistic creation (Vygotsky, 2004 p. 67).

The following data is based on (1) rich documentation, notes, photos, video clips and artifacts from the project that were collected by the teachers and the atelierista; (2) the teachers'/atelierista's pedagogical documentation; (3) interviews that the research team carried out with the teachers and the atelierista and; (4) field notes from visits to class by the researchers.

The teaching team was interested in exploring questions regarding relationships between narrative and play: What stories are created in the children's play? What stories inspire play? Where do the children find inspiration when the play changes? What additions does the material make to the energy of the play/the stories? Which literacy activities/tracks/symbols are created in the play? During the academic year the teachers and the children explored these relationships, and in the following description we focus on sequences in the evolution of their sub-project of making animated movies.

This initiative emerged from the teachers' documentation of children's play in the school forest. The teachers took notes during the children's play, and based on that documentation the teachers performed a small theatrical play for the children in the forest. The play was then re-presented / re-visited. After the first performance the teacher told – or rather convinced – the children that the children had written the play "through their play-ing." One teacher then offered to write down other "play stories" if the children wanted her to do so, and minutes later the story of "The Candytroll and the two hungry boys" was performed by three children and written down by this teacher.

The atelierista and the teachers then offered the children the possibility of making up stories that would be supported by animation. When they told the children that they could create stories in media such as film, and not just through "telling," and that their experiences of play stories could become or be transformed into a movie with clay figures, the children became interested. The atelierista and the teacher only then invited a group of children to conduct the animation project.

The making of a story in stop-motion animation covered several phases:

- **Inventing Characters:** The children's invention of characters went through three steps: Close your eyes and silently imagine one character; Tell each other about your character; Draw your characters and their world. While the children drew their characters on paper, guided by their talk, a narrative, starting with the respective characters and what they liked, or how they lived, began to emerge.
- **Plasticine Figures:** The children made figures of characters in plasticine. The atelierista and teachers guided them one by one. As they usually do when the children make, for example, self-portraits, they asked: What should you start with? Look closely, what does it look like? The children got only the technical assistance that they needed to avoid getting "stuck."
- **Composing a Story:** The children were told that they needed a written story for their film. They were asked: What will the film be about? Do you need a beginning, how does the story continue, and what about the end? The children were invited in pairs to narrate one part of the story us-

ing their characters. Based on the narrative parts, developed by pairs of children, the atelierista provided a suggested script. The adults then made a storyboard of a short animated film as an illustration for the children.

- **Making Moving Images:** The teacher guided the children through the steps of the animation production: Rehearsing and moving clay figures; focusing and shooting images with a DSLR camera; and creating an illusion of movement in the camera. The children produced various props for the movie. When they saw the sequences where the figures begin to move, the experience created joy and energy and the desire to continue an otherwise monotonous process. (It takes many pictures to complete a full film as every minute requires 180 photographs.)

- **Recording Voices:** The children rehearsed how to perform the voices of the figures: How should they sound? How surprised should they sound? How happy or how angry? The children recorded their voices, alongside one teacher's voice, on a smartphone. Then they listened to their recording. If they were satisfied, the file was saved and later inserted during the editing of the animated film.

- **Editing:** The teacher edited the film, ensuring that all images were synched with the right sounds. Sometimes the children were present and observing during the editing process. Everybody had the opportunity to see how the computer program worked on the interactive whiteboard. Eventually the film, "Welcome to the Deer Park" was completed and shown to the class. The animation project inspired another group of children, so the teachers decided to offer all children the opportunity to participate in making a film.

- **A Second Film:** Two teachers then initiated a new film project with a new group of children. This work was carried out through the collaboration of children and teachers in a way that was similar, yet had some differences in the use of play and the other "art forms," to that of the first film project. The film "The Bear and That Key" was the result of this second group of children's work.

- **From Preschool to Community:** The idea of showing one of the finished movies at the pre-school film festival was suggested and realized. The idea of producing a manual showing how to make animated films, where children teach children how to do this, and which stresses that it is not hard to make a movie, was suggested by the teachers. Four children accepted this proposal and mimicked the clay figures talking (silent mouth in only two poses, moving back and forth between the two), a form that was inspired by one of the children who chose this method spontaneously during a filming session. Quite unexpectedly, one of the films was nominated to appear in the Stockholm Film Festival and a journalist from the Swedish radio (SR) interviewed the children and the adults about the films.

The syncretism in children's creative work in this project becomes obvious in the descriptions of the project, above. We find this and other aspects of the project, which are discussed below, to be particularly relevant to our understanding, from a CHAT perspective, of the development of creativity.

In the atelierista's descriptions and reflections on the process in the first movie, she especially notices the interplay among modes of creation, changes in the narrative in relation to other forms of art, and changes in the narrative threads of the story. For instance, she writes:

When the image develops, the story develops, and because it is told in words, the words add new ideas for image making.

When the children created their figures from plasticine they also spoke about their characters. They fantasized about what the characters liked to do, or that their characters had large eyes or mouths, or that the baby would be a year old and sit in a carriage.

When they sit down and plan out the start of the story, it is a quiet conversation. When they stand up and start telling by playing and showing with their body, their speech becomes both livelier and more eager. When they tell their story following internal images and their imagination, it seems that (using) the start of the story creates energy. The narrative parts they now are making create a new story that does not resemble the (small) stories that occurred in the joint floor drawing of the figures and their world.

When the children rehearsed moving their clay figure they found out what they thought was better suited to the figures to do or say. The story was partly changed.

The atelierista's reflections about the changes in the narratives depending on various forms of arts or semiotic modes/"languages" relates to her interest in the exploratory learning approach of enabling children's "hundred languages." Changes in art and corresponding changes in the narrative are highlighted.

Vygotsky states that a common root that unites branches of children's art is children's play. Play serves as a preparatory stage for artistic creation. The teachers were interested in learning about the relationship between play and narrative. They chose the children's play as a starting point in the initiation of the project in the forest and then worked to develop the story through children's

play, based on their characters. One could say that they explored Vygotsky's claim that play makes possible other art forms, in this case creative narration. In their pedagogical documentation, which was based on their experiences and observations during the process, they also described and discussed several issues regarding the relationships between play and narrative and their roles as teachers:

We learned from work on the first film that we must have a frame, a script to relate to. If we only focus on the playful, we can be held up for ages. This group of children likes to be in the theater room and playing roleplay, (so) we decided to let them play to develop a script.

The teacher's first try at developing a script-narrative for the film did not work because there were too many themes. Their analysis suggests that teachers have to help children in framing their play:

If play is children's "strong card," then maybe we should dare to go into it? Think about when and how we can help with the frame.

We are considering how we can offer clay figures in any way. The originals can't be played with (too delicate). Can we photograph them and give them to the children that way? We decide to borrow a solution we've seen in the documentation from another group (take pictures and glue the characters to paper rolls that children use as characters).

The teachers changed the play frame. Their choice could be interpreted as rhizomatic:

It is fascinating to see and hear how they sometimes go their own ways in the play, but still manage to tie everything together in the end. However, it seems that it was hard to be as many as four and on top of it all have six characters to keep track of. We can encourage children to play more times, though not so many.

In the overall process of the film project we see that the teachers begin to document aspects of play. They also begin to develop work with the third pedagogue, here defined as the environment, in relation to the development of play and narrative. Furthermore, the film project became a partly-shared imagined world. Based on their experiences in this new situation the teachers wrote the following reflection:

Have different types of play different roles at different stages of a project? The children had difficulty playing all together and building on the beginning of the story when they were asked to go into the role themselves. When they got a figure in their hand and another play frame, it was easier to play and to take different roles. Maybe it's easier to go into the role when the script/frame is finished? A consequence for us teachers would be trying to understand what type of play needs to be focused on right now in order to help the project/story go forward.

In these observations and reflections, the teachers bring up several interesting questions. It seems that they see the syncretic process in relation to play: the film project is born through various play sessions and through artistic creation of content. Another point that they raise concerns the role of an artifact representing a character, compared to the child's own acting. This imagined character may have a pivotal effect as a "preparatory stage" for children's artistic creation. Again, these are several starting points for further discussion. Our central point, here, is that we find support for Vygotsky's concept of syncretism in this example of young children's creative activity.

The Third Case: Play as the First Form of Creative Imagination

The third preschool project that we will discuss is a playworld project within the pedagogy of exploratory learning, here described as an exploratory learning project in which playworld is a tool used to access one (the first or hundred and first?) of the hundred languages: play. This project shows that play can be understood from within the field of education to be, as Vygtosky claimed and as we have discussed, a creative revision of impressions. This project highlights the creativity of play by focusing on conditions that are made possible by the fact that play is creative, and which are essential to the creation of the shared responsibility for directing the adult-child joint play that is at the heart of playworlds. Again: Adults in a playworld enter fully into children's play by taking on roles, putting on costumes and entering character. Children as well as adults co-construct the environment in which play takes place; and the play activity of playworlds is grounded in children's literature, i.e. texts that address dilemmas that are of great interest to many people in a variety of life stages.

When this project began it was up to each teacher team to decide on the content of their project. In one of the two and three year old classrooms at least one of the teachers was already particularly interested in play and already playing with the children. The "playworld researchers" had been invited to consult with the teachers during the previous spring semester, when the preschools were still outside of their play-themed year. At this time we encouraged the teachers to play with the children while the teachers were in role. In the spring we supported teacher-in-role play that was already happening in the classroom and discussed the teachers' commitment to not imposing a prewritten and adult-written story that might override the children's interests. This discussion helped us to negotiate differences between pedagogies/approaches and issues of trust between teachers and researchers.

The playworld began anew after the spring play and the summer break. One of the teachers decided that she would go into role in her play with the children. This teacher did not consider herself to be an expert player with the children and her play with the children in the spring and before the spring had predominantly resembled theater. But when she chose to go into role in this playworld she went into role 'for all she was worth,' fulfilling one of our three conditions for creating a playworld: adults enter fully into children's play by taking on play roles, putting on costumes and entering character.

This teacher chose to be a princess from a series of books, one of which was popular with the children. In this book a princess is not scared of a noise in the dark but gets out of bed with her sword to investigate and finds a basement troll, whom she eventual puts to sleep with the help of her newfound friends. The choice of literature fulfilled another of the conditions: the play of playworlds is grounded in works of children's literature that address dilemmas of great interest to people in a variety of life stages. Of course this is possible because children are capable of addressing these questions creatively.

Another teacher first read the book out loud to the class. The next week, the teacher mentioned above appeared outside the preschool window unexpectedly one morning as the princess. After she acted on her own for a while the children just as unexpectedly put on their boots on their own, ran out and joined her. The princess was wearing a wonderful costume, which included a golden crown. She had with her a large suitcase with a golden crown emblem on its side and she carried a sword.

The teacher reflected that the process was fun but that she did not have that playing experience/feeling where reality disappears:

I felt like I was playing and the kids were curious about what I was playing, but not as if it was a common play in which they participated fully. They participated but based on what I said and how I acted. More like a play in which they had to step into the scene and participate than a playworld where anything is possible and they can influence the play.

After several adjustments, including having another teacher on hand to take care of non-play issues and limiting the number of children with whom she was playing, and with the passage of time plus several events in which the children were shown, worked with and responded to documentation of their own play, something that looked more like the adult-child joint play of a playworld emerged.

The children painted and drew the princess and the basement troll in the atelier and built things for the play in the construction room. This activity enriched their play and shows how bodily experiences through play informed their work in other "languages." Several of the props and characters crossed the spaces in the room/"languages." Boots, water and keys were often represented and explored. The suitcase took on a life of its own as it became the "portal" of the playworld. We believe that this appreciation had to do with the princess's convincing and moving performance of sleeping under a blanket that she took from her suitcase in her first performance and in several subsequent performances. The children and the adults have spent a lot of time sleeping in suitcases in this playworld, magical sleeps that remind the researchers of Shakespeare's "A Midsummer Night's Dream."

This activity fulfilled a third of our three conditions: children and adults co-construct the environment in which play takes place. And, of course, this behavior was possible because neither the adults nor the children were passive or rote players. All playworld participants, children and adults, created the play itself by creating the space for the play. Further analysis, after the project is complete, should provide support for Vygotsky's understanding of play as an early but creative form of imagining.

There are two observations that are useful concerning the project, as it continues as we write. At one point the teachers felt that they needed fuel for the play and also that they needed to challenge the children. They interviewed the children about the characters that were present in their play. Their choice of action is in accord with the exploratory learning approach, although here it was used to build a playworld. The teachers asked the children individually such questions as: Where does the princess live?; and Where do the princess and the basement troll play? This initiative brought energy to the joint play and helped the teachers reflect on the children's play competences:

Ability to work/play many together. To hang in, playing for a long time and adding new ideas to hold their own and others interests. Found a way to get into play, for example, by bringing a dog, say you bleed, sleep or invite to a party. When the play may be developed, the children receive new experiences and thoughts that they take with them into the next play occasion. Likewise, the play influences the children's expressions in the atelier. Lessons from different occasions enrich each other. What we played we take with us into the atelier and then with new ideas and experiences go into the play again.

The teachers related the creative activity of adult-child joint play to exploratory learning. They quoted a text where rhizomatic learning is addressed and also discussed our initial claim of the research project, i.e. that something about the relationship between learning and play can be found in the meeting of exploratory learning and playworlds:

Skill and ability: "This can be understood as a non-linear way of thinking in which children's learning takes new paths and takes place inter-laced with the outside world, like a loop spirit rhizome." Skolverket (2012, p. 27) ...

Familiarity: The play has evolved but the children have had a shared attitude and the confidence that they had a common framework. To begin the play with everyone putting on boots, or picking up your suitcase, has created a code and community. We have become close to the children in a new way. We are invited, empowered and equal in play.

Fantasy: Truths/facts meets fantasy in play in an elated and liberating way.

Also, in the teachers' documentation we recognize the characteristic that Vygotsky points to in play, i.e. that meaning dominates over objects and actions:

When the play has ended and we are on our way into a new play or a different activity, one child takes command and starts a story time. He says: "Now you sit down and I'll tell you a story!" and then he brings the fairy bag with the fairytale about the three goats that one teacher told yesterday. He unfolds the green cloth that looks like grass and another fabric that looks like water. "This is water!" he says. Then he builds up a house of bricks for a troll.

"Now I'll make a pretend story," he says and starts to narrate: "Once upon a time there was a troll who would go out." The teacher asks, "What happened?"

The child answers, " It was somebody knocking," (He is knocking on the floor). "They hear with their ears! It's the cars," says the child. All are listening intently to his tale. Suddenly, he stops and moves away to get a maracas and starts to play and sing. "The others may also want to have an instrument to play with," says the teacher. The child then hands out instruments to all of his friends who are sitting and listening. He sings and everyone plays together his song." It thunders all day long! Koackakakoackaka."

CONCLUSION

The purpose of the chapter has been to shed light on educational activities guided by the idea of creativity. We have done this through thick descriptions of three preschool projects. We have related concepts that are significant in the conceptual framework that Vygotsky developed. We have discussed creativity and the creation of the "new."

In this chapter we have examined creativity using "project" (Blunden, 2010) as the unit of analysis. We have done so because the project is a preferred form in education for emphasizing children's creative problem solving, experimentation and exploration. Conducting a research project in the form of a formative intervention enabled us to investigate educational projects as part of the preschools' ongoing activity. Research questions were formed in collaboration with the teachers and they were based on their current projects.

The research project had as a broad purpose to understand what happens in an encounter between exploratory learning and playworlds. In the first project we learned that imagination is tightly connected to realistic thinking, and important in exploratory learning, where children develop hypotheses and theories in order to make sense of physical phenomena such as space, light, sound and time. In the second project we used the concept of syncretism to discuss children's creation of animated films and we stressed the crucial impact of interactions between play, playworld, aesthetic-semiotic means and exploratory learning, and development of various art forms. In the third project we focused on playworlds and children's creative imagining through play.

Relating these concepts to the preschool projects has been an exploratory enterprise. We have experienced a potential for these concepts to function as analytical tools. One overarching,

however still tentative, finding is that based on Vygotsky's thinking, we theorize that in play meaning dominates over object and action, while during exploration, at least initially, object dominates over meaning. However, play and exploration appear to be in a dialectical relationship, suggesting that exploration requires imagination in the form of hypotheses and theories, and play requires the material world and embodiment. This statement leads to the hypothesis that in exploration, meaning making is supported by play, and meaning making in play is supported by exploration. We consider play and exploration to be unique activities, yet learning processes are going on in both.

This piece of work has also taken us into dialogue with approaches to learning in which creative learning is described as "rhizomatic" and where children are understood as creative explorers and knowledge producers. These projects, guided in their creation by both CHAT and postmodern theories, and then understood and presented in this chapter from a CHAT understanding in dialogue with several postmodern theories, move CHAT towards developing a much-needed understanding of creativity within educational practices. It is in this way that we address the lacuna within CHAT within the field of education, which we pointed to at the start of the chapter: the fact that creativity does not hold a prominent place in second or even third generation cultural historical activity theory (CHAT) within the field of education. We believe that is it time for contemporary CHAT to emphasize creativity in education.

REFERENCES

Alnervik, K. (2013). *"Men så kan man ju också tänka!" Pedagogisk dokumentation som förändringverktyg i förskolan.* Retrieved from http://hj.diva-portal.org/smash/record.jsf?pid=diva2:659182

Barad, K. (2007). *Meeting the Universe Halfway: Quantum Physics and the Entanglement of Matter and Meaning.* Durham, NC: Duke University Press. doi:10.1215/9780822388128

Blunden, A. (2010). *'Collaborative Project' as a Concept for Interdisciplinary Human Science Research.* Retrieved July, 31, 2014, from https://www.academia.edu/2365533/Collaborative_Project_as_a_Concept_for_Interdisciplinary_Human_Science_Research

Connery, C., John-Steiner, V., & Marjanovic-Shane, A. (Eds.). (2010). Vygotsky and Creativity: A Cultural-Historical Approach to Play, Meaning-Making and the Arts. New York: Peter Lang.

Dahlberg, G., & Lenz Taguchi, H. (1994). *Förskola och skola: om två skilda traditioner och om visionen om en mötesplats.* Stockholm: HLS.

Dahlberg, G., Moss, P., & Pence, A. (2007). *Beyond quality in early childhood education and care: Postmodern perspectives.* London: Falmer Press.

Deleuze, G., & Guattari, F. (1987). *A thousand plateaus: Capitalism and schizophrenia.* London: Continuum.

Elfström, I. (2013). *Uppföljning och utvärdering för förändring: Pedagogisk dokumentation som grund för kontinuerlig verksamhetsutveckling och systematiskt kvalitetsarbete i förskolan.* (Unpublished doctoral thesis). Stockholm University, Stockholm, Sweden.

Engeström. (2007). *From community of practice to mycorrhizae.* Open University, Open CETL. Retrieved July, 31, 2014, from http://www.open.ac.uk/opencetl/resources/pbpl-resources/engestr%C3%B6m-y-2007-communities-practice-mycorrhizae

Engeström, Y. (1987). *Learning by expanding.* Helsinki: Orienta-Konsultit.

Engeström, Y. (2008). *The Future of Activity Theory.* Paper presented at the Second Congress of the International Society for Cultural and Activity Research. San Diego, CA.

Ferholt, B. (2009). *Adult and child development in adult-child joint play: The development of cognition, emotion, imagination and creativity in Playworlds.* (Unpublished doctoral thesis). University of California, San Diego, CA.

Ferholt, B., & Lecusay, R. (2010). Adult and child development in the zone of proximal development: Socratic dialogue in a Playworld. *Mind, Culture, and Activity, 17*(1), 59–83. doi:10.1080/10749030903342246

Fleer, M. (2011). Kindergartens in Cognitive Times: Imagination as a Dialectical Relation Between Play and Learning. *International Journal of Early Childhood Education, 43*(3), 245–259. doi:10.1007/s13158-011-0044-8

John-Steiner, V. (2000). *Creative collaboration.* New York: Oxford University Press.

Lentz Taguchi, H. (2009). *Varför pedagogisk dokumentation?* Stockholm: Stockholms universitets förlag. (Why pedagogical documentation?)

Lentz Taguchi, H. (2010). *Going Beyond the Theory/Practice Divide in Early Childhood Education: Introducing and intra-active pedagogy.* New York: Routledge.

Lindqvist, G. (1995). *The Aesthetics of Play. A Didactic Study of Play and Culture in Preschools. Acta Universitatis Upsaliensis.* Stockholm, Sweden: Almqvist & Wiksell International.

Lindqvist, G. (2001). When small children play: How adults dramatize and children create meaning. *Early Years, 21*(1), 7–14. doi:10.1080/09575140123593

Marjanovic-Shane, A., Ferholt, B., Nilsson, M., Rainio, A. P., & Miyazaki, K. (2011). Playworlds: An Art of development. In C. Lobman & B. O'Neill (Eds.), Play and Culture (pp. 3–32). Association for the Study of Play (TASP).

Olsson, L. M. (2009). *Movement and Experimentation in Young Children's Learning: Gilles Deleuze and Felix Guattari in Early Childhood Education*. London: Routledge.

Pramling Samuelsson, I., & Asplund Carlsson, M. (2003). Det lekande lärande barnet i en utvecklingspedagogisk teori. Stockholm: Liber.

Säljö, R. (2010). *Lärande i praktiken – ett sociokulturellt perspektiv*. Nordstedts.

Skolverket. (2010). Läroplan för förskolan Lpfö 98 Reviderad 2010. Stockholm: Fritzes.

Stetsenko, A. (2014). Transformative activist stance for education: The challenge of inventing the future in moving beyond the status quo. In T. Corcoran (Ed.), *Psychology in Education* (pp. 181–198). Boston: Sense Publishers. doi:10.1007/978-94-6209-566-3_12

Vallberg-Roth, A-C. (2014). *Nordisk komparativ analys av riktlinjer för kvalitet och innehåll i förskola*. .NA2013:92710.6027/NA2013-927

Vygotsky, L. S. (1971). *The Psychology of Art*. Cambridge, MA: M.I.T. Press.

Vygotsky, L. S. (1978). *Mind in society: the development of higher psychological processes*. Cambridge, MA: Harvard University Press.

Vygotsky, L. S. (1987). Imagination and its development in childhood. In R. W. Rieber & A. S. Carton (Eds.), *The collected works of L. S. Vygotsky* (Vol. 1, pp. 339–350). New York: Plenum Press.

Vygotsky, L. S. (2004). Imagination and Creativity in Childhood. *Journal of Russian & East European Psychology, 42*(1), 7–97.

ADDITIONAL READING

Elkonin, B. D. (2005). The psychology of play. *Journal of Russian & East European Psychology, 43*(1), 1–98.

Gadamer, H. (1975). *Truth and method*. New York: Seabury.

Hakkarainen, P. (1999). Play and Motivation. Y. Engeström, R. Miettinen & R.-L. Punamäki (Eds.), Perspectives on Activity Theory (pp. 231-249). New York: Cambridge University Press.

Hakkarainen, P. (2004). Narrative Learning in the Fifth Dimension. *Outlines: Critical Social Studies, 6*(1), 5–20.

Hakkarainen, P., Bredikyte, M., Jakkula, K., & Munter, H. (2013). Adult play guidance and children's play development in a narrative play-world. *European Early Childhood Education Research Journal, 21*(2), 213–225. doi:10.1080/135029 3X.2013.789189

Hakkarinen, P., & Bredikyte, M. (2008). The zone of proximal development in play and learning. *Cultural-historical Psychology, 4*(5), 2–11.

Lindqvist, G. (1989). Från fakta till fantasi. Lund: Studentlitteratur. (From Facts to Fantasy)

Lindqvist, G. (1992). Ensam i vida världen. Lund: Studentlitteratur. (Lonely in the wide world)

Lindqvist, G. (1996). Lekens möjligheter. Lund: Studentlitteratur. (The possibilities of play)

Lindqvist, G. (2000). Historia som tema och gestaltning. Lund: Studentlitteratur. (History as theme and gestalt)

Lindqvist, G. (2002). Lek i skolan. Lund: Studentlitteratur. (Play in school)

Nilsson, M. (2010). Creative Pedagogy of Play - The Work of Gunilla Lindqvist. *Mind, Culture, and Activity, 17*(1), 14–22. doi:10.1080/10749030903342238

Rainio, A. P. (2008a). From Resistance to Involvement: Examining Agency and Control in Playworld Activity. *Mind, Culture, and Activity*, *15*(2), 115–140. doi:10.1080/10749030801970494

Rainio, A. P. (2008b). Developing the Classroom as a Figured World. *Journal of Educational Change*, *9*(4), 357–364. doi:10.1007/s10833-008-9083-9

Rinaldi, C. (2004). *In dialogue with Reggio Emilia: listening, researching and learning*. London: Routledge Falmer.

Rodari, G. (1996). *The grammar of fantasy: An introduction to the art of inventing stories*. New York, NY: Teachers & Writers Collaborative.

KEY TERMS AND DEFINITIONS

Creativity: According to Vygotsky, the creative act is "(a)ny activity that gives rise to something new" (2004, p. 2). In "reproductive" activity "nothing new is created," but, instead, there is "a repetition of something that already exists" (2004, 2). In creative activity: "I never actually saw this remote past, or this future; however, I still have my own idea, image, or picture of what they were or will be like." (2004, p. 4) This basic distinction defines creativity because it allows one who is engaged in creative activity to produce something novel.

Exploratory Learning: Loris Malaguzzi was the motivator for the founding of the municipal preschools of Reggio Emilia, where the pedagogical ideas/concepts of exploratory learning and its accompanying pedagogy of listening were first developed. He considered the preschool to be a multicultural arena or a "town square," perceiving the preschool as a player in a democratic society. Exploratory learning and its accompanying pedagogy of listening are based in a perception of children as creative members of democracies,

and Malaguzzi explained that spoken and written "languages" are just two of the many ways that children express themselves and make sense of the world: The other 98 or 99 "languages" include, for example, dancing, drawing, singing, painting, sculpting, etc., i.e. aesthetical forms of different kinds. In Sweden, exploratory learning understands children to have and develop theories and hypotheses about the world that should be considered to be equally possible to those of adults (Lentz Taguchi, 2009).

Imagination: Vygotsky (1971, 1978, 1987, 2004) states that the processes of imagination and of realistic thinking develop as a unity and that there is no essential independence of the two. According to Vygotsky, imagination is not what in everyday life is referred to as "not true," but is the basis for all creative activity. Imagination is an essential aspect of all thought.

Playworld: The term "Playworld" was developed by Swedish scholar Gunilla Lindqvist (1995) to name the activity that is a central component of her "creative pedagogy of play." Playworlds consist of adults and children creating a common fantasy together through a combination of adult forms of creative imagining, which require extensive experience (art, science, etc.), and children's forms of creative imagining, which require embodiment of ideas in the material world (play) (Ferholt, 2009, 2010; Marjanovic-Shane et al., 2011). Lindqvist (1995) used playworlds to explore what she described as the common denominator of play and art, but playworlds have been adopted by scholars in Sweden, Serbia (the former Yugoslavia), Japan, Finland, Lithuania and the United States to study many topics, from narrative competencies to agency, and motivation to creativity (Marjanovic-Shane et al., 2011 for references to relevant studies). These scholars have been, like Lindqvist, inspired by Vygotsky's (1971, 1978, 1987, 2004) theories of both play and art, as well as by diverse theories and traditions of play and art creation (Marjanovic-Shane et al., 2011). There is currently a resurgence of interest in the playworld activity amongst Swedish preschools due to current international playworld research in Sweden.

Syncretic: Vygotsky (2004) argues that children's creative work in a variety of art forms is syncretic, that is, interrelated to each other in several ways. Firstly, individual types of art are not clearly separated or specialized. Secondly, Vygotsky also claims a broader syncretism where different modes of art are united in one single artistic endeavor. Thirdly, he sees this syncretism as an indication of the relationships of children's creative arts and play.

Chapter 17
Acculturation Processes and Expatriate Behavior

Laurie Watts
Blekinge Institute of Technology, Sweden

Beata Gullberg
Blekinge Institute of Technology, Sweden

ABSTRACT

Understanding the expatriate's acculturation process (i.e. a process of learning and acquiring workplace-related skills to successfully inhabit a foreign cultural realm) is essential in an increasingly international labour market. By using a mixed-methods approach, measuring Work Locus Of Control (WLOC), acculturation strategies, and socio-cultural adaptation by quantitative data, the authors pursue that ambition. They apply phenomenographic method and interpret the results using Cultural-Historical Activity Theory (CHAT). Results show that WLOC and choice of acculturation strategy affect the acculturation process. Expatriates view acculturation in terms of intertwined relationships. This study contributes to expanded knowledge on the acculturation process on the role of work in expatriate acculturation.

INTRODUCTION

Working abroad is a global trend (Toiviainen, 2014). Cross-border assignments have become frequent and so has research on what makes a successful expatriate. Acculturation of employees used to be an issue for international corporations, but today a mobile international workforce has a wide impact on e.g. academia. Employees initiate overseas employment by applying for jobs in foreign countries. Self-initiated expatriates appear to be more successful and satisfied with their international employment (Holopainen & Björk-

man, 2005; Selmer & Lauring, 2012). Expatriate assignments at an individual level cover some developmental career stages, providing access to travelling and adventure. At an organizational level expatriate assignments assist in knowledge transfer between jobs and companies and building a common corporate culture. Sending someone overseas for a job is expensive and premature repatriation makes the economic cost substantial. Despite the assumption that personality traits and individual attitudes toward other cultures is cogent with individual success, selection strategies between candidates are based on personal

DOI: 10.4018/978-1-4666-6603-0.ch017

recommendation or business-based evaluations (Abbott, Stening, Atkins, & Grant, 2006; Holopainen & Björkman, 2005). Personality traits are individually hosted values. They are psychological by nature and they affect people's learning processes, learning experiences and adaptation to and interactions with the environment (Cole & Wertsch, 1996; Rotter, 1966; Vygotsky, 1978). Research on personality traits and aptitude for expatriation revolves around the Big Five personality traits (Holopainen & Björkman, 2005; Taras, Rowney, & Steel, 2009). Lack of knowledge on traits outside the Big Five and their possible connection to successful expatriation, cause costly mistakes e.g. in the recruiting process (Flytzani & Nijkamp, 2008; Peltokorpi & Froese, 2014). Even though previous studies show that there seems to be a connection between locus of control and the ability to cope with cultural adjustment, this area needs thorough research (Yamazaki & Kayes, 2004). The outcome of the acculturation process has been more thoroughly researched than the effect of the subjective experience on the process. The scarcity of research becomes obvious in the field of locus of control. Research (Berry, 1997) indicates that the underlying and/ or obvious reasons to expatriate affect people's acculturation experience. There are several indirect connections to explore between job satisfaction and successful adaptation to a new culture (Peltokorpi & Froese, 2014; Reio & Sutton, 2006; Taras et al., 2009). Acculturation is the process of learning and acquiring the requisite skills to successfully inhabit a new cultural realm (Sam & Berry, 2010). There are influences, changes and outcomes experienced by an individual while interacting in a different cultural environment. The process affects the expatriate's preferences for the home culture and the host culture (Abbott et al., 2006). In this study acculturation is a synonym for sociocultural adaptation.

PROBLEM AND PURPOSE

When moving to a new country and encountering a new culture, expatriates go through a process of socialisation called acculturation. Some individuals harbour personality traits which enable for them to cope better than others with a change in their private and working life environment. But what exactly is the impact of those specific traits? There is a need to study the influence of Work locus of control (WLOC) related to individual acculturation strategies and sociocultural adaptation. There is another need to study the subjective experience of the acculturation process. In order to understand the acculturation process, we examine connections between successful acculturation, work locus of control, acculturation strategies and the working expatriates' experiences of the process.

Motivating the Study

We believe there will be correlation between acculturation strategy and individual WLOC. The integration group will have an internal WLOC while the assimilation group will have a central WLOC. (1) *Is there a connection between which acculturation attitude one has and their work locus of control?* We want to learn if acculturation strategy predicts personal behaviours when in contact with the host culture. It seems reasonable to assume that there should be correlation between acculturation strategy and sociocultural adaptation, and that 'Integrators' and 'Assimilators' will adapt easier than the 'Marginalisers' and 'Separationists'. (2) *Is there a connection between which acculturation strategy one has and their sociocultural adaptation?* We also want to examine if WLOC predicts personal behaviours when in contact with the host culture, and hypothesise a correlation between low (internal), central (neither internal nor external) WLOC and sociocultural adaptation.(3) Is there a connection between WLOC and sociocultural adaptation?

International experience (Holopainen & Björkman, 2005) shows positive effect and adjustment that wear off after the first couple of months. Berry (1997) and Selmer & Lauring, (2012) show that the original purpose of expatriating is a factor that affects adjustment in a foreign, dominant culture. (4) *Is there a connection between the demographics and acculturation attitude, work locus of control and sociocultural adaptation?* Taras et al. (2009) reached the conclusion that in researching culture, it is a good idea to include descriptions of experienced acculturation and adaptation. It is relevant to qualitatively explore the expatriate's perceived experience of the acculturation process and how WLOC and acculturation strategy colour the individual experience. (5) *How does the individual experience the acculturation process?*

THEORETICAL FRAMEWORK

From a cultural-historical perspective (Vygotsky, 1978) culture is a major factor in individual development. We all develop as individuals within a cultural context. Our experiences affect learning and development in all aspects. We acquire not just the content of our thinking, or what to think, but also our processes, or how to think it. Cole and Wertsch (1996, p. 252) frame the process as culture and cultural heritage that in fact "exists in the present to coordinate people with each other and the physical world". Once an individual is displaced from his home culture meeting with a different set of norms, values, and history, his cultural heritage is inappropriate or even in opposition with the current culture. When an individual interacts with the environment his actions are dependent on the sociocultural context. As the expatriate learns to negotiate this new environment, cultural mediation occurs and a process of socializing takes place (Cole & Wertsch, 1996; Vygotsky, 1978). The individual learns to understand and eventually take part in the cultural heritage connected to the new context. Vygotsky (1978) inspired a first

theory of activity and learning, Cultural-Historical Activity Theory (CHAT). Using activity as the smallest unit of analysis, he brought together the mediating tools, the subject and the object. Tools are physical or psychological items, the subject is an actor performing an activity, and object is the task at hand. This construct is often represented as a triangle diagram, with the mediating tools at one point and the subject and object at the others. Second generation activity theory added another layer to the triangle (Engeström & Kerosuo, 2007; Engeström, 1987) in order to provide a comprehensive relationship between the activity, plus the social and collective contextual factors which are an integral part of the activity – here defined as a systemic unit. These additional items are the rules and regulations that limit the activity, the community and division of labour. The rules and regulations node provides limiting factors while the community node recognizes the fact that few activities are performed by the individual in isolation from the context. Division of labour describes the stratification of the activity in relation to the overall object. Even more important than the nodes themselves is Engeström's (1987) emphasis on their interrelatedness between nodes and relations operating in/on any activity. Third generation activity theory (Engeström & Kerosuo, 2007; Engeström, 1987) recognizes that activities rarely occur in isolation. The theory is extended to include at least one other activity that is interacting with the first.

The sociocultural viewpoint has a clear focus of the social and contextual factors of learning, emphasizing how they affect the individual. The individual learns what is absolutely necessary to be able to manage the activity, such as in our case, the requisite skills to navigate a new culture (Säljö, 2001). While activity theory is an acknowledged theory for studying social and cultural aspects of learning, Marton (2000) argues that the theory neglects individual differences in social practices. Säljö(2001) rebukes the argument by saying that while activity theory does focus on the activity as a social learning process, the role of the individual depends on the circumstances. If individual differences were important to the activity, they should be studied accordingly. Since previous research suggests that individual differences play a role in acculturation, we will use Engeström's (1987) interpretation of the Vygotskian original to interpret the integrated results from our study. We will also keep in mind relations between activities from third generation activity theory (Engeström & Kerosuo, 2007). CHAT provides us a way to visualize and analyze the qualitative experience of the expatriates in the context of different activities undertaken during their individual acculturation processes.

Work Locus of Control

Spector (1988, p. 335) defines the personality trait locus of control as "a generalized expectancy that rewards, reinforcements or outcomes in life are controlled either by one's own actions (internality) or by other forces (externality)." An individual with an internal locus of control is prone to be proactive, to be open to taking actions s/he considers advantageous. S/he is likely to be open to learning about the new surrounding culture. Conversely someone with a central locus of control is likely to try to get along with everyone, and exhibit similar behaviours. Someone with an external locus of control may conclude that nothing they do matters anyway, and become passive observers. Rotter (1966) predicts four results for people with an internal locus of control (and the converse for those with an external locus of control). They are alert to aspects of the environment; they take steps to improve their environment; they value reinforcements that can be attributed to skill or behaviour; they are concerned with their ability; they are resistant to subtle attempts to influence their behaviour. Of these outcomes the first two seem to be the most relevant ones to our study. We also use specifically the work locus of control, a domain specific measure of the locus of

control personality trait, developed by Spector (1988) in response to the general nature of the original, i.e. Rotter's (1966) I-E scale of general locus of control. Spector et al., (2001) found that the work locus of control measure correlates with the general locus of control, but better predicts workplace behaviour.

Acculturation Strategy

Contemporary international mobility has made immigration more likely to occur at individual level than before. Current societies have backed away from assimilation as a goal, favouring inter- and multiculturalism or cultural plurality. Assimilation is now but one acculturation strategy of many. Berry's (1997) model of acculturation consists of a two-dimensional matrix divided into four groups that each represents a particular acculturation strategy to guide their behaviour. These groups are *Integration*, *Assimilation*, *Separation* and *Marginalization*. Individuals fall into groups depending on their attitude to the value of maintaining their distinct cultural identity and characteristics, and also their appreciation of the value of creating and maintaining relationships within the dominant culture (Berry & Sam, 1997). People classified as Integrators find positive value in both directions, while those who are less invested in their cultural identity but willing to invest in the dominant society are Assimilators. Separationists value keeping to their own culture and exclude the dominant culture. Marginalisers are unable to maintain their cultural identity and are excluded from the dominant society. Marginalization and Separation would rarely categorize voluntary expatriates, as the group is mostly associated with refugees and minority groups subject to exclusion or discrimination (Berry, 1974; Sam & Berry, 2010). Integration is often held to be a worthy ideal, but depending on the context, assimilation or separation can be viable strategies. For example if the expatriate sojourn is of limited duration and there is a strong expatriate community, a separatist strategy might work because there is little need to socialise or even interact with people in the local culture. Conversely, when the expatriate holds low expectations of returning home, assimilation may be a successful strategy (Berry, 1974, 1997). Berry's model, particularly as used by Ward and colleagues (Berry & Sam, 1997; Berry, 1997; Ward & Kennedy, 1999; Ward, 2008) focuses on sociocultural rather than psychological adaptation, making it directly relevant to our research, providing the convenient groupings for quantitative analysis and selecting participants for qualitative interviews.

METHODOLOGY

We chose a mixed method design (Niglas, 2009), because while it is supported that qualitative research on the acculturation process would add validity and a new perspective, most studies to date only use quantitative data out of convenience (Taras et al., 2009). We believe that this is neglecting the personal experience of the process, hence the mixed methods approach. While quantitative analysis is generalizable and organises individuals into comparable groups, phenomenography will help us see each individual's breadth of experience regarding the acculturation process (Dahlgren & Johansson, 2009). The study is a mixed method non-experimental design, with the aim of examining the relationship between work locus of control, acculturation strategies, sociocultural adaptation and the working expatriate's subjective experience of the acculturation process. The quantitative data was collected with the help of a survey, including items like "People who perform well on their jobs generally get rewarded". *SPSS* analysis provided statistical results, from which we created an interview guide, including questions like "What was your biggest surprise, the thing that made you most say 'wait, what?' when you started working here?" The qualitative data was collected from semi-structured interviews, and

analysed phenomenographically in *ATLAS.ti*. Lastly, the quantitative and the qualitative results were interpreted together with CHAT, combining the individual differences with the social context.

There are no standard paradigms yet for how to combine quantitative and qualitative methods, but mixed method research is becoming common. Our use of quantitative survey combined with interviews, while unconventional in the same study, is an acknowledged approach (Niglas, 2009). The interpretation using CHAT places the individual within the social context, where the individual differences are indeed relevant for the activity and should be studied accordingly (Säljö, 2001). During analysis we attempted to bear in mind that we were establishing second order categories of description rather than ways of experiencing (Marton, 1981, 2000; Säljö, 1997, 2001). Säljö argues that we can't know how the respondents experience a phenomenon, only what they say about it, and a feeling of obligation to answer or a wish to save face may affect answers. We attempted to respond to Säljö's objections by reducing the situational effects for our interviews.

Context of Investigation

Sixty-three expatriates, young and old, men and women participated in the study. The majority of respondents travelled alone rather than with their family. Most of them were self- initiated expatriates who either moved after finding a job on their own or moved first and then found a job. The typical respondent participant of the study is a 26 year old woman from the United States, carrying out her second overseas assignment on a job she found herself. She travelled there alone without a family, and she has spent a total of four years abroad, the last three of them at her current job in Spain. While participation in the study is anonymous, referral tracking on the survey link indicates that about half of the participants found the study through online postings, and the remainder of the participants found it by word

Figure 1. Mixed methods design

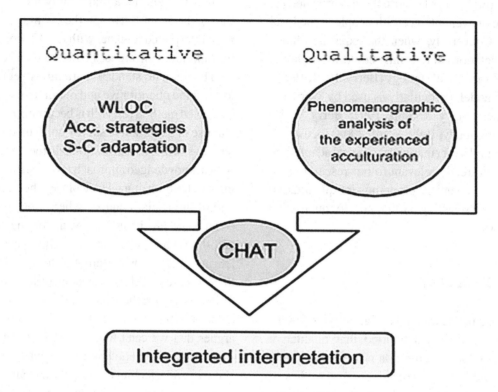

of mouth. All participants were informed of the general subject of our study. We also guaranteed anonymity. Two weeks after posting the survey on web forums we closed the data collecting process. Based on the result of the quantitative analysis we chose respondents for further study. We adjusted the interview guide based on cumulative results because we wanted to explore and learn about the factors mentioned by earlier participants. The qualitative data consists of transcriptions from five semi-structured interviews. We recorded the interviews via webcam on *Skype*. One researcher acted as interviewer and the other researcher acted as observer. At the end of each session the main interviewer invited the observer into the conversation to ask follow-up questions. The interviews were transcribed afterwards, and the transcriptions were used for analysis.

Context of Justification

There is a *first sequence* for analysing quantitative data. The WLOC subscale provides a single score, in the range of 8 to 48, with lower scores being internal WLOC and higher being external WLOC. Berry's acculturation strategy model provides one of four discrete results. The SCAS subscale provides a mean score overall, which we refer to as SCAS 22, and a sub-score for the standard adjustment questions that are commonly used in all applications of the SCAS measure, which we refer to as SCAS 10. In both cases, a higher score on a scale of 1-5 indicates that adjustment was easier. The subscales were analysed for internal reliability with Cronbach's alpha. Scores on the WLOC and Berry's model were analysed for correlations. Scores on the WLOC and Berry's model were further analysed together with the SCAS scores using two-way between-subjects ANOVA or MANOVA, with Tukey's HSD post-hoc tests if applicable. The final survey question asks if they are willing to participate in follow-up interviews, and to provide a point of contact if so. Initial analysis grouped the survey respondents into up to four groups on the basis of Berry's model. From each group, we aimed to find a couple of participants for a follow-up interview, however our data was heavily weighted towards integrators and assimilators, so we interviewed three assimilators and two integrators. There is a *second sequence* for analysing qualitative data. We used phenomenography to analyse our interview transcripts with the purpose of discovering and organizing the different opinions, perspectives, and experiences the participants have about the acculturation process (Cohen, Manion, & Morrison, 2011; Dahlgren & Johansson, 2009). The breadth of differences in these perspectives is the outcome space of the phenomenon, and the different categories that arise from this outcome space is the result of the analysis. Studying the understanding and experience of a phenomenon, and not directly the phenomenon itself, provides a second order analysis. With phenomenography, we strive to describe the meaning of the phenomenon "acculturation process", and this meaning can change over time due to learning processes that provoke a change of understanding in the individual (Dahlgren & Johansson, 2009; Larsson, 2010). For our study that means that the individual will experience the acculturation process differently the more she acculturates. We applied a software called ATLAS.ti to analyse the interviews separately. Then we compared and merged the results, to be able to take advantage of being two researchers while analysing (Dahlgren & Johansson, 2009). First we analysed and compared the results of the two first interviews. After merging our results, we repeated the first step with the third and fourth interview, and after merging our results again, we analysed the fifth interview. During this process, we recoded the material several times, exchanging code lists, discussing possible meanings of quotes, while we

became familiar with the data. A number of possible category schemes were discarded due to lack of differences and big overlaps, until we realized that the "why" was the key; the perceived reason for doing something seemed to give us different groups with few overlaps, which made us look at the data in a new way, with a new understanding. The fourth and last step was to re-code all of the interviews with these categories, to test their inter-category differences and to define the subcategories by merging closely related codes under each category from our final code list.

SURVEY RESULTS

We hypothesized correlation between acculturation strategy and WLOC. We also hypothesized that integrators would have an internal WLOC and that assimilators would have a central WLOC. Results show that the sample is heavily skewed towards internal and central WLOC. We found a significant difference in WLOC scores with Assimilators having a higher score than Integrators. However, the difference was too small for one to predict the other, so this hypothesis is marginally supported.

We expected to find a correlation between WLOC and sociocultural adaptation, specifically that internal and central WLOC would correlate with SCAS. We found that although both groups scored quite highly on the SCAS 22, indicating fairly easy adaptation, the internal WLOC group had a significantly easier time adapting to the new culture than had the central WLOC group. However they show marginal correlations between all the WLOC scores and SCAS scores. We find this hypothesis partially supported: Although the groups were different, the correlations of the scores were far from significant. There were large variances in the individual answers to specific questions. Due to this fact we carried out additional tests.

Finally we explored connections between demographics and acculturation strategy, WLOC and sociocultural adaptation. Although we tested every demographic variable in our data, we found only one significant, relevant and non-ambiguous result, albeit an interesting one: The central WLOC group had an easy time adjusting to the foreign culture when travelling with their family. The internal WLOC group had an easy time travelling alone. Overall results suggest there are weak relationships between the demographic variables and the WLOC, acculturation strategy and the ease of sociocultural adaptation.

Additional survey results suggest there are distinct differences in the respondents' answers to individual questions, so we did additional tests against the questions themselves. One way MANOVA results between acculturation strategy and the SCAS scores show that the *marginalisation* group differed significantly from the other two groups in the sample. Our choice of theory and formulation of our hypotheses predicted this result. Additional results show that the *assimilation* group had by a significant margin the easiest time dealing with unsatisfactory service, adapting to local etiquette and dealing with people of higher status. The *integration* group had a significantly more difficult time dealing with these same items. The *assimilation* group also did much better on accepting and understanding the local political system. The *marginalisation* group found most items difficult to deal with, but significantly so items dealing with going to food outlets and interacting with authority. Then we used independent t-tests in order to analyse internal vs. central WLOC groups, looking for differences on individual SCAS questions. We found that individuals with an internal WLOC scored significantly higher, i.e. found it easier, dealing with several of the items on the SCAS scale; going shopping, dealing with people in authority, understanding the local's worldview and going to coffee shops and other food outlets.

INTERVIEW RESULTS

Our final hypothesis and corresponding research question focused on individual experiences of the acculturation process. We explored the research question by gathering interview data and interpreting the data by phenomenographic method assisted by a software packet called *ATLAS.ti*. Analysis shows that respondents express their experiences of acculturation in terms of distinct relationships between themselves and work, culture as a concept, people outside of work, and self-identity. These categories are conceptually different and mutually exclusive but connected as influences on the acculturation process, and each has several *subcategories*, italicised in the text.

Relationship to Work

The expatriates expressed that their workplaces reflect both the host culture and the *universal structure* of an office. This combination brings familiarity, stability, and support to the expatriates, allowing them to adjust more easily in the workplace than outside it. The workplace also actively facilitated the process by providing *support* in the initial phase.

At work, I still am a little crazy, and I haven't forgotten my [native] work ethic [...] I still feel like I should demand a certain amount of professionalism, that sometimes I don't get from people, but I mean, I still expect it and will demand it. There's an office culture and office mentality [...] the rules and the regulations of an office that means that everyone is more or less taught certain types of behaviours [...]. It makes it easier to adjust to.

There is a tendency for the expatriates to *identify more with the home culture* at work, holding on to their native ideas and values much longer than they did outside of work. The smooth adaptation mentioned above could reflect less need to adapt in the universal office environment than the local culture outside work. This results in cultural clashes when they meet local cultural norms in the workplace.

It's a real etiquette clash for me with meetings. For example my boss tend to arrive very late to meetings, then allow them to run very late, or allow them to run over lunch, which for me... I have to remind myself that he doesn't mean to be rude.

When the expatriates adjust to the culture, the *facilitating means* for doing so relates to *food* rather than to actual work. For example, one expatriate mentions a change from having lunch at her desk, to actually socializing with colleagues during the lunch hour. The self-initiated expatriates also mention that they see their *foreignness as a resource* and work as *a means to an end* to stay in the country of their choice.

Relationship to Culture as an Everyday Concept

Respondents express their opinions about culture as a concept, distinct from social relationships. They see culture as something to be learnt, understood and that takes *effort*, but *adaptation as something that just happens over time*, without connecting the two. *Language, food* and *relationships with the locals* are repeatedly mentioned as tools to gain insight into the culture. The expatriates are aware of the importance of learning the new culture. They are aware of the danger of isolating themselves from the host culture if they socialize with expatriates alone.

When I first got here I made a pretty conscious decision to live with [local] people, that was mostly for language purposes so that I could learn quicker, but also for culture, so that I could understand you know, what they cook, and how they cook it, and when they cook. You know, those types of things, like everyday stuff that might seem unimportant,

but it actually is something different from life in [native country].

Language barriers pose a major hindrance. Most of the respondents say language issues are more difficult than expected. They explain how frustrating inability to communicate properly can be. Another hindrance is *everyday things* that seem similar enough on the surface, like grocery shopping and going to the gym. They describe how small cultural variances clash with the expatriates' expectations on how to go about everyday life.

I'm not in my, how do you say, my comfort zone. You are completely out. In the beginning I was thinking 'Ok, this is easy, that is easy', but I was learning a lot of things, and somehow I was feeling overwhelmed after a month or something [...] Even going to the gym, or going to the swimming pool, you have to learn all that.

These differences were absent in respondents with *previous experience* from expatriation. More bureaucratic *systemic differences*, such as paying a visit to the tax office, were consistent source of frustration and difficulty for most respondents.

Relationship to People Outside of Work

The respondents express the importance of maintaining social relationships outside of work. They know that *making friends takes active effort*, and regardless if this comes naturally for the expatriates, they consciously work to meet and connect with new people. Communicative *language* competence is important for making *local friends* outside of work. Many respondents use social gatherings outside established social networks, such as sport clubs, language exchanges and other social events. They stress the importance of being open to invitations from acquaintances.

I don't just go out with all my western friends, I go, I made friends with local residents and I go out and spend time with them, I go eat their food, I go eat with them, uhm, so I make the effort to sort of say "yes" to everything. [...] once you make the mental shift to be able to do it, it's, it's fine.

Relationships with other expatriates are both easy and common, but the reasons vary. For instance, it can be because of common language, because they are most easily accessed in the case of foreigner-dense neighbourhoods, and sometimes because the shared experience of expatriation provides a bond.

If you also have expat friends who are in a similar situation with the same interest, who are also driven to integrate, I feel like you can open up that door and you can all integrate together.

They observe that socialising exclusively with other expatriates hinders adaptation, and those who avoid adapting in this manner, are unhappy with their expatriate experience.

Relationship to Self-Identity

Being an expatriate has an effect on the respondents' view of themselves, and there is a strong time-based component which many of the respondents are well aware of and able to articulate. Culture shock during the initial phase comes unexpectedly and the expatriates are let down by their idealized expectations. For instance, they harbour an illusion that everything will be easy, or they think they are proficient in the foreign language. Consequently they find reality a frustrating surprise.

I remember the very beginning, the first sort of, maybe two-three months, I found it quite hard to adjust. That was actually quite a surprise as well, I hadn't ... For some reason I hadn't foreseen that I'd have any kind of culture shock.

Over time the *host culture feels like home*, becoming the new normal, and respondents experience that the *home culture seems foreign* when they return home. Sometimes in the case of serial expatriates, this leads to homesickness for the last country they were accustomed to rather than their home country.

If I go back to [hometown] for Christmas or something, I find myself not in agreement with the way of life there.

There is a clear expression of *flipping a switch*; once a commitment to stay in the new country is made, a distinct decision to increase effort towards acculturation occurs. This is expressed in various ways, from an increased interest in politics, in learning the language or being open to finding a local partner.

I felt like I kind of had to choose to stay here and embrace [...] life here, and embrace the culture here, or whether to just [...] go home, as it was then, back to the [native country], and treat this as if it were, you know, a fun interlude, and get back to you know, my real life.

Once the respondents begin to feel like a native, they noticed how the *language affected identity* in some ways. A direct language may lead to a more direct way of expressing oneself even when switching back to the native language. They also expressed awareness that how they see themselves (native) is not always how others see you (foreigner).

I forget sometimes that I'm foreign here. I mean, other people don't forget that, because I don't look [host nationality] and I don't sound [host nationality].

The expatriates mentioned several ways that the experience of being an expatriate lead to *personal growth*, becoming more open and tolerant.

While building tolerance for accepting different cultures might be expected, this expanded tolerance extends to accepting that life has taken an unexpected turn, for instance that this is not the career they planned.

INTERPRETING QUANTITATIVE DATA

At first glance, the difference between the acculturation strategies of integration or assimilation is small. WLOC means differ between them by less than one point. However, assimilators score higher on sociocultural adaptation than integrators, and so did expatriates with internal WLOC compared to central WLOC. The differences in sociocultural adaptation scores for WLOC and acculturation strategy are on different SCAS items. This suggests that the combination of an assimilator with an internal WLOC would score better on all those items, adapting more easily than any other combination. From a company perspective of hiring staff, different profiles might suit different situations. The assimilator who voluntarily downplays her home culture in order to embrace the foreign culture, might be the best expatriate if the purpose is to bring someone to your company from another country to stay there permanently (Berry, 1997). However, if you want to send an employee on an overseas assignment, and after a year send them on to another country or bring them home, the assimilator might have difficulties repatriating. In this case integrators might be suitable candidates, they do not merge as wholeheartedly into a new culture as assimilators. The fact that marginalisers and separationists are underrepresented in our sample suggests that expatriates are generally integrators or assimilators. Also between Assimilators and Integrators our sample was heavily skewed towards Integrators and low WLOC, suggesting that this is the most common profile for successful self-initiated expatriates. This conclusion is in line with what the theory predicts (Rotter, 1966). The lack of

significant results on demographic variables can be interpreted a result in itself. WLOC and acculturation strategies appear to be highly individual and only weakly affected by demographics. The one significant result we did find was the interaction effect of WLOC and whether the expatriate moved to the country alone or with a family. This might be because the individual with internal WLOC believes outcomes, in this case of the acculturation process, are decided by her own actions (Spector, 1988), thus the influence of a family might limit the individual's ease of acculturation. Meanwhile someone with central WLOC might embrace the fact that there are several people partaking in this process.

INTERPRETING QUALITATIVE DATA

The categories we discovered by means of phenomenographic method each represent the main characteristics of a unique activity. The expatriates described their experience of the acculturation process through relationships to and interactions with work, to the culture, to people outside of work and their identity. We performed our interpretation from a second generation activity theory standpoint, because focus of research is on individual experiences and reported perceptions of those experiences. We did so bearing in mind the third generation viewpoint that activities are rarely performed in isolation (Engeström & Kerosuo, 2007; Engeström, 1987). While the activity delimits a social context, individual differences affect how the subject chooses to act within that context, given the tools and rules at hand (Marton, 2000).

Table 1 shows that each main category is an activity with the expatriate acting as subject exposed to influences of tools, rules, community, division of labour and most importantly objects/objectives. The objects constitute the objective of the activity and define qualitative differences between the categories.

Table 1. The CHAT activity object for each of the four phenomenographical categories

Category	Object of the Activity
Work	Fulfill work obligations
Culture	Act according to the local culture
People outside of Work	Social integration
Identity	Evaluate ones place in the world

Workplace Activity

Focus of the study is on acculturation process at the workplace. Results show that there are three main differences in workplace acculturation processes. Outside of work there are other processes going on. Firstly a familiar and universal office environment at work makes adjustment seem easy. Secondly the expatriate tends to hold on to native values and ideas to a greater extent at work, and thirdly they do so for a longer time compared to outside of work. Regarding the first process, the universal structure of the workplace is a part of the rules, i.e. formal and informal limiting factors (Engeström & Kerosuo, 2007; Engeström, 1987). Since workplace (often office) structures are familiar to the expatriates, their acting and adjustment as the subject in the activity poses a comparative mild challenge. During the second process, expatriate actors use the mediating tools they consider to be the most efficient ones to complete the objective. According to the results of this study they seem to consist of familiar home-culture tools. However, in many cases the hosting country and home culture tools together are reasonably similar. An effect of the similarity between tools is that our approach cloaks minor differences and highlight major differences. An example of this phenomenon is an expatriate complaining about long, late and delayed hours in tedious meetings - a different approach to time punctuality, duration and priority. Finally the masking effect of the familiar office structure and the fact that equally familiar home-culture tools produces accept-

able results also delays the expatriates' adoption of local mediating tools at the workplace. The community and the social context consist of colleagues and managers. Their support during the initial phase of the expatriation process is a tool for the expatriate to feel integrated. Division of labor reflects the expatriates' role in the overall workplace activity (Engeström & Kerosuo, 2007; Engeström, 1987). This is a role that most expatriates experience as important, possibly because they brought international expertise and language skills to the company. Apart from this purely work focussed activity, we found a cultural aspect to the workplace; food and language were the main tools to integrate socially. Further integration in the workplace increased the satisfaction at work and generally in life. Aside from performing well at work, a desirable outcome for the expatriates was that they could stay on and continue working in the country of their choice. The job environment becomes a tool for working abroad.

Language and Food Related Activities

Work is easier to adjust to culturally, however when the interviewees were able to come up with specific work-related incidents where they felt pressure from colleagues, the triggers were cultural rituals rather than work-task related. Food in particular is a major tool for socializing newcomers into the national and local culture of the workplace. When, what, where and with whom you eat is expressed in terms of culture rather than in terms of work. Most of the interviewees say they understand the importance of food and the surrounding rituals. Food is a means for fitting in with the community, and they must go to pains to learn about it. The role of these cultural rituals changes, all depending on the object of the activity. When learning about the culture the expatriates realize that although food and language are nominally included in that object, they can also be mediating tools. Language informs when learning about food, and rituals related to food help understand culture. The expatriates' lack of fluent language is a constraining rule, limiting the expatriate's informal learning process. Language constraints as rules and regulations become salient when expatriates socialize outside of work. Several participants mention lack of communicative competence as a show-stopper when they are making friends with the locals. Food is also a regulation in this activity. What, but most importantly when and how people eat becomes a separating factor between expatriates and locals, limiting the social interaction. In relationship to identity, language becomes a tool for personal change. Several of the interviewees mention how the culture and tone of the new language changed them, for instance making them more direct in their approach to others. They experienced this change to be salient, deep and far-reaching even when they switched back to their native tongue.

Change in Activities and Support of Activities

Even though the activities, and so the categories, are qualitatively distinct, they still interact in a social context, according to the third generation of activity theory (Engeström & Kerosuo, 2007; Engeström, 1987). The most prominent example we found is how learning about culture as a concept can become a mediating tool for the relationships with people outside of work, and vice versa. When discussing learning about culture as the object of the activity, the interviewees mention getting to know people as a mediating tool. They might live with the locals in order to learn about their eating habits. Similarly, when talking about getting to know people and make friends as the object of the activity, they mention that they use learning about the culture as the mediating factor, such as when they join a language exchange in order to meet people. These similar objects are tightly intermingled, but perceptually the respondents

see them as two different goals. Social relationships also belong to the community point of the activity triangle for both activities. Relationships between activities suggest that all four activities are important for successful acculturation. To be able to work in a host environment with a minimal number of clashes, and to interact with local clients, one needs to learn about culture as a concept. In order to be able to do so successfully, social relationships with people outside of work is an important tool.

INTEGRATED INTERPRETATION

The traits of WLOC and which acculturation strategy the subject uses affect the activity as a whole. We mentioned earlier that assimilators and people with internal WLOC adapted more easily than others, which suggests that their activity is slightly more efficient than other profiles', and that these traits have an effect on the other variables as well. In the interviews, we saw this expressed in the way they discussed their own place in the division of labour in the organisation. Several expressed that they got the job by virtue of speaking another language, or having particular experience that locals could not provide. They saw neither foreignness nor newness as a hurdle, and instead an advantage, by providing a different insight. They saw themselves as valuable members of the organisation right from the beginning. This expressed sense of self-efficacy combined with the feeling that work provides structure and security, might be a further explanation of the feeling of swift adjustment at work. Individuals with an internal WLOC tend to be instinctively proactive, while those with a more central WLOC are also proactive but on a more conscious level (Rotter, 1966; Spector, 1988). Our results show that all our interviewees use proactivity and active effort as a tool in learning about the culture they are surrounded by. However they see the outcome of the activity, that is actually adjusting to the culture, as a natural process that happens over time, quite disconnected from their own engagement in the activity. In fact, the longer the respondent had been an expatriate, the more they expressed how things came naturally. Despite the fact that adjustment and adaptation require learning, expatriates do not see it that way and distinguish the two as separate processes.

Assimilators and integrators differ in their degree of commitment to the new culture, with assimilators making the leap more wholeheartedly, more or less as predicted in Berry (1997). Adapting to local etiquette and accepting or understanding the local political system were two of the items from SCAS 22 that came significantly easier to assimilators than integrators. These two items were explicitly mentioned in the context of "flipping the switch", the decision to make an increased effort towards acculturation, showing a clear agreement between the quantitative data and the subjective experience. This change in attitude is essentially a change in the identity activity, whose object is to evaluate one's place in the world. The rules, more specifically the informal restrictions the individual creates herself, may change when further acculturated, allowing the individual to evaluate her place in the world more freely, not automatically referring back to her native roots. Individuals with different WLOC scores adapt differently depending on their family status at the time of expatriation. This finding introduces the possibility of analysing how the family affect the activity as depending on the subject. While the family will always be part of the community of the activity, the family might be an additional tool for the subject with central WLOC, and instead a restricting rule for the subject with internal WLOC. From a central WLOC perspective, being single could mean that you have one less tool at your disposal than when you have a family. From an internal WLOC perspective being single might mean fewer factors to have to account for than when you have family.

DISCUSSING THE RESULT

Previous research assumes that successful acculturation leads to a successful expatriate employee experiences (Holopainen & Björkman, 2005; Peltokorpi & Froese, 2014). Failure to acculturate newly arrived members of staff leads to emotional and economic loss for all parties (Selmer & Lauring, 2012). Some informants illustrate a failure to adapt to the new culture and unhappiness about the total experience. Other informants experience minor problems on the way and adapt well. Internal or central locus of control supposedly leads to a smooth adaptation process. So do acculturation strategies of assimilation and integration (Berry, 1997; Flytzani & Nijkamp, 2008; Rotter, 1966; Spector, 1988). Bearing in mind the studied sample consists of successful expatriates, the strong skew in our results towards these properties agrees with previous research. Berry (1997) and Selmer and Lauring (2012) suggest that reason of expatriation is a relevant phenomenon to study. The respondents of this study consistently describe their decision to expatriate in positive terms. They think of it as a decision to move *to* a welcoming new country, rather than *away from* their home culture. Time spent in the host country normally shows an upward curve on SCAS results (Ward & Kennedy, 1999). For this study, the qualitative interviews verified SCAS results. Holopainen and Björkman (2005) mention a honeymoon period of a month or two, and then a culture shock phase sets in, as seen in our interview results. Demographic factors have been found to predict expatriate success, for instance when expatriates marry and bring the family along (Abbott et al., 2006). Our results did not bear on demographic predictions. We suspect this is due to the authors' predominant focus on corporate assignees. Our sample of informants predominantly consists of self-initiated expatriates. Ward and Kennedy (1999) and Holopainen and Björkman (2005) suggest differences relate to the country of origin and cultural fit between home and host cultures. We suggest that globalization, multicultural employment practices and international mobility create a global office culture with a distinct and universal nature of its own, mediating the difference between home and host cultures.

Adaptation at work comes first. With the familiar structure and support of colleagues, integration is considerably easier to accomplish than outside of work. However, since acculturation activities are closely intertwined, the company must support newly arrived expatriates in their adjustment outside of work as well. During acculturation processes food and language play an important and varying role. Joining sport teams and other pre-organised groups was also mentioned to facilitate socialisation in our interviews. Expatriates should accept offers of social interaction. Proactive and conscious expatriate efforts influence the result of this study significantly. Expatriates who describe the acculturation process as natural and easy, also say they made conscious efforts to meet with people, to be involved with others and to learn. The difference between the effort they put in to socializing behaviour and the outcome explains why previous research failed to see socializing as a factor. Put differently, successful integration of expatriates requires a self-initiating and proactive nature in the subject. We relate this to WLOC because internal locus of control highlights pro-activity. Our sample of informants consists of predominantly successful self-initiated expatriates. They lean strongly towards internally controlled behaviour on the WLOC scale.

The mixed-methods research design proved to be valuable. By conducting interviews we gained qualitative data that shed light on the survey results. Surveys generating quantitative data tend to capture spontaneous responses. This became obvious for us once we saw the qualitative data that came out of the interviews. In several cases, the interviewees answered questions one way. Then, when invited to explore their experience, they spoke about the same experiences in opposite terms (Hansson 2014). For instance, a response express-

ing that acculturation is easy, was followed by a list of reasons why it is difficult. The expatriates were unaware of the ambiguity until we brought it up during interviews. The complementary data from both sources affirms the utility and potential of mixed methods in studying culture.

SUGGESTION FOR FURTHER RESEARCH

Future research could investigate the acculturation process from a community of practice perspective. Just like CHAT, Lave and Wenger's (1991) work is grounded in sociocultural theory. However in CHAT the community aspect is a part of the activity system that forms the unit of analysis. From a community of practice point of view, performing the activity is itself part of the process of socialisation into the existing community. Further research should study the effect of company arrangements related to food themes and language events as a means for supporting expatriates socializing processes in and outside of work. Another way of expanding the body of research on expatriate acculturation is to focus on self-initiated rather than corporate assigned expatriates. Relevant research could investigate a spectrum of expatriates, e.g. those who struggle in a new country, and learn how their acculturation processes differ from successful expatriates'. The interaction effect found on WLOC and family status is another thing for further investigation. Finally, it is worth researching change over time on expatriates' experiences of acculturation.

CONCLUSION

We found different profiles of expatriates adjust easier to some assignments than others. This could be used as a candidate screening strategy to help reduce costly expatriation failures, such as early repatriation. We also found that the self-initiated expatriates have a more proactive profile than the corporate assignees from previous research. Expatriates experience of their workplace as the easiest place for adjustment, with a universal office culture providing a bridge between the native culture and the host culture. However, failing to acculturate outside of work, resulted in an overall unhappy expatriate experience. Food, language and activities are tools for the next step of adjustment, as mediators to learn about the culture outside of work and to socialize. Food and language therefore are ready-made tools that the workplace can use to ease acculturation through language education, food events or sport events for coworker-gatherings. By using a mixed methods approach, we got both the individual traits of WLOC and acculturation strategy, and the spectrum of perceived experiences of the individuals. CHAT and phenomenography are traditionally considered to be strange bedfellows, but we found them complementary when studying the individual's adjustment to culture. CHAT made it possible to view the entire outcome space of perceived experience and individual traits in a social context.

REFERENCES

Abbott, G. N., Stening, B. W., Atkins, P. W. B., & Grant, A. M. (2006). Coaching expatriate managers for success: Adding value beyond training and mentoring. *Asia Pacific Journal of Human Resources, 44*(3), 295–317. doi:10.1177/1038411106069413

Berry, J. W. (1974). Psychological Aspects of Cultural Pluralism: Unity and Identity Reconsidered. *Topics in Culture Learning, 2*(6), 17–22. Retrieved from http://files.eric.ed.gov/fulltext/ED100159.pdf

Berry, J. W. (1997). Immigration, Acculturation, and Adaptation. *Applied Psychology, 46*(1), 5–34. doi:10.1080/026999497378467

Berry, J. W., & Sam, D. L. (1997). Acculturation and Adaptation. In J. W. Berry, Y. H. Poortinga, & J. Pandey (Eds.), Handbook of Cross-Cultural Psychology. Academic Press.

Cohen, L., Manion, L., & Morrison, K. (2011). *Research methods in education* (7th ed.). London: RoutledgeFalmer.

Cole, M., & Wertsch, J. V. (1996). Beyond the individual-social antinomy in discussions of Piaget and Vygotsky. *Human Development, 39*(5), 250–256. doi:10.1159/000278475

Dahlgren, L. O., & Johansson, K. (2009). Fenomenografi. In A. Fejes & R. Thornberg (Eds.), Handbok i kvalitativ analys. Stockholm: Liber.

Engeström, Y. (1987). *Learning by Expanding*. Helsinki: Orienta-Konsultit Oy. Retrieved from http://lchc.ucsd.edu/MCA/Paper/Engestrom/expanding/

Engeström, Y., & Kerosuo, H. (2007). From workplace learning to inter-organizational learning and back: The contribution of activity theory. *Journal of Workplace Learning, 19*(6), 336–342. doi:10.1108/13665620710777084

Flytzani, S., & Nijkamp, P. (2008). Locus of control and cross-cultural adjustment of expatriate managers. *International Journal of Foresight and Innovation Policy, 4*(1/2), 146. doi:10.1504/IJFIP.2008.016911

Hansson, T. (2014). Modeling and analyzing contextual influences. In T. Hansson (Ed.), Contemporary Approaches to Activity Theory: Interdisciplinary Perspectives on Human Behavior. Hershey, PA: IGI Global.

Holopainen, J., & Björkman, I. (2005). The personal characteristics of the successful expatriate: A critical review of the literature and an empirical investigation. *Personnel Review, 34*(1), 37–50. doi:10.1108/00483480510578476

Johansson, K. (2014). Collaborative music making and artistic agency. In T. Hansson (Ed.), Contemporary Approaches to Activity Theory: Interdisciplinary Perspectives on Human Behavior. Hershey, PA: IGI Global.

Larsson, S. (2010). *Kvalitativ analys.* Lund: Studentlitteratur.

Lave, J., & Wenger, E. (1991). *Situated learning: Legitimate peripheral participation.* Cambridge University Press. doi:10.1017/CBO9780511815355

Linge, A. (2014). Creative musical practice in an educational context. In T. Hansson (Ed.), Contemporary Approaches to Activity Theory: Interdisciplinary Perspectives on Human Behavior. Hershey, PA: IGI Global.

Marton, F. (2000). The Practice of learning. *Nordisk Pedagogik, 20*(4), 230–236.

Niglas, K. (2009). How the novice researcher can make sense of mixed methods designs. *International Journal of Multiple Research Approaches, 3*(1), 34–46. doi:10.5172/mra.455.3.1.34

Peltokorpi, V., & Froese, F. (2014). Expatriate personality and cultural fit: The moderating role of host country context on job satisfaction. *International Business Review, 23*(1), 293–302. doi:10.1016/j.ibusrev.2013.05.004

Reio, T. G., & Sutton, F. C. (2006). Employer assessment of work-related competencies and workplace adaptation. *Human Resource Development Quarterly, 17*(3). doi:10.1002/hrdq

Rotter, J. B. (1966). Generalized expectancies for internal versus external control of reinforcement. *Psychological Monographs, 80*(1), 1–28. doi:10.1037/h0092976 PMID:5340840

Säljö, R. (2001). The individual in social practices. *Nordisk Pedagogik, 1*(21), 108–116.

Sam, D. L., & Berry, J. W. (2010). Acculturation: When Individuals and Groups of Different Cultural Backgrounds Meet. *Perspectives on Psychological Science, 5*(4), 472–481. doi:10.1177/1745691610373075

Selmer, J., & Lauring, J. (2012). Reasons to expatriate and work outcomes of self-initiated expatriates. *Personnel Review, 41*(5), 665–684. doi:10.1108/00483481211249166

Spector, P. E. (1988). *Development of the Work Locus of Control Scale.* Academic Press.

Spector, P. E., Cooper, C. L., Sanchez, J. I., O'Driscoll, M., Sparks, K., Bernin, P., ... Yu, S. (2001). Do national levels of individualism and internal locus of control relate to well-being: an ecological level international study. *Journal of Organizational Behavior, 22*(8), 815–832. doi:10.1002/job.118

Taras, V., Rowney, J., & Steel, P. (2009). Half a century of measuring culture: Review of approaches, challenges, and limitations based on the analysis of 121 instruments for quantifying culture. *Journal of International Management, 15*(4), 357–373. doi:10.1016/j.intman.2008.08.005

Toiviainen, H. (2014). Interventions for learning at global workplaces. In T. Hansson (Ed.), Contemporary Approaches to Activity Theory: Interdisciplinary Perspectives on Human Behavior. Hershey, PA: IGI Global.

Vygotsky, L. S. (1978). Interaction Between Learning and Development. In M. Cole, V. John-Steiner, S. Scribner, & E. Souberman (Eds.), Mind and Society (pp. 79–91). Cambridge, MA: Harvard University Press.

Ward, C. (2008). Thinking outside the Berry boxes: New perspectives on identity, acculturation and intercultural relations. *International Journal of Intercultural Relations, 32*(2), 105–114. doi:10.1016/j.ijintrel.2007.11.002

Ward, C., & Kennedy, A. (1999). The measurement of sociocultural adaptation. *International Journal of Intercultural Relations, 23*(4), 659–677. doi:10.1016/S0147- 1767(99)00014-0

Yamazaki, Y., & Kayes, D. C. (2004). An experiential approach to cross-cultural learning: A review and integration of competencies for successful expatriate adaptation. *Academy of Management Learning & Education, 3*(4), 362–379. Retrieved from http://amle.aom.org/content/3/4/362.short

ADDITIONAL READING

Åsberg, R., Hummerdal, D., & Dekker, S. (2011). There are no qualitative methods – nor quantitative for that matter: the misleading rhetoric of the qualitative–quantitative argument. *Theoretical Issues in Ergonomics Science, 12*(5), 408–415. Retrieved from 07/10/2013 doi:10.1080/1464536X.2011.559292

Bartel-radic, A. (2006). Intercultural Learning in Global Teams. *Management International Review, 46*(October 2003), 647–677.

Berry, J. W. (2009). A critique of critical acculturation. *International Journal of Intercultural Relations, 33*(5), 361–371. Retrieved from 10/10/2013 doi:10.1016/j.ijintrel.2009.06.003

Chevrier, S. (2003). Cross-cultural management in multinational project groups. *Journal of World Business, 38*(2), 141–149. Retrieved from 10/10/2013 doi:10.1016/S1090-9516(03)00007-5

Collings, D. G., Scullion, H., & Morley, M. J. (2007). Changing patterns of global staffing in the multinational enterprise: Challenges to the conventional expatriate assignment and emerging alternatives. *Journal of World Business, 42*(2), 198–213. Retrieved from 10/10/2013 doi:10.1016/j.jwb.2007.02.005

Fee, A., & Gray, S. J. (2011). Fast-tracking expatriate development: the unique learning environments of international volunteer placements. *The International Journal of Human Resource Management, 22*(3), 530–552. Retrieved from 07/10/2013 doi:10.1080/09585192.2011.543631

Foldy, E. G. (2004). Learning from Diversity: A Theoretical Exploration. *Public Administration Review, 64*(5), 529–538. doi:10.1111/j.1540-6210.2004.00401.x

Holland, W., & Salama, A. (2010). Organisational learning through international M&A integration strategies. *The Learning Organization, 17*(3), 268–283. doi:10.1108/09696471011034946

John-Steiner, V., & Mahn, H. (1996). Sociocultural Approaches to Learning and Development. *Educational Psychologist, 31*(3/4), 191–206. doi:10.1080/00461520.1996.9653266

Roth, W.-M., Radford, L., & Lacroix, L. (2012). Working With Cultural-Historical Activity Theory. *Forum Qualitative Sozial Forschung, 13*(2).

Seaman, J. (2008). Adopting a Grounded Theory Approach to Cultural-Historical Research: Conflicting Methodologies or Complementary Methods? *International Journal of Qualitative Methods, 7*(1), 1–17.

Suutari, V., & Brewster, C. (2000). Making Their Own Way: Through Self-Initiated Foreign. *Journal of World Business, 35*(4), 417–436. doi:10.1016/S1090-9516(00)00046-8

Taras, V., Rowney, J., & Steel, P. (2013). Work-related acculturation: change in individual work-related cultural values following immigration. *The International Journal of Human Resource Management, 24*(1), 130–151. Retrieved from 07/10/2013 doi:10.1080/09585192.2012.672446

Ward, C., & Kus, L. (2012). Back to and beyond Berry's basics: The conceptualization, operationalization and classification of acculturation. *International Journal of Intercultural Relations, 36*(4), 472–485. Retrieved from 07/10/2013 doi:10.1016/j.ijintrel.2012.02.002

Yamazaki, Y., & Kayes, D. C. (2004). An experiential approach to cross-cultural learning: A review and integration of competencies for successful expatriate adaptation. *Academy of Management Learning & Education, 3*(4), 362–379. Retrieved from 07/10/2013 doi:0.5465/AMLE.2004.15112543

KEY TERMS AND DEFINITIONS

Acculturation Strategy: The method an expatriate uses to adapt to a new culture. Based on the value they place on adopting the host culture versus their investment in their home culture, they may choose to integrate both, assimilate into the host culture, remain separate, or become isolated.

Acculturation: The process of learning and acquiring the requisite skills to successfully inhabit a new cultural realm.

Activity Theory (CHAT): A theoretical framework based in the cultural historical school who considers the learning activity the smallest unit of analysis. A subject (individual or group) acts within the frame of the community, rules and division of labour, using mediating tools to reach its objective.

Expatriate: The dictionary definition of expatriate is any person living outside their home country, however in common usage, and in the existing body of research, the term implies skilled workers living abroad for employment purposes, and this is the definition we use here. Expatriates are also commonly called sojourners in literature.

Phenomenography: A theory and methodology that is used to analyse qualitative data in order to find the differences in how a phenomenon is perceived and conceived.

Sociocultural Adaptation: Acculturation consists of psychological and sociocultural adaptation. While psychological adaptation is related to coping skills and stress levels, sociocultural adaptation consists of behaviours, cultural learning through interaction and identification with the host culture.

Work Locus of Control: Locus of control (LOC) is a personality trait defined by how much one feels their own actions affect rewards and outcomes (internal) or that other forces such as fate or luck are responsible (external). Work Locus of Control is a domain specific measurement of LOC that correlates with the generalised personality trait, but better predicts workplace behaviour.

Chapter 18
Constitution of Objects in DWR Activity

Inger Eriksson
Stockholm University, Sweden

ABSTRACT

A shared research object between teachers and researchers in Developmental Work Research (DWR) aims at development of teaching practices and forming of subject-specific knowledge. Currently, design experiments, action research, and formative interventions are used in educational research. A multitude of approaches show an overarching interest in developing teaching and learning practices. Action research and formative interventions include and empower teachers. However, in many DWR projects, teachers and researchers have different objects. In a tradition where teachers are regarded as learners, a shared research object is of interest. This chapter problematizes the relationship between teachers and researchers with the help of three DWR projects. It is challenging to establish a DWR project in which teachers and researchers aim at realising the same object. However, when this is a case, such projects may contribute to new knowledge that enhances student learning and educational, clinical, and subject-matter research.

INTRODUCTION

This chapter is based upon a keynote speech at the Sixth Nordic Conference on Cultural and Activity Research, Nordic ISCAR 2013 (Knutagård, Krantz & Jedemark, 2013) discussing the significance of a shared research object between teachers and researchers in developmental work research (DWR) projects. The purpose is to develop teaching and learning practices as well as subject-specific knowledge (Carlgren, 2012). There is a considerable body of literature discussing the teachers' role

in educational research that focuses on development of teaching and/or teachers' professional development (Carlgren, 2012; Carr & Kemmis, 1986; Chaiklin, 2010; Elliot, 1991; Somehk & Zeichner, 2009). There are also research approaches that address the means for developing teaching and learning, both in general terms and in relation to subject-specific research. Many of these contributions address issues of teacher participation. Action research may be regarded as an umbrella term for a variety of approaches, such as teacher research (Cochran-Smith & Lytle,

DOI: 10.4018/978-1-4666-6603-0.ch018

1999; Stenhouse, 1981) or lesson study (Lewis, 2002). Teachers possess the power of formulating a problem and research questions themselves, or in collaboration with researchers. In other approaches to development of teaching and learning e.g. design experiment, design-based research (Anderson & Shattuck, 2012; Brown, 1992; Cobb, Confrey, diSessa, Lehrer & Schauble, 2003), or developmental research (van der Acker, 1998) the research issue is commonly formulated as a theoretical basis and defined by the researchers.

My interest in collaborative practice DWR relates to the need for a subject-specific knowledge base that can be used as a source of expansion of teaching and students' learning (Carlgren, 2012). Most of the mentioned research approaches aim at improving teaching and developing new knowledge. Many of them take the teachers' everyday problems related to student learning as a source of formulation of research questions (Cochran-Smith & Lytle, 1999; Zeichner & Noffke, 2001). However, another discourse focuses on necessary changes in terms of teachers' learning, collegial learning, cooperative learning, teachers' professional development (Ball & Cohen, 1999; Carlgren, 2012). Within this discourse focus is primarily on teachers, their learning and development – not on the development of a professional, subject-specific knowledge base. Learning as an outcome of a research project is not a problem *per se* and it does not imply that there is no knowledge production of importance for the development of the core activity. However, focusing on teacher learning may blur our vision: if teacher learning is in focus, does research or the teachers perceive teachers as the problem or the solution? If teacher learning is in focus, do researchers and teachers perceive teachers' professionalism, or lack of it, as the problem? If teacher learning is in focus, do researchers or teachers perceive of teachers' collegial collaboration, or lack of it, as the problem? In any collaborative research project the participants have to challenge what appears to

be a culturally-developed perception of *teacher learning as the object* and not *students learning as the teachers' object*. If we were to expand student learning, teachers would need to be part of, and in the long run be responsible for, systematic knowledge production where student learning of specific knowings (Dewey & Bentley, 1960) is the object. Researchers as well as teachers would have to envision teachers as knowledge producers. With reference to medical clinical research, Bulterman-Bos (2008) argues for development of educational research where teachers have a dual role as clinical teachers-researcher and produce practice-relevant research that helps improve education. Carlgren (2012, p. 2) argues in a similar manner, for clinical research in general and especially for "clinical subject matter-didactic research", suggesting application of research approaches like e.g. learning study where teachers, in collaboration with researchers create knowledge of importance for student learning. What is to be known? What can enhance the development of such knowing? What creates difficulties in learning a specific knowing? (Carlgren, *et al,* in press).

By taking an activity theoretical perspective to such developmental research, the relationship between teachers and researchers cannot be restricted to issues concerning relations between the involved individuals, or to issues concerning power, authority and status. There is a third party involved, namely the object of the activity that the participants direct their actions towards (Engeström, 2011; Engeström & Sannino, 2010). If the aim were to develop a joint research activity, the research object needs to be shared between the teachers and the researchers. In many cases however, both in relation to action research and to design experiments, there are different objects involved. If the project is meant to be a collaborative project with a common research object there are many demands, constraints and contradictions that may cause problems in establishing and maintaining a common object of research.

With reference to activity theory, issues related to collaborative research in schools conducted in teacher-researcher partnership have been addressed and discussed by researchers as Wolff-Michael Roth, Kenneth Tobin and Andrea Zimmerman and Yrjö Engeström. Roth and colleagues (2001) frame these types of issues within the concept of co-teaching and generative dialogue. Engeström (2011) discusses these types of issues in relation to formative interventions. Framed by the concept of co-teaching and generative dialogue, Roth and colleagues (2001) discuss the necessity of cooperation between researchers and teachers, supervisors and teacher educators in the everyday teaching activity, and thereby assist in the development of the learning environment. They stress the importance of breaking with what they describe as a situation where educational researchers distance themselves from daily praxis by residing in their ivory towers.

Our methodology breaks with past traditions, taking us (researchers) into the front lines of the daily work of schools and, thereby, assisting in bringing about change. Our choices to undertake research in this way are based on our values and commitments. With Gramsci, we believe in the unity of understanding and changing of praxis and its political dimension. Whereas previous historical developments brought about a divide between educational theory and educational praxis, and a physical move of the former out of school, co teaching/co generative dialoguing returns university-based researchers to their historical origins to become significant partners in educational praxis. That is, we ask ourselves about the extent to which our work in schools has emancipatory practical value to those whose life world we share. (p. 24)

Engeström (2011) argues for a break in traditional research that puts researchers in a position of knowing what changes are necessary and how to achieve them. He claims that much of today's interventional research is framed by linear research-led logic that needs to be altered. It is in the light of this contention the concept of formative interventions is to be understood. Engeström (2011, p. 606) specifies the difference between linear logic and formative interventions.

- **Starting Point:** In linear interventions, the contents and goals of the intervention are known ahead of time by the researchers, /.../ In formative interventions, the participants /.../ face a problematic and contradictory object, embedded in their vital life activity, which they analyze and expand by constructing a novel concept, the contents of which are not known ahead of time to the researchers.

- **Process:** In linear interventions, the participants, typically teachers and students are expected to execute the intervention without resistance. /.../. In formative interventions, the contents and course of the intervention are subject to negotiation and the shape of the intervention is eventually up to the participants. Double stimulation as the core mechanism implies that the participants gain agency and take charge of the process.

- **Outcome:** In linear interventions, the aim is to complete a standardized solution module, typically a new learning environment /.../. In formative interventions, the aim is to generate new concepts that may be used in other settings as frames for the design of locally appropriate new solutions. A key outcome of formative interventions is agency among the participants.

- **Researcher's Role:** In linear interventions the researcher aims at control of all the variables. In formative interventions, the researcher aims at provoking and sustaining an expansive transformation process led and owned by the practitioners.

In acknowledging the importance of everyday activity and the practitioners' power and agency, we need to clarify how the research object becomes a shared object related to teachers' professional object. Research by Roth and colleagues (2001) refers to participating in the everyday activity, understanding and sharing teachers' work, and assisting them in efforts at change of the activity. Engeström (2011) on the other hand argues that the practitioners need to own the process, negotiating with others on what to achieve. Taking part in the practitioners' life and/or empower them is different from joint development of knowledge in relation to the teachers' professional object. The *research object* of these examples is not necessarily developed and maintained in relation to the teachers' professional object. Whatever the intentions built into such an approach to collaboration between teachers and researchers, there are several issues that may influence these ambitions.

THREE PROJECTS

Over the past years, I have been personally involved in interventional projects aiming at developing teaching and students' learning at school. In relation to my experience of collaborative research projects for developing knowledge relative to teachers' professional object, there are some significant aspects that needs to be analysed. First, who takes the initiative for the project and with what motive? Second, who defines the problem of the DWR project? Third, who suggests the changes to be tested? Fourth, who masters the theoretical tools used? Fifth, what type of division of labour is established throughout the project cycle? These questions form an analytical tool for examining what happened to the research object in Farsta Project (2004-2006), Botkyrka Project (2009-2010) and Lidingö Project (2010-2012-2014). These collaborative research projects were framed by different research and developmental models. One common feature has been collaboration with teachers and an initial idea of a research object related to qualifying teaching and student learning. Each project initially aimed at creating a collaborative knowledge activity related to an object of teaching and learning.

The Farsta Project

The Farsta Project was the first of three developmental research projects on mathematical learning in grades 1-6 in compulsory schools. The other researchers were Ingrid Carlgren, as acting project leader, Seth Chaiklin, and Viveca Lindberg. The research team partially included Torbjörn Tambour as expert in mathematics. The aim of the project was to develop knowledge about how to design teaching that would realise the long-term goals in mathematics stated in the previous Swedish national curriculum (1994-2010). At the beginning of 2000 there were several indicators showing that the design of teaching was not carried out in relation to the long-term goals, but to the short-term goals (Eriksson *et al* 2004). The research community considered this as problematic since focusing only on the short-term goals appeared to lead to a narrow and restricted learning environment (Carlgren, 2009; Eriksson, 2009). Against this background Carlgren took the initiative for a research project to explore possible ways of designing teaching that would realise the subject-specific, long-term goals in mathematics. The researchers wrote an application for the project and, when the project was funded, searched for teachers who were interested in participating.

For two school years the research team worked together with two teams of teachers. The first project year the team consisted of eight teachers in grades 1-6 in four compulsory schools. The second project year the team consisted of six teachers in grades 7-9. Their work is left out from this analysis. Participating teachers were financed by the project at 10% of fulltime and organised so that all eight teachers during the first project year could participate in the project every Thursday afternoon. Time was organised as full-group meetings between the researchers and the eight teachers; the eight teachers together; and the teachers within their own schools. The full-group meetings were held every two or three weeks throughout the whole school year. In the first part of the project with the teachers from grades 1-6, began by discussing the different goals in the curriculum in order to establish a common understanding of the problem related to the teaching of mathematics – a problem that was already defined in the research plan. In this discussion it became clear to the teachers (and researchers) that they, for many years, had "read" the curriculum and related goals somewhat erroneously. The researchers stressed that this type of misreading was culturally common among more or less all the teachers in the country and that this was the motive for the collaboration i.e. can we together explore the meaning of the long-term goals in relation to specific content and further develop a model of how to design teaching that can realise these goals?

The teachers reported that their students had problems in operating measurement, especially in relation to volume. The students' learning of measurement of volumes was determined as the core of the project. The long-term goals in mathematics gave no directions for how this content could be taught in order to realise these goals. This created the necessity of elaboration of the meaning of measuring volumes. When struggling with this "meaning" Chaiklin early on in the project introduced some of the principles of developmental teaching following Vasilii V. Davydov (Chaiklin, 2007, 2010). In this example he introduced the term germ cell as an analytical term related to questions such as: Which historical activities involving measurement can be discerned? What artefacts are connected to this knowledge and how are they used? The teachers became interested in this and asked for more information. At the next meeting Seth presented an analysis of measuring and gave an example of how to organise teaching in relation to this. The example and the organisational principles

were drawn from Davydov's work. An ontological assumption was that if a germ cell could be identified then it would be possible to develop what we called a key task, i.e. an assignment that could create a situation where the students' need for knowledge was likely to develop. Further, a key task allows students to participate in an activity in which their knowledge gradually develops. As such, a key task is possible to use as a didactical starting point and how the task develops is related to what the students do or avoid doing (Eriksson & Lindberg, 2007; Lindberg, 2010).

The teachers were interested in designing a key task and develop a sequence of eight lessons. However, since the Davydov model was totally new to the teachers, they asked for guidance in their planning. Four different designs centred round the common key task were tested – two of them were more in line with the Davydov model than the other two.

A contradiction, related to the planning of the key task and the design of lessons, was that teachers and researchers drew upon different traditions in didactical design. Teachers related their analysis to their actual groups and what tasks they thought the students could manage while the researchers began their analysis related to the what knowing was asked for in relation to the content at a principle level. For the researchers the formation of the key task was dependent on the first analysis. This contradiction led to the development of a model of "teaching planning". In this model, planning was illustrated as a process that could be divided into two steps, firstly a step in which the concepts and its conceptual relations and student knowing is reciprocally analysed in terms of what the students are supposed to learn. This is a procedure that was entitled content analysis. The content analysis provided a deeper understanding what knowing the students needed to develop, so a second planning phase became possible – creating a key task that could be used as a central tool for the final design of the lesson. This model was mostly used as a tool by the researchers during the project (Chaiklin, 2010; Eriksson & Lindberg, 2007; Lindberg, 2010).

Aspects of the Farsta Project

When analysing the project in relation to the five analytical questions given, the results can be illustrated as in Table 1.

Table 1 shows how the planned collaborative project was transformed into a situation where the teachers learnt how to interpret and work in relation to the national curriculum. They learnt about the importance of analysing the content historically as a basis for designing a teaching sequence that could realize the long-term goals in the curriculum. The researchers ended up with a deep understanding of the Swedish teaching tradition, the concept of key task and a

tentative design model. The researchers gained new insights related to the concept of practice developmental research (Chaiklin, 2010). There are of course many, contradictions, tensions and situations that contributed to the transformation of the initial object and constrained the collaboration. The relationship that established can only be described as asymmetrical – the researchers had in many aspects the power over the content, the solutions and the theoretical tools. The intended research object was never fully established as a common object.

If we take the outcomes of the project as indicator of the objects established during the project, we can identify traces of two different objects and thereby the collaborative project from an activity theoretical perspective can be understood as two interlaced, but separate, activities (Table 2).

Table 1. The Farsta project in relation to the five questions

	Whose Initiative?	**Who Defined the Problem?**	**Who Developed the Solution?**	**Who Mastered the Theoretical Tools?**	**DofL**
Farsta (Design based & Davydov)	The researchers: Initiated the research project and formulated the motive for it.	The researchers: Formulated the problem and presented it to the teachers.	The researchers: Gave the idea for a solution and guided the teachers.	The researchers: Mastered the theoretical tool used and guided the teachers.	Asymmetric: The researchers took a teaching role and the teachers credited the researchers' competences and placed themselves in a learning position.

Table 2. Traces of two different objects and two different activities

	The Object of Researchers' Activity Indicated in Terms of Outcome	**The Object of the Teachers' Activity Indicated in Terms of Outcome**
Farsta (Design based & Davydov)	*Intended:* Exploring the meaning of the long-term goals and developing a model of how to design teaching that can realise these goals. *Realised:* Knowledge about teachers' understanding of the long term goals. The concept of key task was established. Teachers found they need further mathematical knowledge.	*Intended:* Exploring the meaning of the long-term goals and developing a model for how to design teaching that can realise these goals. *Realised:* Teachers learned how to interpret the curriculum and to design teaching that is in line with the long-term goals and further developed a need for deeper mathematical knowledge.

The Botkyrka Project

This project will only be briefly sketched to illustrate some core aspects of relevance for this chapter. The research group consisted of Ylva Ståhle and Inger Eriksson. We consulted with Torbjörn Tambour and Mona Hverven from the Department of Mathematics and Science Education. The numbers of participating teachers varied during the project between three and six. In the role of researchers, we were contacted by two of the teachers and asked to plan and conduct a collaborative research project addressing students' mathematics learning. The Principal approved the two teachers' project idea. The municipally was willing to finance such a project as a means to improving student results in mathematics. The project was rather well established and had gained high priority. Furthermore the two teachers who took the initiative for the project had, in their plan, decided that they wanted to use the *learning study* model – a model that they had tried in another project. It was, however, only the two teachers that knew about learning study. A core idea of learning study is that teaching needs a learning theory as a tool for design and analysis. The most common theory used in a learning study is variation theory. The entire team of teachers was unfamiliar with variation theory. Learning study is a model in which one lesson is designed and then iteratively revised, often in a cycle of three lessons.

At the beginning of the project, the municipal education board had pointed out geometry as a target area for the project. The teachers were not convinced that it was the students' knowledge of geometry that was the biggest problem. Instead they perceived the students' understanding of the meaning of measurement as a bigger problem. In Swedish, the word *measurement* is often connoted with measuring length. The teachers saw this as a potential problem for the students when they were supposed to understand measuring as a principle related to different phenomena such as volume, weight, time i.e. not only length. In a

learning study, teachers play a crucial role since it presupposes that the learning problem in focus has to be something that teachers experience as difficult for their students to learn. This is called the object of learning. From an activity theoretical perspective the term object in a learning study is used in a narrower fashion. In the Botkyrka Project, the object of learning was defined as students' understanding of the meaning of measurement: so that they would be able to understand that measurement could be something more than just measuring length. The object of learning was analysed by subject-specific researchers (Tambour and Hverven) and then discussed with the teachers. The content analysis was not an issue for the teachers. The learning study model, however, assigned much power to the teachers to design, at least the first two research lessons in relation to their experience of the students' prior knowledge, but with continuous support from the researchers. The third revised lesson plan was established more cooperatively.

Aspects of the Botkyrka Project

The researchers supported the designs since the teachers were unfamiliar with the theory of variation. The relationship established between researchers and teachers must, as in the Farsta Project, be described as asymmetrical as researchers, in many aspects, had power over the understanding of the content and the theory used. The solutions, the research lessons designed, were developed much more collaboratively as compared to the Farsta Project. The teachers learned the model. Until last year the teachers still use the model for local development work. The teachers also learned much about the content that the researchers were analysing as they also felt that their lack of mathematical knowledge was limiting the project. The researchers developed a deeper understanding of possible contradictions in relation to this type of developmental research, especially in relation to teachers' subject knowledge and the Swedish

Table 3. The Botkyrka project in relation to the five questions

	Whose Initiative?	Who Defined the Problem?	Who Developed the Solution?	Who Mastered the Theoretical Tools?	DofL
Botkyrka (Learning study & variation theory)	The teachers: Took the initiative and formulated the motive for the project (together with the school head).	The teachers: Identified the problem based on their experience. The object of learning was then elaborated collaboratively with the researchers.	Collaboratively: The teachers and the researchers collaboratively analysed, revised and designed the three iteratively-conducted lessons.	The researchers: Were responsible for the use of variation theory in the iterative process.	Asymmetric: From time to time the researchers took a teaching role and the teachers mostly credited the researchers competences and placed themselves in a learning position.

Table 4. Traces of two different objects and two different activities

	The Object of Researchers' Activity Indicated in Terms of Outcome	The Object of the Teachers' Activity Indicated in Terms of Outcome
Botkyrka (Learning study & variation theory)	*Intended:* Knowledge about students' understanding of measuring. *Realised:* Knowledge about what is necessary to use learning study as a research approach, e.g. teachers' mathematical knowledge related to the research object.	*Intended:* Knowledge about students' understanding of measuring. *Realised:* Teachers learned how to use learning study as a tool for developing their teaching and further developed a need for deeper mathematical knowledge.

teaching tradition. When analysing the project in relation to the five questions the pattern is slightly different compared to the Farsta Project.

As in the Farsta Project there were several contradictions that contributed to how the Botkyrka Project took form, and its outcomes. The initial object of the collaborative research project was hard to establish as a common object since the researchers and the teachers reciprocally interpreted a need for teacher learning.

If the outcomes of the project are taken as indicators of the quality of the routines that were established during the project, we could identify traces of two different objects in a similar way as in the Farsta project. However, we only partly gained knowledge of the type described as the intended research object. This indicates that the Botkyrka Project from an activity theoretical perspective can also be understood as two interlaced but separate activities (Table 4).

The Lidingö Project

The third collaborative project used in this chapter was the Lidingö Project. Since this project, at least in some aspects, can be understood as a collaborative project with one common research object, the description will be more elaborated than the previous two. The Lidingö Project can be divided into two projects or stages. The first project (that perhaps should not be described as a developmental research project) was initiated, formulated and led locally by a teacher Adolfsson-Boman and her Principal. A group of teachers in her school had chosen to work with a developmental model called lesson study. This model is similar to the learning study model mentioned earlier – however in a lesson study no specific theory of learning must be used. During their project I was invited by the teachers to act as their mentor.

One of the results of this initial step was that the teachers began to question how they introduced students to mathematics in grade one. In most textbooks, first-graders are introduced to practical and laboratory mathematics with simple arithmetical exercises using whole numbers from 1-20. These teachers experienced that this tradition created problems in student learning – a belief they felt was supported by many tests, both national and international. During the lesson study project we had several discussions about how mathematics is introduced in other settings and in relation to that they were informed about some of the basic principles of the Davydov curriculum, where students are introduced to algebraic thinking before they start to work with numbers (Davydov, 2008; Dougherty, 2004; Schmittau, 2004; Schmittau, 2005; Sophian, 2007). Adolfsson-Boman initiated a discussion (at that time she was writing her BA based upon the lesson study project) about starting a new project where we could introduce the students to algebra in grade one. After a discussion with her Principal, the second project was planned. The project was named Development of Mathematical Thinking – Expanded Tasks in Primary Education and was scheduled over the first term for first-graders in the autumn of 2012. One of the aims was to collaboratively design some tasks that would make it possible to introduce students to algebraic reasoning and especially the understanding of the equals sign and the concept of equality. In the design some of the principles in Davydov's curriculum (2008) would be used, but also the concept of key tasks as developed in the Farsta Project as a design tool. Further we were interested in what could be counted as indicators of emerging algebraic reasoning among the students.

The Principal allocated two hour every two weeks for the teachers in the school who wished to participate in the project. In total seven out of ten class teachers and two remedial teachers participated, as did the principal whenever possible. Adolfsson-Boman was responsible for the project at school level and the experiment was carried out

in her class of 28 first graders. The teacher in the parallel class taught her students using conventional methods and thereby served as a reference class. In total, the entire research group consisted of approximately ten teachers (Adolfsson-Boman, two remedial teachers, a parallel teacher and a teacher from grade two participated throughout the project) and four researchers from Stockholm University. The researchers varied in fields of knowledge; mathematics (Tambour), mathematics education (Hverven), educational sciences (Jansson and Eriksson). Tambour supported the group with discussions about mathematical content concerning equality in a mathematical sense and in analysis of student reasoning. Mona participated at the beginning of the project in discussions about task design. Anders participated mostly in relation to the interviews and the analytical work. In establishing the research group we tried to take advantage of our different knowledge and experience. However, our aim was to avoid a situation where the teachers could be regarded as the implementers of a research design. One aspect of this was that teachers needed to develop some understanding of the researchers' perspective as well as the mathematical content. Before the project started the teachers read relevant literature, some of which was suggested by the researchers. To balance this, it is important to mention that all the researchers have a background as teachers in compulsory school with the exception of Tambour. In particular Hverven has a background as maths teacher in primary school. The data in the following examples is based on five recorded, planning meetings, one follow-up discussion with Adolfsson-Boman, and videoed interviews with 16 of the 28 students in November. Adolfsson-Boman and I have been responsible for most of the documentation during the project. In total the bulk of data consists of different documentation items like video and/or photographs of the lessons held during the autumn, students' work and a follow-up interview with all students in both Adolfsson-Boman's class and the parallel class.

In the following, focus will be on the design of the three key tasks used during the first three months as they may be regarded as one of the outcomes of the Lidingö Project. At the end of this description, some examples of our initial analysis will be given.

Key Tasks

From project start, the teachers had a clear picture that the students in Adolfsson-Boman's class would meet mathematics without traditional operations with digits and numbers. Together we discussed the formation of key tasks. In the Lidingö Project the key tasks had the potential to be used as a learning task in what Davydov (2008) call a learning activity. Designing a key task in relation to the ideas of a learning activity, the students should be able to develop a need or a motive and become involved in an activity. A learning activity is not to be confused with a teaching activity – there could be a teaching activity going on without giving the students the opportunity to be engaged in a learning activity. However, a learning activity is vulnerable and often temporary. In a classroom of many students, some may not be engaged in a learning activity even though they participate in the classroom activity. A learning activity is not only a reconstruction of knowledge historically developed in society. It is also an example of the reconstruction of, as Davydov (2008, p. 117) says, "historically formed capacities (reflection, analysis, and thought experiment) that are the basis of theoretical consciousness and thinking." With this definition in mind, we analysed all proposed tasks and asked if the task is historically rich and complex enough and if it is designed in such a way that it will provide the opportunity for students to develop a motive to explore the content that is made available in the task. Since we were drawing upon the Davydov program we did not conduct a content analysis as we did in both the Farsta and Botkyrka projects. Instead we used the analysis presented by Davydov (Kinard & Kozulin, 2008; Schmittau, 2004). Inspired by

Davydov's work and the few examples we had from School 91 in Moscow, the teachers decided that one of the key-tasks would concern how to express equivalence in an algebraic form – in this case by the use of letters.

By developing number from the measurement of quantities, Davydov's curriculum also breaks with the common practice of beginning formal mathematical study with numbers. Observing that culturally and in individual development, the concept of quantity is prior to that of number; he indicted the rush to number as a manifestation of ignorance of the real origins of concepts /.../.
(Schmittau, 2005, p. 18)

The dice game: In the discussions about the concept of equivalence and the equal sign Mona suggested that they could start with the signs 'less than' through a game using dice. If the students only are given the sign for 'less than' and are told to place their dice so that the sign so to say 'tells the truth'. Sooner or later some of the students will throw a double. And then it was a given situation for discussion. "What shall we do now? Can we use the sign meaning *less than*? Is there another sign that we can use?" The teachers saw this as a perfect start. Since the teachers believed that the students, at least from preschool, were familiar with the equals sign and its function, this game was considered more as a warm-up task than a key task. However, the students' response was unexpected! When some of the students had thrown a double and the teacher asks "Can you use the sign 'less than' now" the students answer no! But when asked if they knew another sign that they could use they said that they did not! Well, what shall we do now? The students solved the problem: "We'll throw the dice again!" One of the students suggested that they could use the 'less than' sign but draw it the opposite way – with those two signs you have a sign that shows that it is equal on both sides. Not until the second group did two students say that they knew a sign for showing

313

equality – the equals sign. Realising that students' familiarity with the equals sign did not transfer from their previous work with operational tasks to a different situation prompted the research group to expand the dice task and design it as a key task. Adolfsson-Boman developed the task in different ways and they continued to work with this task for several weeks.

The King's servants: One other aspect that we saw in the Davydov tradition was the idea of creating a situation that could draw upon historical development of measuring things and deciding equivalences. During the summer, Adolfsson-Boman had read about Dagmar Neuman's mathematical programme called *Landet länge sen* or *The Long Ago Country*. The programme is developed around a fantasy world where mathematics does not exist as there are neither digits nor numbers. The King's servants were paid with gold sand and fine oils. The problem was that the servants were always suspicious, doubting if they were paid equally. Since Neuman's programme is directed towards an arithmetic understanding, Adolfsson-Boman adjusted it in relation to the object of our project. Instead of having the students develop a need for numbers Adolfsson-Boman adjusted it to prompt a need for deciding equivalences or un-equivalences. The students met this problem in different ways. Sometimes it was clear that the amount of gold sand was distributed very unequally – but when the students found a way to measure the gold sand they could see that even if it seemed unequal it may be equal. In other situations they could explore the opposite, that even though it seemed equal it was not always so. In this task the students also had the opportunity to develop an understanding of measurement and units.

A+B=C and Cuisinaire-rods: In the third key task the students had the opportunity to construct and represent different equivalences with the help of relational material. In this task Adolfsson-Boman chose to work with Cuisinaire rods. These rods were common during the 1960s and 70s as practical material often used in reme-

dial teaching – at that time the rods were used to represent numbers in order to visualise arithmetical operations. Adolfsson-Boman introduced the rods in a way that allowed the students to express different equivalences. The teacher suggested that they could use letters to name the rods when they represented different algebraic expressions. The students suggested the rods could have their initials – so William used W to denote one of the rods he used in an expression. At the end of November, Anders and I interviewed 16 of Adolfsson-Boman's students. At the interview the students were shown a card that said A=B+C and we asked the students if it was possible to express things like this – "is it possible to write in such a way?" The students told us that "yes of course" and they said that they could show us if they could use the Cuisinaire rods and the equals sign and the sign for addition. The table was full of different signs on small cards and different materials including the rods. At the time of the interview the students had only worked with the rods three or four times and they had not previously met any algebraic expressions in written form. During interviews the students gave many examples of their ability to handle different algebraic expressions and they expanded the expressions that I presented to them in different ways. Their emerging algebraic reasoning was evident in the interview situation. When we interviewed 16 of the students in the parallel class and showed them the same card (A=B+C) we also got answers that confirmed that it was OK to write so since "the expression could be read ABC as in the alphabet".

Aspects of the Lidingö Project

The Lidingö Project was realised as a small-scale pilot project and the only financing involved was the time the Principal had allocated to the teachers. The project was, in many aspects, realised as a genuine collaborative project where the teachers and the researchers participated with a common object – student learning. The teachers – espe-

Table 5. The Lidingö project in relation to the five questions

	Whose Initiative?	Who Defined the Problem?	Who Developed the Solution?	Who Mastered the Theoretical Tools?	DofL
Lidingö (Design based research & Davydov)	Collaboratively: The initiative and motive grew from a dialogue.	Collaboratively: The problem was identified in a dialogue.	Collaboratively: The solutions – the key task was suggested in dialogue, tested and analysed collaboratively.	Collaboratively: The theoretical perspective was known by the researchers but a deeper understanding and concretisation of it emerged in dialogue, informed by our experiments.	Complementary: The teachers, e.g. Marianne, took responsibility for the design and the iterative revisions of the key tasks. The researchers had overall responsibility for the final analysis and writing the article. However, in each part of the project the teachers and the researchers were dependent on each other.

Table 6. Traces of a shared object and one activity

	The Object of Researchers' Activity Indicated in Terms of Outcome	The Object of Teachers' Activity Indicated in Terms of Outcome
Lidingö (Design based research & Davydov)	*Intended & realised:* Knowledge about how to design teaching that enhances students' theoretical understanding of the equals sign. Development of subject-specific key tasks.	

cially Adolfsson-Boman – and the researchers participated in different roles at different times. At the beginning of the project the researchers had more power over the theoretical tools and the teachers were aiming to understand the basic theoretical principles. At the beginning the researchers also had more influence on the design of the first key task. Gradually this was changed and at the end of the project both the researchers and the teachers were reciprocally dependent on each other's work in order to realise the intended object. Adolfsson-Boman designed and iteratively revised the tasks supported by her fellow teachers and the researchers. This presupposed that she continuously analysed student learning. Much of this work had to be done between scheduled meetings with the researchers. The five analytical questions in the Lidingö Project can be described in the following manner (Table 5):

In relation to how the project took form and developed and in relation to the preliminary results it is possible to describe the Lidingö Project as a research project where the teachers' professional object was shared by both the researchers and the teachers. This is illustrated in Table 6.

The Lidingö Project continued after the project period had ended. In 2013 we wrote a peer-reviewed article that has now been published (Adolfsson-Boman et al, 2013). Adolfsson-Boman, Jansson and Eriksson with two doctoral students also visited School Nr 91 in Moscow and this visit has led to a research application where a continuation of the project has been planned and submitted to the Swedish Research Council. At her school, Adolfsson-Boman has continued to develop and expanded the key tasks both in her own class and in other classes. Together with one doctoral student, Adolfsson-Boman has presented her work with the key task at one national conference for mathematics educational research. Adolfsson-Boman is still producing data that she shares with us as researchers.

Discussion

With reference to Engeström (2011) both the Botkyrka and the Lidingö projects may be described as a formative intervention – neither the researchers nor the teachers "had any answers" to implement and try out. Rather, the object of the two DWR projects was by nature problematic and complex. However, in the Botkyrka Project the teachers were mostly in a learning position whereas in the Lidingö Project the teachers especially Adolfsson-Boman played a role as (co-) researchers. Every step in the intervention was collaboratively negotiated, the research object evolved and expanded collaboratively during the project. Teachers and researchers contributed with their competences in planning, in realisation including documentation and analysis. In the Lidingö Project one of the results was the tentative key tasks that may function as a tool for didactical design. In the Botkyrka Project, no tool to be used in the teaching activity was developed. The teachers learned a model to be used, but the model was given in the project (it was however used after the project ended). The fourth aspect of the characteristic of formative intervention is not as applicable to the Lidingö Project as it may be for the Botkyrka project. The researchers were not trying to control any variables but neither did they attempt to provoke any. Whereas in the Botkyrka Project, different contradictions led to the project realising two different objects and the teachers had no opportunities to challenge their own understanding of their role in DWR projects. The Lidingö Project was realised in relation to one common research object, explored and expanded collaboratively. What perhaps is of greater importance is that the shared research object was clearly related to the teachers' professional work and took its starting point in a problem of students' subject-matter learning identified by the teachers at school. The Lidingö Project can also be understood as an example of clinical, subject matter-didactical research as argued by Carlgren

(2012). Action research, design experiment and formative interventional research are examples of research traditions where a practice is to be qualified, expanded and developed. However, if we wish to develop educational research that aims to produce knowledge that expand student learning of specific knowing and everyday teaching practice we perhaps, as Carlgren (2012) with reference to researchers as Bulterman-Bos (2008) argue, need another label and another focus in order to overcome the cultural understanding of teachers' learning. Clinical, subject matter-didactical research is of course a very verbose "label" but in order to change our understanding perhaps we need to label our activity in a way that places the focus on what knowledge is to be produced – not the form for producing it. Clinical, subject matter-didactical research is of course not in its form contradictory to action research, design experiment as well as formative interventional research – all these traditions can provide useful tools and strategies but, as in the Lidingö Project, the motive and the object should be student learning of specific knowing and a teaching who can realise that. I think that we need to take the research object as the "third party" in collaborative projects seriously.

CONCLUSION

Today, teachers are exposed to considerable pressures, not only from governmental level but also from different experts who knows a lot about children's development, their social and medical aspects. This may lead to a situation where the teachers are blamed for different failures without being given the power or tools to develop their own subject-matter professional knowledge base. Collaborative clinical research may contribute to knowledge production that may change this picture. I think that in relation to interventional research using activity theory it is of great importance to further problematize the relationship between practitioners and researchers. And to problematize how and by whom research issues develop. And who sets the aims of the research. In relation to teachers' roles in research, I argue that teachers need to be not only collaborators, but also colleagues – or that we participate in their projects. With reference to Carlgren, it is possible to see Adolfsson-Boman's work as emerging clinical subject matter-didactical research – where the object is the expansion of students' opportunities to learn.

Over the last few years subject matter-didactical clinical research has evolved in which teachers are involved in doctoral programmes – researching their own teaching practice (Nyberg, 2014; Tväråna, 2014). My ambition is to contribute to the discussion about an alternative picture to the mainstream where teachers are regarded as learners and often as the problem, to a picture where teachers are regarded as credible and legitimate knowledge producers. So, the issue that Seth Chaiklin (2010) raised with his title Educational research and educational practice: Why can't we be friends? Could perhaps be rephrased: Educational research and educational practice: Why can't we be colleagues – focusing on the same research object, student learning of specific knowledge and expanded teaching?

REFERENCES

Adolfsson Boman, M., Eriksson, I., Hverven, M., Jansson, A., & Tamobour, T. (2013). Kollaborativ utveckling av uppgifter för algebraiskt arbete i en årskurs 1 – exemplet likhetstecken. *Forskning om undervisning och lärande,* (10), 29-49. Retrieved from http://www.forskul.se/

Anderson, T., & Shattuck, J. (2012). Design-based research: A decade of progress in education research? *Educational Researcher, 41*(1), 16–25. doi:10.3102/0013189X11428813

Ball, D. L., & Cohen, D. K. (1999). Developing practice, developing practitioners: toward a practice-based theory of professional education. In L. Darling-Hammond & G. Sykes (Eds.), *Teaching as the learning profession: Handbook of policy and practice* (pp. 3–32). San Francisco: Jossey-Bass.

Brown, A. (1992). Design experiments: Theoretical and methodological challenges in creating complex interventions in classroom settings. *Journal of the Learning Sciences, 2*(2), 141–178. doi:10.1207/s15327809jls0202_2

Bulterman-Bos, J. (2008). Will a clinical approach make education research more relevant for practice? *Educational Researcher, 37*(7), 412–420. doi:10.3102/0013189X08325555

Carlgren, I. (2009). The Swedish comprehensive school-lost in transition? *Zeitschrift für Erziehungswissenschaft., 12*(4), 633–649. doi:10.1007/s11618-009-0103-1

Carlgren, I. (2012). The Learning Study as an approach for research. *International Journal for Lesson and Learning Studies, 1*(2), 3–16. doi:10.1108/20468251211224172

Carlgren, I., Ahlstrand, P., Björkholm, E., & Nyberg, G. (in press). The meaning of knowing what is to be known. *Education & Didactiques.*

Carr, W., & Kemmis, S. (1986). *Becoming critical: education, knowledge and action research.* Basingstoke: Falmer Press.

Chaiklin, S. (2010). Educational research and educational practice: Why can't we be friends?. In I. Eriksson, V. Lindberg, & E. Österlind (Eds.), Uppdrag undervisning: Kunskap och lärande. Lund: Studentlitteratur.

Cobb, P., Confrey, J., diSessa, A., Lehrer, R., & Schauble, L. (2003). Design experiments in educational research. *Educational Researcher, 32*(1), 9–13. doi:10.3102/0013189X032001009

Cochran-Smith, M., & Lytle, S. (1999). The teacher research movement: A decade later. *Educational Researcher, 28*(7), 15–25. doi:10.3102/0013189X028007015

Cochran-Smith, M., & Lytle, S. (1999). The teacher research movement: A decade later. *Educational Researcher, 28*(7), 15–25. doi:10.3102/0013189X028007015

Davydov, V. V. (2008). *Problems of developmental instruction: a theoretical and experimental psychological study*. New York: Nova Science Publishers, Inc.

Dewey, J., & Bentley, A. F. (1960). *Knowing and the known*. Boston: Beacon Press.

Dougherty, B. (2004). Early algebra: Perspectives and assumptions. *For the Learning of Mathematics, 24*(3), 28–30.

Elliot, J. (1991). *Action research for educational change*. Milton Keynes, UK: Open University Press.

Engeström, Y. (2011). From design experiments to formative interventions. *Theory & Psychology, 21*(5), 598–628. doi:10.1177/0959354311419252

Engeström, Y., & Sannino, A. L. (2010). Studies of expansive learning: Foundations, findings and future challenges. *Educational Research Review, 5*(1), 1–24. doi:10.1016/j.edurev.2009.12.002

Eriksson, I. (2009). Re-interpreting teaching: A divided task in self-regulated teaching practices. *Scandinavian Journal of Educational Research, 53*(1), 53–70. doi:10.1080/00313830802628331

Eriksson, I., & Lindberg, V. (2007). *Matematikundervisningens innehåll. Avrapportering av ett kollaborativt forskningsprojekt om att utveckla redskap och innehåll i arbetet med att realisera "strävansmålen" i matematik*. Lärarhögskolan i Stockholm & Stockholms stad. Retrieved from http://www.stockholm.se/Extern/Templates/InfoPage.aspx?id=42882

Eriksson, I., & Ståhle, Y. (2010). *Mätandets idé - En learning study i Botkyrka kommun*. Stockholms universitet: Institutionen för didaktik och pedagogiskt arbete, (working paper).

Kinard, J. T., & Kozulin, A. (2008). *Rigorous mathematical thinking: conceptual formation in the mathematics classroom*. Cambridge, UK: Cambridge University Press. doi:10.1017/CBO9780511814655

Knutagård, H., Krantz, B., & Jedemark, M. (Eds.). (2013). A Nordic Perspective on the Cultural and Activity Approach in Theory and Practice. Kristianstad: Kristianstad University Press.

Lewis, C. (2000). *Lesson Study: The core of Japanese professional development*. Paper presented at the American Educational Research Association Meetings. New Orleans, LA.

Lindberg, V. (2010). Skolans kunskapsinnehåll i ljuset av elevers uppgifter – Exemplet matematik. In I. Eriksson, V. Lindberg, & E. Österlind (Eds.), Uppdrag undervisning: Kunskap och lärande. Lund: Studentlitteratur.

Neuman, D. (1986). *Räknefärdighetens rötter*. Stockholm: Utbildningsförlaget.

Nyberg, G. (2014). *Ways of knowing in ways of moving: A study of the meaning of capability to move*. (dissertation). Centre for Teaching and Learning in the Humanities, Stockholm University, Stockholm, Sweden.

Roth, W.-M., Tobin, K., & Zimmermann, A. (2002). Coteaching/cogenerative dialoguing: Learning environments research as classroom praxis. *Learning Environments Research, 5*(5), 1–28. doi:10.1023/A:1015662623784

Schmittau, J. (2004). Vygotskian theory and mathematics education: Resolving the conceptual-procedural dichotomy. *European Journal of Psychology of Education, 19*(1), 19–43. doi:10.1007/BF03173235

Schmittau, J. (2005). The development of algebraic thinking. A Vygotskian perspective. *ZDM*, *37*(1), 16–22.

Sophian, C. (2007). *The origins of mathematical knowledge in childhood*. Lawrence Erlbaum Associates.

Stenhouse, L. (1981). What counts as research? *British Journal of Educational Studies*, *29*(2), 103–114. doi:10.1080/00071005.1981.9973589

Tväråna, M. (2014). *Rikare resonemang om rättvisa. Vad kan kvalificera deltagande i samhällskunskapspraktiken?* (Licentiate Thesis). Department of Education, Stockholm University, Stockholm, Sweden.

van den Akker, J. (1998). The science curriculum: Between ideals and outcomes. In B. Fraser & K. Tobin (Eds.), International Handbook for Science Education. Dordrecht, The Netherlands: Kluwer Academic Publishers.

Zeichner, K., & Noffke, S. (2001). Practitioner research. In V. Richardson (Ed.), Handbook of research on teaching. Washington, DC: American Educational Research Association.

ADDITIONAL READING

Chaiklin, S. (2002). *A developmental teaching approach to schooling. Learning for life in the 21st century*. Oxford, UK: Blackwell Publishers.

Chaiklin, S. (2013). Research knowledge production and educational activity. V. Farnsworth & Y. Solomon (Eds.), Reframing educational research: Resisting the 'what works' agenda. Abingdon: Routledge. 166-181.

Engeström, R., Batane, T., Hakkarainen, K., Newnham, D. S., Nleya, P., Senteni, A., & Sinko, M. (2014). Reflections on the use of DWR in intercultural collaboration. *Mind, Culture, and Activity*, *21*(2), 129–147. doi:10.1080/1074903 9.2013.879185

Engeström, Y. (1999). Innovative learning in work teams: Analyzing cycles of knowledge creation in practice. Y. Engeström, R. Miettinen., & R-L. Punamäki (Eds.). Perspectives on Activity Theory. Cambridge University Press.

Engeström, Y. (2008). *From teams to knots: activity-theoretical studies of collaboration and learning at work*. Cambridge: Cambridge University Press. doi:10.1017/CBO9780511619847

Kaptelinin, V. (2005). The object of activity: Making sense of the sense-maker. *Mind, Culture, and Activity*, *12*(1), 4–18. doi:10.1207/s15327884mca1201_2

Lagemann, E. C. (2008). Education research as a distributed activity across universities. *Educational Researcher*, *37*(7), 424–428. doi:10.3102/0013189X08325558

Morris, A., & Hiebert, J. (2011). Creating shared instructional products: An alternative approach to improving teaching. *Educational Researcher*, *40*(1), 5–14. doi:10.3102/0013189X10393501

Noffke, S. E. (2008). Research relevancy or research for change? *Educational Researcher*, *37*(7), 429–431. doi:10.3102/0013189X08325680

Roth, W.-M., Lawless, D. V., & Tobin, K. (2000). {Coteaching|Cogenerative Dialoguing} as praxis of dialectic method. *Forum Qualitative Sozialforschung/Forum: Qualitative Social Research*, *1*(3). Retrieved from 28/05/2014 http://www.qualitative-research.net/index.php/fqs/article/view/1054/2283

Stetsenko, A. (2005). Activity as object-related: Resolving the dichotomy of individual and collective planes of activity. *Mind, Culture, and Activity*, *12*(1), 70–88. doi:10.1207/s15327884mca1201_6

Zaritsky, R., Kelly, A., Flowers, W. W., Rogers, E., & O'Neill, P. (2003). Clinical design sciences: A view from sister design efforts. *Educational Researcher*, *32*(1), 32–34. doi:10.3102/0013189X032001032

Zeichner, K. (1995). Beyond the divide of teacher research and academic research. *Teachers and Teaching: Theory and Practice*, *1*(2), 153–172. doi:10.1080/1354060950010202

KEY TERMS AND DEFINITIONS

Clinical Research: Refers to medical research where medical doctors conduct research in relation to problem they meet in their daily practice. Bulterman-Bos (2008) argues there is a need for educational clinical research in which teachers can play a dual role as teachers-researchers in order to produce practice-relevant research that aims to improve education.

Clinical Subject Matter-Didactic Research: Aims to produce subject-matter knowledge that can expand teaching and student learning (Carlgren, 2012). Teachers identified problems related to student learning as something specific that needs to be in focus. What is to be known? What can enhance the development of sought knowledge? What creates difficulties in learning a specific knowing? (Carlgren, et al, in press).

Co-Teaching and Generative Dialogue: With help of the concepts of co-teaching and generative dialogue Wolf-Michael Roth, Kenneth Tobin and Andrea Zimmerman (2001) illuminate and discuss the necessity of cooperation between researchers and teachers, supervisors and teacher educators in the everyday teaching activity, and thereby assist in the development of the learning environment.

They stress the importance of breaking with what they describe as a situation where educational researchers distance themselves from daily praxis by residing in their "ivory towers".

Developmental Teaching: Developed by Vasilii V. Davydov (2008) drawing upon Lev Vygotsky's legacy. Central to developmental teaching and learning are the students' theoretical learning as an engine for development. Theoretical knowledge is culturally and historically developed and it should be used as a source for creating a curriculum – a curriculum that is realized in relation to concepts such as learning activity and tool-mediated joint actions.

Developmental Work Research (DWR): Has its roots in the CHAT tradition and is conceptualized by Yrjö Engeström and his research group. DWR is an interventionist approach to research and development. Central to DWR is the idea that every human activity is motive driven and tool mediated. The concept of object and contradictions are of importance to DWR. The aim is to support collective change (expansions) in work.

Formative Intervention: Formative intervention is a model and a concept that Engeström (2011) contrasts with research-led logic that needs to be altered. First of all, the researcher aims to provoke and sustain an expansive transformation process led and owned by the practitioners (2011, p. 606). Focus should be on addressing a problematic and contradictory object of the activity, embedded in the studied practitioners' activity. The content and the course of the intervention are subject to negotiation and the shape of the intervention is eventually up to the participants to decide. The aim is to generate new concepts that may be used in other settings as frames for the design of new, locally-appropriate solutions. A key outcome of formative interventions is agency among the participants.

Key Task: An assignment that could create a situation where the students' need for knowledge is likely to develop. A key-task allows the students to participate in an activity in which their knowledge gradually develops. Such a key task is possible to use as a didactical starting point and the task develops differently depending on what the students do (Eriksson & Lindberg, 2007; Lindberg, 2010).

Learning Activity: A special form of activity. The goal is the development of students' capability to act and participate in a new and independent way in a different activity (Davydov 2008). A learning activity can be planned, but there is no guarantee that learning will occur (Repkin, 2003). In order for the students to become involved in a learning activity they need to develop a motive, a desire and a goal that will drive them to transform the problem into a learning task and to search for tools that help them to solve the problem through joint actions (Davydov 2008; Rubtsov 2013; Zuckerman 2004). The problem must be framed in a specially-constructed situation that hinders the students from using familiar solutions. The problem must be intriguing enough for them to try to solve it by joint actions or as Repkin (2003:27) puts it "a problem in the sense that the available modes of actions are unsuitable and there are no others. In other words, new modes of actions are needed".

Learning Study: A research model, often described as a combination of the Japanese lesson study (Lewis, 2000) and design experiment (Brown, 1992). It is a research model in which an object of learning and its critical aspects are explored in a collective iterative and cyclical process. For example, a lesson is designed and then iteratively revised, often in a cycle of three lessons. In managing a learning study, teachers play a crucial role since it presupposes that the learning problem in focus is something (the object of learning) that teachers experience as difficult for their students to learn. A learning study is an inquiry into classroom practice from the point of view of learning something specific. Central to the learning study is the use of a theory of learning as a tool for design and analysis. Variation theory (Marton, 2005) is a commonly used theory used in a learning study.

Object of the Activity: A central concept in activity theory (Leontiev, 1978) suggesting that every activity is object-oriented and driven by its motive. Consequently there is no such thing as an unmotivated activity. A frequently cited quote by Leontiev is that the motive is the true object of the activity. Any activity is a historically shaped phenomenon that enables for solving a collectively or societally-developed problem of a kind that cannot be solved by individual action. In order to solve a problem people look for something that can help solve the problem. This search activates an investigation of what 'raw-material' (material and/or ideas) to use and transform in a way that will meet our needs. After identifying a suitable raw material and forming ideas of what it could be transformed into – we have an object of the activity. The idea of a transformed object as a means of solving the problem provides us with a motive to act (Stetsenko, 2005), e.g. on a research activity. If the aim is to develop a joint research activity, the research object must be shared between teachers and researchers.

Section 5
Philosophy of Activity Theory

Chapter 19
Vygotsky, Heidegger, and Gadamer on Moral Development

Leena Kakkori
University of Eastern Finland, Finland

Rauno Huttunen
University of Turku, Finland

ABSTRACT

The authors present a Heideggerian-Gadamerian interpretation of Vygotsky from the point of view of moral learning. In doing so, they introduce a new concept called Hermeneutic Zone of Proximal Development (HZPD). They also connect HZPD to the self-education of one's moral voice and lifelong moral learning. Adult self-education includes activities like reappraisal of moral choices, improving moral imagination, especially concerning fellow feeling, and dissimulating unproductive moral feelings in order to convert them into productive moral feelings. The purpose of critical self-reflection of one's moral voice is to transform "everyday morality" into "deliberative morality."

INTRODUCTION

Is language a simple tool which we use for communication or is it an advanced instrument for expressing our thoughts? According to the hermeneutic notion, language is something more than an instrument of communication. The hermeneutic notion of language matches with Lev Semjonovitš Vygotsky's socio-cultural theory of language, in which language and thought are intertwined units of analysis. The problems of dealing with dichotomized concepts like thinking and language, thought and world, have been basic philosophical issues since the beginning of

Western thought. Martin Heidegger considered it to be his main task to overcome the Cartesian dichotomy. Thinking and language play an essential role, especially in his later philosophy. Hans-Georg Gadamer, emphasises in a Vygotskian manner the role of dialogue in constructive thinking and hermeneutical experience. In Lev Vygotsky's view, language and thought have different origins but are interconnected and interwoven inseparably. His view is close to a hermeneutical approach to understanding of language. This approach provides a possibility of interconnecting language to the development of the human being, including moral development. According to the hermeneutic no-

DOI: 10.4018/978-1-4666-6603-0.ch019

tion, language is something more than a tool or instrument of communication. The hermeneutic notion of language matches with Vygotsky's (1986) socio-cultural theory of language, in which language and thought are intertwined.

The relation of thought to word is not a thing but process, a continual movement back and forth from thought to word and from word to thought. In that process, the relation of thought to word undergoes changes that themselves may regard as development in the functional sense. Thought is not merely expressed in words; it comes into existence through them. (p. 218)

Vygotsky claims that contemporary psychology was in a state of profound crisis. He quotes Brentano's words (Vygotsky 1986, p.13) saying there are many psychologies, but there is no one, unified psychology. Our conclusion is that the situation is same in our days. The duality of body and mind is one indication of the crisis. Piaget tries to escape this fatal duality by remaining strictly in the realms of facts. Vygotsky (1986, p. 14) claims that Piaget fails to solve the Cartesian dualism. Vygotsky offers his socio-cultural approach to solve the crisis of psychology and the problem of Cartesian dualism. There are interesting relations between Vygotsky's thinking and Martin Heidegger's philosophy (Pacher & Goicoechea, 2000).

PURPOSE OF THE STUDY

Problems of thinking and language, thought and world, have been basic philosophical issues since the beginning of Western thought. Heidegger's (1992, p. 41- 49) main objective was to overcome Cartesian dichotomy. Thinking and language play an essential role in that respect. Heidegger's student, Hans-Georg Gadamer (1998, p. 186-188; p. 362-379; p. 383-389) emphasises the role of dialogue in thinking and hermeneutical experi-

ence. The purpose of this chapter is to present a Heideggerian-Gadamerian interpretation of Vygotsky from the point of view of adult moral learning.

VYGOTSKY AND HEIDEGGER

Vygotsky realizes that solving the problem of thought and language requires two kinds of methods at the opposite end of the scale. The first one offers identification of thought and language and the second one absolute disjunction of thought and language. There is no problem left with the first one. The second method explains properties of verbal thought by breaking it up into its two elements, thought and word. Vygotsky claims that we cannot separate thought and word because they form an integrated whole. We cannot break language into thought and word in the same way in which chemical analysis breaks water down into hydrogen and oxygen. When language is analysed in this manner, a large amount of empirical information is gained, but the basic phenomenon is left out of the equation. This kind of analysis does not provide an adequate basis for the study of relationships between thought and language in general, or the development of language, and we would add moral development. Heidegger's criticism against so-called calculative thinking resembles Vygotsky's argument. Heidegger uses an example of the heaviness and hardness of rock. We cannot understand what rock is, when heaviness and shine are described by numbers. Such analyses leads to generalisation, which does not tell about the properties of the studied entity (Vygotsky 1986, p. 2-3; p. 211- 213, Heidegger 1966; 2002, p. 21-22). As an alternative method to such analyses Vygotsky presents an approach of his own. He replaced analysis of elements with analysis of units. Vygotsky' s method combines the advantages of analysis and synthesis, and permits adequate study of the complex as a whole. Units are the product of analysis which corresponds to

Figure 1. Relation of thinking and language in adults according to Vygotsky (1986, p. 88)

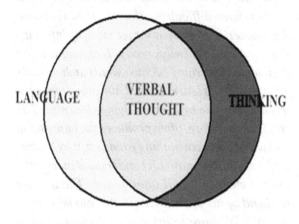

specific aspects of the phenomena under investigation (Vygotsky, 1986, p. 211-213). Vygotsky comes to the same conclusion as Wittgenstein and Heidegger concerning the social nature of language. In answering the question if speech and thought were originally the same thing, Vygotsky says no. Figure 1 describes thought and speech schematically as two intersecting circles.

The overlapping parts of the two circles in Figure 1 presents verbal thought as a field where thinking and language connect. Vygotsky emphasises that this image of verbal thought only includes some forms of thinking and speech. The roots and developmental course of intellectual thinking differ from those of speech, but at a certain point the lines of development meet. Then speech becomes rational and thinking verbal. The primary function of speech is communication and honouring a social contact. This goes for children as well as for adults. There is a question which remains for the researcher to answer: What kind of relation is there between speech and thinking? For example, does inner speech equal thinking? The answer to the question is complex. Vygotsky admits that inner speech is one of the most difficult phenomena to investigate (Vygotsky 1986, 98-99). The question of inner speech is also crucial to the theory of moral development. What we tend to call conscience is actually inner moral speech.

The genesis of morality is the genesis of inner moral speech. That is why a theory of the genesis of speech is elementary to understanding a theory of morality and moral development.

For Heidegger and Gadamer, language constitutes the world. The verbal thought-section of this chapter corresponds with the Vygotskian ideas about relations. The major difference is that Heidegger and Gadamer do not have a theory of the genesis and development of language. According to Heidegger and Gadamer we always find ourselves *in-the-world* with language and with others. Outside the world is nothingness. Nevertheless Heidegger comes close to Vygotsky when he says that the little child takes part in the mother's *being-in-the-world* because the child is a *being-in-the-world*. At the same time the child is tied to the ways of another human being's *being-in-the-world*. This, if anything, is the social start of human development, analogous to Vygotsky's idea of the development of social speech (Heidegger 2001, p. 163).

Vygotsky presents a theory of the genesis of speech, saying the child's earliest speech is essentially social. The argument for this bold statement is that at any given age the primary function of speech is social. Very soon social speech turns into egocentric speech and communicative speech. Eventually egocentric speech leads to inner speech, which serves thinking. The schema of development is first social speech, then egocentric speech and third inner speech. Inner speech is speech for oneself and external speech is for the benefit of others. Inner speech and outer speech have different kinds of structure. Inner speech is, in a sense, the opposite of external speech. External speech means the turning of thoughts into words, their formulation, materialisation and objectification. With inner speech, the process is reversed, going from the outside to the inside. Vygotsky (1986, 225-227) describes this change of direction saying "overt speech sublimates into thought".

The focus of research into human development changes from biological to socio-historical and problems of thought and language expand beyond the limits of natural science. Verbal thought is an artificial form of behavior, meaning that people learn in a more or less natural way. Heidegger (2004, p. 3) expresses a similar opinion, saying: "We come to know what it means to think when we ourselves are thinking. If our attempt is to be successful, we must be ready to learn thinking". And just like verbal thought is an unnatural form of behavior, morality and moral awareness are unnatural forms of learning behavior but we need thinking, language and concepts. Heidegger (2004, p. 17) defines thinking as a process similar to for example the practical building a house.

We must keep our eyes fixed firmly on the true relation between teacher and taught—if indeed learning is to arise in the course of these lectures. We are trying to learn thinking. Perhaps thinking, too, is just something like building a cabinet. At any rate, it is a craft, a 'handicraft. (p. 17)

Heidegger asked in a lecture in Freiburg in 1951: *Wass Heisst Denken? - What is called thinking?* (Heidegger, 2004). He did not actually answer this question. It seems that questioning is more important to Heidegger than answering; the path of thinking is more important than the result, dynamic is better than static. If you give a perfectly accurate and all-inclusive answer to the question, you need not think any more. And that is a wilful contention.

The question of thinking is a peculiar one. When we ask 'what is thinking' or, like Heidegger, demand that we must learn to think, we are already thinking. Only by thinking can we say something about thinking, and only by speaking can we study language. Thinking is a social act: it cannot be learned without other people. The same pattern goes for moral thinking. To put Heidegger's (2004) lecture in a nutshell, his argument is that we must learn to think, because we are not yet capable of thinking. Learning to think is difficult, but teaching to think is even more difficult.

Teaching is even more difficult than learning. We know that; but we rarely think about it. And why is teaching more difficult than learning? Not because the teacher must have a larger store of information, and have it always ready. Teaching is more difficult than learning because what teaching calls for is this: to let learn. Indeed, the proper teacher lets nothing else be learned than— learning. His conduct, therefore, often produces the impression that we really learn nothing from him, if by 'learning' we now automatically understand merely the procurement of useful information. The teacher is ahead of his apprentices in this alone, that he has still far more to learn than they—he has to learn to let them learn. (p.15)

'Letting people learn' can be regarded as Heideggerian formulation of Vygotsky's *zone of proximal development, ZPD*. Letting learn defines the boundaries of teaching and learning: these bounds are our *being-in-the-world within-others*. You are never just a teacher or just a learner, but both.

Language speaks, says Heidegger and this means that language does not have any other ground than itself (Heidegger, 1971, p. 198). Language is not the production of a need for communication. Neither is it based on thinking. Is thinking based on language? Heidegger did not take a stance on this question. Heidegger (2004, p. 16) wrote: "And only when man speaks, does he think – not the other way round". Without speaking, whether it is Vygotskian inner silent speaking or ordinary loud speaking, there is no thinking.

Vygotsky describes the development of verbal thought by showing how spontaneous concepts, as opposed to everyday and scientific concepts, develop. The development of a child's spontaneous concepts proceeds upward and the development of scientific concepts moves downward. The origin of an everyday concept can be traced to a concrete situation, where we are confronting different things. A scientific concept, on the other hand, involves a mediated attitude toward its object. Even if concepts are developing in opposite directions, the two processes are closely connected. The everyday concept must have reached a certain level of maturity before the child can absorb a related scientific concept. The two conceptual systems are in essence interrelations between actual development and the zone of proximal development (Vygotsky, 1986, p. 194-195).

The division between everyday concepts and scientific concepts can also be applied to moral thinking. We do not support the notion of "scientific morality" but we can make a division between "everyday morality" (ordinary moral attitude; moral virtues; morality as *ready-to-handen*) and "deliberative morality" (morality as principles; reflective moral virtues; morality as *present-at-handen*. In our interpretation, Vygotsky's everyday language and scientific language are analogous to Heidegger's *ready-to-hand* and *present-at-hand* (Zuhanden and Vorhanden). Vygotsky's use of Claparède's law of consciousness supports this interpretation, especially when we consider Heidegger's hammer illustration of *ready-to-hand* and *present-at-hand*. Claparède's "law of consciousness" states that the conscious realization of a problem occurs when automatic adaptation of one's action fails to achieve its goal. Heidegger says that when we are hammering, we do not think about hammer, but the hammer is ready-to-hand, and we know how to use it without making it an object. But if hammer is lost or it is broken, or out of sight, it becomes our object through present-at-hand awareness. (Heidegger, 1992, p. 98; p. 100-101; Vygotsky, 1986, p. 48 – 49). Social speech happens *in-the-world* in a Heideggerian sense and it can only exist on the condition of *being-with* other *Daseins*, with "other social speakers". Vygotsky (1998) defines his concept of the social situation of development in a Heideggerian manner.

The social situation of development represents the initial moment for all dynamic changes that occur in development during the given period. It determines wholly and completely the forms and the path along which the child will acquire ever newer personality characteristics, drawing them from the social reality as from the basic source of development, the path along which the social becomes the individual. (p. 198)

One of the most important elements in Heidegger's philosophy is *Ereignis,* meaning that everything in life has the nature of a happening. There are no static meanings or objects, but happening of truth and Being. Vygotsky sees similarly that the relation of thought to word is a process, movement back and forth from thought to word and from word to thought. According to Vygotsky thought happens in words and in speech. This movement is happening of truth in the Heideggerian sense. Something emerges in the world in a back-and-forth-movement between thought and word. And, like Heidegger, Vygotsky assumes that poetry and art possess other than aesthetic value, because art is more part of this kind of oscillation (back-and-forth-movement) than normal language. Also, moral innovation happens in words and likewise moral feelings come true in words. Morality as a social phenomenon has emerged into the world through the process of happening or moral action. At some point in human history, language users have come to the point where moral aspects or dimensions come to light (Vygotsky 1986, 213-214).

In *Being and Time* (1986), Heidegger explains that our being in the world discloses accordingly our *state-of-mind* (*Befindlichkeit*), our *attunement* (*Gestimmheit*) and our *mood* (*Stimmung*) (Heidegger 1992, p. 172). The *state-of-mind* is an *existentiale* in Heidegger's thinking. Human beings and *Dasein*, which is Heidegger's counterpart to human beings in *Sein und Zeit*, have a different mode of being in the world than any other entity. Heidegger calls this different kind of being *existentiale* (Mulhall 1966, 76-77). Heidegger states that there are three fundamental *existentialia* – care, understanding and *state-of-mind*. These *existen-*

tialia are fundamental, and the main purpose is to ask the question of the meaning of Being. "They" and das Man is a special kind of *existentiale*, because it describes a primordial phenomenon. Truth is an *existentiale* if understood in the most primordial way (Heidegger, 1986, p. 167). Other *existentialia* are worldhood, making-room, solicitude, end, totality, and de-severance. Accordingly we are always attuned to a *state-of-mind existentiale*: the world is disclosed in some way and this makes mood possible. Dreyfus (1991, p. 168) argues that the best translation of *Befindlichkeit* is "Being found in a situation where things and options already matter". This is an informative translation, but we must settle for *state-of-mind*. We always find ourselves *being-in-the world* in some way already attuned, and the manifestation of *attunement* and *state-of-mind* is *mood*. Heidegger (1992, p. 174) says: "In a state-of-mind Dasein is always brought before itself, and has always found itself, not in the sense of coming across itself by perceiving itself, but in the sense of finding itself in the mood that it has."

Heidegger uses *attunement* and *state-of-mind* like synonyms. The mood discloses the world and makes it possible to direct oneself towards things (Heidegger 1992, p. 176). The *state-of-mind* directs how the mood discloses the world.

There is a kind of passivity in Heidegger's way of thinking. We cannot force the happening of truth in the work of art; we cannot understand Being with hard work. This is why it is surprising and contradictory, when Heidegger (1992, p. 175) writes: "Factically, Dasein can, should, and must, through knowledge and will, become master of its moods; in certain possible ways of existing, this may signify a priority of volition and cognition." Still, Heidegger (1992, p. 175) stresses: "Only we must not be mislead into denying that ontologically mood is a primordial kind of being of Dasein, in which Dasein is disclosed to itself prior to all cognition and volition, and beyond their range of disclosure." In order to become master of our mood we can control our mood by free will and

cognition. We are always thrown into the world at a certain time and place, or, as Vygotsky would say, a certain socio-cultural situation; we have the possibility of mastering how the world is opening to us. It is the teacher's task to let children learn how to master mood in a way that makes expansion of the ZDP possible.

Vygostsky uses Stanislavsky's model of instructions in the play *Woe from Wit* as an example of "scaffolding" motivation. In this illustration the task is to master mood in a way that makes expanding of the ZDP possible. Stanislavsky gives instruction to actors in their attempt to reveal motives behind words (Vygotsky, 1986, 252-253) and master one's mood. According to Vygotsky, to understand another person's thoughts requires more than understanding another's words. One must also understand his thought and motivations (Vygotsky, 1986, p. 253). Actors using Stanislavsky's method are doing exactly that. Furthermore the actor is mastering his or her mood (*Stimmung*) in order to expand his or her ZPD as an actor. (Vygotsky, 1986, p. 252-253). First there is the text of the play. Then there is an outline of parallel motives (in parenthesis):

SOPHYA: O, Chatsky, but I am glad you've come. (Tries to hide her confusion)

CHATSKY: You are glad, that's very nice: But gladness such as yours not easily one tells. It rather seems to me, all told, that making man and horse catch cold. I've pleased myself and no one else. (Tries to make her feel guilty by teasing her). *Aren't you ashamed of yourself!* (Tries to force her to be frank about it)

LIZA: There, sir, and if you'd stood on the same landing here. Five minutes, no, not five ago. You'd heard your name clear as clear. You say, Miss! Tell him it was so. (Tries to calm him) (Tries to help Sophya in a difficult situation)

SOPHYA: And always so, no less, no more. No, as to that. I'm sure you can't reproach me.

(Tries to reassure Chatsky. I am not guilty of anything!)

CHATSKY: Well, let's suppose it's so. Thrice blessed who believes. Believing warms the heart. (Let us stop this conversation, etc.)

VYGOTSKY, GADAMER, AND MORAL LEARNING

The *zone of proximal development* (ZPD) is an important concept for adult learning and studies of moral growth in adults. ZPD connects with Gadamer's philosophical hermeneutics in an interesting way. Vygotsky defines ZPD as "the distance between the actual developmental level as determined by independent problem solving and the level of potential development as determined through problem solving under adult guidance or in collaboration with more capable peers" (Vygotsky 1978, p. 86). Vygotsky's notion of ZPD can be linked to Gadamer's (1998) notions of hermeneutic experience, hermeneutic circle and fusion of horizons. According to Gadamer, hermeneutic experience broadens our horizon and enables us to see something differently than we did in the past. The hermeneutic experience is essentially negative in nature. It breaks down typical or restricted ways of seeing things. It is not just that we first had a deceptive view and "now we know better"; rather, we have constructed a new and wider perspective on other things and other people. Gadamer (1998, p. 353) says: "… we use word 'experience' in two different senses: the experience that conforms to our expectation and confirm it and the new experiences that occur to us. This latter – 'experience' in the genuine sense – is always negative."

To put it into educational terminology, ordinary experience happens in the comfort zone and this mode conforms to the person's expectations. The hermeneutic experience is a shaking learning experience and it widens the person's comfort zone and ZPD. Trivial experiences do not make

us more "experienced" in the Gadamerian sense (*Erfahrener*) and we do not learn anything new. Trivial experiences do not widen comfort zone and ZPD. According to Gadamer, experienced people have been through a series of hermeneutical experiences, which have widened their horizon, their comfort zone and ZPD. The hermeneutic experience is a world-shaking experience. After having a hermeneutic experience one looks at the world through different eyes. One sees new things that one has not seen before or paid attention to. Also the agent (experiencer; *Dasein*) changes because of the power of hermeneutic experience. Imagine reading a book that has shaken your world view. After the reading it your world (horizon) changes and so do you. Gadamer preserves the term hermeneutic experience for this kind of experience.

In Gadamer's philosophical hermeneutics, the idea of the hermeneutic experience is connected with the concept of horizon. When a person remains in a comfort zone – for example because of the mood – and securely locked up in his or her preunderstanding, the hermeneutic experience or the expansion of the horizon will not happen. Heidegger says truth will not happen (*Ereignis*). Section 1 in Figure 1 illustrates the agent's comfort zone or preunderstanding (current understanding, knowledge, and skills). This comfort zone and preunderstanding includes the mood (*Stimmung*) and facilitate a situation where hermeneutical experience could happen. Gadamer (1998, p. 302) says: "We define the concept of 'situation' by saying that it represents a standpoint that limits the possibility of vision. Hence essential part of the concept of situation is the concept of 'horizon'. The horizon is the range of vision that includes everything that can be seen from a particular vantage point in space. Applying this line of reasoning to the thinking mind, we speak of narrowness of horizon, of possible expansion of horizon, of opening of new horizon, and so forth. Since Nietzsche and Husserl, the word has become accustomed to philosophical ways to characterize how thought is tied to its finite determinacy, and how one's range of vision is gradually expanded. A person without a horizon does not see very far and hence overvalues what is closest to him. On the other hand, 'to have a horizon' means not being limited to what is nearby, but to being able to see beyond it. A person who has a horizon knows the relative significance of everything within this horizon, weather it is near or far, great or small. Similarly, working out the hermeneutical situation means acquiring the right horizon of inquiry.

With suitable preunderstanding, situation and mood (*Stimmung*), the hermeneutic experience could expand the existing horizon. Everything that one could understand with one's current preunderstanding is within one's ZPD and horizon. The limits of the ZPD are also the limits of language and the world (as we know it). One cannot speak or even think of things that are beyond those limits (Section 3 in Figure 1). The sections in the spiral are moving forwards. Sometimes movement is slow and at other times it is rapid. Sections marked a, b, c and d signify earlier pre-understanding,

ZPD and things currently beyond reach. ZPD is also a place for dialogue with teachers, mentors, friends, strangers, traditions, other cultures, etc. Preunderstanding, mood (*Stimmung*) and the hermeneutical situation expand the range of such dialogue. When dialogue – often in a playful manner – is fruitful, hermeneutic experience and fusion of horizons might occur. Then the limits of language and the world move.

After a series of hermeneutical experiences, people turn their attention to the nature of the events of this experience and become aware of their ability to attain transformative experiences. Those people are reflectively aware about their ability to learn new things and widen their perspective. Gadamer (1998, p. 354) comments on their competency to learn: "The experiencer has become aware of his experience; he is 'experienced'. He has acquired a new horizon within which something can become an experience for him". In educational literature such a person is referred to as a "reflective learner"

Figure 2. The spiral of hermeneutic experiences and the limits of language and the world

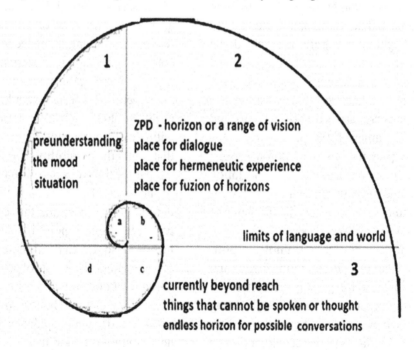

(Ertmer & Newby 1996), an expert in learning who possesses good metacognitive skills.

For Gadamer, an experienced person (*Erfahrener*) refers to life experiences, reminding us of Aristotle's notion of *megalopsyche* (great spirit). The nature of adult learning is different from the cases that Vygotsky discusses. Vygotsky is interested in children's learning and development. Gadamer's *Erfahrener* and Aristotle's *megalopsyche* refer to learning in adult age. Therefore, we would like to introduce a concept of the *hermeneutic zone of proximal development* (HZPD) in order to signify those learning processes or hermeneutical experiences that lead the way to the experienced person in the Gadamerian sense (*Erfahrener*). When we speak about learning in

adult age or learning from life, it might be that the term 'development' is not appropriate. Vygotsky relates the ZPD to children's development. With the notion of the HZPD we do not refer to development precisely in the Vygotskian manner, but nevertheless hermeneutic experience is a learning experience. As a learning experience, hermeneutic experience widens a person's horizon, and the HZPD is the zone in which this widening occurs.

The *Erfahrener,* or experienced person in the Gadamerian sense of the word has a wide HZPD. In contrast to the *Erfahrener* we can postulate the experienced person in the Shakespearian sense with a narrow HZPD. This is a person who has a long, deep and wide life experience, but thinks that there is "nothing new under the sun". Such

Figure 3. The experienced person in the Shakespearian sense

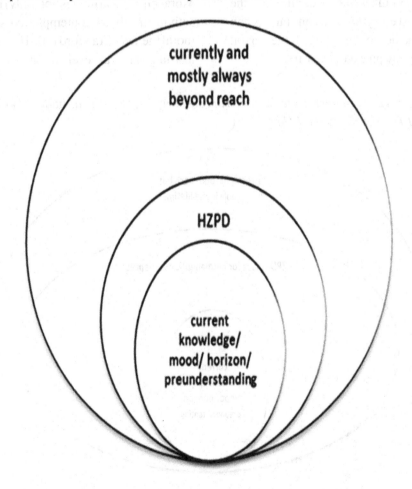

a person could say that "I have seen it, done it, been through it, so there is nothing new for me to experience.

Experienced people in the Shakespearian sense are immune to new learning experiences. So they have a great current horizon owing to their life experience, but their *hermeneutical zone of proximal development* is very narrow. Consequently many skills, knowledge, ideas, points of view and moral stances remain beyond reach. Put in Heideggerian terminology, the experienced person in the Shakespearian sense has the wrong mood (*Stimmung*) for further learning or hermeneutic experiencing. They have prejudices (*Vorurteil*) which effectively restrict their HZPD. The experienced person in the Gadamerian sense, on the other hand, has just the right mood (*Stimmung*) to benefit from hermeneutic experiences. The *Erfahrener* is a kind of reflective learner in learning from life. For the *Erfahrener*, almost everything that one human can grasp in a lifetime lies in the zone that the person can learn during any phase of their life.

The distinction between the experienced person in the Gadamerian and Shakespearean senses (Bang 2014) also concerns moral learning. In the field of morality there is the possibility that a person gains the *Erfahrener*-level of moral cognition and sensitivity of moral feelings. *Erfahrener*-level moral learning happens in adult years. *Erfahrener*-level is the phase that Paul Duncan Crawford (2001) calls "genuinely moral conduct". We would like to think that "higher moral learning" happens at the *Erfahrener*-level or in genuinely moral conduct but of course we cannot be sure, because we are not there yet personally. Moral higher learning involves Socratic knowledge of morality (moral issues; moral aspects) – knowing that there is so much to learn in the field of morality. We support Crawford's (2001) notion of morality (moral ability) as dialogical meaning-creating activity. Moral higher learning is not (only) rule-following activity or solitary contemplation of sophisticated moral themes. Crawford (2001) claims that moral learning or moral development is Vygotskian style

Figure 4. The experienced person in the Gadamerian sense with a Socratic attitude: "I know That There is so Much that I Do Not Know but I Can Learn"

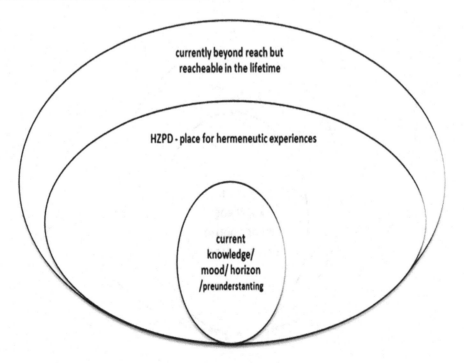

of socio-cultural meaning-making activity that facilities a personal way of *being-in-the-world* in the Heideggerian sense (Crawford 2001, p. 118). Moral learning is "the quintessential sociocultural activity" (Moll 1990, p. 1) where fusion and expansion of horizons happen. Like all kinds of learning, meaning-making activity in the moral sphere, is essentially dialogical. So in a sense one cannot have "private morality" like one cannot have "private language" (Candlish & Wrisley 2012; Wittgenstein 2001, §243, §244-§271 and §256-§271).

Dialogical meaning-making on moral issues belongs to the sphere of outer speech. Concurrently people carry out an internal dialogue or inner speech, listening to their moral voice. One's own moral voice is actually the instance which is busy learning in the *hermeneutical zone of proximal development*. The most important task in adult and lifelong learning is self-education of one's moral voice. Moral self-education (*Moralische Selbstbildung*) includes critical self-reflection on moral judgements, moral virtues and moral feelings. Higher level (adult age) moral self-education includes such activities as re-appraisal of moral choices, improving moral imagination, especially concerning fellow feeling and dissimulating unproductive moral feeling in order to convert them into productive moral feelings (Maxwell & Reichenbach 2007). The purpose of critical self-reflection of personal morality (moral voice) is to transform "everyday morality" (ordinary moral attitude; un-reflective moral virtues; morality as ready-to-hand/*Zuhanden*) into "deliberative morality" (defined as principles; reflective moral virtues; morality as present-at-hand/*Vorhanden*). Moral self-education implies growth going from morality as ready-to-hand to morality as present-at-hand. For Adam Smith, the elementary concept in moral self-education is cultivation of the sense of propriety (TMS i.1.3.-4.). Tronto (1993) explains Smith's sense of propriety.

Propriety refers to the sentiment we share, being by nature sociable, that makes us eager to be sure that others perceive us as proper. If we did not develop a sense of propriety, perhaps we would be able to ignore the situations of others. But our desire to be accepted, our sense of propriety, causes us to develop an ability to put ourselves in others' positions. (p. 46)

The sense of propriety is related to Smith's idea of the impartial spectator. If we are engaged in moral conflict, our instant moral feelings might be more or less biased by the situation at hand. The task of moral self-education is to learn to imagine the reaction of others who have no particular favourable emotion towards any engaged party. We should learn to imagine what kind of moral feelings the impartial spectator would feel (TMS, iii.2.31-31). As a moral maxim, it sounds like an easy thing to accept, but such relations, qualities and and behaviors are extremely difficult to carry out. It takes a life time to really learn to feel moral feelings that an impartial spectator would feel. According to Erich Fromm, to learn to really love impartially and in a non-egoistic way is a rare achievement (Fromm 1956, p. vii). The starting point of Fromm's school of love is to learn how to love oneself in non-egoistical manner. A person cannot truly love another person if that person does not love mankind or himself. To do that, one must be a master of love (Fromm 1956, ch. III). To be a master of love is the ultimate goal when cultivating a sense of propriety of another person rather than to prove their love. This moral self-education – cultivation of the sense of propriety and love and critical self-reflection on moral judgements – is a never-ending task. In this way Aristotle understood Oracle's maxim in Plato's Phaedrus: "know thyself". For Nietzsche, this maxim means that one should overcome oneself by becoming what one is. Knowing oneself is a process of self-transcendence. We would like to modify this maxim: "Know your hermeneutical zone of proximal development in the moral sphere"!

CONCLUSION

Vygotsky, Heidegger and Gadamer agree that language is something other than an instrument for communication. They support a socio-cultural theory of language, in which language and thought are closely intertwined. Relations between thought and word cover dynamic process where a continual movement goes back and forth from thought to word and vice versa. This is a dialogical process. Relations between language and thought is a continuous process going from external speech to thinking (internal speech) and from thinking to external speech. The same dialectic applies to human morality (moral thinking and moral speech). Morality emerges from oscillation between individual internal world and public external world. Morality exists only as movement in a shared social world. We call this oscillation play acting in the Gadamerian sense and a happening of truth in the Heideggerian sense. Dialogue is the genesis of thinking and morality. Inner speech or inner dialogue is essential for adult morality. The main purpose of moral learning in adult age is self-education of one's moral voice or inner speech. With the right kind of attitude and mood (*Stimmung*) a person controls a wide *hermeneutical zone of proximal development* in the sphere of morality. Such a person is experienced in Gadamerian sense of the word. Experienced people in the Gadamerian sense have an ability to manage their mood in a Stanislavskian manner. Such people possess just right mood for moral higher learning in an extremely wide *hermeneutical zone of proximal development*. We would like to think that the truest form of moral learning happens in adult age. This is so because moral learning is connected to learning from life. If a person considers there is nothing much to learn about moral sensitivity, moral judgment, moral motivation and moral character (Rest, 1994, p. 9), then this person is only experienced in the Shakespearian sense. Improving these dimensions of morality is a lifelong task (task of lifelong learning). There is always a possibility to meet with a mind blowing hermeneutical experience of the kind that it widens the limits of moral action, language and the world.

REFERENCES

Bang, L. (2014). Mapping [Capital v.2.0] – An encounter of thoughts. In T. Hansson (Ed.), Contemporary Approaches to Activity Theory: Interdisciplinary Perspectives on Human Behavior. Hershey, PA: IGI Global.

Candlish, S., & Wrisley, G. (2012). Private Language. In N. Zalta (Ed.), *The Stanford Encyclopedia of Philosophy*. Retrieved October 4, 2013, from http://plato.stanford.edu/archives/sum2012/entries/private-language/

Crawford, P. (2001). Educating for Moral Ability: Reflections on Moral Development Based on Vygotsky's Theory of Concept formation. *Journal of Moral Education*, *30*(2), 113–129. doi:10.1080/03057240120061379

Dreyfus, H. (1991). *Being-in-the-World: A Commentary on Heidegger's Being and Time, Division I*. Boston, MA: MIT Press.

Ertmer, P., & Newby, T. (1996). The Expert Learner: Strategic, self-regulated and reflective. *Instructional Science*, *24*(1), 1–24. doi:10.1007/BF00156001

Fromm, E. (1956). *The Art of Loving*. New York: Harper & Row.

Gadamer, H.-G. (1998). *Truth and Method* (2nd rev. ed.). New York: Continuum.

Hegel, G. W. F. (2013). *The Phenomenology of Mind – Introduction*. Retrieved April 15, 2013, from http://www.marxists.org/reference/archive/hegel/works/ph/phintro.html

Heidegger, M. (1986). *Sein und Zeit*. Tübingen: Max Niemeyer Verlag.

Heidegger, M. (1992). *Being and Time*. Oxford, UK: Blackwell.

Heidegger, M. (2001). *Zollikon Seminars: Protocols—Conversation—Letters*. Evanston, IL: Northwestern University.

Heidegger, M. (2002). The Origin of the Work of Art. In J. Young (Ed.), Martin Heidegger: Off the Beaten Track (pp. 1-56). Cambridge University Press.

Heidegger, M. (2004). *What is called thinking?* New York: Harper Perennial.

Maxwell, B., & Reichenbach, R. (2007). Educating Moral Emotions: A Praxiological Analysis. *Studies in Philosophy and Education, 26*(2), 147–163. doi:10.1007/s11217-006-9020-4

Moll, L. (1990) Introduction. In L. Moll (Ed.), Vygotsky and Education: Instructional Implications and Applications of Sociohistorical Psychology (pp. 1–27). New York: Cambridge University Press.

Mulhall, S. (1996). *Heidegger and Being and Time*. London: Routledge.

Packer, M. J., & Goicoechea, J. (2000). Sociocultural and Constructivist Theories of Learning: Ontology, Not just Epistemology. *Educational Psychologist, 35*(4), 227–241. doi:10.1207/S15326985EP3504_02

Rest, J. (1994). Background: Theory and research. In J. R Rest & D. Narvaez (Eds.), Moral development in the professions: Psychology and applied ethics (pp. 1-26). Hillsdale, NJ: Erlbaum.

Smith, A. (1976). *TMS* [The Theory of Moral Sentiments]. Oxford, UK: Oxford University Press.

Tronto, J. (1993). *Moral Boundaries: A Political Argument for an Ethic of Care*. Academic Press.

Vygotsky, L. (1986). *Thought and Language*. Cambridge, MA: MIT Press.

Vygotsky, L. (1998). The collected works of L.S. Vygotsky: Child Psychology (vol. 5). New York: Plenum Academic.

Vygotsky, L. S. (1978). *Mind in Society: The Development of Higher Psychological Processes*. Cambridge, MA: Harvard University Press.

Wittgenstein, L. (2001). *Philosophical Investigations*. Oxford, UK: Blackwell Publishing.

Wood, D. J., Bruner, J. S., & Ross, G. (1976). The Role of Tutoring in Problem Solving. *Journal of Child Psychiatry and Psychology, 17*(2), 89–100. doi:10.1111/j.1469-7610.1976.tb00381.x PMID:932126

KEY TERMS AND DEFINITIONS

Dasein: The most important term in Martin Heidegger's opus magnum Being and Time. Dasein is human being, but only in that sense, that human being has relation to its own being. Dasein is not an anthropological term. Dasein is a being that can ask its own being.

Existentiale: Heideggerian term. We always already are in the world and existentiale is the way of the being in the world. Also being-in-the world is existentiale, other existentialia are for example understanding, being–in, worldhood, they, truth.

Experienced in Gadamerian Sense: Characterized not by a particular amount of experience but by radical openness to new experience (*Offenheit für Erfahrung*). The experienced person in Gadamerian sense possess extremely wide zone of proximal development.

Experienced in Shakespearean Sense: The Shakespearian sense thinks that there is nothing new under the sun and she or he has seen it all. This kind of person is not sensitive to new (learning) experiences. They have a great current horizon owing to their life experience, but the person's ability to learn and see new things is very narrow.

Hermeneutical Experience: A shaking learning experience and it widens the person's ZPD. Trivial experiences do not make us more "experienced" in the Gadamerian sense and we do not learn anything new. According to Gadamer, experienced persons are individuals who have experienced a series of hermeneutical (dialectical) experiences. The hermeneutic experience is a world-shaking experience. After hermeneutic experience one looks at the world through different eyes. One sees new things that one has not seen before or paid attention to. Also the agent (experiencer; Dasein) changes because of the power of hermeneutic experience.

Hermeneutical Zone of Proximal Development: A new Vygotskian concept introduced by Kakkori and Huttunen in this volume. When speaking about learning in adult age or learning from life, the plain term 'development' is not appropriate. Vygotsky relates the ZPD to children's development, suggesting it means the difference between what a learner can do without help and what he or she can do with help. With the notion of the HZPD Kakkori & Huttunen do not refer to development precisely in the Vygotskian manner, but nevertheless hermeneutic experience is a learning experience. As a learning experience, hermeneutic experience widens a person's horizon, and the HZPD is the zone in which this widening occurs.

Language: In the Heideggerian-Gadamerian sense everything what we can understand is language. Language is not only tool of communication, it is also an existentiale.

Mood (Stimmung): Heideggerian term. Mood determinates how we are in the world and how the world is opening to us.

Present-at-Hand (Vorhanden): A thing, that is understood as an object in our environment. According to Heidegger's example, an entity can come to our object when it is missing or broken. If a hammer is not where it should be, when we are needing it, it comes to our object, present-at-hand.

Ready-to-Hand (Zuhanden): Being, which is not understood through theoretical interpretation and is not under objective consideration. Ready-to-hand is as it is in its own being. Heidegger's example of ready-to-hand is hammer. When we are hammering, we do not think about hammer, but the hammer is ready-to-hand, and we know how to use it without doing it an objective.

Chapter 20
Mapping [Capital v.2.0]:
An Encounter of Thoughts

Lars Bang
Aalborg University, Denmark

ABSTRACT

This chapter explores the benefits of a theoretical and methodological encounter between Bourdieu's concepts of capital, Deleuze's line of thought, and Marxist activity theory, particularly the Russian strand by Ilyenkov and Leontjev. Bourdieu, Deleuze, and Ilyenkov share a common denominator in Marx. In a contemporary light, Bourdieu's sociological concepts reflect an effort to readdress issues of class and practice as raised by Marx. The author claims that development of Marxist activity theory benefits from such an encounter, especially in educational research. The expanded concept of capital is exemplified through the optic of an educational Danish project. The author intends to show how the expanded concept of capital resonates with the theoretical framework of activity theory. He also shows how development of Marxist activity theory benefits from the methodological construct of capital. Bourdieuian and Deleuzian perspectives lead to the construction of a new structural map of events.

UPTAKE IN SCIENCE EDUCATION: A QUESTION OF CAPITAL

A literary reference to Shakespearian drama introduces the theme of this chapter, that is, human activity related to notions of *capital*, value, and ownership and descriptions of how they are connected.

This kindness will I show.
Go with me to a notary, seal me there
Your single bond, and, in a merry sport,
If you repay me not on such a day,

In such a place, such sum or sums as are
Expressed in the condition, let the forfeit
Be nominated for an equal pound
Of your fair flesh, to be cut off and taken
In what part of your body pleaseth me.

(Shylock, Merchant of Venice, Shakespeare, 2003 p.89)

This is 2014 and a Danish administrative region suffers from a structural educational problem. Problems of low uptake into science, technology, engineering, and mathematics (STEM) begin in

DOI: 10.4018/978-1-4666-6603-0.ch020

upper secondary schools (gymnasium/STX). The problems continue as poor uptake into university. The facts and figures of the studied region do not match the desired political goal of uptake in tertiary education. There are specific social problems in neighbouring municipalities regarding parental background and educational mobility (Lange, Johannesen & Henriksen, 2010). A regional council associated with the troubled educational system has funded the Youth-to-Youth Project. The purpose is to bridge transfer from primary school to upper secondary school and from upper secondary school to university studies. The goal of the bridging effort is to provide youths with lacking interest and performance in STEM and tertiary education unlikely, a new *foreground* (Alrø, Skovmose & Valero, 2007) related to information and experiences of studying at upper secondary school and university levels means. To implement this scaffolding project, a network was established between teachers and classes from upper primary school (seventh to eighth grades) to upper secondary school, as was a network between students in upper secondary school and university mentors. The main project idea was that relations between youths 'one step ahead' in the educational system have a potential to provide another new insights into what it means to study in upper secondary school and at university. The intent was an attempt at dealing with reproduction in the educational system, especially related to STEM areas, facilitating an educational trajectory. This is 2014 and a structural event, an uneven distribution and positioning of interest, has occurred – but only on the surface of the structures, substructures, and strata of a spatio-temporal location in Denmark: *In such a place, such sum or sums as are. Expressed in the condition, let the forfeit. Be nominated for an equal pound* (Shakespeare, 2003).

This chapter aims at outlining how the structural problem in education requires a specific conceptualization of *capital* that rests on Marxism, activity theory, and dialectical materialism. Then we will be able to make sense of and topologi-cally map the problem. This specific methodology has been explored previously in relation to the notions of *field* and *power* through an encounter with Pierre Bourdieu and Michel Foucault (Bang, 2014a). I argue that educational researchers need a double movement and construction of *capital* to capture the various ways capital differentiates and manifests between past, current and future activities. The first part of the movement is the construction of a conceptualization of *capital* which lies close to sociology. Bourdieu's methodology helps educational researchers chart relatively valid and measureable factors in different forms of *capital*. Cultural capital and science capital are especially critical to the mapping of the referred structural problem in education. The second part of the movement is inspired by Gilles Deleuze. A conceptualization of capital related to Deleuze's reading of structuralism leads to the creation of a map of events – combining strata of discourse, thought, and history to Bourdieu's axis of cultural and economical capital. Bourdieu's and Deleuze's methodologies have a common denominator in Marx. My aim is to show how the encounter between systems of thought benefits theoretical and methodological research. I use Marxist activity theory and supply a necessary element of a specific kind of structuralism extracted from Bourdieu and Deleuze. However, before I vivisect the body of educational institutions and study their functions, structures and objectives, which explain the given regional 'defect' and ultimately help create a productive map of events, I turn to the concept of *capital*.

CAPITAL: A CONCEPT BEYOND MONEY

The concept of *capital* was at the centre of Marx's analysis and it lies at the very roots of Marxist thought. Examining the consequences of *capital* during the industrial revolution in England gave birth to *The Capital*. Marx and Engels' (1904) careful structural and economical examination paved the way for a new philosophy and way of thought. It is strange that *capital* has somewhat vanished from contemporary activity theory. Now we have to turn elsewhere to conceptualize it. I will readdress and expand the Marxist concept of *capital* to a concept that can be used for analyzing learning and education. In other words, I bring *capital* to the forefront of research grounded in educational and activity theory.

In the first movement Bourdieu's conceptualizations encounter general approaches to activity theory. It is important to emphasize the specific nature of the encounter between views and conceptualizations this chapter attempts to construct. The theoretical encounter is an *affirmation of measurement* in the Deleuzian sense. This choice does not pose critique toward Marx, Ilyenkov, Bourdieu or Deleuze. It rather suggests a necessary movement and expansion of measurement of *capital* across strata, which again posit various perspectives with different roles and ultimately assisting each other in constructing the necessary map of events. But why do educational researchers, especially researchers oriented towards activity theory and dialectical thought, need the concept of *capital*? The answer is a simple one: they need an expanded conceptualization of capital in order to address and topologically visualize the basic and imbedded social structural inequality (*class*) hidden in learning. Specifically, a learning theory based on a Marxist theoretical foundation needs expanded concepts of *capital* and *class* to address and frame the social dimensions of teaching and learning. Vygotsky (1997, p. 345) elaborates on the theme, saying: "'that psychology needs its own Das Kapital'. He [Vygotsky] did not want to gather psychological illustrations to the well-known theses of materialistic dialectics, but *to apply these theses as tools which allow us to reform the investigative process from inside* and compared to which other methods of obtaining and organizing knowledge are powerless." Vygotsky and related researchers say the methodological

approach of *The Capital* (Marx & Engels, 1904) constitutes the very cornerstone of a dialectical material approach in activity theory. There is a need to develop a notion of *capital* that addresses this aspect of the dialectic. There are no *capital*-free cultural domains or institutions and *capital* is a part of and the background of thought, as well as an analytical tool for describing learning and activity. Capital is conceptualized as a structural element and as such the concept covers a real aspect, an imaginary aspect, and a symbolic aspect operating in response to how we recognize structuralism and what structuralism 'is' (Deleuze, 2004, p. 170-192). These aspects are similarly manifested in various ways in Bourdieu's nomenclature.

Contemporary society differs in several ways from the conditions that people met in early industrial society, the environment which Marx analysed in *The Capital*. The concept of *capital* includes the contingency and temporal singularity of cultural historical development. Today *capital* signifies money, which contains virtual, fluid, imaginary and symbolic qualities. Capital is an abstraction deployed to connect different forms of sedimented labour in the form of material products and knowledge organized in a stratum of distribution. David Harvey (2010) emphasizes earlier problems of 'countering' capitalism and, in a way, the rationale behind the expansion of *capital* outlined in this chapter:

Previous attempts to create a communist or socialist alternative fatally failed to keep the dialectic between the different activity spheres in motion and also failed to embrace the unpredictabilities and uncertainties in the dialectical movement between the spheres. Capitalism has survived precisely by keeping that dialectical movement going and by embracing the inevitable tensions, including crisis that result. (p. 228-229)

The nature of capitalism is a warped and monstrous form of dialectical movement and educational researchers need to conceptualize and visualize this monstrous aspect of *capital* in late market-oriented capitalism and the very fluid forms of life and behaviour it requires and adopts.

THE FIRST MOVEMENT: BOURDIEU MEETS ILYENKOV

Ilyenkov is a Russian thinker who emphasized the specific relation between science and *capital* in a Marxist perspective. It would be helpful turning to him to obtain a glimpse of how the relations between science and *capital* are structured. The particular relation between science, education, and *capital* is crucial to understanding the aforementioned problematic situation in a region of Denmark. In an elaboration of Hegel, Ilyenkov (1977) highlights the relation between forms of *capital*, which is similar to the conceptualizations proposed by Bourdieu (emphasis by this author):

Just as accumulated labour concentrated in machines, in the instruments and products of labour functions in the form of capital, in the form of 'self-expanding value', for which the individual capitalist functions as the 'executor', so too scientific knowledge, i.e. the accumulated mental labour of society functions in the form of science, i.e. the same sort of impersonal and featureless anonymous force. [...] He does not think here as such – Knowledge, which has taken root in his head during his education, 'thinks'. (p. 79)

Capital is frozen, or sedimented, labour often appearing in the form of commodities and attributed symbolic value. In its physical or pure economical form capital can mean money, products or commodities. In its *mental form* capital covers forms of knowledge and education. The logic of *capital* is metamorphosed into other areas of human activity, very much above and beyond the field of economics and monetary exchange value. This does not mean, though, in Ilyenkov's or Marx's sense, that an investigation of the forms

of *capital* must solely be in 'general terms', just because the particular historic investigation of specific forms of *capital* is both general and particular. The 'nature' of capital is measureable, and even as capital differentiates and shifts form the quality of a quantifiable element remains, capital thus escapes the standard methods of measurement of the social sciences. This appropriation of the concept is very much akin to Gabriel Tarde's description and expansion of what one needs to measure beyond simple wealth, the classical way of measuring capital (Latour & Lepinay, 2009; Tarde, 1902). Emphasis on the above dimensions and aspects of capital suggests a particular role for producing social science knowledge. It relates to the role that *capital* plays as a special form of 'accumulated mental labour' and 'impersonal and featureless anonymous force' Ilyenkov (1977, p. 79). Capital, practice, and similar notions are general abstractions indeed and according to Ilyenkov (ibid., p. 117), for them to make sense if regarded from a cultural historical perspective, there should be a general and a particular form of expression, saying: "The essence of human nature in general can only be brought through a scientific, critical analysis of the 'whole ensemble', of man's social and historical relations to man, through concrete investigation and understanding of the patterns with which the process of the birth and evolution both of human society as a whole and of the separate individual has taken place and is taking place." The quote shows how activity theory and Ilyenkov are in line with Bourdieu's conceptualizations and methods. When Ilyenkov mentions 'The essence of human nature' he remains safely positioned in a theoretical setting dominated by a dialectical 'whole ensemble' perspective rather than essentialism. In the context of this quote, Bourdieu constructed sociological concepts in order to be able to explore particular and general levels of investigation, preferably concrete sociological analyses of sedimented labour or commodities in physical and mental form. Bourdieu's (1986) overall conceptualization of capital is similar to that of Ilyenkov and Marx.

Capital is accumulated labor (in its materialized, 'incorporated' or embodied form) which, when appropriated on a private, i.e. exclusive, basis by agents or groups of agents, enables them to appropriate social energy in the form of reified or living labor. It is a vis insita, a force inscribed in objective or subjective structures, but it is also a lex insita, a principle underlying the immanent regularities of the social world. (p. 1)

Capital as a 'force inscribed in objective or subjective structures' and 'principle underlying the immanent regularities of the social world' is very much definitions of the role the concept takes on in contemporary institutions. Only through analysis of capital in its *expanded form* can one understand the social world. Bourdieu (ibid., p. 1) says "It is in fact impossible to account for the structure and functioning of the social world unless one reintroduces capital in all its forms and not solely in the one form recognized by economic theory". To summarize the contents of this section, the object of activity theory is mediated in thought and as a tool, but in the same dialectical movement the object of activity is a product of labour and ultimately a form of *capital*. To forget the *capital* inherent in the object of thought and activity and that thought *ipso facto* is a product of mental labour and *capital* subsequent practices related to this *capital* would, in other words, be to forget the lesson that Marx and his dialectical movement teach.

VIVISECTING CLASS AND CAPITAL

In order to properly reintroduce *capital* to contemporary activity theory, one needs in a first movement to turn to Bourdieu's reflexive sociology and his version of structuralism. This combination precisely reintroduced *capital* in various forms of analyses into society. Bourdieu (1984, p. 95) developed different concepts in which the following relation takes centre stage: [(Habitus) (Capital)] + Field = Practice. The relation in brackets between *habitus* and *capital* contains a crucial dialectic dimension and facilitates attempts at bridging notions of society to mind and overcome various dualistic dichotomies regarding subject and object, man and society and so forth. Bourdieu (ibid.) descibes habitus.

The habitus is both the generative principle of objectively classifiable judgements and the system of classification (principium divisionis) of these practices. It is in the relationship between the two capacities which define the habitus, the capacity to produce classifiable practices and works, and the capacity to differentiate and appreciate these practices and products (taste), that the represented social world i.e., the space of lifestyles, is constituted. (p. 170).

Bourdieu (1984, p. 172) describes the crucial dialectic between capital and habitus as: "The dialectic of conditions and habitus is the basis of an alchemy which transforms the distribution of capital, the balance-sheet of a power relation, into a system of perceived differences, distinctive properties, that is, a distribution of symbolic capital, legitimate capital, whose objective truth is misrecognized." Bourdieu's concepts of habitus and capital indicate where the premise of Marxist activity theory is most vibrant and I will in the following show how Vygotsky's notion of double-stimulus and mediation is visible in Bourdieu's sociological notion of habitus. Bourdieu's (1977, p.72) overall theory of practice describes a way: "... to construct the theory of practice, or, more precisely, the theory of the mode of generation of practices, which is the precondition for establishing an experimental science of the dialectic of the internalization of externality and the externalization of internality, or, more simply, of incorporation and objectification." Isn't the dialectic of 'the internalization of externality and the externalization of internality' precisely what Vygotsky investigated in his research regarding double-stimuli? Bourdieu (1977, p. 79) emphasizes the overarching role mediation plays in his concept of habitus:"The habitus is the universalizing mediation which causes an individual agent's practices, without either explicit reason or signifying intent, to be none the less "sensible" and "reasonable". Furthermore Bourdieu (ibid.) highlights habitus as an acquired system akin to the role systems of activity plays in activity theory.

Through the habitus, the structure which has produced it governs practice, not by the processes of a mechanical determinism, but through the mediation of the orientations and limits it assigns to the habitus's operations of invention. As an acquired system of generative schemes objectively adjusted to the particular conditions in which it is constituted, the habitus engenders all the thoughts, all the perceptions, and all the actions consistent with those conditions, and no others. (p. 95)

In other words there seems to be a fertile ground for an encounter between Bourdieu's conceptualizations and research and research in activity theory. Bourdieu's conceptualizations are inspired by anthropology and traditional sociology, especially the works of Max Weber and Emile Durkheim. But contrary to theirs, Bourdieu's concepts are developed with a dialectical and Marxist orientation. Therefore it would seem productive to set up an encounter with Bourdieu to see how his conceptualizations resonate with the Marxist premise of activity theory as expressed in the Feuerbach theses (Marx & Engels, 1978, p. 143-145). Bourdieu (1990, p. 49) wanted to escape from being called a Marxist sociologist and similar labels, saying about affinity with Marxist ideology: "There may be impassable philosophies, but there is no impassable science. By definition, science is there to be surpassed. And since Marx went to such lengths to claim the title of scientist, the only

fitting homage to pay him is to use what he did, and what others have done with what he did, so as to surpass what he thought he did." Bourdieu draws attention to mediations at a 'macro' or class structural level between man, physical objects and activity. His structural macro-perspective is often neglected as a fundamental background for any kind of 'micro' activity. Bourdieu positions himself at the same structural class level as Antonio Gramsci and Marx, but with an additional set of conceptualizations devised to explain interactions between individual and society. Another ambition is to show how practices change and form parts of belonging to a particular place in the social field.

Contemporary activity theory research often focuses on micro perspectives of how learning takes place in various settings and how learning begets various practices, unfortunately often forgetting the Marxist heritage of activity theory (Roth, 2004). Activity theory is more than a theory of learning. It is an attempt at dialectically understanding the relation between subject and object, man and culture, and similar general relations combined with practical considerations. There is a philosophical line, or thread of thought, going from Spinoza to Marx and, further on, from Marx to Vygotsky and Leontjev (Ilyenkov, 1977). Bourdieu brings the latter line of thought into his reflexive sociology and constructs concepts that shed new light on the relation between man and objects and showing how they structure class and practice. In this capacity, Bourdieu revitalizes Marx's concept of *class and capital,* since he brings the dichotomy to the forefront through empirical analyses. Bourdieu's relations between key concepts of *capital, habitus, field,* and *practice* emphasize why any understanding of practice is interdependent of a complementary understanding of *capital.* Capital must in a first movement combine with notions of *habitus* or *field.* I focus on the relation between a specific form of *capital* and specific forms of practice, reflecting how Bourdieu's concept supplements the current framework of activity theory. Though

Bourdieu's conceptualization of *capital* is an abstraction and suited for sociological analyses, the argument is that concrete activity-theoretical analyses of learning suffer from lack of insights into the Marxist inheritance. They would also suffer from lack of insights into the significance (analytical power) of Bourdieu's additional strata or theoretical fields.

ON CAPITAL AND SCIENCE

Akin to Francis Bacon's (2010) famous premise that knowledge is power, one should recognize that knowledge becomes a form of *capital* if applied to conditions and operations in the social field. Just like wealth, knowledge is a measureable entity. Bourdieu proposes three forms of *capital*: 1) economic *capital*, 2) cultural *capital* and 3) social (symbolic) *capital*. These forms of capital are, of course, interrelated and Bourdieu's (1986) notion of transubstantiation between various forms stressing that economic *capital* is the primary form. The other general aspects of a structural element – the real, the imaginary, and the symbolic – are found in all three forms of capital, such that symbolic capital in Bourdieu's sense is not purely social/symbolic. The differentiated forms of *capital* are thus akin to Ilyenkov's conceptualizations, since they are both general and particular at the same time and always a product of some kind of labour activity. There is an intricate relationship between these forms of capital and only through a combination of micro and macro studies, observations of practice and analyses of the particular institutions can we understand the workings of forms of capital and the specific forms in which they manifest themselves, or are actualized, in the field.

As emphasized in the Ilyenkov quote above, a very particular relationship exists between *capital* and science. Especially in what (Zizek, 2012) terms *late capitalism* there is a crucial relation between economic and cultural *capital* and science. Others have termed relations between economic *capital*

and science/academia a new type of post-academic science (Ziman, 1995; 1996). Bourdieu uses three *fields* to examine education, academia and science. He describes them as the educational *field,* the academic *field* and the scientific *field* (Bourdieu, 1988; 1998; 2004; Bourdieu & Passeron, 1990). An alternative way of defining them would be by use of terms of an overall field (like education) and various related subfields. It is important to note the Marxist premise of the notion of *field –* every *field* is a *field* of struggle (Bourdieu, 1984). The notion of strata is used here to describe the different structural layers in the field, a particular notion and use inspired by Deleuze's (1986; 2004) reading of Foucault and of the work with Felix Guattari (1987). Bourdieu's field(s) is thus in a way inserted in Deleuze and Guattari 's notion of strata (Deleuze & Guattari, 1987 p. 39-74) as measurable structures on the various stratums.

In the educational *field,* knowledge of science is a specific form of cultural *capital*. If you have knowledge, aptitude and skill in science, you are likely to score high in tests and other forms of assessment and examination. This knowledge is partly reproduced, handed down or inherited. In other words, if you come from an educated family, chances are that the length of your parents' bookshelf influences how easily you learn science at school. This general mode of reproduction or inheritance is a well established fact in sociology (Archer et al., 2012; Bourdieu & Passeron, 1990; Osborne & Dillon, 2008). Cultural *capital* is, however, more, than accumulated knowledge and it is interdependent of *habitus* to enact this specific form of *capital*. It is through the concept of *habitus* or "sense of the game" that the agent exchanges his or her cultural capital to academic recognition and various positions, or grades in the field. Without *habitus* institutions and agents in the educational field will not recognize the actual form of behaviour or *capital* as legitimate. The dialectic between *habitus* and *capital,* between *sense* and *structure,* is obvious in Bourdieu's (2004, p. 35) terminology in outlining the role played by proponents of the scientific field: "The specificity of the scientific field is partly due to the fact that the quantity of accumulated history is especially great, owing in particular to the 'conservation' of its achievements in a particularly economical form, with for example organization into principles and formulae or in the form of a slowly accumulated stock of calibrated actions and routinized skills."

To explore this specific field and its influence on the field of upper secondary education, one needs a concept of *capital* expanded beyond the scientific *capital*. Bourdieu (2004, p. 55) says: "Scientific capital functions as a symbolic capital of recognition that is primarily, sometimes exclusively, valid within the limits of the field (although it can be converted into other kinds of capital, economic capital in particular)." What is not emphasized in this conceptualization is transference of *capital* from other *fields into* the scientific *field*, especially regarding knowledge. In order to explore the mentioned regional problem in Danish education, the relation between cultural capital and scientific capital needs to be enunciated.

To explore scientific practices and knowledge in upper secondary school and the aforementioned problem regarding uptake into STEM areas and into the educational field in general, it would seem advantageous to conceptualize a specific form of scientific *capital* as a sub form of cultural *capital* divided into light/minor scientific *capital* compared to the proper scientific *field* and scientific *habitus*. This latter concept was previously dubbed *Homo Empiricus* (Bang, 2014b). The last critical conceptualization stems from the Bourdieuian notion of *field* and how the scientific *field* called proper science at universities influences the educational *field*. This latter field specifically relates to the upper secondary *subfield*, i.e. gymnasiums.

Specific scientific *capital* and subsequent *habitus* is produced and exchanged in particular educational institutions in the educational *field* and problems regarding poor uptake in a specific region in Denmark closely relates to scientific *capital* and

habitus. This institutional manifestation and the forms of *capital* and *habitus* therein materialize as 'reflection' or perhaps a light version of true scientific institutions in the educational field. The scientific *capital* and *habitus* in the upper secondary subfield of education are produced with the goal of transference into academia and university. The accumulation, distribution, and production of scientific *capital* and *habitus* undergo transference to other institutions and related subfields in the educational *field*. This transference has critical implications for reproduction and the educational trajectory in the educational *field,* as shown in Bourdieu (1998) and Bourdieu and Passeron (1990). In the following text I emphasize cultural *capital* (science *capital*) and *habitus* related to a specific type of institution (gymnasium in Denmark) in the educational field and related to a specific subject matter and practice (science). But, first, the relationship between *capital*, *habitus,* and the traditional activity-theoretical concept of learning must be demarcated.

DIFFERENTIATION OF CULTURAL CAPITAL

Bourdieu (1986) proposes that cultural *capital* covers an embodied state, an objectified state, and an institutionalized state. These states are, in this conceptualization, all states of the real. The three states are important additions and not a direct break to the traditional learning focus of activity theory. Bourdieu (1986, p. 3) says: 'This starting point implies a break with the presuppositions inherent both in the commonsense view, which sees academic success or failure as an effect of natural aptitudes, and in human capital theories'. Cultural capital is actualized in all three states and a study of learning, sedimented labour in the form of knowledge, traverses all three states. A study of learning is the study of a particular cultural *capital* enacted through a particular class *habitus* with a specific temporality and spatiality, that is, a localized position in the stratum. To solely focus on aspects of learning in the traditional sense disavows learning as a neutral process. Therefore one should always consider it enmeshed in a dialectic of specific cultural structures (an assemblage) and their relative localization in time and space in the stratum – often reproducing the same distribution. Learning is not purely the domain of psychology or pedagogy but should, in the same methodological movement, be analysed from the perspective of sociology.

Returning to the problem regarding uptake into the natural sciences in the gymnasium in a Danish region, the above considerations need to be taken into account if one were to propose a dialectical material approach to studying the problem, particularly one oriented towards activity and practice. One could falsely propose that the problem is merely related to specifically *learning* in the natural sciences and that this is why the students are not interested or motivated to choose science as a career or educational trajectory. Then the solution would be to develop teaching practices and adopt an overall focus on the micro situation of teaching and learning and interest/motivation in the sciences. With such a demarcation the researcher overlooks structural circumstances, localization and distribution of the strata and conditions inherent in the acquisition of cultural *capital*. The choice of career in science should be carefully examined regarding learning conditions within the classroom/laboratory and similar micro-settings of specific practices (Latour & Woolgar, 1986; Roth & Lee, 2004). These practices will have tell-tale-signs of manifested *habitus* and forms of *capital,* thereby grounding Bourdieu's macro conceptualizations regarding class and practice.

Keeping in mind the lessons of Marx, Ilyenkov, and Bourdieu, in the same investigation it is, however, necessary to examine a *general structural view*. In this general view, cultural *capital* is a product of family/class conditions or the lay of the land and spatial temporality surrounding the gymnasium. A study of learning and unequal distribution of opportunities requires a socioeconomic analysis coupled with an analysis of cultural *capital* akin to those exemplified by Bourdieu (1984; 1998) and Bourdieu and Passeron (1990). In summary, an overall analysis of cultural capital contains at least two specific perspectives: one perspective including analysis of concrete learning practices in the classroom, manifested as cultural *capital* and *habitus*. The analysis should also cover a perspective for examining the structures surrounding the institution or family or similar larger structures, that is, an assemblage of various manifested forms of *capital, habitus* and *practices*. The following shows the second movement and how the above conceptualizations and movement between Bourdieu and Ilyenkov translates to a methodology of mapping events, which outlines the investigation of the problem regarding uptake in a region in Denmark. Results of the second movement point to areas where analysis of Marxist activity theory benefits from double movements.

THE SECOND MOVEMENT: EVENTS AND ASSEMBLAGES OF ACTIVITY

The second movement affirms the previous measurements by Bourdieu and his system of concepts (*capital, habitus, field* and *practice*) as well as Marxist activity theory. Taken together they become the necessary tools and conceptualizations for constructing some of the strata which I will mention in the succeeding text. The measurement needs to go 'deeper' and 'higher' akin to Gabriel Tarde's sociology (Latour & Lepinay, 2009; Tarde, 1893) and in the last movement presented here various other measurements or quantifiables supplements the construction of the map of events. The map of events is a form of mapping and measurement, which replaces substances with events in a Deleuzian approach. We thus expand and affirm the traditional view of the dialectic in favor of Deleuze's (1994) approach which always inserts multiplicity, dx/dy between two concepts or notions.

Activity theory understood as Leontyev's systems of activity (Leontev, 1998) is in this movement seen in a Deleuzian way as assemblages of activity connecting concrete activity, thought and practice to various strata. The second movement is a process of taking the first movement of Bourdieu and activity theory through a theoretical movement of Deleuze with a specific interest in his reading of structuralism (Deleuze, 2004). The map of events is similarly influenced by Tarde and Foucault. The following text outlines exploration of science in upper secondary school. The approach is informed by conceptualizations in the first movement, as seen through the lens of a concrete project and line of research activity. The Danish Youth-to-Youth Project consisted of five gymnasiums; ten primary schools, each connected to one of the five gymnasiums; and one university, from which a body of mentors was recruited.

The data collected by this author focused on the five gymnasiums and the students therein. My ambition was to construct a whole ensemble of data in line with Ilyenkov's recommendations so as to map the problem regarding uptake in science. Various types of data were collected in concert with project activities. Examples of the data types are interviews with gymnasium students and university mentors, a large-scale longitudinal survey on attitude, socio-economic, and biographical data, observations gathered from project students, mentors, and teachers, and historical documentation about the region and the structures surrounding the five gymnasiums. This process covered a mixture of qualitative and quantitative data ranging from 2011 to 2014. It was gathered directly by this author and indirectly through interviews, observations and documents. The survey included an account from the majority of all the students

in the five gymnasiums in the period 2011-2014, i.e. four generations of students. The survey is an example of types of measurements and connected strata which enables for investigation and analysis of capital. I employed a statistical method called Latent Class Analysis (Collins & Lanza, 2010) for analyzing the dataset. This method for analyzing the data opened up for a new relational perspective where unobserved (latent) relations could be drawn between the variables.

These four types of data also allowed the researcher to construct a map of various structural levels, or strata, which was again a step in analyzing the problem of uptake in science. Among these strata there is the stratum of science *capital,* in which the researcher connected various factors to each agent as part of the data on collective qualities. The stratum of science *capital* is interrelated with the other strata in the exploration. For example, strata of activities like sports, music/art and leisure, strata of economy, strata of aesthetics and so forth. Categorization of strata offers a way of capturing an expansion of measurement. A method which Tarde (1902) calls for in Psychologie économique because it is needed when capital/capitalism expands and colonizes other strata (Deleuze & Guattari, 1987). This author draws carefully on strata of science *capital* but also on related strata, which were determined in the exploration. But a break occurs where the above typical forms of data take on a different meaning due to the specific theoretical position invoked here. *The strata of science capital are not strata of human properties, attributes, or any kind of individual essences, but connected to a map of events and assemblages of activity.* This map of events and assemblages of activity is relational and the measured *capital* is never located inside the individual but relationally placed in an assemblage of different structures and potentials within singular events. These events are both quantitative and qualitative entities (Deleuze, 2004). In fact my ambition is to map the symbolic and imaginary aspects of capital with several survey variables seen in an imaginary and symbolic light. Similarly, this map shows various forms of labour surrounding and creating the agent's relative position in the map of science *capital*. Bourdieu (Bourdieu, 1984; Lebaron, 2009) used measurement of the participants' objects in their surveys. They attributed the typical class objects to specific clusters in the social field. This kind of relative measurement of objects was not used in this author's exploration due to considerations regarding the concrete case; *the fact that the youths live with their parents* so any objects accounted for in the above describe the parents' *capital/habitus* form. Therefore, some general pieces of information on education and the partent's types of employment was considered to be sufficient. This author's approach to mapping *capital* as a map of events and knots of assemblages of activity reveals another theoretical point. Deleuze's (1994) distinction and rendering of different strata follows Foucault's line of thought and identifies the archive, the map, and the diagram. Deleuze (ibid.) instigated the particular mapping used above. In the map, youth with a potentially high relational amount of science *capital* and subsequent *habitus* were surrounded by the following assemblages of activity: parents with a career in science or higher education and/or who had also attended a gymnasium, siblings who had also attended a gymnasium, high test scores in science and related science subjects as part of their curriculum in a gymnasium, and generally positive high-ranking interest in science and pursuit of a career in STEM areas.

These four points describing the enunciation of relations for a relative high amount of science *capital* are an assemblage of different forms of activity. The first and second points are a relative indicator of the milieu surrounding home activity, where inherited forms of labour affect the actual activity of the youth. The youth can get help with homework, become adept at mathematics/physic/

chemistry, and receive a huge amount of help and scaffolding to grasp the meaning of abstract natural sciences. The remaining points are a relative indicator of the youth's activity at the gymnasium, where the former is a relative indicator of the *habitus* or skill in science and the latter a relative indicator of a discursive formation in which the youth positions himself or herself within a specific community of the gymnasium, labelled nerds, mathematicians, experts and so forth.

The given display of a specific case lies within a map of events constructed as a virtual/actual form of science capital. The display suggests there is a relation between this map of events and the possibilities of the trajectories of the youths. It also suggests that they can only be explored after a certain time has passed. Elements of force and power in the various strata shape the youth's trajectories as series of singular events. However, this quality does not become visible solely from the point of view of science capital. Structure, on contrary, consists of enacting effects on structure, strata upon strata or diagram influencing the map and the archive. Bourdieu's (1984) analysis used an axis of economic capital and cultural capital to create a social field of dispositions. Here, other axes or strata are connected to the axis of science capital, in addition to the axis of economic capital. For example, the axis of geography shows the agents' placement in the geography of the studied region. In other words, through depiction of various axes or strata, the researcher constructs a map of events pointing towards the problem of uptake into STEM, without indicating causality or a set of determinisms from this limited event in time. The described process of constructing a map of events illustrates an attempt to outline the construction of a new kind mapping, in which this author tries to implement Deleuze's imaginary, real and symbolic dimensions of structuralism. One can now return to the ramifications of seeing a mapping of assemblages of activities as a mapping of events in a dialectical light.

A MAP OF EVENTS: CAPITAL BEYOND ESSENCE

The notion of essence has plagued and continues to plague dialectical thought, but Deleuze (1994) shows there is a way out, an escape route through a new dialectical line of thought. His philosophical line of thought shares many similarities with the 'necessity of dialectical monism' proposed by Smith (2009). Monism is closely related to Spinoza and Leibniz and it is a crucial element of such an ontology. Marx's sixth Feuerbach thesis (Marx & Engels, 1978) shows that dialectical thought must go beyond essentialist thinking:

Feuerbach resolves the religious essence into the human essence. But the human essence is no abstraction inherent in each single individual. In its reality it is the ensemble of the social relations. Feuerbach, who does not enter upon a criticism of this real essence, is consequently compelled: (1) Abstract from the historical process and to fix the religious sentiment as something by itself and to presuppose an abstract – isolated – human individual. (2) The human essence, therefore, can with him be comprehended only as "genus," as an internal, dumb generality which merely naturally unites the many individuals. (p. 145).

Deleuze (1990) proposes a new ontology based on the sense-event. For him sense takes on a role similar to the notion of *habitus* put forth by Bourdieu. For Deleuze, however, sense develops and expands in a philosophical line of thought. Deleuze's (2004) new reading of structuralism, and in accordance to his notion of event, what structure consists of, and how we recognize structuralism is of critical importance for taking "*Das Kapital* into psychology" and also for bridging various fields of knowledge. As a structural element, *capital* consists of real, imaginary and symbolic aspects. During the process of mapping the influence and topology of various forms of capital in human assemblages of activity, theses aspects need to be

taken into account. Deleuze (2004) comments on the notion of the empty square or the paradoxical element form a critically new structural element in the map of events.

All structures are infrastructures. The structural orders—linguistic, familial, economic, sexual, etc.—are characterized by the form of their symbolic elements, the variety of their differential relations, the species of their singularities, finally and, above all, by the nature of the object = x that presides over their functioning.(…) In each structural order, certainly, the object = x is not at all something unknowable, something purely undetermined; it is perfectly determinable, including within its displacements and by the mode of displacement that characterizes it.(…) As a result, for each order of structure the object = x is the empty or perforated site that permits this order to be articulated with the others, in a space that entails as many directions as orders. The orders of the structure do not communicate in a common site, but they all communicate through their empty place or respective object = x. (p. 188).

At this stage one needs to affirm and expand the concepts, models and arguments as supplied by Marx and Bourdieu. Standard socioeconomic analyses and similar statistical forms of measurement will only reveal to the educational researcher's an inadequate map of the whole ensemble. Such ways of working often tend to reduce the complexity of the problem of education to crude caricatures with obscure denominators, categories, universals and topologies of types of students, families, settings or other. Such research returns to an essentialist view of knowledge and mental labour. To explore educational contexts properly is to take on the challenge of gazing at structural complexity. Unravelling the contents of such fields requires an effective way of mapping and measuring, to go beyond essence, to obtain a n-dimensional (real, imaginary, symbolic) image of the highlighted structures. More specifically, the particular connection between Deleuze's thinking and the heritage of Marx allows for a crucial bridging and encounter for reintroducing *capital* and a specific form of structuralism - transcendental empiricism and complementing activity theory. Put differently, analytical advantages emerge from bringing Deleuze's version of the empty square and paradoxical element into resonance with dialectical materialism. I hope that this contention enunciates the importance of efforts at bridging French thought by Bourdieu and Deleuze in this case with Marx.

CONCLUSION

The ultimate purpose of this chapter is to integrate *capital* into psychology and activity theory. The map of *capital* illustrates a map of events and in its pure sense it is a map of a *stunted game* with locked structures and numbed causalities, ultimately removed from pure chance. Deleuze (1990) comments on the stunted game.

The characteristics of normal games are therefore the preexisting categorical rules, the distributing hypotheses, the fixed and numerically distinct distributions, and the ensuing results. The games are partial in two ways: first they characterize only one part of human activity, and second even if they are pushed to the absolute, they retain chance only at certain points, leaving the remainder to the mechanical development of consequences or to skill, understood as the art of causality. (p. 69–70)

This display of the researcher's process of mapping events is an attempt at revealing stunted as well as normal games going on between people, to vivisect and reveal inner causality and logic related to late capitalism among citizens in contemporary society. Even today, the notion of capital carries with it, as Shakespeare wrote "of your fair flesh to be cut off and taken" and equally a part of thought, body, and activity.

REFERENCES

Alrø, H., Skovsmose, O., & Valero, P. (2007). Inter-viewing foregrounds. *Working Papers on Learning and Philosophy*, 2007(5), 1-23.

Archer, L., DeWitt, J., Osborne, J., Dillon, J., Willis, B., & Wong, B. (2012). Science Aspirations, Capital, and Family Habitus How Families Shape Children's Engagement and Identification With Science. *American Educational Research Journal*, 49(5), 881–908. doi:10.3102/0002831211433290

Bacon, F. (2010). *Meditationes Sacrae and Human Philosophy*. London: Kessinger Publishing.

Bang, L. (2014a). Between the Cat and the Principle: An encounter between Foucault's and Bourdieu's conceptualisations of power. *Power and Education*, 6(1), 18–31. doi:10.2304/power.2014.6.1.18

Bang, L. (2014b). *Welcome to school - welcome to the Empire-Building Business: an exploration and expansion of Bourdieu's notion of field. Waikota Journal of Education*.

Bourdieu, P. (1977). *Outline of a Theory of Practice*. Cambridge, UK: Cambridge University Press. doi:10.1017/CBO9780511812507

Bourdieu, P. (1984). *Distinction: A Social Critique of the Judgement of Taste* (N. Richard, Trans.). London: Routledge.

Bourdieu, P. (1986). The forms of capital. In J. Richardson (Ed.), Handbook of theory and research for the sociology of education. New York: Greenwood

Bourdieu, P. (1988). *Homo academicus*. Cambridge, MA: Polity Press.

Bourdieu, P. (1990). *In other words: Essays towards a reflexive sociology*. Stanford, CA: Stanford University Press.

Bourdieu, P. (1998). *The state nobility: Elite schools in the field of power*. Stanford, CA: Stanford University Press.

Bourdieu, P. (2004). *Science of science and reflexivity*. Cambridge, UK: Polity Press.

Bourdieu, P., & Passeron, J.-C. (1990). *Reproduction in education, society and culture*. Cambridge, UK: SAGE.

Collins, L. M., & Lanza, S. T. (2010). *Latent class and latent transition analysis: With applications in the social, behavioral, and health sciences* (Vol. 718). John Wiley & Sons.

Deleuze, G. (1990). *The logic of sense*. New York: Columbia University Press.

Deleuze, G. (1994). *Difference and repetition*. London: Contiuum Group.

Deleuze, G. (2004). *Desert Islands: And Other Texts, 1953--1974*. New York: Semiotext.

Deleuze, G., & Guattari, F. (1987). *A thousand plateaus: Capitalism and schizophrenia*. Minneapolis, MN: University of Minnesota Press.

Ilyenkov, E. (1977). *Dialectical Logic: Essays on its Theory and History*. Moscow: Progress.

Kakkori, L., & Huttunen, R. (2014). Vygotsky, Heidegger and Gadamer on moral development. In T. Hansson (Ed.), Contemporary Approaches to Activity Theory: Interdisciplinary Perspectives on Human Behavior. Hershey, PA: IGI Global.

Lange, T., Johannesen, K., & Henriksen, T. H. (2010). *De unges veje gennem uddannelsessystemet i Nordjylland*. Region Nordjylland.

Latour, B., & Lepinay, V. A. (2009). *The Science of Passionate Interests-An Introduction to: Gabriel Tarde's Economic Anthropology*. Chicago: Prickly Paradigm Press.

Latour, B., & Woolgar, S. (1986). *Laboratory life: The construction of scientific facts*. Princeton, NJ: Princeton University Press.

Lebaron, F. (2009). How Bourdieu "Quantified" Bourdieu: The Geometric Modeling of Data. In K. R. a. C. Sanders (Ed.), Quantifying Theory: Pierre Bourdieu (pp. 11-29). London: Springer Science + Business Media B.V

Leontyev, A. N. (1978). *Activity, Consciousness, Personality* (M. J. Hall, Trans.). Prentice Hall.

Marx, K., & Engels, F. (1904). *Das Kapital: Kritik der politischen Ökonomie* (Vol. 3). Hamburg, Germany: Meissner.

Marx, K., & Engels, F. (1978). *The Marx-Engels Reader*. New York: W. W. Norton & Company.

Osborne, J., & Dillon, J. (2008). *Science education in Europe: Critical reflections*. London: Nuffield Foundation.

Roth, W.-M. (2004). Activity Theory and Education: An Introduction. *Mind, Culture, and Activity*, *11*(1), 1–8. doi:10.1207/s15327884mca1101_1

Roth, W.-M., & Lee, S. (2004). Science education as/for participation in the community. *Science Education*, *88*(2), 263–291. doi:10.1002/sce.10113

Smith, M. E. (2009). Against dualism: Marxism and the necessity of dialectical monism. *Science and Society*, *73*(3), 356–385. doi:10.1521/siso.2009.73.3.356

Shakespeare, W. (2003). *The Merchant of Venice* (M. M. Mahood, Ed.). Vol. 26). Cambridge: Cambridge University Press.

Tarde, G. (1893). *Monadologie et sociologie* (E. Alliez, Ed.). Paris: Inst. Synthélabo pour le Progrès de la Connaissance.

Tarde, G. (1902). *Psychologie économique* (F. Alcan, Ed.). Paris: Ancienne Libr. Germer Baillière et Cie.

Vygotsky, L. S. (1997). The collected works of LS Vygotsky: Problems of the theory and history of psychology (vol. 3). (R. V. d. Veer, Trans.). New York: Plenum Press.

Ziman, J. (1995). Postacademic Science: Constructing Knowledge with Networks and Norms. In U. Segerstråle (Ed.), Beyond the science wars: The missing discourse about science and society. Albany, NY: State University of New York Press.

Ziman, J. (1996). Is science losing its objectivity? *Nature*, *382*(6594), 751–754. doi:10.1038/382751a0

Zizek, S. (2012). *Organs without bodies: On Deleuze and consequences*. London: Routledge.

ADDITIONAL READING

Bourdieu, P. (1986). The forms of capital, J. Richardson (Ed.). Handbook of theory and research for the sociology of education. New York: Greenwood.

Grenfell, M. (2008). *Pierre Bourdieu: key concepts*. Durham: Acumen Publishers.

Harvey, D. (2010). *A companion to Marx's capital*. Lonson: Verso Books.

Parr, A. (2010). *The Deleuze dictionary*. Edinburgh: Edinburgh University Press.

Stolze, T. (1998). Deleuze and Althusser: Flirting with structuralism. *Rethinking Marxism*, *10*(3), 51–63. doi:10.1080/08935699808685540

KEY TERMS AND DEFINITIONS

Assemblages of Activity: Akin to Leontjev's systems of activity, activity is seen here from Deleuze's point of view as an assemblage and connected ad infinitum to related activities in the strata. A concrete activity such as laboratory work in a science class is connected to activities in many other strata, not directly but in an assemblage.

Capital: The researcher here sees capital as a relative indication of a structural disposition and potential in a temporal and spatial stratum. Capital is beyond money and represents various forms of value and sedimented labour.

Field: The researcher uses Bourdieu's definition of field as a specific temporal and spatial place where the above capital and habitus dispositions manifest themselves. The researcher uses the word strata as a new concept evoked in the encounter and movement of Bourdieu and Deleuze.

Forms of Capital: The researcher uses Bourdieu's differentiation of capital in economic, cultural, and symbolic/social capital. The researcher has conceptually explored scientific capital as a specific differentiation of cultural capital.

Habitus: The researcher uses Bourdieu's definition in the 'sense of the game', a concept encompassing the knowledge and skill (and within the realm of cognition and very much connected to activity) of how to use the specific disposition given or attained in the field (the specific form of capital). Habitus has no meaning without the concept of capital, since the two concepts are structurally entwined. Habitus is brought here into an encounter and movement with Deleuze's concept of sense, which expands it and brings it into philosophical line regarding sense.

Map of Events: The topological kind of structural mapping Bourdieu put forth in his analyses encounters here Deleuze's concept of event. This means that the map proposed in this chapter's outlined methodology is a map of virtualities that are actualized in various parts of the strata. The quantitative and qualitative data gathered take a new meaning as actualized manifestations of the events plotted in the map. The map of events connects discourse, various structural elements such as forms of capital, and other kinds of structural instances to topologically mapped events.

Strata: The various planes, or fields, in which the structural elements manifest themselves in various forms. The term strata is used as a concept arising from the encounter between Bourdieu's concept of field and Deleuze.

Structural Element: Capital is seen as a structural element with a real aspect, an imaginary aspect, and a symbolic aspect.

Chapter 21
Reflections on the Theory of Activity

Regi Theodor Enerstvedt
Oslo University, Norway

ABSTRACT

Activity theory is a "productive" resource for shedding light on the functioning of traditional and innovative activities. In discussing theoretical-methodological problems related to a valid theory of activity, the author puts forward the hypothesis that singular references to the Vygotskian school lead to an unproducive confinement of activity theory. First of all, there are problems concerning terminology and concepts. Second, there are issues related to the roots of the activity theory and the cultural-historical school. It is a common mistake in Western Europe and in the United States to regard cultural-historical psychology as the basis for critical psychology and to regard both schools as identical with activity theory. Embracing such a point of view is a mistake and a serious matter.

INTRODUCTION

There is a lot to be said about critical psychology, cultural-historical psychology, cultural-historical school and activity theory. In Western Europe and in the USA miscellaneous psychological currents develop and thrive. Proponents coin and use a variety of terms and concepts. This development is part and parcel of a broad liberation movement, e.g. student riots in Paris in 1968. On the one hand, the terms and concepts demonstrate a productive variety and diversity. On the other hand, people communicate easily in everyday life by using the same words for the same concepts. This human convention or semantic agreement of ours is required in order to enable for scientific discussion, cooperation and development of a research community and a research tradition. Such is the situation today as we attempt to create a basis for understanding what activity theory means and what it is. A common vocabulary is a prerequisite to the achievement of a developed scientific level of discussion eventually enabling for us to see the rise and successful implementation of a (new) paradigm. Of course we use different words for the concept of *activity* in different languages. But the crucial question remains to be answered: What is activity?

DOI: 10.4018/978-1-4666-6603-0.ch021

CONCEPTUAL ANALYSIS

The English word *activity* is a general term and there are many conflicting activity theories around. Due to these facts, the terminology reflects an unfortunate choice. Etymologically, the German word "Tätigkeit" means "doing" in English. The latter term was embraced by Dewey's pragmatism, for example as in Learning by Doing. In Scandinavia, *activity* translates "virksomhet", "verksamhet" etc. However, for some Scandinavian researchers the word activity is similar to or the same as "aktivitet". Here I discuss the theoretical implications of crucial phrases, expressions and utterances – for example concepts like activity theory, cultural-historical school, internalization and interchange. I also argue that the concepts enable for different approaches, analyses and understandings in the scientific community. Fortunately, in Scandinavia we use the word "aktivitet" (*activity*) to denote that life is activity as well as movement. When I use the word "virksomhet" I do so with the purpose to describe a particular contextualized human activity. The theory I have in mind is the one Scandinavians label "virksomhetsteori" or "verksamhetsteori". I propose that we use this term rather than the translation from English, "aktivitetsteori".

PROBLEM STATEMENT

Most of the literature on cultural-historical psychology and activity theory in Western Europe and the USA refer to Vygotskian ideas as the only historical source worth mentioning. Furthermore, activity theorists argue the hypothesis that Vygotskij is the one and only reference to activity theory. However, in the former Soviet Union there was S. L. Rubinstein's school of activity theory too. Also, there is a discussion of fundamental theoretical-methodological problems in the theory of activity, mainly the Rubinstein – Leontjev controversy on internalization. Finally, there

are relations to explore between dialectics and activity theory. It takes a comprehensive model of the individual and society defined as activity to clarify the relation.

ACTIVITY THEORY AND THE CULTURAL-HISTORICAL SCHOOL

I start off with a reference to Karl Marx (1818-1883). The Feuerbach Theses has had an undisputed impact on contemporary understanding of activity theory. The connection between Marx and Feuerbach is well known. It is, however, important to emphasize that there are different lines of reasoning about Marx. One of them suggests a structural interpretation called "the logic of capital", i.e. an alternative interpretation of the human subject understood as object of capital. Another line of reasoning emphasizes the subject in capitalism, the creative, active personality operating in/on suppressing market-controlled conditions. In order to separate between the double lines of reasoning, the Feuerbach theses suggest that by changing the world, surroundings, environment, context, setting etc. man is able to change identity and personality. Marx's interpretation forms a foundation for, or a cornerstone of activity theory.

Origins

Very few people would contest the proposition that activity theory and the cultural-historical school originated and developed in the Soviet Union. But the question remains: by whom? Let's have a look at the Marxist theory of Psychology in the former Soviet Union. Vygotskij's school of activity theory emerged in the 1920s. His contribution to social science formed far from a homogeneous, negotiated, agreed and institutionalized paradigm. It was more like miscellaneous and temporary cooperative initiatives among several researchers. On this basis, however, close teamwork developed – for example between Luria (1902-1977),

Leontjev (1903-1979) and Vygotskij (1896-1934). They labeled themselves "troika"; they met and discussed fundamental problems of psychology like perception, mind, memory, language, learning etc. The main achievement of the Vygotskian School, or cultural-historical psychology, known in German as "die Kulturhistorische Schule", is that proponents emphasize the power of social determination in human beings. Their emphasis implicated the emergence of a new understanding of human biology, nature and personality.

A methodological hallmark lies in highlighting the so-called interiorization or internalization process. Everyone experiences this process on a daily basis. A good example from my experience is when I practiced driving a car in order to get a driver's license. This is an experience I think most people with a license remember and relate to. When the instructor and I arrived at the first intersection something frightening happened. I was to simultaneously look to the right and left while clutching, shifting, and braking. This was a scary experience for me and I was certain I would never learn to drive. On my behalf, every little act of crossing the intersection was extended over time in a most conscious process. But as every driver knows, in a relatively short period of time those over-conscious individual acts become unconscious mental operations – looking, clutching, gearing, braking and navigating are internalized as driving. Generally speaking everybody recognizes the shift from conscious to unconscious behavior. Leontjev (1974-1975) provides a similar example of an activity containing a motive which leads to outer actions structured by goals and accomplished by the actor's operations which are eventually internalized to the mental operations. Another, almost forgotten, contemporary tradition is Rubinstein's (1889-1960) school. Already in 1922 Rubinstein (1968, p. 115) spoke of the principle of creative spontaneous activity and also – of the principle of unity of consciousness and activity. Rubinstein created innovative psychological theories of personality, thinking, emotion, memory and speech as processes, i.e. activity. One famous proposition is that outer, external impact and incitement have an effect only via internal mental processes. The external operations are refracted by inner conditions and processes that constitute a foundation of development. Another important achievement by Rubinstein and followers like Brushlinski, Shorokova, and Budilova was directed towards understanding the crucial impact of relations opening up between human beings and environment. He labels such relations interchange (Wechselwirkung) and interaction. The relations in fact define activity as interchange, interplay, interdependence, interaction, intermediation rather than one-directional internalization. Hence, Rubinstein refutes the thesis that the development of an individual is exclusively determined by external influences. He also refutes the argument that inner mental conditions exclusively determine development.

The Emergence of Critical Psychology

It is possible to trace the chronological historical development of activity theory and cultural-historical psychology in Europe and the US after 1945, but I refrain from doing so here. Soviet psychology harbors the legacy of European and US currents and movements, but in studying such historical currents, we come across a strange discovery. We have presented the two great traditions in Soviet psychology of activity theory and the cultural-historical approach to psychology. However, only one of these traditions seems to constitute the foundation of activity theory and the cultural-historical approach. I have scrutinized books, articles and entries in encyclopedias. With very few exceptions, Rubinstein's work is left behind, quietly positioned outside public attention and recognition. An example illustrating a variety of sources of information is an introduction of the entry *Tätigkeitstheorie* in German Wikipedia (Translation by this author).

Activity theory (....) is a psychological theory, developed in the 1930s in Charkov by Alexei Nikolajevits Leontjev and co-workers. It is a further development of the works which in the 1920s originated in the context of the cooperation among the psychologists Lev Semjonovitsj Vygotsky (....) Alexander Romanovitsj Luria (....) and Alexei Nikolajevitsj Leontjev, referred to today as the cultural-historical school.

A similar lack of attention and recognition applies for entries on critical psychology, activity theory and cultural historical psychology in English Wikipedia plus for entries on Kritische Psychologie, Tätigkeitstheorie and Kulturhistorische Schule in German Wikipedia.

NAME-DROPPING VS. ARGUMENTATION

So what does it matter if one school of thought outscores the other. It could well be that my insistence on paying tribute to Rubinstein is merely a matter of name-dropping. Vygotskij and Leontjev may be considered to be the founders of the cultural-historical school. Contrary to that view I argue and support the claim that Rubinstein is the true-real-actual founder of activity theory. Already at the beginning of the 20s, he used the corresponding Russian term for activity. *The Principles of General Psychology* by Rubinstein in 1940 was the first and foremost basic compulsory work in Psychology at Soviet universities. During The Cold War, Rubinstein was officially denounced as a major anti-patriot (cosmopolitan) and consequently stripped of his positions in psychology. After Stalin's death, his rights were gradually restored.

The preclusion and exclusion of Rubinstein was a serious mistake which resulted in a limited comprehension of the meaning of the concept, theory and use of activity. This is a sad story because there were knowledgeable people around. Today

leading European activity and cultural-historical psychologists are the followers and successors of Vygotskij, Leontjev and Luria rather than of Rubinstein. One reason is that they agree with Vygotskij and Leontjev in the theory of internalization and hence in their criticism of Rubinstein. For me, personally, Rubinstein's great work called *The Principles of General Psychology*, brought about a revolutionary change in my understanding, and led the way to a theory of activity. A long time passed, however, before I became acquainted with Rubinstein's theory in 1968. I made the discovery in the German Democratic Republic through a German-language translation called *Grundlagen der allgemeinen Psychologie*.

Fundamental Theoretical-Methodological Problems in the Theory of Activity

A. N. Leonjtev (1903-1979) criticized Rubinstein, well aware of his proposition regarding inner refraction, commuting and altering of outer influences. Leontev regards Rubinstein's arguments as an attempt to solve an old problem of the stimulus-response paradigm by introducing intervening variables. In short, Rubinstein claims there is No Stimulus-Response, but an S-Intervening variable-R. Find two quotes as given in Leontjev's (1974-75) and Leontjev's (1979) words.

S. L. Rubinstein expressed this position in a formula, which stated that "External causes act through internal conditions." Indeed, this formula is quite indisputable. If, however, we include in the "internal conditions" those states evoked by an influence, this formula adds nothing new, in principle, to the S —> R formula. (p. 6-7)

Indeed, non-living objects also undergo various changes of state as a result of their interactions with other objects: footprints will be clearly imprinted in soft, wet earth- but not in dry, caked ground. This is all the more clear in animals and human beings: a hungry animal will respond to a food stimulus quite differently from one that is full, and a football fan will respond to a report of a score quite differently from a person indifferent to football. (p. 77-78)

Now, I'd like to turn to Rubinstein's criticism of internalization theory. A starting point would be Vygotskij's (1978, p. 56) unconditional statement that "We call the internal reconstruction of an external operation *internalization*." The renowned and debated part of Vygotskij's (1978) propositions goes as follows.

An interpersonal process is transformed into an intrapersonal one. Every function in the child's cultural development appears twice: first on the social level, and later, on the individual level; first, between people (interpsychological) and then inside the child (intrapsychological). This applies equally to voluntary attention, to logical memory, and in the formation of concepts. All the higher functions originate as actual relations between human beings. (56-57).

In several of his works, Rubinstein provides a fundamental critique of Vygotskij's position, refuting the idea of internalization as given and understood in Vygotskij's interpretation. In a Russian publication from 1960, Budilova (1975) quotes Rubinstein twice on the matter.

The correct standpoint regarding the question of the social determination of human thinking and the human faculties is in the theory of internalization overlaid by the mechanical notion of the social determination in this theory. The theory of internalization tears apart every interdependent connection and every interrelation of the external and the internal, and eradicates every dialectic relation between the external and the internal, the social and the natural (p. 275).

There is another telling quote by the same reference in Budilova (1975).

To "refute" our characterizing of the theory of internalisation could be argued that according to this theory the internalisation of the external is mediated through the activity of the subject in his acquisition of the external circumstances. This fact, however, in no way abolishes the mechanical character of this view of the personality and the development of the individual faculties, since the subject's activity itself is conceived as determined merely through the object, merely (italics in original) from the outside. (p. 275).

Leontjev's criticism of Rubinstein's proposition of interchange is hardly a just critique, basically because Rubinstein is far from thinking according to a conventional S-R, or S-I-R pattern. Vygotskij, Leontjev and son, (A. A. Leontjev 1936-2004), go so far as to speak of different approaches to psychology by Rubinstein on one side and the other researchers on the opposing side. A. A. Leontjev states, in a discussion with Lomov, that Rubinstein's approach could be called the theory of interchange (Wechselwirkung), and Vygotsky's approach could be called theory of activity (Leontjev 1980). This is a telling example of the heated controversy. In the 1970s a young Norwegian psychologist, Jan Nordal Høie, succeeded – through many discussions – to convince me that Rubinstein had the deepest understanding of psychological processes. Give credit where credit is due! It remains, of course, for people to decide if Rubinstein's criticism of Vygotskij's and Leontjev's theory of internalization is correct. Based on succeeding arguments, I think Rubinstein is right in criticizing Vygotskij and Leontjev. He has the deepest understanding of activity theory. The opposite conclusion as provided by Leontjev and son is correct too: Internalization by inter-intra relations is impossible without a simultaneous externalization by *intra-inter* relations. That is, we have to stay clear of negated descriptions like "neither interchange *nor* activity". The reason is that *activity is to be understood as interchange*. Various psychological approaches lead to new sets of concepts for understanding and describing the nature of human beings. They also lead to different humanistic education and ethically sound pedagogical approaches. Followers of Vygotskij and Leontjev like Galperin developed theories of how to succeed in getting students to concur with a solution already found in society (like Socrates' majeutic approach). Followers of Rubinstein concentrate on leading the students toward posing new questions and solving new problems.

DIALECTICS AND ACTIVITY THEORY

When I wrote my doctoral dissertation labeled *The Human Being as Activity* at the beginning of the 80s, my main problem was to understand the relationship between individual and society. The reason was that although Soviet researchers of activity like Rubinstein, Vygotskij, Leontjev and Luria were great philosophers, they were psychologists as well. They studied the foundations of individual mind, memory, perception, feeling, brain, personality etc. Society was not at any point their focus of interest. For example they stayed clear of political issues like working conditions, citizen freedom etc. It is obvious that sociology, psychology and similar social science disciplines suffered in the former Soviet Union. There was a tendency to regard the interrelationship between individual and society as an external relation. This is obviously the case in Vygotskij's famous thesis. A consequence of this fact is that for a long time the problem of blurred relations between human nature and society could not be posed or clarified in a productive way.

Another unresolved issue emerges because of the absence of an activity approach adapted to the study of society. While I was giving a lecture in Norway on activity theory for students in education, one of them asked: what about communi-

cation? I failed to come up with an answer, but I was tempted to say: communication is also an activity. It is an activity, of course, but it is futile to give a simple-minded answer to a question which requires and deserves a complex answer. Everything is explained by the concept *activity*, and if activity - defined in a narrow sense - explains everything, the logical conclusion is that it explains nothing. Fortunately for me, I was interested too and published a book on dialectics. When I tried to learn and acquire a theory of activity, dialectics was intrinsically connected to, or an internal part of my understanding of Rubinstein's theory of activity. On that basis, I always try to understand phenomena in their contradictory and identical essence. Contrary to my line of thinking, Karl Popper considers dialectics to be nonsense because, in his opinion, dialectics is an antinomy, an inconsistent creation of the mind incompatible with the logical law of contradiction. I feel he is wrong, because dialectics is a mental process helping people to come to logical operations and conclusions. Therefore the concept of *process* is extremely relevant for activity theory, while activity is the dimension of a process. For example, Vygotskij (1978, p. 60) stresses the importance of a dialectical method when he discusses "problems of method" in *Mind in Society*.

Relationships "Individual-Society" and "Nature-Society"

Now I'd like to open a discussion about the nature of communication. This has been a recurring and perhaps under-emphasized theme in my writing. An article of mine called *Pedagogy and the Concept of Activity* (Enerstvedt 1988), contains an example of how to separate between kinds of relations.

The general concept of the relation between human activity and communication is derived from Marx's understanding of the relation between productive forces and production relations. Marx speaks clearly of this relation as a substance-form relation. The productive force is the relation between subject and object in production of goods - the substance. The production relation is the form of this substance, it is a subject-subject relation, for instance as capitalist-worker relation. The question is then, could this conception of the relation between productive force and production relation be generalized also to other spheres of life?

This is precisely my assertion. I don't mean the contents of the quote in the sense that all human relations are identical to the production of goods. I mean it in the sense, however, that human activities like labor, play, and learning are activities of subjects directed towards objects in a subject-subject relation. Today I would rather have it that what I wrote in 1988 was an example of abduction, as coined by Peirce (1997), rather than an example of generalization. I favor the hypothesis that all human relations are a substance-form-relation (Inhalt-Form). And accordingly, the relation can — at individual level as well as at societal level — be characterized as a substance activity in the form of communication. When I speak of *communication* I use the word as a term for material and ideal interaction. Stated differently, communication implies practical (buses, cars, parks etc.) and intellectual (attention, interest, agreement etc.) interaction. Generally speaking, the extension will be the material and ideal cooperation (*Verkehr* – as coined by Marx). The mode of existence for individual and society is activity as a substance in a communicative form in which people produce or use objects. Those objects are objectified activity like streets, houses, cars, etc.

Individual, Society, and Human Nature

Society *sui generis* resides inside the sphere of individual activity. *Society* is the *cooperative, collective activity of individuals*. Individual and collective subjects are merely different modali-

ties of human activity. Put differently, society and the individual define each other. This means that human nature can only be conceived of as social. People, i.e. human nature and the human organism, is produced in phylogenetic development, especially in the anthropogenesis, which is the period in which man in society emerges. Nor can human nature be reduced to "social" when people falsely conceive of the concept as something external to the individual. That also means that the social is not internalized in the individual. Both the social and the nature of the human being simultaneously originate from and exist in interchange, interplay and interaction. The process ranges from the breathing of the organism to the activity of the personality. The individual is anything but a closed monad, it is the relationship between an organism and the surroundings. And society is internal to that relationship understood as cooperation of between people of flesh and blood. Figure 1 describes inner relations of nature, society, groups and individuals.

As stated in Figure 1, human activity – regardless if defined by individuals or society - is a relation between natural organisms and a particular environment. The mode of existence of individual and society is activity defined as interchange. I argue that we could understand those relations by applying Rubinstein's theory of interchange (Wechselwirkung).

CONCLUSION

A model in my article (Enerstvedt 1988) visualizes activity at individual and the societal level. Figure 2 describes the individual's and society's mode of existence.

In principle, I am against using visual models of verbal statements like in Figure 2. However, this model is attractive because of its simplicity. So, an explanation is appropriate. This is not a model of a dyad. It is intended to visualize certain fundamental relations. The notion of the M-dyad

Figure 1. The inner relations of nature, society, groups, individuals

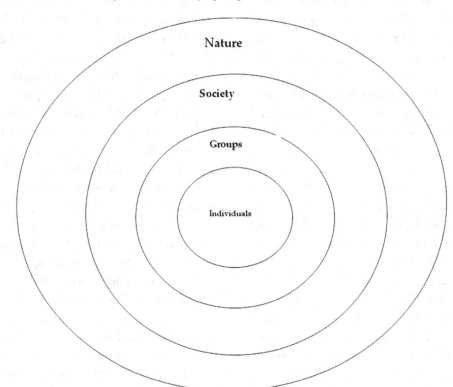

Figure 2. Model of activity

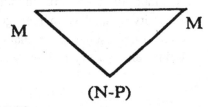

(N-P)

M=Man
M-M=Material and ideal communication (interaction, co-operation)
N= Nature
P= Produced objects
(N and P) = the natural and created world
M-(N and P) = the creating process, man's transformation of nature

as the foundation and the emergence of modern society is merely a development of the legend of Adam and Eve. See for example Engels's (1820-1895) criticism of Dühring (1833-1921) on this matter. However, the religious legend is folklore rather than social science. So I have come to the conclusion that we should abandon either-or thinking altogether. Instead we should consider interchange or activity. Then we may adopt a both-and way of thinking. I put forward the following proposal for the purpose of discussion: Internalization *yes* – but only in the context of Rubinstein's understanding of activity.

REFERENCES

Budilova, J. A. (1975). *Philosophische Probleme in der sowjetischen Psychologie*. Berlin: VEB Deutscher Verlag der Wissenschaften.

Enerstvedt, R. Th. (1969). *Dialektikk og samfunnsvitenskap*. Oslo: Forlaget Ny Dag.

Enerstvedt, R. Th. (1988). Pedagogy and the Concept of Activity. *Multidisciplinary Newsletter for Activity Theory, 1988*(1/2). Retrieved from http://folk.uio.no/regie/litteratur/index.htm

Enerstvedt, R. Th. (2011). *Spiller Gud terning likevel?* Oslo: Marxist Forlag.

Leontjev, A. A. (1980). Tätigkeit und Kommunikation. *Sowjetwissenschaft, 5.*

Leontjev, A. N. (1979). *Tätigkeit-Bewusstsein-Persönlichkeit. Volke und Wissen.* Berlin: Volkseigener Verlag.

Leontjev, A. N. (1974-75). The Problem of Activity in Psychology. *Soviet Education, 8*(2).

Lomov, B. F. (1980). Die Kategorien Kommunikation und Tätigkeit in der Psychologie. *Sowjetwissenschaft, 5.*

Peirce, C. S. (1997). Pragmatism as a Principle and Method of Right Thinking. In P. A. Turrisi (Ed.), *The 1903 Harvard Lectures on Pragmatism.* Albany, NY: State University of New York Press.

Rubinstein, S. L. (1968). *Grundlagen der allgemeinen Psychologie: Volk und Wissen.* Berlin: Volkseigener Verlag.

Rubinstein, S. L. (1969). *Prinzipien und Wege der Entwicklung der Psychologie.* Berlin: Akademie-Verlag.

Rubinstein, S. L. (1976). *Væren og bevidsthed.* Copenhagen: Gyldendal.

Vygotskij, L. S. (2001). *Tenkning og tale.* Oslo: Gyldendal.

Vygotsky, L. S. (1978). *Mind in Society: The Development of Higher Psychological Processes.* Cambridge, MA: Harvard University Press. Retrieved from http://de.wikipedia.org/wiki/T%C3%A4tigkeitstheorie

ADDITIONAL READING

Damianova, M. K., & Sullivan, G. B. (2011). Rereading Vygotsky's Theses on Types of Internalization and Verbal Mediation. *Review of General Psychology, 15*(4), 344–350. doi:10.1037/a0025627

Kohlberg, L. (1971). From 'is' to 'ought': How to commit the naturalistic fallacy and get away with it in the study of moral development. T. Mischel (Ed.). Cognitive Development and Epistemology. New York: Academic Press. 151–284.

Kohlberg, L. (1973). The Claim to Moral Adequacy of a Highest Stage of Moral Judgment. *The Journal of Philosophy, 70*(18), 630–646. doi:10.2307/2025030

Meissner, W. W. (1981). *Internalization in Psychoanalysis.* New York: International Universities Press.

Nonaka, I., & Nishiguchi, T. (Eds.). (2001). *Knowledge emergence: Social, technical, and evolutionary dimensions of knowledge creation.* New York: Oxford University Press.

Nonaka, I., & Takeuchi, H. (1995). *The knowledge-creating company.* New York: Oxford University Press.

Rowlands, S. (2000). Turning Vygotsky on His Head: Vygotsky's "Scientifically Based Method" and the Socioculturalist's "Social Other". *Science & Education, 9*(6), 537–575. doi:10.1023/A:1008748901374

Van der Veer, R., & Valsiner, J. (1991). *Understanding Vygotsky. A quest for synthesis.* Oxford: Basil Blackwell.

Van der Veer, R., & Zavershneva, E. (2011). To Moscow with Love: Partial Reconstruction of Vygotsky's Trip to London. *Integrative Psychological & Behavioral Science, 45*(4), 458–474. doi:10.1007/s12124-011-9173-8 PMID:21626140

Vygotsky, L. S. (1978). *Mind in society*. Cambridge, MA: Harvard University Press.

Wallis, K. C., & Poulton, J. L. (2001). *Internalization: The Origins and Construction of Internal Reality*. Buckingham, Philadelphia: Open University Press.

Wertsch, J. V. (1985). *Vygotsky and the social formation of mind*. Cambridge, MA: Harvard University Press.

Zinchenko, V. P. (2007). Thought and word: The approaches of L. S. Vygotsky and G. G. Shpet. In H. Daniels, M. Cole, & J. V. Wertsch (Eds.), The Cambridge companion to Vygotsky (212–245). England: Cambridge University Press.

KEY TERMS AND DEFINITIONS

Abduction: Is the researcher's method for exploring data, finding patterns and suggesting plausible hypotheses. The goal is conceptual understanding of a phenomenon.

Activity Theory: Is a descriptive meta-theory for influencing and analyzing human practices, defined as work/activity system (including teams, organizations, etc.) that beyond the thinking and doing of individual actors. Activity theoretical approaches to influencing and analyzing activities accounts for contexts, people, historical development, culture, artifacts, motivation and dialectic complexity. AT bridges the conceptual gap between the individual subject and social structures by means of analyzing mediating activity defined as object-oriented, collective and culturally mediated activity system. The objective of activity theoretical analysis is to understand and describe consciousness and activity as a conceptual pair.

Consciousness: The term qualifies a state of mind or the degree to which a person is aware of an external object or some quality in self. The nature of consciousness and its essential properties is hard to grasp. Philosophers argue whether the concept is valid, how to explain/recognize consciousness in mechanistic or in (bio)logical terms, if kinds of consciousness exist; relations between consciousness and language; if language is part of a dualistic distinction between mental and physical states or properties and so on. At best there is a shared intuition about what consciousness represents.

Convention: Is a concept meaning a number of things: e.g. an agreement between nations; a free-floating or arranged gathering of people. A human convention is a long term agreement, a custom, a tradition or a standard of conduct like driving on the right hand side of the road or using first language expressions.

Environment: The concept defined as by systemic qualities means the physical and biological factors along with their chemical interactions that affect and control organisms. Other definitions apply for natural (humans and plants), social (culture, humans plus interactions with institutions) plus physical environment (material things).

Feuerbach Theses: Karl Marx wrote eleven philosophical notes as an outline for a chapter of another book. After Marx's death Fredrick Engels published the theses as an appendix to a pamphlet by himself on motivation, activity, consciousness and personality. The political message of one famous thesis is that philosophers should try and change the world rather than merely describe it.

Generalization: The concept has broad applications in the social sciences as researchers study specialized contexts or meanings. Generalization signifies extension of an original concept to less contextualized criteria. Generalization by logic and human reasoning presupposes the unity of a given set of individual elements, but also some common characteristics differentiating between those elements. Related concepts are external validation, universals and abstraction.

Interchange: The definition covers an exchange or a place where elements or people meet to allow exchange from one to the other, e.g. two people discussing a party or the junction between railway lines.

Internalization: Usually defines as the opposite process to externalization. People relate internalization to moral behavior as well as to learning and using new ideas as well as new skills.

Psychology: Involves the study of human mental functions with an objective to understand human behavior. Psychologists argue general principles and research specific cases. Professional practitioners can be classified by practices. Social, behavioral or cognitive psychologists try to understand the role of mental functions in individual and collective behavior. Typical concepts related to research and practices are perception, cognition, attention, emotion and behavior.

Compilation of References

Abbott, G. N., Stening, B. W., Atkins, P. W. B., & Grant, A. M. (2006). Coaching expatriate managers for success: Adding value beyond training and mentoring. *Asia Pacific Journal of Human Resources, 44*(3), 295–317. doi:10.1177/1038411106069413

Abbott, A. D. (2004). *Methods of Discovery: Heuristics for the Social Science*. New York: Norton.

Åberg, A., & Lenz Taguchi, H. (2005). *Lyssnandets pedagogik – Etik och demokrati. In Pedagogiskt arbete*. Stockholm: Liber.

Abrams, Z. I. (2002). Surfing to cross-cultural awareness: Using internet-mediated projects to explore cultural stereotypes. *Foreign Language Annals, 35*(2), 141–153. doi:10.1111/j.1944-9720.2002.tb03151.x

Adolfsson Boman, M., Eriksson, I., Hverven, M., Jansson, A., & Tamobour, T. (2013). Kollaborativ utveckling av uppgifter för algebraiskt arbete i en årskurs 1 – exemplet likhetstecken. *Forskning om undervisning och lärande,* (10), 29-49. Retrieved from http://www.forskul.se/

Akkerman, S., Admiraal, W., Simons, R. J., & Niessen, T. (2006). Considering diversity: Multivoicedness in international academic collaboration. *Culture and Psychology, 12*(4), 461–485. doi:10.1177/1354067X06069947

Alasoini, T. (2009). Alternative Paths for Working Life Reform? A Comparison of European and East Asian Development Strategies. *International Journal of Action Research, 5*(2), 155–183.

Allsup, R. E. (2008). Creating an educational framework for popular music in public schools: Anticipating the second-wave. *Visions of Research in Music Education, 12*(1-2).

Alnervik, K. (2013). *"Men så kan man ju också tänka!" Pedagogisk dokumentation som förändringverktyg i förskolan*. Retrieved June 6, 2014, from http://hj.diva-portal.org/smash/record.jsf?pid=diva2:659182

Alrø, H., Skovsmose, O., & Valero, P. (2007). Interviewing foregrounds. *Working Papers on Learning and Philosophy, 2007*(5), 1-23.

Anastasiades, S. P., Filippousis, G., Karvunis, L., Siakas, S., Tomazinakis, A., Giza, P., & Mastoraki, H. (2010). Interactive Videoconferencing for collaborative learning at a distance in the school of 21st century: A case study in elementary schools in Greece. *Computers & Education, 54*(2), 321–339. doi:10.1016/j.compedu.2009.08.016

Anderson, T., & Shattuck, J. (2012). Design-based research: A decade of progress in education research? *Educational Researcher, 41*(1), 16–25. doi:10.3102/0013189X11428813

Andersson, F. (2007). *Att utmana erfarenheter: Kunskapsutveckling i en forskningscirkel*. (Doctoral thesis). Stockholm University, Stockholm, Sweden.

Andersson, F., & Sundh, S. (2013). *GOTKALC.COM: Young Learners on Gotland and in Kaliningrad in Communication in English with the Use of Digital Tools – the Pilot Study*. Visby: Gotland University.

Andreasen, K. E. (2012). *VIU: Projekt VIrtuel Undervisning: Rapport fra følgeforskningen*. Aalborg Universitet: Institut for Læring og Filosofi.

Andreasen, K., & Rasmussen, P. (2014). Video mediated teaching and learning in Adult Education. In T. Hansson (Ed.), Contemporary Approaches to Activity Theory: Interdisciplinary Perspectives on Human Behavior. Hershey, PA: IGI Global.

Andreasen, K. E., & Hviid, M. K. (2011). *Evalueringsrapport: Projekt Parallel Pædagogik - Et udviklingsarbejde med VUC Sønderjylland og VUC Fyn & Fyns HF-kursus.* Aalborg Universitet og UC Syd.

Andreasen, K. E., & Rasmussen, P. (2013). Videomedieret parallelundervisning: Som rum for læring ved Almen Voksenuddannelse i udkantsområder. *Læring & Medier, 11*, 1–22.

Anh, D. T. K., & Marginson, S. (2013). Global learning through the lens of Vygotskian sociocultural theory. *Critical Studies in Education, 54*(2), 143–159. doi:10.1 080/17508487.2012.722557

An, K. (2006). An investigation of error correction in the zone of proximal development: Oral interaction with beginning learners of Chinese as a foreign language. *Dissertation Abstracts International. A, The Humanities and Social Sciences, 67*(6), 2026–2027.

Archer, L., DeWitt, J., Osborne, J., Dillon, J., Willis, B., & Wong, B. (2012). Science Aspirations, Capital, and Family Habitus How Families Shape Children's Engagement and Identification With Science. *American Educational Research Journal, 49*(5), 881–908. doi:10.3102/0002831211433290

Arnkil, T. E., Eriksson, E. & Saikku, P. (1998). Huolen harmaa vyöhyke. [The grey zone of the worry, in Finnish]. *Dialogi, 1998*(7), 8-11.

Asplund, J. (1980). *Socialpsykologiska studier* [sociopsychological studies]. Stockholm: Awe/Glebers.

Austin, J. L. (1962). *How to do things with words.* Oxford University Press.

Ax, J., & Ponte, P. (2008). *Critiquing Praxis: Conceptual and Empirical Trends in the Teaching Profession.* Rotterdam: Sense.

Bacon, F. (2010). *Meditationes Sacrae and Human Philosophy.* London: Kessinger Publishing.

Baden-Fuller, C., & Haefliger, S. (2013). Business models and technology innovation. *Long Range Planning, 46*(6), 419–426. doi:10.1016/j.lrp.2013.08.023

Bakhurst, D. (2009). Reflection on activity theory. *Educational Review, 61*(2), 197–210. doi:10.1080/00131910902846916

Ball, D. L., & Cohen, D. K. (1999). Developing practice, developing practitioners: toward a practice-based theory of professional education. In L. Darling-Hammond & G. Sykes (Eds.), *Teaching as the learning profession: Handbook of policy and practice* (pp. 3–32). San Francisco: Jossey-Bass.

Bang, L. (2014). Mapping [Capital v.2.0] – An encounter of thoughts. In T. Hansson (Ed.), Contemporary Approaches to Activity Theory: Interdisciplinary Perspectives on Human Behavior. Hershey, PA: IGI Global.

Bang, L. (2014). Between the Cat and the Principle: An encounter between Foucault's and Bourdieu's conceptualisations of power. *Power and Education, 6*(1), 18–31. doi:10.2304/power.2014.6.1.18

Bang, L. (2014). *Welcome to school - welcome to the Empire-Building Business: an exploration and expansion of Bourdieu's notion of field. Waikota Journal of Education.*

Barab, S., Dodge, T., Ingram-Goble, A., Pettyjohn, P., Peppler, K., Volk, C., & Solomou, M. (2010). Pedagogical dramas and transformational play: Narratively rich games for learning. *Mind, Culture, and Activity, 17*(3), 235–264. doi:10.1080/10749030903437228

Baskerville, R. L., & Wood-Harper, A. T. (1996). A Critical Perspective on Action Research as a Method for Information Systems Research. *Journal of Information Technology, 3*(11), 235–246. doi:10.1080/026839696345289

Bateman, B. (2002). Promoting openness toward culture learning: Ethnographic interviews for students of Spanish. *Modern Language Journal, 86*(3), 318–331. doi:10.1111/1540-4781.00152

Beckett, G. H. (1999). *Project-based instruction in a Canadian school's ESL classes: Goals and evaluations.* (Unpublished doctoral dissertation). University of British Columbia, Canada.

Beckett, G. H. (2006). Beyond second language acquisition: Secondary school ESL teacher goals and actions for project-based instruction. In G. H. Beckett & P. Miller (Eds.), Project-based second and foreign language education: Past, present, and future (pp. 55-70). Greenwich, CT: Information Age Publishing, Inc.

Beckett, G. H. (2002). Teacher and student evaluations of project-based instruction. *TESL Canada Journal, 19*(2), 52–66.

Beckett, G. H. (2005). Academic language and literacy socialization of secondary school Chinese immigrant students: Practices and perspectives. *Journal of Asian Pacific Communication, 15*(1), 191–206. doi:10.1075/japc.15.1.12bec

Beckett, G. H., & Slater, T. (2005). The Project Framework: A tool for language and content integration. *The English Language Teaching Journal, 59*(2), 108–116. doi:10.1093/eltj/cci024

Bedny, G. Z., & Harris, S. (2005). The systemic-structural theory of activity: Applications to the study of human work. *Mind, Culture, and Activity, 12*(2), 128–147. doi:10.1207/s15327884mca1202_4

Bennett, D. (2008). *Understanding the classical music profession: The past, the present and strategies for the future*. Farnham, UK: Ashgate.

Bernard, R. H. (1995). *Research methods in anthropology: Qualitative and quantitative approaches*. Thousand Oaks, CA: Sage.

Berry, J. W. (1974). Psychological Aspects of Cultural Pluralism: Unity and Identity Reconsidered. *Topics in Culture Learning, 2*(6), 17–22. Retrieved from http://files.eric.ed.gov/fulltext/ED100159.pdf

Berry, J. W. (1997). Immigration, Acculturation, and Adaptation. *Applied Psychology, 46*(1), 5–34. doi:10.1080/026999497378467

Berry, J. W., & Sam, D. L. (1997). Acculturation and Adaptation. In J. W. Berry, Y. H. Poortinga, & J. Pandey (Eds.), Handbook of Cross-Cultural Psychology. Academic Press.

Bibliography of Research on Chinese Language. (2008). *Education University of British Columbia Center for Research in Chinese Language and Literacy Education*. Retrieved from http://crclle.lled.educ.ubc.ca/bibliography.html

Björnsdóttir, A. (2009). Fjarnemar [Distance students]. University of Iceland.

Blair, D. V. (2009). Stepping aside: Teaching in a student-centered music classroom. *Music Educators Journal, 95*(3), 42–45. doi:10.1177/0027432108330760

Blunden, A. (1997). Vygotsky and the dialectical method. *Lev Vygotsky Archive*. Retrieved from 28/08/2006 http://www.marxists.org/archive/vygotsky/index.htm

Blunden, A. (2010). *'Collaborative Project' as a Concept for Interdisciplinary Human Science Research*. Academic Press.

Bodrožić, Z. (2008). *Post-industrial intervention. An activity-theoretical expedition tracing the proximal development of forms of conducting interventions*. Helsinki: University of Helsinki, Department of Education.

Boellstorff, T., Nardi, B., Pearce, C., & Taylor, T. L. (2013). Words with Friends: Writing Collaboratively Online. *Interaction, 20*(5), 58–61. doi:10.1145/2501987

Boltanski, L., & Chiapello, E. (2005). *The new spirit of capitalism*. London: Verso.

Borg, S. (2003). Teacher cognition in language teaching: A review of research on what language teachers think, know, believe and do. *Language Teaching, 36*(2), 81–109. doi:10.1017/S0261444803001903

Bourdieu, P. (1986). The forms of capital. In J. Richardson (Ed.), Handbook of theory and research for the sociology of education. New York: Greenwood

Bourdieu, P. (1977). *Outline of a Theory of Practice*. Cambridge, UK: Cambridge University Press. doi:10.1017/CBO9780511812507

Bourdieu, P. (1984). *Distinction: A Social Critique of the Judgement of Taste* (N. Richard, Trans.). London: Routledge.

Bourdieu, P. (1988). *Homo academicus*. Cambridge, MA: Polity Press.

Bourdieu, P. (1990). *In other words: Essays towards a reflexive sociology*. Stanford, CA: Stanford University Press.

Bourdieu, P. (1998). *The state nobility: Elite schools in the field of power*. Stanford, CA: Stanford University Press.

Bourdieu, P. (2004). *Science of science and reflexivity*. Cambridge, UK: Polity Press.

Bourdieu, P., & Passeron, J.-C. (1990). *Reproduction in education, society and culture*. Cambridge, UK: SAGE.

Braund, M., & Reiss, M. (2006). Validity and worth in the science curriculum: Learning school science outside the laboratory. *Curriculum Journal, 17*(3), 213–228. doi:10.1080/09585170600909662

Braun, V., & Clarke, V. (2006). Using thematic analysis in psychology. *Qualitative Research in Psychology, 3*(2), 77–101. doi:10.1191/1478088706qp063oa

Brinkman, D. J. (2010). Teaching creatively and teaching for creativity. *Arts Education Policy Review, 111*(2), 48–50. doi:10.1080/10632910903455785

Brown, A. (1992). Design experiments: Theoretical and methodological challenges in creating complex interventions in classroom settings. *Journal of the Learning Sciences, 2*(2), 141–178. doi:10.1207/s15327809jls0202_2

Brown, R. (1992). Managing the "S" curve in innovation. *Journal of Business and Industrial Marketing, 7*(3), 41–52. doi:10.1108/08858629210035418

Brown, S. P., Cron, W. L., & Slocum, J. W. (1998). Effects of traint competitiveness and perceived intraorganizational competition on sales-person goal setting and performance. *Journal of Marketing, 62*(4), 88–98. doi:10.2307/1252289

Bruner, J. S. (2006). *In Search of Pedagogy: The Selected Works of Jerome Bruner*. London: Routledge.

Budilova, J. A. (1975). *Philosophische Probleme in der sowjetischen Psychologie*. Berlin: VEB Deutscher Verlag der Wissenschaften.

Bulterman-Bos, J. (2008). Will a clinical approach make education research more relevant for practice? *Educational Researcher, 37*(7), 412–420. doi:10.3102/0013189X08325555

Burke, K. (1962). *A Grammar of Motives and A Rhetoric of Motives*. New York.

Burke, K. (1970). *The Rhetoric of Religion: Studies in Logology*. London: University of California Press.

Burnard, P., & White, J. (2008). Creativity and performativity: Counterpoints in British and Australian education. *British Educational Research Journal, 34*(5), 667–682. doi:10.1080/01411920802224238

Burnard, P., & Younker, B. A. (2008). Investigating children's musical interactions within the activities systems of group composing and arranging: An application of Engestrom's Activity Theory. *International Journal of Educational Research, 47*(1), 60–74. doi:10.1016/j.ijer.2007.11.001

Burns, A. (1999). *Collaborative action research for English language teachers*. Cambridge, UK: Cambridge University Press.

Burns, A. (2005). Action research: An evolving paradigm? *Language Teaching, 38*(02), 57–74. doi:10.1017/S0261444805002661

Caillois, R. (2001). *Man, Play and Games*. Wantage: University of Illinois Press.

Cairns, L., & Malloch, M. (2011). Theories of work, place and learning: New directions. In M. Malloch, L. Cairns, K. Evans, & B. N. O'Connor (Eds.), The SAGE Handbook of Workplace Learning (pp. 3-16). London: Sage Publications Ltd.

Candlish, S., & Wrisley, G. (2012). Private Language. In N. Zalta (Ed.), *The Stanford Encyclopedia of Philosophy*. Retrieved October 4, 2013, from http://plato.stanford.edu/archives/sum2012/entries/private-language/

Carlgren, I. (2009). The Swedish comprehensive school-lost in transition? *Zeitschrift für Erziehungswissenschaft., 12*(4), 633–649. doi:10.1007/s11618-009-0103-1

Carlgren, I. (2012). The Learning Study as an approach for research. *International Journal for Lesson and Learning Studies, 1*(2), 3–16. doi:10.1108/20468251211224172

Carlgren, I., Ahlstrand, P., Björkholm, E., & Nyberg, G. (in press). The meaning of knowing what is to be known. *Education & Didactiques*.

Carr, P. R., & Thésée, G. (2012). Discursive epistemologies by, for and about the de-colonizing project. In A. A. Abdi (Ed.), Decolonizing Philosophies of Education (pp. 15–28). Rotterdam: Sense Publishers. doi:10.1007/978-94-6091-687-8_2

Carr, W. (2006). Philosophy, methodology and action research. *Journal of Philosophy of Education, 40*(4), 421–435. doi:10.1111/j.1467-9752.2006.00517.x

Carr, W., & Kemmis, S. (1986). *Becoming critical: education, knowledge and action research.* Basingstoke: Falmer Press.

Castells, M. (Ed.). (1999). *Critical education in the new information age.* Lanham, MD: Rowman & Littlefield Publishers Inc.

Chaiklin, S. (1999). Developmental teaching in upper-secondary school. In Learning activity and development (pp. 187-210). Aarhus University Press.

Chaiklin, S. (2010). Educational research and educational practice: Why can't we be friends?. In I. Eriksson, V. Lindberg, & E. Österlind (Eds.), Uppdrag undervisning: Kunskap och lärande. Lund: Studentlitteratur.

Chaiklin, S. (2011). Social scientific research and societal practice: Action research and cultural-historical research in methodological light from Kurt Lewin and Lev S. Vygotsky. *Mind, Culture, and Activity, 18*(2), 129–147. doi:10.1080/10749039.2010.513752

Chamot, A., Barnhardt, S., & Dirstine, S. (1998). *Conducting action research in the foreign language classroom.* Washington, DC: National Capital Language Resource Center.

Chapelle, C. A. (2007). Technology and second language acquisition. *Annual Review of Applied Linguistics, 27,* 98–114. doi:10.1017/S0267190508070050

Christensen, V. L., & Hansen, J. J. (2010). Innovativ læremiddelkultur. In K. Gynther (Ed.), Didaktik 2.0. Akademisk Forlag. København.

Christiansen, B. R., & Gynther, C. (2010). Didaktik 2.0 - didaktisk design for skolen i vidensamfundet. In K. Gynther (Ed.), Didaktik 2.0. Akademisk Forlag. København

Chu, C. (1990). Semantics and discourse in Chinese language instruction. *Journal of the Chinese Language Teachers'. Association, 25,* 15–29.

Chu, M. (1990). Teaching Chinese as a functional language. *Journal of the Chinese Language Teachers Association, 25,* 93–96.

Claxton, G. (2002). Education for the learning age: a sociocultural approach to learning to learn. In G. Wells & C. Claxton (Eds.), Learning for Life in the 21st Century: Sociocultural Perspectives on the Future of Education. Blackwell Publishing.

Clot, Y. (2009). Clinic of activity: the dialogue as instrument. In A. Sannino, H. Daniels, & K. D. Gutiérrez (Eds.), Learning and expanding with activity theory (pp. 286-302). Cambridge, UK: Cambridge University Press.

Clot, Y. (2009). Clinic of activity: The dialogue as instrument. In A. Sannino, H. Daniels, & K. Gutierrez (Eds.), *Learning and expanding with activity theory* (pp. 286–302). Cambridge, UK: Cambridge University Press. doi:10.1017/CBO9780511809989.019

Cobb, P., Confrey, J., diSessa, A., Lehrer, R., & Schauble, L. (2003). Design experiments in educational research. *Educational Researcher, 32*(1), 9–13. doi:10.3102/0013189X032001009

Cochran-Smith, M., & Lytle, S. (1999). The teacher research movement: A decade later. *Educational Researcher, 28*(7), 15–25. doi:10.3102/0013189X028007015

Cohen, L., Manion, L., & Morrison, K. (2011). *Research methods in education* (7th ed.). London: RoutledgeFalmer.

Cole, M., & Engeström, Y. (1993). A cultural-historical approach to distributed cognition. In G. Salomon (Ed.), Distributed Cognitions: Psychological and Educational Considerations. Cambridge, UK: Cambridge University Press.

Cole, M., & Engeström, Y. (2007). Cultural-Historical Approaches to Designing for Development. In J. Valsiner, & A. Rosa (Eds.), The Cambridge handbook of sociocultural psychology (pp. 484-507). Cambridge, UK: Cambridge University Press.

Cole, M. (1986). Toward a cultural psychology of human activity systems. An interview. *Nordisk Pedagogik, 6*(1), 25–32.

Cole, M. (1996). *Cultural psychology: A once and future discipline.* London: The Belknap Press of Harvard University Press.

Cole, M. (2005). Cross-Cultural and Historical Perspectives on the Developmental Consequences of Education. *Human Development*, *48*(4), 195–216. doi:10.1159/000086855

Cole, M. (2010). What's culture got to do with it? Educational research as a necessarily interdisciplinary enterprise. *Educational Researcher*, *39*(6), 461–470. doi:10.3102/0013189X10380247

Cole, M., & Bruner, J. S. (1971). Cultural differences and inferences about psychological processes. *The American Psychologist*, *26*(10), 867–876. doi:10.1037/h0032240

Cole, M., & Engeström, Y. (1993). A cultural historical approach to distributed cognition. In G. Salomon (Ed.), *Distributed cognitions: Psychological and educational considerations* (pp. 1–46). Cambridge, UK: Cambridge University Press.

Cole, M., & Wertsch, J. V. (1996). Beyond the individual-social antimony in discussions of Piaget and Vygotsky. *Human Development*, *39*(5), 250–256. doi:10.1159/000278475

Coleman, J. A. (1992). Project-based learning, transferable skills, information technology and video. *Language Learning Journal*, *5*(1), 35–37. doi:10.1080/09571739285200121

Collins, L. M., & Lanza, S. T. (2010). *Latent class and latent transition analysis: With applications in the social, behavioral, and health sciences* (Vol. 718). John Wiley & Sons.

Craft, A. (2003). The limits to creativity in education: Dilemmas for educator. *British Journal of Educational Studies*, *51*(2), 113–127. doi:10.1111/1467-8527.t01-1-00229

Crawford, P. (2001). Educating for Moral Ability: Reflections on Moral Development Based on Vygotsky's Theory of Concept formation. *Journal of Moral Education*, *30*(2), 113–129. doi:10.1080/03057240120061379

Crawley, E., Malmqvist, J., Östlund, S., & Brodeur, D. (2010). *Rethinking engineering education: The CDIO approach*. Springer.

Cropley, A. J. (2010). The dark side of creativity: what is it? In D. H. Cropley, A. J. Cropley, J. C. Kaufman, & M. A. Runco (Eds.), The dark side of creativity (pp. 1-14). Cambridge, UK: Cambridge University Press. doi:10.1017/CBO9780511761225

Csikszentmihalyii, M. (2006). *Flow: Den optimala upplevelsens psykologi*. Stockholm: Natur och kultur.

Cusumano, M., Suarez, F. F., & Kahl, S. (2008). *Product, process and service: A new industry lifecycle model* (MIT Working Paper). Retrieved May 5, 2014, from http://web.mit.edu/sis07/cusumano.pdf

Cusumano, M. (2004). *The business of software: What every manager, programmer, and entrepreneur must know to thrive and survive in good times and bad*. New York: Free Press.

Dahlberg, G., & Lenz Taguchi, H. (1994). *Förskola och skola: om två skilda traditioner och om visionen om en mötesplats*. Stockholm, Sweden: HLS.

Dahlberg, G., Moss, P., & Pence, A. (2007). *Beyond quality in early childhood education and care: Postmodern perspectives*. London, UK: Falmer Press.

Dahlgren, L. O., & Johansson, K. (2009). Fenomenografi. In A. Fejes & R. Thornberg (Eds.), Handbok i kvalitativ analys. Stockholm: Liber.

Damvad. (2013). *Nye udfordringer for VUC? Fokus på Almen Voksenuddannelse (AVU)*. Lederforeningen for VUC og VUC Videnscenter.

Danermark, B. (2003). *Att förklara samhället*. Lund: Studentlitteratur.

Daniels, H. (2004). Activity theory, discourse and Bernstein. *Educational Review*, *56*(2), 121–123. doi:10.1080/0031910410001693218

Daniels, H. (2008). *Vygotsky and research*. London: Routledge.

Daniels, H., & Edwards, A. (Eds.). (2004). Sociocultural and activity theory in educational research. *Educational Review*, *56*(2).

Danmarks Evalueringsinstitut. (2011). *E-læring og blended learning på VEU-området. Undersøgelse af e-læring og blended learning på enkeltfag på VUC, VVU på erhvervsakademier og diplomuddannelser på professionshøjskoler.* Danmarks Evalueringsinstitut.

Danmarks Statistik. (2012). Forberedende voksenundervisning, almen voksenuddannelse og hf-enkeltfag mv. 2010/2011. *Nyt fra Danmarks Statistik, 122,* 9.

Danmarks Statistik. (2013). Kursister ved voksen- og efteruddannelse, VUC 2011/2012. *Nyt fra Danmarks Statistik, 71.*

Davidov, V. V. (1988). *La enseñanza escolar y el desarrollo psíquico: investigación teórica y experimental.* Moscú: Editorial Progreso.

Davidson, J. W., & Good, J. M. M. (2002). Social and musical co-ordination between members of a string quartet: An exploratory study. *Psychology of Music, 30*(2), 186–201. doi:10.1177/0305735602302005

Davydov, V. V. (1990). Types of Generalisation in Instruction. In Soviet studies in mathematics education (Vol. 2). Reston, VA: National Council of Teachers of Mathematics.

Davydov, V. V. (1999). The content and unsolved problems of activity theory. In Y. Engeström, R. Miettinen, & R.-L. Punamaki (Eds.), Perspectives on activity theory. New York: Cambridge University Press.

Davydov, V. (1990). *Types of generalization in instruction: logical and psychological problems in the structuring of school curricula. (Soviet studies in mathematics education* (J. Kilpatrick, Ed.). Reston, VA: National Council of Teachers of Mathematics.

Davydov, V. V. (1990). *Types of generalization in instruction: Logical and psychological problems in the structuring of school curricula.* Reston, VA: National Council of Teachers of Mathematics.

Davydov, V. V. (2008). *Problems of developmental instruction: a theoretical and experimental psychological study.* New York: Nova Science Publishers, Inc.

del Rio, P., & Álvares, A. (2002). From activity to directivity: the question of involvement in education. In G. Wells & C. Claxton (Eds.), *Learning for Life in the 21st Century. Sociocultural Perspectives on the Future of Education* (pp. 59–72). Oxford, UK: Blackwell Publishing. doi:10.1002/9780470753545.ch5

Deleuze, G. (1990). *The logic of sense.* New York: Columbia University Press.

Deleuze, G. (1994). *Difference and repetition.* London: Contiuum Group.

Deleuze, G. (2004). *Desert Islands: And Other Texts, 1953--1974.* New York: Semiotext.

Deleuze, G., & Guattari, F. (2004). *A thousand plateaus: Capitalism and schizophrenia.* London: Continuum.

Deresky, H. (2011). *International management. Managing across borders and cultures: Text and cases* (7th ed.). Boston, MA: Pearson.

Deutsch, M. (2000). Cooperation and competition. In M. Deutsch & P. Coleman (Eds.), *The handbook of conflict resolution: Theory and practicee* (pp. 21–40). San Francisco: Jossey-Basss.

Dewey, J. (1910). *How we Think.* Boston: Heath and Company. doi:10.1037/10903-000

Dewey, J. (1934). *Art as experience.* New York: Minton, Balch & Company.

Dewey, J., & Bentley, A. F. (1960). *Knowing and the known.* Boston: Beacon Press.

Dickinson, E. (2009). The Montana-meth project: Applying Burke's dramatistic pentad to a persuasive anti-drug media campaign. *Communication Teacher, 23*(3), 126–131. doi:10.1080/17404620902974824

Dillenbourg, P., Baker, M., Blaye, A., & O'Malley, C. (1996). The evolution of reserarch on collaborative learning. In P. Reimann & H. Spada (Eds.), *Learning in humans and machines* (pp. 189–205). Oxford, UK: Elsevier.

Dillon, J., Rickinson, M., Teamey, K., Morris, M., Choi, M. Y., Sanders, D., & Benefield, P. (2006). The value of outdoor learning: Evidence from research in the UK and elsewhere. *The School Science Review, 87*(320), 107.

Dodgson, M. (1993). Learning, Trust, and Technological Collaboration. *Human Relations*, 46(1), 77–95. doi:10.1177/001872679304600106

Doherty, D., & Eyring, J. (2006). Instructor Experience with Project work in the Adult ESL classroom: A Case Study. In Project-Based Second and Foreign Language education: Past, present, and future. Greenwich, CT: Information Age Publishing.

Döhrmann, M., Kaiser, G., & Blömeke, S. (2012). The conceptualisation of mathematics competencies in the international teacher education study TEDS-M. *ZDM Mathematics Education*, 44(3), 325–340. doi:10.1007/s11858-012-0432-z

Dougherty, B. (2004). Early algebra: Perspectives and assumptions. *For the Learning of Mathematics*, 24(3), 28–30.

Dreyfus, H. (1991). *Being-in-the-World: A Commentary on Heidegger's Being and Time, Division I*. Boston, MA: MIT Press.

Edge, J. (Ed.). (2001). *Action research. Case studies in TESOL practice*. Alexandria, VA: TESOL.

Edwards, A. (2009). From the systemic to the relational: relational agency and activity theory. In A. Sannino, H. Daniels, & K. Gutiérrez (Eds.), Learning and expanding with activity theory (pp. 197-211). Cambridge, UK: Cambridge University Press.

Elfström, I. (2013). *Uppföljning och utvärdering för förändring: Pedagogisk dokumentation som grund för kontinuerlig verksamhetsutveckling och systematiskt kvalitetsarbete i förskolan*. Avhandling, Stockholms Universitet.

Eliam, G. (2003). The philosophical foundations of Alexander R. Luria's neuropsychology. *Science in Context*, 16, 551–577. PMID:15025065

Elkonim, D. B. (1998). *Psicologia do Jogo*. São Paulo: Martins Fontes.

Elkonin, B. D. (2005). The psychology of play. *Journal of Russian & East European Psychology*, 43(1), 1–98.

Elliot, D. J. (1995). *Music matters: A new philosophy of music education*. New York: Oxford University Press.

Elliot, J. (1991). *Action research for educational change*. Milton Keynes, UK: Open University Press.

Ellis, R. (1992). Learning to communicate in the classroom. *Studies in Second Language Acquisition*, 14(1), 1–23. doi:10.1017/S0272263100010445

Ellis, R., & Barkhuizen, G. (2005). *Analysing Learner Language*. Oxford, UK: Oxford University Press.

Ellis, V. (2011). Reenergising professional creativity from a CHAT perspective: Seeing knowledge and history in perspective. *Mind, Culture, and Activity*, 18(2), 181–193. doi:10.1080/10749039.2010.493595

Enerstvedt, R. (1971). *Vetenskap som pedagogic: En analys av vetenskapens medel och mål*. [Science and pedagogy: Analysis of means and ends in science]. Verdandi debatt.

Enerstvedt, R. Th. (1988). Pedagogy and the Concept of Activity. *Multidisciplinary Newsletter for Activity Theory*, 1988(1/2). Retrieved from http://folk.uio.no/regie/litteratur/index.htm

Enerstvedt, R. (1977). *Mennesket i et fylogenetisk og ontogenetisk perspektiv* [Human beings in a phylogenetic and ontogenetic perspective]. Oslo: Forlaget Ny Dag.

Enerstvedt, R. Th. (1969). *Dialektikk og samfunnsvitenskap*. Oslo: Forlaget Ny Dag.

Enerstvedt, R. Th. (2011). *Spiller Gud terning likevel?* Oslo: Marxist Forlag.

Engeström, Y. (1987). *Learning by Expanding*. Helsinki: Orienta-Konsultit Oy. Retrieved from http://lchc.ucsd.edu/MCA/Paper/Engestrom/expanding/

Engeström, Y. (1990). Developmental work research as activity theory in practice: Analyzing the work of general practitioners. In Y. Engeström (Ed.), Learning, Working and Imagining (pp. 69-106). Helsinki: Orienta-Konsultit OY.

Engeström, Y. (1999). Activity Theory and individual and social transformation. In Y. Engeström, R. Miettinen, & R. L. Punamäki (Eds.), Perspectives on Activity Theory (Learning in Doing: Social, Cognitive and Computational Perspectives). Cambridge, UK: Cambridge University Press.

Engeström, Y. (1999). Innovative learning in work teams: Analyzing cycles of knowledge creation in practice. In Y. Engeström, R. Miettinen, & R.-L. Punamäki (Eds.), Perspectives on activity theory (pp. 377-404). Cambridge, UK: Cambridge University Press.

Engeström, Y. (2007). Putting Vygotsky to work: the Change Laboratory as an application of double stimulation. In H. Daniels, M. Cole, & J. Wertsch (Eds.), The Cambridge companion to Vygotsky (pp. 363-382). Cambridge, UK: Cambridge University Press.

Engeström, Y. (2009). The future of activity theory: a rough draft. In A. Sannino, H. Daniels, & C. Gutierrez (Eds.), Learning and expanding with activity theory (pp. 303-328). Cambridge, UK: Cambridge University Press.

Engeström, Y. (2009). *Expansive concept formation at work*. CRADLE. Retrieved from http://www.helsinki.fi/behav/tiedepaiva/2009/CONCEPT%20FORMATION%20PLAN.pdf

Engeström, Y. (2010). *In From Teams to Knots Activity-Theoretical Studies of Collaboration and Learning at Work*. Cambridge Books Online. Retrieved from http://ebooks.cambridge.org

Engeström, Y., & Kallinen, T. (1988). Theatre as a Model System for Learning to Create. *The Quarterly Newsletter of the Laboratory of Comparative Human Cognition, 10*(2).

Engeström, Y., Engeström, R., & Suntio, A. (2002). Can a school community learn to master its own future? An activity-theoretical study of expansive learning among middle school teachers. In G. Wells & G. Claxton (Eds.), Learning for Life in the21st Century: Sociocultural perspectives on the future of education. Oxford, UK: Blackwell.

Engeström, R. (2009). Who is acting in an activity system? In A. Sannino, H. Daniels, & K. Gutierrez (Eds.), *Learning and expanding with activity theory*. Cambridge, UK: Cambridge University Press. doi:10.1017/CBO9780511809989.017

Engeström, R., Batane, T., Hakkarainen, K., Newnham, D. S., Nleya, P., Senteni, A., & Sinko, M. (2014). Reflections on the use of DWR in intercultural collaboration. *Mind, Culture, and Activity, 21*(2), 129–147. doi:10.1080/10749039.2013.879185

Engeström, Y. (1987). *Learning by expanding. An activity-theoretical approach to developmental research.* Helsinki: Orienta-Konsultit.

Engeström, Y. (1992). *Interactive expertise studies in distributed working intelligence. Research Bulletin No. 83.* Helsinki: University of Helsinki, Department of education.

Engeström, Y. (1999). Activity theory and individual and social transformation. In Y. Engeström, R. Miettinen, & R. L. Punamäki (Eds.), *Perspectives on Activity Theory* (pp. 19–38). Cambridge, UK: Cambridge University Press. doi:10.1017/CBO9780511812774.003

Engeström, Y. (2001). Expansive learning at work: Toward an activity theoretical reconceptualization. *Journal of Education and Work, 14*(1), 133–156. doi:10.1080/13639080020028747

Engeström, Y. (2004). New forms of learning in co-configuration work. *Journal of Workplace Learning, 16*(2), 11–21. doi:10.1108/13665620410521477

Engeström, Y. (2005). *Developmental work research. Expanding activity theory in practice* (Vol. 12). Berlin: Lemanns Media.

Engeström, Y. (2007). Enriching the theory of expansive learning: Lessons from journeys toward coconfiguration. *Mind, Culture, and Activity, 14*(1/2), 23–39. doi:10.1080/10749030701307689

Engeström, Y. (2008). *From teams to knots: Activity-theoretical studies of collaboration and learning at work.* Cambridge, UK: Cambridge University Press. doi:10.1017/CBO9780511619847

Engeström, Y. (2009). The future of activity theory: a rough draft. In A. Sannino, H. Daniels, & K. Gutierrez (Eds.), *Learning and expanding with activity theory.* Cambridge, UK: Cambridge University Press. doi:10.1017/CBO9780511809989.020

Engeström, Y. (2011). From design experiments to formative interventions. *Theory & Psychology*, 1–31.

Engeström, Y., Engeström, R., & Kärkkäinen, M. (1995). Polycontextuality and boundary crossing in expert cognition: Learning and problem solving in complex work activities. *Learning and Instruction, 5*(4), 319–336. doi:10.1016/0959-4752(95)00021-6

Engeström, Y., & Kerosuo, H. (2007). From workplace learning to inter-organizational learning and back: The contribution of activity theory. *Journal of Workplace Learning, 19*(6), 336–342. doi:10.1108/13665620710777084

Engeström, Y., & Middleton, D. (Eds.). (1996). *Cognition and Communication at Work.* Cambridge, UK: Cambridge University Press. doi:10.1017/CBO9781139174077

Engeström, Y., Rantavuori, J., & Kerosuo, H. (2013). Expansive learning in a library: Actions, cycles and deviations from instructional intentions. *Vocations and Learning, 6*(1), 81–106. doi:10.1007/s12186-012-9089-6

Engeström, Y., & Sannino, A. (2010). Studies of expansive learning: Foundations, findings and future challenges. *Educational Research Review, 5*(1), 1–24. doi:10.1016/j.edurev.2009.12.002

Engeström, Y., & Sannino, A. (2011). Discursive manifestations of contradictions in organizational change efforts. A methodological framework. *Journal of Organizational Change Management, 24*(3), 368–387. doi:10.1108/09534811111132758

Engeström, Y., & Sannino, A. (2012). Whatever happened to process theories of learning? *Learning. Culture and Social Interaction, 1*(1), 45–56. doi:10.1016/j.lcsi.2012.03.002

Engeström, Y., Virkkunen, J., Helle, M., Pihlaja, J., & Poikela, R. (1996). The change laboratory as a tool for transforming work. *Lifelong Learning in Europe, 2*, 10–17.

Eriksson, I., & Lindberg, V. (2007). *Matematikundervisningens innehåll. Avrapportering av ett kollaborativt forskningsprojekt om att utveckla redskap och innehåll i arbetet med att realisera "strävansmålen" i matematik.* Lärarhögskolan i Stockholm & Stockholms stad. Retrieved from http://www.stockholm.se/Extern/Templates/InfoPage.aspx?id=42882

Eriksson, I., & Ståhle, Y. (2010). *Mätandets idé - En learning study i Botkyrka kommun.* Stockholms universitet: Institutionen för didaktik och pedagogiskt arbete, (working paper).

Eriksson, E., & Arnkil, T. E. (2009). *Taking up one's worries.* National Institute for Health and Welfare.

Eriksson, I. (2009). Re-interpreting teaching: A divided task in self-regulated teaching practices. *Scandinavian Journal of Educational Research, 53*(1), 53–70. doi:10.1080/00313830802628331

Ertmer, P., & Newby, T. (1996). The Expert Learner: Strategic, self-regulated and reflective. *Instructional Science, 24*(1), 1–24. doi:10.1007/BF00156001

Estling Vannestål, M. (2007). *A University Grammar of English with a Swedish Perspective.* Lund: Studentlitteratur.

Eyring, J. L. (1989). *Teacher experience and student responses in ESL project work instruction: A case study.* (Unpublished doctoral dissertation). University of California Los Angeles, Los Angeles, CA.

Eyring, J. L. (1997). *Is Project Work Worth It?.* Distributed by ERIC Clearinghouse.

Ferholt, B. (2009). *Adult and child development in adult-child joint play: The development of cognition, emotion, imagination and creativity in Playworlds.* (Doctoral Thesis). University of California, San Diego, CA.

Fernández-Vara, C., & Tan, P. (2008). The Game Studies Practicum: Applying Situated Learning to Teach Professional Practices. In *Proceedings of the 2008 Conference on Future Play: Research, Play, Share.* ACM. doi:10.1145/1496984.1496990

Fleer, M. (2011). Kindergartens in Cognitive Times: Imagination as a Dialectical Relation Between Play and Learning. *International Journal of Early Childhood Education, 43*(3), 245–259. doi:10.1007/s13158-011-0044-8

Flytzani, S., & Nijkamp, P. (2008). Locus of control and cross-cultural adjustment of expatriate managers. *International Journal of Foresight and Innovation Policy, 4*(1/2), 146. doi:10.1504/IJFIP.2008.016911

Folkestad, G. (2006). Formal and informal learning situations or practices vs formal and informal ways of learning. *British Journal of Music Education, 22*(2), 135–145. doi:10.1017/S0265051706006887

Folkestad, G. (2008). Review article. *Music Education Research, 10*(4), 499–503. doi:10.1080/14613800802547755

Foot, K. A. (2002). Pursuing an Evolving Object: A Case Study in Object Formation and Identifi cation. *Mind, Culture, and Activity, 9*(2), 132–149. doi:10.1207/S15327884MCA0902_04

Forsgren, T., & Johansson, R. (2004). *Fysikundervisning utomhus. (Unpublished undergraduate thesis).* Umeå University, Umeå, Sweden.

Foster, S. (1989). Streetwise physics. *The School Science Review, 70*(254), 15–17.

Fragoulis, L. (2009). Project-Based Learning in the Teaching of English as A Foreign Language in Greek Primary Schools: From Theory to Practice. *English Language Teaching, 2*(3), 113–119.

Francke, M.G. (2014). Ett högt spel. *Sydsvenskan* (sidor B4-B9), 2014-01-14.

Freeland, R. F. (1997). Culture and Volition in Organizational Decision-Making. Review Essay. *Qualitative Sociology, 20*(1), 127–137. doi:10.1023/A:1024772516671

Freire, P. (1993). *Pedagogy of the city.* New York: Continuum.

Friedman, T. (2007). *The World is Flat: A Brief History of the Twenty-first Century.* New York, NY: Farrar, Straus and Giroux.

Friesen, N. (2009). Discursive psychology and educational technology: Beyond the cognitive revolution. *Mind, Culture, and Activity, 16*(2), 130–144. doi:10.1080/10749030802707861

Frisk, H. (2008). *Improvisation, computers, and interaction: rethinking human-computer interaction through music.* Malmö Academy of Music, Lund University.

Fromm, E. (1956). *The Art of Loving.* New York: Harper & Row.

Fülöp, M. (2002). *Competition in educational settings.* Paper presented at the Faculty of Education, University of Ljubljana. Ljubljana, Slovenia.

Fülöp, M. (1999). Students' perception of the role of competition in their respectivwe contries: Hungary, Japan, and the USA. In A. Ross (Ed.), *Young citizens in Europe* (pp. 95–219). London: University of North London.

Fülöp, M. (2004). Competition as a culturally constructed concept. In C. Baillie, E. Dunn, & Y. Zheng (Eds.), *Travelling facts: The social construction, distribution, and accumulation of knowledge* (pp. 124–128). Frankfurt, Germany: Campus Verlag.

Gadamer, H.-G. (1975). *Thruth amd Method.* Seabury Press.

Gadamer, H.-G. (1998). *Truth and Method* (2nd rev. ed.). New York: Continuum.

Gammelby, M. (2012). *Plads til barndommen. En undersøgelse af sammenhænge mellem plads, rum og pædagogisk praksis i børnehaven. (Ph.d.-afhandling).* Aalborg Universitet, Institut for Læring og Filosofi.

Gärdenfors, P. (2010). *Lusten att förstå: Om lärande på människans villkor.* Stockholm: Natur & Kultur.

Gardner, D. (1995). Student produced video documentary provides a real reason for using the target language. *Language Learning Journal, 12*(1), 54–56. doi:10.1080/09571739585200451

Gaunt, H. (2008). One-to-one tuition in a conservatoire: The perceptions of instrumental and vocal teachers. *Psychology of Music, 36*(2), 215–245. doi:10.1177/0305735607080827

Gee, J. P. (2008). A Sociocultural Perspective on Opportunity to Learn. In P. A. Moss, D. C. Pullin, J. P. Gee, E. H. Haertel, & L. J. Young (Eds.), Assessment, Equity, and Opportunity to Learn (pp. 76-108). Cambridge, UK: Cambridge University Press.

Gee, J. P. (2006). Are Video Games Good for Learning? *Nordic Journal of Digital Literacy, 1*(3), 172–183.

Gee, J. P. (2007). *What Video Games Have to Teach Us about Learning and Literacy.* New York: Palgrave/Macmillan.

Geertz, C. (1973). *The interpretation of cultures: selected essays.* New York: Basic Books.

Georgii-Hemming, E., & Kvarnhall, V. (2011). YouTube som musikalisk erfarenhet. In C. Ericsson & M. Lindgren (Eds.), Perspektiv på populärmusik och skola. Lund: Studentlitteratur.

Giddens, A. (1984). *The constitution of society*. Cambridge, MA: Polity.

Giest, H., & Lompscher, J. (2003). Formation of learning activity and theoretical thinking in science teaching. In A. Kozulin, B. Gindis, V. S. Ageyev, & S. M. Miller (Eds.), Vygotsky's Educational Theory in Cultural Context. Cambridge, UK: Cambridge University Press.

Gjøsund, G., & Huseby, R. (2010). *Gruppe og samspil. 2. reviderede udgave*. København: Hans Reitzels forlag.

Glaser, B. G. (2010). *Att göra grundad teori: problem, frågor och diskussion*. Mill Valley, CA: Sociology Press.

Glaser, B. G. (1978). *Theoretical sensitivity: Advances in methodology of grounded theory*. Mill Valley, CA: Sociology Press.

Glasgow, N. A., Cheyne, M., & Yerrick, R. K. (2010). *What Successful Science Teachers Do: 75 Research-Based Strategies*. Thousand Oaks, CA: Corwin Press Inc.

Gleick, J. (1992). *Genius: The Life and Science of Richard Feynman*. New York, NY: Pantheon Books.

Goehr, L. (1992). *The imaginary museum of musical works: An essay in the philosophy of music*. Oxford, UK: Clarendon.

Goffman, E. (1959). *The Presentation of Self in Everyday Life*. Anchor Books.

Gravem Johansen, G. (2013). *Å øve på improvisasjon: Ein kvalitativ studie av øvepraksisar hos jazzstudentar, med fokus på utvikling av imporivsasjonskompetanse* [To practise improvisation: A qualitative study of practising practices among jazz students, with a particular focus on the development of improvisation competence]. Oslo: Norges Musikkhøgskole.

Green, L. (1997). *Music, gender, education*. Cambridge, UK: Cambridge Univ. Press. doi:10.1017/CBO9780511585456

Green, L. (2008). *Music, informal learning and the school: A new classroom pedagogy*. Aldershot, UK: Ashgate.

Greiner, C., & Sakdapolrak, P. (2013). Translocality: Concepts, Applications and Emerging Research Perspectives. *Geography Compass*, 7(5), 373–384. doi:10.1111/gec3.12048

Grotjahn, R. (1991). The research programme subjective theories: A new approach in second language research. *Studies in Second Language Acquisition*, 13(2), 187–214. doi:10.1017/S0272263100009943

Gruber, H., & Harteis, C. (2011). Researching Workplace Learning in Europe. In M. Malloch, L. Cairns, K. Evans, & B. N. O'Connor (Eds.), The SAGE Handbook of Workplace Learning (pp. 224-235). London: Sage Publications Ltd.

Gu, P. (2002). Effects of project-based CALL on Chinese EFL learners. *Asian Journal of English Language Teaching*, 12, 195–210.

Gupta, A., & Ferguson, J. (1992). Beyond "Culture": Space, Identity, and the Politics of Difference. *Cultural Anthropology*, 7(1), 6–23. doi:10.1525/can.1992.7.1.02a00020

Gustavsen, B. (2007). Work Organization and 'the Scandinavian Model'. *Economic and Industrial Democracy*, 28(4), 650–671. doi:10.1177/0143831X07082218

Gutierréz, K. (2007). Commentary. In C. Lewis, P. Enciso, & E. Moje (Eds.), Reframing Socioclultural Research on Literacy: Identity, Agency and Power. Routledge.

Gutierrez, K., & Larson, J. (1995). Script, counterscript, and underlife in the classroom: James Brown versus Brown v. Board of Education. *Harvard Educational Review*, 65(3), 445–471.

Guttmann, A. (1978). *From ritual to record: The nature of modern sports*. New York: Columbia University Press.

Gynther, K. (2009). *Parallel undervisning – Videokonferencer i et remedierings- og re-didaktiseringsperspektiv*. Retrieved from http://ucsj.dk/fileadmin/user_upload/FU/IT_og_laering/Parllel_undervisning_og_videokonferencer.pdf

Gynther, C. (2005). *Blended learning: IT og læring I et teoretisk og praktisk perspektiv*. København: Unge Pædagoger.

Haapasaari, A., Engeström, Y., & Kerosuo, H. (2014). The emergence of learners' transformative agency in a change laboratory intervention. *Journal of Education and Work*, 1–31. doi:10.1080/13639080.2014.900168

Hakkarinen, P., & Bredikyte, M. (2008). The zone of proximal development in play and learning. *Cultural-historical Psychology, 4*(5), 2–11.

Hammersley, M., & Atkinson, P. (1997). *Ethnography: Principles in practice*. London: Routledge.

Hampel, R., & Stickler, U. (2012). The use of video-conferencing to support multimodal interaction in an online language classroom. *ReCALL, 24*(2), 116–137. doi:10.1017/S095834401200002X

Hansson, T. (2014). Modeling and analyzing contextual influences. In T. Hansson (Ed.), Contemporary Approaches to Activity Theory: Interdisciplinary Perspectives on Human Behavior. Hershey, PA: IGI Global.

Hansson, T. (2014). Social science universals. In T. Issa, P. Isaias, & P. Kommers (Eds.), Multicultural Awareness and Technology in Higher Education: Global Perspectives. Hershey, PA: IGI-Global.

Hargreaves, D. J., & North, A. C. (n.d.). *The Social Psychology of Music*. Oxford, UK: Oxford University Press.

Hargreaves, A. (2004). *Läraren i kunskapssamhället: I osäkerhetens tidevarv*. Lund: Studentlitteratur.

Harrison, S., Tatar, D., & Sengers, P. (2007). The Three Paradigms of HCI. In *Proceedings of CHI 2007*. ACM.

Hatch, J. A. (2002). *Doing qualitative research in education settings*. Albany, NY: SUNY.

Hatchuel, A. (2001). Towards design theory and expandable rationality: The unfinished program of Herbert Simon. *Journal of Management and Governance, 5*(3/4), 260–273. doi:10.1023/A:1014044305704

Hawhee, D. (2004). *Bodily arts: Rhetoric and athletics in ancient Greece*. Austin, TX: University of Texas Press.

Head, B. W. (2008). Assessing network-based collaborations. Effectiveness for whom? *Public Management Review, 10*(6), 733–749. doi:10.1080/14719030802423087

Hedegaard, M. (1990). The zone of proximal development as basis for instruction. In L. C. Moll (Ed.), Vygotsky and education: Instructional implications and applications of sociohistorical psychology. Cambridge, UK: Cambridge University press.

Hedegaard, M. (2005). Strategies for dealing with conflicts in value positions between home and school: Influences on ehtnic minority students' development of motives and identity. *Culture and Psychology, 11*(2), 187–205. doi:10.1177/1354067X05052351

Hedegaard, M. (2012). Analyzing children's learning and development in everyday settings from a cultural-historical wholeness approach. *Mind, Culture, and Activity, 19*(2), 127–138. doi:10.1080/10749039.2012.665560

Hedegaard, M., & Chaiklin, S. (2005). *Radical-local teaching and learning: A cultural historical approach*. Aarhus: Aarhus University Press.

Hedestig, U., & Kaptelinin, V. (2005). Facilitator's Roles in a Videoconference Learning. *Information Systems Frontiers, 7*(1), 71–83. doi:10.1007/s10796-005-5339-6

Hedge, T. (2002). *Teaching and learning in the language classroom*. Oxford, UK: OUP.

Hegel, G. W. F. (2013). *The Phenomenology of Mind – Introduction*. Retrieved April 15, 2013, from http://www.marxists.org/reference/archive/hegel/works/ph/phintro.html

Hegel, G. W. F. (1996). *Science of Logic*. Allen & Unwin.

Heidegger, M. (2001). *Zollikon Seminars:Protocols—Conversation—Letters*. Evanston, IL: Northwestern University.

Heidegger, M. (2002). The Origin of the Work of Art. In J. Young (Ed.), Martin Heidegger: Off the Beaten Track (pp. 1-56). Cambridge University Press.

Heidegger, M. (1986). *Sein und Zeit*. Tübingen: Max Niemeyer Verlag.

Heidegger, M. (1992). *Being and Time*. Oxford, UK: Blackwell.

Heidegger, M. (2004). *What is called thinking?* New York: Harper Perennial.

Heikinheimo, T. (2009). *Intensity of interaction in instrumental music lessons*. Helsinki: Sibelius Academy.

Heikkilä, H. (forthcoming in 2014). *The dialectics between transformative agency and work-related well-being in network activity*. Manuscript under elaboration.

Heikkilä, H., & Seppänen, L. (2014) Examining developmental dialogue: the emergence of transformative agency. *Outlines – Critical Practice Studies*, *15*(2), 5-30.

Henry, J. (1994). *Teaching through projects. Open and distance learning series*. London: Kogan Page.

Hilton-Jones, U. (1988). *Project-based learning for foreign students in an English-speaking environment* (Report No. FL017682). Washington, DC: US Department of Education.

Hodkinsson, P., Biesta, G., & James, D. (2008). Understanding learning culturally: Overcoming the dualism between social and individual views of learning. *Vocations and Learning*, *1*(1), 27–47. doi:10.1007/s12186-007-9001-y

Hofstede, G. (1984). *Culture's Consequences: International Differences in Work-Related Values (Abridged edition)*. London: SAGE.

Holland, D., & Cole, M. (1995). Between discourse and schema: Reformulating a cultural-historical approach to culture and mind. *Anthropology & Education Quarterly*, *26*(4), 475–489. doi:10.1525/aeq.1995.26.4.05x1065y

Holopainen, J., & Björkman, I. (2005). The personal characteristics of the successful expatriate: A critical review of the literature and an empirical investigation. *Personnel Review*, *34*(1), 37–50. doi:10.1108/00483480510578476

Hu, G. (2002). Potential cultural resistance to pedagogical imports: The case of communicative language teaching in China. *Language, Culture and Curriculum*, *15*(2), 93–195. doi:10.1080/07908310208666636

Huizinga, J. (1945). *Den lekande människan*. Stockholm: Natur och kultur.

Hultberg, C. (2010). *Vem äger lärandet?* [Students ownership of learning]. Stockholm: Myndigheten för nätverk och samarbete inom högre utbildning.

Hultberg, C. (2005). Practitioners and researchers in cooperation – method development for qualitative practice-related studies. *Music Education Research*, *7*(2), 211–224. doi:10.1080/14613800500169449

Hviid, M. K., Keller, H. D., Rasmussen, A., Rasmussen, P., & Thøgersen, U. (2008). *Kompetenceudvikling i udkantsområder: Almen og praksisnær kompetenceudvikling for voksne*. Aalborg: Aalborg Universitetsforlag.

Ilyenkov, E. V. (1977). *The concept of the Ideal*. Retrieved from http://www.marxists.org/archive/ilyenkov/works/ideal/ideal.htm

Ilyenkov, E. V. (2008). *The dialectics of the abstract and the concrete in Marx's Capital*. Delhi: AAKAR books.

Ilyenkov, E. (1977). *Dialectical Logic: Essays on its Theory and History*. Moscow: Progress.

Ingold, T. (2006). Walking the plank: meditations on a process of skill. In J. R. Dakers (Ed.), *Defining technological literacy: Towards an epistemological framework* (pp. 65–80). New York: Palgrave Macmillan.

Ingold, T. (2010). The textility of making. *Cambridge Journal of Economics*, *34*(1), 91–102. doi:10.1093/cje/bep042

Inkpen, A., & Currall, S. (2004). The Coevolution of Trust, Control, and Learning in Joint Ventures. *Organization Science*, *15*(5), 586–599. doi:10.1287/orsc.1040.0079

Jackson, P. (2012). How we think we think. *Teachers College Record*, *114*(2). Retrieved from http://www.tcrecord.org

Jahreie, C. F., & Ottesen, E. (2010). Learning to become a teacher: Participation across spheres for learning. In V. Ellis, A. Edwards, & P. Smagorinsky (Eds.), *Cultural-historical perspectives on teacher education and development* (pp. 131-145). London: Routledge.

Janzen, K., Perry, B., & Edwards, M. (2011). Aligning the quantum perspective of learning to instructional design: Exploring the seven definite questions. *International Review of Research in Open and Distance Learning*, *12*(7).

Jin, H. G. (2005). Form-focused instruction and second language learning: Some pedagogical considerations and teaching techniques. *Journal of Chinese Language Teaching Association*, *40*(2), 43–66.

Jóhannsdóttir, T. (2010). Deviations from the conventional: Contradictions as sources of change in teacher education. In V. Ellis, A. Edwards, & P. Smagorinsky (Eds.), Cultural-historical pespectives on teacher education and development (pp. 163-279). London: Routledge.

Jóhannsdóttir, T. (2010). *Teacher education and school-based distance learning: individual and systemic development in schools and a teacher education programme.* (PhD Doctoral thesis). University of Iceland. Retrieved from http://hdl.handle.net/1946/7119

Johansson, K. (2013). Musical creativity and learning across the individual and the collective. In A. Sannino & V. Ellis (Eds.), Learning and collective creativity: Activity-theoretical and socio-cultural studies (pp. 23-39). London: Routledge.

Johansson, K. (2013). (Re)thinking organ improvisation: Revisiting musical practice. In H. Frisk & S. Östersjö (Eds.), (re)thinking improvisation: artistic explorations and conceptual writing. Malmö: Malmö Academy of Music.

Johansson, K. (2014). Collaborative music making and artistic agency. In T. Hansson (Ed.), Contemporary Approaches to Activity Theory: Interdisciplinary Perspectives on Human Behavior. Hershey, PA: IGI Global.

Johansson, K. (2008). *Organ improvisation - activity, action and rhetorical practice.* Malmö: Lund University.

Johansson, K. (2012). Experts, entrepreneurs and competence nomads: The skills paradox in higher music education. *Music Education Research*, *14*(1), 47–64. do i:10.1080/14613808.2012.657167

Johansson, K. (2013). *Walking together with music: Teachers' voices on the joys and challenges of Higher Music Education.* Malmö: Malmö Academy of Music.

Johansson, K. (2013). Undergraduate students' ownership of musical learning: Obstacles and options in one-to-one teaching. *British Journal of Music Education*, *30*(2), 277–295. doi:10.1017/S0265051713000120

Johnson, D. W., & Johnson, R. T. (1994). Learning together and alone: cooperative, competitive and individualistic learning. Needham Heights, MA: Allyn and Bacon.

Johnson, D. W., & Johnson, R. T. (1989). *Cooperation and competition: Theory and research.* Edina, MN: Interaction.

Johnson, D. W., Johnson, R. T., & Roseth, C. J. (2012). Competition and performance: More facts, more understanding? Comment on Murayama and Ellion (2012). *Psychological Bulletin*, *138*(6), 1071–1078. doi:10.1037/a0029454 PMID:23088571

John-Steiner, V. (2010). *Vygotsky and Creativity: A Cultural-historical Approach to Play, Meaning Making, and the Arts.* New York: Peter Lang.

Jonasson, C. (2013). Defining boundaries between school and work: teachers and students' attribution of quality to school-based vocational training. *Journal of Education and Work,* 1-21.

Jonasson, C. (2013). *Trust in vocational schools?* Paper presented at the JVET 10th International Conference 2013. Oxford, UK.

Jonasson, C. (2013). Why stay in school: Student retention processes in vocational schools. Germany Scholars' Press.

Jónasson, J. (2001). *On-line distance education – A feasible choice in teacher education in Iceland?* (Master of Philosophy Thesis). University of Strathclyde. Retrieved from https://notendur.hi.is/jonjonas/skrif/mphil/

Jonasson, C. (2012). Teachers and students' divergent perceptions of student engagement: Recognition of school or workplace goals. *British Journal of Sociology of Education*, *33*(5), 723–741. doi:10.1080/01425692.2012.674811

Jónasson, J. (1996). *Spurningalisti nemenda 1996* [Questionnaire for students 1996]. Iceland University of Education. Reykjavík.

Jorgensen, E. R. (2003). *Transforming music education.* Bloomington, IN: Indiana Univ. Press.

Jung, T. (2010). Citizens, co-producers, customers, clients, captives? A critical review of consumerism and public services. *Public Management Review*, *12*(3), 439–446. doi:10.1080/14719031003787940

Juslin, P. (2001). Communication of emotion in music performance. In P. Juslin & J. A. Sloboda (Eds.), Music and emotion. Oxford, UK: Oxford University Press.

Kajamaa, A., Kerosuo, H., & Engeström, Y. (2008). Työelämän kehittämisprojektien seuraamusten jäljillä - Uusi näkökulma arviointitutkimukseen. *Hallinnon Tutkimus, 26*(4), 61-79.

Kakkori, L., & Huttunen, R. (2014). Vygotsky, Heidegger and Gadamer on moral development. In T. Hansson (Ed.), Contemporary Approaches to Activity Theory: Interdisciplinary Perspectives on Human Behavior. Hershey, PA: IGI Global.

Kaptelinin, V. (2013). Activity Theory. In *The Encyclopedia of Human-Computer Interaction* (2nd ed.). Aarhus, Denmark: The Interaction Design Foundation. Retrieved from http://www.interaction-design.org/encyclopedia/activity_theory.html

Kaptelinin, V., & Nardi, B. (2012). *Affordances in HCI: Toward a Mediated Action Perspective.* Paper presented at the Conference of CHI 2012. Austin, TX. doi:10.1145/2207676.2208541

Kaptelinin, V., & Nardi, B. (2006). *Acting with Technology: Activity Theory and Interaction Design.* Cambridge, MA: The MIT Press.

Karlsson, J. (2008). *A novel approach to teaching emotional expression in music performance.* Uppsala: Acta Universitatis Upsaliensis.

Katznelson, N. et al. (2009). *Vejen mod de 95% (del I). En erfaringsopsamling fra projektet Ungdomsuddannelse til alle.* København: Danmarks Pædagogiske Universitetsskole. Kommunernes Landsforening. Undervisningsministeriet.

Katznelson, N. et al. (2010). *Vejen mod de 95% (del II). In Erfaringsopsamling fra projektet Ungdomsuddannelse til alle.* København: Danmarks Pædagogiske Universitetsskole. Kommunernes Landsforening. Undervisningsministeriet.

Kaufman, J. C., & Beghetto, R. A. (2009). Beyond big and little: The four c model of creativity. *Review of General Psychology, 13*(1), 1–12. doi:10.1037/a0013688

Keating, C. B., Kauffmann, P., & Dryer, D. (2001). A framework for systemic analysis of complex issues. *Journal of Management Development, 20*(9), 772–784. doi:10.1108/02621710110405479

Ke, L. (2010). Project-based College English: An Approach to Teaching Non-English Majors. Chinese. *Journal of Applied Linguistics, 33*(4), 99–112.

Kennaraháskóli Íslands. (2005). *Kennaraháskóli Íslands, ársskýrsla 2004* [Iceland University of Education, yearly report 2004]. (S. Kaaber & H. Kristjánsdóttir, Eds.). Reykjavík: Kennaraháskóli Íslands.

Kerosuo, H. (2006). *Boundaries in action. An activity-theoretical study of development, learning and change in health care for patients with multiple and chronic illnesses.* University of Helsinki.

Kerosuo, H. (2006). *Boundaries in action: An activity-theoretical study of development, learning and change in health care for patients with multiple and chronic illnesses.* Helsinki: University of Helsinki, Department of Education.

Kinard, J., & Kozulin, A. (2008). *Rigorous Mathematical Thinking: Conceptual Formation in the Mathematics Classroom.* Cambridge, UK: Cambridge University Press. doi:10.1017/CBO9780511814655

Kirkeby, I. M., Gitz-Johansen, T., & Kampmann, J. (2004). Samspil mellem fysisk rum og hverdagsliv i skolen. In K. Larsen (Ed.), Arkitektur, krop og læring. København: Hans Reitzel.

Kirkeby, I. M. (2004). *Skolen finder sted (Arbejdsrapport).* København: Statens Byggeforskningsinstitut.

Kirkeby, I. M., Iversen, O. S., & Martinussen, M. (2009). *Fremtidens hybride læringsrum. På vej mod en forståelsesramme for hvordan skolens it-berigede rum kan støtte arbejdsprocesser og skift mellem forskellige arbejdsprocesser.* Statens Byggeforskningsinstitut, Aalborg Universitet.

Kloetzer, L. (2008). *Analyse de l'homélie de la messe dominicale: Langage et conflits de métier dans l'activité des prêtres: La part de Dieu, la part de l'homme.* (Doctoral thesis in Psychology). CNAM, Paris, France.

Kloetzer, L., & Seppänen, L. (2014). Dialogues and interactions as "the nursery for change". *Outlines - Critical Practice Studies, 15*(2), 1-4.

Kloetzer, L. (2012). Development of professional concepts through work analysis: Tech Diving under the loop of Activity Clinic. *Mind, Culture, and Activity, 20*(4), 318–337. doi:10.1080/10749039.2012.688087

Knutagård, H., Krantz, B., & Jedemark, M. (Eds.). (2013). A Nordic Perspective on the Cultural and Activity Approach in Theory and Practice. Kristianstad: Kristianstad University Press.

Knutagård, H. (2002). *Introduktion till verksamhetsteori*. Lund: Studentlitteratur.

Kohn, A. (1986). *No contest: The case against competition*. Boston, MA: Houghton-Mifflin Company.

Kopnin, P. V. (1978). *A dialética como lógica e teoria do conhecimento*. Rio de Janeiro: Civilização Brasileira.

Kosik, K. (1976). *Dialética do Concreto*. Rio de Janeiro: Paz e Terra.

Kostulski, K. (2011). Formes et fonctions psychologiques des réalisations langagières: Vers une psychologie concrète du langage. In Note de synthèse en vue de l'obtention de l'Habilitation à Diriger des Recherches. Université de Paris 8.

Kostulski, K., & Kloetzer, L. (2014). Controversy as a Developmental Tool in Cross-Self Confrontation. *Outlines: Critical Practice Studies, 15*(2), 54–73.

Kratus, J. (1990). Structuring the music curriculum for creative learning. *Music Educators Journal, 79*(9), 33–37. doi:10.2307/3401075

Krüger, T. (1998). Teacher practice, pedagogical discourse and the construction of knowledge: Two case studies of teachers at work. Bergen University College.

Kupferberg, F. (2003). Kritik, tilpasning, autencitet og kommunikation. Kreativitetsregimer i moderniteten. *Dansk Sociologi, 14*(3), 43–62.

Kuutti, K. (1996). Activity Theory as a potential framework for human-computer interaction research. In B. Nardi (Ed.), Context and Consciousness: Activity Theory and Human Computer Interaction. Cambridge, MA: MIT Press.

Kwami, R. M. (2001). Music Education in and for a pluralist society. In C. Plummeridge & C. Philpott (Eds.), Issues in music teaching. London: RoutledgeFalmer.

Laclau, E. (1990). *New reflections on the revolution of our time*. London: Verso.

Lai, C., Zhao, Y., & Wang, J. (2011). Task-Based Language Teaching in Online Ab Initio Foreign Language Classrooms. *Modern Language Journal*, 9581–103.

Lange, T., Johannesen, K., & Henriksen, T. H. (2010). *De unges veje gennem uddannelsessystemet i Nordjylland*. Region Nordjylland.

Larsson, S. (2010). *Kvalitativ analys*. Lund: Studentlitteratur.

Latour, B. (1987). *Science in action*. Cambridge, MA: Harvard University Press.

Latour, B. (2000). When things strike back: A possible contribution of science studies to the social sciences. *The British Journal of Sociology, 51*(1), 107–123. doi:10.1080/000713100358453

Latour, B., & Lepinay, V. A. (2009). *The Science of Passionate Interests-An Introduction to: Gabriel Tarde's Economic Anthropology*. Chicago: Prickly Paradigm Press.

Latour, B., & Woolgar, S. (1986). *Laboratory life: The construction of scientific facts*. Princeton, NJ: Princeton University Press.

Laurillard, D. (2002). *Rethinking university teaching*. London. Falmer: Routledge. doi:10.4324/9780203304846

Lave, J. (2011). *Apprenticeship in critical ethnographic practice*. Chicago: Chicago University Press. doi:10.7208/chicago/9780226470733.001.0001

Lave, J. (2012). Changing practice. *Mind, Culture, and Activity, 16*(2), 156–171. doi:10.1080/10749039.2012.666317

Lave, J., & Wenger, E. (1991). *Situated learning: legitimate peripheral participation*. Cambridge, UK: Cambridge University Press. doi:10.1017/CBO9780511815355

Lavie, D., Stettner, U., & Tushman, M. L. (2010). Exploration and exploitation within and across organizations. *The Academy of Management Annals, 4*(1), 109–155. doi:10.1080/19416521003691287

Lawson, T., Comber, C., Gage, J., & Cullum-Hanshaw, A. (2010). Images of the future for education? Video-conferencing: A literature review. *Technology, Pedagogy and Education, 19*(3), 295–314. doi:10.1080/147593 9X.2010.513761

Lebaron, F. (2009). How Bourdieu "Quantified" Bourdieu: The Geometric Modeling of Data. In K. R. a. C. Sanders (Ed.), Quantifying Theory: Pierre Bourdieu (pp. 11-29). London: Springer Science + Business Media B.V

Lee, I. (2002). Project work made easy in the English classroom. *Canadian Modern Language Review, 59*, 282–290. doi:10.3138/cmlr.59.2.282

Lee, M.-H., Wu, Y.-T., & Tsai, C.-C. (2013). Research trends in science education from 2003 to 2007: A content analysis of publications in selected journals. *International Journal of Science Education, 31*(15), 1999–2020. doi:10.1080/09500690802314876

Lee, Y.-J., & Roth, W.-M. (2008). How activity systems evolve: Making saving salmon in British Columbia. *Mind, Culture, and Activity, 15*(4), 296–321. doi:10.1080/10749030802391211

Leffler, E., & Lundberg, G. (2012). Att vilja lära språk är entreprenöriellt lärande. *Lingua*, (2), 15–21.

Leitsch, D. (2011). Vygotsky, consciousness, and the German psycholinguistic tradition. *Mind, Culture, and Activity, 18*(4), 305–318. doi:10.1080/10749031003713815

Lektorsky, V. A. (2009). Mediation as a means of collective activity. In A. Sannino, H. Daniels, & K. Gutiérrez (Eds.), *Learning and expanding with activity theory*. Cambridge, UK: Cambridge University Press. doi:10.1017/CBO9780511809989.006

Lentz Taguchi, H. (2009). *Varför pedagogisk dokumentation?* Stockholm: Stockholms Universitets Förlag.

Lentz Taguchi, H. (2010). *Going Beyond the Theory/Practice Divide in Early Childhood Education. Introducing and intra-active pedagogy*. New York, NY: Routledge.

Leont'ev, A. N. (1981). The problem of activity in psychology. In J. Wertsch (Ed.), The Concept of Activity in Soviet Psychology (pp. 7-71). New York, NY: M.E. Sharpe Inc.

Leontev, A. (1977). Activity and consciousness. Moscow: Progress Publishers; Retrieved from http://www.marxists.org/archive/leontev/works/1977/leon1977.htm

Leont'ev, A. N. (1978). *Activity, consciousness, and personality*. Englewood Cliffs, NJ: Prentice-Hall.

Leontev, A. N. (2002). *Virksomhed, bevisthed og personlighed* [Activity, Consciousness and Personality]. København: Hans Reizels Forlag.

Leontev, A. N., & Luria, A. R. (1968). The psychological ideas of L. S. Vygotsky. In B. B. Wolman (Ed.), *The historical roots of contemporary psychology* (pp. 338–367). New York: Harper & Row.

Leontiev, A. (1983). *Actividad, Consciencia y Personalidad*. Havana: Pueblo y Educación.

Leontiev, A. N. (1978). *Activity, consciousness, and personality*. Prentice Hall. Retrieved from http://www.marxists.org/archive/leontev/works/1978/index.htm

Leontiev, A. N. (1981). *Problems of the development of the mind*. Moscow: Progress.

Leontjev, A. A. (1980). Tätigkeit und Kommunikation. *Sowjetwissenschaft*, 5.

Leontjev, A. N. (1974-75). The Problem of Activity in Psychology. *Soviet Education, 8*(2).

Leontjev, A. N. (1979). *Tätigkeit-Bewusstsein-Persönlichkeit. Volke und Wissen*. Berlin: Volkseigener Verlag.

Leontyev, A. N. (1978). *Activity, Consciousness, Personality* (M. J. Hall, Trans.). Prentice Hall.

Levine, G. S. (2004). Global simulation: A student-centered, task-based format for intermediate foreign language courses. *Foreign Language Annals, 37*(1), 26–36. doi:10.1111/j.1944-9720.2004.tb02170.x

Lewis, C. (2000). *Lesson Study: The core of Japanese professional development*. Paper presented at the American Educational Research Association Meetings. New Orleans, LA.

Lin, C.T. (2009). *Chinese Guest Teacher Program*. Paper presented at New York College Board. New York, NY.

Lindberg, V. (2010). Skolans kunskapsinnehåll i ljuset av elevers uppgifter – Exempel matematik. In I. Eriksson, V. Lindberg, & E. Österlind (Eds.), Uppdrag undervisning: Kunskap och lärande. Lund: Studentlitteratur.

Lindberg, V. (2003). Learning practices in vocational education. *Scandinavian Journal of Educational Research*, *47*(2), 157–179. doi:10.1080/00313830308611

Lindberg, V. (2003). Vocational knowing and the content in vocational education. *International Journal of Training Research*, *1*(2), 40–61. doi:10.5172/ijtr.1.2.40

Lindqvist, G. (1989). *Från fakta till fantasi (From Facts to Fantasy)*. Lund: Studentlitteratur.

Lindqvist, G. (1992). *Ensam i vida världen (Lonely in the wide world)*. Lund: Studentlitteratur.

Lindqvist, G. (1995). *The Aesthetics of Play: A Didactic Study of Play and Culture in Preschools*. Stockholm, Sweden: Almqvist & Wiksell International.

Lindqvist, G. (1996). *Lekens möjligheter (The possibilities of play)*. Lund: Studentlitteratur.

Lindqvist, G. (2000). *Historia som tema och gestaltning (History as theme and gestalt)*. Lund: Studentlitteratur.

Lindqvist, G. (2001). When small children play: How adults dramatize and children create meaning. *Early Years*, *21*(1), 7–14. doi:10.1080/09575140123593

Lindqvist, G. (2001). The Relationship between Play and Dance. *Research in Dance Education*, *2*(1), 41–53. doi:10.1080/14647890120058302

Lindqvist, G. (2002). *Lek i skolan (Play in school)*. Lund: Studentlitteratur.

Lindqvist, G. (2003). Vygotsky's theory of creativity. *Creativity Research Journal*, *15*(4), 245–251. doi:10.1080/10400419.2003.9651416

Linge, A. (2013). *Svängrum: För en kreativ musikpedagogik*. (Dissertation). Malmö: Malmö högskola.

Linge, A. (2014). Creative musical practice in an educational context. In T. Hansson (Ed.), Contemporary Approaches to Activity Theory: Interdisciplinary Perspectives on Human Behavior. Hershey, PA: IGI Global.

Ljungar-Chapelon, A. (2008). *Le respect de la tradition Om den franska flöjtkonsten: Dess lärande, hantverk och estetik i ett hermeneutiskt perspektiv*. Malmö: Lund University.

Lögdlund, U. (2010). Constructing learning spaces? Videoconferencing at local learning centres in Sweden. *Studies in Continuing Education*, *32*(3), 183–199. doi:10.1080/0158037X.2010.517993

Lomov, B. F. (1980). Die Kategorien Kommunikation und Tätigkeit in der Psychologie. *Sowjetwissenschaft, 5.*

Lompsher, J. (1999). Learning activity and its formation: Ascending from the abstract to the concrete. In M. Hedegaard & J. Lompscher (Eds.), Learning activity and development. Aarhus, Denmark: Aarhus University Press.

Lorino, P., Tricard, B., & Clot, Y. (2011). Research methods for non-representational approaches to organizational complexity: The dialogical mediated inquiry. *Organization Studies, 32*(6), 769–801. doi:10.1177/0170840611410807

Lu, M. (2012). *Using the learners-as-ethnographers approach to enhance intercultural learning among American college students learning Chinese as a foreign language* (dissertation). Retrieved from http://search.proquest.com/docview/1038368174?accountid=2909. (1038368174).

Lucas, N. (2007). Rethinking initial teacher education for further education teachers: From standards-led to a knowledge-based approach. *Teaching Education*, *18*(2), 93–106. doi:10.1080/10476210701325077

Lukács, G. (1979). *Ontologia do Ser Social: Os princípios ontológicos fundamentais de Marx*. São Paulo: Livraria Editora Ciências Humanas.

Lundberg, D., Malm, K., & Ronström, O. (2000). *Musik, medier, mångkultur: Förändringar i svenska musiklandskap*. Hedemora: Gidlund.

Lurija, A. R. (1979). *The making of mind: a personal account of Soviet psychology*. Cambridge, MA: Harvard U.P.

Lurija, A. R. (1981). *Language and cognition*. Washington, DC: Winston.

Madsen, U. A. (2003). *Pædagogisk etnografi*. Aarhus: Forlaget Klim.

Mäkitalo, J. (2005). *Work-related well-being in the transformation of nursing home work.* (Doctoral dissertation). University of Oulu, Oulu, Finland. Retrieved from http://herkules.oulu.fi/isbn9514277678/isbn9514277678.pdf

Mäkitalo, Å. (2012). Professional learning and the materiality of social practice. *Journal of Education and Work,* *25*(1), 59–78. doi:10.1080/13639080.2012.644905

Mäkitalo, A., & Säljö, R. (2009). Contextualizing social dilemmas in institutional practices: Negotiating objects of activity in labour market organizations. In A. Sannino, H. Daniels, & K. Gutierrez (Eds.), *Learning and expanding with activity theory* (pp. 112–128). New York: Cambridge University Press. doi:10.1017/CBO9780511809989.008

March, J. (1991). Exploration and exploitation in organizational learning. *Organization Science, 2*(1), 71–87. doi:10.1287/orsc.2.1.71

Marjanovic-Shane, A., Ferholt, B., Nilsson, M., Rainio, A. P., & Miyazaki, K. (2011). Playworlds: An Art of development. In C. Lobman & B. O'Neill (Eds.), *Play and Culture.* TASP.

Markham, T. (2011). Project based learning: A bridge just far enough. Teacher Librarian (Vancouver), 39 (2), 38.

Marková, I. (2000). Amédée and how to get rid of it: Social representations from a dialogical perspective. *Culture and Psychology, 6*(4), 419–460. doi:10.1177/1354067X0064002

Marková, I. (2012). Objectification in common sense thinking. *Mind, Culture, and Activity, 19*(3), 207–221. doi:10.1080/10749039.2012.688178

Markström, P., & Cedergren, A. (2005). *Praktisk fysik i grundskolans tidigare år. (Unpublished undergraduate thesis).* Umeå University, Umeå, Sweden.

Martin, D., & Peim, N. (2009). Critical perspectives on activity theory. *Educational Review, 61*(2), 131–138. doi:10.1080/00131910902844689

Marton, F. (2000). The Practice of learning. *Nordisk Pedagogik, 20*(4), 230–236.

Marx, K. (1909). *Capital* (Vol. 1). London: William Glaisher.

Marx, K. (1996). *O Capital* (Vol. 1). São Paulo: Nova Cultura.

Marx, K. (2011). *Grudrisse: Manuscritos econômicos de 1857-1858; esboços da crítica da economia política.* São Paulo: Boitempo.

Marx, K., & Engels, F. (1904). *Das Kapital: Kritik der politischen Ökonomie* (Vol. 3). Hamburg, Germany: Meissner.

Marx, K., & Engels, F. (1978). *The Marx-Engels Reader.* New York: W. W. Norton & Company.

Marx, K., & Engels, F. (2007). *A ideologia alemã.* São Paulo: Boitempo.

Mateas, M. (2008). Procedural Literacy: Educating the New Media Practitioner. In Beyond Fun: Serious Games and Media. ETC Press.

Maxwell, B., & Reichenbach, R. (2007). Educating Moral Emotions: A Praxiological Analysis. *Studies in Philosophy and Education, 26*(2), 147–163. doi:10.1007/s11217-006-9020-4

McDonell, W. (1992). The role of teacher in the cooperative learning classroom. In C. Kessler (Ed.), Cooperative Language Learning: A Teacher's Resources Book. Englewood Cliffs, NJ: Prentice Hall Regents.

McGrath, R. G. (2010). Business models: A discovery driven approach. *Long Range Planning, 43*(2-3), 247–261. doi:10.1016/j.lrp.2009.07.005

McGroarty, M. (1989). The benefits of cooperative learning arrangements in second language instruction. *Journal of the National Association for Bilingual Education, 13,* 127–143.

McNiff, J., & Whitehead, J. (2006). *All You Need To Know About Action Research.* London: SAGE Publications.

Mercer, N. (2005). Sociocultural discourse analysis: Analysing classroom talk as a social mdoe of thinking. *Journal of Applied Linguistics, 1*(2), 137–168. doi:10.1558/japl.2004.1.2.137

Mertler, C. A., & Charles, C. M. (2008). *Introduction to educational research.* Boston: Allyn & Bacon.

Miettinen, R., Toikka, K., Tuunainen, J., Freeman, S., Lehenkari, J., Leminen, J., & Siltala, J. (2008). *Informaatiotekninen kumous, innovaatiopolitiikka ja luottamus* (Vol. 234/2008. sivu 3, 9.6.2008). Helsinki: Tekesin katsaus 234/2008.

Miettinen, R. (2005). Object activity and individual motivation. *Mind, Culture, and Activity*, *12*(1), 52–69. doi:10.1207/s15327884mca1201_5

Miettinen, R. (2006). The Sources of Novelty: A Cultural and Systemic View of Distributed Creativity. *Creativity and Innovation Management*, *15*(2), 173–181. doi:10.1111/j.1467-8691.2006.00381.x

Miles, M., & Huberman, M. A. (1994). *Qualitative Data Analysis*. London: Sage.

Ministry of Social Affairs and Health. (2010). *Socially sustainable Finland 2020*. Strategy for social and health policy, Ministry of Social Affairs and Health. Retrieved from http://www.stm.fi/c/document_library/get_file?folderId=2765155&name=DLFE-15321.pdf

Moll, L. (1990) Introduction. In L. Moll (Ed.), Vygotsky and Education: Instructional Implications and Applications of Sociohistorical Psychology (pp. 1–27). New York: Cambridge University Press.

Moran, S., & John-Steiner, V. (2003). Creativity in the making: Vygotsky's contemporary contribution to the dialectic of development and creativity. In R. K. Sawyer (Ed.), Creativity and development (pp. 61-90). Oxford, UK: Oxford University Press.

Moran, R. T., Harris, P. R., & Moran, S. V. (2011). *Managing Cultural Differences: Global Leadership Strategies for Cross-cultural Business Success* (8th ed.). Burlington, MA: Elsevier/Butterworth-Heinemann.

Mulhall, S. (1996). *Heidegger and Being and Time*. London: Routledge.

Murayama, K., & Elliot, A. J. (2012). The competition-performance relation: A meta-analytic review and test of the opposing processes model of competion and performance. *Psychological Bulletin*, *138*(6), 1035–1070. doi:10.1037/a0028324 PMID:23088570

Narayan, U. (1998). Essence of Culture and a Sense of History: A Feminist Critique of Cultural Essentialism. *Hypatia*, *13*(2), 86–106. doi:10.1111/j.1527-2001.1998.tb01227.x

Nardi, B. (2007). Placeless Organizations: Collaborating for Transformation. *Mind, Culture, and Activity*, *14*(1-2), 5–22. doi:10.1080/10749030701307663

Nersessian, N. (2012). Engineering concepts: The interplay between concept formation and modeling practices in bioengineering sciences. *Mind, Culture, and Activity*, *19*(3), 222–239. doi:10.1080/10749039.2012.688232

Neuman, D. (1986). *Räknefärdighetens rötter*. Stockholm: Utbildningsförlaget.

Nielsen, K. (2000). Musikalisk mästarlära. In K. Nielsen & S. Kvale (Eds.), Mästarlära: Lärande som social praxis. Lund: Studentlitteratur.

Niglas, K. (2009). How the novice researcher can make sense of mixed methods designs. *International Journal of Multiple Research Approaches*, *3*(1), 34–46. doi:10.5172/mra.455.3.1.34

Nilsson, P., Pendril, A.-M., & Pettersson, H. (2006). Learning physics with the body. In R. Janiuk & E. Samonek-Miciuk (Eds.), Science and Technology Education of a Diverse World: Dilemmas, Needs and Partnerships. Lublin, Poland: Marie Curie-Sklodowska University Press.

Nilsson, K. A. (2003). Enklare och nyttigare? Om metodiken för ämnes- och programutvärderingar[On methods for evaluating courses and programmes]. *National Agency for Higher Education Report*, *2003*, 17.

Nilsson, M., & Wihlborg, M. (2011). Higher Education as Commodity or Space for Learning: Modelling contradictions in educational practices. *Power and Education*, *3*(2), 104. doi:10.2304/power.2011.3.2.104

Niskala, A. (2010). Mallinnus sosiaalityön kehittämisen välineenä [Modeling as a tool in developing social work, in Finnish]. Asiakkuus sosiaalityössä. Gaudeamus Helsinki University Press.

Nolen, A. L., & Putten, J. V. (2007). Action research in education: Addressing gaps in ethical principles and practices. *Educational Researcher*, *36*(7), 401–407. doi:10.3102/0013189X07309629

Normann, R. (2001). *Reframing business: When the map changes the landscape*. Chichester, UK: John Wiley & Sons. Ltd.

North, A. C. (2008). *The social and applied psychology of music*. New York: Oxford University Press. doi:10.1093/acprof:oso/9780198567424.001.0001

Nussbaumer, D. (2012). An overview of cultural historical activity theory (CHAT) use in classroom research 2000 to 2009. *Educational Review*, *64*(1), 37–55. doi:10.1080/00131911.2011.553947

Nyberg, G. (2014). *Ways of knowing in ways of moving: A study of the meaning of capability to move*. (dissertation). Centre for Teaching and Learning in the Humanities, Stockholm University, Stockholm, Sweden.

OECD Competency Framework. (n.d.). Retrieved February 25, 2014, from http://www.oecd.org/careers/oecd%20level%201_v1.pdf

Ollman, B. (2003). *Dance of the dialects: Steps in Marx's method*. Champaign, IL: University of Illinois Press.

Olsson, L. M. (2009). *Movement and Experimentation in Young Children's Learning. In Early Childhood Education*. London: Routledge.

Orland-Barak, L., & Becher, A. (2011). Cycles of action through systems of activity: Examining an action research model through the lens of activity theory. *Mind, Culture, and Activity*, *18*(2), 115–128. doi:10.1080/10749039.2010.484099

Osborne, J., & Dillon, J. (2008). *Science education in Europe: Critical reflections*. London: Nuffield Foundation.

Östersjö, S. (2008). *Shut up 'n' play! Negotiating the musical work*. Malmö: Lund University.

Packer, M. J., & Goicoechea, J. (2000). Sociocultural and Constructivist Theories of Learning: Ontology, Not just Epistemology. *Educational Psychologist*, *35*(4), 227–241. doi:10.1207/S15326985EP3504_02

Pastré, P. (2005) Analyse d'un apprentissage sur simulateur: de jeunes ingénieursaux prises avec la conduit d'une central nucléare. In Apprendre par la simulation. Toulouse: Octarés.

Pastré, P. (1999). La conseptualisation dans l'action: Bilan et nouvelles perspectives. *Education Permanente*, *139*(2), 13–35.

Peirce, C. S. (1997). Pragmatism as a Principle and Method of Right Thinking. In P. A. Turrisi (Ed.), *The 1903 Harvard Lectures on Pragmatism*. Albany, NY: State University of New York Press.

Peltokorpi, V., & Froese, F. (2014). Expatriate personality and cultural fit: The moderating role of host country context on job satisfaction. *International Business Review*, *23*(1), 293–302. doi:10.1016/j.ibusrev.2013.05.004

Perdue, C. (2000). Organizing principles of learner varieties. *Studies in Second Language Acquisition*, *22*(3), 299–305. doi:10.1017/S0272263100003016

Perez, C. (2005). *Respecialization and the deployment of the ICT paradigm: An essay on the present challenges of globalization*. Paper for the IPTS FISTERA Project, Nov 2005. Retrieved May 6, 2014, from http://www.carlotaperez.org/papers/PEREZ_Respecialisation_and_ICTparadigm.pdf

Perez, C. (2014). *Green and socially equitable direction for ICT paradigm*. Working Paper 2014-01. Globelics, working paper series. The global network for economics of learning, innovation, and competence building systems. Chris Freeman Memorial Lecture GLOBELICS 2012. Hangzhou, P.R. China. Rev. March 2014. Retrieved May 7, 2014 from http://www.globelics.org/wp-content/uploads/2014/04/wpg1401.pdf

Perez, C. (2002). *Technological revolutions and financial Capital: The dynamics of bubbles and golden ages*. Cheltenham, UK: Edward Elgar Publishing Limited. doi:10.4337/9781781005323

Pless, M., & Hansen, N.-H. M. (2010). HF på VUC – et andet valg. CeFU - Center for Ungdomsforskning. København.

Poikela, R. (2010). *Asiakassuunnitelma asiakaslähtöistä auttamista tavoitteellistamassa*. [From a client plan to user perspective in multi-professional social work. A method of emerging object with multiple voices. In Finnish, abstract in English]. Valtiotieteellinen tiedekunta. Helsinki, Helsingin yliopisto. Väitöskirja.

Popov, O. (2014). Outdoor science in teacher education. In T. Hansson (Ed.), Contemporary Approaches to Activity Theory: Interdisciplinary Perspectives on Human Behavior. Hershey, PA: IGI Global.

Popov, O., & Tevel, I. (2007). Developing prospective physics teachers' skill of independent experimental work using outdoors approach. *Baltic Journal of Science Education, 6*(1), 47–57.

Popper, K. R. (1999). *All life is problem solving*. London: Routledge.

Potter, T. (2003). From chamber to concert hall. R. Stowell (Ed.), The Cambridge companion to the string quartet (pp. 41-59). Cambridge, UK: Cambridge University Press.

Prahalad, C. K., & Krishnan, M. S. (2008). *The new age of innovation: Driving co-created value through global networks*. New York: The McGraw-Hill Companies Inc.

Pramling Samuelsson, I., & Asplund Carlsson, M. (2003). *Det lekande lärande barnet i en utvecklingspedagogisk teori*. Stockholm: Liber.

Putney, L. G., & Frank, C. R. (2008). Looking through ethnographic eyes at classrooms acting as cultures. *Ethnography and Education, 3*(2), 211–228. doi:10.1080/17457820802062482

Raisch, S., Birkinshaw, J., Probst, G., & Tushmann, M. L. (2009). Organizational ambideterity: Balancing exploitation and exploration for sustained performance. *Organization Science, 20*(4), 685–695. doi:10.1287/orsc.1090.0428

Rasmussen, I., & Ludvigsen, S. (2009). The hedgehog and the fox: A discussion of the approaches to the analysis of ICT reforms in teacher education of Larry Cuban and Yrjö Engeström. *Mind, Culture, and Education, 16*(1), 83–104. doi:10.1080/10749030802477390

Reason, P., & Bradbury-Huan, H. (Eds.). (2007). Handbook of action research: Participative inquiry and practice. London: Sage Publications.

Regelski, T. A. (2007). Music Education: What is the 'value added' for self and society?. In B. Stålhammar (Ed.), Music and human beings: Music and identity. Örebro: Örebro Universitet.

Regelski, T. A., & Gates, T. (2009). Preface and introduction. In T. A. Regelski & T. Gates (Eds.), Music education for changing times: Guiding visions for practice. Dordrecht, The Netherlands: Springer.

Reimer, B. (2003). *A philosophy of music education: Advancing the vision*. Upper Saddle River, NJ: Prentice Hall.

Reio, T. G., & Sutton, F. C. (2006). Employer assessment of work-related competencies and workplace adaptation. *Human Resource Development Quarterly, 17*(3). doi:10.1002/hrdq

Reiserer, M., Ertl, B., & Madl, H. (2002). Fostering collaborative knowledge construction in desktop videoconferencing: effects of content schemes and cooperation scripts in peer teaching settings. In *Proceedings of the Conference on Computer Support for Collaborative Learning: Foundations for a CSCL Community*. International Society of the Learning Sciences. doi:10.3115/1658616.1658670

Renshaw, P. (2011). *Working together. An enquiry into creative collaborative learning across the Barbican–Guildhall Campus*. London: Barbican Centre and Guildhall School of Music and Drama.

Rest, J. (1994). Background: Theory and research. In J. R Rest & D. Narvaez (Eds.), Moral development in the professions: Psychology and applied ethics (pp. 1-26). Hillsdale, NJ: Erlbaum.

Robinson, K. (2011). *Out of our minds*. Chichester, UK: Capstone.

Roblyer, M. D., Edwards, J., & Havriluk, M. A. (1997). *Integrating educational technology into teaching*. Upper Saddle River, NJ: Prentice-Hall.

Rose, M. (2012). Rethinking remedial education and the academic-vocational divide. *Mind, Culture, and Activity, 19*(1), 1–16. doi:10.1080/10749039.2011.632053

Roth, W.-M. (2004). Activity Theory and Education: An Introduction. *Mind, Culture, and Activity, 11*(1), 1–8. doi:10.1207/s15327884mca1101_1

Roth, W.-M., & Lee, S. (2004). Science education as/for participation in the community. *Science Education, 88*(2), 263–291. doi:10.1002/sce.10113

Roth, W.-M., & Lee, Y.-J. (2007). 'Vygotsky's neglected legacy': Cultural-historical activity theory. *Review of Educational Research*, 77(2), 186–232. doi:10.3102/0034654306298273

Roth, W.-M., Lee, Y.-J., & Hsu, P.-L. (2009). A tool for changing the world: Possibilities of cultural-historical activity theory to reinvigorate science education. *Studies in Science Education*, 45(2), 131–167. doi:10.1080/03057260903142269

Roth, W.-M., Tobin, K., & Zimmermann, A. (2002). Coteaching/cogenerative dialoguing: Learning environments research as classroom praxis. *Learning Environments Research*, 5(5), 1–28. doi:10.1023/A:1015662623784

Rotter, J. B. (1966). Generalized expectancies for internal versus external control of reinforcement. *Psychological Monographs*, 80(1), 1–28. doi:10.1037/h0092976 PMID:5340840

Rubinstein, S. L. (1968). *Grundlagen der allgemeinen Psychologie: Volk und Wissen*. Berlin: Volkseigener Verlag.

Rubinstein, S. L. (1969). *Prinzipien und Wege der Entwicklung der Psychologie*. Berlin: Akademie-Verlag.

Rubinstein, S. L. (1976). *Væren og bevidsthed*. Copenhagen: Gyldendal.

Rückheim, G. (2009). Digital technology and mediation: A challenge to activity theory. In A. Sannino, H. Daniels, & K. Guiterrez (Eds.), *Learning and expanding with activity theory* (pp. 88–111). Cambridge, UK: Cambridge University Press.

Rueckert, W. H. (1963). *Kenneth Burke and the Drama of Human Relations*. Minneapolis, MN: Academic Press.

Ruotsala, R. (2014). Developing a tool for cross-functional collaboration: the trajectory of an annual clock. *Outlines – Critical Practice Studies*, 15(2), 31-53.

Ruotsala, R. (2014). Developing a tool for cross-functional collaboration: The trajectory of an annual clock. *Outlines. Critical Practice Studies*, 15(2), 31–53.

Russell, B. (1969). *On education*. London: Unwin Books.

Saar, T. (1999). *Musikens dimensioner: En studie av unga musikers lärande*. (Dissertation). Göteborg: Göteborgs Universitet.

Säljö, R. (1991). Learning and mediation: Fitting reality into a table. *Learning and Instruction*, 1(3), 261–272. doi:10.1016/0959-4752(91)90007-U

Säljö, R. (1997). Talk as data and practice – a critical look at phenomenographical inquiry and the appeal to experience. *Higher Education Research & Development*, 16(2), 173–190. doi:10.1080/0729436970160205

Säljö, R. (2000). *Lärande i praktiken: ett sociokulturellt perspektiv*. Stockholm: Prisma.

Säljö, R. (2001). The individual in social practices. *Nordisk Pedagogik*, 21(2), 108–116.

Säljö, R. (2009). Learning, theories of learning, and units of analysis in research. *Educational Psychologist*, 44(3), 202–208. doi:10.1080/00461520903029030

Säljö, R. (2010). *Lärande i praktiken – Ett sociokulturellt perspektiv*. Nordstedts.

Säljö, R. (2013). *Lärande och kulturella redskap: om lärprocesser och det kollektiva minnet*. Lund: Studentliteratur.

Sam, D. L., & Berry, J. W. (2010). Acculturation: When Individuals and Groups of Different Cultural Backgrounds Meet. *Perspectives on Psychological Science*, 5(4), 472–481. doi:10.1177/1745691610373075

Samurçay, R., & Rogalski, R. (1992). Formation aux activités de gestion d'environnements dynamiques: Concepts et methods. *Activités (Vitry-sur-Seine)*, 8(2), 4–31.

Sanjek, R. (1990). *Fieldnotes: The Makings of Anthropology. Uthaca*. Cornell University Press.

Sannino, A. (2013). Critical transitions in the pursuit of a professional object: Simone de Beauvoir's expansive journey to become a writer. In V. Ellis & A. Sannino (Eds.), Learning and collective creativity: Activity-theoretical and sociocultural studies. London: Routledge.

Sannino, A. (2014). *Double stimulation as anchoring forward: The unity of conceptualization and agentive action*. Paper presented in the 11th International Congress on the Learning Sciences. Boulder, CO.

Sannino, A. (2008). From talk to action: Experiencing interlocution in developmental interventions. *Mind, Culture, and Activity*, 15(3), 234–257. doi:10.1080/10749030802186769

Sannino, A., & Sutter, B. (2011). Cultural-historical activity theory and interventionist methodology: Classical legacy and contemporary developments. *Theory & Psychology*, *21*(5), 557–570. doi:10.1177/0959354311414969

Satka, M. (2010). Varhainen puuttuminen ja sosiaalityö. In M. Laitinen & A. Pohjola (Eds.), *Asiakkuus sosiaalityössä* (pp. 181–276). Helsinki: Gaudeamus Helsinki University Press.

Sawyer, R. K. (2003). *Group creativity: Music, theater, collaboration*. Mahwah, NJ: Erlbaum.

Sawyer, R. K. (2007). *Group genius: the creative power of collaboration*. New York: Basic Books.

Sayer, A. (1992). *Method in social science: A realist approach*. London: Routledge.

Schaupp, M. (2011). From function-based development practices to collaborative capability building: an intervention to extend practitioners' ideas. In R.F. Poell & M. van Woerkom (Eds.), Supporting Workplace Learning: Towards Evidence-based Practice (pp. 205-224). Dordrecht, The Netherlands: Springer.

Schaupp, M., Seppänen, L., Korpelainen, E., Kira, M., & Toiviainen, H. (2013). *Yhdessä vihreälle alueelle. Kohaus-hankkeen raportti eroperheiden palveluverkostosta. Julkaisematon raportti*. Helsinki: Työterveyslaitos.

Scherer, M. (2002). Do Students Care About Learning? A Conversation with Mihaly Csikszentmihalyi. *Educational Leadership, 60*(1), 12-17.

Schmittau, J. (2004). Vygotskian theory and mathematics education: Resolving the conceptual-procedural dichotomy. *European Journal of Psychology of Education*, *19*(1), 19–43. doi:10.1007/BF03173235

Schmittau, J. (2005). The development of algebraic thinking. A Vygotskian perspective. *ZDM*, *37*(1), 16–22.

Schrier, L. L. (1993). Prospects for the professionalization of foreign language teaching. In *Developing language teachers for a changing world*. Lincolnwood, IL: National Textbook.

Schwaber, K. (2004). *Agile Project Management with Scrum*. Microsoft Press.

Schwille, J., & Dembélé, M. (2007). *Global perspectives on teacher learning: Improving policy and practice*. UNESCO: International Institute for Educational Planning. Retrieved from http://www.unesco.org/iiep/eng/publications/recent/rec7.htm

Searle, J. R., & Vanderveken, D. (1985). *Foundations of illocutionary logic*. Cambridge, UK: Cambridge University Press.

Seikkula, J., & Arnkil, T. E. (2005). *Dialoginen verkostotyö*. Tammi.

Seikkula, J., Arnkil, T. E., & Eriksson, E. (2003). Postmodern society and social networks: Open and anticipation dialogues in network meetings. *Family Process*, *42*(2), 185–203. doi:10.1111/j.1545-5300.2003.42201.x PMID:12879593

Selander, S., & Kress, G. R. (2010). *Design för lärande: Ett multimodalt perspektiv*. Stockholm: Norstedts.

Selmer, J., & Lauring, J. (2012). Reasons to expatriate and work outcomes of self-initiated expatriates. *Personnel Review, 41*(5), 665–684. doi:10.1108/00483481211249166

Senge, P. (1990). *The fifth discipline: The art and practice of the learning organization*. New York: Doubleday.

Seppänen, L. (2009). Kuvia ja näkökulmia perheneuvolatyön lähikehitykseen. *KONSEPTI - Toimintakonseptin Uudistajien Verkkolehti, 5*(2). Retrieved from www.muutoslaboratorio.fi

Seppänen, L., & Kloetzer, L. (2014). A micro-analysis of professional and hybrid concepts in social work: How to develop mediations for networking? In T. Hansson (Ed.), Contemporary Approaches to Activity Theory: Interdisciplinary Perspectives on Human Behavior. Hershey, PA: IGI Global.

Seppänen, L., Ala-Laurinaho, A., Launis, K., & Schaupp, M. (August 2009). *Representing changes in work in and for developmental interventions*. Paper presented at the 17th World Congress on Ergonomics: Changes, Challenges and Opportunities. Beijing, China.

Seppänen, L., Cerf, M., & Toiviainen, H. (2013). *Multivoiced customer understanding in the zone of proximal development of public service networks*. Paper presented at the EGOS 2013 Conference. New York, NY.

Seppänen, L., Schaupp, M., Toiviainen, H., Ala-Laurinaho, A., Heikkilä, H., Kira, M., et al. (2012). *Palveluverkostojen asiakasymmärryksen tutkimuslähtökohtia: Konseptimuutosten haasteet ja työhyvinvointi* Retrieved from https://helda.helsinki.fi/handle/10138/32393

Seppänen, L., Toiviainen, H., & Kira, M. (2014). Palveluverkostojen asiakasymmärrys muutoksessa. In T. Pakarinen & T. Mäki (Eds.), *Henkilöstöjohtaminen kurkiauran kärkeen: Uudistumisen sykettä palveluihin* (pp. 135-150). Helsinki: Edita.

Sewell, W. Jr. (1996). Historical events as transformation of structures: Inventing revolution at the Bastille. *Theory and Society*, *25*(6), 841–881. doi:10.1007/BF00159818

Shaffer, D. W. (2006). *How Computer games help children learn*. New York: Palgrave Macmillan. doi:10.1057/9780230601994

Shayer, M. (2003). Not just Piaget, not just Vygotsky, and certainly not Vygotsky as alternative to Piaget. *Learning and Instruction*, *13*(5), 465–485. doi:10.1016/S0959-4752(03)00092-6

Sheridan, S., & Williams, P. (2006). Constructive competition in preschool. *Journal of Early Childhood Research*, *4*(3), 291–310. doi:10.1177/1476718X06067581

Sheridan, S., & Williams, P. (2011). Developing individual goals, shared goals, and the goals of others: Dimensions of constructive competition in learning contexts. *Scandinavian Journal of Educational Research*, *55*(2), 145–164. doi:10.1080/00313831.2011.554694

Shi, L. (2006). The successors to Confucianism or a new generation? A questionnaire study on Chinese students' culture of learning English. *Language, Culture and Curriculum*, *19*(1), 122–147. doi:10.1080/07908310608668758

Shulman, L. S. (1987). Knowledge and teaching: Foundations of new reform. *Harvard Educational Review*, *57*, 1–22.

Siedentop, D. (2002). Content Knowledge for physical education. *Journal of Teaching in Physical Education*, *21*, 368–377.

Skolverket. (2010). *Läroplan för förskolan Lpfö 98 Reviderad 2010*. Stockholm: Fritzes.

Skolverket. (2011). *Curriculum for the compulsory school, preschool class and the recreation center 2011*. Stockholm: Skolverket.

Slingsby. (2006). The future of school science lies outdoors. *Journal of Biological Education*, *40*(2), 51-52.

Sloboda, J. A. (2005). *Exploring the musical mind: Cognition, emotion, ability, function*. Oxford, UK: Oxford University Press.

Smagorinsky, P. (2011). Vygotsky's stage theory: The psychology of art and the actor under the direction of Perezhivaine. *Mind, Culture, and Activity*, *18*(4), 319–341. doi:10.1080/10749039.2010.518300

Small, C. (1998). *Musicking: The meanings of performing and listening*. Hanover, NH: Univ. Press.

Smilde, R. (2008). Lifelong learners in music; research into musicians' biographical learning. *International Journal of Community Music*, *1*(2), 243–252. doi:10.1386/ijcm.1.2.243_1

Smith, A. (1976). *TMS* [The Theory of Moral Sentiments]. Oxford, UK: Oxford University Press.

Smith, M. E. (2009). Against dualism: Marxism and the necessity of dialectical monism. *Science and Society*, *73*(3), 356–385. doi:10.1521/siso.2009.73.3.356

Smith, W. K., Binns, A., & Tushman, M. L. (2010). Complex business models: Managing strategic paradoxes simultaneously. *Long Range Planning*, *43*(2-3), 448–461. doi:10.1016/j.lrp.2009.12.003

Smith, W. K., & Lewis, M. W. (2011). Towards a theory of paradox: A dynamic equilibrium model of organizing. *Academy of Management Review*, *32*(2), 381–403. doi:10.5465/AMR.2011.59330958

Snyder, K. (2007). *Dietrich Buxtehude. Organist in Lübeck*. Rochester, NY: University of Rochester Press.

Somekh, B., & Nissen, M. (2011). Cultural-historical activity theory and action research. *Mind, Culture, and Activity*, *18*(2), 93–97. doi:10.1080/10749039.2010.523102

Sophian, C. (2007). *The origins of mathematical knowledge in childhood*. Lawrence Erlbaum Associates.

Sosna, M., Trevinyo-Rodríguez, R. N., & Velamuri, S. R. (2010). Business model innovation through trial-and-error learning: The Naturhouse case. *Long Range Planning*, *43*(2-3), 383–407. doi:10.1016/j.lrp.2010.02.003

Spector, P. E. (1988). *Development of the Work Locus of Control Scale*. Academic Press.

Spector, P. E., Cooper, C. L., Sanchez, J. I., O'Driscoll, M., Sparks, K., Bernin, P., ... Yu, S. (2001). Do national levels of individualism and internal locus of control relate to well- being: an ecological level international study. *Journal of Organizational Behavior, 22*(8), 815–832. doi:10.1002/job.118

Spradley, J. P. (1980). *Participant observation*. New York: Holt Rinehart and Winston.

Spring, J. (2008). Research on Globalization and Education. *Review of Educational Research*, *78*(2), 330–363. doi:10.3102/0034654308317846

Stacey, R. D. (1995). The science of complexity: An alternative perspective for strategic change processes. *Strategic Management Journal*, *6*(6), 477–495. doi:10.1002/smj.4250160606

Stenhouse, L. (1981). What counts as research? *British Journal of Educational Studies*, *29*(2), 103–114. doi:10.1080/00071005.1981.9973589

Sterman, J. D. (2001). System dynamics modeling: Tools for learning in a complex world. *California Management Review*, *43*(4), 8–25. doi:10.2307/41166098

Stesenko, A. (2003). Alexander Luria and the cultural historical activity theory: Pieces for the history of an outstanding collaborative project in psychology. *Mind, Culture, and Activity*, *10*(1), 93–97. doi:10.1207/S15327884MCA1001_10

Stetsenko, A. (2005). Activity as object-related: Resolving the dichotomy of individual and collective planes of activity. *Mind, Culture, and Activity*, *12*(1), 70–88. doi:10.1207/s15327884mca1201_6

Stetsenko, A., & Arievitch, I. (2004). The self in cultural-historical activity theory: Reclaiming the unity of social and individual dimensions of human development. *Theory & Psychology*, *14*(4), 475–503. doi:10.1177/0959354304044921

Stödberg, U., & Orre, C. J. (2009). It's not all about video-conferencing. *Campus-Wide Information Systems*, *27*(3), 109–117. doi:10.1108/10650741011054410

Stoller, F. (2006). Establishing a theoretical foundation for project-based learning in second and foreign language contexts. In G. H. Beckett & P. C. Miller (Eds.), Project-Based Second and Foreign Language education: Past, present, and future (pp. 19-40). Greenwich, CT: Information Age Publishing.

Stoller, F. L. (1997). Project work: A means to promote language content. *English Teaching Forum*, *35*(4), 2-9.

Suchman, L. (2007). *Human-machine reconfigurations: Plans and situated actions*. Cambridge, UK: Cambridge University Press.

Sundh, S. (2003). *Swedish School Leavers' Oral Proficiency in English. In Acta Universitatis Upsaliensia 123*. Uppsala: Almqvist&Wiksell.

Sundqvist, P. (2009). *Extramural English Matters – Out-of-School English and Its Impact on Swedish Ninth Graders' Oral Proficiency and Vocabulary*. Karlstad: Karlstad University Studies.

Suter, W. N. (2006). *Introduction to educational research: A critical thinking approach*. Thousand Oaks, CA: Sage.

Svensson, L., Brulin, G., & Ellström, P.-E. (2002). Interaktiv forskning - För utveckling av teori och praktik. [Interactive research – Development of theory and practice]. (Ö Widegren, Ed.). Media-Tryck. Arbetsliv i omvandling.

Sverin, T. (2011). *Open-ended problems in physics: Upper secondary technical program students' ways of approaching outdoor physics problems* (Student research paper). Umeå Universitet.

Swedish Higher Education Ordinance. (n.d.). *Learning outcomes and terms for qualifications in the fine, applied and performing arts*. Author.

Takahashi, K., & Hirai, M. (2010). Toward a New Stage of Cross-Cultural Studies: Ordinary People in Individual by Culture Interactions: Essay Review of Women and Family in Contemporary Japan by Susan D. Holloway. *Human Development*, *53*(6), 361–365. doi:10.1159/000321890

Taleb, N. N. (2007). *The black swan: The impact of the highly improbable*. New York: Random House Publishing Group.

Taras, V., Rowney, J., & Steel, P. (2009). Half a century of measuring culture: Review of approaches, challenges, and limitations based on the analysis of 121 instruments for quantifying culture. *Journal of International Management, 15*(4), 357–373. doi:10.1016/j.intman.2008.08.005

Tarde, G. (1893). *Monadologie et sociologie* (E. Alliez, Ed.). Paris: Inst. Synthélabo pour le Progrès de la Connaissance.

Tarde, G. (1902). *Psychologie économique* (F. Alcan, Ed.). Paris: Ancienne Libr. Germer Baillière et Cie.

Tarufi, J. (2006). Processes and teaching strategies in musical improvisation with children. In I. Deliége & G. A. Wiggings (Eds.), Musical creativity: Multidisciplinary research in theory and practice. Hove, UK: Psychology Press.

Teräs, M. (2007). *Intercultural learning and hybridity in the culture laboratory*. Helsinki: University of Helsinki.

Teräs, M. (2012). Learning in "Paperland": Cultural tools and learning practices in Finland. *Scandinavian Journal of Educational Research, 56*(2), 183–197. doi:10.1080/00313831.2011.581682

Tilling, S., & Dillon, J. (2007). *Initial Teacher Education and the Outdoor Classroom: Standards for the Future: A Report on the Training of Pre-Service Teachers to Support the Development of Outdoor Teaching in Secondary Science Education. Field Studies Council*. Association for Science Education.

Toiviainen, H. (2014). Interventions for learning at global workplaces. In T. Hansson (Ed.), Contemporary Approaches to Activity Theory: Interdisciplinary Perspectives on Human Behavior. Hershey, PA: IGI Global.

Toiviainen, H. (2003). *Learning across levels: Challenges of collaboration in a small-firm network*. Helsinki: University of Helsinki.

Toiviainen, H., & Kerosuo, H. (2013). Development curriculum for knowledge-based organizations: Lessons from a learning network. *International Journal of Knowledge-Based Organizations, 3*(4), 1–18. doi:10.4018/ijkbo.2013070101

Toiviainen, H., Kerosuo, H., & Syrjälä, T. (2009). "Development Radar": The co-configuration of a tool in a learning network. *Journal of Workplace Learning, 21*(7), 509–524. doi:10.1108/13665620910985513

Toiviainen, H., Lallimo, J., & Hong, J. (2012). Emergent learning practices in globalizing work – The case of a Finnish-Chinese project in a Finnish technology consulting firm. *Journal of Workplace Learning, 24*(7/8), 509–527. doi:10.1108/13665621211261016

Tolman, C. (1981). The metaphysics of relations in Klaus Riegel's "Dialectics" of human development. *Human Development, 24*(1), 33–51. doi:10.1159/000272623

Tornberg, U. (2007). Vem äger språkundervisningens språk?. In T. Englund (Ed.), Utbildning som kommunikation: Deliberativa samtal som möjlighet (pp. 361-379). Göteborg: Daidalos.

Trognon, A., & Kostulski, K. (1999). Éléments d'une théorie sociocognitive de l'interaction conversationnelle. *Psychologie Française, 44*(4), 307–318.

Tronto, J. (1993). *Moral Boundaries: A Political Argument for an Ethic of Care*. Academic Press.

Tväråna, M. (2014). *Rikare resonemang om rättvisa. Vad kan kvalificera deltagande i samhällskunskapspraktiken?* (Licentiate Thesis). Department of Education, Stockholm University, Stockholm, Sweden.

Vallberg-Roth, A-C. (2014). *Nordisk komparativ analys av riktlinjer för kvalitet och innehåll i förskola*. doi:10.6027/NA2013-927

van de Ven, A. (1992). Suggestion for studying strategy process: A research note. *Strategic Management Journal, 13*(S1), 169–188. doi:10.1002/smj.4250131013

van den Akker, J. (1998). The science curriculum: Between ideals and outcomes. In B. Fraser & K. Tobin (Eds.), International Handbook for Science Education. Dordrecht, The Netherlands: Kluwer Academic Publishers.

Vandebocoeur, J., & Collie, R. (2013). Locating social and emotional learning in schooled environments: A Vygotskian perspective on learning as unified. *Mind, Culture, and Activity, 20*(3), 201–225. doi:10.1080/107 49039.2012.755205

Vargo, S. L., & Lusch, R. F. (2008). From goods to service(s): Divergences and convergences of logics. *Industrial Marketing Management, 37*(3), 254–259. doi:10.1016/j.indmarman.2007.07.004

Victor, B., & Boynton, A. C. (1998). *Invented here: Maximizing your organization's internal growth and profitability.* Boston, MA: Harvard Business School Press.

Vidal-Gomel, C., & Rogalski, J. (2007). La conceptualization et la place des concepts pragmatiques dans l'activité professionnelle et le developpement des compétences. *Activités (Vitry-sur-Seine), 4*(1), 49–84.

Vigotski, L. S. (2001). *Psicologia da Arte.* São Paulo: Martins Fontes.

Vigotski, L. S. (2009). *A construção do pensamento e da linguagem.* São Paulo: Martins Fontes.

Vigotsky, L. S. (2004). *Imaginación y creación en la edad infantil.* Havana: Pueblo y Educación.

Virkkunen, J. & Virkki, M. (2014, in process). *Transformative organizational learning as a process of ascending from the abstract to the concrete: The creation of the business model for Kemira Grow How.* Academic Press.

Virkkunen, J. (2007). Collaborative development of a new concept for an activity. *@ctivités, 4*(2), 158-164.

Virkkunen, J., Pihlaja, J., & Ristimäki, P. (2010). Tuotteesta palveluun – Liiketoiminnan kehityksen epäjatkuvuuden hallinta ohjelmistoyrityksessä. In Hyötyläinen & Nuutinen (Eds.), Mahdollisuuksien kenttä: Palveluliiketoiminta ja vuorovaikutteinen johtaminen (pp. 72-88). Helsinki: Teknologiainfo Teknova Oy.

Virkkunen, J., & Newnham, D. S. (2013). *The Change Laboratory: A Tool for Collaborative Development of Work and Education.* Rotterdam: Springer. doi:10.1007/978-94-6209-326-3

Virkkunen, J., Newnham, D., Nleya, P., & Engeström, R. (2012). Breaking the vicious circle of categorizing students in school. *Learning. Culture and Social Interaction, 66*(3-4), 183–192. doi:10.1016/j.lcsi.2012.08.003

Virkkunen, J., & Ristimäki, P. (2012). Double stimulation in strategic concept formation: An activity-theoretical analysis of business planning in a small technology firm. *Mind, Culture, and Activity, 19*(3), 273–286. doi:10.108 0/10749039.2012.688234

Virtanen, P., Suoheimo, M., Lamminmäki, S., Ahonen, P., & Suokas, M. (2011). *Matkaopas asiakaslähtöisten sosiaali- ja terveyspalvelujen kehittämiseen.* Helsinki: Tekesin katsaus 281/2011.

von Hippel, E., & Tyre, M. J. (1995). How learning by doing is done: Problem identification in novel process equipment. *Research Policy, 24*(1), 1–12. doi:10.1016/0048-7333(93)00747-H

Vygotski, L. S. (1995). *Obras Escogidas* (3 vols.). Madri: Visor.

Vygotskij, L. (1978). *Mind in Society.* Cambridge, MA: Harvard University Press.

Vygotskij, L. (2001). *Tänkande och språk.* Göteborg: Daidalos. (Original work published 1934)

Vygotskij, L. S. (2001). *Tenkning og tale.* Oslo: Gyldendal.

Vygotsky, L. (1986). *Thought and Language.* Cambridge, MA: MIT Press.

Vygotsky, L. (1987). Thinking and speech. In R. W. Rieber & A. S. Carton (Eds.), The collected works of L. S. Vygotsky: The fundamentals of defectology. New York: Plenum.

Vygotsky, L. (1994). Imagination and the creativity of the adolescent. In R. van der Veer & J. Valsiner (Eds.), The Vygotsky Reader. Oxford, UK: Blackwell.

Vygotsky, L. (1998). The collected works of L.S. Vygotsky: Child Psychology (vol. 5). New York: Plenum Academic.

Vygotsky, L. S. (1978). Interaction Between Learning and Development. In M. Cole, V. John-Steiner, S. Scribner, & E. Souberman (Eds.), Mind and Society (pp. 79–91). Cambridge, MA: Harvard University Press.

Vygotsky, L. S. (1978). *Mind in Society: The Development of Higher Psychological Processes*. Cambridge, MA: Harvard University Press. Retrieved from http://de.wikipedia.org/wiki/T%C3%A4tigkeitstheorie

Vygotsky, L. S. (1997). The collected works of LS Vygotsky: Problems of the theory and history of psychology (vol. 3). (R. V. d. Veer, Trans.). New York: Plenum Press.

Vygotsky, L. (1994). Imagination and the creativity of the adolescent. In R. van der Veer & J. Valsiner (Eds.), *The Vygotsky reader* (pp. 266–288). Oxford, UK: Blackwell.

Vygotsky, L. (1997). *Educational psychology*. Boca Raton, FL: St. Lucie Press.

Vygotsky, L. (2004). Imagination and creativity in childhood. *Journal of Russian & East European Psychology*, *42*, 7–97.

Vygotsky, L. S. (1971). *The Psychology of Art*. Cambridge, MA: M.I.T. Press.

Vygotsky, L. S. (1978). *Mind and Society*. Cambridge, MA: Harvard University Press.

Vygotsky, L. S. (1978). *Mind in Society: The Development of Higher Psychological Processes*. Cambridge, MA: Harvard University Press.

Vygotsky, L. S. (1978). *Mind in society: The psychology of higher mental functions*. Cambridge, MA: Harvard University Press.

Vygotsky, L. S. (1987). *Imagination and its Development in Childhood. In The collected works of L. S. Vygotsky*. New York: Plenum Press.

Vygotsky, L. S. (1987). *Thinking and Speech. The collected works of L.S. Vygotsky* (R. W. Rieber & A. S. Carton, Eds.). New York, London: Plenum. (Original work published 1934)

Vygotsky, L. S. (1995). *Fantasi och kreativitet i barndomen*. Göteborg: Daidalos.

Vygotsky, L. S. (2004). Imagination and Creativity in Childhood. *Journal of Russian & East European Psychology*, *42*(1), 7–97.

Walden, R. (2009). The School of the Future: Conditions and Processes – Contributions of Architectural Psychology. In R. Walden (Ed.), Schools for the future: design proposals from architectural psychology. Hogrefe: Cambridge.

Walford, G. (2008). The Nature of educational ethnography. In G. Walford et al. (Eds.), How to do Educational Ethnography. The Tufnell Press.

Walford, G. (2009). For ethnography. *Ethnography and Education*, *4*(3), 271–282. doi:10.1080/17457820903170093

Wallace, M. (1991). *Training foreign language teachers*. Cambridge, UK: Cambridge University Press.

Wang, L., & Higgins, L. T. (2008). Mandarin teaching in the UK in 2007: A brief report of teachers' and learners' views. *Language Learning Journal*, *36*(1), 91–96. doi:10.1080/09571730801988504

Wang, S. C. (2007). Building societal capital, Chinese in the US. *Language Policy*, *6*(1), 27–52. doi:10.1007/s10993-006-9043-2

Ward, C. (2008). Thinking outside the Berry boxes: New perspectives on identity, acculturation and intercultural relations. *International Journal of Intercultural Relations*, *32*(2), 105–114. doi:10.1016/j.ijintrel.2007.11.002

Ward, C., & Kennedy, A. (1999). The measurement of sociocultural adaptation. *International Journal of Intercultural Relations*, *23*(4), 659–677. doi:10.1016/S0147- 1767(99)00014-0

Waterman, D. (2003). Playing quartets: A view from the inside. In R. Stowell (Ed.), The Cambridge companion to the string quartet (pp. 97-126). Cambridge, UK: Cambridge University Press.

Weisberg, R. W. (1993). *Creativity: Beyond the myth of genius*. New York: Freeman.

Welch, G. F. (2011). Culture and gender in a cathedral music context: An activity theory exploration. In M. S. Barrett (Ed.), A cultural psychology of music education (pp. 225-258). Oxford, UK: Oxford University Press.

Welch, G. F. (1998). Early childhood musical development. *Research Studies in Music Education*, *11*(1), 27–41. doi:10.1177/1321103X9801100104

Welch, G. F. (2007). Addressing the multifaceted nature of music education: An activity theory research perspective. *Research Studies in Music Education*, *28*(1), 23–37. doi: 10.1177/1321103X070280010203

Wells, G. (2011). Integrating CHAT and action research. *Mind, Culture, and Activity*, *18*(2), 161–180. doi:10.1080/10749039.2010.493594

Weman, L. (2008). "...världens skridskotystnad före Bach" historiskt informerad uppförandepraxis ur ett kontextuellt musikontologiskt perspektiv, belyst genom en fallstudie av Sonat i E-dur, BWV 1035, av J S Bach. Luleå tekniska universitet, Luleå.

Wen, X. (2009). Teaching listening and speaking: An interactive approach. In M. E. Everson & Y. Xiao (Eds.), Teaching Chinese as a Foreign Language. Boston: Cheng & Tsui.

Wenger, E. (2006). Social læringsteori – Aktuelle temaer og udfordringer. In K. Illeris (Ed.), Læringsteorier: Seks aktuelle forståelser. Roskilde Universitetsforlag. Frederiksberg.

Wenger, E. (2006). *Communities of practice. A brief Introduction*. Retrieved from http://wenger-trayner.com/wp-content/uploads/2012/01/06-Brief-introduction-to-communities-of-practice.pdf

Wenger, E. (2010). Communities of practice and social learning systems: The career of a concept. In C. Blackmore (Ed.), Social learning systems and communities of practice. Springer Verlag and The Open University.

Wenger, E., McDermott, R., & William Snyder, W. (2002). Cultivating Communities of Practice: A Guide to Managing Knowledge. Harvard Business Press.

Wenger, E. (1998). *Communities of Practice: learning, meaning, and identity*. Cambridge, UK: Cambridge University Press. doi:10.1017/CBO9780511803932

Wenger, E. (2004). *Praksisfællesskaber*. København: Hans Reitzels Forlag.

Wertsch, J. V. (1998). *Mind as action*. New York: Oxford University Press.

Wertsch, J. (1991). *Voices of the mind: A sociocultural approach to mediated action*. London: Harvester Wheatsheaf.

Wertsch, J. (2007). Mediation. In H. Daniels, M. Cole, & J. Wertsch (Eds.), *The Cambridge Companion to Vygotsky* (pp. 178–192). Cambridge, UK: Cambridge University Press. doi:10.1017/CCOL0521831040.008

Wertsch, J. V. (1998). *Mind as action*. New York: Oxford University Press.

Wertsch, J. V., del Rio, P., & Alvarez, A. (1995). *Sociocultural Studies of Mind*. Cambridge University Press. doi:10.1017/CBO9781139174299

Westerlund, H. (2002). *Bridging experience, action, and culture in music education*. Helsinki: Sibelius Academy.

Wilkerson, S. J. (1991) And then they were sacrificed: the ritual ballgame of Northeastern Mesoamerica through time and space. In The Mesoamerican Ballgame. Tucson, AZ: University of Arizona Press.

Williams, P., & Sheridan, S. (2010). Conditions for collaborative learning and constructive competition in school. *Educational Research*, *52*(4), 335–350. doi:10.1080/00131881.2010.524748

Wittchen, M., Krimmel, A., Kohler, M., & Hertel, G. (2013). The two sides of competition: Competition-induced effort and affect during intergroup versus inter-individual competition. *British Journal of Psychology*, *104*(3), 320–338. doi:10.1111/j.2044-8295.2012.02123.x PMID:23848384

Wittgenstein, L. (2001). *Philosophical Investigations*. Oxford, UK: Blackwell Publishing.

Wolff, J. (1987). Foreword: The Ideology of Autonomous Art. In R. Leppert & S. McClary (Eds.), Music and Society: The Politics of Composition, Performance and Reception. Cambridge, UK: Cambridge University Press.

Wood, D. J., Bruner, J. S., & Ross, G. (1976). The Role of Tutoring in Problem Solving. *Journal of Child Psychiatry and Psychology*, *17*(2), 89–100. doi:10.1111/j.1469-7610.1976.tb00381.x PMID:932126

Worthen, H. (2008). Using activity theory to understand how people learn to negotiate the conditions of work. *Mind, Culture, and Activity*, *15*(4), 322–338. doi:10.1080/10749030802391385

Wu, S., & Meng, L. (2010). The integration of inter-culture education into intensive reading teaching for English majors through Project-based Learning. *US-China Foreign Language*, *8*(9), 26–37.

Yamazaki, Y., & Kayes, D. C. (2004). An experiential approach to cross-cultural learning: A review and integration of competencies for successful expatriate adaptation. *Academy of Management Learning & Education*, *3*(4), 362–379. Retrieved from http://amle.aom.org/content/3/4/362.short

Yanow, D. (2000). Seeing organizational learning: A 'cultural' view. *Organization*, *7*(2), 247–269. doi:10.1177/135050840072003

Zeichner, K., & Noffke, S. (2001). Practitioner research. In V. Richardson (Ed.), Handbook of research on teaching. Washington, DC: American Educational Research Association.

Zhang, L. (2004). Stepping carefully into designing computer-assisted learning activities. *Journal of Chinese Language Teaching Association*, *39*(2), 35–48.

Zhao, H., & Huang, J. (2010). China's Policy of Chinese as a Foreign Language and the Use of Overseas Confucius Institutes. *Educational Research for Policy and Practice*, *9*(2), 127–142. doi:10.1007/s10671-009-9078-1

Ziman, J. (1995). Postacademic Science: Constructing Knowledge with Networks and Norms. In U. Segerstråle (Ed.), Beyond the science wars: The missing discourse about science and society. Albany, NY: State University of New York Press.

Ziman, J. (1996). Is science losing its objectivity? *Nature*, *382*(6594), 751–754. doi:10.1038/382751a0

Zizek, S. (2012). *Organs without bodies: On Deleuze and consequences*. London: Routledge.

About the Contributors

Thomas Hansson is Docent in Pedagogy at Blekinge Institute of Technology. He took a Dr Ph at Luleå University of Technology. At University of Southern Denmark, he led several Nordic Council projects on Values in Teacher Education. He worked as assessment expert, project manager, and educational consultant (2004-2008) of Socrates/Erasmus (EAC/60/02OJ 2002/C 211/02), European Commission (KA3-ICT) (DG EAC/30/2007), and Comenius (EACEA/P1/BH/cs(2007)D102812). Research interests relate to applications of activity theory, developmental intervention, and moral values. Besides tutoring on workplace learning, he has written ISI articles plus chapters in books. He has authored/edited books on teaching and learning, project management, ICT, and vocational training.

* * *

Karin Alnervik is an assistant professor Early Childhood Education at Jönköping University, Sweden. She holds a Ph.D. in Education from Jönköping University. Her research interests include pedagogical documentation, exploratory learning, and pedagogical transformation in preschools.

Fia Andersson was a primary and secondary teacher for some 25 years. From 1995, she was a lecturer in Teacher Education followed by a PhD degree in Education at Stockholm University in 2007. Her study describes and analyses the process and content in a research circle with teachers working with multilingual children diagnosed within the autism spectrum. Since 2008, she has been a senior lecturer first at Stockholm University, with a special focus on Special Educational Needs, then at Uppsala University, where she lectures in courses in teacher education and for studies in Game Design. She has also been responsible for research circles with teachers in various types of schools and cooperates on studies in Participatory Action Research with universities in Sweden, in Nordic countries, and in Russia.

Karen Egedal Andreasen is PhD in Education and associate professor in Education and Pedagogical Assessment at the Department of Learning and Philosophy, Aalborg University. Karen Egedal Andreasen is a member of the research group Centre for Education Policy Research and is doing research within the area of education. Her main interests are socialisation, social mobility, and processes in communities, such as school classes with a focus on inclusion and exclusion and marginalization in different educational contexts. In her recent research, she has focused on the role of assessment in the comprehensive school and on innovation projects focusing on the development of educational opportunities for marginalized young adults.

Lars Bang is a PhD student at the Institute of Learning and Philosophy, Aalborg University in Denmark. This chapter is related to a research methodology and theoretical framework applied in the Youth-to-Youth Project, an educational bridge-building project with a specific interest in science education. He has background as a teacher in special education and holds a Master's degree in Educational Psychology. His current research and teaching interests include science education, educational research, Marxism, and the philosophy of science.

Regi Theodor Enerstvedt became a student at Oslo University in 1957. In 1983, he became Ph Dr in Political Science. Then he introduced activity theory to a Western audience by publishing a dissertation and books on dialectics in the '70s (e.g. on a fylogenetic and ontogenetic perspective on man [1976]). Since the '80s, RTE has been working at Skådalen Resource Center as research and development leader. He is currently Professor Emeritus of Sociology at the Department of Sociology and Human Geography, Oslo University, and is also busy composing a book on philosophical problems tentatively called *Dialectics*. Other characteristic titles of his are *The Problem of Validity in Social Science and Pedagogy* and the *Concept of Activity*. His research interests cover philosophical problems, language, deviation from norms, and issues of deaf-blindness.

Inger Eriksson is Professor of Education at Stockholm University. Her research interest is related to teaching and learning. In earlier research projects, her focus was on classroom learning, given different teaching and learning practices. Currently, she is engaged in projects on developing teaching and learning where teachers are involved as co-researchers. One specific interest is development of a mathematical teaching practice where algebraic reasoning is made available to grade one pupil following Davydov's conceptual work. During the last few years, IE has initiated collaboration with researchers at Moscow State University of Psychology and Education and School Nr 91. In line with this work, she is involved in a national PhD programme for Learning Study in which some of the PhD students have framed their projects in either activity theoretical or socio-cultural perspectives. IE is one of the coordinators of the national CHAT seminar in Stockholm.

Beth Ferholt is an assistant professor in the Department of Early Childhood and Art Education at Brooklyn College, City University of New York. She holds a Ph.D. in Communication from the University of California, San Diego. Her research interests include early childhood education, emotional and cognitive development, imagination, creativity and qualitative methods.

Beata Gullberg is a bachelor's degree graduate in Social Science at Blekinge Technological Institute, Sweden, where she has been focusing her degree on intercultural communication and expatriation. She has combined her degree with professional basketball and language studies in Spain, coaching kids on the side. Further research interests are cultural studies combined with inequality and female empowerment.

Rauno Huttunen is a Marxist philosopher and a sociologist of education. He is adjunct professor (docent) of philosophy of education at the University of Jyväskylä. Currently, he works as senior lecturer of education at the University of Turku. Huttunen is member of editorial board of an open access refereed publication called *Encyclopedia of Educational Philosophy and Theory*. In 2009, Huttunen published a book called *Habermas, Honnet, and Education*. On the back cover of the book, Carlos Alberto Torres writes: "Rauno Huttunen shows that he knows the research tradition, and has a very solid theoretical background. Huttunen has mastered the craft of research at all levels, from the design to the scientific proof, from the theory and method to the bibliographical critical analysis of the material."

Anders Jansson was an assistant professor of Educational Science at Jönköping University and is currently an assistant professor of Special Education at Stockholm University. He holds a Ph.D. in Didactic Science from Stockholm University. His research interests include change and didactical development, learning, creativity and narrativity.

Thurídur Jóhannsdóttir is a senior lecturer in educational studies at University of Iceland, School of Education. Her research interest has been on the development of teaching and learning with the use of Internet and the possibilities and implications for teacher education and teacher development. She has published research on school-based teacher education where the academic part of a teacher qualification is provided for through distance or blended learning focusing attention on the relationship between teacher education and school development. In her research, Thurídur has applied cultural-historical activity theory to shed light on interconnections between professional development of teachers as individuals and collectives and systemic development in schools and teacher education programmes. Recently, she has focused on Vygotsky's concept of experiencing [perezivanie] as a unit of analysis for the wholeness of person-in-environment development, thereby enriching understanding of teacher development. Her research includes development of educational opportunities in rural communities by looking at person-environment transactions with reference to critical place-based education and the role of ideology for directing activities.

Karin Johansson is a Reader and the Director of artistic research in Music at the Department of Music Education and Performance, Malmö Academy of Music, Lund University. After her PhD thesis, *Organ Improvisation: Activity, Action, and Rhetorical Practice* (2008), she worked with the projects *(Re)thinking Improvisation*, funded by the Swedish Research Council, *Students' Ownership of Learning* based at the Royal Academy of Music, Stockholm, and in the international research network *Choir in Focus*, funded by Riksbankens Jubileumsfond. She is a performing organist with a special interest in early and contemporary music.

Charlotte Jonasson, PhD, is Assistant Professor at Department of Psychology and Behavioral Sciences, Aarhus University, Denmark. Her research interests are retention and drop out in vocational education and training, student engagement and competition and learning from errors in school-based vocational training. She has published articles in *British Journal of Sociology of Education* and *Journal of Education and Work*.

Leena Kakkori has worked in University of Jyväskylä as senior assistant and lector of philosophy. In addition, she has lectured at University of Eastern Finland on topics like Global Ethics and Phenomenological Research Method. Her major research interest is Martin Heidegger's philosophy, hermeneutical interpretation of Heidegger's philosophy of time, hermeneutics and philosophy of education. Leena Kakkori has brought up problems of hermeneutical-phenomenological research method during her studies. Together with Dr. Rauno Huttunen, she has also published articles about pedagogical friendship and Aristotle.

Laure Kloetzer is Associate Professor in Psychology at CNAM, Paris, France. Her PhD investigated language in preaching with a work psychology perspective. She did a post-doc at Geneva University on learning and creativity in Citizen Science. Among her research interests are learning and development at work, the potential of talk for the development of thinking, new approaches of social science for social transformation, and the psychology of art. She joined the CNAM in 2013, teaching Psychology and contributing to the research of the Activity Clinic group.

Hans Kyhlbäck is Assistant Professor in computer science at Blekinge Institute of Technology, Sweden. His research and teaching interests include human-computer interaction, interaction design, and "documents at work." Hans has done research about wound care treatment in public healthare, and about high precision metal cutting in automotive industry. Currently, he is involved in education and research on digital game construction in higher education.

Anna Linge has over 20 years of experience as a music teacher and violinist for different ages and in different contexts. She worked as a violin teacher at municipal culture centres and music schools. She has a Master's degree in Library and Information Science. Currently, Anna works at Kristianstad University College. She is a senior lecturer in Education and teaches music for preschool student teachers. Anna's research interest lies in creative teaching contributions to general skills and teaching and learning. In addition to her dissertation, Anna has published peer-reviewed contributions and articles. Anna is a member of a research team in Aesthetics and Media at Malmö University College.

Carolina Picchetti Nascimento was a Physical Education teacher in Kindergarten and in primary school. She took her Doctoral degree at the University of São Paulo (2010-2014) with an internship period at the University of Bath. Since 2004, she is the member of two research groups focused on the study of Activity Theory and Cultural Historical Theory. They are Research group on Pedagogical Activity (GEPAPe), at the College Education of the University of São Paulo, and Inter-institutional Laboratory of School and Educational Psychology- LIEPPE, at the Institute of Psychology at the University of São Paulo. Research interests relate to teaching and learning of school subject matter, theoretical and philosophical framework of cultural historical theory, and methodology of educational research.

Monica Nilsson is an associate professor of Preschool Didactics at Jönköping University, Sweden. She holds a Ph.D. in Education from Helsinki University. Her research interests include educational institutional change and development, learning and play in preschools, and more particularly exploratory learning and playworlds, a form of adult-child joint play. Since 1996 MN has been affiliated with Laboratory of Comparative Human Cognition vid University of California San Diego, USA.

Oleg Popov is Associate Professor in Physics Education at the Department of Science and Mathematics Education at Umeå University. He has over 30 years of experience working in the fields of science education and curriculum development. OP started as a high school teacher of Physics and Mathematics at a rural school in Siberia in 1980. After finishing his PhD in Physics in Moscow, he went to Africa, Mozambique, in 1989. There he worked as curricular adviser in science education and as lecturer-consultant in theoretical physics. Since 1994, he has been living and working in Sweden. His research interests lie mainly in the field of science education, curriculum development, and inter-cultural studies related to which he has over 50 publications. He also worked as a guest professor at Tokyo Gakugei University in Japan, the University of South Africa, and the Federal University of Bahia in Brazil.

Palle Rasmussen is Professor of Education at the Department of Learning and Philosophy, Aalborg University. His research areas include educational policy in national and international contexts, sociological theories of education and learning, educational evaluation, professional education, and lifelong learning in education and work contexts. He teaches full-time and part-time Master's students in study programmes on learning and innovative change. He has broad experience with evaluation and development projects in collaboration with partners in business and public services. He has participated in several international research networks and has published extensively in his research fields. A recent publication is "Lifelong Learning Policy in Two National Contexts," *International Journal of Lifelong Education, 33*(3), 2014. He is a member of the Danish research council for Culture and Communication and a member of the board of the North Denmark College of General Adult Education.

Päivi Ristimäki is Master of Science (Econ. and Bus. Adm.) and affiliated PhD Candidate for the Center for Research on Activity, Development, and Learning at the University of Helsinki. During 2007-2012, she worked as project researcher at CRADLE in two research projects titled: 1) ServO – Interactive Organisation and Management in Service Business and 2) Learning Production Concepts (OT) – Tools for Management of Networked Activity. Her research interest involves learning and concept formation embedded in organizational and business transformation. PR has over 20 years of work experience from business development and entrepreneurship. She has worked for several service business companies. At present, she is working in the field of adult education and finishing her dissertation of a longitudinal and multidisciplinary study concerning Finnish technology firm's efforts to change business logic.

Riikka Ruotsala, MEd, is a researcher at the Finnish Institute of Occupational Health. She has over ten years of experience in research and development projects in the field of occupational safety and work-related well-being. She has conducted developmental work research-based interventions in workplaces and in cross-organizational network settings. Her research interests relate to collective learning processes, intervention methods, and collaborative development practices at workplaces. She has carried out her Doctoral studies at the University of Helsinki, in the Center for Research on Activity, Development, and Learning (CRADLE). She is currently preparing her Doctoral thesis on the role of cross-functional collaboration in promoting safety and well-being at work.

Laura Seppänen works as a Senior Research Scientist at the Finnish Institute of Occupational Health and has made her PhD on learning challenges in organic vegetable farming at the Center for Activity Theory and Developmental Research, University of Helsinki. Her main research interest is how changes at work are conceptualized and how the changes can be represented in workplace contexts for the purpose of learning and development. Recently, she was leading a research project on changing concepts, tools, and well-being in client-oriented service networks. Seppänen also carries out developmental interventions both within and outside research.

Stellan Sundh was an upper secondary teacher and a headmaster for some 20 years. Then he obtained his PhD degree in English Linguistics at Uppsala University in 2003 in a study on Swedish School-Leavers' Oral Proficiency in English. Since 2005, he has been a senior lecturer at Uppsala University where he lectures on Intercultural Communication and Academic Writing. He is engaged in teacher education, in courses about the teaching and learning of English, and with a special interest in young learners of English as a foreign language. He has produced study material on intercultural communication in English between Russia and Sweden and cooperates with universities in the Baltic Region.

Hanna Toiviainen, PhD, Docent of Developmental Work Research is affiliated to the Center for Research on Activity, Development, and Learning (CRADLE), Institute of Behavioral Sciences, University of Helsinki, Finland. She graduated from the Doctoral school for Developmental Work Research and Adult Education in 2003. The dissertation and the publications in international journals and edited books deal with multi-level learning, tool-mediation, and pedagogic modeling for inter-organizational networks. In the post-doctoral research project of Academy of Finland, she analyzed multi-mediation in a regional learning network and in a globally networked consulting and engineering company and got interested in emergent learning practices in global work. Research partnerships have focused on the learning-oriented production concepts of industrial networks and activity concepts for customer understanding and learning in service networks. Hanna is Finland's contact person of the ISCAR Nordic-Baltic-Polish membership 2011-2014.

Laurie Watts has completed a BSSoc in Education at Blekinge Technical Institute, and is about to complete a BS in Psychology at the same school. She is an expatriate who has lived in and worked in several countries before settling down in Sweden. This combined with a long-time involvement in open source development are the driving forces behind research interests in the multicultural workplace and community development.

Juanjuan Zhao is a doctoral candidate in Educational Studies at the University of Cincinnati, USA. She received her Master's and bachelor's degrees in English Language and Literature at Shandong University (Weihai), China. While working on her PhD degree, she taught Chinese as a foreign language at a local U.S. high school. She also taught English to adult learners and college students for five years before pursuing her PhD in Education. Her current research interests include cultural challenges facing international foreign language teachers in U.S., application of activity theory in second language teaching and learning, and research methodology including educational action research.

Index